AGAINST A HINDU GOD

Against a Hindu God

BUDDHIST PHILOSOPHY OF RELIGION IN INDIA

Parimal G. Patil

DEV PUBLISHERS & DISTRIBUTORS
New Delhi

Published by:
DEV PUBLISHERS & DISTRIBUTORS
2nd Floor, Prakash Deep,
22, Delhi Medical Association Road,
Darya Ganj,
New Delhi-110002
Phone : 011-4357 2647, 98102 36140
e-mail: devbooks@hotmail.com
website: www.devbooks.co.in

ISBN 978-93-81406-03-8
This edition, 2012

Printed in India.

For A, B, and M, and all those who have called Konark *home*

CONTENTS

ABBREVIATIONS

AJP	*Anekāntajayapatākā* (Haribhadra Sūri) in Kāpādia 1940/1947
AP	*Apohaprakaraṇa* (Jñānaśrīmitra) in Thakur 1987
AP-D	*Apohaprakaraṇa* (Dharmottara) in Frauwallner 1937
AR	*Anupalabdhirahasya* (Jñānaśrīmitra) in Thakur 1987, Kellner 2007
AS	*Apohasiddhi* (Ratnakīrti) in Thakur 1975
BCA	*Bodhicaryāvatāra* (Śāntideva) in Shastri 1988
BhK1	*Bhāvanākrama 1* (Kamalaśīla) in Adam 2002, Tucci 1986
BhK2	*Bhāvanākrama 2* (Kamalaśīla) in Adam 2002
BKNCT	*Bulletin of Kochi National College of Technology*
CAPV	*Citrādvaitaprakāśavāda* (Ratnakīrti) in Thakur 1975
DhPr	*Dharmottarapradīpa* (Durvekamiśra) in Malvania 1971
DvāṬ	*Dvādaśaśatikā* (Dignāga) in Jambuvijayaji 1966–1978
HB	*Hetubindu* (Dharmakīrti) in Steinkellner 1967
HBṬ	*Hetubinduṭīkā* (Arcaṭa) in Sanghavi 1949
HBṬĀ	*Hetubinduṭīkāloka* (Durvekamiśra) in Sanghavi 1949
ĪSD	*Īśvarasādhanadūṣaṇa* (Ratnakīrti) in Thakur 1975
JNĀ	*Jñānaśrīmitranibandhāvali* (Jñānaśrīmitra) in Thakur 1987
KāVṛ	*Kāśikāvṛtti* (Vāmana and Jayāditya) in Sharma 1969–1985
KBhA	*Kṣaṇabhaṅgādhyāya* (Jñānaśrīmitra) in Thakur 1987 and Kyuma 2005

KKBhS	*Kāryakāraṇabhāvasiddhi* (Jñānaśrīmitra) in Thakur 1987
KSA	*Kṣaṇabhaṅgasiddhi Anvayātmika* (Ratnakīrti) in Thakur 1975
KSV	*Kṣaṇabhaṅgasiddhi Vyatirekātmika* (Ratnakīrti) in Thakur 1975
KTBh	*Tarkabhāṣā* (Keśavamiśra) in Gajendragadkar and Karmarkar 1934
LPrP	*Laghuprāmāṇyaparīkṣā* (Dharmottara) in Krasser 1991
MBh	*Mahābhāṣya* (Patañjali) in Kielhorn 1962–1973
MTBh	*Tarkabhāṣā* (Mokṣākaragupta) in Iyengar 1952
N1	*Apohasiddhi* (Ratnakīrti), ms. 5–256 from the National Archives of Nepal
N2	*Apohasiddhi* (Ratnakīrti), ms. 3–696 from the National Archives of Nepal
N3	*Apohasiddhi* (Ratnakīrti), ms. 764d (running number) from the National Archives of Nepal
NB	*Nyāyabindu* (Dharmakīrti) in Malvania 1971
NBh	*Nyāyabhāṣya* (Vātsyāyana) in Thakur 1997b
NBhū	*Nyāyabhūṣaṇa* (Bhāsarvajña) in Yogindrananda 1968
NBṬ	*Nyāyabinduṭīkā* (Dharmottara) in Malvania 1971
NBṬ-Vi	*Nyāyabinduṭīkā* (Vinītadeva) in Gangopadhyaya 1971
NBṬṬ	*Nyāyabinduṭīkāṭippaṇa* in Shastri 1984
NCV	*Nayacakravṛtti* (Siṃhasūri) in Jambuvijayaji 1966–1978
NK	*Nyāyakoṣa* in Jhalakīkar 1996
NKaṇ	*Nyāyakaṇikā* (Vācaspatimiśra) in Stern 1998
NM	*Nyāyamañjarī* (Jayantabhaṭṭa) in Varadacharya 1969/1983
NS	*Nyāya-sūtra* (Gautama) in Thakur 1997b
NSū	*Nyāya-sūtra* (Gautama) in Thakur 1997b
NV	*Nyāyabhāṣyavārttika* (Uddyotakara) in Thakur 1997a
NVTṬ	*Nyāyavārttikatātparyaṭīkā* (Vācaspatimiśra) in Thakur 1996a
NVTṬP	*Nyāyavārttikatātparyaṭīkāpariśuddhi* (Udayana) in Thakur 1996a
PAP	*Pramāṇāntarbhāvaprakaraṇa* (Ratnakīrti) in Thakur 1975
PS 1	*Pramāṇasamuccaya* (Dignāga) in Steinkellner et al. 2005
PSṬ	*Pramāṇasamuccayaṭīkā* (Jinendrabuddhi) in Steinkellner et al. 2005
PSV	*Pramāṇasamuccayavṛtti* (Dignāga) in Steinkellner et al. 2005
PV 1	*Pramāṇavārttika*, Svārthānumāna (Dharmakīrti) in Gnoli 1960
PV 2	*Pramāṇavārttika*, Pramāṇasiddhi (Dharmakīrti) in Miyasaka 1971/2
PV 3	*Pramāṇavārttika*, Pratyakṣa (Dharmakīrti) in Miyasaka 1971/72
PV 4	*Pramāṇavārttika*, Parārthānumāna (Dharmakīrti) in Miyasaka 1971/72, Tillemans 2000
PVABh	*Pramāṇavārttikālaṅkārabhāṣya* (Prajñākaragupta) in Sāṃkṛtyāyana 1953

PVin 1	*Pramāṇaviniścaya* 1 (Dharmakīrti) in Vetter 1966
PVin 2	*Pramāṇaviniścaya* 2 (Dharmakīrti) in Steinkellner 1973
PVinṬ	*Pramāṇaviniścayaṭīkā* (Dharmottara) in Krasser and Steinkellner 1989
PVKP	*Pramāṇavārttikakroḍapatra*, printed as an appendix to Sāṃkṛtyāyana 1938–1940
PVSV	*Pramāṇavārttikasvavṛtti* (Dharmakīrti) in Gnoli 1960
PVSVṬ	*Pramāṇavārttikasvavṛttiṭīkā* (Karṇakagomin) in Sāṃkṛtyāyana 1943
PVṬ	*Pramāṇavārttikaṭīkā* (Śākyabuddhi) in Kellner 1999.
PVV	*Pramāṇavārttikavṛtti* (Manorathanandin) in Sāṃkṛtyāyana 1938–1940
RNĀ	*Ratnakīrtinibandhāvali* (Ratnakīrti) in Thakur 1975
SāmP	*Sāmānyaparīkṣā* (Dignāga) in Jambuvijayaji 1966–1988
SD	*Santānāntaradūṣaṇa* (Ratnakīrti) in Thakur 1975
SP	*Saptapadārthī* (Śivāditya) in Jetly 2003
SS	*Sarvajñasiddhi* (Ratnakīrti) in Thakur 1975, Bühneman 1980
SSD	*Sthirasiddhidūṣaṇa* (Ratnakīrti) in Thakur 1975, Mimaki 1976
SSS	*Sākārasiddhiśāstra* (Jñānaśrīmitra) in Thakur 1987
ŚV	*Ślokavārttika* (Kumārila) in Ray 1993
ŚVK	*Ślokavārttikakāśikā* (Sucaritamiśra) in Śāstri and Rāmasvāmi Śāstri 1926–1943
TS	*Tarkasaṃgraha* (Annaṃbhaṭṭa) in Bhattacharya 1976
TS/TSP	*Tattvasaṃgraha/Tattvasaṃgrahapañjikā* (Śāntarakṣita/Kamalaśīla) in Shastri 1981
VC	*Vyāpticarcā* (Jñānaśrīmitra) in Thakur 1987, Lasic 2000a
VN	*Vyāptinirṇaya* (Ratnakīrti) in Thakur 1975, Lasic 2000b
VNV	*Vādanyāyaṭīkā, Vipañcitārtha* (Śāntarakṣita) in Shastri 1972
WSTB	*Wiener Studien zur Tibetologie und Buddhismuskunde*
WZKM	*Wiener Zeitschrift für die Kunde des Morganlandes*
WZKS	*Wiener Zeitschrift für die Kunde Südasiens*
WZKSO	*Wiener Zeitschrift für die Kunde Süd- und Ostasiens*
YN	*Yoginirṇayaprakaraṇa* (Jñānaśrīmitra) in Thakur 1987
YTBh	*Tarkabhāṣā* (Yaśovijaya) in Bhargava 1973

AGAINST A HINDU GOD

Introduction

CHAPTER I
Comparative Philosophy of Religions

THIS BOOK IS ABOUT THE PHILOSOPHICAL CONTENT of an interreligious debate between Buddhist and Hindu intellectuals in premodern India. Its central concern is the range of arguments that an eleventh-century Buddhist intellectual named Ratnakīrti employed to criticize the beliefs of his non-Buddhist, Nyāya, interlocutors regarding the existence of a God-like being called "Īśvara."[1] What is so exciting about these arguments is that they provide a window into Buddhist, Hindu, and

---

1. For what little historical information is known about Ratnakīrti (ca. 1000–1050 C.E.), and for more on his dates and those of his contemporaries, see Thakur 1975, Bühneman 1980, Kajiyama 1965, Lasic 2000b, Mimaki 1976, Woo 1999, and the references contained therein. The term "Nyāya" refers to a "Hindu" philosophical system that is based on the *Nyāya-sūtra* and its commentaries. Philosophers working within this text tradition are referred to as "Naiyāyikas." Throughout this book the terms "Nyāya" and "Naiyāyikas" will be used to refer to the intellectuals whom Ratnakīrti considers to be his interlocutors. Moreover, whenever phrases such as "according to the Naiyāyikas" are used, what is referred to is the Nyāya viewpoint as reported by Ratnakīrti. Although Ratnakīrti's characterizations of Nyāya philosophy are generally fair and accurate, this work will not concern itself with demonstrating that this is so. Instead, it will concern itself with Ratnakīrti's Naiyāyikas and their arguments.

Jaina intellectual practices and serve as concrete examples of one way in which the philosophy and intellectual history of religions was practiced in premodern South Asia.[2] In interpreting and critically explaining these arguments, I am moving beyond the usual historical and philological task of restating, in English, complex arguments formulated in Sanskrit. I am committed to viewing these arguments not just as historical artifacts from someone else's intellectual past but as an interculturally available source from which we can learn today. What is at stake for Ratnakīrti (and I hope for some of us) in these arguments is nothing less than the nature of rationality, the metaphysics of epistemology, and the relevance of philosophy to the practice of religion. Written during the final phase of Buddhism in India, Ratnakīrti's work also provides us with a unique perspective on the centuries-long series of debates among Buddhist and Hindu philosophers of religion and shows us what was intellectually important to one of the famed "gate-keepers" at the international Buddhist university of Vikramaśīla.[3] As I hope to show, work like Ratnakīrti's effectively challenges the widespread notion that the intellectual world of premodern India is irrelevant to more contemporary concerns in the study of religion, philosophy, and South Asian studies.

Given that scholarship on Ratnakīrti and his Nyāya interlocutors is still in its very early stages, I have tried in this book to balance the historical and philological methods that are necessary for accurately interpreting Sanskrit texts with the philosophical concerns that motivate Ratnakīrti's (and my own) interest in the material. I have also tried to support my interpretations by citing and translating in the notes the texts on which they are based and to explain my use of technical terms by providing extended definitions of them, also in the notes. This book will not be successful if either Ratnakīrti's arguments are misinterpreted or their significance for him, and for us, is not brought into view.

---

2. For a brief discussion of why I think Buddhist intellectuals like Ratnakīrti could be considered "intellectual historians" see McCrea and Patil 2006 and Patil 2007.

3. "Vikramaśīla" is the name of the Buddhist monastic and educational complex where Ratnakīrti and his teacher, Jñānaśrīmitra (whose work will be discussed, briefly, in chapter 6), are said to have lived and worked. Both are called "gate-keepers" of this complex. Vikramaśīla is generally supposed to have been founded by the Pāla king Dharmapāla (ca. 775–820 C.E.) and was located in the Bhagalpur district of modern-day Bihar. For more on Vikramaśīla see Chattopadhyaya and Chattopadhyaya 1970, Asher 1975, and Ghosh 1989.

In introducing this book, I want to begin by situating my project within the contemporary academy, in order to argue that what is needed to properly accommodate it is a specifically "comparative approach" to the philosophy of religions. While such methodological remarks are often thought to be unnecessary, for projects such as mine, which tend to disappear into the gaps between existing disciplinary frameworks, a methodological introduction is helpful for establishing an intellectual context and indeed for justifying their very existence.[4] For those who do not share my methodological interests or disciplinary concerns it may be helpful to skip ahead to section 4, where I provide an outline of the book and briefly discuss its central arguments.

1. Disciplinary Challenges

I consider this book to be "transdisciplinary." Unlike inter- and multidisciplinary works, which often do not have a proper academic home, I intend this study to fit, even if uncomfortably, within the three disciplinary frameworks mentioned above. In this introduction I will argue that in order to create a transdisciplinary space for work such as this what is needed is a properly comparative approach to the philosophy of religions that in part undermines the traditional disciplinary boundaries between the study of religion, philosophy, and South Asian studies. In my view, it is only through a rethinking of these disciplinary boundaries that the study of South Asian intellectual practices will be able to occupy its proper place in the academy, and to be taken seriously by those who do not specialize in South Asian texts and textual traditions.[5] In providing a specific example of how this can be

---

4. Compare, for example, the introductions to Chakrabarti 1997, Phillips and Tatacharya 2004, Siderits 2003, and Taber 2005—which are written by individuals located in philosophy departments—with those in Arnold 2005, Cabezón 2004, Dunne 2004, and Griffiths 1986—which are written by those in, generally speaking, religious studies departments. Also see Williamson 2007, especially his introduction and afterword, for a discussion of methodological issues in philosophy.

5. This is, of course, only one way to imagine such a "transdisciplinary" space. For an outstanding example of another work on South Asian intellectual practices that occupies a very different—but in my view still "transdisciplinary"—space see Pollock 2006. By "South Asian intellectual practices" I mean, in general, the disciplines picked out by the term "*śāstra*," e.g., grammar, hermeneutics, philosophy, literary theory, etc. For more on this see Pollock 1989, and my brief discussion in chapter 6.

done, this book argues for a new kind of philosophy of religions.[6] Before I attempt to define this intellectual space, it may be helpful to outline some of the reasons for the project's somewhat uncomfortable fit within current disciplinary frameworks.

The religious studies subfields of South Asian religions and Buddhist studies are currently suffering from what may be called a tyranny of social and cultural history, and a closely related distrust of philosophy.[7] The idea that it is only the social, cultural, and political "outsides" of texts that are of real relevance to the study of religions has resulted in a decades-long shift away from the study of intellectual practices and/or their histories.[8] While this may have been a necessary corrective to previous scholarship, the pendulum has swung too far in this direction and there has been a systematic neglect of Buddhist, Hindu, and Jaina thought. Projects such as mine, which focus on arguments, are often dismissed as being irrelevant to a field which has "rightly" committed itself to the lived outsides of texts and text traditions. In contrast, philosophy departments have, for the most, ignored the study of Indian philosophy.[9] This is sometimes due to an accident of history, but more often to the still widespread belief that Indian "philosophy" is too soft, and either is not really philosophy at all or is at best a part of someone else's philosophical past and therefore irrelevant to us.[10] Compounding this

---

6. The kind of philosophy of religions that I am arguing for here can be helpfully viewed as an intellectual descendant of the "Towards a Comparative Philosophy of Religions" conference series that took place at the University of Chicago, now almost twenty years ago. For an account of this project, see Bantly 1990. For some of the work that has resulted from it, see the work published by SUNY Press in the book series of that name. For more recent work that is consistent with the objectives of this project see Arnold 2005, Clooney 1999, Ganeri 2007, Gold 2007, and Neville 2001a, 2001b, and 2001c.

7. I consider the terms "study of religion" and "religious studies" to be equivalent.

8. For two strong and well-argued statements for the priority of textual "outsides" see Schopen 1987 and Davidson 2002. For a sophisticated account of how textual "outsides" and "insides" can be studied together see Collins 1998.

9. There are, of course, some noteworthy exceptions, e.g., Illinois State University; University of Hawaii, Manoa; University of New Mexico; University of Texas, Austin; and University of Sussex.

10. For example, compare and contrast the very critical stance of Rorty (1989, 1992a, 1992b) and D. Davidson (as referred to in Mohanty 1992b:401–404) with that of Strawson. In his reply to Chakrabarti 1998, Strawson (1998:327) helpfully concludes, "His [Chakrabarti's] paper demonstrates vividly how one and the same philosophical issue can be a matter of contention in philosophical centers entirely distinct from each other, widely separated in time

fact is the relative neglect of philosophy of religions, which itself is often viewed as not being properly or interestingly philosophical.[11] Projects such as this, which focus on the philosophical work of Buddhist and Hindu intellectuals, are therefore routinely dismissed as being beyond the scope of philosophy proper, and ironically are thought to belong to religious studies or South Asian studies. Many South Asian studies programs, however, are "presentist" in orientation and align themselves with recent trends in the social sciences and humanities, in which the importance of premodern intellectual contexts and the textual production of elites (especially religious elites) is devalued, when considered at all. Others, particularly in Europe and Japan, are informed by classical Indology, where what is privileged is the "literal," in the form of critical editions of texts and very specific studies of topics that all too often are accessible only to other specialists who have knowledge of the primary languages. While the intellectual values that inform each of these versions of South Asian studies are crucial to the field and its future, they are incomplete, and leave almost no room for the kind of work that I am trying to do.

One way of describing this project with respect to these contemporary disciplinary frameworks is to suggest that its specific subject matter, and the language and style in which it is discussed, belongs primarily to philosophy, and more specifically to the subfield of epistemology; its texts primarily to South Asian studies and Indology; and its overall intellectual context to religious studies, especially the subfields of Buddhist studies, South Asian religions, and philosophy of religions.[12] This description is, of course, a contingent feature of the contemporary Euro-American academy, which is based upon a conception of these disciplinary frameworks that this project seeks to undermine. By constructing a transdisciplinary space for a properly comparative approach to the philosophy of religions, I hope to be able to draw from and contribute to each of these disciplinary frameworks, without having to choose any one of them. More specifically, I hope that by self-consciously

---

and space, and belonging to quite disparate cultures. And this in turn provides a compelling argument for two things: first, for the genuine universality of some major philosophical problems; and, second, for the desirability of further comparative study of the respects in which the two philosophical traditions in question may illustrate this universality."

11. For a discussion of this issue see Taliaferro 2005.

12. I take this final point to be the case given my focus on Buddhist and Hindu arguments about the nature and existence of Īśvara.

situating this project within such a transdisciplinary framework I will enable it to find a home in all three, even as it challenges their self-conceptions. Central to my conception of this transdisciplinary space is its comparative aspect.

2. A Grammar for Comparison

One way to envision the comparative philosophy of religions is to first think of comparative work more generally. In my view, it is instructive to think of such work on the model of a grammatical event, and more specifically one that can be analyzed in the vocabulary of the Sanskrit grammatical theory of "event-makers" (***kāraka***).[13] The theory of event-makers identifies six semantic relations between the components of a given sentence and the event that is expressed by the main verb of that sentence. In so doing, it provides a conceptual vocabulary for analyzing the event. Through an understanding of these semantic relations in the sentence, it is possible to understand the semantic structure of the sentence as a whole. For example, in the sentence, "In the kitchen, Rāma cooks food for Sītā with firewood from the forest," the event is cooking.[14] According to the theory, this cooking event can be analyzed in terms of the other sentence-components' relations to it. More specifically, the event can be understood through its agent, Rāma; patient, rice; instrument, firewood; source, forest; beneficiary, Sītā; and location, kitchen. It is through these relational components that the event itself is individuated, and thereby defined. For our purposes, the vocabulary provided by this theory can help us to understand the various components of comparative projects and thereby develop a more sophisticated notion of in exactly what sense(s) a given project is "comparative." Given the vocabulary of the theory of event-makers, in describing the structure of a comparative project it is necessary to identify its various components; describe how they are related to one another; and specify the ways in which the comparison is

---

13. For a discussion of the theory of event-makers and references to primary and secondary sources see chapter 2. I think that it is possible to develop a rigorous and complete theory of comparison that is based upon conceptual resources provided by the theory of event-makers. It is, however, beyond the scope of this introduction to make all of the necessary arguments to support this claim. All that I am doing here is providing a preliminary description of such a theory.

14. This example is taken from Ganeri 1999a:52.

supposed to be of value and for whom. In this section, I will describe the various components of my comparative project and some of the ways in which they are related to one another. In section 3, I will discuss its value.

2.1. *Event*

It is helpful to think of the event in question as being "to study comparatively," even though precisely what this means and why it is different from the event of studying more generally will not be clear until section 3, once the framework has been developed a bit further.

2.2. *Agent*

The agent of this particular study is, of course, me. There are, however, other agents that are relevant for this book—most notably, Ratnakīrti and his interlocutors. Each of them is an agent of an event that can also be analyzed in terms of the theory of event-makers. For example, as a result of his engagement with the work of his Nyāya opponents and Buddhist predecessors, Ratnakīrti himself can be understood as the agent of his own "comparative" project. In addition, it is worth noting that Ratnakīrti's texts can be helpfully thought of as "complex agents" in their own right.[15]

2.3. *Patient*

The patient, or primary object of study, is Ratnakīrti and his Nyāya interlocutors' *arguments* regarding the existence of a God-like being called Īśvara. In this work, I will argue that these arguments are best understood on a continuum, from those that are explicit, and obviously present in the texts, to those that are at best implicit, but as I will show also present in the texts. It is the arguments themselves and their philosophical significance both for him and for us that comprise the subject matter of this book.

Of course, the patient of this book could have been very different, even given my specific interest in the work of Ratnakīrti and his interlocutors. For example, the patient could have been the more focused philological context of

---

15. See Inden 1990 for an extremely sophisticated, and relevant, discussion of agency and complex agency.

Ratnakīrti's texts themselves; the much broader South Asian intellectual context leading up to Ratnakīrti's work; the sociopolitical context in which Ratnakīrti's work was produced and consumed; or Ratnakīrti's critique of Nyāya theism as it relates to Euro-American arguments against the existence of God, etc. While each of these projects is interesting, important, and not entirely unrelated to my own, my specific interest in this book is in Ratnakīrti's arguments and what I am calling their philosophical significance for him and for us.[16]

2.4. *Instrument*

The instruments for this study are the conceptual and disciplinary resources that I use to study Ratnakīrti's arguments. There are three sets of such conceptual resources: (1) those that Ratnakīrti himself identifies and/or uses, such as his Nyāya opponents' epistemology and his own theory of mental content; (2) those to which he himself does not appeal, though he could do so, such as the theory of event-makers; and (3) those to which he could not appeal, such as those of contemporary philosophy. There are also two sets of disciplinary resources: (1) those associated with the historical and philological study of Sanskrit texts; and (2) those associated with the study of Euro-American philosophy. Instruments belonging to each of these categories and disciplines will be used, to varying degrees, in each chapter of this book. The instrument, like the patient, can be multivalent.[17]

---

16. My interest in this dual significance is both similar to and different from that delineated in Smith 2004:10, where he characterizes his later work in terms of a "double archaeology of situating a text or artifact both in 'their' history and in 'ours.'" Where my interest differs from that of Smith is in his emphasis on, and understanding of, "history," which he takes to be the "meaning within the cultures that produced the text or artifact in question" in the case of "'*their* history,'" and the "history of scholarship" in the case of "'*our*'" history. In my case, "their history" corresponds to Ratnakīrti's thought and its significance for him. "Our history" relates not only to *us* as scholars, occupying a particular disciplinary or transdisciplinary space, but also as individuals for whom Ratnakīrti's questions are also our own. In this sense, as I see it, "their history" can also be "our history." These issues are also helpfully discussed in terms of the "beneficiary" and "location." For more on this see below, where I discuss location 3. It is worth noting that Smith (2004:11) recognizes the relationship between what I am calling the patient and the beneficiary and location, and discusses it in terms of a "double pedagogical intent."

17. Cf. Smith 1980, where he first uses the term "polythetic," and his discussion of related issues in Smith 1988.

2.5. *Source*

The source is where the instrument(s) come from. There are both textual and disciplinary sources. The textual sources for this work can be divided into four groups: source I consists of Ratnakīrti's written work, and more specifically seven of Ratnakīrti's ten extant texts;[18] source II consists of the texts directly referred to by him, most notably those of his teacher, Jñānaśrīmitra, and those of his (primarily) Nyāya opponents;[19] source III consists of texts, commentaries, and secondary sources to which Ratnakīrti does not refer (although much of this work postdates his work, it is nevertheless helpful for understanding and interpreting Ratnakīrti's arguments and those of his opponents);[20] and source IV, which consists of contemporary philosophical literature that I have found helpful in interpreting and writing about Ratnakīrti's arguments and their philosophical significance. The disciplinary sources are the disciplinary resources of religious studies, philosophy, and South Asian studies/Indology.

Given these sources, it may be helpful to briefly think back on the instruments and some of the ways in which they are related. Some of the instruments, such as those in (1), can be thought of as being "inherited" by

---

18. Source I: Ratnakīrti's extant work: [1] "The Refutation of Arguments for Establishing Īśvara [*Īśvarasādhanadūṣaṇa*, ĪSD]"; [2] "An Inquiry Into Inference-Warranting Relations [*Vyāptinirṇaya*, VN]"; [3] "A Demonstration of Exclusion [*Apohasiddhi*, AS]"; [4] "The Doctrine of Multifaceted Nonduality [*Citrādvaitaprakāśavāda*, CAPV]"; [5] "The Refutation of Other Mental Continua [*Santānāntaradūṣaṇa*, SD]"; [6] "A Treatise on the Accepted Instruments of Warranted Awareness [*Pramāṇāntarbhāvaprakaraṇa*, PAP]"; [7] "Demonstrating Omniscience [*Sarvajñasiddhi*, SS]"; [8] "A Refutation of the Proof of Enduring Entities [*Sthirasiddhidūṣaṇa*, SSD]"; [9] "The Proof of Momentary Destruction, Negative Concomitance [*Kṣaṇabhaṅgasiddhi, vyatirekātmikā*, KSV]"; and [10] "The Proof of Momentary Destruction, Positive Concomitance [*Kṣaṇabhaṅgasiddhi, anvayātmikā*, KSA]." This book is based primarily on the first three essays. Selected passages from essay 4, essay 6, essay 7, essay 8, essay 9, and essay 10 will also be discussed.

19. The most important texts from source II are those written by Ratnakīrti's teacher, Jñānaśrīmitra, and the work of Dharmakīrti and his commentators; Vācaspatimiśra's commentary on Maṇḍanamiśra's *Vidhiviveka*; and the *Nyāyabhūṣaṇa* of Bhāsarvajña and Vācaspatimiśra's commentary on the *Nyāya-sūtras*.

20. The most useful texts from source III are sections from the so-called *Nyāya-sūtra* corpus (see chapters 2 and 3), Śāntarakṣita's *Tattvasaṃgraha* and its commentary by Kamalaśīla (see chapter 6), Udayana's *Ātmatattvaviveka* and *Nyāyakusumāñjali* (see chapter 2), Mokṣākaragupta's *Tarkabhāṣā* (see chapters 2–4), the "Īśvarānumāna" section of Gaṅgeśa's *Tattvacintāmaṇi* (see chapter 2), and Keśavamiśra's *Tarkabhāṣā* (see chapters 2 and 3).

me from source I, in the sense that I am making use of instruments that Ratnakīrti himself makes use of. Others, such as those in (2), may be thought of as being "discovered" by me in texts from source groups II and III, in the sense that I am identifying and using as instruments conceptual resources that Ratnakīrti could have used, but did not. Still others, such as those in (3), may be thought of as being "constructed" by me from source IV, in the sense that I am using conceptual resources that Ratnakīrti not only did not use but could not have used.

2.6. Beneficiary

The beneficiary is the intended audience of this work. As I will discuss further below, I intend this work to be of interest and use to readers who locate themselves in one or more of the three disciplinary frameworks referred to above. Such "beneficiaries" can be individuated and identified through the specific features of the multivalent patient, instrument, and source that are of greatest interest to them. In my view, disciplinary frameworks can also be beneficiaries. Attention to the beneficiaries of comparative projects—regardless of whether they are types of individuals or disciplines—is of particular importance in determining the value, or "ends," of comparison.[21] The various forms of comparative analysis used in this book should make it possible for each of the attendant beneficiaries to derive some value/benefit from it.

For example, I hope first that my focused attention on the philosophical content and significance of Ratnakīrti's arguments will remind historians of religion of the importance of intellectual contexts to the study of religion. All too often, intellectual and intertextual contexts are not recognized as being legitimate contexts of study in their own right, and instead are thought to be of interest only insofar as they help us better understand the sociopolitical contexts of which they are thought to be artifacts. In such a framework, it is only the outsides of texts that are taken to be relevant to a historian of religion. I hope that this book will help to remind those of us situated in religious studies that intellectual and intertextual contexts are also *contexts*, and that the content of philosophical texts cannot be so easily reduced to, or explained merely in terms of, social, cultural, or political contexts. Both the outsides of

---

21. Determining this is the third of the three tasks outlined above (see the beginning of section 2).

texts and their insides should be of importance. This book attempts to illustrate the benefit of studying the insides of South Asian texts, and in so doing gestures to the need to create a space in religious studies for the intellectual history of religions, as well as for the "historicist" approach to the philosophy of religions that is being described here, and will be described in greater detail below.

Second, I hope that my focus on the Īśvara-inference will remind philosophers of religion—in both religious studies and philosophy—of the relevance of Buddhist, Hindu, and Jaina intellectual practices to the field.[22] For too long the philosophy of religions has been defined by questions and concerns that are drawn almost exclusively from Christian texts and textual traditions.[23] While there is an increasing openness to the work of non-Christian philosophers, there is still very little work that is accessible to philosophers of religion who are interested in thinking about the relevance of Sanskrit philosophy to the field. By analyzing the Īśvara-inference through the religious epistemology that is used to defend and critique it, I hope to contribute to a description and understanding of the philosophy of religion in the final phase of Buddhism in India, and in so doing to introduce to the field questions and concerns that are drawn from Sanskrit texts and text traditions. This is, I hope, a preliminary step in re-envisioning what the philosophy of religions can (and should) be.

Third, I hope that this book will make it possible for professional philosophers unfamiliar with Sanskrit philosophical material to develop a more accurate conception of "Indian philosophy"—a conception that I trust will force us all to confront the troubling (and embarrassing) question of why the history of philosophy in India is not a proper part of philosophy.

Fourth, I hope that this book will provide my colleagues in South Asian studies with a new model for thinking about the "relevance" of the field. For many, what makes South Asian studies relevant is what it can tell us about South Asia and/or South Asians today. It is worth noting, however, that one does not have to be interested in Europe or Europeans, from any time period, to find the work of Aristotle, Kant, Hegel, Foucault, or even Shakespeare to be relevant and of value. Why then is it so often thought that the

---

22. For a very interesting "anthropology" of the so-called APA (American Philosophical Association) and AAR (American Academy of Religion, Philosophers of Religion) see Quinn 1996, and the other essays in Wainwright 1996, notably Wainwright's introduction.

23. This is, fortunately, beginning to change.

work of premodern South Asian intellectuals can only be of relevance to those interested in premodern South Asia? There are metrics of relevance that are, in my view, all but ignored by so many in the field. In treating Ratnakīrti and his interlocutors as philosophers in their own right, I want to suggest that even those who have no interest in South Asia can find relevance in the content and quality of the thought of Sanskrit intellectuals.[24] Like the work of Euro-American intellectuals, the work of Sanskrit intellectuals can be a source of genuine theoretical insight that may be of transhistorical and transcultural value.

Finally, I hope that my colleagues on the Indological side of South Asian studies will come to see value in a work that tries to come to terms with the thought of a Sanskrit philosopher long before what they take to be the "necessary prerequisites" for such work have been completed. While critical editions, translations, and very specialized studies of individual concepts and texts are absolutely essential to the study of South Asian philosophers and their intellectual practices, there is a desperate need for new models of how to present this work in a manner that will be useful to others without such philological skills. In my view, it is our responsibility to encourage and create space for such work while still maintaining our standards. This book attempts to strike this balance and to provide an example of how to study the work of a Sanskrit philosopher in a manner that is historically and philologically responsible and yet accessible and meaningful to those outside the field.

2.7. Location

The locations for my particular study of Ratnakīrti's arguments are the intellectual contexts in which, and with respect to which, his arguments will be studied, interpreted, and/or written about.[25] Often these contexts are associated with a particular disciplinary framework (and, alternatively, the transdisciplinary space that I am seeking to create). The locations for this study are therefore multiple, and necessarily so. The following three loca-

24. This point has also been made recently in Cabezón 2006a and 2006b:46, where he writes, "We should resort to non-Christian theories not because they are non-Christian, and not because they are religious, but because, quite simply, they illuminate the phenomenon that is being subjected to scrutiny—to put it more bluntly, they work." See also Cabezón 2006a:22 n. 2.

25. "Interpreting" and "writing about" are, in this construal, aspects of "studying."

tions, in descending order of significance, are relevant for this particular project. It is the relative importance of the first of these locations that led me to describe this work earlier as an example of a "historicist" approach to the philosophy of religions.[26]

Location 1 and Its Instruments

The primary location for this study is the intellectual world in which Ratnakīrti's work was produced. This includes not only the world of Buddhist scholasticism, but also the worlds of Ratnakīrti's primarily Nyāya interlocutors.[27] More specifically, this location is defined by the texts to which Ratnakīrti explicitly and implicitly refers—that is, by the texts that make up the first two groups of source texts described above (see section 2.5). The effort to interpret Ratnakīrti's arguments as a part of this intellectual and intertextual context recognizes the importance of trying to understand these arguments as Ratnakīrti and the other Sanskrit philosophers of his time did. This requires training oneself to think, along with Ratnakīrti and his interlocutors, in the technical vocabulary and style of Sanskrit philosophy; understanding the intellectual and intertextual space in which they produced their work; and trying to identify their own philosophical concerns.[28] This is primarily a historical and philological mode of inquiry.[29]

---

26. For the idea of a historicist approach to the philosophy of religions see Bowlin 1999. For some excellent recent examples of historicist approaches to Sanskrit philosophy see Dunne 2004, Phillips and Tatacharya 2004, and Taber 2005.

27. See Cabezón 1994 for the significance of using the term "scholasticism."

28. For some recent examples that set the standards for such work see Dunne 2004, Kapstein 2001, Katsura 2004, Kellner 1997a, Krasser 1999, Lasic 2000a, Taber 2005, and Tillemans 2000. For a clear statement of this approach to the study of Sanskrit philosophers see Hayes 1988:2.

29. Careful historical and philological work is absolutely necessary, since, given the state of scholarship on Ratnakīrti and his interlocutors, it is still too easy for one's interpretation of a Sanskrit text to be so shaped by contemporary concerns that a modern reading of it would be unrecognizable and unacceptable to its original producers and consumers. Although such work is, in this sense, "primary," it is not the only necessary mode of inquiry. As Ruegg (1986:236) points out, "One must guard against anachronistically transposing and unsystematically imposing concepts of modern semantics and philosophy, which have originated in the course of particular historical developments, on modes of thought that evolved in quite different historical circumstances, and which have therefore to be interpreted in the first place in the context of their own concerns and the ideas they themselves developed."

In studying Ratnakīrti's arguments in this location, and to these ends, the primary instruments will be those conceptual resources "inherited" from Ratnakīrti's own work and sources, and those methodological resources inherited from classical Indology.[30] In my view, careful historical and philological work is absolutely necessary if we are to understand what Ratnakīrti's arguments meant to him and his peers.[31] In recognition of this necessity, I have tried to provide philological support for my interpretation of Ratnakīrti's arguments by providing translations of, and detailed references to, the texts being interpreted. Since my primary interest in this work is Ratnakīrti's arguments (the patient of this work is, as I explained earlier, Ratnakīrti's arguments and *not* the historical context in which they were produced), I have noted to a lesser extent the historical precedents of the arguments being considered, and have virtually ignored any discussion of the broader historical context and background of Ratnakīrti's debate with the Naiyāyikas.[32] Rather than beginning my analysis of his arguments with a discussion of previous Buddhist and Nyāya debates about the nature and existence of Īśvara, for

---

Similarly, Halbfass (1992:15) says, "Nor should we use Indian and other texts . . . as mere occasions for the employment and display of the 'latest achievements' in logic and epistemology. Clarity and precision are indispensable; yet they have to be pursued with caution and discretion. Analysis and the search for conceptual precision can be obtrusive and interfere with the task of translating and understanding, and with our obligation to respect the Indian tradition in its own context and dimensions. A certain well-tempered vagueness may, indeed, be a hermeneutic virtue." For other examples of such caution and criticism see Bronkhorst 1989 and Franco 1997.

30. In my view, the danger of not being sufficiently grounded in the texts themselves is that what is potentially unique about Sanskrit philosophy and the work of Sanskrit intellectuals will be lost. As Smith often points out, "difference should not be overcome" (Smith 2000:239).

31. It is often remarked (especially by my colleagues in religious studies and South Asian studies) that understanding what texts "meant" to authors from different times and places is theoretically impossible. This is a view that I do not share. Unfortunately, it is beyond the scope of this project to argue against it philosophically. The best that I can do here is to provide an interpretation of Ratnakīrti's thought with which I believe he would concur. One could disagree with this interpretation by declaring, for example, that I cannot, for theoretical reasons, provide such an interpretation or that I have misunderstood Ratnakīrti's arguments and therefore have provided an interpretation with which he would not concur.

32. For a short but extremely useful summary discussion of Ratnakīrti's intellectual context see Granoff 1978:1–2; also see Thakur 1975.

example, I have chosen to begin chapter 2 by directly introducing the Naiyāyikas' inferential argument, as Ratnakīrti himself does.[33]

It is equally important to recognize that while Ratnakīrti's work may be of historical interest to many, it is certainly not the case that it was merely of historical interest to him or his interlocutors. As works of philosophy, Ratnakīrti's texts and the arguments that constitute them were intended to be much more than just historical artifacts.[34] As a result, when they are studied in this location it is not sufficient to treat them as such. The danger in doing so is that lively and important philosophical and theological arguments will be reduced to conversations about the meanings of technical terms and concepts, and that the diverse and varied history of these arguments will be reduced to exercises in intellectual archaeology, where one's primary task is to uncover layers of argument and counterargument until their "origin" is discovered. As mentioned above, such work is necessary, but far from sufficient.[35] Acknowledging this recognizes and takes seriously the normative dimensions of Ratnakīrti's work.[36]

As this book will make clear, Ratnakīrti's texts (and those of his interlocutors) are characterized by philosophical arguments that were supposed to be both valid and sound. Moreover, Ratnakīrti and his interlocutors considered themselves to be arguing for positions that could be supported by

---

33. I have also chosen to begin in this way since much of the "historical work" has been done elsewhere and does not need to be repeated. See, for example, Jacobi 1923, Glasenapp 1954, Bechert et al. 1966, Chattopadhyaya 1969, Bhattacharya 1961, Bulcke 1947, Chemparathy 1965, Oberhammer 1965, Chemparathy 1968, Gonda 1968, Chemparathy 1969a, Chemparathy 1969b, Chemparathy 1972, Hayes 1988, Vattanky 1984, Jackson 1986, Carman 1994, Bronkhorst 1996, Van den Bossche 1998, Clooney 1997, Griffiths 1999b, Krasser 1999, and esp. Krasser 2002.

34. For an interesting and thoughtful discussion of this see McClintock 2002.

35. Oetke 1993:196: "I regard it as unavoidable to carry out philosophically oriented studies on non-European philosophies in combination with philological investigations at the present stage of research but on the other hand deny that the historical-philological perspective must be *guiding* for all investigations of this kind. In particular, there seems to be no compelling reason why *all* questions that might be of interest from a philological-historical point of view have to be dealt with in studies whose primary aim lies elsewhere."

36. For a powerful, and therefore controversial, statement on the pervasive but hidden forms of "anxious" normativity in the study of religion see Griffiths 2006a and Griffiths 2006b.

persuasive if not demonstrative arguments. We do his work and the Sanskrit philosophical tradition more generally a great disservice if we do not consider these arguments with the same philosophical seriousness with which they were offered.[37] Acknowledging this requires that we also study the arguments made by both Ratnakīrti and his interlocutors philosophically; that is, with instruments—conceptual resources and methodologies—from sources I–IV (see section 2.5) and, more important, the discipline of philosophy. Such philosophical work is a necessary part of the more historical and philological task of accurately understanding and interpreting Ratnakīrti's texts even in his world, since it is through such work that the normative dimensions and significance of his arguments can be understood.[38] With these instruments, new perspectives on Ratnakīrti's arguments emerge and it becomes possible to see more clearly what is at stake in them, and to better appreciate the consequences of his views.[39] Conceptual and methodological instruments constructed from source IV are particularly important, since it is almost impossible to accurately describe Sanskrit philosophical arguments in English without an awareness of philosophical vocabulary in English. If for no other reason, it is because of this that those of us who are interested in Sanskrit

---

37. For more on this see chapter 6. Cf. Griffiths 1999b.

38. Oetke (1993:197) claims that "it is not merely desirable but even imperative to bring philosophy in general, and therewith also modern Western philosophy, into play when studying non-European philosophical traditions—at least if it is granted that investigations of foreign philosophical or religious doctrines are worthwhile at all. This is, however, not meant in the sense that reference to the background of Western philosophy is indispensable in every single case of investigation but means that the study of Indian or other non-European philosophy as a whole cannot be profitably carried out unless it is related in some way to the subject matter of philosophy and even to the most recent developments of Western thought. One reason for this lies in the fact that in the same manner as also in other fields of study *competence in the respective subject matter* is more essential for research in the field than it seems to have been widely assumed in Oriental studies." Taber (2001:74, in a review of Kellner 1997b) remarks, "While her interpretive study provides an accurate account of the details of the debate between Śāntarakṣita and Kumārila, one misses the big picture. What is really going on here? What is at stake? Why would Kumārila and Śāntarakṣita take up the positions that they do? In order to see that one must understand their positions in relation to other doctrines of their systems, and one must also, at least to some extent, reflect philosophically on the problem of non-being itself."

39. Halbfass (1992:14) interestingly suggests that the proper use of contemporary philosophical resources can function as a "microscope" for viewing Indian texts and traditions.

philosophical texts are justified in using contemporary philosophical vocabulary to describe and think about Sanskrit philosophy. In making use of such vocabulary in nearly every chapter of this book, my intention is to bring out the philosophical structure of the arguments being considered, irrespective of whether these arguments have contemporary parallels. As will become clear in what follows, some arguments have such parallels while others do not.

Location 2 and Its Instruments

In addition to the intellectual world in which Ratnakīrti's work was produced, a second location for this study is the contemporary Euro-American academy, and more specifically the three disciplinary frameworks referred to in this introduction. While the first location informs my understanding of Ratnakīrti's arguments and their significance, this second location shapes the ways in which I write about both. To some extent, it also determines the project's beneficiaries. The instruments used to write about (and study) Ratnakīrti's arguments in this multidisciplinary location are based on the genre conventions of contemporary academic discourse; the conceptual and methodological expectations of each discipline (including my own, insofar as I am formally located in the disciplines of religious studies and South Asian studies/Indology and subject to their disciplinary demands); and my transdisciplinary goals.

In attending to this location, I have chosen to present Ratnakīrti's work by reconstructing and highlighting those features of his texts that are the most relevant to his critique of the Nyāya argument for the existence of Īśvara. In some cases, this requires bringing together arguments from texts that are topically distant from each other, and selecting and highlighting only some of Ratnakīrti's arguments while ignoring others. For example, while Ratnakīrti's remarks on "inference-warranting relations" are directly related by him to his critique of the Naiyāyikas' argument, his remarks on "exclusion" and "mental content" are discussed more fully in other contexts and are, at best, only indirectly applied by him to this problem. In my work, however, these remarks will be brought together in order to explain dimensions of Ratnakīrti's critique of the Nyāya arguments that he himself does not choose to discuss explicitly. This kind of constructive representation of Ratnakīrti's views is designed to facilitate a description of Ratnakīrti's arguments that is faithful to his texts and intellectual concerns, and yet meaningful to those who do not have a detailed knowledge of Sanskrit philosophy. It is worth noting that such a rational reconstruction is not unprecedented in Sanskrit philosophy itself. In fact, the style of Sanskrit philosophy is such that the sort of rational reconstruction described here is pervasive.[40] In an important sense, this method also claims sources I and II (i.e., texts from Ratnakīrti's world) as its own.

The "disciplinary expectations" that come from studying Ratnakīrti's arguments in this location are reflected in the content of some of the chapters: for example, this introduction, which addresses the disciplinary expectation that projects in religious studies be methodologically self-conscious, and many of the footnotes, in which the disciplinary expectations of classical Indology are addressed. The multidisciplinary location that I am describing here is also closely related to the transdisciplinary space that I am seeking to create, in that this space is constructed out of religious studies, philosophy, and South Asian studies. It is the demands and expectations of this transdisciplinary location, as I understand it, that guide how the body of the text has been written.[41]

Location 3 and Its Instruments

In addition to the two locations just described, there is a third location in which my study of Ratnakīrti's arguments should take place. This location is one that I imagine myself to share with Ratnakīrti and his interlocutors. As such, it is neither *my* context, location 2, nor *their* context, location 1, but an imagined "our" context. In this location, my understanding and interpretation of Ratnakīrti's arguments become vulnerable to an imagined critique by him. It is also here that his arguments and counterarguments place de-

---

40. In his *Tarkabhāṣā*, for example, the Buddhist scholastic Mokṣākaragupta includes Ratnakīrti's arguments on inference-warranting relations and mental content in his discussion of the Naiyāyikas' argument for the existence of Īśvara. In addition, large parts of Ratnakīrti's own work can be seen to be rational reconstructions of the work of his teacher, Jñānaśrīmitra. For an excellent illustration of this compare Lasic 2000a with Lasic 2000b. More generally, many philosophical commentaries are either themselves rational reconstructions of earlier texts or contain such reconstructions. For a very useful discussion of the styles of commentaries see Griffiths 1999a. For a discussion of "rational reconstruction" as a kind of philosophical method see, for example, Bennett 2001 and Arnold 2005:11ff.

41. There are, of course, many other ways of meeting these transdisciplinary demands and expectations. This book is intended as just one example of how this can be done.

mands on me by requiring, for example, that I respond to them.[42] In my view, studying Ratnakīrti's arguments in such a location is necessary for properly situating his work (and that of Sanskrit intellectuals more generally) in the life of the academy, since it is here that a "normative" context is recognized in which it becomes possible to learn from Sanskrit philosophers in some of the same ways in which we currently learn from Euro-American ones.[43] As mentioned above, this book takes only a few preliminary steps toward studying Ratnakīrti's arguments in such a location. Although while reading and writing about Ratnakīrti's work I have participated in his philosophical project, by taking his arguments and conclusions seriously and making judgments as to their success and failure, I have chosen not to include these judgments in this work. I have, however, tried to make explicit the philosophical issues on which the success and failure of his arguments depend. A final evaluation of Ratnakīrti's arguments and the constructive work that I believe should accompany such evaluations is, unfortunately, beyond the scope of this more "historicist" project. What is presented here, however, is a necessary part of such a project and one that I hope will contribute to such work in the future.[44]

3. *Comparative* Philosophy of Religions

In identifying the six components through which this study is defined, I have not yet described why this work is comparative, as there is nothing in the *structure* of the theory of event-makers that requires that it be so. What makes this project specifically comparative, in my view, is the self-conscious

---

42. For some examples of what this context might look like see Krishna, Rege, Dwivedi, and Lath 1991, Chakrabarti 2005a, and Tatacharya 2005. There is a great deal of skepticism about both the possibility and desirability of such work. See, for example, Bronkhorst 1993 and Bronkhorst 1989, in which he reviews Oetke 1988. Also see Oetke's response in Oetke 1993. For an excellent example of what he calls "fusion philosophy" see Siderits 2003. Note that, in my view, Siderits' project could also be "comparative." Cf. Ganeri 2001.

43. For a powerful statement of this position see Cabezón 2006a, and for some excellent examples of how this can be done with Sanskrit philosophical texts, see the work of Arindam Chakrabarti, esp. Chakrabarti 1992, Chakrabarti 1997:211–245, and Chakrabarti 2004; Jonardon Ganeri, esp. Ganeri 2001; and Mark Siderits, esp. Siderits 2003.

44. For an interesting discussion of a "collegial" approach to the history of early modern philosophy that overlaps in interesting ways with my proposal see Bennett 2001:1–9.

bringing together of two or more components that are generally taken to be different.[45] This "bringing together" can be understood either as the bringing together of different components (e.g., two "different" patients or a patient with a "different" instrument) or as the bringing together of different features of a single, multivalent component, or both.[46] More specifically, what "brings" these different elements together is the fact that they are all related by an agent to a single event, which in such a context becomes, by definition, a comparative one.[47] The self-consciousness of this process is also significant, since what counts as "different" in such contexts is contingent: what is different for one agent may not be different, and therefore "comparative," for another. In fact, if this project is fully successful, it will someday no longer be viewed as one in the comparative philosophy of religions, but rather as one in the philosophy of religions without qualification. Most simply, what is "compared" in this book—that is, self-consciously brought together—are "different" instruments, sources, and locations in relation to a single patient (Ratnakīrti's arguments) and a single comparative event.[48]

There are three features of this comparative framework that are worth noting. The first is that it allows for both "narrow" and "broad" comparisons. By "narrow comparisons" I mean comparisons in which the elements that are brought together "touch" one another historically; for example, concepts, methods, or texts from sources I and II. That they "touch one another his-

---

45. In my view, it is "difference" that needs to be privileged when conceptualizing comparison. This is the case even if one is ultimately interested in pointing to similarities; cf. Smith 1982, Poole and Porter 1986, Mack 1996, Smith 2000:237–239. "Comparison requires the postulation of difference as the grounds of its being interesting . . . and a methodological manipulation of difference, a playing across the 'gap' in the service of some useful end" (Smith 1982, as quoted in Smith 2000:239). See also Smith 2004:20, a quotation from Smith 1986–1987:13–14.

46. For a similar idea regarding the multiplicity of what is to be compared see Smith 2004:23, where he also endorses Poole's remark that "Comparison does not deal with phenomena *in toto* or in the round, but only with aspectual characteristics of them." In my view, it is not phenomena that are most directly being compared, but components or "aspects" of them.

47. The qualification "by an agent" is necessary for the requirement that comparison be "self-conscious." In this view, one cannot produce properly comparative work without intending—in this minimal sense—to do so.

48. Although I speak of different instruments, beneficiaries, locations, etc., it is also possible to imagine each of these "different" components as being subcomponents of a single compound instrument, beneficiary, location, etc.

torically" means simply that there is a known (or plausible) historical connection between the elements in question. By "broad comparison" I mean comparisons in which the elements that are brought together have nothing to do with one another historically; for example, concepts, methods, and texts from source I and source IV.[49] Both kinds of comparison will be used in this book. A second feature of this comparative framework is the diversity in what can be "compared," that is, the *exempla*.[50] The *exempla* need not be merely religious traditions, practices, phenomena, ideas, texts/text-traditions, or individuals. Rather, the framework allows for comparisons between, and within, any component or set of components, regardless of what they are. Thus, not only can patients be compared with one another, but patients can be compared with instruments, and instruments with other instruments, beneficiaries, locations, etc.[51] From this it should be clear that the framework allows for a comparison not only of components but also of processes.[52] In each chapter of this book, different *exempla* are brought together with respect to the same patient. Thus, each chapter can be understood to exemplify a different form of comparison in what is still a single comparative study.[53] Finally, this framework allows for a complex metric for assessing the value of

---

49. Smith 2004:24–25, paraphrasing Owen 1843, writes "For Owen, homology, resemblances explained by common descent, were 'real.' That is to say, they were the sorts of genealogical comparisons favored by historians in order to demonstrate filiation, contact, diffusion. Analogies, by contrast, are 'ideal.' That is to say, they are mental constructions, they rest on postulated relations stipulated with respect to particular points of interest." Smith discusses this issue to signal his shift from homological to analogical comparison. This distinction is also used in Smith 1971 and developed further in Smith 1990:47–48 and Smith 2000:238, 240–241 n. 8. Also see Holdrege 2000.

50. For a related use of the term *exempla* in the context of comparison see Smith 2000:239.

51. Too often "comparative religion" is understood in terms of the bringing together of two or more *exempla*—that is, patients—from different religious traditions. This is, it seems, what justifies calling the comparison in question a work of comparative *religion*. In my view, however, this is a mistake. As my framework suggests, such a view is far too limiting. Like comparative work more generally, comparative religion requires neither that two patients be brought together nor that they be indexed to religious traditions. Instead, it could be the disciplinary location or beneficiary that makes a comparative study a work of comparative religion. Shifting attention away from a patient as being the only relevant kind of *exemplum* does not, however, simplify what is required of a comparativist.

52. See Smith 1987:85, where he makes a similar point.

53. For more on this see section 4 of this introduction.

a comparative study, in that the beneficiaries, whether groups of individuals or disciplinary frameworks, may be multiple.[54]

While I have devoted a considerable amount of space in this introduction to developing a framework of comparison, and to explaining how and why this particular project should be thought of as one in the comparative philosophy of religions, I will not discuss these issues explicitly in the chapters that follow. Instead, as I will explain below, these chapters are intended as examples of this framework at work. I hope that their success and/or failure will speak to the success and/or failure of this method and the desirability of the transdisciplinary space that I am trying to create. In the final section of this introduction, I want to turn to the structure of this book, its central arguments, and some of the ways in which its various chapters exemplify the comparative framework outlined here.

4. Content, Structure, and Arguments

In addition to this introductory chapter, this book is divided into two parts, each containing two chapters, and a conclusion. In part 1 I focus on Ratnakīrti's interpretation and critique of his Hindu opponents'—the Naiyāyikas'—most important argument for the existence of Īśvara. In chapter 2 I provide an introduction to religious epistemology in classical India. More specifically, I introduce the technical vocabulary on the basis of which all Buddhist, Hindu, and Jain theories of inferential reasoning were developed and provide an interpretation of specifically Nyāya epistemology. Particular attention is paid to the extremely sophisticated theory of defeaters, which has not yet received the attention that it deserves. The purpose of this chapter is

---

54. It is worth noting that here I differ from Smith, in that my view allows for and accepts what Smith takes to be of value in comparative work, but also allows for and accepts results that Smith does not choose to discuss. See, for example, his discussion of the "end of comparison" (Smith 2000:239), where he writes, "With at least two exempla in view, we are prepared to undertake their comparison both in terms of aspects and relations held to be significant, and with respect to some category, question, theory, or model of interest to us. The aim of such a comparison is the redescription of the *exempla* (each in light of the other) and a rectification of the academic categories in relation to which they have been imagined."

to provide a relatively detailed yet accessible introduction to the epistemological framework within which Ratnakīrti and his opponents debate the inferential argument for the existence of Īśvara (and nearly every other topic of philosophical interest). The patient of this specific chapter is the Naiyāyikas' Īśvara-inference, as it is understood by Ratnakīrti. The location with respect to which it will be studied is, primarily, location 1—Ratnakīrti's intellectual world. The instruments used, however, will include those that I have "inherited" from source I—Ratnakīrti's texts, and especially his conceptual vocabulary—but also those that I have "discovered" and "constructed" in sources II and IV—that is, both the texts to which Ratnakīrti directly refers and contemporary sources to which he could not. As with the chapters that follow, a scale of beneficiaries is intended, ranging from those who are most interested in the specific (and literal) details of Ratnakīrti's work, to those who are interested in its significance for him and those who are concerned with its significance for us.

In chapter 3 I discuss Ratnakīrti's critique of the Naiyāyikas' inferential argument. Here the patient is Ratnakīrti's most important arguments against the Īśvara-inference, as it was understood by Ratnakīrti himself. As in chapter 2, location 1 is primary, and I appeal to a wide range of instruments, sources, and beneficiaries. For most of this chapter it is instruments from source I that are of primary importance. Near the end of the chapter, however, and especially in section 5, the location shifts to location 2 (our intellectual world), and the instruments to those that I have "constructed" from source IV (contemporary Euro-American philosophy). Taken together, chapter 2 and chapter 3 argue that in addition to the Naiyāyikas' specific argument for the nature and existence of Īśvara, the target of Ratnakīrti's critique is the epistemological theory that supports nearly all forms of Nyāya religious reasoning.

Although Ratnakīrti's argument is presented as an "internal critique" of the Naiyāyikas' arguments, it is actually supported by specifically Buddhist philosophical principles. In part 2 of this book I focus on the Buddhist philosophical theories that underlie Ratnakīrti's critique of Nyāya epistemology. Through this I am able to provide a more comprehensive account of Ratnakīrti's thought and to illustrate the very close connection between Buddhist theories of mind, language, and epistemology. In chapter 4 I discuss the Buddhist theory of exclusion and argue that it is best understood as a theory of conceptual content, that is, as a theory of what our thoughts are about. I also show that it is the basis for Ratnakīrti's views of epistemic necessity, inference-warranting relations, and the problem of negative existential statements, central themes in his critique of the Īśvara-inference. In this chapter the patient is a theory that is neither obviously nor directly related by Ratnakīrti himself to his discussion of the Īśvara-inference. As in chapters 2 and 3, in studying this patient—that is, the theory of exclusion—I appeal to a wide range of instruments, sources, and beneficiaries. Like in chapter 3, it is instruments inherited from source I and those constructed from source IV that are the most significant. In this chapter, however, the location is defined more narrowly, by a single text from source I, namely, Ratnakīrti's "Demonstration of Exclusion." What is different about this chapter (and also the next two) is that its specific patient is transformed from being the subject of a specific chapter to being an *instrument* for studying Ratnakīrti and his Nyāya interlocutors' arguments about the Īśvara-inference, that is, the patient of the work as a whole.

While the process of transforming the theory of exclusion from a patient to an instrument begins in chapter 4, it is completed in the next chapter. In chapter 5, I show how Ratnakīrti uses ten key concepts to construct his view of the world and the kinds of entities in it. On the basis of this, I argue that Ratnakīrti's overall philosophical (and religious) project is to show how mind, language, and world together create mind, language, and world. The theory of exclusion is central to this. Ratnakīrti's worldview is fundamentally different from that of his Nyāya opponents, and in this chapter I try to show how (and why) there is no room in it for the Naiyāyikas' Īśvara. Chapter 5 also describes the metaphysics of modality (and epistemology) in a way that directly relates this issue to Ratnakīrti's arguments in part 1. As in chapter 4, the specific subject of this chapter—Ratnakīrti's account of mental images (*ākāra*)—is neither obviously nor directly related by Ratnakīrti (or his interlocutors) to his discussion of the Īśvara-inference. Unlike in chapter 4, however, where the location is defined by a single text from source I, here the location is Ratnakīrti's corpus as a whole. The instruments used to study Ratnakīrti's account of mental images in this location are primarily those inherited from source I and those constructed from source IV. It is in the concluding sections of this chapter (sections 5 and 6) that the transformation of Ratnakīrti's theory of exclusion and account of mental images from patient to instrument is complete, and its significance for studying the Īśvara-inference becomes apparent.

In chapter 6, the concluding chapter of the book, I argue for the religious significance of Buddhist logic and epistemology. Although there has been considerable interest in the relationship (or lack thereof) between Buddhist philosophy and Buddhist forms of religious practice, theories of liberation, etc., very little work has been done on the ways in which Buddhists like Ratnakīrti considered Buddhist philosophy to be of religious significance. In this chapter I provide an extended account of how Ratnakīrti's view of its soteriological significance relates to those of his predecessors. Based on Ratnakīrti's work, and that of his teacher, Jñānaśrīmitra, I also show how Buddhist logic and epistemology can itself be viewed as a kind of religious practice, and more specifically why it was believed by Ratnakīrti and his predecessors to be of soteriological value.[55]

55. As in chapters 4 and 5, in this chapter the patient—the religious significance of Buddhist logic and epistemology—is transformed from being a patient that is studied in location 1, defined by Ratnakīrti's text-tradition, to an instrument that is used to study Ratnakīrti's critique of the Īśvara-inference in multiple locations.

PART I

Epistemology

CHAPTER 2

Religious Epistemology in Classical India

In Defense of a Hindu God

PHILOSOPHICAL ARGUMENTS FOR AND AGAINST THE existence of God-like beings such as Īśvara have been important to the study of philosophy and religion in both Euro-American and South Asian contexts. This is in part because there is often much more at stake in such arguments than just the existence of an entity of one kind or the other—also at stake are both the worldview within which an Īśvara-like being is supposed to play a (central) role and the sense of self and way of life recommended by it. While such concerns may have informed Ratnakīrti's arguments with the Naiyāyikas, his texts are interestingly silent on the matter. For the most part, this is also the case with the writings of his Nyāya interlocutors. For both Ratnakīrti and his interlocutors, the significance of arguments about the nature and existence of Īśvara appears to lie elsewhere. In this chapter and the next, I explore what Ratnakīrti's texts explicitly and implicitly tell us about their debate and its significance. Along the way, I also provide an introduction to Nyāya epistemology and an analysis of Ratnakīrti's interpretation and critique of the Īśvara-inference.

For someone approaching Sanskrit philosophical texts for the first time, what is most striking and difficult to grasp is the language and style of Sanskrit epistemology. The technical terms and concepts that comprise this philosophical language were generally shared by Buddhist, Hindu, and Jaina intellectuals, even though their precise interpretations were often (if not always) highly contested.[1] As a result, it was often through discussions of specific technical terms and concepts that Sanskrit philosophers chose to express their views on very basic philosophical problems. This is particularly true for the terms and concepts used in theories of inferential reasoning (*anumāna*) in "classical" and "late premodern/early modern" India.[2] In Ratnakīrti's interpretation and critique of the Naiyāyikas' most important argument for the existence of Īśvara, he relies heavily on the technical philosophical vocabulary that he shared with other Sanskrit philosophers. The dialogical style and essay-like format in which he presents his arguments also assume a familiarity with the technical issues in terms of which the Īśvara-inference was debated.[3] It is not at all surprising, therefore, that Ratnakīrti's critical engagement with the Naiyāyikas' arguments often focuses on very specific, and seemingly trivial, logical and epistemological issues. Familiarity with the philosophical language and style of Sanskrit epistemology reveals, however, that Ratnakīrti and his interlocutors used this technical language to discuss very basic philosophical differences, whose significance extends well beyond the Īśvara debate. Without understanding this technical language, it is simply impossible to appreciate and understand even the general character of Sanskrit philosophy of religion, let alone the specific details of interreligious debates between Buddhist and Nyāya philosophers.

The purpose of this chapter is to provide an introduction to the philosophical language and style of Sanskrit epistemology, and to Buddhist and Nyāya theories of inferential reasoning more specifically. I seek to develop a conceptual vocabulary for understanding both the philosophical details of Ratnakīrti's debate with his Nyāya opponents and what is at stake in it. One

---

1. Compare and contrast, for example, the Nyāya *Tarkabhāṣā* of Keśavamiśra (ca. thirteenth century), KTBh, which is translated in Gajendragadkar and Karmarkar 1934; the Jaina *Tarkabhāṣā* of Yaśovijaya (ca. seventeenth century), YTBh, which is translated in Bhargava 1973; and the Buddhist *Tarkabhāṣā* of Mokṣākaragupta (ca. twelfth/thirteenth century), MTBh, which is translated in Kajiyama 1998. Also see Matilal 1986:22–26, 35–38.

2. I don't have much at stake in either the periodization or the conceptual commitments that may be implied by these terms. I am using them simply for convenience to refer to the period from (roughly) the fifth to the eighteenth/nineteenth centuries C.E. Cf. Pollock's use of "premodern" in Pollock 2006:1–36.

3. This style is not unique to Ratnakīrti, and in fact characterizes many Sanskrit intellectual practices, such as philosophy, theology, and literary theory.

of the methodological arguments being made in this chapter, and the next, is that it is only by paying attention to these philosophical details that we can discover what philosophical debates in classical and early modern India were really about. In providing an introduction to the language and style of Sanskrit epistemology, I hope to enable us to think with Sanskrit philosophers in their own idiom. To do this, I often follow their texts rather closely and try not to "prepackage" their arguments by interpreting them in terms of contemporary philosophical *debates*. At the same time, the issues that Ratnakīrti and his Nyāya opponents are writing and thinking about are not unique to Sanskrit philosophy. And while it is necessary to pay close attention to what makes their work distinct, it is also important to recognize what makes their work more universal. For this reason, I also interpret their arguments in more familiar philosophical *vocabulary* and, when appropriate, relate their work to more contemporary topics in Euro-American epistemology. A second methodological argument being made in this chapter (and the book as a whole) is that without our doing so Sanskrit philosophical texts will remain imprisoned in someone else's philosophical past. By attending to the details of Sanskrit philosophy in this way, I argue that it becomes possible to better appreciate what is at stake, explicitly, and to discover what is at stake, implicitly, in Buddhist-Nyāya debates about the nature and existence of Īśvara.

What is most obviously and explicitly at stake in these debates is the existence of Īśvara, and more generally the kind of being/object whose existence can and cannot be established through inferential reasoning. As I will argue, what is also at stake—though not quite so obviously—is the Nyāya approach to religious epistemology more generally. In this chapter I focus specifically on Ratnakīrti's presentation of the Nyāya position, and argue that the Naiyāyikas' argument is best thought of in terms of both the cosmological argument and the argument from design.[4] I argue further that the epistemological framework within which this argument is presented and defended is best understood as a "bivalent epistemology" in which knowledge and justification/reflective-knowledge are treated separately.[5]

4. These arguments are discussed briefly in section 2.1 and again in section 4.

5. My use of the term "reflective-knowledge" is based on Sosa 1991 and Sosa 1997. In Sosa 1991:143–145, he contrasts reflective-knowledge with "animal knowledge." He says that *animal knowledge* is a true, apt belief, where "apt" refers to a belief that is produced by an "intellectual virtue," i.e., a cognitive faculty that reliably produces true-beliefs for an agent

More specifically, I point out that the Nyāya theory of knowledge is a version of externalism, and in particular a kind of reliabilism.[6] In contrast, their theory of justification is best interpreted as a kind of "internalist foundationalism."[7] Understanding the Naiyāyikas' argument in these

---

(usually a normal human being) in a specific environment (usually our normal environment). In contrast, Sosa says that *reflective-knowledge* is a true, apt, and justified belief. For Sosa, a belief is justified only if it fits within a coherent set of beliefs, including a perspective on one's first-order belief as deriving from an intellectual virtue. A concept like this has also been used to discuss aspects of Nyāya epistemology; see, for example, Phillips and Tatacharya 2004:9, where Phillips uses the term "conscious justification," and Ganeri 1999a:152, where he refers to Sosa 1991:240. Note, however, that my interpretation differs from that of Sosa in that I attribute a foundationalist, rather than a broadly coherentist, account of justification to Ratnakīrti's Naiyāyikas. The specific form of the Naiyāyikas' epistemological "bivalence" will be discussed in greater detail in section 1.3.

6. The semantic range of the terms "externalism" and "reliabilism" can be quite broad, and, as with many philosophical terms, their precise meaning is often theory dependent and contested. In general, an account of an epistemic state such as "knowledge" or "justification" can be called an "externalist" account when it asserts that the absence or presence of that state depends on facts/features that are not "internally available" to the person in question.

By "reliabilism," I generally mean a Nyāya version of "process reliabilism." In general, according to process reliabilists, whether or not a belief is justified is a function of the reliability of the processes through which that belief was produced. In general, one doesn't have to know how a belief was produced for the belief to be justified, nor does one have to have any evidence that that belief was produced by a reliable process. According to process reliabilists, a belief is justified just so long as it was in fact produced by a reliable process. A belief-forming process is generally taken to be "reliable" to the extent that it tends to produce true beliefs. Some belief-forming mechanisms yield beliefs as output only when they're given other beliefs as inputs (e.g., inferential reasoning). Such belief-forming mechanisms are often said to be "conditionally reliable," since they tend to produce true beliefs when the beliefs they're given as inputs are themselves true. My view is that the Naiyāyikas are externalists and reliabilists about knowledge, but not justification.

7. I take this term from BonJour, in BonJour and Sosa 2003: part 1, and Fumerton 2006: chap. 4. As mentioned above, there is rarely (if ever) consensus on the precise meaning of technical philosophical terms such as "internalism" and "foundationalism," let alone "internalist foundationalism." On my use of the term, "foundationalism" refers to the view that there is a kind of justification for beliefs that does not require other justified beliefs—that is, there is noninferential, immediate justification. By "internalism," I generally mean a strong version of "access internalism," according to which the conditions that constitute having justification must be conditions that the believer has access to (and is aware of). Here "access" is understood to be the result of "apperception/introspection," which is itself taken to be direct and immediate, and therefore "foundational." There is, of course, a great deal of

terms—and more accurately, according to their interpretation of these terms—makes it possible to discover the technical philosophical issues on which its success depends and on which Ratnakīrti's critique is based.

Attention to Ratnakīrti's presentation of the Nyāya argument within this broader epistemological context also gives us insight into what is implicitly at stake in his debate with the Naiyāyikas. As I will argue, this has to do with the value of epistemology, and especially the value of justification. What emerges from an understanding of the details of Ratnakīrti's debate with the Naiyāyikas is his interest in the nature of philosophical arguments and the value of epistemology; the nature and epistemic significance of religious disagreements; and the soteriological significance of epistemology. The first two issues will be introduced in this chapter, and discussed at greater length in chapter 3. The third issue will be discussed in part 2, and especially chapter 6.

1. Interpreting Nyāya Epistemology

Sanskrit epistemology is concerned, most generally, with sources of knowledge—that is, with how we know what we in fact know—and with what it means to know at all. Throughout part 1 of this book, I will refer to these sources of knowledge as "instruments for warranted awareness" (*pramāṇa*) and to knowledge itself as "warranted awareness" (*pramā*).[8]

---

controversy about all of this. It is worth noting that in my view in order to be justified one must be aware that one is justified. This is discussed in greater detail in section 1.3.

In BonJour and Sosa 2003:7, BonJour provides a typology of accounts of justification, including internalist foundationalism: "On the one hand, there is the dichotomy between *foundationalist* and *coherentist* accounts of epistemic justification. Does such justification derive ultimately from 'foundational' beliefs whose justification somehow does not depend at all on that of other beliefs, or does it derive instead from relations of coherence or agreement or mutual support among beliefs, with no appeal to anything outside of the system of beliefs? On the other hand, there is the dichotomy between *internalist* and *externalist* accounts of such justification. Must epistemic justification depend on elements that are internal to the believer's conscious states of mind in a way that makes them accessible to his conscious reflection (at least in principle), or might it derive instead from factors that are external to those states of mind, entirely outside the scope of his conscious awareness? These two dichotomies cut across each other, so as to generate four prima facie possible overall positions: internalist foundationalism, externalist foundationalism, internalist coherentism, and externalist coherentism."

8. I intend the term "instrument" to be neutral in regard to the interpretations of "*pramāṇa*" as either a "means" (*pramīyate anena iti pramāṇam*) or an "event" (*pramā iti pramāṇam*).

Given the centrality of knowledge-sources to Sanskrit epistemology, one way to characterize and differentiate between rival Sanskrit epistemological theories is in terms of the number and nature of the instruments for warranted awareness.[9] This is especially so for the Nyāya and Buddhist theories that inform Ratnakīrti's work. Naiyāyikas and Buddhists disagree not only on the number of instruments for warranted awareness, but also on the proper interpretation of the terms "instrument," "warrant," and "awareness." As an introduction to Sanskrit epistemology—and the Naiyāyikas' argument for the existence of Īśvara—it is important to consider how these terms were interpreted by Nyāya philosophers, since this points to the bivalent epistemological theory within which Nyāya inferential arguments, such as the Īśvara-inference, are presented and defended.[10]

My use of the terms "instrument" and "sources of knowledge" is thus supposed to apply to the diverse interpretations of "*pramāṇa*" found in Sanskrit sources. In part 1 of this book I will generally use the term "*warranted* awareness" to translate the Sanskrit term "*pramā*." In part 2, however, in discussing Ratnakīrti's own view, I will generally use the term "*valid* awareness" (to translate "*pramā/pramāṇa*").

9. For Ratnakīrti's discussion of this issue see RNĀ (PAP 96–105) and Kajiyama 1998:30–38.

10. My interpretation of the "Nyāya" theory of epistemology is based on Keśavamiśra's *Tarkabhāṣā* and Ratnakīrti's own presentation and discussion of the theory. Whenever possible I have supported my interpretation by citing passages from the KTBh, and in many cases have also cited relevant secondary scholarship. In some cases the secondary scholarship treats Nyāya theories that significantly postdate Ratnakīrti's own work, and therefore it should be consulted with care. Unfortunately, it is beyond the scope of this chapter to fully defend my interpretation of Nyāya epistemology, which would require a systematic analysis of the *Nyāya-sūtra* (NS) corpus at least up to and including Udayana (ca. eleventh century) and the work of Bhāsarvajña (ca. 860–920).

The KTBh is an introductory text, or "handbook," of Nyāya philosophy. It was composed in the latter half of the thirteenth century, but reflects the viewpoint of an earlier period of Nyāya thought. It represents a point of view that is not, for example, overly influenced by the "new school" of Nyāya. The general theoretical framework discussed in this text is therefore closer to the viewpoint of Ratnakīrti's Naiyāyikas than to that discussed in other such texts, e.g., Annaṃbhaṭṭa's *Tarkasaṃgraha* (TS). It provides a convenient "baseline" interpretation of Nyāya epistemology, and in my view reflects the general viewpoint of the specific Naiyāyikas discussed by Ratnakīrti. I have supplemented the KTBh discussion when necessary. The account of Nyāya epistemology discussed in the following section is not, therefore, the theory of any particular Naiyāyika. Instead, it is a reconstruction and interpretation that is primarily based upon the KTBh.

1.1. The Theory of Event-Makers

Naiyāyikas (and Buddhists) interpret the idea of instruments for warranted awareness in terms of the Sanskrit grammatical theory of "event-makers" (*kāraka*).[11] As briefly discussed in the introduction, this grammatical theory provides a conceptual vocabulary for developing a general theory of "events" (*kriyā*) and does so by describing six semantic relations (*kāraka*) between the nouns in a given sentence and the event that is expressed by the main verb in that sentence.[12] This is important for Nyāya and Buddhist epistemology since both Naiyāyikas and Buddhists understand warranted awareness (*pramā/pramāṇa*) to be a mental event that is denoted by the verb "to know" (*pra+√mā*). Of the six semantic relations, or "semantic roles," described in the theory, three are especially important for Nyāya and Buddhist epistemology: the "patient" (*karman*); the "agent" (*kartṛ*); and the "instrument" (*karaṇa*).

Consider the sentence "Devadatta cuts the tree with an axe."[13] In this sentence the event is the action denoted by the verb "to cut." The Naiyāyikas

---

11. For the Grammarians' description of this theory see the "*kārakāhnika*" of Patañjali's *Mahābhāṣya* (MBh 1.4.23ff) and the "*Kārakaprakaraṇa*" of Bhaṭṭoji Dīkṣita's *Siddhāntakaumudī* in Bhattacharya 1974. For the Naiyāyikas' use of this theory see NBh, NV, NVTṬ, and NVTṬP *ad* NS 2.1.15–2.1.16. Also see Biardeau 1964:30ff, Cardona 1974:231ff, Ganeri 1999a:51–72, Kiparsky and Staal 1969, and Matilal 1985:372–389.

It is interesting (and important) to note that while contemporary epistemologists often appeal to ethical, metaphysical, psychological, semantic, or social-scientific theories to interpret epistemological concepts, Sanskrit philosophers almost always appeal to grammatical ones. For more on "background theories" in contemporary epistemology see Zagzebski 1999.

12. The "six semantic relations" are: (1) *kartṛ* (agent); (2) *karman* (patient); (3) *karaṇa* (instrument); (4) *sampradāna* (target, beneficiary); (5) *apādāna* (donor, source); (6) *adhikaraṇa* (place, location). For the description of these relations as "semantic" consider Cardona 1974:231, who writes, "Things are *kārakas* when they play certain roles in the accomplishment of an action. A thing may be classified in one way if it functions in a certain way with respect to any activity at all; or it may belong to a certain *kāraka* class if it functions in a given way with respect to a particular activity; and a *kāraka* classification may apply only if a certain action is denoted by particular items." Also see Vātsyāyana's discussion in his *Nyāyabhāṣya* (NBh *ad* NS 2.1.16), which is translated in Matilal 1990:43 and Ganeri 1999a:52.

13. KTBh 13–14. This example is also referred to at RNĀ (ĪSD 34.06–34.16) but in a different, though related, context. My discussion of the theory of "event-makers" is based on Pietroski 1998 and Pietroski 2000, and more specifically his analysis of agency, thematic roles, and actions. The relevance of Pietroski's proposals to Nyāya epistemology has been very helpfully discussed in Ganeri 1999a: chap. 2.

analyze this event as being constituted by two subevents, an intermediary, or "functioning," event (*vyāpāra*) and a final, or "culminating," event (*phala*). The final, or culminating, event is, in this case, the cutting of the tree. This is the event in which we are most interested. It is helpful to think of it as the final effect of the action expressed by the verb. Since the tree is the locus of this final effect, it is said to be the patient of the event.[14] The functioning event is an intermediary event in the causal chain that begins with the agent's effort (*kṛti*) and culminates in the final effect.[15] This event is usually represented by the initial contact (*saṃyoga*) of the axe with the tree.[16] According to the Naiyāyikas, the agent of an event is the one who performs the action that is the first member in the causal chain that culminates in the final effect of the event. This action is sometimes described as the "effort" (*prayatna*) motivated by a specific desire (*icchā*) of the agent. It is also described as what instigates (*pra+√yuj*) the event. In the above sentence, the agent is Devadatta. According to the Naiyāyikas, the instrument is the cause par excellence (*sādhakatama*) of the event.[17] It is usually represented by the axe. On this view, the instrument (i.e., the axe) is the cause whose functioning (i.e., contact with the tree) culminates in the final effect of the event (i.e., the cutting of the tree). Given this interpretation, an instrument is closely associated with a functioning event and, in an important sense, it is the instrument

---

14. "Final effect" also includes a change in the state of the patient (e.g., the softening of rice) or a change in its location. See Ganeri 1999a:56.

15. Ganeri 1999a:56. Also see Matilal 1986: chap. 4.

16. Functioning event: "A functioning intermediary is a producer of a *y* that is produced by *x*: Just as the contact of an axe with a tree is produced by the axe (*x*) [and] produces a cutting (*y*) that is produced by the axe" (*tajjanyas tajjanako 'vāntaravyāpāraḥ | yathā kuṭhārajanyaḥ kuṭhāradārusaṃyogaḥ kuṭhārajanyacchidājanakaḥ*) (KTBh 15 n. 1). Usually, functioning intermediary (*vyāpāra*) is defined as: "A producer of a *y* that is produced by *x*, given that it itself is produced by *x*" (*tajjanyatve sati tajjanyajanakah*) (KTBh 137). Given this definition, the functioning intermediary is that which produces the culminating effect, the cutting of the tree (*y*), given that it has the property of being produced by the instrument, the axe (*x*).

17. The term "par excellence" is interpreted in various ways. Some Naiyāyikas, for example, maintain that an instrument (*karaṇa*) is the cause that finally produces the event; the cause that seizes the effect (*phalopādhāyakaṃ kāraṇam*); or the cause that is excluded from a nonconnection with the culminating effect (*phalāyogavyavacchinnakāraṇam*). Given these interpretations, the contact of the axe with the tree would be the instrument. Also see NK (s.v. *karaṇa*), KTBh 113, ŚV Pratyakṣa vv. 74–75, Matilal 1985:373, and Ganeri 1999a:61. For more on this see below.

that functions.[18] An instrument can be described, therefore, as a cause whose functioning is just the intermediary event that culminates in the final effect. Given this conceptual vocabulary, the Naiyāyikas argue as follows: The complex event denoted by the verb "to cut" is constituted by an intermediary event "e" (i.e., the axe's contact with the tree) and a final event "f" (i.e., the cutting of the tree). Devadatta is the agent of "e" and the tree is the patient of "e." The axe is the instrument whose functioning produces the intermediary event that culminates in the final event "f."[19]

The conceptual framework provided by the theory of event-makers is directly applied by the Naiyāyikas to the mental event denoted by the verb "to know."[20] Consider, for example, the sentence "Devadatta knows 'p' by means

---

18. There are at least three different Nyāya views regarding the instrument (*karaṇa*). See Matilal 1985:372–378.

(1) The first view, which is usually associated with the older Nyāya school (*prācīnanyāya*), is that the instrument is the cause par excellence of the event. On this view, the instrument is the most excellent cause. See KTBh 3.10–3.11: "What is the instrument? It is the most effective instrument. 'Most effective' is the preeminent effective thing, which means that it is the most excellent cause" (*kiṃ punaḥ karaṇam | sādhakatamaṃ karaṇam | atiśayitaṃ sādhakaṃ sādhakatamaṃ prakṛṣṭaṃ kāraṇam ity arthaḥ*). It is also explained that what makes the cause "preeminent" and "most excellent" is that it "possesses the functioning intermediary." See KTBh 137 where it is said, in the notes, that the term "preeminent" (*atiśaya*) means "possesses the functioning" (*vyāpāravat*). Thus, the instrument is a cause that possesses the functioning (*vyāpāravat-kāraṇaṃ karaṇam*).

(2) The second view, which is usually associated with the new Nyāya school (*navyanyāya*), is that the instrument is, as discussed in KTBh 137, "that which is excluded from a non-connection with the culminating effect" (*phalāyogavyavacchinna*) and "that which does not produce the relevant effect with delay" (*yadvilambāt prakṛtakāryānutpādaḥ*). This same idea is expressed at KTBh 12.06 as "the cause which seizes hold of the culminating effect" (*phalopādhāyakakāraṇam*). Also see Matilal 1985:373. On this view what I am calling the functioning intermediary is itself the instrument. In the context of our example, this means that the contact of the axe with the tree, and not the axe, would be the instrument.

(3) The third view seems to be the view of Jayantabhaṭṭa (ninth century C.E.), who argues that the entire causal complex that produces the culminating effect is the instrument. Jayantabhaṭṭa thus rejected previous approaches to the problem by rejecting the distinction between a "most excellent" cause and subsidiary or contributing causes. See Matilal 1985:376 and, for a much fuller treatment of Jayantabhaṭṭa's views, Shah 1992:20–26 and NM 25–28.

19. Although cumbersome, this way of describing the event is supposed to make clear the various components of its definition, and also to make it easier to compare my discussion with that of Pietroski 1998 and Pietroski 2000.

20. See KTBh 14, and my earlier references to the NS corpus.

of 'I.'" In this sentence, the event is the awareness-event denoted by the verb "to know." Knowing-events, like cutting-events, are understood in terms of two subevents, an intermediary or functioning event and a culminating event. The culminating event is the warranted awareness (*pramiti*) that "p," where "p" is the object or content of that state of awareness. As such, "p" is taken to be the locus of the culminating event and is therefore the patient of the event. The functioning intermediary of the event is associated with the instrument "I" and is an intermediary in the causal chain that begins with the action of an agent and culminates in the final effect. A more specific description of the intermediary event will depend upon the nature of the specific instrument. For the Naiyāyikas, there are four instruments whose functioning could culminate in the final effect of warranted awareness. In addition to inferential reasoning (*anumāna*), the Naiyāyikas argue that perception (*pratyakṣa*), verbal testimony (*śabda*), and comparison (*upamāna*) are also accredited instruments for warranted awareness.[21] Associated with each of them is a somewhat different functioning intermediary. The agent of the event is, as before, Devadatta. With this conceptual vocabulary, the Naiyāyikas interpret the event denoted by the verb "to know" (*pramā*) as follows: They say that knowing-events are constituted by an intermediary event "e" and a culminating event 'f.' Devadatta is the agent of "e" (*pramātṛ*) and "p" is the patient (or object) of "e" (*prameya*). Warranted awareness is the culminating event "f" (*pramiti*). "I" is the instrument (*pramāṇa*) whose functioning produces the intermediary event that culminates in the final effect "f."

1.2. A Causal Theory of Warranted Awareness

The above analysis describes the basic structure of a knowing-event (*pramā*), by identifying a set of event-making components; by defining the relevant relationships between them; and by explaining how they come together to constitute the event. This structure is important since it reveals the broadly causal features of Nyāya epistemology, and the Nyāya theory of knowledge more specifically. As the above paraphrase suggests, in the Nyāya view, the final effect/event and the instrument are distinct, in that they are related

---

21. The instrument (*karaṇa*) of inferential reasoning will be discussed in detail in sections 2.2 and 2.3.

to one another as effect and cause. It is the aetiology (or causal history) of a state of awareness that determines whether or not that state of awareness is a knowing-event. The Nyāya theory of knowledge is thus best viewed as a causal theory of knowledge and, as mentioned earlier, a version of externalism.[22]

More specifically, the Naiyāyikas are "extrinsicists" about knowledge: What makes an awareness-event a knowing-event is the presence of an "epistemically special property" (*guṇa*) among the generic causal factors that bring about the event. This property is a necessary, but not sufficient, condition for it to be a *knowing*-event. Similarly, it is the presence of an "epistemically negative property" (*doṣa*) among the generic causal factors that leads to a nonknowing-event. This position is referred to as "extrinsicism," since both of these properties are external to (*parataḥ*) the collection of generic causal factors that are necessary for an *awareness*-event as such.[23] Unlike epistemically negative properties, the epistemically special property is almost always a property of the instrument. For example, if the "generic causal factors" that bring about the cutting-event described earlier include the agent, axe, swinging of the axe, tree, etc., then the special property that leads to a cutting-event (rather than a hitting-event) would be something like the axe's "making proper contact with the tree," "having a sharp enough blade," etc. Epistemically negative properties might be the agent's "lack of skill in wielding an axe," the axe's "having a dull blade," its "being swung with insufficient velocity," etc. As this example suggests, both positive and negative epistemic properties are often defined relative to an instrument and are, to a significant degree, instrument specific.

In contrast to Nyāya extrinsicism about knowledge, "intrinsicists" about knowledge argue that awareness-events that do not have an epistemically negative property among their generic causal factors—that is, a property that interferes with its causes and conditions—are knowing-events.[24] Awareness-

---

22. See Goldman 1992: chap. 4, for a reprint of an early version (1967) of his "causal theory of knowledge." For a more recent statement see Goldman 1999, in which he discusses his causal/reliabilist theory of justification. It is worth repeating that in my view the Naiyāyikas are not externalists or reliabilists about justification, but rather are so about knowledge. Given their bivalent epistemology, knowledge is an epistemic state distinct from being justified. For a discussion of a reliabilist theory of knowledge, see Dretske 1981.

23. For a discussion of this issue with textual references see Mohanty 1966:58–71, Phillips and Tatacharya 2004:10, Potter 1977:158–160, and Matilal 2002:154–159.

24. In addition to the references cited above, many of the relevant issues are discussed in Taber 1992.

events that are not knowing-events occur only because an external factor interferes with the causes and conditions that are otherwise necessary and sufficient for it to be a knowing-event. Unlike the intrinsicists, Naiyāyikas maintain that there is a basis for knowing-events, epistemically special properties. Like the intrinsicists, they maintain that there is also a basis for nonknowing-events—negative epistemic properties.

This analysis of a knowing-event in terms of the theory of event-makers describes the basic architecture of the Nyāya theory of knowledge. A more adequate analysis requires (at least) an account of "warranted awareness" and a more detailed analysis of "instrument." Attention to the Nyāya interpretation of these terms is especially important since it reveals the sense in which Nyāya epistemology is bivalent, and thus leads to a more nuanced understanding of the Naiyāyikas' interpretation of knowledge as warranted awareness, and to their theory of justification.

1.3. A Bivalent Epistemology

According to most Sanskrit philosophers, it is awareness-events/episodic states of awareness (*jñāna*)—rather than beliefs—that are the primary objects of epistemic analysis. Belief-episodes are generally understood as a special sort of awareness-event.[25] The Nyāya typology of awareness-events thus

---

25. See Heil 1999:44–48 for an account of "belief" and Matilal 1986:101–107 and Mohanty 1992a:134–135 for a discussion of the differences between "beliefs" and "awareness" (*jñāna*). Also see Shukla 1991 for a discussion of why Naiyāyikas have no room for a "third realm" of propositions. In general, for Naiyāyikas, awareness (*jñāna*) is a quality (*guṇa*) that is located in a soul (*ātman*). Unlike other "qualities" that are located in the soul—e.g., desire, aversion, pleasure, pain, etc.—awareness is directed towards an object (*arthapravaṇa*). Thus, desire, aversion, pleasure, and pain are not themselves awareness-events, even though we can become aware of them. For three very useful "charts" of Praśastapāda's (ca. sixth century), Udayana's (ca. eleventh century), and Annaṃbhaṭṭa's (ca. seventeenth century) typologies of awareness-events, see Nyman 2005:554, 556. KTBh 59–61, 74 discusses the soul. For more on the soul see Mishra 2006:301–330.

Although I will not argue for it here, I understand the verb "to believe" to mean "to think with assent"; see Zagzebski 1999:93 n. 4. For the Naiyāyikas, the phrase "awareness-event" (*jñāna*) refers to a much broader range of mental events that includes (i) dreams (*svapnajñāna*), which are usually classified as memory-awareness that is not in accordance

provides the conceptual context within which their account of warranted awareness, and beliefs, is developed.

According to the Naiyāyikas, there are two classes of awareness-events: presenting-awareness (*anubhava*) and memory (or re-presenting awareness) (*smṛti*). It is important that, for the Naiyāyikas, every awareness-event is intentional (*arthapravaṇa*), and that most are either in accordance with their object (or content) (*yathārtha*) or not in accordance with their object (or content) (*ayathārtha*).[26] The Nyāya position is also that the object of an awareness-event is distinct from the awareness-event itself.[27] Knowledge, according to them, is simply warranted awareness (*pramā*)—that is, presenting-awareness that is in accordance with its object (*yathārthānubhava*). Presenting-awareness is usually defined negatively as any awareness-event that is not a memory-episode. Memory-episodes are described as awareness-events in which the intentional object is one about which we were already aware, or as awareness-events that are produced from mental impressions alone (*saṃskāramātrajanya*).[28] When used in the context of presenting-awareness-events, the phrase "in accordance with its object" describes an awareness-event that is not produced through suppositional reasoning (*tarka*) and in which there is neither doubt (*saṃśaya*) nor error (*viparyaya*).[29]

---

with its object (*ayathārtha-smṛti*); (ii) memory (*smṛti*); (iii) awareness produced through "suppositional reasoning" (*tarka*); (iv) mislocation (or misobservation) (*viparyaya*); and (v) doubt (*saṃśaya*) (these latter three states of awareness are classified as presenting-awareness that is not in accordance with its object [*ayathārtha-anubhava*]); finally, there is (vi) warranted awareness (*pramā*). See KTBh 127.

26. See KTBh 86: "Awareness manifests an object" (*arthaprakāśo buddhi*), and KTBh 94.09–94.10: "All awareness is marked by an object since it is available to the mind only if it is connected with an object" (*sarvaṃ jñānam arthanirūpyam arthapratibaddhasyaiva tasya manasā nirūpaṇāt*); see also Potter 1984. For a useful discussion of "in accordance with its object" see Nyman 2005, who also refers to Goldman's "causal theory of knowing."

27. This refers to the idea that awareness is imageless (*jñānaṃ nirākāram*). KTBh 94.07–94.08 explains: "Moreover, all awareness is in fact imageless, and it is not the case that in awareness an object produces an image of itself" (*sarvaṃ ca jñānaṃ nirākāram eva | na tu jñāne 'rthena svasyākāro janyate*).

28. KTBh 94 and KTBh 128. For an excellent discussion of memory, with references, see Mohanty 1966:36–37 and Mishra 1934:177–186. See also the helpful discussion in Granoff 1978 and Perry 1995.

29. For suppositional reasoning, see KTBh 101.11–102.10: "Suppositional reasoning is reasoning to an undesired consequence. Moreover, it has the form of reasoning to an undesired

A presenting-awareness-event that is in accordance with its object is also described, more positively, as an awareness-event that is produced by a functioning instrument. According to the Naiyāyikas, a "functioning instrument" must be one of the four accredited instruments mentioned above and must be free from any defects (*aduṣṭa*). Let us refer to a nondefective, accredited instrument as a "well-functioning instrument." A knowing-event, then, is any awareness-event that is in accordance with its object and is produced by a well-functioning instrument. Since, in the Nyāya view, a well-functioning instrument necessarily produces a presenting-awareness-event that is in accordance with its object, a knowing-event can be described, more simply, as any awareness-event that is produced by a well-functioning instrument. For the Naiyāyikas, then, "knowledge" is warranted awareness, that is, a presenting-awareness-event that is in accordance with its object or, equivalently, any awareness-event that is produced by a well-functioning instrument.

According to this analysis, any awareness-event that is in fact produced by a well-functioning instrument will be in accordance with its object and will be a knowing-event. As I have presented it, the Nyāya theory of knowledge may naturally be interpreted as a version of reliabilism.[30] According to

---

pervader through the [provisional] acceptance of the pervaded when pervasion between the two properties is known" (*tarko 'niṣṭaprasaṅgaḥ | sa ca siddhavyāptikayor dharmayor vyāpyāṅgīkāreṇāniṣṭavyāpakaprasañjanarūpaḥ*). The idea is that if there were the absence of a pervader (e.g., fire) in the site of an inference, as an opponent claims, then there would also have to be the absence of the pervaded (e.g., smoke). But, there is not the absence of the pervaded. Thus the opponent's supposition is incorrect. One reason the Naiyāyikas consider this to be awareness that is not in accordance with its object (*ayathārtha*) is that the provisionally accepted awareness that the pervader is absent is known by the person entertaining it to be incorrect. Other Sanskrit philosophers, however, consider this awareness to be in accordance with its object (*yathārtha*). Although Naiyāyikas identify eleven different varieties of "suppositional reasoning" (*tarka*), KTBh discusses only one of them: the variety called reasoning to "an object that is defeated by an instrument of warranted awareness" (*pramāṇabādhitaviṣaya*). My translation of "*tarka*" as "suppositional reasoning" is intended to capture this use of the term. For more on "*tarka*" see the excellent discussion in Bagchi 1953; see also Davis 1981 and Patil (forthcoming, a).

For doubt, see KTBh 97.05–97.10: "Doubt is the awareness of there being incompatible properties in a single locus" (*ekasmin dharmiṇi viruddhanānārthāvamarśaḥ saṃśayaḥ*).

For error, see KTBh 94.01–94.03: "And error is grasping *x* when there is non-*x*" (*viparyayas tv atasmins tadgrahaḥ*).

30. For a brief description of "reliabilism" see note 6. See also Matilal 1985:70–72, Matilal 1986:138–140, and Ganeri 1999a:66 n. 26. On my use of the term, reliabilist theories of

most versions of reliabilism, knowledge is any true belief that is produced by a reliable belief-forming mechanism. In the context of Nyāya epistemology, we might say that on this interpretation a knowing-event is any awareness-event that is in accordance with its object (the truth component) and produced by a well-functioning instrument (the reliability component).[31] Notice, however, that for the Naiyāyikas, there cannot be a state of awareness that is both produced by a well-functioning instrument and not in accordance with its object. This is because the property "being produced by a well-functioning instrument" entails that awareness will be "in accordance with its object."[32] This is what allows for the simplified description that knowledge is, for the Naiyāyikas, any awareness-event that is produced by a well-functioning instrument.[33]

---

knowledge assert that what makes a true belief an instance of knowledge is that it was formed by a reliably truth-producing process, e.g., sense perception. According to reliabilist theories of justification, what makes a belief justified (or warranted) is that it was formed by a reliably truth-producing process. In most versions of reliabilism, it is not necessary that the reliability of "the process" be cognitively accessible to the agent. As a result, reliabilism is usually taken to be a form of externalism. See Zagzebski 1999:617–622. The Nyāya view, however, is not an example of "simple reliabilism," which also asserts that reliability is both necessary and sufficient for knowledge. One well-known problem with simple reliabilism is that it does not rule out, as instances of knowledge, beliefs that are accidentally produced by reliable processes or faculties. See Plantinga 1993a and Zagzebski 1999:620. In my view, the Nyāya theory should not be considered a version of simple reliabilism, since built into their theory that reliability is necessary and sufficient for knowledge is also an account of what makes a process reliable *in the right way*. See below.

31. See Nyman 2005.

32. This seems to be a somewhat controversial claim. My view is that according to Ratnakīrti's Naiyāyikas, there cannot be awareness that is in accordance with its object but not produced by a well-functioning instrument. One cannot, in other words, come to have warranted awareness accidentally. All putative cases of accidental warranted awareness are in fact the result of instruments that are, for one reason or the other, not well-functioning. For very useful work on this issue see Matilal 1986: chap. 6, Matilal 1990:65–68, 72–74, Matilal 2002:159–160, 177–180, Phillips and Tatacharya 2004:9–10. Consider, for example, that correct memory is an example of an awareness-event that is in accordance with its object, but not an instance of warranted-awareness. It is, therefore, clear that not every awareness-event that is in accordance with its object must be warranted. One reason for this is that such awareness-events are not "presenting-awareness-events" (*anubhava*). In my view, this means that awareness-events such as memory (and accidentally warranted awareness-events) are not produced "in the right way."

33. Zagzebski (1999:99–104) argues that it is a desideratum of any definition of knowledge that there not be a "gap" between the truth component of knowledge (for the Naiyāyikas,

Assumed in the typology presented above is another dimension to how awareness-events are characterized. Awareness-events may be either "unnoticed" or "noticed."[34] Unnoticed awareness-events are mental events that we are aware of only in the sense that we have them. Such awareness-events are mental happenings, even though they may escape our notice. Noticed awareness-events are awareness-events that do not escape our notice—we are aware that we have them. There are two sorts of unnoticed awareness-events: those that have nonconceptual content (*nirvikalpaka*, A_0) and those that have conceptual content (*savikalpaka*, A_c).[35] The content of nonconceptual awareness-events is taken to be, in principle, nonpredicative, inexpressible, and inaccessible to any form of apperception/introspection.[36] The fact

---

the "in accordance with its object" component) and the element that is added to it in the definition of knowledge, for example, justification (for the Naiyāyikas, the element "being produced by a well-functioning instrument"). She argues that closing this gap is the only way to avoid Gettier counterexamples. Entailment of truth by the second element is, she suggests, one way in which this gap could be closed.

34. My use of these concepts is based, loosely, on BonJour and Sosa 2003:120–121, where Sosa draws a distinction between "n(oticing)-awareness and e(xperiential)-awareness," interestingly, in order to argue against BonJour's "internalist-foundationalism." Here Sosa also makes the point that from the fact that one is e-aware of something it does not follow that one is n-aware of it. BonJour (BonJour and Sosa 2003:190) helpfully glosses this by saying that this is "a distinction between two sorts of awareness that one might have of a feature of one's experiences: (1) intellectual awareness or noticing ('n-awareness'), which involves believing or judging that feature to be present, and further requires that the belief in question be in some way justified or reasonable; and (2) experiential awareness ('e-awareness'), the sort of awareness that one has of the content of one's experience simply in virtue of having or undergoing it." This distinction is also relevant to the issue of "luminosity," which is discussed below in note 44.

35. For a discussion of this distinction see Bhattacharya 1996:25–34, Chatterjee 1978:-189–204, Mohanty 1966, Phillips 1995:122–125, Phillips and Tatacharya 2004, and Potter 1977:147–153.

36. Recently there has been a lively debate regarding whether unnoticed awareness-events with nonconceptual content are necessary for Nyāya. For arguments in support of the view that they are unnecessary see Chakrabarti 2000 and the response in Phillips 2001. Also see Chadha 2001 and the responses in Siderits 2004 and Phillips and Tatacharya 2004. It is worth noting that in a series of articles Arindam Chakrabarti takes a position on the following three issues in the philosophy of perception that are indirectly related to the issues that I am discussing in this section. For a discussion of (1) whether there are perceptual awareness-events with nonconceptual content, see Chakrabarti 2000; (2) whether there are awareness-events that are not self-luminous, see Chakrabarti 2003; and (3) whether there are nonlinguistic

that there are such states of awareness is established inferentially.[37] Moreover, these awareness-events are, unlike all other awareness-events, neither in accordance with their objects nor not in accordance with their objects—they are neither warranted nor unwarranted—and cannot be (what I am calling) a knowing-event. The content of unnoticed awareness-events with conceptual content (A_c) is taken to be a triad made up of a subject locus, a property, and a relation that connects the property to the subject locus.[38] The content of such awareness-events is predicative, in that the subject component of content is always propertied, verbally expressible, and accessible through apperception/introspection.[39] Moreover, unnoticed conceptual awareness-events must be either in accordance with or not in accordance with their objects—that is, they must be either warranted or nonwarranted. They are, therefore, the kind of awareness-event with which the Nyāya theory of knowledge is most concerned. When verbalized, the content of basic unnoticed conceptual awareness-events is expressible as "That (the subject component) is (the relation component) *F* (the property component)," e.g., "That is a pot." It may be helpful to think of such awareness-events as nonoccurrent belief-episodes.

According to the Naiyāyikas, it is not necessary that unnoticed awareness-events be noticed.[40] Nonconceptual awareness-events (A_0) are, for example, never noticed, even though they play a causal role in the production of other awareness-episodes. And although unnoticed conceptual awareness-events (A_c) are noticeable, it is not always the case that they are noticed. There are, according to the Naiyāyikas, many conceptual awareness-events that pass unnoticed.[41] Conceptual awareness-events are not self-luminous or self-intimating. Those conceptual awareness-events that are noticed, however, are noticed in virtue of becoming the object (content) of illuminating-awareness—a secondary, meta-awareness-event that results from the instrument of apperception

---

forms of conceptualization, see Chakrabarti 1998. For a brief introduction to these three issues, see Chakrabarti 2004. See also Kellner 2004a.

37. For an interesting discussion of this see Chakrabarti 2004. See also Potter 1977:161–168 and Bhattacharya 1996:26–28 for a brief, but useful, discussion of this issue in both the "old" and "new" schools of Nyāya.

38. See Bhattacharya 1996:26–28, 36–45; Mohanty 1966:30–34; and Potter 1993:24–33 for a discussion of, and references to, this characteristic description of the constituents of the content of conceptual awareness-events according to the later Nyāya school.

39. See Gupta 2006:176–179, Potter 1977:160, Matilal 1986:143–144.

40. For a useful discussion of this issue see Chakrabarti 2003.

41. See Matilal 1986: chap. 5.

(*anuvyavasāya*), a variety of perception. Illuminating-awareness (A_i) is a second-order apperceptive awareness-event.[42] When verbalized, the content of such awareness-events is expressible as "I am aware that that (the subject component) is (the relation component) *F* (the property component)," e.g., "I notice that that is a pot." It may be helpful to think of such awareness-events as occurrent belief-episodes. Both unnoticed and noticed belief-episodes can be either in accordance with their objects or not in accordance with their objects, and thus can be either warranted or unwarranted. It is, then, only such belief-episodes—that is, conceptual awareness-events—that can be candidates for being knowledge-episodes, regardless of whether they are unnoticed or noticed.[43]

This distinction between unnoticed awareness-events and noticed awareness-events reveals another aspect of Nyāya extrinsicism: in addition to being extrinsicists about what makes a conceptual awareness-event a knowing-event, they are also extrinsicists about what makes us aware of conceptual awareness-events. Conceptual awareness-events are not self-luminous or self-intimating. In order to notice them—that is, be aware that we have them—another awareness-event, illuminating-awareness, is necessary. This is also the case for knowing-events. It is not a part of the Nyāya view of knowledge that one must *notice* that one knows. Like awareness-events in general, conceptual awareness-events and knowing-events are not self-luminous.

---

42. By the term "apperceptive awareness-event," I mean a higher-order noticed awareness-event that takes a first-order unnoticed awareness-event as its object, but is separate and distinct from it. See NK (s.v. *anuvyavasāya*) for references to this concept in Nyāya texts. For my purposes, "apperception" may also be thought of in terms of "introspection" or "reflective awareness." For useful discussions of "apperception" and "introspection" see BonJour and Sosa 2003: part 1, chap. 4. For more on this see below.

43. This is based on the view that in order for an awareness-event to be "in accordance with its object" (*yathārtha*) it must, by definition, be an awareness-event that has as its content the three specific constituents discussed above. While nonconceptual awareness-events, like all awareness-events, are said to have the general constituent of "being about an object" (*viṣayatā*), only the content of conceptual awareness-events is constituted by all three specific constituents. For a very helpful discussion of this see Bhattacharya 1976:148–155, Bhattacharya 1996:36–44, Mohanty 1966:32–34, and Potter 1993:24–33. This way of speaking about awareness-events is primarily found in texts belonging to the "new" Nyāya school, and I will not go into further details here. Related to this issue is the idea that nonconceptual awareness-events cannot be the objects of apperception/introspection (*anuvyavasāya*): nonconceptual awareness-events are never illuminated and their contents go unnoticed. What we know about them, we know inferentially. See Mohanty 1966:32.

It is also not a part of the Nyāya view of knowledge that one must *know* that one knows. For the Naiyāyikas, knowing is not self-luminous either.[44] In order to know that one knows, one has to know either that the awareness-event in question is a presenting-state of awareness that is in accordance with its object or that the instrument that produced it is well-functioning. All that is required for warranted awareness, however, is that the awareness-event be a presenting-state of awareness that is in accordance with its object or, equivalently, that it be produced by a well-functioning instrument. There is nothing in the Nyāya account of warranted awareness that requires that one actually know, for example, that the instrument that produced it is well-functioning. In order to know that one knows, the Naiyāyikas insist, another knowing-event is necessary. This reveals a third dimension to Nyāya extrinsicism: the causes and conditions that result in our having an unnoticed knowing-event and those that result in our noticing this awareness-event do not result in our unnoticed or noticed awareness of it as a knowing-event. For this, another awareness-event is necessary. While our awareness of a knowing-event as an *awareness-event* is said to be the result of illuminating-awareness, our awareness of a knowing-event as a *knowing-event* is, according to the Naiyāyikas, the result of a certification-inference, a second-order knowing-event, which I will refer to as reflective-knowledge (A_r). Noticing that we have reflective-knowledge is said to be the result of illuminating-awareness. It is these two knowing-events,

---

44. My use of the term "luminous" is based on Williamson 2000: chap. 4, where he argues that hardly any mental states are *luminous*, in the sense that if one were in such a state one would invariably be in a position to know so. The issue of luminosity is, in the Sanskrit philosophical context, often associated with a variety of externalism. In this context the term "externalism" labels the idea that to have a state of awareness "*x*" does not entail an awareness of having that state of awareness "*x*." A state of awareness that is "external to" or different from the state of having "*x*" is necessary for an awareness of having that state "*x*." The Nyāya view is, as is Williamson's, opposed to what is usually referred to as the "KK-thesis." For the classic statement of the thesis see Hintikka 1962. For Williamson's discussion see Williamson 2000:114–117. As Mohanty (1999:197) describes the Nyāya view, "if K1 is knowledge of the object 'O' at time t1, K1 itself is not known at t1. K1 can be known, and is usually known, by another cognition K2 occurring at the succeeding moment t2." Also see Matilal 1986:138–140, Matilal 1990:70–72, and Ganeri 1999a:67 n. 26, where, summarizing Matilal's view, he writes, "Someone who by chance comes to believe truly that *p*, and so 'knows' that *p*, will not be in a position to know that he knows that *p*, i.e., truly believe that he truly believes that *p*." For some excellent work on Williamson's anti-luminosity arguments see Brueckner and Fiocco 2002, Weatherson 2004, and Ramachandran 2006.

knowledge and reflective-knowledge, that define the Naiyāyikas' bivalent epistemology.

There are two important differences between knowledge/warranted awareness and reflective-knowledge: warranted awareness is rarely voluntary, and its intentional object does not have to be an awareness-event. As a second-order awareness-event, "reflective-knowledge" is defined relative to a first-order knowing-event and does not itself refer to a different *kind* of knowing-event: every reflective knowing-event can itself be the object of a subsequent reflective knowing-event and thus, relative to it, a first-order knowing-event.

1.3.1. Reflective-Knowledge and Justification

This third dimension of Nyāya extrinsicism is directly related to "iterative awareness"—that is, whether and how one knows that one knows or, for the Naiyāyikas, is aware that one's awareness is warranted.[45] For convenience, let us stipulate that while warranted awareness has to do with knowledge, iterative awareness has to do with reflective-knowledge, both unnoticed and noticed. Let us stipulate further that having unnoticed reflective-knowledge is just what it means to have justification and that having noticed reflective-knowledge is being aware of this.[46] When verbalized, the content of unnoticed reflective knowing-events is expressible as "My awareness 'That is *F*' (subject component) is (the relation component) warranted (the property component)," e.g., "My awareness 'That is a pot' is warranted." Noticed reflective knowing-events can be expressed as "I am aware that 'That is F' is warranted," e.g., "I notice that 'That is a pot' is warranted."

For the Naiyāyikas, "justification" is not a necessary condition for a first-order awareness-event (A_c) to be warranted.[47] Rather, justification is closely tied to reflective-knowledge, the second-order awareness-event (A_r) that provides us with an epistemic perspective on the first-order awareness-event by certifying that the instrument that produced it was well-functioning.

---

45. This use of "iterative awareness" is a modification of "iterative knowledge" in Klein 1996:101.

46. The issue of "iterative awareness" is widely discussed in Sanskrit philosophy and has to do with much more than what I am calling "justification." See Matilal 1986:141–179 and Mohanty 1966:9ff.

47. BonJour 1985:8: "Epistemic justification is therefore in the final analysis only an instrumental value, not an intrinsic one." See also Sartwell 1992.

Justification is a "criterion" rather than a condition for knowledge; that is, it is a test for determining whether or not an awareness-event is warranted.[48] The Nyāya theory of justification, then, has to do with specifying and satisfying criteria through which one can determine whether or not an instrument of awareness is well-functioning. I will refer to these criteria as defining an instrument's "certification conditions" (C, see figure 1, p. 64).[49] Although some of the certification conditions provide a general account of what it means for an instrument in general to be well-functioning, these conditions are, for the most part, instrument specific, and need to be discussed separately in the context of each accredited instrument for warranted awareness.

Given the Nyāya position on iterative awareness, justification is not necessary for warranted awareness. It is only needed when there is legitimate doubt about whether a particular awareness-event is warranted.[50] Legitimate doubt can be raised either by oneself or by another person. In either case, justification is needed to remove it. According to the Naiyāyikas, removing this doubt entitles one to claim that the first-order awareness-event is a knowing-event and that the instrument that produced it is well-functioning. For the Naiyāyikas, justification is a kind of voluntary epistemic activity: while it is not necessary for warranted awareness itself, it is necessary for us to know that a particular awareness-event is warranted. When it has been determined that an instrument's certification conditions have been adequately defined and satisfied, let us stipulate that that instrument has been "certified."[51] A certified instrument is, therefore, one that has been shown, by an agent, to be well-functioning.[52] An agent who has certified an instrument in this way

48. Sartwell 1992:174: "By a criterion, I mean a test for whether some item has some property that is not itself a logically necessary condition of that item having that property."

49. This terminology is derived from Oetke 1994a:849 and Oetke 1991:471.

50. See Matilal 1986:165 and Perry 1995:157 n. 138.

51. For a use of this term in the context of Nyāya epistemology see Phillips and Tatacharya 2004:9.

52. There are two "levels" at which this determination takes place. Arguments about whether a particular instrument (such as a particular case of sense perception) is justified usually presuppose arguments about whether that type of instrument is an accredited instrument of warranted awareness. Unlike the Naiyāyikas, for example, Buddhists argue that only perception (*pratyakṣa*) and inferential reasoning (*anumāna*) are such instruments. In their view, verbal testimony (*śabda*) and comparison (*upamāna*) are reducible to inferential reasoning (*anumāna*). Since both Naiyāyikas and Buddhists agree that inferential reasoning (*anumāna*) is an instrument of warranted awareness, however, their arguments focus on the

is "justified," in the sense that this agent has fulfilled her epistemic obligations. "Being justified" is, therefore, the result of an epistemic practice and is, most directly, a property of an agent and only derivatively a property of an awareness-event.

As mentioned above, Naiyāyikas maintain that it is the presence of special properties among the causes and conditions that lead to an awareness-event that make it a knowing-event, and the presence of negative properties that lead to it not being a knowing-event. In addition to their causal role, these properties are also indicators that the instrument in question is either well-functioning or defective. These properties thus have an "evidential role" in that it is through an awareness of their presence that one is able to determine whether or not an instrument was well-functioning, and whether or not the awareness-event that was produced by it is warranted. The certification process can be understood, therefore, as being directed toward detecting the presence of these epistemically positive and negative properties.

Although the Nyāya theory of justification will be discussed in greater detail in what follows, it is worth noting here that it has the strong "internalist" requirement that an agent satisfy a set of "certification conditions (C)." It is also "proceduralist" in that it is the conduct of persons that is, in the first instance, justified or unjustified.[53] First-order awareness-events are justified only in the sense that the instruments that produced them have been certified by a person. As will become clear in what follows, this certification procedure is fallible.[54] As the Naiyāyikas themselves recognize, certification conditions are instrument specific, and, as a result, they must be discussed in the context of a specific instrument. The certification process as a whole, however, is itself taken to be a kind of instrument that is, most often, classified as an inference.

1.3.2. Certification and the Īśvara-Inference

The Naiyāyikas defend their inferential argument for the existence of Īśvara by showing that the instrument used to produce the awareness that Īśvara exists satisfies a set of certification conditions that are specific to the instrument,

---

certification conditions for that type of instrument and on whether the certification conditions that are specific to it have been satisfied.

53. My use of the term "proceduralist" is based on Rosenberg 2002:101–132, 203–248.

54. See Phillips and Tatacharya 2004:11–12 and Potter 1977:158.

inferential reasoning. Ratnakīrti's critique of the Naiyāyikas' argument focuses on showing that they have not satisfied these certification conditions and that they in principle cannot do so. On this interpretation, Ratnakīrti's debate with the Naiyāyikas is about the certification of the instrument used to produce the awareness that Īśvara exists. The Naiyāyikas claim that they have certified the instrument and that they are, therefore, justified in claiming that their first-order awareness of the existence of Īśvara is warranted. Ratnakīrti argues, however, that they have not done so and cannot do so. Their debate is framed, therefore, as a debate about whether or not the Naiyāyikas are, or even can be, justified. Before turning to the Naiyāyikas' specific argument for the existence of Īśvara, it is important to consider how the Naiyāyikas describe the instrument of an inferentially produced knowing-event (*anu*+√*mā*) more generally. The certification conditions for this instrument will be discussed in the next section.

1.4. Inferential Reasoning

Inferential reasoning has been referred to as the instrument of an inferentially produced knowing-event (*anu*+√*mā*). More precisely, the Naiyāyikas identify the instrument of this event with what is, strictly speaking, a component of inferential reasoning. This component is called the "special consideration of the reason property" (*liṅgaparāmarśa*).[55] This is a technical term that is itself defined in terms of two other technical terms, "special consideration" (*parāmarśa*) and "reason property" (*liṅga*). "Special consideration" is also called the "third awareness" (*tṛtīyajñāna*) of the reason property, and is among the epistemically special properties that account for inferential reasoning being a source of knowledge.

The standard example that is used to illustrate what this all means is the inference of fire on a mountain from the presence of smoke. In this example, the event being analyzed is an inferentially produced knowing-event whose

55. KTBh 120.08–120.10. Although somewhat infelicitous, I have chosen to translate "*parāmarśa*" as "special consideration" for two reasons: First, there is a long history of using the term "consideration" in the translation of this term. See, for example, Athalye and Bodas 1974:279, "consideration (of the sign)"; Ingalls 1951:30, 32, "consideration (of the middle term)"; Varadachari 1977:669, "consideration (of the mark)"; Matilal 1977:459, "synthetic consideration"; and Phillips and Tatacharya 2004. Second, by using the term "special" I hope to have marked that according to the Naiyāyikas it is not consideration as such.

culminating effect is the inferential awareness (*anumiti*) that there is fire on that mountain. The reason property is said to be smoke or the awareness of smoke. The instrument of the event is the special consideration, or third awareness, of the reason property. The reason why the term "special consideration" is described as a "third awareness" is that the event is usually analyzed in terms of three distinct awareness-episodes of the reason property. It is only the third awareness of the reason property that is taken to be the instrument of the event. Consider the following scenario: (1) Devadatta works in a kitchen with a wood-burning stove and repeatedly observes that wherever he sees smoke he sees fire. He observes, therefore, that smoke is pervaded by fire—that is, that wherever there is smoke there is fire. He commits this concomitance between smoke and fire to memory. This awareness of smoke in the kitchen is the first of the three awareness-episodes of smoke; (2) Sometime later, on a weekend camping trip, Devadatta wonders if there is fire on a nearby mountain after noticing that there is smoke there. This is his second awareness of smoke; (3) After recalling the previously observed concomitance of smoke and fire, Devaḍatta is again aware of smoke rising above the mountain. On this occasion, however, his awareness is that the smoke on the mountain is pervaded by fire. This awareness of smoke, which is his "third awareness" of it, immediately results in the awareness that there is fire on that mountain. It is this awareness that is called the "special consideration of the reason property" and is, strictly speaking, the instrument of an inferentially produced knowing-event.

Previously I defined an instrument of an event as "a cause whose functioning culminates in the final effect."[56] As described here, however, special consideration (*parāmarśa*) is itself the instrument. According to this interpretation, the instrument of the cutting-event described earlier would be the contact (*saṃyoga*) of the axe with the tree and not the axe. Earlier, however, the axe was interpreted as the instrument and, more specifically, as the "cause component" of the instrument. Its contact with the tree was interpreted as its "functioning component." On this "two component" interpretation of an instrument—according to which an instrument is "a cause that *has* a functioning" (*vyāpāravat kāraṇaṃ karaṇam*)—the reason property is the cause component of the instrument and its special consideration is the functioning component.[57] This

56. See section 1.1.

57. KTBh 137, quoted in section 1.1.

is in contrast to the interpretation of the instrument as the "special consideration of the reason property" (*liṅgaparāmarśa*)—which follows what may be called the "single component" interpretation. The term "special consideration of the reason property" can be reinterpreted, however, in accordance with the two component view such that an instrument of inferential awareness is a cause (the reason property) whose functioning (whose special consideration) directly produces the culminating effect (warranted inferential awareness). This modified interpretation is the one that I will follow in discussing the Naiyāyikas' argument.[58]

Naiyāyikas (and Buddhists) notice that there are two different inferential contexts in which a reason property can function as an instrument. In one context, the instrument is used to produce an inferential awareness for oneself. This inferential context is called "inferential reasoning for one's own sake" (*svārthānumāna*).[59] Since in this inferential context the inference itself is internal to the agent, it is said to have the nature of awareness (*jñānātmaka*). In the second context, the instrument is used to produce inferential awareness in another person. This inferential context is called "inferential reasoning for the sake of another" (*parārthānumāna*).[60] Since, in this case, the instrument is being used to convince someone else of what has already been inferred by oneself, the inference needs to be made explicit to that other person. It is therefore said to be linguistic in nature (*śabdātmaka*). More specifically, the inference is described as a compound sentence (*mahāvākya*) consisting of five parts (*pañcāvayava*). This compound sentence is the

58. See section 1.1.

59. KTBh 25.07–26.03: "Having grasped, by just oneself, through a special kind of perception, the concomitance between smoke and fire in a kitchen, someone who has gone to the mountains sees an unbroken column of smoke stretching from a mountain up to the clouds and wonders if there is fire present there. From seeing the smoke, a mental impression arises [and] he remembers the concomitance [relation], 'Where there is smoke there is fire.' Then he realizes, 'Here, too, there is smoke.' Therefore, he realizes just for himself that 'On this mountain, there is fire too.' That is inferential reasoning for one's own sake" (*svayam eva mahānasādau viśiṣṭena pratyakṣena dhūmāgnyor vyāptiṃ gṛhītvā parvatasamīpaṃ gatas tadgate cāgnau saṃdihānaḥ parvatavartinīm avicchinnamūlām abhraṃlihāṃ dhūmalekhāṃ paśyan dhūmadarśanāc codbuddhasaṃskāro vyāptiṃ smarati yatra dhūmas tatrāgnir iti tato 'trāpi dhūmo 'stīti pratipadyate | tasmād atra parvate 'gnir apy astīti svayam eva pratipadyate tat svārthānumānam*).

60. For a critical discussion and overview of these two inferential contexts see Prets 1992 and Tillemans 1984.

standard form in which Naiyāyikas present inferential arguments that are designed to convince others of what they themselves have already inferred to be the case.[61] It is, therefore, the form of the Naiyāyikas' inference for the existence of Īśvara and the kind of inferential argument that they defend in their work. What follows is an introduction to Ratnakīrti's discussion of this argument and the philosophical language and style in which it was presented and defended by his Nyāya interlocutors. It is through Ratnakīrti's presentation of this argument that the details of the certification process and the Nyāya theory of justification become apparent.

2. The Nyāya Argument for the Existence of Īśvara

Ratnakīrti's "Refutation of Arguments for Establishing Īśvara" (*Īśvarasādhanadūṣaṇa*) begins with a long introductory section in which he sets out the Nyāya position.[62] Here he presents their most important argument for the existence of Īśvara and describes, in some detail, their defense of it.[63] He does so by providing what could be described as a Buddhist perspective on the long history of Buddhist-Nyāya debates on this issue: he rehearses many of the arguments offered by his Buddhist predecessors; quotes, at length, the responses given by numerous Nyāya authors; and in some cases furthers an argument on behalf of his Nyāya opponents.[64] The purpose of this section of his essay is to present his opponents' position and highlight the issues that he takes to be most important for a successful defense (and critique) of it. It is important to note that although Ratnakīrti refers to and reproduces the views of specific Naiyāyikas, his discussion does not exclusively reflect the views of any one of them. Ratnakīrti's opponent can be described, therefore, as a "generic" Naiyāyika whom he rationally reconstructs from the long

---

61. KTBh 26.06–26.10: (i) This mountain possesses fire (*parvato 'yam agnimān*); (ii) On account of possessing smoke (*dhūmavattvāt*); (iii) Whatever possesses smoke possesses fire, like a kitchen (*yo yo dhūmavān sa so 'gnimān yathā mahānasaḥ*); (iv) And this [mountain] is like that (*tathā cāyam*); (v) Therefore, it is so (*tasmāt tathā*).

62. RNĀ (ĪSD 32.07–40.16).

63. For a discussion of the variety of arguments that Naiyāyikas use to establish the existence of Īśvara, see Chemparathy 1972.

64. For a discussion of these debates see Bhattacharya 1961, Bulcke 1947, Chemparathy 1972, Glasenapp 1954, Hayes 1988, Jackson 1986, Krasser 1999, Krasser 2002, Taber 1986, Van den Bossche 1998, Vattanky 1993, and Vetter 1997.

history of Buddhist-Nyāya debates.[65] What follows, then, is an introduction to this Naiyāyika's argument, as it is understood and interpreted by Ratnakīrti.

2.1. *Inferring the Existence of Īśvara: An Informal Description*

Ratnakīrti's Naiyāyika's argument for the existence of Īśvara is usefully interpreted in terms of both the "cosmological argument" and the "argument from design," or "design inference."[66] As with versions of the cosmological argument, the Nyāya version can be understood to have two parts.[67] In the Nyāya version, the first part of the argument seeks to prove that the world (*jagat*) was constructed by an intelligent agent/maker (*buddhimat-kartṛ*).[68]

---

65. For a very interesting discussion of this issue see Kellner 1997b:xxvii–xxviii.

66. The terms "cosmological argument" and "argument from design"—which is sometimes called the "teleological argument"—refer, strictly speaking, to two families of arguments. For a "history" of cosmological arguments see Craig 1980. For more contemporary versions see Gale 1991: chap. 7, Gale and Pruss 1999, Gale and Pruss 2005, Koons 1997, Koons 2001, Mackie 1982: chap. 5, Oppy 2006a, Oppy 2006b: chap. 3, Pruss 2006, Reichenbach 1972, Reichenbach 2004, and Rowe 1975. For a discussion of arguments from design/teleological arguments and the "design inference" see Behe 2001, Dembski 1998, Dembski 2002, Fitelson et al. 1999, Habermas et al. 2005 (where Flew, a prominent atheist, says that he now accepts a form of the argument from design), Leslie 1988, Manson 2000a, the articles in Manson 2003, McPherson 1972, Oppy 2006b: chap. 4, Priest 1981, Ratzsch 2003 (who argues that design can be perceived), Sober 2004, Swinburne 1968, Swinburne 1979: chaps. 1–6, 8, and Swinburne 1994: chaps. 1–4. For a useful anthology of relevant literature see Gale and Pruss 2003.

Potter (1977:101–107) insightfully refers to the Nyāya argument as a "cosmo-teleological argument." For an excellent discussion of the Nyāya argument as a "causal argument with *cosmological, moral, and teleological* variants," see Chakrabarti 1989:22. More recently, Collins (2003) considers it to be an "argument from design." K. K. Chakrabarti 1999:159–174 contains a useful comparative analysis of the Nyāya argument with some well-known historical versions of both cosmological and design arguments.

67. See Rowe 1997:331: "Within the philosophy of religion, a cosmological argument is understood to be an argument from the existence of the world to the existence of God. Typically, such arguments proceed in two steps. The first step argues from the existence of the world to the existence of a first cause or necessary being that accounts for the existence of the world. The second step argues that such a first cause or necessary being has, or would very likely have, the properties associated with the idea of God."

68. In what follows I will use the terms "maker" and "agent" interchangeably, and sometimes will also use the term "designer," depending on context.

In the Nyāya version, however, it is not argued that because there is a world—i.e., a something rather than a nothing—there must be a first-cause or self-existent being who created it, but rather that because the world has an apparent design—i.e., it appears to be an artifact—there must be an intelligent designer who made it.[69] In this respect it is unlike cosmological arguments and more like arguments from design. Unlike versions of the argument from design, however, where the complexity of the artifact is the basis for inferring an intelligent designer, in the Nyāya version it is not the complexity of the world, but rather the fact that the world is made up of parts, that is the basis for the inference. It is helpful, therefore, to think of the first part of the Nyāya argument as a kind of "hybrid" argument that draws upon elements from both the "cosmological argument" and the "argument from design." The second part of the Nyāya argument seeks to prove that the intelligent agent/maker/designer who constructed the world has the qualities that identify him as the God-like being called "Īśvara." These qualities include being single (*eka*), omnipresent (*vibhu*), omniscient (*sarvavid*), and eternal (*śāśvata*).[70] Since such considerations are usually taken to be beyond the scope of the design inference, the Nyāya argument is structurally more similar to the cosmological argument.[71] As with more familiar versions of the cosmological argument, relatively more attention is devoted to part 1. In Ratnakīrti's text, for example, issues pertaining to part 2 are usually discussed only in the context of defending part 1. This is, therefore, how the two parts of the argument will be discussed in what follows.

This initial description of the Nyāya argument has been very informal and for the most part neutral with regard to the epistemological contexts in which it is usually described, defended, and critically assessed. The Naiyāyika's own description of the argument is presented more formally, in the

---

69. Since Nyāya philosophers, and almost all other philosophers in classical India, believed that the most basic (usually atomic) constituents of the world are beginningless, the issue of how they came into being does not usually arise. Instead, the question is how to account for the construction of the world from the eternal things that existed prior to it.

70. RNĀ (ĪSD 32.07–32.12).

71. This is, for example, the view of Dembski (2002), the most prominent defender of the design inference. Paley 1890/1805 also suggests that this is beyond the scope of his analogical version of the argument from design. It is worth noting, however, that some defenders of the cosmological argument also insist that this step is beyond the scope of their argument. See, for example, Reichenbach 1972. This issue will be discussed in greater detail in section 4.

technical vocabulary of Sanskrit philosophy and in the distinctive form in which only Naiyāyikas present inferential arguments. Understanding this distinctively Nyāya form of the argument is essential for understanding Ratnakīrti's critique of it. I will return to my description of it as a "hybrid" argument in section 4.

2.2. *The Īśvara-Inference*

When the Naiyāyikas are asked how they prove the existence of Īśvara, Ratnakīrti writes that "they present this argument (*sādhana*):

(i) The object under discussion (*vivādādhyāsita*) [i.e., our world/the earth (or anything like it)] has been constructed by an intelligent agent (*buddhimaddhetuka*).
(ii) On account of being an effect (*kāryatva*).
(iii) Each and every effect has been constructed by an intelligent agent, just like a pot.
(iv) And, the [world/earth] is an effect.
(v) Therefore, it has been constructed by an intelligent agent."[72]

It is understood that the "intelligent agent" referred to in the argument will later be shown to be Īśvara. This five-part inference is the standard form in which Naiyāyikas (and not Buddhists) present inferential arguments. Each step in the argument is interpreted as a separable part of a single compound sentence that, strictly speaking, constitutes an inference-for-the-sake-of-another. This compound sentence is helpfully interpreted as a conjunction of the five subexpressions that are the steps of the argument. The purpose of the argument is to produce for/in another person the warranted awareness that the world is constructed by an intelligent agent.[73] In order to interpret this argument, it is helpful to first describe it in terms of its five steps and the five technical terms that, for the most part, constitute them.

72. RNĀ (ĪSD 32.14–32.18): *vivādādhyāsitaṃ buddhimaddhetukam | kāryatvāt | yat kāryaṃ tad buddhimaddhetukam iti | yathā ghaṭaḥ | kāryaṃ cedam | tasmād buddhimaddhetukam iti.*

73. This raises the question of the relationship between these verbal expressions and the states of awareness that are supposed to be produced upon hearing and understanding them.

The first step in the argument states what the person presenting the argument has already inferred to be the case through an inference-for-one's-own-sake.[74] The term "the object under discussion" marks the "site of the inference" (*pakṣa*), which in this case is the world. The site of an inference is generally defined as "a property possessor in which there is doubt about a target property" (*sandigdhasādhyadharmā dharmī*).[75] More simply, it is that about which there is some kind of doubt or disagreement. In this case, the doubt or disagreement is about whether or not the world has been constructed by an intelligent agent. The term "constructed by an intelligent agent" is what is to be proved (*sādhya*). It is also described as the "target property" (*sādhya-dharma*), and thus expresses (in part) what is supposed to be inferred by someone about the site of the inference.[76] The term "on account of being an effect" is called the "reason property" (*hetu, liṅga*). As mentioned above, this is the instrument of the knowing-event that is supposed to be produced through the five steps of the argument. The second step of the argument is interpreted as asserting that the reason property is present in the site of the inference. It is often said that this step asserts that the reason property is a "property of the site" (*pakṣadharmatā*).[77] The third step of the

---

74. This step is named the "Hypothesis" (*Pratijñā*). It is defined in KTBh 100.10 as follows: "The Hypothesis is a statement which explains that a property possessor is characterized by the property which is to be proved" (*sādhyadharmaviśiṣṭadharmipratipādakaṃ vacanaṃ pratijñā*). This step is also described as: "The statement that the site of the inference has the target property" (*sādhyavattvena pakṣavacanam*).

75. KTBh 34.12. The terms "property" and "property possessor" will be interpreted on the "property-location" model developed by Matilal (1998:19, 143–165). This model interprets the terms "property" (*dharma*) and "property possessor" (*dharmin*) as they are used by Sanskrit philosophers. Briefly, Matilal's model recognizes that the relationship between "property" and "property possessor" is much broader than the subject/predicate relationship with which it is usually compared. For example, properties (*dharma*) include qualities (e.g., color, shape), attributes (e.g., motion of a body), universals (e.g., cow-ness, fire-ness), general terms (e.g., fire), and individuals (e.g., a pot). Property possessors (*dharmin*) are any locus in which such properties can be present.

76. See Mohanty 1992a:104ff. and Nieuwendijk 1992:411. This term is variously described in Ratnakīrti's text, e.g., "intelligent-maker," "intelligence-possessor," "intelligent cause," "person," etc.

77. The term "*hetu*" (reason property) is usually used to name this step of an inferential argument, while the term "*liṅga*" (reason property) is used to name the reason property. Since Ratnakīrti uses the term "*hetu*" to refer to the reason property, I will not follow the

argument states the inference-warranting relation called "pervasion" (*vyāpti*) and provides an "example" (*dṛṣṭānta*) of a locus where this relation is instanced.[78] In this case, the example is a "positive example," which is defined as "a property possessor in which the target property has been clearly ascertained" (*niścitasādhyadharmā dharmī*). In order to function as an example, however, the locus cited must be one about which both the proponent of the argument and the "beneficiary" of the argument agree. The fourth step of the inferential argument is similar to step ii, in that it too is one in which the presence of the reason property in the site of the inference is expressed. This step is interpreted, however, as expressing the "special consideration" (*parāmarśa*), or third awareness, of the reason property. Step ii expresses that the reason property is a property of the site of the inference. Step iv expresses that the reason property that is a property of the site of the inference is pervaded by the target property. In other words, step iv is what I described earlier as the "functioning intermediary" (*vyāpāra*), and here will call the "functioning component," of the instrument.[79] The fifth step of the argument states the conclusion of the inference and expresses the culminating effect (*phala*) of the event.[80] By following the steps of this argument, a person

---

usual Nyāya convention. When I refer to step (ii) of an inferential argument, however, I will capitalize the term, i.e., *Hetu*.

Given this, this step is named the "Reason" (*Hetu*). KTBh 101.01 explains that: "The Reason (*Hetu*) is the statement in which the reason property is explained" (*liṅgapratipādakaṃ vacanaṃ hetuḥ*). This step is also described in the SP as: "The Reason is the statement that the reason property is a property of the site of the inference" (*liṅgasya pakṣadharmatvavacanaṃ hetuḥ*).

78. This step is named the "example" (*udāharaṇa*)." KTBh 101.03 says that: "The example is a statement of an example together with pervasion" (*savyāptikaṃ dṛṣṭāntavacanam udāharaṇam*).

79. This step is named the "application" (*upanaya*). KTBh 101.04 says that: "The application is a statement which draws together the reason property and the site of the inference" (*pakṣe liṅgopasaṃhāravacanam upanayaḥ*). The SP says: "The application is a statement of the special consideration [of the reason property]" (*parāmarśatvavacanam upanayaḥ*). The phrase "This is like that" (*tathā cāyam*) is the standard form in which this step is usually expressed. "Like that" (*tathā*) refers to the reason property's being pervaded by the target property. "This" refers to the site of the inference.

80. This step is named the "conclusion" (*nigamana*). KTBh 101.10 says that: "The conclusion is a statement which sums up what is to be proved" (*sādhyopasaṃhāravacanaṃ nigamanam*).

is supposed to conclude that the world was constructed by an intelligent agent.[81]

The structure of the Nyāya argument may (initially) seem unnecessarily complex; for example, from the perspective of first-order predicate logic, steps ii and iii alone could yield, by *modus ponens*, the conclusion expressed in step v.[82] Rival Sanskrit philosophers also considered the Nyāya argument to involve far too many steps, and argued variously that steps i, iv, and v were unnecessary. Buddhists, for example, thought that steps ii and iii alone were jointly necessary and sufficient for an inference-for-the-sake-of-another.[83] That the Naiyāyikas chose to retain their five-part inferential structure in opposition to such critics reveals that their theory of inferential reasoning is interestingly different from those of their Buddhist opponents, and suggests that it might work against some of our contemporary intuitions about what should constitute a good inferential argument. What most Sanskrit philosophers agreed upon, however, was the importance of steps ii and iii. These two steps can be interpreted as constituting the instrument of inferential awareness, as understood by the Naiyāyikas. Step ii, the step in which the reason property is stated, can be interpreted as the "cause component" of the instrument and step iii—as a necessary part of step iv—can be interpreted as the "functioning component." It is not surprising, therefore, that disagreements about this and almost all inferential arguments focused on the nature of the instrument. Since, in my "two-component" interpretation, it is the reason property that functions, I will refer to it as the instrument.

2.3. *Certification Conditions*

According to the Naiyāyikas, a reason property must have five characteristics (*pañcarūpāṇi*, P) if it is to be a well-functioning instrument of inferential awareness (*anumiti-karaṇa*).[84] Without even one of these characteristics, a

---

81. "Following" the steps requires hearing and (properly) understanding, in sequence, the five verbal expressions that constitute the argument.

82. See Mohanty 1992a: chap. 4.

83. See Kajiyama 1998:72–75 and Mookherjee 1975:356ff.

84. KTBh 31.10–33.07: "Moreover, these five characteristics are (P1) 'being a property of the site of the inference'; (P2) 'being present in a similar case'; (P3) 'being excluded from dissimilar cases'; (P4) 'having an undefeated object'; (P5) 'not having a rival'" (*tāni pañcarūpāṇi tu pakṣadharmatvaṃ sapakṣe sattvaṃ vipakṣād vyāvṛttir abādhitaviṣayam asatpratipakṣatvaṃ*

proposed reason property is said to be a "non-reason" (*ahetu*) or one that only appears to be a reason.[85] Naiyāyikas further describe such reasons as being defective (*duṣṭa*) and identify five specific defects, whose presence indicates that the proposed reason property is not a well-functioning instrument. These five "defects of a reason property" (*hetvābhāsa*, H) are loosely linked with the absence of at least one of the five characteristics.[86] Determining that a particular instrument of inferential awareness is well-functioning requires determining that none of the five possible defects apply to the proposed reason property/instrument. Earlier, this was referred to as satisfying a set of certification conditions (C) for the instrument. Although this is phrased in terms of the elimination of defects, it is important to note that the elimination of some of these defects is taken to reveal the presence of some of the epistemically special properties that are necessary for knowing-events.

According to the Naiyāyikas, the satisfaction of a set of certification conditions shows that a reason property is not defective, and therefore that the instrument that is defined by it is well-functioning and the awareness-event that is produced by it is a knowing-event. Certifying an instrument in this way is also how the Naiyāyikas defend the inferential argument of which it is a part. In order to understand how the Naiyāyikas defend their argument for the existence of Īśvara, it is necessary to first consider why the Naiyāyikas believe that certifying an instrument is sufficient for both defending an inferential argument and being justified in believing that the awareness-event produced by it is a knowing-event.

Although the five defects referred to above are defined as defects of a reason property, they can be usefully divided into three sets of certification conditions that are individuated according to how they relate to the argument as a whole. Certification conditions (C), then, are also the conditions that must be satisfied in order to properly defend an inferential argument.

---

ceti). These five characteristics are, strictly speaking, only required for reason properties that have both positive and negative concomitance with a target property (*anvaya-vyatirekī hetuḥ*). Those that have only positive concomitance (*kevalānvayī*) require P1, P2, P4, and P5. Those that have only negative concomitance (*kevalavyatirekī*) require P1, P3, P4, and P5. Since the reason property in the Naiyāyikas' argument is of the first type, I will only consider reason properties that have both positive and negative concomitance with the target (*anvaya-vyatirekī hetuḥ*).

85. KTBh 34.05: *hetuvad ābhāsate*.

86. For a useful survey of the different Buddhist and Nyāya accounts of these "defects" see Gokhale 1992: chaps. 5–6 and Pandeya 1984.

Since certification conditions are themselves defined in terms of the defects of a reason property (H), *showing* that a certification condition has been satisfied requires showing that the defects of the reason property that define it do not apply. By showing that none of the five possible defects of a reason property apply to a particular reason property, the Naiyāyikas are thus able to show

FIGURE 1. Certification Conditions

C1: Performance Conditions

P1
H1a: "unestablished in the site of the inference" (*āśraya-asiddha*)

C2: Instrument Conditions/Triple Conditions

C2.1: P1, T1
H1b: "unestablished in itself" (*svarūpa-asiddha*)

C2.2: P2, T2, V
H2: "opposed" (*viruddha*) [a direct defeater]
H3b: "uncommon" (*asādhāraṇa-anaikāntika*)
H3c: "not universal" (*anupasaṃhārin*)

C2.3: P3, T3, V
H2: "opposed" (*viruddha*) [an indirect defeater]
H3a_1: "generally inconclusive" (*sādhāraṇa-anaikāntika*) [a direct defeater]
H3a_2: "generally inconclusive" (*sādhāraṇa-anaikāntika*)
[an underminer called "doubt about the exclusion of the reason property from dissimilar cases" (*sandigdha-vipakṣa-vyāvṛtti*)]
H3c: "not universal" (*anupasaṃhārin*)

U:
H1c: "unestablished in being pervaded" (*vyāpyatva-asiddha*)

C3: Argument Conditions

P4:
H4: "equal in scope" (*prakaraṇasama*)

P5:
H5: "too late" (*kālātyāpadiṣṭa*)

C = certification condition; H = defects of a reason property (*hetvābhāsa*); P = one of the five characteristics of a reason property (*pañcarūpa*); T = triple condition (*trairūpya*); U = additional condition (*upādhi*); V = deviation (*vyabhicāra*).

that the certification conditions for the argument as a whole have been satisfied, and therefore that the awareness-event that is produced by it is a knowing-event. The Naiyāyikas' account of certification, for both the reason property/instrument and the inferential argument as a whole, can be understood in terms of three sets of certification conditions (C), the five characteristics of a reason property (P), and the five associated defects (H) (figure 1).

2.3.1. C1: Performance Conditions

The first set of certification conditions are "performance conditions" (C1).[87] These conditions have to do with whether an inferential argument is presented correctly, that is, with whether there are the requisite number of steps, whether the terms of the argument are satisfactory, etc. Strictly speaking, this condition is not necessary, since if the second and third sets of certification conditions are satisfied C1 will also be satisfied.[88] This may account for why only one such condition is usually specified, even though in principle there could be conditions for each and every step and term of an inferential argument. The performance condition most often specified and discussed is defined in terms of the first characteristic of a reason property (P1): A reason property must be known to be a property of the site of the inference. A reason property that lacks this property is said to be "unestablished" (*asiddha*, H1).[89] This defect has at least three subtypes that are individuated by the different ways in which a reason property may not be a property of the site of the inference.[90] Certification condition C1, however, is defined in terms of just the first major subtype (H1a), which is called "unestablished in the site of the inference" (*āśraya-asiddha*). A reason property is said to have this defect when the site of the inference in which it is supposed to be located is known not to exist.[91] Although this subtype of

87. Oetke 1994a:849.

88. Oetke 1994b also makes this point.

89. KTBh 35.07–38.04 and KTBh 104.02–113.01.

90. KTBh 105.08: *āśraya-asiddha* (H1a); KTBh 105.09–107.02: *svarūpa-asiddha* (H1b); KTBh 107.03–110.05, of which there are four subtypes; and KTBh 110.07–113.02: *vyāpyatva-asiddha* (H1c), of which there are two subtypes. H1c will be discussed in chapter 3.

91. KTBh 106.01 gives the following definition and example. Df (H1a): "A reason property which is known to not be in the site is [called] 'unestablished in the site'" (*tatra yasya*

the defect is defined in terms of the reason property, it is more easily understood as a necessary condition for the site of an inference: it specifies that the site of an inferential argument must be known to exist. The absence of defect H1a is most usefully interpreted, therefore, as a performance condition (C1) of the argument.

2.3.2. C2: Instrument Conditions

The second set of certification conditions are "instrument conditions" (C2), or the "triple conditions" (*trairūpya*, T), of a reason property.[92] These three conditions are defined in terms of defects associated with the first (P1), second (P2), and third (P3) characteristics of a reason property. The presence of these defects directly prevents a reason property from being a well-functioning instrument of awareness, since each one directly prevents the special consideration, or third awareness, that is its functioning. For example, a reason property cannot be a well-functioning instrument without the functioning component that directly results in its culminating effect, inferential awareness. As I mentioned above, this functioning component is the special consideration, or third awareness, of the reason property, and is primarily represented by step iv of the inferential argument. There are two necessary subcomponents of this functioning: step ii, the first awareness of the reason property, in which the reason property is known to be a property of the site of the inference (the "site subcomponent"), and step iii, the "second" awareness of the reason property, in which the reason property is

---

hetor āśrayo nāvagamyate sa āśrayāsiddhaḥ). Example: "A sky-lotus [site] is fragrant [target] on account of being a lotus [reason], like a water-lotus" (*gaganāravindaṃ surabhi | aravindatvāt | sarojāravindavat*).

92. The secondary literature on the "triple conditions" is extensive. See, for example, Franco 1984, Katsura 1983, Katsura 1985, Katsura 2004, Nenninger 1992, Oetke 1994b (and the numerous references contained therein), Patil (forthcoming, a), and Tachikawa 1971. Some of the best recent work on these conditions can be found in Katsura and Steinkellner 2004. In my discussion of these conditions, I will follow the "epistemic" rather than the "ontic" interpretation, and also in its "strongest version." See Oetke 1994a:846, where he describes the strongest version of the epistemic interpretation of the conditions as follows: (T1') the reason property must be known to occur in the site of the inference; (T2') it must be known that the reason property occurs together with the target property in some locus other than the site of the inference; (T3') it must be known that the reason property does not exist in any dissimilar locus and there is a locus in which neither the reason property nor the target property are present.

shown to be one of the terms in the inference-warranting relation of pervasion (the "pervasion subcomponent"). Interestingly, it is toward the satisfaction of the three instrument conditions that the Naiyāyikas direct most of their attention, and where Ratnakīrti chooses to direct his criticism.

The first of the three triple-conditions (T1) is defined in terms of the second major subtype (H1b) of the defect "unestablished." This subtype is called "unestablished in itself" (*svarūpa-asiddha*) and applies to a reason property that is itself known not to be present in the site of the inference.[93] The presence of this defect directly prevents the reason property from being a well-functioning instrument, since without being a property of the site of the inference a reason property will not possess one of the necessary subcomponents for its functioning. H1b thus blocks the proper functioning of the instrument and defeats the argument.

The second triple-condition (T2) is defined in terms of the second characteristic (P2) of a reason property: A reason property (*hetu*) must be known to exist in a similar case (*sapakṣa*); that is, a locus other than the site of the inference in which the target property is also present. An instrument that lacks this property is said to be "opposed" (*viruddha*) (H2).[94] More precisely, the presence of this defect is defined in terms of a reason property that is known to be pervaded by the absence of the target property. This establishes that the reason property is not present in a single similar case (*sapakṣa*) and that it is present in at least one dissimilar case (*vipakṣa*).[95] A reason property with this defect is said to be "opposed" since it proves what is *opposed to* what is to be proved (*sādhya-viparyaya*). It directly prevents the functioning of the instrument since it defeats the second subcomponent of its functioning—i.e., pervasion. It does so by establishing, first, that the reason property is not known to occur together with the target property in some locus other than the site of the inference and, second, that it is present in a dissimilar case. A second defect associated with the absence of this characteristic (P2) is a subtype of the defect known as incon-

93. KTBh 107.03–110.05 gives the following definition. Df (H1b): "A reason property which is itself known to not be present in the site is said to be 'unestablished in itself'" (*yo hetur āśraye naivāgamyate sa svarūpāsiddha ucyate*).

94. See RNĀ (ĪSD 33.21). KTBh 113.04–113.08 gives the following definition and example. Df (H2): "A reason property that is pervaded by what is opposed to the target property is 'opposed'" (*sādhyaviparyayavyāpto hetur viruddhaḥ*), e.g., "sound [site] is permanent [target] on account of being an effect [reason]" (*śabdo nityaḥ | kṛtakatvāt*).

95. The presence of this defect also shows that T3 cannot be satisfied.

clusive (*anaikāntika*, H3).[96] This subtype is called "uncommon" (*asādhāraṇa*, H3b), since a reason property with this defect is known only to be present in the site of the inference: it is excluded from all similar and dissimilar cases.[97] These two defects (H2, H3b) prevent a reason property from being a well-functioning instrument since their presence establishes that the reason property is not present in a single similar case. The presence of this defect blocks step iii by showing that the positive form of pervasion (*anvaya*) is not known.

The third triple-condition (T3) is defined in terms of the third characteristic of a reason property (P3): a reason property must be known to be excluded from all dissimilar cases (*vipakṣa*). A reason property that lacks this property is said to be a subtype of the defect "inconclusive." This subtype is called "common/general" (*sādhāraṇa*, H3a), since a reason property with this defect is known to be present in the site of an inference, a similar case, and a dissimilar case.[98] The presence of this defect prevents the reason property from being well-functioning since it defeats the pervasion subcomponent by showing that there is a locus in which the target property is absent but in which the reason property is present. A third subtype, which is called "not universal" (*anupasaṃhārin*, H3c), applies to reason properties in which both the second (P2) and the third (P3) characteristics are absent.[99] The presence of each of these defects blocks step iii by showing that the negative form of pervasion (*vyatireka*) is not known.

2.3.3. C3: Argument Conditions

Certification conditions of the third set are "argument conditions" (C3). These conditions have to do with factors that are external to the argument

96. KTBh 113.10–115.02 gives the following two definitions: Df.1 (H3): "That which deviates [from the target property]" (*savyabhicāraḥ*); Df.2 (H3): "A reason property for which there is doubt about [its concomitance with] the target property" (*sādhyasaṃśayahetuḥ*). Note: "deviates" and "doubt" are technical terms. See section 3.2.2.

97. KTBh 114.07–114.10 gives the following definition. Df (H3b): "One that is excluded from similar and dissimilar cases, and is present only in the site of the inference" (*yaḥ sapakṣavipakṣābhyāṃ vyāvṛttaḥ pakṣa eva vartate*).

98. KTBh 113.09–114.01 gives the following definition. Df (H3a): "One that is present in the site of the inference, a similar case, and a dissimilar case" (*pakṣasapakṣavipakṣavṛttiḥ*). I will usually refer to this defect with the term "generally inconclusive" (*sādhāraṇānaikāntika*).

99. This subtype is not discussed in the KTBh, but is discussed at RNĀ (ĪSD 36.21–36.23).

itself but nevertheless defeat it. They are defined in terms of the fourth (P4) and fifth (P5) characteristics of a reason property. The fourth characteristic of a reason property (P4) is that a reason property must be known to not have a rival that proves the absence of what it seeks to prove. A reason property that lacks this property of "not having a rival" has the defect called "equal in scope" (*prakaraṇasama*, H4).[100] The fifth characteristic of a reason property (P5) is that its final effect must be known not to be contradicted by another well-functioning instrument such as perception. A reason property that lacks this property has the defect called "too late" (*kālātyāpadiṣta*, H5).[101] It is interesting to note that a reason property with defects H4 and H5 could satisfy all three of the instrument conditions (C2) and still not produce warranted awareness. Although satisfying the instrument conditions may be necessary for showing that an instrument is well-functioning, it is clear that it is not sufficient.

3. Defending the Nyāya Argument

Ratnakīrti's Naiyāyikas defend their argument for the existence of Īśvara by showing that none of the five defects discussed in section 2 applies to the reason property "on account of being an effect" (or, more simply, "being an effect"). In so doing, they satisfy the three sets of certification conditions and thus certify the instrument and defend their argument. In Ratnakīrti's

---

100. KTBh 39 gives the following definition. Df.1 (H4): "Equal in scope is a reason property for which there is another reason property that proves the opposite of the target property" (*prakaraṇasamas tu sa eva yasya hetoḥ sādhyaviparītasādhakaṃ hetvāntaram vidyate*). KTBh 115.03–116.08 gives the following Df.2 (H4): "That for which there is another reason property that is a rival is called 'equal in scope,' which is, 'one for which there is a rival'" (*yasya pratipakṣībhūtaṃ hetvāntaraṃ vidyate sa prakaraṇasamaḥ | sa satpratipakṣaḥ*). Note: "rival" is a technical term. The text says, "A rival is said to be another inferential argument of equal strength that proves the opposite of the target property" (*sādhyaviparītasādhakaṃ samānabalam anumānāntaraṃ pratipakṣa ity ucyate*). For a very interesting discussion of this see Oetke 1994b.

101. The term "*kālātyāpadiṣṭaḥ*" literally means "that which was pointed out long after its time." KTBh 117.01–118.11 gives the following definition. Df.1 (H5): "That for which it has been determined, through perception etc., that the target property is absent in the site of the inference is 'too late.' It is also said to be 'that whose object is defeated'" (*yasya pratyakṣādipramāṇena pakṣe sādhyābhavaḥ paricchinnaḥ sa kālātyāpadiṣṭaḥ | sa eva bādhitaviṣaya ity ucyate*).

presentation of the Nyāya argument, his Naiyāyikas follow this procedure by systematically showing that none of the five defects applies to the reason property being considered.[102] They focus their effort, however, on showing that the "instrument conditions" (C2) have been satisfied.[103] Ratnakīrti similarly focuses on these conditions in his critique of their argument.[104] What follows is a discussion of the Naiyāyikas' attempt at satisfying the instrument conditions (C2) for the reason property "being an effect" and an introduction to the issues that frame Ratnakīrti's critique. My discussion will focus, more specifically, on how the Naiyāyikas show that neither H2 ("opposed") nor H3a ("generally inconclusive") applies to this reason property. This selectivity is warranted because it is their discussion of these two defects that introduces the issues on which Ratnakīrti focuses his own arguments.

What directly and explicitly emerges from this discussion are the specific philosophical issues in terms of which the Naiyāyikas themselves frame the Īśvara debate. This discussion also provides a clear picture of the "inside-out" style of philosophical arguments in classical India, in which broader philosophical issues are introduced through very focused technical discussions. What is revealed, indirectly, is the epistemological significance of the dialogical context of an inference-for-the-sake-of-another, and the relevance of this context to the Nyāya theory of justification/certification. Attention to how the Naiyāyikas show that neither H2 nor H3a applies to the reason property in the Īśvara-inference also points to the deontological aspects of Nyāya internalism. Taken together, these two sets of issues lay the groundwork for the broader epistemological issues that are at stake in the Īśvara debate, for both Ratnakīrti and the Naiyāyikas. I will pick up on some of these issues in section 4.

3.1. Satisfying C2.2, H2

As discussed above, the presence of the defect called "opposed" (*viruddha*, H2) blocks the functioning of a reason property and thus prevents it from

---

102. See RNĀ (ĪSD 32.19–39.01). For H1, RNĀ (ĪSD 32.22–33.20); H2, RNĀ (ĪSD 33.21–36.20); H3, RNĀ (ĪSD 36.21–38.13); H4, RNĀ (ĪSD 38.14–38.18); H5, RNĀ (ĪSD 38.19–38.13).

103. See RNĀ (ĪSD 33.21–38.13).

104. Ratnakīrti's arguments will be discussed in detail in chapter 3.

being a *well*-functioning instrument of awareness.[105] In order to certify the instrument "being an effect," therefore, the Naiyāyikas must show that its functioning is not blocked by defects such as H2. Ratnakīrti's Naiyāyikas address this issue by first describing the defect and then explaining why it does not apply to the reason property in the Īśvara-inference. They say,

> It is well-known that a [reason property] that exists in only dissimilar cases proves what is opposed to the target property, through its being pervaded by the absence of the target property, and that it is named "opposed" (*viruddha*). . . . But this [reason property, "being an effect"] is not like that, since it is observed to really exist in similar cases such as a pot, for which a maker is well known.[106]

According to Ratnakīrti's Naiyāyikas, the reason the reason property "being an effect" is not opposed is that it is known, through observation, to be present in a similar case, such as a pot. Since it is well known that pots are effects and that they are made by an intelligent agent (they are routinely observed to be made by potters), the Naiyāyikas reason that both parties must agree that a pot is in fact a similar case. Given this, it must also be accepted that the reason property is not present in just dissimilar cases, and therefore that it is not defective because of the presence of H2. To illustrate this further, the Naiyāyikas choose to defend their position against an opponent who insists that the presence of the reason property in a pot-locus is not sufficient for showing that it is not defective because of the presence of H2.

3.1.1. Three Reasons

An opponent provides three related reasons the Naiyāyikas' position is not tenable. He explains that:

> (a) Given that what is to be proved is an omniscient cause, pervasion is not apprehended in even a dream. Since potters and the like are not

105. See 2.3.2.

106. RNĀ (ĪSD 33.21–33.24): *{tathā hi} yo vipakṣa eva vartate sa khalu sādhyaviparyaya-vyāpteḥ sādhyaviruddhaṃ sādhayan viruddho 'bhidhīyate | {yathā nityaḥ śabdaḥ kṛtakatvād iti}| na cāyaṃ tathā, prasiddhakartṛkeṣu ghaṭādiṣu sapakṣeṣu sadbhāvadarśanāt.*

omniscient, the example does not have the target property [and therefore is not a proper example or a similar case].

(b) Moreover, the reason property is opposed, since in the case of things like pots, only the pervasion of "being an effect" by "having a ***non***-omniscient cause" is apprehended.

(c) And it is not correct that the scope of the reason property is an intelligent-cause-in-general, and that the special characteristic, "being an omniscient cause," is proven on the basis of it, even though it is not within its scope.[107]

The opponent reasons that if what is to be proved is that the world has an intelligent maker who is Īśvara, then in order to satisfy certification condition C2.2, the Naiyāyikas must show that the reason property is present in a locus that is known to have Īśvara, or an Īśvara-like entity, as its cause. Since Īśvara is by definition omniscient, the opponent argues that this locus must be known to have an omniscient agent as its cause. This issue is suppressed in the Naiyāyikas' statement of the inferential argument and in their description of the target property as an "intelligent agent." As mentioned earlier, in order for a locus to be a similar case, both parties must agree that the target property is present there. This kind of intersubjective agreement is necessary if the argument is to be rhetorically effective. The Naiyāyikas example of a pot, however, is now not a similar case, since, as the opponent implies, neither party would agree that potters are omniscient (passage *a*). As a result, the presence of the reason property in such a locus does not show that H2 does not apply to it.

The opponent continues by arguing that not only have the Naiyāyikas not shown that the reason property is present in a similar case, but their example suggests that the reason property is pervaded by a property that is opposed to the target property (passage *b*). After all, it is well known that potters are not omniscient. The opponent insists, therefore, that the reason property is opposed. The problem, as the opponent sees it, is that a reason property must have within its scope the target property as defined by its special characteristics (passage *c*). It must, in other words, have these special characteristics (*viśeṣa*) within its reach. This requires attention to exactly

107. RNĀ (ĪSD 33.26–33.29): *sarvajñapūrvakatve {tu} sādhye vyāptiḥ svapne 'pi nopalabdhā | dṛṣṭāntaś ca sādhyahīnaḥ, kulālādīnām asarvajñatvāt | viruddhatā ca hetor asarvajñapūrvakatve-naiva kumbhādau kāryatvasya vyāpter upalabdheḥ | na copalabdhimatpūrvakatvamātraṃ sādhanaviṣayaḥ, tadviśeṣasya tu sarvajñapūrvakatvasyātadviṣayasyāpi tataḥ siddhir {iti sāmpratam}.*

what it is that is being proved, the scope of the reason property, and whether or not the target property is within its scope. In this case, the opponent argues that the reason property should prove not just that the world is constructed by an intelligent agent, but that it is constructed by an intelligent agent who has the special characteristic of being omniscient (*sarvajñatva*). The reason property "being an effect" is opposed, according to the opponent, since this special characteristic of the target property is not within its scope, and a characteristic that is opposed to it, "being non-omniscient" (*asarvajñatva*), appears to pervade it. The example cited by the Naiyāyikas is therefore not a similar case, and so the presence of the reason property in it cannot show that H2 does not apply. The opponent concludes, therefore, that the reason property is defective and cannot be a well-functioning instrument of warranted awareness.

3.1.2. Nyāya Response: Being a Property of the Site

The Naiyāyikas first respond to this series of arguments by explaining how in noncontroversial inferential arguments a reason property has special characteristics of the target property within its scope. They then show why the reason property "being an effect" and the target property "having an intelligent agent/maker" are similar to the terms in noncontroversial inferences. According to the Naiyāyikas, this analysis shows both that the example cited by them is a similar case and that the reason property "being an effect" can have the property "being omniscient" within its scope. From this they conclude that H2 does not apply to their reason property. They explain:

> An inference definitely has special characteristics within its scope. This is because, although there is pervasion just between general-terms, since [one of them, the reason property,] is a property of the site of the inference, there is, for that possessor of the target property, an inference of the general-term and its special characteristics. If this were not the case, there would be the unwanted consequence of the failure of all inferential arguments.[108]

---

108. RNĀ (ĪSD 33.32–34.05): *{ucyate}*| ***sāmānyamātravyāptāv apy antarbhāvitaviśeṣasya sāmānyasya pakṣadharmatāvaśena sādhyadharmiṇy anumānād viśeṣaviṣayam anumānaṃ bhavaty eva | itarathā sarvānumānocchedaprasaṅgāt.***

Consider the inference of fire from smoke mentioned earlier.[109] In the inference-warranting relation in that argument, as the Naiyāyikas now tell us, the reason property is "smoke-in-general" and the target property is "fire-in-general." Included within the scope of these "general terms" are necessary characteristics, such as "being caused by fire" (in the case of smoke) and "having the capacity to burn" (in the case of fire).[110] The purpose of the inference, however, is not to prove that there is fire-in-general, but that there is fire-on-the-mountain.[111] One way to interpret this is to insist that what is being inferred in this case is inclusive of a special, though contingent, characteristic of fire-in-general—that is, the characteristic of "being on the mountain." The issue, then, is whether or not the reason property "smoke-in-general" is able to prove this, and if so, how. It is important to note that the Naiyāyikas' identification of a kitchen as a similar case shows that in order for a locus to be a similar case it is only necessary that the "generic form" of the target property, i.e., fire-in-general, be known to be present there.[112] It is not necessary, for example, that "fire-on-the-mountain" be present there. H2 does not then apply to the reason property "smoke-in-general" because it is present in a similar case—that is, a locus in which the "generic form" of the target property "fire-in-general" is also known to be present.

Although both terms in the inference-warranting relation are general terms *(sāmānya)* and refer to the generic forms of the reason and target properties, the Naiyāyikas argue that a reason property can have within its scope a special characteristic of the target property. More important, they argue that this special characteristic, "being on the mountain," need not characterize the "generic form" of the target property as it is present in the similar case. They reason that since it is known that the reason property "smoke-in-general" is pervaded by fire, step iii, ***and*** that it is a property of the site of the inference, i.e., that it is present on the mountain, it is also known that the "fire-in-general" that is concomitant with it must be present on the mountain.[113] It isn't just fire-in-general that is inferred, but fire that has the special

109. See 1.4.

110. For more on "general terms" see chapter 3.

111. Matilal 1968; NV, NVTṬ, NVTṬP ***ad*** NS 1.1.5 and NS 2.1.46.

112. See 1.5.

113. KTBh (33.09–34.02).

characteristic of "being present on that mountain" or, more generally, "being located in the site of the inference."[114] Given this, the Naiyāyikas argue that a reason property must have at least one special characteristic of the target property within its scope: the characteristic of being a property of the site of the inference (*pakṣadharāmatā*). If this were not the case, they assert, inferential reasoning would be impossible—a consequence that is equally unacceptable to the opponent. This approach to showing that a special characteristic of the target property can be within the scope of the reason property is significant for the Naiyāyikas' discussion of H2, since it explains how a reason property that is present in a similar case that is defined by the "generic form" of the target property can have a "specific form" of it within its scope.

The Naiyāyikas also maintain, however, that a reason property can have more than this one special characteristic within its scope. They argue, for example, that a reason property can have within its scope also those special characteristics of the target property that are implied by its having the special characteristic of being present in the site of the inference. In responding to the opponent, the Naiyāyikas apply this reasoning to their inference for the existence of Īśvara. They insist, for example, that the site of their inference, "the world," is such that only an omniscient maker could have created it. Although the general form of the target property is "an intelligent-maker-in-general," it is known, in virtue of its being a property of the site of the inference, that this intelligent-maker-in-general has the property "being the maker of the world." According to the Naiyāyikas, this implies that this maker must be omniscient, since only such a maker could create an artifact such as the world.[115] This line of reasoning is relevant to showing that H2 does not apply to the reason property "being an effect," since it enables the Naiyāyikas to claim both that a pot-locus is a similar case (since both the reason property and the target property are known to be present there) and that a reason property has those special characteristics within its scope that are implied by the target property being a property of the site of the inference. The first part of their argument shows that H2 does not apply to their reason property, and the second part shows why the opponent's

114. Matilal 1968:152.

115. This point is not only asserted—it is argued for. See RNĀ (ĪSD 56.14–56.25).

objection to their identification of a pot-locus as a similar case does not apply either.

There are, then, three issues that are raised in the Naiyāyikas' discussion of C2.2, each of which has to do with various aspects of the target property. The first has to do with the proper description of the target property. What is to be proved: that the world was constructed by an intelligent-agent-in-general, or that it was constructed by an omniscient agent? Related to this is the question of whether it is possible to establish an inference-warranting relation once the proper description of the target property has been determined. A second issue has to do with whether the example cited in the inferential argument is in fact a locus to which the pervasion relation between the reason property and the target property applies—that is, with whether it is a similar case. A third issue has to do with how the scope of the reason property relates to what can be proved, and more specifically, with how special characteristics of the target property can be established.

Ratnakīrti's Naiyāyikas address each of these issues and claim to have satisfied C2.2 by showing that H2 does not apply to the reason property "being an effect." They show this by (1) identifying a similar case in which the reason property is present and defending their identification of it against an opponent who argues that it is not a suitable example and (2) arguing that some special characteristics of a target property are within the scope of what can be proved, since they are entailed by the target property being located in the site of the inference. In making these arguments, Ratnakīrti's Naiyāyikas explain how a reason property that is known to be pervaded by a "generic form" of the target property can have a specific form of it within its scope. In each of their arguments, the intersubjective context of the certification process is never far from view.

3.2. *Satisfying C2.3, H3a*

The Naiyāyikas' discussion of the defect "inconclusive" (***anaikāntika***, H3) focuses on the subtype called "generally inconclusive" (***sādhāraṇa-anaikāntika***, H3a).[116] The presence of this subtype—which itself has two subtypes—blocks the functioning of an instrument by affecting its pervasion subcomponent in

116. RNĀ (ĪSD 36.26–38.13).

one of two ways.[117] It either "defeats" it, by identifying a locus in which the reason property is known to be present but the target property is known to be absent (H3a_1), or it "undermines" it, by raising doubt about whether the reason property is excluded from all dissimilar cases (H3a_2).[118] In the first case, the defect is detected through the identification of a specific locus (i.e., a dissimilar case) that is a "counterexample" to the general rule of pervasion. In the second case, it is detected through doubt about pervasion and, more specifically, about the contraposed form of it.[119] In this case, it is the possibility, rather than the actual identification, of a dissimilar case that explains why the defect applies. The Naiyāyikas assert, however, that neither variety of H3a applies to their reason property, since it is known that their reason property is excluded from all dissimilar cases. This rules out a counterexample and also eliminates doubt regarding the possibility of one.[120] They defend this through critically engaging an opponent who argues both that there is a counterexample to pervasion and that the Naiyāyikas' counterargument reveals a much deeper problem with how they think pervasion relations can be established. It is through this exchange that the Naiyāyikas try to show that the instrument condition that is defined in terms of defect H3a (i.e., C2.3) is satisfied.

3.2.1. A Dissimilar Case

An opponent argues that H3a applies to the reason property "being an effect" by proposing a counterexample to pervasion, that is, by identifying

---

117. See section 2.3.2.

118. The first of these "two ways" should not be confused with defect H2, which applies to a reason property that is known to be pervaded by what is opposed to the target property (*sādhya-viparyaya*). Although the same locus may be used to illustrate each of these defects (i.e., H2, H3a), the reason why it is used will differ. With respect to H2 such a locus may be referred to by someone who argues that the reason property being considered is pervaded by the opposite of what is to be proved, while with respect to H3a it may be referred to by someone who argues that it just is a locus in which the reason property is present but the target property is not. The issue of whether or not the reason property is pervaded by the opposite of the target property need not arise.

119. The "contraposed" form of pervasion (*vyāpti*) is expressed, in this context, as the exclusion of the reason property (*hetu*) from loci in which the target property (*sādhya*) is not present.

120. RNĀ (ĪSD 37.12–37.16).

a locus in which the reason property is known to be present but in which the target property, "having an intelligent maker," is known to be absent. The locus proposed by the opponent is growing grass. The opponent says,

> In seeing grass grow without the activity of a person, people will definitely not accept the inference-warranting relation, "effects-in-general [i.e., all effects] are caused by a person [i.e., an intelligent maker]."[121]

According to the opponent, growing grass is a dissimilar case (*vipakṣa*), since it is a locus in which the reason property "being an effect" is known to be present and the target property "having an intelligent maker" is known to be absent. Given such a counterexample, the inference-warranting relation of pervasion is defeated. And since pervasion—one of the subcomponents necessary for an instrument to function—has been defeated, the instrument is shown to be defective, and therefore cannot be considered a well-functioning instrument for warranted awareness. The opponent concludes, therefore, that since C2.3 has not been satisfied the instrument has not been certified and the Naiyāyikas are not justified.

The Naiyāyikas respond to this by questioning whether growing grass is really a dissimilar case. They argue that the criteria that the opponent relies on to determine that it is are too rigid, since their application would invalidate/defeat even well-known and noncontroversial inferences. The issue, then, is whether or not the locus, growing grass, is a genuine defeater of the inference-warranting relation, and therefore of the pervasion subcomponent of the instrument. The Naiyāyikas argue,

> If this were so, then even well-known inferences would be offered a handful of water [and thereby given their last rites]. This is because, even when pervasion is being determined in such cases, it is possible to say that "there is smoke without the activity of fire, in a faraway place filled with lions and the like," or that "in the past, a pot was made without the activity of a person." [Thus] people will not even admit the

121. RNĀ (ĪSD 36.26–36.27): *{nanu} puruṣavyāpāram antareṇa tṛṇādīn udayamānān avalokayaṃl lokaḥ kāryamātraṃ puruṣapūrvakam iti vyāptim eva na pratipadyata {iti cet}*.

inference-warranting relation "smoke-in-general [i.e., all smoke] is caused by fire" or "pots-in-general [i.e., all pots] are caused by a person."[122]

The opponent's reason for considering growing grass to be a dissimilar case is that even though it is seen to grow and is known to be an effect, it is not seen to have a person as its cause. It is therefore a dissimilar case, since it is known to be an effect that is not caused by a person or any intelligent agent. The Naiyāyikas respond to this by arguing that nonobservation is not always an appropriate criteria for determining whether or not a property is present in a particular locus. Even in well-known inferences, for example, a reason property, e.g., smoke, could be observed in a locus in which its target property, e.g., fire, is not observed to be present. In a passage immediately following this one, it is explained that such a locus need not be a genuine defeater, since the nonobservation of the target property, e.g. fire, in such a locus could be due to its being "spatially remote" (*deśa-viprakṛṣṭa*), i.e., in a faraway place.[123] Similarly, pots are often observed without the potter who made them being observed. Here too the well-known pervasion relation between pots and a potter is not defeated, since in this case the potter who made them could be "temporally remote" (*kāla-viprakṛṣṭa*), e.g., he may be long dead. The Naiyāyikas argue that the maker of growing grass may be remote in a relevantly similar way. Unlike fire or the potter, the maker of growing grass is said to be "essentially remote" (*svabhāva-viprakṛṣṭa*), which means that relative to a normal observer this maker is unobservable. Nonobservation is not, therefore, suitable for determining his absence. In order for a locus to be a genuine defeater, then, it is not sufficient to simply identify a locus in which the reason property is observed to be present but the target property is not, since that target property may be either spatially, temporally, or essentially remote (*deśa-kāla-svabhāva-viprakṛṣṭa*).[124] Not recognizing the significance of the "theory of remoteness" to the identification of

---

122. RNĀ (ĪSD 36.27–36.31): *evaṃ tarhi prasiddhānumānasthitir api dattajalāñjaliḥ | tatrāpi hi vyāptipratītikāla eva vyāghrādiparyākulātidurgapradeśe vahnivyāpāram antareṇa dhūmaṃ puruṣavyāpāraṃ vinā pūrvaṃ siddhaṃ ghaṭaṃ vā vilokayan loko dhūmamātraṃ vahnipūrvakam iti vyāptim eva na pratipadyata iti vaktuṃ śakyatvāt.*

123. RNĀ (ĪSD 37.01–37.04).

124. For more on the "theory of remoteness" and related issues see Kellner 1997a: n. 165, 1999, Steinkellner 1967, and Tillemans 1995. This issue is also discussed in chapter 3.

genuine defeaters will, the Naiyāyikas argue, result in the identification of "genuine" defeaters even for the pervasion subcomponents of the instruments of well-known inferential arguments. The significance of this is that by not recognizing that a maker of growing grass could be "essentially remote" the opponent is relying on an approach through which even well-known inferential arguments would be invalidated.

The criterion used to identify growing grass as a genuine defeater is therefore too rigid, and is not a legitimate way of showing that H3a applies. As a result, the opponent has not, according to the Naiyāyikas, shown that the pervasion subcomponent of the reason property has been defeated, and there is no reason, therefore, to question their initial assertion that C2.3 has been satisfied.

3.2.2. Deviation

At this point, the opponent chooses to concede the point and raises a new, though related, set of objections.[125] These objections have to do with doubt about whether the reason property is known to be excluded from *all* dissimilar cases (P3). The opponent agrees that growing grass may not be a genuine defeater, but insists that the Naiyāyikas' theory of inference-warranting relations does not rule out the possibility of there being a different one.[126] This possibility is referred to as the possibility of deviation (*vyabhicāra*), that is, the possibility that a reason property deviates from the pervasion rule according to which it is known that wherever the reason property is present the target property is present (positive concomitance, *anvaya*) and wherever the target property is absent the reason property is absent (negative concomitance, *vyatireka*).[127] In the opponent's view, since the Naiyāyikas cannot rule out the possibility of deviation, there could be a locus that deviates from the rule. Such a locus would be a genuine defeater for the pervasion subcomponent, and therefore for the functioning of the instrument. The doubt that this generates is significant enough that, in their opinion, it undermines pervasion, by specifically undermining the negative concomitance between the two terms. Their worry is that there may be a locus in which the target

---

125. RNĀ (ĪSD 37.12–38.13).

126. This theory will be discussed in chapter 3.

127. "Deviation" (or wandering) is a technical term that will be discussed in greater detail in chapter 3. Briefly: A property H deviates from a property S just in case H is located somewhere S is not. See Ganeri 1999a:68.

property is absent but the reason property is present. This worry undermines any claim to C2.3 being satisfied, and even to its being satisfiable. The issues that are raised in this discussion have to do with the epistemic significance of doubt, the nature of pervasion, its scope, and the adequacy of the Nyāya method of determining it. The initial exchange is as follows:

> [*Opponent*] Nondeviation is not ascertained through mere observation and nonobservation in similar and dissimilar cases, since there isn't a nondeviation rule for [reason properties that are] neither of the same nature [as the target property] nor produced from it. So, since there is doubt about its exclusion from dissimilar cases, "being an effect" is not a reason property.
>
> [*Naiyāyika*] About this it is said: There is no doubt about the exclusion of the reason property from dissimilar cases, since an effect-cause relationship, which is established through observation and nonobservation, is established for an effect [the reason property] and an intelligence-possessor [the target property], as it is for smoke [the reason property] and fire [the target property].[128]

The opponent begins by stating that the nondeviation rule (*avyabhicāra-niyama*) applies only to two sorts of relations: those in which the two terms are "of the same nature" and those in which the two terms are related as "effect and cause." Let us refer to these as the "identity-mode" (*tādātmya*) and the "production-mode" (*tadutpatti*) of pervasion.[129] The opponent further asserts that in the Naiyāyikas' theory, the inference-warranting relation is neither of these two types and so is not a relation for which deviation can be ruled out. There is, therefore, doubt about the exclusion of the reason property from dissimilar cases (*sandigdha-vipakṣa-vyāvṛtti*). The Naiyāyikas respond,

---

128. RNĀ (ĪSD 37.12–37.16): *{syād etat}| na sapakṣāsapakṣayor darśanādarśanamātreṇa avyabhicāraniścayaḥ, atadātmano 'tadutpatteś cāvyabhicāraniyamābhāvāt | tad idaṃ kāryatvaṃ sandigdhavipakṣavyāvṛttikatvenāsādhanam | atrocyate nāsti vipakṣāddhetor vyāvṛttisandehaḥ, dhūmānalayor iva kāryabuddhimator upalambhānupalambhasādhanasya kāryakāraṇabhāvasya siddhatvāt.*

129. The secondary literature on these two modes of pervasion is extensive. See, for example, Kajiyama 1989, Katsura 1986a, Katsura 1992a, Lasic 2000a, Lasic 2000b, Steinkellner 1971, Steinkellner 1974, Gillon and Hayes 1991, Hayes 1988, Goekoop 1967, Wada 1990, and Wada 2007. For more on this see chapters 4 and 5.

however, by asserting that the two terms in the inference-warranting relation for the existence of Īśvara are related as effect and cause, just like the two terms in the inference-warranting relation between smoke and fire. They assert further that the relation is established, in part, through the observation (*upalambha*) of the reason property in a finite number of loci in which the target property is known to be present, and the nonobservation (*anupalambha*) of it in a finite number of loci in which the target property is known to be absent, just like in the inference of fire from smoke. The opponent's argument is therefore irrelevant according to the Naiyāyikas, since the nondeviation rule is known to apply to the inference-warranting relation in their argument for the same reasons that it is known to apply to the reason property in very well known, and noncontroversial, inferences.

3.2.3. Scope of the Reason Property

The opponent chooses, at this point, to accept the Naiyāyikas' claim that the inference-warranting relation is an effect-cause relation and that, in general, such relations can be established through observation and nonobservation (*upalambhānupalambha*). The opponent instead directs his attention to showing how the scope of the terms in well-known inference-warranting relations is different from the scope of the terms in the inference-warranting relation in the Naiyāyikas' argument. According to the opponent, the significance of this is that, given the scope of the reason property that is required for the Naiyāyikas' inference, it is not possible, given their own criteria, for them to establish pervasion through observation and nonobservation. The opponent says,

> Only a specific class of effects is proven to be caused by it [i.e., an intelligent maker], not effects-in-general. Just as it is not ascertained that [a property] such as "being a thing," which is present in smoke, etc., is produced from fire.[130]

The inference-warranting relation in the Naiyāyikas' argument is "Each and every effect has been constructed by an intelligent agent, just like a pot."[131] In other words, the terms of the relation are "effects-in-general"—i.e.,

---

130. RNĀ (ĪSD 37.17–37.18): *kāryaviśeṣasyaiva tadutpādasiddhir na kāryasāmānyasya, yathā dhūmādivartino vastutvāder nānalādijanyatvaniścaya iti {cet}.*

131. See 2.1.

all effects—and "being constructed by an intelligent agent." In the passage cited above, however, the opponent implies that in the well-known inference-warranting relation between smoke and fire, the relation is between a restricted class of effects (*kārya-viśeṣa*), namely smoke and its cause, and not all effects (*kārya-mātra*).[132] Moreover, it is only specific classes of effects that can be shown through observation and nonobservation to be constructed by an intelligent agent. The Naiyāyikas' view that the inference-warranting relation in their argument for the existence of Īśvara is an effect-cause relation that can be determined through observation and nonobservation requires (at least) that the scope of the reason property be restricted to specific, observable classes of effects. If, in general, the scope of a reason property is taken to be unrestricted, then as the opponent points out, even properties of smoke such as "being a thing" could be taken to be pervaded by fire. Since both parties agree that pervasion is between "smoke" and "fire" and not between "smoke-and-all-of-its-properties" and "fire," the opponent presses the Naiyāyikas to explain how the pervasion relation between an unrestricted class of "effects-in-general" (i.e., any effect) and an "intelligent agent" can be determined. The Naiyāyikas' response is to provide an example. They say,

> An effect, such as a piece of cloth, is seen to have a material cause. And a different effect, whose material cause is unobserved, is established as being an effect that has a material cause. Similarly, that very effect, cloth, etc., is observed to have a maker. Therefore that [thing], whose maker is not observed, is established as having a maker, on account of [its] being an effect. This is because the positive and negative concomitance of a maker with an effect is like that of a material cause. . . . Therefore, just as it is not possible to doubt that there could be an effect without a material cause, since a material cause-in-general produces an effect-in-general, similarly, it must not be doubted that there could be an effect without a maker, since there isn't a relevant difference in proving that a maker-in-general produces an effect-in-general.[133]

---

132. That this, and what follows, is implied by the passage is clear from the Naiyāyikas' response to it and the subsequent discussion of the passage later in the text. See chapter 3, section 2.

133. RNĀ (ĪSD 37.20–37.26): *{yathā hi} kāryaṃ vastrādy upādānavad dṛṣṭam, kāryāntaram apy adṛṣṭopādānam upādānavat kāryatvādy upasthāpyate tathā tad eva kāryaṃ vastrādi dṛṣṭa-kartṛkam ity adṛṣṭakartṛkam api kāryatvāt kartṛmad vyavasthāpyate | upādānasyeva kartur api*

The Naiyāyikas' approach is to again compare the inference-warranting relation in their inference to a noncontroversial case—here, the relation between effects, such as a piece of cloth, and their having a material (or primary) cause (*upādāna-kāraṇa*). Although the pervasion relation is determined through the observation of a specific class of effects and those effects having a material cause, both parties agree that the relation is more general, and that it applies to effects-in-general. On the basis of this relation it is possible to infer that effects whose material cause has not been observed nevertheless do have a material cause. From the observation of a specific class of effects, such as pieces of cloth, pots, etc., it is similarly possible, the Naiyāyikas maintain, to determine an effect-cause relation between effects-in-general and an unobserved maker.

The opponent is not convinced by the comparison, however, and insists that pervasion can be determined only for a specific class of effects and its cause. In rephrasing the objection, the opponent specifies the property that he believes restricts the scope of the Naiyāyikas' reason property when it is properly formulated. He says:

> You may say anything, still, there is not the inference of an intelligent agent from effects-in-general. On the contrary, it is only from specific effects, from the observation of which there could be an awareness of them having been made, even for one who did not observe them being made.[134]

The reason property should be limited, according to the opponent, to those classes of effects that could be observed to be the products of an intelligent agent. This would distinguish between effects such as pots and buildings, for which pervasion with a maker has been (and can be) observed, and those such as grass and trees, for which it has not (and cannot) be observed. The opponent suggests that the reason property should be limited to just a specific class of effects, namely, those with the property "being an effect from the observation of which there could be an awareness of its having been

---

kāryeṇānukṛtānvayavyatirekatvāt | {tanmātranibandhanatvāc ca sarvatra kāryakāraṇavyavahārayoḥ} | tasmād yathā kāryaṃ ca syān nirupādānaṃ ceti na śakyam āśaṅkitum, kāryamātrasya upādānamātrād utpādasiddhes tathā ca bhaved akartṛkaṃ ceti nāśaṅkanīyaṃ kāryamātrasya kartṛmātrād utpādasiddher aviśeṣāt.

134. RNĀ (ĪSD 37.27–37.29): *{nanu} brūyā nāma kiñcit | tathāpi na kāryamātrād buddhimadanumānam, api tu kāryaviśeṣād eva | yaddarśanād akriyādarśino 'pi kṛtabuddhiḥ syāt.*

made, even for one who did not observe its being made." The pervasion relation that can be established through observation and nonobservation is not, as the Naiyāyikas assume, between "effects-in-general" (i.e., all effects) and "being made by an intelligent agent," but between "specific-effects" and "being made by an intelligent agent." What makes such effects "specific," moreover, is the special characteristic of "being an effect from the observation of which there could be an awareness of its having been made, even for one who did not observe its being made." Given this, the opponent claims that the Naiyāyikas' reason property is inconclusive, since pervasion can be established only for this specific class of effects and not for effects-in-general.

The presence of the subtype of the defect "generally inconclusive" (H3a_2) is detected through the opponent's doubt about the Naiyāyikas' ability to establish pervasion. The basis for this doubt is the opponent's view that the scope of the unrestricted form of the reason property "effects-in-general" includes classes of effects about which it cannot be known through observation whether they have been constructed by an intelligent agent. Given the Naiyāyikas' view that pervasion is established through observation and nonobservation, the opponent argues that there will always be epistemically significant doubt about pervasion. The opponent concludes, therefore, that the Naiyāyikas have not shown that this subtype of the defect "generally inconclusive" does not apply to the reason property in the Īśvara-inference.

The Naiyāyikas defend themselves by first providing an analysis of the limiting phrase "an awareness of having been made." They then try to show that there is no interpretation of it that undermines the pervasion subcomponent of the instrument in their argument. They ask,

> Moreover, what is this "awareness of having been made"? Is it the determination that the activity of something else was needed? Or is it the ascertainment that it came from a person, i.e., was made by a person?[135]

According to the Naiyāyikas, it is necessary to further analyze the terms in the phrase "an awareness of having been made." In their view, the opponent could either mean that an effect that has this characteristic is an effect about

135. RNĀ (ĪSD 37.30–37.32): *api ca kā punar iyaṃ kṛtabuddhiḥ, kim apekṣitaparavyāpārāvasāyo 'tha puruṣakṛtam etad iti pauruṣeyatvaniścaya iti.*

which it has been determined that its production depends upon the activity of something other than itself (*apekṣitaparavyāpāra*), or that it has been made by a person (*puruṣa-kṛta*). The first interpretation, which just specifies what it means for something to be "made" (*kṛta*), applies equally well to effects such as pots and the earth, since both parties would agree that "being an effect" is (at least) "being something whose production depends upon something other than itself."[136] Both the Naiyāyikas and the opponent agree that the class of effects that includes pots and the class that includes the earth are effects in this sense. There is not, therefore, a relevant distinction between these two classes of effects. As a result, the Naiyāyikas reason that this cannot be the opponent's interpretation of the limiting property, since it does not distinguish between what the opponent takes to be the problematic case and the well-known one. The second interpretation focuses on the term "awareness" (*buddhi*) and, according to the Naiyāyikas, needs to be specified further still. The Naiyāyikas suggest that the awareness that an effect "was made by a person" is the awareness either of someone who knows the pervasion relation between "being an effect" and "being made by a person" or of someone who does not.[137] They argue further that for someone who knows the relation there will certainly be the awareness of an intelligent agent from an effect-in-general, and so this cannot be what the opponent has in mind. For someone who does not know the pervasion relation, however, they concede that the inference is impossible. Given this criterion, however, even well-known inferences would be suspect, since it is never the case that someone who does not know pervasion can know, through inferential reasoning, what is to be proved.

According to the Naiyāyikas, there are two problems with the opponent's argument. The first is that the characteristic that the opponent claims is necessary for limiting the scope of the reason property does not limit it in the manner required by him. The second is that the opponent's doubt about being able to establish pervasion between general terms (*sāmānya*) through observation and nonobservation is not epistemically significant, since after considering well-known inferences it is clear that pervasion can be established between general terms, and through this method. The Naiyāyikas conclude that the opponent's attempts at showing that the pervasion compo-

136. RNĀ (ĪSD 38.01).
137. RNĀ (ĪSD 38.03).

nent has been undermined by doubt have not been successful and therefore that $H3a_2$ does not apply to the reason property "being an effect."

While the issues raised in the Naiyāyikas' discussion of C2.2 were framed in terms of the target property, the issues raised here have to do with the reason property. There are two specific issues that are raised. The first concerns the problem of "deviation" and whether the reason property is known to *actually* deviate from the target property, to *possibly* deviate from it, or to *not* deviate from it at all. In discussing this issue, the Naiyāyikas focused their attention on the criteria for identifying a "counterexample," and the significance of the "theory of remoteness" (*viprakṛṣṭa*) for making this identification. The second issue has to do with the scope of the reason property (*hetu-viṣaya*) and the related issue of how pervasion is supposed to be established. Most central to this discussion is the nature of pervasion and whether or not, given the proper description of the reason property, observation and nonobservation is an adequate method for establishing it.

The Naiyāyikas' discussion of C2.3 thus shows how issues having to do with the reason property are closely linked to those having to do with pervasion. Unlike their discussion of H2, however, here the Naiyāyikas show that H3a does not apply to the reason property by defending their claim that the reason property is known to be excluded from all dissimilar cases. They do so by (1) appealing to the "theory of remoteness," in order to discuss how the absence of a property in a particular locus should not be determined; (2) comparing their argument with well-known and therefore paradigmatic inferences, to show that the opponent's arguments are such that even well-known inferences would be invalidated by them; and (3) exposing internal inadequacies in the opponent's account of the limiting property "an awareness of having been made."

4. Conclusion: Shifting the Burden of Proof

Ratnakīrti's Naiyāyikas frame their discussion of the Īśvara-inference by first identifying a set of potential defeaters for their argument, and then arguing that none of them apply to its reason property, "being an effect." I have argued that these defeaters are best understood as defining a set of certification conditions for the instrument and that, from their perspective, the Naiyāyikas' argument is about showing that these certification conditions have been satisfied.[138] The certification conditions that are most important for the Naiyāyikas' Īśvara-inference are the instrument conditions (C2), and more specifically those defined by defects H2 (C2.2) and H3a (C2.3)—the defects that affect the functioning component of the instrument, by either defeating or undermining its pervasion subcomponent. It is primarily in showing that H2 and H3a do not apply to "being an effect" that the Naiyāyikas take themselves to have successfully defended their Īśvara-inference. Moreover, given that the Īśvara-inference is an "inference-for-the-sake-of-another," by defending it in this way, Ratnakīrti's Naiyāyikas expect their opponents to concede that the instrument is well-functioning, and that, as a result, the awareness-event that is produced by it is a knowing-event. In concluding this chapter, and before turning to a more detailed discussion of the Naiyāyikas' arguments in the context of Ratnakīrti's critique of them, I want to briefly return to the question of what Ratnakīrti's Naiyāyikas' tell us is at stake, both explicitly and implicitly, in their argument for the existence of Īśvara.

4.1. The Īśvara-Inference as a Hybrid Argument

In section 2.1 I suggested that the Īśvara-inference is helpfully thought of as a "hybrid" argument that makes use of elements from both cosmological arguments and arguments from design.[139] As a way of exploring what Ratnakīrti's Naiyāyikas tell us is explicitly at stake in their defense of this argument, it may be helpful to think of it further in terms of such a hybrid, and therefore in what may be more familiar terms. What follows, however, is not a detailed comparative analysis of the Īśvara-inference that is systematically informed by the extensive (and very sophisticated) philosophical literature on cosmological arguments and arguments from design, but rather an attempt at providing an alternative framework and vocabulary for seeing what Ratnakīrti's Naiyāyikas take to be their most pressing philosophical concerns in defending the Īśvara-inference.[140] This alternative framework

---

138. The fact that the argument is "about this" is due to its being an "inference-for-the-sake-of-another," in which case it is necessary that the inference-instrument be certified.

139. See the notes to section 2.1, and below, for references to helpful secondary literature on these two types of arguments.

140. There are two reasons I am not providing a more systematic treatment of this issue: first, such a discussion deserves a book-length study of its own; second, an analysis of this

and vocabulary also provides a slightly different perspective on my discussion of the Īśvara-inference in this chapter, and highlights the kinds of issues that will be discussed in greater detail in chapter 3.

The structure of the Naiyāyikas' hybrid cosmological/design argument can be understood in terms of the following three steps, which have been used to characterize both cosmological arguments and arguments from design.[141] Each of these arguments can be understood to begin with a contingent (and usually noncontroversial) existential fact, such as the existence of the universe or of complex well-functioning lifeforms. One way that cosmological and design arguments differ with respect to this existential fact is that in cosmological arguments this fact is often "nonnormative," while in design arguments it is often "normative."[142] In the Nyāya case, the existential

---

issue should be based on the Naiyāyikas' own arguments and not those of Ratnakīrti's Naiyāyikas. Vattanky 1984 provides a translation and commentary on the Nyāya philosopher Gaṅgeśa's discussion of the Īśvara-inference, and could serve as the basis for such a study. Ideally, however, such a study would be based on the work of Gaṅgeśa's predecessor, Udayana. For "translations" of his work see Dravid 1995, Dravid 1996, Laine 1993, and Laine 1998, and the excellent discussion in Chemparathy 1972.

141. For such a characterization see Gale 1991:239, and especially the excellent discussion in Gale and Pruss 2005:117–118, which is what my own discussion is based upon. Here is how they describe the three steps in a typical cosmological argument: (1) a contingent value-neutral existential fact; (2) a version of the PSR [Principle of Sufficient Reason] that requires that every fact of this kind have an explanation; and (3) an explanatory argument to show that the only possible explanation of this fact is in terms of the intentional actions of a supernatural, God-like being. They describe a typical teleological/design argument as follows: (1') a contingent valuable existential fact; (2') some principle of inductive reasoning; and (3') an explanatory argument to show that the probable explanation of this fact is in terms of the intentional actions of a supernatural, God-like being.

There are a number of well-known "hybrid" arguments for the existence of God, including those discussed by Koons 1997 and Koons 2001 (which is also helpfully discussed in Pruss 2006 and Oppy 2006b:125–130) and Gale 2000, who calls his hybrid argument a "cosmological cum ontological cum teleological argument." Gale's argument is essentially an ontological argument (which is based on a slighter weaker version of the well-known S5 modal ontological argument) in which a possible-worlds version of the cosmological argument is used to support its most controversial premise and a design argument is used to solve the "gap-problem."

142. A "nonnormative" existential fact is one that is value-neutral, in the sense that there are very few, if any, features of it that one might take to be valuable, e.g., beauty, simplicity, widespread law-like regularity, etc. A "normative" existential fact is one that is valuable. For this distinction see Gale and Pruss 2005:117, 128.

fact that is expressed in the first step of the argument is that things like the world/earth (the site of the inference) are effects (the reason property), in the sense that they have been constructed out of preexisting parts. As Ratnakīrti's Naiyāyikas seem to interpret it, this fact is both more normative than those that are appealed to in traditional versions of the cosmological argument, and less normative than those with which more familiar versions of the design argument begin.[143]

The second step in these arguments states a principle that, in some relevant way, is supposed to account for the existential fact in step 1. In many cosmological arguments, this principle is some version of either the "Causal Principle" (e.g., every thing that comes into existence has a cause/every contingent event has a cause) or the "Principle of Sufficient Reasoning" (e.g., all true propositions have explanations or all contingently true propositions have explanations). In most design arguments, this principle is a nondeductive principle of reasoning such as analogy, inference to the best explanation, likelihood, prior probabilities (i.e., Bayes' Theorem), or an anthropic principle of one sort or the other, as in arguments based on "fine-tuning."[144] It is

---

143. Gale and Pruss 2005:128, for example, suggest that the fact about design must be "a morally desirable one. Otherwise, nothing could be inferred about the goodness, as contrasted with the intelligence and power, of the person who brings about this fact. Moreover, if the design explanation is to be satisfactory, the existential fact should be one that an intelligent person would not be too unlikely to desire: if we have a group of stones strewn about apparently at random, we would not expect that an intelligent person desired precisely that combination."

144. For brief, but very useful, discussions of arguments based on analogy see Gale 2007:47–50, Le Poidevin 1996:44–47, Mackie 1982:133–145, Oppy 2006b:174–200, Rowe 1978: chap. 4, and Sober 1993:30–36; for those based on inference to the best explanation/abduction see Gale 2007:50–52, Swinburne 1968, and Swinburne 1979; for those based on likelihood see Sober 2004; for those based on prior probabilities/Bayes' Theorem see Swinburne 1979: chap. 8 (which is criticized in Mackie 1982: chap. 8); for those based on anthropic principles/fine-tuning see Craig and Sinnot-Armstrong 2004, Gale 2007:52–55, Le Poidevin 1996:54–69, Leslie 1988, Manson 2003, Oppy 2006b:201–228, and Swinburne 1968. It may be helpful to note that other than the arguments based on analogy, design arguments are generally probabilistic. For an example of how probability theory has been used to defend the design inference see Dembski 1998 and Dembski 2002. For excellent work on the uses and misuses of probability theory in such arguments, including Dembski's, see Mellor 1969, and especially Fitelson et al. 1999, and Sober 2004. For a short discussion of the contrast between "traditional" and "modern" teleological arguments see Le Poidevin 1996:47.

worth noting that there are also deductive versions of the argument from design.[145] Regardless of the specific principle that is appealed to in such arguments, their function is essentially the same—to provide a basis for recognizing the marks of intelligent design in what is referred to in step 1.[146] In the Naiyāyikas' hybrid argument, the relevant principle is expressed by the inference-warranting relation of pervasion, which is most naturally interpreted as a version of the causal principle. As stated by Ratnakīrti's Naiyāyikas, it is: Each and every effect is constructed by an intelligent agent, just like a pot.

The third step in these arguments is generally an explanatory argument to the effect that the fact expressed in step 1 is to be finally accounted for by the intentional actions of a God-like being. Defenders of both the cosmological and the design argument seem to differ on whether or not this step is really within the scope of their argument. In the Nyāya case it is clearly included, as indicated by the Naiyāyikas' defense of their argument in section 3.1. When the Naiyāyikas' Īśvara-inference is viewed as such a hybrid argument, the following issues are seen to be central to their defense of it.

Ratnakīrti's Naiyāyikas recognize that one obvious and important issue that must be addressed in defense of their hybrid argument has to do with exactly what the target property of their argument is supposed to be: an agent-in-general, an intelligent agent, and/or an intelligent agent who is Īśvara. They clearly recognize that their opponent might accept that there is an "intelligence-possessing" maker of the world/earth, but deny that this maker is Īśvara.[147] The Naiyāyikas recognize that they need to account for the apparent "gap"

---

145. See Smart and Haldane 2003, for a Thomistic style deductive design argument. Deductive versions of the argument are also discussed briefly in Reichenbach 2004 and Swinburne 1979, who rejects them.

146. See Gale and Pruss 2005:129. Le Poidevin 1996:44 contrasts the second step in cosmological and design/teleological arguments by suggesting that "whereas for the cosmological argument the crucial notion is that of causality, for the teleological argument the crucial notion is that of purpose [i.e., design]. We can make something intelligible by pointing to its antecedent cause, or we can make intelligible its existence by pointing to the purpose for which it was made, provided of course that we are talking about artifacts, i.e., things which are constructed by a conscious agent."

147. Interestingly, Ratnakīrti suggests that he too could accept this. For a discussion of this issue see chapter 5, section 6.

between the intelligent agent that is the target property of their argument and Īśvara. In my hybrid version of the argument, this "gap" is reflected in the differences between what can be concluded on the basis of steps 1 and 2, and what is supposed to be concluded with the addition of step 3. In one sense, the "gap" that needs to be closed is between the cause/intelligent agent in step 2 and the God-like being referred to in step 3.

In showing that H2 does not apply to the reason property "being an effect," Ratnakīrti's Naiyāyikas address this issue explicitly. In the voice of their opponent, they consider the proposal that the only way to close the gap is to build into step 2 the condition that the cause/agent that is referred to there be one that has the qualities of the God-like being referred to in step 3, e.g., omniscience. As the Naiyāyikas point out, however, this radically alters the causal principle in step 2, to the extent that it becomes much more difficult to prove, and, given the Naiyāyikas' specific theory about how such principles can be proven, almost impossible. As a result, the Naiyāyikas refuse to accept this solution to the gap-problem, and argue that there is another way of addressing the issue. They argue that the gap can by closed by recognizing that, given steps 1 and 2, it can be established that effects like the earth have an intelligent cause. They further argue that, given what we know about the earth, we can conclude its cause/agent must have very special qualities, such as omniscience, which uniquely belong to Īśvara. The Naiyāyikas' proposal is to solve the gap-problem with a design argument in step 3.[148]

In showing that H3a doesn't apply to the reason property "being an effect," Ratnakīrti's Naiyāyikas highlight, again in the voice of an opponent, their awareness of a second set of issues. These issues have to do with the Naiyāyikas' version of the "causal principle" in step 2, and its supposed strength. Often the strength of a causal principle can be traced through the scope of its terms and the closely related epistemic burden that it places on its defenders. For example, a "strong" version of the causal principle might require that whatever exists have a cause, while a "weaker" version might

148. For more on this see chapter 3, section 4, where this issue will be discussed in terms of the "site subcomponent" of the inference. A similar strategy seems to be at work in Koons 1997. As Gale and Pruss (2005:135–136) have noted, cosmological arguments and arguments from design are both susceptible to (or as Gale writes, "infected" by) the gap-problem.

require that whatever comes into existence have a cause.[149] In restricting the scope of the existential facts (or types of existential facts) that are to be accounted for, weaker versions of the causal principle can ease the epistemic burden on its defenders. The Naiyāyikas' version of the causal principle is therefore "strong," in the sense that it requires that each and every thing that comes into existence have a cause, but also "weak" in the sense that it doesn't require that whatever exists have a cause, only that each and every thing that comes into existence does. On the other hand, the Naiyāyikas' version of the causal principle significantly restricts the kind of "cause" that is relevant, by ruling out non-intelligence-possessing ones. In this case, restricting the scope of what counts as the right kind of cause/agent for the causal principle strengthens it, in the sense that it increases the epistemic burden on its defenders, even while it lessens the gap between the cause/agent in the causal principle and the God-like being referred to in step 3.

In showing that H3a doesn't apply to "being an effect," Ratnakīrti's Naiyāyikas highlight their awareness of the interrelationship between the scope of the terms referred to in steps 1 and 2, the strength of the causal principle, and their epistemic burden. It is clear from their discussion that defending their causal principle is one of their central concerns. As is well known, this is also one of the central concerns for defenders of the cosmological argument.[150] The Naiyāyikas' strategy in defending their causal principle is to first respond to the charge that there are actual counterexamples to it by arguing, partly on the basis of their "theory of remoteness," that the criteria that the opponent uses to identify "actual" counterexamples would result in counterexamples to the causal principles of arguments that even they accept. More specifically, the Naiyāyikas argue that not observing that some effect has an intelligent agent as its cause does not mean that it does not have such an agent as its cause, since its cause could be remote, and similarly, neither does never observing that effects of some type have an intelligent agent as their cause mean that effects of that type do not have such an agent as their cause. Again, the basis for the Naiyāyikas' argument is that the opponent's

---

149. This issue parallels discussions of "strong" and "weak" versions of the "Principle of Sufficient Reason" (PSR). For references, see below.

150. See Gale and Pruss 1999, Gale and Pruss 2005, Oppy 2006a, Oppy 2006b, Reichenbach 2004:98–103, Rowe et al. 1998:60–114, and Pruss 2006 (a very helpful book-length treatment of PSR).

critique is equally applicable to some of the opponent's own arguments. As Ratnakīrti's Naiyāyikas present it, this argument silences their opponent. In arguing against there being actual counterexamples to their causal principle, the Naiyāyikas thus take themselves to have provided indirect support for it.

In responding to the opponent's charge that there are possible counterexamples to their causal principle, however, the Naiyāyikas explicitly address the issue of the kinds of positive arguments that can be offered in direct support of it. They insist that their causal principle is in fact a version of a principle accepted by the opponent, and that it is established in the same way as the effect-cause relationship between smoke and fire, which the opponent grants does not have any possible counterexamples. The Naiyāyikas then go on to argue that their causal principle is a "nondeviation rule" that can be established empirically, just like the nondeviation rule for smoke and fire. Again, the Naiyāyikas' strategy is to compare both the causal principle in their argument and the positive arguments they use to support it with the causal principle that the opponent accepts and the positive arguments she uses to support them. The issue of exactly what sort of relation the Naiyāyikas' causal principle expresses, and what sorts of arguments they use to defend it, will be discussed in great detail in chapter 3.

At this point in their discussion, however, Ratnakīrti's Naiyāyikas have the opponent resist their analysis, by arguing that there is a deep disanalogy between the causal principle in the Naiyāyikas' argument and those in noncontroversial ones. To support this point, they have their opponent argue that the disanalogy is due to a suppressed difference in the scope of the fact/effect that is assumed in the different versions of the causal principle. The opponent's proposal is that the Naiyāyikas' positive argument can support only a much weaker version of the causal principle, since it can support only the principle that each and every effect "from the observation of which there could be an awareness of its having been made, even for one who did not observe its being made," has been constructed by an intelligent agent. The opponent's strategy is to try to undercut the Naiyāyikas' earlier appeal to the theory of remoteness, by eliminating the possibility that the intelligent agent in question could be "essentially remote." Their proposal is effectively to insist that (given the Naiyāyikas' reliance on observation) the only kinds of effects that anyone can take to exhibit the marks of having been made by an intelligent agent are those that can be seen to have been made by such an agent, e.g., a person. As the opponent sees it, what is essential to inferring an intelligent maker in ordinary contexts is that we have seen that effects with a certain degree of complexity and scale have been made by such an agent. While this new version of the causal principle lessens the epistemic burden, it does not (according to the opponent) apply to the existential fact in step 1 of the Naiyāyikas' argument, and thus does not provide any basis for an inference from it.

As discussed in section 3.2.3, however, the Naiyāyikas reject the disanalogy, and in so doing clearly show that they recognize both the force of such arguments and the need to formulate an adequate response to them.[151] The Naiyāyikas' general strategy for rejecting the disanalogy is to work with what they present as shared intuitions about the kinds of similarities and dissimilarities that are relevant to the argument. These "shared intuitions" are arrived at by examining those arguments that are accepted by everyone, including the opponent. On the basis of this, the Naiyāyikas then insist that the opponent's argument for a weaker causal principle that can support the inference of an intelligent maker for only a restricted class of effects is actually based on intuitions that are in fact opposed to what she herself takes to be the case. This strategy is reflected in the Naiyāyikas' assessment of the proper interpretation of the "effect-term" in their causal principle, and the closely related issue of the positive support that can be given to it through observation, as compared with the "proper" scope and support through observation of the casual principle in noncontroversial inferences.

As they present the "disanalogy" issue, it is about whether the observability of the cause/agent is the property in virtue of which the causal principles in the two arguments are to be compared. In interpreting the disanalogy issue in this way, they reject the opponent's attempt at trying to restrict the scope of the effect-term, and instead accept the epistemic burden of establishing their less restricted version of the causal principle. Ratnakīrti's Naiyāyikas thus deflect the kinds of disanalogy arguments that have been used primarily against analogical versions of the argument from design, by shifting (or twisting) it away from disanalogies between the effects/artifacts whose causes/makers can be determined and the effect/artifact cited in step 1, to the cause/maker of these effects/artifacts. For the Naiyāyikas, the only relevant "mark of design" is that both sets of effects/artifacts are things "from

---

151. Cf. Gale 2007:48–49, where he criticizes one of Hume's arguments that there is a decisive disanalogy at work.

the observation of which there could be an awareness of its having been made, even for one who did not observe its being made." (Differences between such effects/artifacts are deemed to be irrelevant.) It should come as no surprise that this issue is explicitly raised again by Ratnakīrti in his critique of the Naiyāyikas' response; it will be discussed in greater detail in chapter 3.

4.2. Satisfaction, Certification, and Justification

When it is understood as a hybrid version of the cosmological and design argument, what Ratnakīrti's Naiyāyikas tell us is explicitly at stake in their Īśvara-inference is a closely related set of issues that parallel, in interesting ways, the kinds of issues that frame (and have framed) debates about both arguments. Through a constructed dialogue with an opponent, the Naiyāyikas highlight the importance of both the gap-problem and the relationship between the scope of the terms in their causal principle and the epistemic burden that this places on them. They clearly recognize that the scope of the reason and target properties account for a trade-off between the force of the gap-problem and the epistemic burden problem. This recognition is important, since it may help to explain their decision to specify that the target property is an *intelligent*-agent and not just a cause or agent-in-general.

In discussing these issues, however, Ratnakīrti's Naiyāyikas also point to what is *implicitly* at stake for them in their argument. As I have pointed out, Ratnakīrti's Naiyāyikas often respond to their opponents by comparing controversial features of the Īśvara-inference to similar features in arguments that are known to be accepted by them. In addition, as Ratnakīrti's Naiyāyikas present it, the transition from argument to argument is often marked by the opponent's seeming acceptance of their analysis. This rhetorical context is epistemically significant, and hardly incidental. As I hope to show, it suggests that Ratnakīrti's Naiyāyikas are aware, at least implicitly, that what is at stake in their argument is their entire epistemology, and especially their approach to certification.

The specific dialogical features of the Naiyāyikas' discussion suggest that Ratnakīrti's Naiyāyikas understand the certification process in terms of fulfilling an epistemic obligation to their epistemic peers.[152] This obligation is

152. My use of this term is based on Gutting 1982:83, where the term is used to refer to those individuals who are like us with respect to "intelligence, perspicacity, honesty, thoroughness, and other relevant epistemic virtues." Kelly 2005 extends Gutting's notion to re-

defined through their theory of defeaters, and is introduced into their argument through the dialogical framework of the text. Specific obligations are met by addressing the philosophical issues that arise in fulfilling what they see as their prima facie responsibility to show their opponent that no known defeaters apply to the reason property in question. A further responsibility is to respond to their opponent's counterarguments, until that opponent's reasonable, and epistemically significant doubts, have been resolved. In an important sense it is peer disagreement that drives the debate by shifting the burden of proof back and forth until it has been lifted. In Ratnakīrti's text, there is never an explicit stalemate.

The certification process thus has built into it what I earlier referred to as both "deontological" and "procedural" dimensions. The deontological dimension is evident from the fact that Ratnakīrti's Naiyāyikas assume that they have a prima facie epistemic responsibility to show their opponent that none of the known defeaters apply to the reason property in the Īśvara-inference. This is evident from the structure of their argument, as is their further obligation to respond to all of the opponent's reasonable doubts.[153] It is only once these epistemic responsibilities have been fulfilled that certification follows. The procedural dimension is evident from the Naiyāyikas' insistence that it is the activity and epistemic practice of certification—i.e., the practice of showing that a set of defects does not apply to a particular inference instrument—that not only precedes the reflective knowing-event itself (A_r) but is in fact what that event is based upon. A first-order awareness-event (A_c) is thus certified only insofar as an epistemic agent has herself

---

quire, in addition, that our epistemic peers be like us with respect to "their exposure to evidence and arguments which bear on the question at issue." Such a peer is one over whom we "claim no epistemic advantage." The Naiyāyikas' opponent seems to be an epistemic peer who is in between that of Gutting and Kelly. More specifically, while Ratnakīrti's Naiyāyikas seem to view their opponent as being an epistemic peer with respect to Gutting's criteria, it does not seem to me that they would go as far as to say that they have no epistemic advantage over their opponent, e.g., that they have not given greater attention and thought to the arguments at hand. As Kelly 2005 sees it, the Naiyāyikas' opponent is an epistemic peer with respect to his criterion ii, but not with respect to his criterion i.

153. See Alston 1989:74–75 and chaps. 4–5, where Alston discusses and rejects what he calls the "deontological" concept of justification and argues in support of an "evaluative" conception of justification which is "just reliability of belief formation with evaluative frosting" (Alston's concession to his moderate internalism). See Alston 1989:96–109.

shown that the instrument that produced it is well-functioning.[154] Certification is how an agent comes to know that a particular first-order awareness-event is warranted. As a result of it, both the agent and the first-order knowing-event itself are "justified."

Given the Naiyāyikas' understanding of certification and justification, this is exactly what one should expect. Ratnakīrti's Naiyāyikas take themselves to have shown that a relevant set of defects does not apply to a specific inference-instrument, once they have met their prima facie epistemic obligations and have responded to and resolved the legitimate doubts that are raised by their epistemic peers. Once these obligations have been met and the doubts have been resolved, the Naiyāyikas are, in their view, entitled to claim that the first-order awareness-event (A_c) that was produced by that instrument is a knowing-event, since the instrument that produced it has been certified, and thereby shown to be well-functioning. Doxastic ascent is thus stopped once legitimate doubt has been resolved through the certification process.

As before, let us refer to the first-order awareness-event as a "knowing-event" (A_c) and the higher-order awareness-event that results from certification as "reflective-knowledge"/"a reflective knowing-event" (A_r).[155] My noticed awareness of this reflective knowing-event is a "certifying-event," which is itself self-luminous, since it is an illuminating awareness-event (A_i). The content of this certifying awareness-event, which has the reflective knowing-event as its object, provides us with an epistemic perspective on the first-order knowing-event by enabling us to notice the content of the reflective knowing-event. There are two constituents of its content: the first is the content of the knowing-event itself, e.g., "Īśvara is the maker of our world,"

---

154. For a discussion of proceduralism see Rosenberg 2002, esp. chap. 3, where he develops his own position by critically engaging Alston 1989 in support of what he takes to be broadly Sellarsian insights, which he says are "proceduralist only by implication."

155. The certification process, which is itself broadly inferential, produces this second-order knowing-event, about which no further legitimate doubt has been raised. As a result, reflective-knowledge is not itself in need of certification, even though in principle further legitimate doubt could be raised, in which case it too would be an awareness-event for which certification is sought. According to Ratnakīrti's Naiyāyikas, reflective-knowledge cannot be undermined by mere possibilities, but only by those possibilities for which there are strong positive reasons to suppose they actually obtain. Thus, though defeasible, a reflective knowing-event is not itself in need of certification. For an interesting discussion of this with regard to knowledge, see Rosenberg 2002: chap. 1.

and the second is the epistemic perspective on that knowing-event, e.g., "I have certified that the inference-instrument that produced that awareness-event is well-functioning."[156] It may be helpful to think of this second constituent as the assertive-content of that awareness-event. It is this assertive-content that is the source of the agent's "epistemic perspective" on her first-order awareness-event. More specifically, with this assertive-content comes a kind of confidence in the content of the first-order knowing-event. While the first-order knowing-event itself comes with the absence of doubt/uncertainty, the certifying-event comes with confidence, which is one reason it has differential epistemic value as compared with the first-order knowing-event itself. Whether this differential epistemic value is added or simply additional epistemic value will depend on context.

The dialogical form of the text thus indicates that the Nyāya epistemic framework provides not only a dialectical context for their defense of the Īśvara-inference but also an epistemological context for it. The Naiyāyikas' deontological, proceduralist, internalist foundationalism thus informs their defense of the Īśvara-inference by quietly specifying the conditions that determine when any such defense is successful. As I hope to show in chapter 3, Ratnakīrti clearly recognizes this, and fashions a critique of the Īśvara-inference that targets both the inference and the epistemology that is used to defend it.

156. The content of the certifying-event is as follows: "I notice that I am aware that the inference-instrument that produced my awareness that Īśvara is the maker of the world (the subject component) is (the relation component) certified/well-functioning (the property component)." See section 1.3.

CHAPTER 3
Against Īśvara
Ratnakīrti's Buddhist Critique

RATNAKĪRTI'S NAIYĀYIKAS DEFENDED THEIR ARGUMENT for the nature and existence of Īśvara by showing that none of the possible defects of the reason property "being an effect" applied to it. They concluded, therefore, that this reason property was a well-functioning instrument for the inferential awareness of Īśvara. Interestingly, in responding to their arguments, Ratnakīrti does not consider each defect in sequence and then argue that it does or does not apply to the reason property. Instead, he reorganizes the Naiyāyikas' presentation of the material and discusses the issues raised in their defense of the argument under three more general section headings: there is a *Section on Pervasion*, in which he discusses the nature of inference-warranting relations and how such relations can be detected; a *Section on the Reason Property*, in which he discusses its proper scope; and finally, a *Section on the Target Property*, in which he discusses the special characteristics of the target property that can and cannot be proven through inferential reasoning.[1] In each of these sections Ratnakīrti brings

1. *Section on Pervasion*, RNĀ (ĪSD 40.17–50.20); *Section on the Reason Property*, RNĀ (ĪSD 50.21–54.04); *Section on the Target Property*, RNĀ (ĪSD 54.05–57.10).

together those aspects of the Naiyāyikas' defense that have to do with the topic being considered, and then in that context discusses their arguments that specific defects such as "opposed" (H2) or "inconclusive" (H3) do not apply.[2] His response to the Naiyāyikas' discussion of a particular defect is, therefore, often distributed throughout the three sections. For example, while his discussion of H2, "opposed," is primarily restricted to the *Section on the Target Property,* his discussion of H3, "inconclusive," is distributed throughout both the *Section on Pervasion* and the *Section on the Reason Property.*

Ratnakīrti's decision to restructure the debate in this way is not insignificant, since it reveals that his critique of the Nyāya argument is supposed to extend to the basic components of the epistemological theory that supports all such inferential arguments. As I will argue, Ratnakīrti uses his critique of the Īśvara-inference to target both the Nyāya theory of inference-warranting relations—that is, their account of the *pervasion subcomponent* of the inference-instrument—and their understanding of the scope of the reason property—that is, their account of the *site subcomponent.* In targeting these two subcomponents of the functioning of the inference-instrument, Ratnakīrti tries to show not only that the Naiyāyikas have not certified the instrument "being an effect," but that their approach to the epistemology of certification in general is untenable. This strategy enables Ratnakīrti to identify the specific philosophical issues on which successful certification of the Īśvara-inference depends, while also pointing to the broader significance of what he sees as the Naiyāyikas' failure to adequately address them. Restructuring the debate in this way thus focuses attention on both the philosophical details that are specific to his critique of the Īśvara-inference and the broader significance of his arguments against it.

In discussing Ratnakīrti's arguments in this chapter, I will follow the order of his critique through each of the three sections, but will selectively focus on those aspects of his discussion that are most relevant to H2 and H3a, "generally inconclusive," and its subtypes. I will begin with Ratnakīrti's discussion of H3a, as it is presented in the first subsection of his essay—the *Section on Pervasion*—and then turn to his discussion of it in the following subsection, the *Section on the Reason Property.* I will then discuss H2 in the *Section on the Target Property.* Before turning to Ratnakīrti's specific discussion of H3a, however, it will be helpful to first consider his account of the

2. See chapter 2, sections 2.3.1, 3.1, and 3.2.

Nyāya theory of inference-warranting relations and his generic critique of it. This rather lengthy discussion is necessary for appreciating both the force of his more specific arguments and their broader philosophical significance.

1. The *Section on Pervasion*: The Trouble with Natural Relations

Ratnakīrti begins the critical part of his "Refutation of Arguments for Establishing Īśvara" (*Īśvarasādhanadūṣaṇa*) with a long *Section on Pervasion* in which he argues that none of the known methods for establishing inference-warranting relations can be used to establish pervasion between effects-in-general (*kārya-mātra*) and an intelligent maker.[3] This is true, he argues, not only for the method favored by the Naiyāyikas, but for all of the methods of which he is aware.[4] Included in his discussion are also more gen-

3. See RNĀ (ĪSD 40.17–50.20).

4. Ratnakīrti considers four alternatives: alternative 1, RNĀ (ĪSD 40.24–43.29); alternative 2, RNĀ (ĪSD 43.30–45.29); alternative 3, RNĀ (ĪSD 45.30–49.12); and alternative 4, RNĀ (ĪSD 49.13–50.04). Ratnakīrti explains that alternative 3 is the Naiyāyikas' view. My discussion focuses on this section of text. In my view, this list of alternatives is intended to exhaust all of the possibilities.

The four alternatives are listed at RNĀ (ĪSD 40.19–40.23): "And how is [pervasion] grasped? There are four possibilities: (1) It is grasped by a warranted mode of awareness that disproves the presence [of the reason property] in dissimilar cases, like in the [inference-warranting] relation between a cause and an effect-in-general; (2) It is known by specific perceptions and nonperceptions that are directed toward grasping a specific [instance] of positive and negative concomitance, like in the [inference-warranting] relation between smoke and fire; (3) It is known by numerous observations [of the reason property] in similar cases and nonobservations in dissimilar cases, as per your position; or (4) It is known by single observation [of the reason property] in a similar case and nonobservation in a dissimilar case" (*sā ca gṛhyamāṇā kim, kāraṇakāryamātrayor iva viparyayabādhakapramāṇabalād grāhyā | yad vāgnidhūmayor iva viśiṣṭānvayavyatirekagrahaṇapravaṇaviśiṣṭapratyakṣānupalambhābhyāṃ boddhavyā | uta svavyavasthayā sapakṣāsapakṣayor bhūyodarśanād darśanādarśanābhyāṃ pratyetavyā | āhosvit sapakṣāsapakṣayoḥ sakṛd darśanādarśanābhyāṃ jñātavyeti catvāro vikalpāḥ*). Alternatives 2 and 3 are also discussed in Ratnakīrti's "Inquiry Into Inference-Warranting Relations" (*Vyāptinirṇaya*, VN). For example, alternative 2, which describes Ratnakīrti's view, is introduced at RNĀ (VN 106.01–106.02) and alternative 3, which is attributed to the Naiyāyikas, is discussed at RNĀ (VN 106.24–108.02; 109.27–

eral remarks about the sorts of relations that can be inference-warranting and the methods that are adequate for detecting them. It is helpful to divide Ratnakīrti's remarks in this section into three groups: the first is directed toward criticizing the Naiyāyikas' analysis of the nature of inference-warranting relations; the second focuses on showing that the method that the Naiyāyikas propose for detecting the presence of such relations is inadequate; and the third extends these critiques to the pervasion subcomponent of the instrument in the Naiyāyikas' argument for the existence of Īśvara. The first two groups of remarks will be discussed together in section 1.1, and will provide the background for the third group of remarks, which will be discussed in greater detail in section 1.2. A useful way of initially thinking about all of these issues is in terms of what I will call "epistemic necessity."

As discussed in chapter 2, an inference-warranting relation is a component of an instrument of inferential-awareness.[5] More specifically, it is one of the two subcomponents of its functioning.[6] This "pervasion" subcomponent is defined in terms of the second (C2.2) and third (C2.3) "Instrument Conditions" and is closely associated with defects such as H2 and H3a. In order for an instrument to be well-functioning, this subcomponent must not be defeated or undermined by either defect. An inference-warranting relation is said to be "defeated" by defect H3a when a locus is identified in which the reason property is known to be present and the target property is known to be absent. In such cases, C2.3 is defeated by $H3a_1$, a subtype of H3a. Defect H2 also defeats an inference-warranting relation, since in directly showing that a reason property is pervaded by the absence of the target property, it shows, indirectly, that the reason property is present in at least one dissimilar case. Let us refer to H2 as a "direct defeater" of C2.2 and

111.24). Interestingly, Ratnakīrti makes use of the similarities between the Nyāya position and the (Bhāṭṭa) Mīmāṃsā position to support his criticism of alternative 3. For his criticism of this position see RNĀ (VN 106.02–106.12; 108.23–109.12). Much of Ratnakīrti's discussion of alternative 3 parallels his discussion in his VN. For an excellent study of Ratnakīrti's VN, see Lasic 2000b.

5. See chapter 2, section 2.3.1.

6. The other subcomponent is defined in terms of T1, which states that a reason property must be known to be present in the site of the inference (*pakṣadharmatva*). The defect associated with T1 is H1b. See chapter 2, section 2.3.1.

an "indirect defeater" of C2.3.[7] It is important to note that as I have interpreted them C2.2 and C2.3 are defined only by their direct defeaters.[8] An inference-warranting relation is "undermined" by H3a when there is doubt about the exclusion of the reason property from all dissimilar cases. In such cases, C2.3 is undermined by H3a_2, a second subtype of H3a. Only a relation that is neither defeated nor undermined can be a subcomponent of a well-functioning instrument of inferential awareness. For the Naiyāyikas, let us stipulate that when it is *known* that none of the defects that could affect the pervasion subcomponent of an instrument apply to it, the pervasion subcomponent of that instrument has "epistemic necessity" and is, therefore, "necessary enough" to be the pervasion subcomponent of a *well*-functioning instrument.[9] In such cases, the relation between the reason property and the target property is known to be "genuinely" inference-warranting and epistemically necessary.

In what I am calling his first set of remarks, Ratnakīrti discusses the Nyāya theory of inference-warranting relations and argues that the conditions in terms of which these relations are defined are too weak to define the pervasion subcomponents of only well-functioning inference-instruments. For convenience, let us refer to the conditions in terms of which the Naiyāyikas define such relations as "pervasion conditions." In his second set of remarks, Ratnakīrti argues that the method that the Naiyāyikas propose for satisfying the pervasion conditions is inadequate. He concludes, therefore, that, given their own criteria, the Naiyāyikas are unable to determine whether or not a proposed relation is genuinely inference-warranting and therefore has epistemic necessity. Before turning to Ratnakīrti's critical remarks, it will be helpful to first consider his account of the Nyāya theory in general.

1.1. The Nyāya Theory: A "Natural-Mode" of Pervasion

Ratnakīrti chooses to describe the Nyāya theory of inference-warranting relations by quoting a number of passages from the work of Naiyāyikas

7. See chapter 2, section 2.3.1.

8. More precisely, C2.2 is defined in terms of H2 and H3b, and C2.3 in terms of H3a and H3b.

9. This condition will be modified, slightly, in section 1.2.

Vācaspatimiśra and Trilocana, his teacher. Ratnakīrti's description focuses on the Naiyāyikas' account of the nature of inference-warranting relations, their analysis of pervasion conditions other than C2.2 and C2.3, and their position on how all such conditions can be satisfied. As a way of providing a context for Vācaspatimiśra and Trilocana's remarks, Ratnakīrti first provides a quick summary of their view. In the voice of a Naiyāyika, he says,

> (a) The connection [between a reason property and its target] is known through repeated observations and nonobservations. But this connection is not understood to be causal but rather natural—[and] it can definitely be detected through observation and nonobservation.[10]

Ratnakīrti then supports this description by referring specifically to the work of Vācaspatimiśra and Trilocana. He explains that,

> (b) Vācaspati says: We do not say that the reason property "being an effect" brings about inferential awareness *because* it is observed [in similar cases] and not observed [in dissimilar cases]. Rather, we say this because there is a natural connection. Now, this very connection is detected by observing [the reason property] in similar cases and not observing [it] in dissimilar cases, as per a method which will be stated. . . . It is correct that when a natural connection between a property *R* and a property *T* is proven to be epistemically necessary, *R* is the reason property and the other relatum, *T*, is its target. That is to say: there is a natural relation between smoke and fire, but not between fire and smoke. This is because [fire] is perceived even without smoke. If fire is put together with wet fuel, however, it will be invariably related with smoke. As a result, the relation of fire [with smoke] is clearly due to the additional condition, wet fuel, but is not natural. Therefore, it is not epistemically necessary. On the other hand, the relation between smoke and fire is natural. This is because an additional condition is not seen [and] deviation is not observed anywhere.[11]

---

10. RNĀ (ĪSD 45.30–45.32): *{nanu} bhūyodarśanādarśanābhyāṃ pratibandhaḥ pratīyata {iti tṛtīya evāsmākaṃ pakṣaḥ} | kevalaṃ sa pratibandho na tadutpattilakṣaṇo grahītavyaḥ | kintu svābhāvikaḥ | sa eva darśanādarśanābhyāṃ pratīyate.*

11. RNĀ (ĪSD 45.32–46.13): *vācaspatiḥ prāha | na sapakṣāsapakṣayor darśanābhyāṃ kārya-*

(c) Vācaspati also said this: It is . . . just a sense faculty, which is assisted by latent cognitive impressions that were produced by numerous observations, that grasps the natural relation of smoke with fire. This is just like [the repeated observations of a jeweler that enable him to determine] that a real [jewel] is different from a fake.[12]

(d) This point was also stated by Trilocana: the well-functioning instrument that removes doubt about the presence of the reason property in dissimilar cases is just perception—called "nonapprehension." This is also the means for ascertaining the absence of an additional condition that has met the requirements for apprehension. This is how a relation is proven to be natural.[13]

These passages outline the Nyāya theory of inference-warranting relations. They do so by defining inference-warranting relations to be "natural relations" (passage *a*/passage *b*); identifying what appear to be two further conditions for pervasion—the absence of an "additional condition" and the absence of "deviation" (passage *b*/passage *d*); and describing a method through which the pervasion conditions can be satisfied (passage *c*/passage *d*). What follows is a brief discussion of each of these components of the Nyāya theory, as it is understood by Ratnakīrti.

---

tvasya gamakatvam api tu svābhāvikapratibandhabalād iti brūmaḥ | sa eva tu sapakṣāsapakṣayor darśanādarśanābhyāṃ vakṣyamāṇena krameṇa pratīyata {iti tadupakṣepo 'pi yuktaḥ} | tena yasyāsau svābhāvikapratibandho niyataḥ siddhaḥ sa eva gamako gamyaś cetaraḥ sambandhīti yujyate | tathā hi dhūmādīnāṃ vahnyādibhiḥ saha sambandhaḥ svābhāviko na tu vahnyādīnāṃ dhūmādibhiḥ | te hi vinā dhūmādibhir upalabhyante | yadā tv ārdrendhanasambandham anubhavanti tadā dhūmādibhiḥ sambadhyante | tasmād vahnyādīnām ārdrendhanādy upādhikṛtaḥ sambandho na tu svābhāvikas tato na niyataḥ | svābhāvikas tu dhūmādīnāṃ vahnyādibhiḥ sambandhaḥ, tadupādher anupalabhyamānatvāt | kvacid vyabhicārasyādarśanāt. See also RNĀ (VN 106.24–107.05) and NVTṬ (135.08–135.14).

12. RNĀ (ĪSD 47.01–47.02): *vācaspatināpīdam uktam abhijātamaṇibhedatattvavad bhūyodarśanajanitasaṃskārasahāyam indriyam eva dhūmādīnāṃ vahnyādibhiḥ svābhāvikasambandhagrāhīti yuktam iti.* See also RNĀ (VN 107.23–107.24) and NVTṬ (136.22–136.23), ŚV: Anumāna 12, ŚVK (3.16, 14–15), and RNĀ (ĪSD 46.21–46.23).

13. RNĀ (ĪSD 46.27–46.31): *trilocanena punar ayam arthaḥ kathitaḥ | {bhūyodarśanena bhūyodarśanasahāyena manasā tajjātīyānāṃ sambandho gṛhīto bhavati | ato dhūmo 'gniṃ na vyabhicarati | tadvyabhicāre 'py upādhirahitaṃ sambandham atikrāmet} hetor vipakṣaśaṅkānivartakaṃ pramāṇam upalabdhilakṣaṇaprāptopādhivirahaniścayahetur anupalambhākhyaṃ pratyakṣam eva | tataḥ siddhaḥ svābhāvikaḥ sambandhaḥ | {tathehāpīti svamataṃ vyavasthāpitam iti}.* See also RNĀ (VN 106.19–106.23).

1.1.1. Natural Relations

Vācaspatimiśra explains that the relation between a reason property and its target is not epistemically necessary simply because the two properties have been repeatedly observed together in similar cases and not observed together in dissimilar cases (passage *b*). Rather, he says that it is because there is a "natural connection" (*svābhāvika-pratibandha*) between them.[14] It is this nonepistemic relation that is taken to underwrite genuinely inference-warranting relations and their epistemic necessity. The patterns of observation and nonobservation to which both Vācaspatimiśra and Trilocana refer are epistemic facts that, like epistemic necessity, supervene on this natural relation.[15] As Vācaspatimiśra points out, according to the Naiyāyikas, natural relations are not identical to causal relations, and so cannot be interpreted in terms of the "production-mode" of pervasion.

Although the class of natural relations may include causal ones, it is clear that it also includes those that are not (passage *a*).[16] Consider, for example, Vācaspatimiśra's example of the jeweler (passage *c*). In this standard example, traditional instruction in gemology, supported by extensive experience with both genuine and fake rubies, enables a jeweler to identify a property unique to genuine rubies—namely, the property "having rainbow-like luster."[17] It is partly on the basis of having seen this property in genuine rubies (C2.2) and not having seen it in any fake ones (C2.3) that an experienced jeweler is able to determine whether a particular stone is a genuine ruby or a fake. According to the Naiyāyikas, the jeweler's observations and nonobservations of this property must also be supplemented with the nonobservation of an "additional condition" and the nonobservation of "deviation" (passage *b*/

---

14. For a discussion of this theory see Oberhammer 1964, Oberhammer 1965, and Vattanky 1984:76–79. The best place to start, however, is Krasser 2001.

15. For them, the epistemically evaluative supervenes on nonevaluative properties. For an interesting discussion of this see Sosa 1991:110 and Sosa 2007.

16. See NB, NV, and NVTṬ *ad* NS 1.1.5 and NS 2.1.37–2.1.38, where, for example, the following inferential arguments are discussed: (1) the prediction of rain from seeing a rising cloud (or from seeing ants scurrying about carrying their eggs); (2) an inference of rain from seeing a full and swiftly flowing river; and (3) an inference of movement from seeing the moon at one place at one time and at a different place at a different time.

17. Ratnakīrti explains this point about "traditional instruction" in gemology and specifies the defining characteristic "rainbow-like luster" at RNĀ (ĪSD 48.14–48.19). This section of text is quoted and discussed in section 1.2.1 below.

passage *c*).[18] It is on the basis of this set of observations and nonobservations that a jeweler can infer that a particular stone (the site of the inference) is a genuine ruby (the target property) because it has rainbow-like luster (the reason property). According to the Naiyāyikas, what accounts for the epistemic necessity of the inference-warranting relation in this argument is that the terms of the relation are known to be naturally related.

In addition to C2.2 and C2.3, Vācaspatimiśra suggests that inference-warranting relations must meet two further conditions, defined in terms of the nonobservation of an additional condition and the nonobservation of deviation (passage *b*/passage *d*). Insofar as these conditions are necessary conditions for natural relations, their satisfaction is a necessary condition for epistemic necessity, and therefore for the pervasion subcomponents of well-functioning instruments of inferential awareness. It is helpful, therefore, to think of the *presence*/awareness of either an additional condition (U) or deviation (V) as a defeater of pervasion/epistemic necessity and of their *absence*/awareness of their absence as a necessary condition for it. Interestingly, according to the Naiyāyikas, U and V are both classified as defeaters of C2.3, and deviation, which is also understood as a defeater of C2.2, is specifically identified with each of the three subtypes of the defect "inconclusive" (H3).[19] Given this, it is important to consider whether U and/or V define pervasion conditions that are distinct from C2.2 and C2.3.

In my view, deviation should not be interpreted as defining a separate pervasion condition, since, according to the Naiyāyikas, "deviation" just refers to a property that is shared by H3a, H3b, and H3c—the three subtypes of the defect "inconclusive" (H3).[20] More specifically, deviation is often de-

---

18. "Additional conditions" and "deviation" will be discussed in section 1.2.2.

19. Since H3c is not discussed in KTBh, "deviation" is only identified with H3a and H3b. My discussion, however, will include H3c, because it is mentioned in RNĀ. This does not constitute a significant departure from KTBh, since what is philosophically significant is that H3 can be completely described in terms of deviation and deviation in terms of H3.

20. KTBh 105.04–105.05 explains the relationship between "deviation" and the defect called "inconclusive" (*anaikāntika*, H3) as follows: "In this way, where instances of (*ādayas*) deviation are like that, they are inconclusive" (*evaṃ yatra vyabhicārādayas tathābhūtās te 'naikāntikāḥ*). KTBh 113.11 states that another name for the defect called "inconclusive" (*anaikāntika*) is "deviating" (*savyabhicāra*): "A reason property that results in doubt about the target property may be called either 'inconclusive' or 'deviating'" (*sādhyasaṃśayahetur anaikāntikaḥ savyabhicāra iti vocyate*).

fined in terms of an epistemological rule which states that in order for a reason property to be well-functioning it must be known to be present in similar cases (C2.2) and excluded from all dissimilar cases (C2.3). This rule is sometimes referred to as the "nondeviation rule" (*avyabhicāra-niyama*).[21] Deviation is defined by the violation of this rule, which is itself defined by C2.2 and C2.3.[22] The property that is shared by H3a, H3b, and H3c may be thought of, therefore, as the property "being a defeater of the nondeviation rule." Thus deviation can be helpfully interpreted as a pervasion-defeating property that is shared, in different ways, by H3a, H3b, and H3c.[23] The requirement that deviation must not be observed in order for a relation to have epistemic necessity is, therefore, equivalent to the requirement that H3a, H3b, and H3c be known to not apply to the reason property being considered; that is, that C2.2 and C2.3 be satisfied. The "nonobservation of deviation," then, refers just to the nonobservation of this property, and is equivalent to showing that these three defects do not apply to a reason property.[24] It is

---

21. See chapter 2, section 3.2.2, where RNĀ (ĪSD 37.12–37.16) is discussed. The term "nondeviation rule" (*avyabhicāraniyama*) is used there.

22. KTBh 114.10–115.02 describes "deviation" as follows: "Now, deviation is defined: The rule is that a reason property, for which a similar and dissimilar case is possible, is well-functioning (*gamakatva*) only [when] it is excluded from dissimilar cases (C2.3) while being present in a similar case (C2.2). 'Deviation' is the absence of this rule for a reason property that is not pervaded by the absence of the target property" (*vyabhicāras tu lakṣyate | saṃbhavatsapakṣavipakṣasya hetoḥ sapakṣavṛttitve sati vipakṣād vyāvṛttir eva niyamo gamakatvāt | tasya ca sādhyaviparītāvyāptasya tanniyamābhāvo vyabhicāraḥ*). Note: the phrase "for a reason property that is not pervaded by the absence of the target property" is added to prevent H2 from being classified as a subtype of H3.

23. For example, H3a—i.e., the defect called "common" (*sādhāraṇa*)—possesses the property "being a nondeviation rule violator," since, although it is present in a similar case (C2.2), it is also known to be present in a dissimilar case; that is, it is known to violate C2.3. Similarly, H3b—i.e., the defect called "uncommon" (*asādhāraṇa*)—violates the nondeviation rule, since it is known not to be present in a similar case, in which case it is known to violate C2.2, or in a dissimilar case, in which case it is known to satisfy C2.3. H3c—i.e., the defect called "not-universal" (*anupasaṃhāra*)—violates the rule by violating both C2.2 and C2.3. What individuates these three defects is how the property they share is instantiated in a particular case.

24. As mentioned earlier, "deviation" can also be used to refer to a locus or property-possessor in which "U" is present. On this use of the term, the "nonobservation of deviation" refers to the nonobservation of a locus of deviation.

this "equivalence" that accounts for the assimilation of deviation into H3, and supports the idea that the nonobservation of deviation should not be interpreted as a pervasion condition that is distinct from C2.2 and C2.3.

1.1.2. Additional Conditions

Interestingly, since the presence of an additional condition (U) is defined as a subtype of the defect "unestablished" (H1), it too can be characterized as a defect of a reason property.[25] However, the Naiyāyikas do not identify the presence of an additional condition with the defects that define either C2.2 or C2.3. This suggests that there is not "closure" with respect to the satisfaction of C2.2 and C2.3, and U—that is, that although it may be known that C2.2 and C2.3 are satisfied, it may not be known that an additional condition is absent; that is, that U is satisfied.[26] In contrast, there is closure with respect to deviation—that is, if it is known that C2.2 and C2.3 are satisfied it is

25. KTBh discusses H1 and its three main subtypes at KTBh 35.07–38.04; 104.05–113.03. Both of these sections associate one subtype of H1c with additional conditions.

KTBh 110.06–111.07 defines H1c, the defect called "unestablished in being pervaded" (*vyāpyatvāsiddha*) as follows: "But where the pervasion of a reason property is not known there is indeed [the defect] 'unestablished in being pervaded.' It is of two sorts. The first is [defined by a reason property which is] not [known to be] accompanied by the target property, and the other is one which is [known to be] related to the target property through an additional condition" (*vyāpyatvāsiddhas tu sa eva yatra hetor vyāptir nāvagamyate | sa dvividhaḥ | ekaḥ sādhyenāsahacaritaḥ | aparas tu sopādhikasādhyasaṃbandhī*).

KTBh 36.07–36.08 also describes the two subtypes of H1c: "'Unestablished in being pervaded' is of two sorts. The first is due to the absence of a well-functioning instrument of awareness that grasps pervasion and the other is due to the presence of an additional condition" (*vyāpyatvāsiddhas tu dvividhaḥ | eko vyāptigrāhakapramāṇābhāvāt | aparas tūpādhisadbhāvāt*). Note: an example of the first subtype of "unestablished in being pervaded" is an inference of the momentariness (*s*) of sound (*p*) from its existence (*h*). In this case, the pervasion of the reason property is said to be unknown because there is not a well-functioning instrument of awareness that can prove its pervasion with the target property. See KTBh 110.08–111.01.

26. The Naiyāyikas do not classify reason properties with additional conditions as being defective because of H2 and H3. As a result, H1c cannot be taken to be a direct defeater of either C2.2 or C2.3. This does not mean, however, that H1c cannot be related to C2.2 or C2.3. For example, although the Naiyāyikas insist that because H1c is not a direct defeater of C2.2 or C2.3 it is not equivalent to H2 or H3, it is still possible for H1c to be interpreted as an indirect defeater of C2.3.

known that deviation is absent; that is, that V is satisfied.[27] It is helpful, therefore, to consider the absence of an additional condition as a *pervasion condition* that is distinct from C2.2 and C2.3. Before considering the significance of this to the Naiyāyikas' account of epistemic necessity, it may be helpful to first consider the Nyāya account of additional conditions in greater detail.

Vācaspatimiśra introduces the idea of an additional condition by pointing to an asymmetry in the relation between fire and smoke, namely, that the relation *of smoke* (the reason property) *with fire* (the target property) is natural, while the relation *of fire* (the reason property) *with smoke* (the target property) is not (passage *b*). Even if it can be shown that C2.2 and C2.3 are satisfied for each relation, Vācaspatimiśra maintains that they are not both inference-warranting. It is explained that the asymmetry is due to the presence of an additional condition, contact with wet fuel, in the relation between fire and smoke.[28] According to the Naiyāyikas, an additional condition

---

27. My use of the term "closure" is related to (though not identical with) the standard use of the term. For example, knowledge is generally said to be "closed" under logical implication in cases in which an S who knows that *p* and also knows that *p* entails *q* is assumed to know that *q*. For the Naiyāyikas, there is nonclosure with respect to the satisfaction of U; that is, although an agent may know that C2.2 and C2.3 are satisfied, and that the satisfaction of C2.2 and C2.3 entails the satisfaction of U, she is not assumed to know that U is satisfied. There is, however, closure with respect to the satisfaction of V; that is, an agent who knows that C2.2 and C2.3 are satisfied, and knows that the satisfaction of C2.2 and C2.3 entails the satisfaction of V, is assumed to know that V is satisfied. For more on "closure" and "nonclosure" see Nozick 1981:172–185, 197–217.

28. This is the standard example of such a condition. In the inference of fire from smoke, for example, the inference-warranting relation is "wherever there is smoke there is fire" (*yatra yatra dhūmas tatra tatra vahniḥ*). This relation is generally taken to be epistemically necessary and, according to the Naiyāyikas, an example of a relation that is "natural." In the inference of smoke from fire, however, the proposed inference-warranting relation is "wherever there is fire there is smoke" (*yatra yatra vahnis tatra tatra dhūmaḥ*). As stated, this relation is neither epistemically necessary nor natural, since it does not satisfy C2.3, as it is known that a red-hot iron bar is a dissimilar case in which the reason property is known to be present. Fire(-in-general) is not, therefore, a well-functioning instrument for the inferential awareness of smoke. It is important to note, however, that although "fire (in-general)" violates C2.3, it is not said, in this context, to be defective because of H3a. Instead, in this context, it is recognized that when fire-in-general is in contact with wet fuel (*ārdrendhana-saṃyoga*), fire can be a well-functioning instrument for the inferential awareness of smoke. The pervasion subcomponent of this well-functioning instrument, however, is not "wherever there is fire there is smoke" (*yatra yatra vahnis tatra tatra dhūmaḥ*) but "wherever there

is a property without which a proposed reason property could not be pervaded by its target. More accurately, such a property is said to be a pervader of the proposed target property and a nonpervader of the proposed reason property.[29] The presence of such a property "U" indirectly defeats C2.3 by directly showing that the epistemic necessity between a proposed reason property and target property depends upon this additional condition. In so doing, it indicates that there are loci in which the proposed reason property is present but the proposed target property is not; that is, it indirectly indicates that the proposed reason property is known to be present in at least one dissimilar case. Like H2, the presence of such a property is helpfully thought of as an indirect defeater of C2.3 but (unlike H2) a direct defeater of the pervasion subcomponent of the proposed instrument itself. As implied in the passages quoted above, it is the absence of such a property (or defeater) that is a necessary condition for pervasion. As Trilocana explains, this condition is satisfied by the nonobservation of "U" (passage *c*).[30]

Interestingly, the Naiyāyikas do not associate the presence of "U" with either defect H2 or H3a, and therefore with either C2.2 or C2.3.[31] Instead, as mentioned earlier, it is usually identified with a subtype of the defect "unestablished" (H1). This subtype is defined as "one in which being pervaded is not established" (*vyāpyatvāsiddha*, H1c) and is said to apply to a proposed reason property that is "related to a target property [only] in virtue of an additional condition."[32] The significance of this for an interpretation of the Nyāya theory of epistemic necessity is twofold. First, it reveals that even though C2.2 and C2.3 state necessary conditions for epistemic neces-

---

is fire in contact with wet fuel there is smoke" (*ārdrendhanasaṃyoge sati yatra yatra vahnis tatra tatra dhūmaḥ*). According to the Naiyāyikas, this shows that the relation of fire with smoke is not natural because it is brought about by an additional condition, contact with wet fuel (and not because of H3a). For other examples see KTBh 111, 229 and Bhattacharya 1976:257–262.

29. KTBh 37.08–37.09: "An additional condition is 'a pervader of the target property that is a non-pervader of the reason property.' This is the defining characteristic of an additional condition" (*sādhyavyāpakatve sati sādhanāvyāpaka upādhir ity upādhilakṣaṇam*). See the excellent discussion in Phillips and Tatacharya 2002.

30. The satisfaction of the pervasion conditions is discussed in section 1.1.3.

31. In my interpretation, this is because "U" is not a "direct defeater" of either C2.2 or C2.3. It is a direct defeater of pervasion itself; that is, the conjunction of C2.2 and C2.3.

32. See earlier note: "*sopādhikasādhyasambandhī*" (*hetuḥ*).

sity, they are not sufficient: it is also necessary to show that an additional condition is absent—that is, that H1c does not apply. Second, it shows that there isn't closure specifically with respect to the satisfaction of C2.3—that is, that although it may be known that a reason property is excluded from dissimilar cases, it must still be shown, through nonapprehension, that an additional condition is absent. Although it indirectly defeats C2.3, property "U" defines a separate pervasion condition. It may be helpful to think of additional conditions as "undercutting" the pervasion of the proposed reason property by its target.[33] Interestingly, in addition to being an undercutting defeater of pervasion, property "U" is also said to be an "effecting/enabling condition" (*prayojaka*) for the proposed relation.[34] This feature of property "U" indicates that given its presence, a proposed reason property would be naturally related to the property that is supposed to be proven by it. In other words, when "U" is conjoined to the proposed reason property, the conjunction of "U" and the proposed reason property would be naturally related to the target property.

The following example (passage *b*) illustrates both features of property "U." Suppose that someone "infers" the presence of smoke—in this case, the target property—from the presence of fire, the reason property. She insists that the relation between the reason property, fire, and the target property, smoke, is a natural relation. She also claims to have satisfied both C2.2 and C2.3, and to have therefore certified that the pervasion subcomponent is well-functioning. According to the Naiyāyikas, this is not sufficient for certification, since in addition to satisfying C2.2 and C2.3, it is also necessary to show that there is not an additional condition: detecting the presence of an additional condition would show that the relation is not natural, and therefore not epistemically necessary. In this case, it is noticed that a property "U," wet fuel, is present in every locus of fire in which smoke is present, and absent from every locus of fire in which smoke is absent. From this, the Naiyāyikas conclude that "U" is a pervader of the proposed target property, smoke. If the relation between the proposed reason property, fire, and the

33. For an extended argument in support of referring to additional conditions as "undercutting conditions" see Phillips and Tatacharya 2002.

34. KTBh 22.01: "It is said that an additional condition is an effecting condition" (*prayojakaś copādhir ity ucyate*). KTBh 37.08: "The sense is that an additional condition is an effecting condition" (*prayojakam upādhir iti yāvat*).

proposed target property, smoke, is really a natural one, "U" should also be a pervader of the proposed *reason* property, fire. This is due to the reflexivity and transitivity of the pervasion relation. If "U" is not a pervader of the proposed reason property, it suggests that there is a locus in which the proposed reason property is present but the proposed target property is absent. As an example of such a locus, the Naiyāyikas often point to a red-hot bar of iron. This is a locus in which the proposed reason property, fire, is present, but the property "U" is not. Thus, in this case "U" is also known to be a nonpervader of the proposed reason property. As a result, its presence defeats the naturalness of the proposed relation and its supposed epistemic necessity. In addition, since a relation between the reason property conjoined with "U'—that is, fire which is in contact with wet fuel—and the target property, smoke, is natural and has epistemic necessity, "U" is an "effecting/enabling condition" for the proposed relation. This means that it is only in virtue of "U" that the relation could be epistemically necessary.

Given this, it should be clear why the Naiyāyikas do not consider the presence of an additional condition to be equivalent to defect H3a, and why I have described property "U" as defining a separate pervasion condition. Defect H3a (i.e., $H3a_1$) is defined in terms of a reason property that is known to be present in at least one dissimilar case. C2.3 is, therefore, directly defeated by the presence of H3a, as is the proposed inference-warranting relation. The presence of property "U," however, does not defeat a proposed inference-warranting relation by directly identifying a dissimilar case in which the proposed reason property is known to be present. Instead, it does so indirectly through the identification of a property "U." In the above example, if the red-hot iron bar were directly cited as a dissimilar case in which the reason property is known to be present, H3a would defeat the relation. As discussed above, however, the counterexample to the proposed pervasion relation is indicated indirectly, through directly detecting the presence of an additional condition, contact with wet fuel. It is the presence of the additional condition that is the defeater, not the presence of the counterexample.

1.1.3. Satisfying C2.2, C2.3, and U

In order for a relation to be genuinely inference-warranting and have epistemic necessity, it is necessary (and sufficient) that it meet three pervasion conditions: C2.2, C2.3, and U. It is through the satisfaction of these conditions that a relation is shown to be inference-warranting, and therefore epistemically necessary. Without an account of how these conditions can be satisfied, however, the Naiyāyikas will not be able to explain how they can determine when these conditions obtain. As Trilocana explains, according to the Naiyāyikas, there is an accredited instrument of warranted-awareness that enables one to know that there is neither deviation nor an additional condition (passage *d*). This Instrument is a form of sense perception called "nonapprehension" (*anupalambha*) by him (passage *d*) and "nonobservation" (*adarśana*) by Vācaspatimiśra (passage *c*). It is through this type of perception that the absence of "V" and "U" is said to be known.[35] According to the Naiyāyikas, the first two conditions, C2.2 and C2.3, can be satisfied through the nonapprehension or nonobservation of deviation (property "V") and the third, U, through the nonobservation or nonapprehension of an additional condition (property "U"). As Vācaspatimiśra also explains (passage

---

35. In more familiar descriptions of the Nyāya view, "nonapprehension" (*anupalabdhi*) is not said to be another *name* for sense perception (*pratyakṣa*), even though nonapprehension (*anupalabdhi*) is understood to be a subtype of perception and not a distinct instrument for warranted awareness. According to the Naiyāyikas, absences are perceived as a result of the various sense faculties being related to them through what they call a "characterized-characteristic relation" (*viśeṣya-viśeṣaṇa-bhāva*), of which there are five subtypes. For example, in a statement such as "There is no pot on the floor," what is characterized (*viśeṣya*) is the floor, and the characteristic (*viśeṣaṇa*) is the absence of a pot. See KTBh 18.03–19.01; 47.11–52.02.

KTBh 18.10–19.01: "So, briefly, an absence is grasped by a sense faculty through the contact relation between the sense faculty and a sense object. This [contact relation] is a 'characteristic-characterized relation' that can be related to any one of the five types of [contact] relations" (*tad evaṃ saṅkṣepataḥ pañcavidhasambandhānyatamasambandhasambaddhaviśeṣaṇaviśeṣyabhāvalakṣaṇena indriyārthasannikarṣeṇābhāva indriyeṇa gṛhyate*). More important, for our purposes, KTBh 48.02–48.03 describes the relationship between sense perception (*pratyakṣa*), nonapprehension (*anupalabdhi*), and suppositional reasoning (*tarka*): "Absence is in fact grasped by perception, which is accompanied by nonapprehension, and assisted by suppositional reasoning; that is, 'If a pot were present [on the floor] it would be observed just as the floor [is observed]'" (*yad yatra ghaṭo 'bhaviṣyat tarhi bhūtalam ivādrakṣyad ityādi tarkasahakāriṇānupalambhasanāthena pratyakṣeṇaivābhāvagrahaṇāt {kim abhāvapramāṇena}*).

It is interesting that Ratnakīrti does not choose to focus on the role that suppositional reasoning plays in the Nyāya theory. KTBh describes the important role that suppositional reasoning plays at KTBh 22.08–22.09: "Thus the absence of an additional condition is determined through perception, which is assisted by suppositional reasoning and nonapprehension" (*tato darśanābhāvān nāstīti tarkasahakāriṇānupalambhasanāthena pratyakṣeṇaivopādhyabhāvo 'vadhāryate*). This passage is quoted in note 37.

c), together with observations of the reason property in similar cases and nonobservations in dissimilar cases, these nonobservations make possible a final observation, through which epistemic necessity is directly grasped. According to Vācaspatimiśra, numerous observations of the reason property in similar cases and nonobservations in dissimilar cases are necessary, but not sufficient, for determining that the relation between a reason property such as "having rainbow-like luster" and its target, "being a genuine ruby," is genuinely inference-warranting and has epistemic necessity. In addition to these observations, and the nonobservation of "V" and "U," there must be a "final observation" in which the apprentice notices that the two properties are naturally related. The epistemic necessity between the two terms is itself grasped through this final observation, which is conditioned by mental impressions that were produced from all of the previous observations and nonobservations described above (passage *d*). This final observation is also understood by the Naiyāyikas to be an instance of perception, and so is also considered to be an instrument for warranted awareness.[36] According to the Naiyāyikas, then, in addition to the observation of the reason property in similar cases (C2.2) and its nonobservation in dissimilar cases (C2.3), the "final observation" also requires the nonobservation of an additional condition (U).[37]

---

36. Kajiyama (1998:97 n. 59) notes Vācaspatimiśra's disagreement with Trilocana about this. According to Trilocana, it is mental-perception that grasps concomitance. According to Vācaspatimiśra, concomitance is grasped either by any of the other subvarieties of sense-perception or by another instrument of warranted awareness. For an oblique reference to this see RNĀ (VN 107.22–107.26).

37. Much of this is also discussed in KTBh 20.06–25.05. Consider the following, KTBh 21.05–23.02: "The natural relation of smoke with fire, 'wherever there is smoke there is fire,' is detected through numerous observations [of the reason property in similar cases and nonobservation of the reason property in a dissimilar case]. Although it is known that there are similarly numerous observations that 'Maitrī's sons are dark skinned,' still the relation between 'being Maitrī's son' and 'being dark skinned' is not natural, but in fact is brought about by an additional condition. This is because an additional condition, 'the digestion of vegetarian food,' is known to exist. To explain: 'Being Maitrī's son' is not an effecting condition for 'being dark skinned.' In fact, the effecting condition is just the change due to the digestion of vegetarian food. And, as it is said, the effecting condition is an additional condition. Furthermore, in the relation of smoke with fire, there are no additional conditions. If there were [an additional condition], it would be either 'capable' or 'incapable' [of being observed]. It is not possible, however, to have doubt about one that is incapable [of being observed], and [here] there is the nonobservation of one that is capable [of being observed]. Wherever there is an additional condition it is apprehended, e.g., 'contact with wet

* * *

For Ratnakīrti's Naiyāyikas, epistemic necessity is grounded in inference-warranting relations that they call "natural." Such relations can be defined in terms of three pervasion conditions (C2.2, C2.3, U) that can be satisfied through a set of observations, most importantly the nonobservation of deviation and an additional condition. In order to show that the pervasion subcomponent of an inference-instrument is well-functioning, it is necessary to show that the inference-warranting relation that is defined by these three conditions is neither defeated, undermined, nor undercut by H2, H3a, or U. Only a relation that has been certified in this way has epistemic necessity. Natural relations are therefore a central element in the Nyāya theory of inference-warranting relations and epistemic necessity, and the primary object of Ratnakīrti's critique.

---

fuel' in the relation of fire with smoke . . . and the 'change due to the digestion of vegetarian food' in the relation of 'being Maitrī's son' with 'being dark skinned.' Now here, with respect to the concomitance of smoke with fire, there is not an additional condition. If there were [an additional condition] it would have been observed. Therefore, because of its nonobservation it does not exist. Thus, the absence of an additional condition is detected through perception itself, which is governed by nonapprehension, with the help of suppositional reasoning. Now, given this, the pervasion of smoke with fire is detected by perception itself, which grasps concomitance with the help of the cognitive impressions produced by grasping the absence of an additional condition and with the help of the cognitive impressions produced through numerous observations. Thus the relation of smoke with fire is, in fact, natural, and not brought about by an additional condition" (*{tena} bhūyodarśanena dhūmāgnyoḥ svābhāvikaṃ saṃbandham avadhārayati, yatra dhūmas tatrāgnir iti | yady api yatra yatra maitrītanayatvaṃ tatra tatra śyāmatvam apīti bhūyodarśanaṃ samānam avagamyate tathāpi maitrītanayatvaśyāmatvayor na svābhāvikaḥ saṃbandhaḥ kintv aupādhika eva | śākādyannapariṇāmasyopādher vidyamānatvāt | tathā hi | śyāmatve maitrītanayatvaṃ na prayojakaṃ kintu śākādyannapariṇatibheda eva prayojakaḥ | prayojakaś copādhir ity ucyate | na ca dhūmāgnyoḥ saṃbandhe kaścid upādhir asti, asti cet yogyo 'yogyo vā, ayogyasya śaṅkitum aśakyatvād yogyasya cānupalabhyamānatvāt | yatropādhir asti tatropalabhyate | yathāgner dhūmasaṃbandha ārdrendhanasaṃyogah | {hiṃsātvasya cādharmasādhanatvena saha saṃbandhe niṣiddhatvam upādhiḥ} | maitrītanayatvasya ca śyāmatvena saha saṃbandhe śākādyannapariṇatibhedaḥ | na ceha dhūmāgnisāhacarye kaścid upādhir asti | yady abhaviṣyat tadādrakṣyat | tato darśanābhāvān nāstīti | tarkasahakāriṇānupalambhasanāthena pratyakṣeṇaivopādhyabhāvo 'vadhāryate | tathā ca sati upādhyabhāvagrahaṇajanitasaṃskārasahakṛtena bhūyodarśanajanitasaṃskārasahakṛtena sāhacaryagrāhiṇā pratyakṣeṇaiva dhūmāgnyor vyāptir avadhāryate | tena dhūmāgnyoḥ svābhāvikaiva saṃbandhaḥ | na tv aupādhikaḥ*).

For more on suppositional reasoning (*tarka*) see section 1.2. For a detailed study see Bagchi 1953.

1.2. Ratnakīrti on Natural Relations

Ratnakīrti focuses his criticism of the theory of inference-warranting relations on the Naiyāyikas' description of pervasion, and their proposed method for showing that its defining conditions can be satisfied. As Ratnakīrti sees it, the Nyāya theory is such that epistemic necessity—that is, the necessity conferred upon such relations by the Nyāya theory—is not "necessary enough" for them to be genuinely inference-warranting.[38] He argues further that the Naiyāyikas cannot even show that the pervasion conditions for such relations are ever satisfied. Although he does not choose to do so, it is useful to interpret Ratnakīrti's critical remarks in two parts, based upon whether his criticism is directed primarily toward how this class of relations is defined (group 1) or how its defining conditions, the three pervasion conditions, are supposed to be satisfied (group 2). These general remarks are important since they support many of his specific arguments against the inference-warranting relation in the Naiyāyikas' argument for the existence of Īśvara.

1.2.1. Defining Natural Relations

According to Ratnakīrti, the Naiyāyikas' claim that epistemic necessity is grounded in relations described as "natural" is not convincing, since even if there were such relations they would be too general to be genuinely inference-warranting. Informing Ratnakīrti's analysis is a view referred to earlier, according to which there are only two possible modes of pervasion: a "production-mode" (*tadutpatti*), which is based on a causal relation, and an "identity-mode" (*tādātmya*), which is based on an identity-relation, perhaps a relation of "token-identity." According to this view, all genuinely inference-warranting relations must be instances of either the production-mode or the identity-mode of pervasion.[39] More specifically, when the *relata* in such genuinely inference-warranting relations are identified as being "different from" or "other than" each other, they can be related only through the production-

---

38. "Epistemic necessity" is indexed to a set of pervasion conditions, as they are defined in a particular theory. It is meaningful, therefore, to speak of epistemic necessity as a kind of necessity that is "conferred upon" inference-warranting relations by a particular theory. The phrase "genuinely inference-warranting" refers to those relations that a particular philosopher takes to be inference-warranting.

39. For a brief discussion of what I mean by "token-identity" see chapter 5.

mode of pervasion.[40] When the two are "nondifferent from" each other, they are said to be related through the identity-mode.[41] The only relations that are epistemically necessary are those in which the *relata* are "different" and "nondifferent" in the manner specified by these two modes of pervasion. This is, of course, not the Nyāya position, since although the class of natural relations includes relations that can be described in terms of these two

---

40. The standard example of an inference-warranting relation in which the two terms are "different-from" each other is the pervasion relation between smoke and fire. Ratnakīrti explains that this relation is the paradigmatic example of the "production-mode" (*tadutpatti*) at RNĀ (VN 106.01–106.02): "The pervasion relation of fire with smoke, an entity that is different [from fire], is defined by the production-mode. And the rule is that [the production-mode of pervasion] is established by specific perceptions and nonperceptions that grasp a specific [instance] of positive and negative concomitance" (*{iha} dahanādinā dhūmader arthāntarasya vyāptis tadutpattilakṣanā | sā ca viśiṣṭānvayavyatirekagrahaṇapravaṇaviśiṣṭapratyakṣānupalambhasādhaneti nyāyaḥ*). In the production-mode of pervasion, the reason property is a property whose presence in a particular locus *causally necessitates* the presence in that locus of the target property. In such inferences, epistemic necessity is identified with causal necessity. In his *Tarkabhāṣā*, Mokṣākaragupta expands this to include other species of "causal relations," such as relations in which both the reason property and the target property are effects of the same causal complex; see MTBh 28.02–28.15. Recently there has been a lively discussion on the production-mode of pervasion in the secondary literature. This discussion has focused both on how it can be known that two items are related as effect and cause and why an effect-cause relation that is established for two items in a particular locus can be generalized. Much of the discussion has focused on the work of Dharmakīrti; see, for example, Gillon 1991, Inami 1999, and Lasic 1999. For more on Ratnakīrti's view see, for example, RNĀ (KS 72.11), RNĀ (SSD 125.22–125.24), and RNĀ (VN 110.32–111.04), where Ratnakīrti suggests that on his view there are a finite number of perceptions and non-perceptions that are needed to establish that two items are related as effect and cause. Once it has been established in a single locus that the two terms are so related, the relation can be generalized beyond the sample locus for which the relation was established. For a discussion of the debate over whether three or five observational events are needed to determine whether two items are related as effect and cause, see Inami 1999, Kajiyama 1963, Lasic 1999, Mimaki 1976:164–167, Mookherjee 1975:67–69, Woo 1999:179–182, and my discussion in chapter 5, section 2.4.

41. The standard example of an inference-warranting relation in which the two terms are "nondifferent from" each other is the pervasion relation between "being a Śimśapa(-tree)" and "being a tree." At RNĀ (KS 69.24) Ratnakīrti refers to this example and explains that the two terms have "different exclusions" (*vyāvṛtti-bheda*). This suggests that when considered as types the two terms are different from each other, as suggested in my interpretation of the identity-mode of pervasion as a relation of "token-identity." This interpretation is also suggested at MTBh 28.16–28.09. For more on the identity-mode of pervasion see, for example, Steinkellner 1971, Katsura 1986a, Steinkellner 1991, Katsura 1992a, and Dunne 1999.

modes of pervasion, it explicitly includes those that cannot.[42] The issue for Ratnakīrti is whether the Naiyāyikas have shown that there is such a class of relations, and if so that they are genuinely inference-warranting.

Against the Nyāya theory, Ratnakīrti first argues that given the Naiyāyikas' account of natural relations any two things could be naturally related and that, as a result, the epistemic necessity that is underwritten by such relations would be too weak to account for only genuinely inference-warranting ones. He says,

> If there could be a natural relation between one thing and another which accompanies it [but is not its cause], everything could be related to everything. And in this way, everything could be inferred from everything.[43]

On this reading, the Naiyāyikas' insistence that the class of natural relations includes those that are not causal suggests that what really defines a relation as "natural" is just that the two *relata* are in some way "other than" each other. Natural relations are therefore nothing but "in-some-way-other-than" relations. And since any two things could be "in-some-way-other-than" each other, any one thing could be, in principle, inferred from any other thing. The Naiyāyikas insist, of course, that this is not the case and argue that just like causal relations, natural relations are also constrained by the nature of things. In other words, they reason that just as the production-mode of pervasion is supposed to be grounded in the way in which some things that are "other than" each other are causally related in the world, the proposed "natural-mode" is grounded in the way in which certain things that are "other than" each other are naturally related in the world. Ratnakīrti argues, however, that this position can only be maintained if, like causal relations, natural relations could be properly defined and then proven to exist through a well-functioning instrument of warranted awareness.[44] Since the Naiyāyikas have neither provided a defining characteristic for such relations nor shown through a well-functioning instrument that such relations exist, he reasons that a characteristic such as "other than" must define the relation.

---

42. See section 1.2.1.

43. RNĀ (ĪSD 46.14–46.16): *{syād etad} anyasyānyena sahakāreṇa cet svābhāvikaḥ sambandho bhavet, sarvaṃ sarveṇa sambadhyeta | tathā ca sarvaṃ sarvasmād gamyeta*. See also RNĀ (VN 107.16–107.17) and NVTṬ 136.03–136.04.

44. RNĀ (ĪSD 47.22–47.26).

Given this, Ratnakīrti argues that such relations are too general to be genuinely inference-warranting. His point is that the Naiyāyikas' theory that epistemic necessity supervenes on such natural relations results in it being too weak to account for only genuinely inference-warranting relations—in other words, for the pervasion subcomponents of only well-functioning instruments of awareness.

Ratnakīrti builds on this line of reasoning by arguing that the Naiyāyikas have not even shown that there are any natural relations. He says,

> There is nothing that is denoted by the term "natural relation" and is proven to exist by a well-functioning instrument for warranted awareness. This is because a defining characteristic has not been established for it. Moreover, it is not the case that if a real thing is established by fiat an unwanted consequence cannot be discussed. This is because there is the unwanted consequence that by merely accepting that something has such a nature everyone would be victorious everywhere.[45]

According to Ratnakīrti, what the Naiyāyikas call "natural relations" have neither been clearly defined nor proven to exist through an accredited instrument for warranted awareness. As a result, the presence of such relations amounts merely to wishful thinking on their part. The existence of so-called natural relations can, it seems, be only stipulated and not proved. And if stipulation is accepted as a method for establishing inference-warranting relations, Ratnakīrti claims that anyone could stipulate that the relation between a proposed reason property and its target is of such and such a type, and therefore genuinely inference-warranting. In such a case, epistemic necessity would be grounded in a stipulative definition and would not supervene on nonepistemic facts as required by the Nyāya theory. The result would be that by creative stipulation "everyone would be victorious everywhere."

In support of his point that there are not any natural relations, Ratnakīrti argues that the inference-warranting relation that enables a jeweler to detect the presence of a real jewel versus a fake is not an instance of a natural relation as suggested by Vācaspatimiśra. He explains that,

---

45. RNĀ (ĪSD 47.28–47.31): *na {caivaṃ} svābhāvikasambandhaśabdavācyo 'rthaḥ pramāṇasiddhaḥ kaścid asti, tallakṣaṇasyāsiddhatvāt | na ca pratijñāsiddhe vastuny atiprasaṅgo nābhidhātavyaḥ, sarveṣāṃ sarvatra tadrūpābhyupagamamātreṇa vijetṛtvaprasaṅgāt.*

> As the result of a tradition of instruction, a defining characteristic such as "rainbow-like luster" is ascertained, with effort, as belonging to a ruby. But the defining characteristic of a natural relation is created by your imagination. It is not ascertained by a well-functioning instrument for warranted awareness, on account of which there could be a situation like this, even for it.[46]

The relation between the reason property, "having rainbow-like luster," and the target property, "being a ruby," is established by showing that the two terms are related as *definiens* and *definiendum*. In other words, the reason property is shown to be a defining characteristic of the target property. Although it is not stated here, the relation between the two terms is an example of the identity-mode of pervasion.[47] This relation does not therefore support the Naiyāyikas' claim that there is a separate natural-mode for pervasion. As Ratnakīrti explains, in this case a particular stone is known to be a ruby only because it is known to have the defining characteristic of a ruby. If a defining characteristic for so-called natural relations were known and it could be shown that a particular relation has that defining characteristic, then the presence of such relations could also be known. Since such a characteristic has not been specified, however, there isn't a good reason to suppose that there is such a class of relations at all.[48]

---

46. RNĀ (ĪSD 48.15–48.19): *{abhijātamaṇibhedatattvaṃ tu parisphuratīti yuktam | tasya hy} upadeśaparamparāto māṇikyavat tenāpi kaṣṭenendradhanurākārajyotirādikaṃ lakṣaṇaṃ niścitam | na caivaṃ svābhāvikasambandhalakṣaṇaṃ tvayā svakalpitaracitam api pramāṇena niścitam | yenāsyāpi tādṛśī vyavasthā syād iti.*

47. Note that when considered as "types" the two properties are distinct, but when considered as tokens they are identical.

48. In addition to this argument, Ratnakīrti argues at RNĀ (ĪSD 48.04–48.07) that on conceptual grounds such relations cannot be defended: "Moreover, what is a 'natural relation'? What does it mean? Is it produced by itself, produced from its own causes, or is it uncaused? These are the three possibilities. Now then, it is not the first option, since it is a contradiction to cause oneself. But if it is the second option there isn't a disagreement, since the relation is accepted as the production-mode, [but] with a different look. And if it is uncaused there is the unwanted consequence of the absence of temporal, spatial, and essential specificity. So, a relation that is 'natural' does not follow" (*kiṃ ca svābhāvikasambandha iti ko 'rthaḥ | kiṃ svato bhūtaḥ svahetuto bhūto 'hetuko veti trayaḥ pakṣāḥ | na tāvad ādyaḥ pakṣaḥ, svātmani karitravirodhāt | dvitīyapakṣe tu tadutpattir eva sambandho mukhāntareṇa svīkṛta iti na kaścid vivādaḥ | ahetukatve tu deśakālasvabhāvaniyamābhāvaprasaṅgād ity asaṅgataḥ svābhāvikaḥ sambandhaḥ*).

1.2.2. Detecting Pervasion

Although there may not be, strictly speaking, a single defining characteristic for natural relations, Ratnakīrti considers the possibility that the presence of such relations could still be detected through observation and nonobservation.[49] The method used for detecting them would thus become their de facto defining feature. For example, as both Vācaspatimiśra and Trilocana imply, natural relations could be defined as relations for which there is neither the observation of an additional condition nor deviation.[50] The defining characteristic of such relations could be the property "being a relation for which there is the nonobservation of an additional condition and deviation." Given the Naiyāyikas' interpretation of "nonobservation," natural relations would be those relations that have the property "being a relation for which there is the absence of an additional condition and deviation."[51] Although such a relation would be by definition "natural," Ratnakīrti argues that according to the Naiyāyikas' own theory, a proposed relation could never be shown to be so. This is because, according to him, nonobservation cannot rule out the presence of an additional condition or deviation as the Naiyāyikas suppose. Despite Trilocana's assertion that nonapprehension is a form of perception, and therefore an accredited instrument for coming to know the absence of "U" and "V," Ratnakīrti argues that this cannot be the case. According to him, it is not possible for the Naiyāyikas to show that a proposed relation is natural and has epistemic necessity through observation and nonobservation. If this is the case, Ratnakīrti recognizes, the Naiyāyikas will rarely be able to certify that a particular reason property is a well-functioning instrument.

The following passages contain two of Ratnakīrti's most important arguments. He writes,

> (a) "The relation between things like smoke and fire is natural because an additional condition is not observed for it [and] because deviation is not

---

49. This possibility is mentioned at RNĀ (ĪSD 48.20–48.21).

50. It is important to note that this is only implied in the passages quoted by Ratnakīrti. Although Vācaspatimiśra does describe a natural relation as a "relation that does not have an additional condition" (*anaupādhikasambandha*), the relationship between natural relations (*svābhāvika-sambandha*), additional conditions, and suppositional reasoning (*tarka*) and deviation and nonobservation (*anupalabdhi*) is not as clear as Ratnakīrti implies.

51. This is clear from KTBh 21.05–23.02, which was quoted earlier, in section 1.1.3.

> observed anywhere." You said that this is its definition. But this is not established since what is meant by the words "additional condition" is that an entity in addition to itself is required. But this additional entity is not invariably observable, since it is also possible for it to be unobservable—i.e., spatially, temporally, or essentially remote. Therefore there could be an additional condition which is not seen, even in the relation between smoke and fire. So, how is it that from nonobservation—by means of which a natural relation is established—it is known that it does not exist?[52]

And,

> (b) What is the meaning of "By not observing deviation there is nondeviation?" Is it because deviation is unobserved that there is nondeviation or because of the absence of deviation? If it is the first alternative there may or may not be deviation. . . . If it is the second alternative, then how is the absence of deviation known? One may say: "From nonobservation." Is this nonobservation-in-general or the nonobservation of an observable? The first is impossible, since it is not possible to say that although there is nonobservation, deviation—like the deviation [in the character] of a woman who died a long time ago—does not exist. This is also because even if there were unobstructed nonobservation, deviation could be observed after a very long interval. Moreover, the second is impossible. This is because if the total causal complex for observing deviation exists, deviation will be observed somewhere, sometime, and by someone. But if the total causal complex for observing it does not exist, either because the other causal factors are weak or because it occurs at a different place or time, deviation will not be observed. This is because there would be the absence of its having satisfied the conditions for being apprehensible. Therefore, given the absence of the total causal complex

---

52. RNĀ (ĪSD 47.03–47.10): *tathā hi, svābhāvikas tu dhūmādīnāṃ vahnyādibhiḥ sambandhas tadupādher anupalabhyamānatvāt | kvacid vyabhicārasyādarśanād iti tvayaivāsya lakṣaṇam uktam | etac cāsiddham | yataḥ, upādhiśabdena svato 'rthāntaram evāpekṣaṇīyam abhidhātavyam | na cārthāntaraṃ dṛśyatāniyatam, adṛśyasyāpi deśakālasvabhāvaviprakṛṣṭasya sambhavāt | tataś ca dhūmasyāpi hutāśena saha sambandhe syād upādhiḥ, na copalakṣyata iti katham adarśanān nāsty eva yataḥ svābhāvikasambandhasiddhiḥ.* See RNĀ (ĪSD 46.08–46.09), RNĀ (VN 109.32), and NVTṬ 135.09–135.14.

for apprehending it, there could be the nonapprehension of deviation, even if deviation exists.[53]

Ratnakīrti first argues that the Naiyāyikas' account of how natural relations are established cannot even account for epistemic necessity in the paradigmatic inference of fire from smoke. His argument is based on his view that the nonobservation of an additional condition (passage *a*) or deviation (passage *b*) cannot prove the absence of either of them. As a result, he concludes that the Naiyāyikas cannot even show that U and C2.3 (V) are satisfied for well-known inferences. In the passages quoted above, he argues that this is the case regardless of whether nonobservation is interpreted as "nonobservation-in-general" (*adarśanamātra*) or as the "nonobservation of an observable" (*dṛśyādarśana*) (passage *b*).[54] In the context of Ratnakīrti's remarks,

---

53. RNĀ (ĪSD 48.28–49.08): *vyabhicārādarśanād avyabhicāra iti cet | nanu vyabhicārādarśanād avyabhicāra iti ko 'rthaḥ | kiṃ vyabhicārādarśanād avyabhicāraḥ, vyabhicārābhāvād vā | prathame pakṣe vyabhicāro bhavatu mā vā vyabhicārādarśanād {evāvyabhicāra iti niṣṇātaṃ paṇḍitam }| atha dvitīyaḥ pakṣaḥ | tadā vyabhicārābhāvaḥ kuto jñātaḥ | adarśanād iti cet | tat kim adarśanamātraṃ dṛśyādarśanaṃ vā | prathamam aśaktam | na hy adarśane 'pi vyabhicāro nāstīty abhidhātuṃ śakyate, cirakālanaṣṭabrāhmaṇīvyabhicāravat | āhatyādarśane 'py aticirakālavyavadhānena vyabhicāradarśanāt | dvitīyaṃ cāsambhavi, kvacit kadācit kenacid vyabhicāradarśanasāmagryāṃ satyāṃ vyabhicāradarśanāt | darśanasāmagryabhāve tu pratyayāntaravaikalyād deśakālāntaravartitvād vā vyabhicārasya sarvaṃ praty upalabdhilakṣaṇaprāptatvābhāvāt* | tasmāt saty api vyabhicāre tadupalambhasāmagryabhāvād vyabhicārānupalambhaḥ | {prakārāntareṇa vā tadutpattilakṣanenāvyabhicāre vyabhicārānupalambha ity ubhayathāpi vyabhicāropalambhanivṛttir astu | tvayā tu yad avyabhicārapratipattinibandhanaṃ darśanādarśanam upavarṇitaṃ tatpārthivatvādau vyabhicārād dhūme 'pi nāvyabhicāranibandhanam iti dhūmo 'pi tvanmate nāśvāsabhājanam iti prasaktam}*. See also RNĀ (VN 110.02–110.06). Unlike the other passages quoted in this section, this passage is from Ratnakīrti's discussion of alternative 2 and not alternative 3. The similarity between the two positions on the point being discussed justifies the use of this passage here.

As Kellner (1999:197) notes, there are two ways of interpreting the phrase "having satisfied the conditions for being apprehensible." Śākyabuddhi PVṬ (9a6f) interprets this to refer to the presence of all of the conditions or causal factors that are different from the object itself (*pratyayāntara*). For a close parallel to this view see PVSVṬ 21.22–21.24, as quoted in Kellner 1999:197 n. 11. Dharmottara (NBṬ 101.7–101.10) interprets this to mean the complete causal complex that is necessary for perception (*janikā sāmagrī*). For Dharmottara, this complete causal complex includes both the "additional causal factors" and the "object itself."

54. There is a long history of Buddhist arguments about "nonobservation-in-general." See the notes to section 2.1.1 for references to Īśvarasena's use of nonobservation in general, and Kellner 1997b.

"nonobservation-in-general" refers to nonobservation that is indifferent to whether the unobserved object is "unobservable" or "observable." As Ratnakīrti explains (passage *a*), an "unobservable" (*adṛśya*) object is one that is spatially, temporally, or essentially remote (*deśa-kāla-svabhāva-viprakṛṣṭa*).[55] And although he does not explain it here, it is understood that "remoteness" is defined relative to a particular kind of observer. For example, although a ghost (*piśāca*) may be essentially remote for a normal human observer, it is not essentially remote for another ghost.[56] Similarly, an "observable" object is one that is, relative to a particular kind of observer, neither spatially, temporally, nor essentially remote. It is an object that, if present, would be immediately and inevitably observed.[57] Ratnakīrti explains that nonobservation in general cannot prove that an object such as "U" or "V" is absent, since that object may have been observable only in the distant past or may be observable only in the distant future (passage *b*). As he mentions (passage *a*), it is always possible that because of remoteness an additional condition is present but unobserved. Ratnakīrti also explains that the nonobservation of an observable cannot prove that "U" or "V" is absent, since even if "U" or "V" is not spatially, temporally, or essentially remote, the total causal complex necessary for observing it may not be complete—for example, there may not be enough light to see it or the observer may not be paying attention (*manaskāra*).[58] As a result, even if deviation were present there could be the nonobservation of it. According to Ratnakīrti, then, the Naiyāyikas cannot satisfy their own pervasion conditions and so cannot even show that the

---

55. For example, the spatially distant Mount Meru [see MTBh 30.18], the future emperor Śaṅkhā [see NB 2.27, PVSV 16.15, VN 6.5, MTBh 30.18], or a ghost [see DhPr 107.30, RNĀ (ĪSD 146.18), MTBh 30.19]. It is also important to note that these three "degrees" of remoteness are always indexed to a specific type of agent.

56. For references to this example see RNĀ (ĪSD 146.18), DhPr 107.30, and VNV 19.27. For a more detailed account of "observable" (*dṛśya*) see Kellner 1999:202.

57. See Kellner 1999:196 n. 7, for references to Dharmakīrti's use of this expression. Kellner notes, for example, that at PVin2 16.12–17.07 and PVSV 102.02–102.11 Dharmakīrti explains that "remote" objects are those that do not inevitably and immediately result in awareness for a particular kind of agent at a particular spatio-temporal location. This suggests that an "unobservable" (*adṛśya*) object is one that cannot be observed by a particular kind of agent because the object in question is spatially, temporally, or essentially remote. The idea is that if such an object were not remote in any of these ways, it would be observed.

58. This example is from Kellner 1999:197, following Śākyabuddhi (PVṬ 9a6f). See Katsura 1992b:228 for a similar analysis.

pervasion subcomponents of well-known inferences have epistemic necessity. Their theory has an inherent weakness.

Ratnakīrti also asks whether nondeviation is supposed to be due to the nonobservation of deviation or the absence of deviation (passage *b*). This question can also be generalized to include the absence of an additional condition. The issue is whether epistemic necessity is supposed to supervene on an epistemic fact, nonobservation, or a nonepistemic fact, absence (*abhāva*). If it is supposed to supervene on the epistemic fact, then given that this fact is based on nonobservation, there will always be the possibility that there was deviation in the past or that deviation will be observed in the future (passage *b*). From nonobservation, one can only conclude that there may or may not be deviation. As a result, if epistemic necessity is supposed to supervene on the epistemic fact of nonobservation, the necessity will be too weak to account for only genuinely inference-warranting relations—there will always be epistemically significant doubt.[59] If it is supposed to supervene on the nonepistemic fact, then because this nonepistemic fact cannot be known, epistemic necessity cannot be known. The reason given for this is that nonobservation cannot establish the absence of an object, since it may be that an object is present but the complete set of causal conditions necessary for its observation is not.

2. Two Arguments

This general criticism of the Nyāya theory of inference-warranting relations is also reflected in Ratnakīrti's more specific discussion of why he believes that the Naiyāyikas cannot show that the defect "generally inconclusive" (H3a) does not apply to the reason property in their argument for the existence of Īśvara. As discussed earlier, H3a blocks the functioning of an instrument by affecting its pervasion subcomponent in one of two ways: it either *defeats* it, through the identification of a locus in which the reason property is present but the target property is absent ($H3a_1$) or it *undermines* it, by raising doubt about whether the reason property is excluded from all dissimilar cases ($H3a_2$).[60] In their defense of the reason property "being an

---

59. The concept of "epistemically significant doubt" will be discussed in section 2.1.

60. See chapter 2, sections 2.3.2 and 3.2, and section 1.1.1 above.

effect," the Naiyāyikas appealed to the theory of remoteness in order to support their argument that the opponent's criteria for identifying a locus of deviation were such that $H3a_1$ would apply to even well-known, and universally accepted, inferential arguments.[61] From this they concluded that the opponent's proposed counterexample, growing grass, was not a suitable example of deviation.[62] Let us refer to this argument as "Argument 1: The Growing Grass Argument." In addition, the Naiyāyikas argued that there isn't epistemically significant doubt about the exclusion of the reason property from all dissimilar cases, since the inference-warranting relation in their argument is as epistemically necessary as the ones in well-known and universally accepted inferences, such as the inference of fire from smoke.[63] Let us refer to this argument as "Argument 2: The Argument from Localized Doubt." In support of this argument, the Nyāya philosopher Trilocana argued further that there is a special type of perception called "nonapprehension," which can prove that a reason property is not present in a single dissimilar case.[64] On the basis of this, Trilocana argued that there isn't epistemically significant doubt about the exclusion of the reason property from all dissimilar cases in the Īśvara-inference. The final argument considered by the Naiyāyikas was the opponent's argument that given the generality and scope of the reason property "being an effect(-in-general)," its pervasion by the target property could never be established. According to the opponent, pervasion can be established only for a more restricted version of the reason property. As the opponent sees it, this reveals that the original reason property is inconclusive. The Naiyāyikas' response to this was to show that the opponent's demand to restrict the scope of the reason property is either unnecessary or unreasonable. Let us refer to this as "Argument 3: The Restricted Scope Argument."

In the critical sections of his essay, Ratnakīrti returns to each of these arguments: he discusses the first two in the *Section on Pervasion* and the third one in the *Section on the Reason Property*. My discussion will follow this order.

---

61. Where "universally accepted" means among those who take inferential reasoning to be a source of knowledge.

62. See chapter 2, section 3.2.1.

63. See chapter 2, section 3.2.2.

64. See section 1.1 passage *d*; the notes to section 1.1.2, where the relationship between perception, nonapprehension, and suppositional reasoning is discussed; and section 2.1, where this alternative is discussed in detail.

Interestingly, in the *Section on Pervasion* he begins with argument 2, for which the burden of proof is easier to meet.

2.1. *The Argument from Localized Doubt, H3a₂*

Ratnakīrti begins his analysis of argument 2 by providing a more nuanced version of the Nyāya position. He writes,

> (a) Vācaspati says: There isn't even the defeater of the reason property called "doubt about its exclusion from all dissimilar cases." How is it set aside? Well, only a reason property that was observed in a dissimilar case disproves what was intended. . . . But how could one which was not observed in a dissimilar case, even though it was searched for with great effort, disprove what is to be proven . . . ?
>
> (b) If this were so, the ghost of doubt, to whom an opportunity is given by overstepping the limits of common sense, would be released. Nowhere would it not exist, and so one would not act anywhere. This is [1] because every object would somehow be a locus of doubt; [2] because on the basis of such unlocalized doubt intelligent people would desist from activity; and [3] because in the end death is observed even for those who consume nutritious food and drink.
>
> (c) Therefore, those who protect the practices of epistemically credible people insist that there can be doubt only in accordance with observation, and not with what has not been already observed.[65]

According to Vācaspatimiśra, not observing a reason property in a dissimilar case cannot lead one to have epistemically significant doubt about its exclusion from such cases (passage *a*). Vācaspatimiśra's analysis is based on the

---

65. RNĀ (ĪSD 42.08–42.17): (a) *atra vācaspatiḥ prāha, sandigdhavipakṣavyāvṛttikatvaṃ nāma hetudoṣa eva na bhavati | tat kathaṃ nirasyate | tathā hi ya eva vipakṣe dṛṣṭo hetuḥ sa eva {prameyatvādivad} abhimataṃ na sādhayet | yas tu mahatāpi prayatnena mṛgyamāṇo 'sapakṣe nopalakṣitaḥ sa kathaṃ sādhyaṃ na sādhayet | {avaśyaṃ śaṅkayā bhāvyaṃ niyāmakam apaśyatām |}* (b) *iti tu dattāvakāśā laukikamaryādātikrameṇa saṃśayapiśācī labdhaprasarā na kvacin nāstīti nāyaṃ kvacit pravarteta | sarvasyaivārthasya kathañcic chaṅkāspadatvād{arśanāt}* | anarthaśaṅkāyāś ca prekṣāvatāṃ nivṛttyaṅgatvāt | antataḥ snigdhānnapānopayoge 'pi maraṇadarśanāt |* (c) *tasmāt prāmāṇikalokayātrām anupālayatā yathādarśanaṃ śaṅkanīyam, na tv adṛṣṭam api*. See RNĀ (VN 107.11–107.13), NVTṬ 135.17–135.22 *ad* NS 1.1.5, PV 1.326c–d, PVin 2.45c–d, and NBṬ 14.01. In support of this decision see NVTṬ 135.19.

Nyāya theory of epistemically significant doubt. According to this theory, doubt (*saṃśaya*) is an awareness-event that, like all awareness-events, must have an object. More specifically, its object must be a specific property-possessor (*dharmī*) about which there is doubt regarding whether it possesses a particular property *F* (*dharma*) or its contrary, non-*F*.[66] In the case of H3a$_2$, the property-possessor in question would be a dissimilar case in which the exclusion of the reason property is said to be in doubt.[67] Vācaspatimiśra agrees that if such a property-possessor were observed and identified, there could be epistemically significant doubt about whether a particular property or its contrary is present in it. The awareness that there is some as yet unobserved and unidentified property-possessor in which a particular property is supposed to be present or absent is not, however, an example of doubt that is epistemically significant. Epistemically significant doubt must be based on the observation of a specific property-possessor or locus. Vācaspatimiśra argues that if epistemically significant doubt could be based on the nonobservation of a specific property-possessor, "the ghost of doubt would be released" (passage *b*) and rational people would be paralyzed. If, for example, pervasion could be undermined by H3a$_2$, without one actually observing a dissimilar locus in which there is doubt about the exclusion of a reason property, there could always be epistemically significant doubt about whether a reason property is excluded from every dissimilar case. As a result, rational people could never base their actions on inferentially produced awareness-

66. In a passage that parallels passage *c* Vācaspatimiśra explains, at RNĀ (VN 107.10–107.13): "Therefore, for those who protect the practices of people who follow the warranted-modes of awareness there should be doubt only in accordance with observation, and never [in accordance with] what was not previously observed. For doubt definitely depends upon a specific memory and does not exist when there isn't memory. And memory cannot exist for an object which was not [previously] experienced" (*tasmāt prāmāṇikalokayātrām anupālayatā yathādarśanam eva śaṅkanīyaṃ na tv adṛṣṭapūrvam api | viśeṣasmṛtyapekṣa eva saṃśayo nāsmṛter bhavati | na ca smṛtir ananubhūtacare bhavitum arhati*). For more on the Nyāya theory of doubt see KTBh 97.05–98.10.

67. It is important to note that in passage *a* Vācaspatimiśra says that the object that must be observed in order for there to be doubt is the reason property. Here I am suggesting that the object that needs to be observed is the locus. This is not inconsistent, because according to the Naiyāyikas the role of property and property-possessor are "interchangeable" in such cases. For example, in this case there is supposed to be doubt about the absence of a reason property from a dissimilar locus. According to Naiyāyikas, the property (*dharma*) could either be the reason property or the absence of a dissimilar locus, and the property-possessor (*dharmin*) could either be the dissimilar locus or the absence of the reason property.

events. After all, Vācaspatimiśra reasons, they would never know whether some as yet unobserved locus will undermine the awareness on which their potential action is based. From such considerations Vācaspatimiśra concludes that the opponent's original argument, that there is epistemically significant doubt about the exclusion of the reason property from dissimilar cases ($H3a_2$), is based on an untenable theory of doubt, and should therefore be dismissed.

Before responding to Vācaspatimiśra's remarks about the theory of doubt that underlies his argument that $H3a_2$ applies to the reason property "being an effect," Ratnakīrti responds to Trilocana and Vācaspatimiśra's claim that nonapprehension and nonobservation can prove that a reason property is excluded from all dissimilar cases. This is important since, if the Nyāya claim is correct, then at least in such cases there cannot be epistemically significant doubt about the satisfaction of C2.3, and thus the question of whether $H3a_2$ applies would not arise.

2.1.1. The Problem with Nonobservation

Ratnakīrti responds to Trilocana and Vācaspatimiśra's claim by adding to his earlier arguments about why nonapprehension and nonobservation cannot prove that a reason property is excluded from all dissimilar cases.[68] For convenience, he uses the term "nonobservation" to refer to both.[69] He writes,

> (a) Now, this is nothing but idle chatter, since negative concomitance cannot be proven by just the nonobservation of a reason property in dissimilar cases—even one which was searched for with great effort.
>
> (b) That is to say: "the reason property is not apprehended in a dissimilar case" means that there isn't a well-functioning instrument of awareness that apprehends it [i.e., there isn't the warranted awareness of it]. Warranted-awareness is the effect of the patient of a knowing-event. This is based on the principle that there isn't an object of awareness without a cause. And given the absence of an effect, it is not the case that one apprehends the absence of a cause: even when there isn't any smoke, there is the apprehension of fire. But if the existence of a patient of a knowing-event were pervaded by the existence of warranted awareness,

68. See section 1.1.3.

69. For a list of synonymous expressions see Kellner 1999.

then it would be correct. However, this very pervasion is not possible, since there would be the unwanted consequence that everything would be observed by everyone. So negative concomitance is not proven by nonobservation alone.

(c) As it was said: "[If you say that negative concomitance can be proven on the basis of] universal nonobservation, then there is doubt. [And if you say] it is [on the basis of] one's own nonobservation, then there is deviation. This is because with respect to proximate times all dissimilar cases are not observed. For example, although a blade of grass in a small hole on the Vindhyā mountains is not seen, it exists."[70]

Vācaspatimiśra had argued that the nonobservation of a reason property in dissimilar cases was sufficient for showing that the defect called "doubt about the exclusion of the reason property from all dissimilar cases" ($H3a_2$) did not apply. According to Ratnakīrti, however, this assumes that nonobservation can prove that a reason property is not present in any dissimilar case. In other words, it assumes that nonobservation can establish negative concomitance (*vyatireka*)—that is, that nonobservation can prove that a reason property is not present in any locus in which the target property is not also present (passage *a*).[71] In these passages Ratnakīrti argues that this cannot be the case. He bases his argument on the Nyāya view that warranted awareness is the culminating effect of a causal complex that includes the patient of that awareness-event (passage *b*). In this case, the proposed awareness-event is the awareness that the reason property is not present in a dissimilar case.

---

70. RNĀ (ĪSD 42.24–43.03): (a) *tad etat pralāpamātram* | *na hi mahatāpi prayatnena vipakṣe mṛgyamāṇasya hetor adarśanamātreṇa vyatirekaḥ sidhyati** | (b) *tathā hi vipakṣe hetur nopalabhyata ity anena tadupalambhakapramāṇanivṛttir ucyate* | *pramāṇaṃ ca prameyasya kāryam, nākāraṇaṃ viṣaya iti nyāyāt* | *na ca kāryanivṛttau kāraṇanivṛttir upalabdhā, nirdhūmasyāpi vahner upalambhāt* | *yadi punaḥ pramāṇasattayā prameyasattā vyāptā syāt, tadā yuktam etat* | *kevalam īyam eva vyāptir asaṃbhavinī, sarvasya sarvadarśitvaprasaṅgāt* | *tan nādarśanamātreṇa vyatirekasiddhiḥ* | (c) *yathoktaṃ sarvādṛṣṭiś ca sandigdhā svādṛṣṭir vyabhicāriṇī* | *vindhyādrirandhradūrvāder adṛṣṭāv api sattvataḥ* || *iti sakalavipakṣasyārvācīnaṃ praty adṛśyatvāt.*
*See RNĀ (ĪSD 42.09) and MTBh 43.05–43.15.

71. Steinkellner (1968/1969) attributes this view to Īśvarasena. For Steinkellner's reconstruction of Īśvarasena's view from HB 28*–35* see Steinkellner 1988. As Steinkellner (1991:310) has argued, Dharmakīrti argues against Īśvarasena's idea that negative concomitance can be established by nonobservation in general. Ratnakīrti's arguments are, to some extent, related to these.

The proposed instrument is nonobservation. The Naiyāyikas' inferential argument is that there is warranted awareness (the site/effect) that the reason property is not present in a dissimilar case (the target property/cause) because there is the nonobservation of the reason property being present in a dissimilar case (the reason property/cause). According to the Naiyāyikas, the nonobservation of a patient "*x*" is supposed to result in the warranted awareness that "not *x*."

Ratnakīrti begins his analysis of this argument by interpreting the "nonobservation" of a reason property in a dissimilar case to mean "the absence of a well-functioning instrument that proves that a reason property is present in a dissimilar case" (passage *b*).[72] Implicit in his interpretation is the idea that since observation is supposed to be a form of perception, nonobservation must be defined in terms of the absence of this form of perception. He thus interprets the nonobservation of some fact "*x*" in terms of the absence of an instrument that proves "*x*." For Ratnakīrti—and not for his Nyāya opponents—warranted awareness is itself the instrument for warranted awareness.[73] As a result, as he sees it, the absence of a well-functioning instrument that establishes some fact "*x*" is merely the absence of the warranted awareness-event that "*x*." The fact "*x*" that is a component in the causal complex that produces this effect is, for the Naiyāyikas, the absence of the reason property from dissimilar cases. In their view, it is because there is not a well-functioning instrument of warranted awareness that proves that the reason property is present in a dissimilar case that they know, with epistemic certainty, that the reason property is not present in a dissimilar

72. This has interesting parallels with the Mīmāṃsā discussion of whether there is a separate instrument for coming to know absences. See, for example, Kellner 1999.

73. This is in contrast with the Nyāya view, which was discussed in chapter 2. According to the Naiyāyikas, the term "instrument of warranted awareness" (*pramāṇa*) is interpreted as meaning "by means of this there is warranted awareness" (*pramīyate anena iti pramāṇam*); the "this" being referred to is the instrument. See, e.g., NM 31.05, 31.13, 38.15, 72.11. According to Buddhists like Ratnakīrti, however, the term "instrument of warranted awareness" (*pramāṇa*) is interpreted to mean "it is warranted awareness" (*pramā iti pramāṇam*); the "it" being referred to is the instrument, which just is warranted awareness itself. The reason for this is that the instrument (i.e., the "*pramāṇa*") and its culminating effect (i.e., the "*pramiti*" or "*pramāṇaphala*") are assumed to be nondifferent. This means that the culminating effect of an instrument's functioning is nothing but the instrument itself. See MTBh 1.06–1.12, 22.17–23.06; and Dunne 1999:77–79, referring to PV 3.213–215 and PV 3.306–320. See also Hattori 1968:97–100 nn. 55–57, and the references contained therein.

case. According to Ratnakīrti, however, this is an illegitimate inference from a cause to an effect: in his view, such an inference requires that the absence of an effect (the knowing-event that "*x*") prove the absence of its cause (fact "*x*"). That such an inference is illegitimate is clear, Ratnakīrti argues, from the well-known example of the "inference" of smoke from its cause, fire. Ratnakīrti agrees, however, that if the patient of an awareness-event (putative fact "*x*"/the cause) were pervaded by the presence of the warranted awareness-event that proves it (the effect), the inference would be legitimate. He reasons, however, that a pervasion relation of this sort is not possible, since it would result in the absurd consequence that everyone would have warranted awareness of every object of awareness (passage *b*). He concludes from this that despite Trilocana and Vācaspatimiśra's assertion to the contrary, since there is always the possibility of an unobserved dissimilar locus (i.e., patient/cause), nonobservation cannot prove negative concomitance, and therefore it cannot be a basis for showing that H3a$_2$ does not undermine pervasion (passage *c*).

Now that Ratnakīrti has shown that nonobservation cannot be used to satisfy C2.3, he returns to the issue of whether there is epistemically significant doubt about it—that is, whether H3a$_2$ applies to the reason property "being an effect."

2.1.2. Ratnakīrti on Localized and Unlocalized Doubt

Vācaspatimiśra's response to the original argument that nonobservation cannot prove that a reason property is excluded from all dissimilar cases was to insist that the opponent's position would result in epistemically significant doubt about all inferentially produced awareness-events.[74] He recognized that even without actually observing a dissimilar locus there could still be, in the opponent's view, doubt about whether a reason property is excluded from such loci. As Vācaspatimiśra sees it, such a position entails that there will always be doubt about whether a reason property is present in some, as yet unobserved, dissimilar locus. Since such a locus need not be the object of an awareness-event, there could be doubt about the presence of the

74. See section 2.1., passage *b*.

reason property in such a possible counterexample for any awareness-event. If this sort of "unlocalized doubt" (*anartha-sandeha*) is supposed to be epistemically significant, Vācaspatimiśra reasoned that not only would the pervasion subcomponent of every proposed instrument of inferential awareness be undermined by $H3a_2$, but every awareness-event could be as well. As a result, the ghost of paralyzing doubt would be released, and rational people would never be able to act. Vācaspatimiśra concluded from this that epistemically significant doubt must be restricted to "localized-doubt" (*artha-sandeha*)—that is, to awareness-events in which there is doubt about whether a specific property-possessor that one is aware of possesses a particular property. This sort of localized doubt, he claimed, has to be based on observation. Since the doubt raised by the opponent is "unlocalized doubt"—that is, an awareness-event in which there is doubt about whether a property-possessor that one is not aware of possesses a particular property—he claims that it is not epistemically significant, and therefore that it does not undermine the pervasion subcomponent of the instrument in the Naiyāyikas' argument for the existence of Īśvara.

Ratnakīrti responds to this argument by first challenging the interpretation of the terms "localized doubt" and "unlocalized doubt." He writes,

> (a) What Vācaspati said—"The ghost of doubt would be released. Nowhere would it not exist, and so one would not act anywhere"[75]—does not follow. For intelligent people, positive activity is definitely not prevented, since "localized doubt" is a basis for activity. Unlocalized doubt can be raised in every case. It was also said that there would not be positive activity "because, in the end, death is observed even for those who consume nutritious food and drink."[76] This is difficult to understand.
>
> (b) That is to say: The terms "localized doubt" and "unlocalized doubt" are not genitive compounds. Rather, "localized doubt" means "doubt which is directed toward an object" and the term "unlocalized doubt" means "doubt which is not directed toward an object." These are compounds in which the middle word has been elided, like the compound "era-king."[77]

---

75. See section 2.1, passage *b*; RNĀ (ĪSD 42.13).

76. See section 2.1, passage *b*; RNĀ (ĪSD 42.15).

77. RNĀ (ĪSD 43.04–43.10): (a) ***yac coktam, saṃśayapiśācī labdhaprasarā na kvacin nāstīti na kvacit pravarteteti | tad asaṅgatam | arthasaṃśayasyāpi prekṣāvatāṃ pravṛttyaṅgatvāt pravṛt-***

Ratnakīrti reasons that the compound words "localized doubt" and "unlocalized doubt" do not describe awareness-events for which there must be a specific and identifiable object that either is or is not the object of that awareness-event. This is because this interpretation presupposes that the compounds are best interpreted as meaning "doubt that has an object" and "doubt that does not have an object"—where "doubt" refers to the awareness-event and "object" refers to the specific and identifiable object (or patient) of that awareness-event. In Ratnakīrti's view, however, these compounds are best interpreted as compounds in which the "middle word" is elided (passage *b*). In Ratnakīrti's interpretation, the compound word "localized doubt" refers to a state of awareness in which there is doubt that is "directed toward" an object—that is, doubt about some object (or property-possessor), but not necessarily about a specific and identifiable one. Ratnakīrti argues that this is the sort of "localized doubt" that is epistemically significant. The compound word "unlocalized doubt" refers, in his view, to doubt that is not directed toward an object—that is, doubt that is not about an object (or property-possessor). Ratnakīrti agrees here with Vācaspatimiśra that "unlocalized doubt" is not epistemically significant, since as Vācaspatimiśra points out it could be raised with respect to any awareness-event (passages *c* and *d*).

Given Ratnakīrti's reinterpretation of these concepts, the examples that the Naiyāyikas originally dismissed as being epistemically insignificant instances of unlocalized doubt can be seen to be epistemically significant instances of localized doubt. According to Vācaspatimiśra, the opponent's argument that $H3a_2$ applies to the reason property "being an effect," since it may be present in an as yet unobserved and unidentified dissimilar case, is based on the assumption that unlocalized doubt is epistemically significant. As Ratnakīrti interprets it, however, this argument has nothing to do with

---

tir avirodhiny eva | *anarthasandehaḥ sarvatra kartuṃ śakyate* | *antataḥ snigdhānnapānopayoge 'pi maraṇadarśanād apravṛttir iti cet* | *durjñānam etat* | (b) *tathā hi, arthasandeho 'narthasandeho veti nāyaṃ ṣaṣṭhīsamāsaḥ* | *kintv arthonmukhaḥ sandeho 'rthasandehaḥ, anarthonmukhaḥ sandeho 'narthasandeha iti śākapārthivādivanmadhyapadalopī samāsaḥ*. See RNĀ (ĪSD 42.13), RNĀ (ĪSD 42.15), and RNĀ (ĪSD 42.08–42.17), quoted earlier.

The example "*śāka-pārthiva*" (era-king) is usually understood as "*śāka-priya-pārthiva*" (era-dear-king), where the elided middle word is "*priya*" (*dear*). The term can be translated as "a king who is dear to the Śākas," i.e., an era-making king. See KāVṛ *ad* Pāṇini 2.1.60 and MBh *ad* Pāṇini 2.1.69. The elided word in the compounds "localized doubt" (*artha-unmukha-sandeha*) and "unlocalized doubt" (*anartha-unmukha-sandeha*) is *unmukha* ("directed toward").

unlocalized doubt. Rather, it is based on localized doubt—that is, doubt that is directed toward an object, i.e., a possible dissimilar locus. For Ratnakīrti, it is not necessary that a specific property-possessor be presented to awareness for there to be epistemically significant doubt about whether it possesses a particular property. All that is necessary is that there be some potential property-possessor about which there is such doubt.[78]

With his interpretation of the terms "localized doubt" and "unlocalized doubt" in place, Ratnakīrti also responds to Vācaspatimiśra's criticism of the opponent's original arguments for why H3a$_2$ applies to the reason property "being an effect." Vācaspatimiśra had argued that the opponent's understanding of epistemically significant doubt was such that if it were taken seriously it would paralyze rational people, and would result in their complete inactivity.[79] To support this claim Vācaspatimiśra argued that: (i) the opponent's view would result in epistemically significant doubt about every awareness-event; (ii) rational people would never act if unlocalized doubt were epistemically significant, as the opponent claims; and finally (iii) the opponent's position cannot account for why rational people act on the basis of widely accepted inferential arguments about which, in the opponent's view, there is epistemically significant doubt. As an example of such an argument he referred to the inference of a long and healthy life (target property) on the basis of consuming nutritious food and drink (reason property).[80]

Ratnakīrti responds to Vācaspatimiśra's arguments by defending the opponent's original insights. More specifically, he argues that not only is it possible to show that H3a$_2$ applies to the reason property "being an effect," but also that the three problematic consequences that Vācaspatimiśra attributes to the opponent's position do not follow from it. In a passage immediately following the one in which he interprets the terms "localized doubt" and "unlocalized doubt," Ratnakīrti explains that,

> (c) in the case of [a reason property] such as "nutritious food and drink," there is indeed localized doubt. This is because in one's own and another's continuum, things that belong to that class are observed to

78. This discussion is related to the issue of "empty subject" terms in logic, which has been discussed in Matilal 1970, McDermott 1969, McDermott 1970, and Chakrabarti 1997:211–245.

79. See section 2.1.

80. See section 2.1, passage *b*.

produce good eye-sight and be nourishing, etc., and unintended things such as death are observed only occasionally, in some cases. Unlocalized doubt is seen to be opposed to this. Therefore, it is indeed difficult to deny that in such cases intelligent people also act from doubt that is directed toward an object, as they do from warranted awareness.[81]

And in a somewhat different context he says,

(d) This is because when there isn't a well-functioning instrument of awareness that is capable of proof or disproof, reasonable doubt is accepted, even by those who act on the basis of well-functioning instruments of awareness. Moreover, the unwanted consequence of total inactivity doesn't follow, since activity is possible on the basis of both a well-functioning instrument of awareness and localized doubt. In addition, unlocalized doubt cannot be raised in every [such] case since, in some cases, localized doubt is seen.[82]

In passage *c*, Ratnakīrti addresses Vācaspatimiśra's concern that the opponent's position cannot adequately explain some widely accepted inferential practices. It is, for example, well known that a diet of nutritious food and drink (the reason property) contributes to a long and healthy life (the target property). It is also observed, however, that some people who maintain such diets occasionally become sick and die. According to the opponent, such a person would be a locus of deviation, since she is a locus in which the target property is absent and the reason property is present. On the basis of having observed such a person, however, the opponent should have epistemically significant doubt about the exclusion of the reason property from all dissimilar cases. Moreover, on this basis, she should conclude that $H3a_2$ applies to the reason property. As a result, she should also conclude that the inference

81. RNĀ (ĪSD 43.10–43.12): (c) *{evaṃ sati} snigdhānnapānādāv arthasandeha eva, tajjātīyasya svaparasantāne dṛṣṭipuṣṭyādyarthasya koṭiśaḥ karaṇadarśanāt, maraṇāder anarthasya kvacit kadācid darśanāt | etadviparīto 'narthasandeho draṣṭavyaḥ | tasmāt pramāṇād ivārthasaṃśayād api prekṣāvatāṃ tatra tatra pravṛttir durvāraiva.*

82. RNĀ (ĪSD 47.19–47.21): (d) *prāmāṇikair eva sādhakabādhakapramāṇābhāve nyāyaprāptasya saṃśayasya vihitatvāt | na ca sarvatrāpravṛttiprasaṅgaḥ, pramāṇād arthasaṃśayāc ca pravṛtter upapatteḥ | na cānarthasandehaḥ sarvatra kartuṃ śakyate, kvacid arthonmukhatāyā eva darśanāt.*

of a long and healthy life from a diet of nutritious food and drink is not a knowing-event, and so should not provide a basis for the actions of rational people. The problem, according to Vācaspatimiśra, is that rational people do not come to this conclusion. That this is the case is clear from seeing that rational people maintain a diet of nutritious food and drink in order to live a long and healthy life. According to Vācaspatimiśra, these sorts of inferential practices cannot be explained by the opponent.

As Ratnakīrti explains in passage *c*, however, from his perspective such practices can be easily explained. Although Ratnakīrti would agree with the opponent that the inference is not certified, he disagrees with Vācaspatimiśra that epistemically significant doubt must result in inactivity. In fact, as this example reveals, according to Ratnakīrti, rational people do act on the basis of unwarranted awareness-events. As a result, Vācaspatimiśra's worry that the opponent's position would result in complete inactivity can be dismissed. In passage *d* Ratnakīrti further explains this point, and extends its significance to the other two problematic consequences that Vācaspatimiśra attributes to the opponent's position. As Ratnakīrti explains, without a well-functioning instrument of awareness to prove or disprove that a particular reason property is excluded from all dissimilar cases, there will inevitably be doubt about whether that reason property is excluded from all such cases. Moreover, this doubt will be epistemically significant, since it will be an instance of localized doubt. As a result, the pervasion subcomponent of the instrument will be undermined, and the awareness-event that is produced by it will not be warranted. In such cases, however, Ratnakīrti says that the doubt is "reasonable," since there is not a well-functioning instrument of awareness that could resolve the matter in one way or the other. And as Ratnakīrti argues, rational people do act on the basis of such reasonable, localized doubt.

As a result of this analysis, which is supported by his critique of nonobservation and his own account of epistemically significant doubt, Ratnakīrti supports the opponent's original insight that not only have the Naiyāyikas not shown that H3a$_2$ does not apply to the reason property in their Īśvara-inference but they have in fact demonstrated that it applies to it.

2.2. *The Growing Grass Argument, H3a$_1$*

In defending their argument from H3a, the Naiyāyikas argued that since there were no known instances of deviation, the defect H3a$_1$ did not defeat the pervasion subcomponent of the instrument defined by the reason property "being an effect."[83] One of the issues raised in their defense concerned the criteria through which instances of deviation could be identified.[84] As previously discussed, an instance of deviation is a locus, other than the site, in which the reason property is known to be present and the target property is known to be absent.[85] When such a locus is identified, the defect is said to apply. Determining that a particular locus is a locus of deviation requires: (1) determining that that locus is not the site; (2) determining the precise nature of the target property; (3) determining that the target property is not present in that locus; (4) determining the precise nature of the reason property; and (5) determining that the reason property is present in that locus.

Through the theory of remoteness, the Naiyāyikas had argued that the opponent could not determine (3)—that is, that the target property was not present in growing grass, the opponent's proposed locus of deviation.[86] On the basis of this, they argued that since defect $H3a_1$ was not shown to apply to "being an effect," C2.3 was in fact satisfied. Of the five issues mentioned above, issues 1–3 are central to Ratnakīrti's arguments in the *Section on Pervasion*. Issues 4–5 are discussed in the *Section on the Reason Property*. Ratnakīrti begins his argument in the *Section on Pervasion* with issue 2, and a brief discussion of the target property.

2.2.1. Two Alternatives

From the Naiyāyikas' inferential argument, it is clear that what they are trying to prove is that an intelligent agent created our world, in the sense that it is Īśvara who put it together.[87] What is not clear, however, is whether this agent is supposed to be observable, unobservable, or contextually observable and unobservable.[88] If this agent is supposed to be observable (alternative 1), Ratnakīrti argues that a locus of deviation can be easily identified, and thus that it can be shown that $H3a_1$ defeats the pervasion subcomponent of the instrument. In support of the opponent's initial argument that growing

83. See chapter 2, section 3.2.

84. See chapter 2, section 3.2.1.

85. Deviation has been discussed in chapter 2, section 3.2.2 and in sections 1.2–1.3 above.

86. See chapter 2, section 3.2.1.

87. See chapter 2, sections 2–2.2.

88. RNĀ (ĪSD 43.31–44.01).

grass is a locus of deviation and a counterexample to pervasion, Ratnakīrti also points to trees. If the agent is supposed to be unobservable or contextually observable and unobservable (alternative 2), Ratnakīrti argues, there will be epistemically significant doubt about the exclusion of the reason property from all dissimilar cases, and therefore that $H3a_2$ can be shown to defeat the pervasion subcomponent of the instrument. In either case, Ratnakīrti argues not only that the Naiyāyikas have not certified that the instrument is well-functioning, but that, since its pervasion subcomponent is defective, the instrument is in fact not well-functioning.

What is specifically at issue for Ratnakīrti is whether, according to the Naiyāyikas, the target property is always, occasionally, or never observable (issue 2), and whether, given the Naiyāyikas' position, pervasion can be established.[89] Given that a dissimilar case must be a locus in which the target property is known to be present, and that according to the Naiyāyikas observation and nonobservation are the instruments most commonly used to detect the presence or absence of a property in a particular locus, the issue of whether the maker is always (i.e., inevitably and immediately) or only occasionally (i.e., neither inevitably nor immediately) observable is significant for the Īśvara-inference. As Ratnakīrti sees it, however, in either case H3a can be shown to apply to the reason property "being an effect."

AN OBSERVABLE ĪŚVARA

Ratnakīrti introduces alternative 1 as follows:

> If it is the first alternative, the reason property is generally inconclusive. . . . This is because [the reason property] "being an effect" is observed in things like trees, which are produced even without a target property like that.[90]
>
> [The Naiyāyikas respond:] Things like trees are included in the site of the inference. How can there be deviation with respect to them? Existing things are of three sorts: either there is doubt about them having a maker, as there is for trees and the like; or a maker is well known, as for pots

---

89. Interestingly, the issue of Īśvara's being in principle unobservable (i.e., never observable) is not discussed in this context. The (mis-)interpretation of "unobservable" as "in principle unobservable" is discussed in Kellner 1999.

90. RNĀ (ĪSD 44.01–44.02): *yady ādyaḥ pakṣaḥ, tadā tathābhūtasādhyam antareṇāpy utpadyamāne viṭapādau kāryatvadarśanāt sādhāraṇānaikāntiko hetuḥ.*

> and the like; or there isn't a maker, like in the case of space and the like. Having accepted, on the basis of perception and nonapprehension, that there is pervasion for things like pots—which have a well-known maker—and having located the reason property "being an effect" in things like trees—loci about which there is doubt—an intelligent agent is inferred. Again, they cannot be a locus of deviation.[91]

In responding to Ratnakīrti's assertion that, like growing grass, trees are a locus of deviation, the Naiyāyikas argue that since trees are a part of the site of the inference they cannot count as examples of deviation (issue 1). The Naiyāyikas defend this view by classifying all objects into three distinct groups, based upon whether the object is known to have an intelligent maker, whether there is doubt about it having such a maker, or whether it is known to not have a maker at all. The site of the inference includes, by definition, only those objects for which there is doubt about their being made by an intelligent agent. Since it is well known, for example, that pots are made by an intelligent agent, they cannot be a part of the site of the inference. Even though Ratnakīrti does not have any doubt about whether trees have such a maker, the Naiyāyikas argue that since they have reasonable doubt about this, it is appropriate for trees to be included in the site of the inference. On this basis, they also argue that things like trees cannot be *known* to be instances of deviation. In response, Ratnakīrti says,

> This is incorrect, since a locus of deviation must not be included in the site of an inference. This is based on the following principle: "In putting forth a reason property when there is doubt, the reason property is without a specific locus." In addition, there *is* a locus of deviation. This is because, in the case of things like growing grass, an intelligent agent-in-general, with the additional property of an observable body, is rejected on the basis of the nonapprehension of an observable. Because of this, it is entirely appropriate to make things like mountains—about which there is doubt regarding a maker—into the site of the inference. Trees, on the other

91. RNĀ (ĪSD 44.03–44.08): *nanu vṛkṣādayaḥ pakṣīkṛtāḥ | kathaṃ tair vyabhicāraḥ | trividho hi bhāvarāśiḥ | sandigdhakartṛko yathā vṛkṣādiḥ | prasiddhakartṛko yathā ghaṭādiḥ | akartṛko yathākāśādiḥ | tatra prasiddhakartṛke ghaṭādau pratyakṣānupalambhābhyāṃ vyāptim ādāya sandehapade kṣmāruhādau kāryatvam upasaṃhrtya buddhimān anumīyate | na punar asau vyabhicāraviṣayo bhavitum arhati*. See NVTṬ 563.11–563.13 *ad* NS 4.1.21.

hand, have a sentient maker, but you don't accept this fourth category of things.[92]

Ratnakīrti implies that by simply asserting that they have reasonable doubt about whether trees have an observable, intelligence-possessing maker, the Naiyāyikas have not shown that their doubt is either reasonable or epistemically significant. He suggests that if one agrees with the Naiyāyikas' line of reasoning almost any proposed locus of deviation could be dismissed by simply asserting that it is a part of the site of the inference. As Ratnakīrti also points out, he could just as easily assert that a locus that he knows to be a locus of deviation cannot be included in the site of an inference, since he knows it to be a locus in which the reason property is present and the target property is absent. Simply asserting that trees are a part of the site of the inference is not, therefore, a proper response to the charge that they are a locus of deviation.

More significantly, Ratnakīrti argues that as in the case of growing grass it can be shown that trees are a locus of deviation. If, for example, the target property is supposed to be observable, it is possible to know that it is not present in a particular locus through the "nonapprehension of an observable" (*dṛśya-anupalambha*).[93] Since both Trilocana and Vācaspatimiśra seem to consider nonapprehension (or nonobservation) to be a type of perception—i.e., an accredited instrument of warranted awareness—Ratnakīrti implies that they too should be able to determine whether growing grass and trees have an observable, intelligent maker. He reasons that since nearly everyone

92. RNĀ (ĪSD 44.08–44.13): *ayuktam etat | na hi vyabhicāraviṣaya eva pakṣe bhavitum arhati, sandigdhe hetuvacanād vyasto hetor anāśraya iti nyāyāt | vyabhicāraviṣayatā ca dṛśyaśarīropādher buddhimanmātrasya tṛṇādyutpattau dṛśyānupalambhena pratikṣiptatvāt | tataś ca kṣmādharādir eva sandigdhakartṛkaḥ pakṣīkartum ucitaḥ kṣmāruhādis tu cetanākartṛka iti caturtho bhāvarāśir neṣṭavyaḥ.* See PV 4.91 and Tillemans 2000:124–129.

93. According to Buddhists like Ratnakīrti, the "nonapprehension of an observable" (*dṛśyānupalabdhi*) is an accredited instrument for establishing the absence of observable objects. In some cases, the term refers to a form of perception. See, for example, JNĀ (AR 79.14–79.16) in Kellner 2007. In most cases, however, the term refers to a reason property (*anupalabdhi-hetu*). In such cases, the "nonapprehension of an observable" is an instrument that justifies the threefold treatment of an object as absent (*asadvyavahāra*). The secondary literature on nonapprehension (*anupalabdhi*) is extensive; see, for example, Katsura 1992b, Kellner 1997a, Kellner 1999, and Steinkellner 1992. Now see too the very helpful discussion in Kellner 2007.

has seen that grass and trees are produced from seeds, soil, sunlight, water, etc., and that an observable, intelligent agent has never been seen to be a part of the causal complex that leads to the production of either object, it should be clear that neither grass nor trees have such a maker. Since no one has ever seen the "causes" of the great mountains, however, there is reasonable and epistemically significant doubt about whether they have an observable and intelligent maker. A maker of things like mountains might, after all, have been observable, but only a very long time ago at the moment of their origin. Since their maker could be temporally remote, it cannot be determined through the nonapprehension of an observable whether or not they have such a maker. Ratnakīrti explains that, as a result of this, things like mountains should be included in the site of the inference. His point is that there is a principled way of determining whether there is reasonable doubt about whether a proposed locus possesses a particular property. Moreover, once this criterion is applied, it is clear that there isn't doubt about whether trees have an observable and intelligent maker, but there is doubt about whether mountains have such a maker. As a result, trees cannot be included in the site of the inference, and thus can legitimately serve as an example of deviation. From this, Ratnakīrti concludes that if the Naiyāyikas' claim that the target property is observable, it can be shown that trees are a locus of deviation, and therefore that $H3a_1$ defeats the pervasion subcomponent of the instrument.

AN UNOBSERVED ĪŚVARA

Ratnakīrti now considers the possibility that the Naiyāyikas take the target property to be an intelligent agent who is not observable (alternative 2). Such a maker might be unobservable, in principle, or only contextually unobservable, as a result of being spatially, temporally, or essentially remote to us (*deśa-kāla-svabhāva-viprakṛṣṭa*). In considering such a possibility, Ratnakīrti writes,

> (a) Now, shocked by deviation, and for the purpose of showing that there are three groups of existing things, they [i.e., the Naiyāyikas] say that it is the second alternative: there is pervasion with an intelligent-maker-in-general who, in virtue of being both observable and unobservable, cannot be rejected on the basis of perception as being the maker of things like trees.
>
> (b) Given this, it is possible that there is an intelligent-maker-in-general for things like trees. Thus we do not say that the reason property

is generally inconclusive. Instead we say that because of the absence of pervasion, there is doubt about the exclusion [of the reason property from dissimilar cases]. The reason for this is that negative concomitance cannot be proven by the nonapprehension of an observable, since what is to be proven, an intelligent agent who is both observable and unobservable, may be unobservable at the time when pervasion is being grasped.

(c) That is to say: If the negative concomitance of a pot is determined prior to the instrumental activity of the potter, it is not possible to determine that the negative concomitance of the pot is due to the absence of the target property [i.e., the potter]. For example, when things like trees were coming into being, it is possible that the intelligent-maker-in-general was present, since in virtue of his being unobservable this cannot be denied. This is also the case for things like pots, since in virtue of being unobservable at the time when negative concomitance is being ascertained, it is possible that the intelligent-maker-in-general was present. Since it has not been proven that the absence of the reason property is dependent upon the absence of the target property, pervasion is absent. How is the reason property not one about which there is doubt regarding its exclusion [from dissimilar cases]? [94]

Given that the target property may be unobservable, it is not possible, through nonobservation, to know that that property is not present in a particular locus (passage *b*). This is because, as a result of remoteness, that property may not be observed even though it is present in that locus. Ratnakīrti agrees that in such cases it cannot be shown that the pervasion relation is defeated by $H3a_1$, the defect called "generally inconclusive" (passage *b*). Instead he argues that in such cases it is defeated by $H3a_2$, the defect called "doubt about the exclusion of the reason property from dissimilar cases"

94. RNĀ (ĪSD 44.16–44.24): (a) *atha vyabhicāracamatkārās trividhabhāvarāśivyavasthāpanārthaṃ ca viṭapādau pratyakṣāpratikṣiptena dṛśyādṛśyasādhāraṇena buddhimanmātreṇa vyāptir avagamyata iti dvitīyaḥ saṅkalpaḥ* | (b) *tadā viṭapādau buddhimanmātrasya saṃbhāvyamānatvān na sādhāraṇānaikāntikatāṃ brūmaḥ* | *kiṃ tarhi, vyāptigrahaṇakāle dṛśyādṛśyasādhāraṇasya buddhimanmātrasya sādhyasya adṛśyatayā dṛśyānupalambhena vyatirekāsiddher vyāpter abhāvāt sandigdhavyāvṛttikatvam ācakṣmahe* | (c) *tathā hi* | *yadā kumbhakāravyāpārāt pūrvaṃ kumbhasya vyatirekaḥ pratyetavyas tadā na sādhyābhāvakṛto ghaṭavyatirekaḥ pratyetuṃ śakyaḥ* | *yathā hi viṭapādijanmasamaye buddhimanmātrasyādṛśyatvena niṣeddhum aśakyatvāt sattvasaṃbhāvanāyām, sādhyābhāvaprayuktasya sādhanābhāvasyāsiddhatvena vyāpter abhāvāt kathaṃ na sandigdhavyatireko hetuḥ.*

(passage *b*). In considering alternative 2, therefore, the discussion shifts from the discussion of $H3a_1$ back to a discussion of $H3a_2$. According to Ratnakīrti, in order for the Naiyāyikas to know that the reason property "being an effect" is not present in any dissimilar locus they must know that the absence of the reason property is *due to* the absence of the target property (passage *c*). What is at issue is negative concomitance and how, according to the Naiyāyikas, it can be established. Since the target property may be unobservable, Ratnakīrti argues that there is no way for the Naiyāyikas to determine negative concomitance through observation and nonobservation (nonapprehension).

What the Naiyāyikas need to show, according to Ratnakīrti, is how pervasion, and especially negative concomitance, can be established when one of the terms in a proposed inference-warranting relation is (at least contextually) unobservable. One way they could do this would be to show how negative concomitance is established in well-known and widely accepted inferences, such as the inference of a potter—who as a result of being temporally or spatially remote may be contextually unobservable—from the presence of pots. In order to show this, the Naiyāyikas must, in accordance with their own theory, explain why the defect called "doubt about the exclusion of the reason property from dissimilar cases" does not apply. More specifically, in the case of a potter and his pots, they must, according to Ratnakīrti, show that the absence of a pot is *due to* the absence of the potter. Ratnakīrti argues that according to their own theory the Naiyāyikas cannot show this. In arguing his point, he makes use of the Naiyāyikas' earlier argument that one cannot know through observation and nonobservation that trees do not have an intelligent maker, since due to remoteness this maker could be unobservable.[95]

Ratnakīrti's point in citing this example is to illustrate that for the Naiyāyikas too the nonobservation (or nonapprehension) of a contextually unobservable maker cannot establish the absence of that maker in a particular locus. As a result, it is always possible that such a maker is present but not seen. Thus the Naiyāyikas cannot show that such a maker is not present. As a result, if the target property is unobservable, there will always be doubt about its exclusion from dissimilar cases. Moreover, this will be the case regardless of whether the target property is a potter or an intelligent maker. As

95. See chapter 2, section 3.2.1.

a result Ratnakīrti concludes that there is epistemically significant doubt about the exclusion of the reason property from dissimilar cases, and therefore that H3a_2 defeats it. The problem, as Ratnakīrti sees it, is that if the target property is not observable, negative concomitance cannot be established, given the Nyāya view. And as a result, it is inevitable that there will be epistemically significant doubt about the exclusion of the reason property from dissimilar cases (C2.3).

2.2.2. A Counterargument from Material Causes

In responding to an earlier objection, however, the Naiyāyikas explained how a pervasion relation that was established between specific and observable classes of effects and specific and observable classes of causes could be used to infer a specific, unobservable cause—an unobserved maker—from the reason property "effects-in-general."[96] In order to illustrate this, the Naiyāyikas provided an example. They argued that since their opponent would agree that pervasion can be established between specific pieces of cloth and their material cause—i.e., threads—he should also agree that there is pervasion between all effects—i.e., effects-in-general—and the property "having a material cause." The assumption underlying this argument is that specific, observed pieces of cloth are known to be pervaded by the property "having a material cause," in virtue of their having the property "being an effect-in-general." The Naiyāyikas reason that since the opponent agrees with the conclusion of this first argument he should also agree with the conclusion of a parallel argument in which the property "having an instrumental cause" is substituted in both steps of the argument for the property "having a material cause." Their imagined opponent, however, rejected the parallel argument. But according to the Naiyāyikas, this rejection entails the rejection of the well-known argument. Since this is not acceptable to the opponent, the Naiyāyikas conclude that he must then accept the parallel argument. These two arguments are important to Ratnakīrti's continuing discussion of H3a_2, since they provide another example of how the Naiyāyikas argue that negative concomitance can be known even when one or both of the terms is not observable.

In responding to this argument, Ratnakīrti rejects both the example and the analysis. He argues,

96. See chapter 2, section 3.2.2.

> So who deceived you in this way? If in this case pervasion is grasped by perception and nonapprehension, how is it proven that an effect-in-general has a material cause? You didn't mention another method for grasping pervasion. And if they are observable and unobservable, it is impossible to rationally arrive at pervasion between an effect-in-general and a material cause by means of perception and nonapprehension, since each must have an observable object.[97]

Ratnakīrti's response to the parallel argument strategy is based on his earlier point about the method that the Naiyāyikas use to establish pervasion. Although Ratnakīrti agrees with the conclusion of the first argument, he does not agree with the Naiyāyikas' theory of pervasion. Thus he rejects both arguments, but only the conclusion of the second one. In the above passage Ratnakīrti repeats his point that it is not possible to establish pervasion for an unobservable object by perception and nonapprehension. The reason he rejects the Naiyāyikas' parallel argument strategy is suggested by his earlier remark, that to establish negative concomitance it is necessary to know that "the absence of the reason property is *due to* the absence of the target property" (*sādhya-abhāva-prayukta*). Neither the Naiyāyikas' theory of inference-warranting relations nor their parallel argument strategy is able to show this dependence.

According to Ratnakīrti, then, the Nyāya theory cannot account for how a pervasion relation that is established for a specific set of observable objects can be extended to objects that are not observable. Without a plausible method for determining pervasion for an unobservable target property, there will always be doubt about the exclusion of the reason property from putatively dissimilar cases, and so $H3a_2$ will be known to apply. As Ratnakīrti sees it, this is a problem not only for the Īśvara-inference, but for every inference in which the target property is unobservable in this way.

---

97. RNĀ (ĪSD 44.25–44.30): *{yathoktam, na ca yathā kāryaṃ ca syān nirupādānaṃ ceti nāśaṅkanīyam, tathā kāryaṃ ca bhaved akartṛkaṃ ceti nāśaṅkanīyam iti, tatrāpi kāryaṃ ca syān nirupādānaṃ ca bhaved iti na vaktavyam iti} kenaivaṃ pratārito 'si | yadi hy atra pratyakṣānupalambhābhyāṃ vyāptir gṛhyate tadā katham upādānapūrvakaṃ kāryamātraṃ sidhyati | vyāptigrahaṇaprakārāntaraṃ ca tvayāpi nopanyastam | dṛśyādṛśyasādhāraṇayor upādānakārya-mātrayor dṛśyaviṣayābhyāṃ pratyakṣānupalambhābhyāṃ vyāpter abhyūhitum aśakyatvāt.*

2.3. *Conclusion: The* Section on Pervasion

In his *Section on Pervasion*, Ratnakīrti considers the Nyāya theory of inference-warranting relations, in order to show why the inference-warranting relation in their argument for the existence of Īśvara is defeated by H3a. In describing the Nyāya theory, he also discusses the three pervasion conditions in terms of which the Naiyāyikas define the natural relation that they insist underwrites the pervasion subcomponent of all well-functioning instruments of inferential awareness. In this section he also provides an account of how the Naiyāyikas propose to satisfy these conditions and thereby show that the inference-warranting relation defined by them is epistemically necessary.

Although Ratnakīrti argues that the Naiyāyikas have neither provided a precise definition of such relations nor proven that such relations exist, his most important criticism of the Nyāya theory is his argument that the Naiyāyikas cannot show by observation and nonobservation that C2.3 (and U) are ever satisfied. According to Ratnakīrti, an inherent weakness in the Nyāya theory is their view that a finite, unspecified number of empirical observations and nonobservations can establish the absence of a reason property in all dissimilar cases (C2.3). As Ratnakīrti argues, the epistemic necessity conferred upon negative concomitance by the Nyāya theory is such that there will always be the possibility that a reason property is present in an as yet unidentified dissimilar case. As a result, Ratnakīrti concludes that the Naiyāyikas cannot show that C2.3 is satisfied and that $H3a_2$ does not apply to a reason property. This is the case, he suggests, not only for the reason property in the Naiyāyikas' argument for the existence of Īśvara but for nearly every inferential argument that is supposed to be certified within the Nyāya epistemological framework. This general criticism of the Nyāya theory of inference-warranting relations and certification informs Ratnakīrti's response to each of the Nyāya arguments discussed in this section.

In discussing "Argument 1: The Growing Grass Argument," Ratnakīrti argued that if the Naiyāyikas suppose that Īśvara is observable then it can be shown through the nonapprehension of an observable that trees and growing grass are instances of deviation, and that they defeat the pervasion subcomponent of the instrument in the Naiyāyikas' argument. This is because, according to both Ratnakīrti and the Naiyāyikas, the epistemic fact of not observing an observable object in a locus establishes the nonepistemic fact of its absence in that locus. If Īśvara is supposed to be an "unobservable," however,

Ratnakīrti argues that the Naiyāyikas cannot prove negative concomitance through nonapprehension or nonobservation, as required by their theory. This is because, as Ratnakīrti has argued, the epistemic fact of not observing an unobservable cannot establish the nonepistemic fact of the absence of that unobservable. More specifically, a finite, unspecified number of nonobservations can never establish that the absence of an unobservable object, such as the target property, is due to the absence of the reason property. The observed instances of negative concomitance could be coincidental. Since negative concomitance cannot be established, Ratnakīrti argues that there will always be epistemically significant doubt about the exclusion of the reason property from all dissimilar cases, and therefore that $H3a_2$ will defeat the reason property.

In his discussion of "Argument 2: The Argument from Localized Doubt," Ratnakīrti considers the Naiyāyikas response to this sort of argument. The Naiyāyikas argue that the epistemic necessity conferred upon inference-warranting relations by their theory is sufficient for ruling out what they consider to be epistemically significant doubt about the presence of the reason property in dissimilar cases. Ratnakīrti dismisses this on the grounds that it is based on an untenable theory of epistemic doubt. According to Ratnakīrti, the problem with the Nyāya theory of doubt is that it considers only available, but not possible, objects to be epistemically significant. As he sees it, the Nyāya view is impoverished by their empiricism. In responding to the Naiyāyikas, Ratnakīrti reinterprets the Naiyāyikas' theory of doubt and shows that his interpretation is more reasonable and that it will not lead to paralyzing doubt, as they suggest. Given his account of reasonable and epistemically significant doubt, Ratnakīrti argues that $H3a_2$ can be shown to defeat the reason property.

3. The *Section on the Reason Property*

In the next section of his essay, Ratnakīrti continues his discussion of $H3a_1$ and $H3a_2$ by focusing on issues that have to do with the scope of the reason property "being an effect."[98] The discussion shifts, therefore, to the specific

98. See chapter 2, section 3.2.2. There are two somewhat different issues that have to do with what I am calling the "scope" of the reason property. The first issue, which will be discussed in this section, concerns the conditions under which, given a particular formulation

nature of the reason property (issue 4) and the related issue of whether it is known to be present in a particular locus (issue 5).[99] While in section 2 of this chapter Ratnakīrti discussed H3a$_1$ and H3a$_2$ primarily in terms of the target property (issue 2, issue 3), here he reconsiders these defects by focusing on the *reason* property. In both cases, however, he is concerned with negative concomitance. In addition, in section 2 Ratnakīrti focused his attention almost exclusively on the pervasion subcomponent of the instrument—that is, on C2.2, C2.3, U, and the defects associated with them (see figure 1 in chapter 2, p. 64). Here his attention to the reason property enables him to expand his analysis to include a discussion of C2.1, which is the instrument condition in terms of which the site subcomponent is defined, and its associated defect, H1b. As discussed earlier, C2.1 states that a reason property must be known to be present in the site of the inference.[100] It is in discussing the nature of the reason property and its proposed negative concomitance that Ratnakīrti provides his response to what I referred to earlier as "the Restricted Scope Argument."[101]

3.1. *The Restricted Scope Argument*

In defending their argument for the existence of Īśvara, Ratnakīrti's Naiyāyikas stated that the reason property "being an effect" should be interpreted as "effects-in-general" so as to include any and all effects.[102] In defending this formulation of the reason property, the Naiyāyikas also responded to an opponent who argued that this version of the reason property is inconclusive, since it is known to be present in dissimilar cases such as growing grass

---

of the reason property, a pervasion relation can be "extended" from a "sample class" for which the co-presence and co-absence of the reason and the target properties have been observed in the "site" of the inference. The second issue, which will be discussed in section 4, has to do with the special characteristics that can and cannot be proven on the basis of knowing that the reason property is a property of the site of the inference. These two issues are related in that they both have to do with the precise formulation of the reason property (i.e., its scope) and with different aspects of instrument condition T1, which states that a reason property must be known to be a property of the site of the inference (*pakṣadharmatā*).

99. See chapter 2, section 3.2.2. All five issues are also listed in section 2.2 above.

100. See chapter 2, section 2.3.1.

101. See chapter 2, section 3.2.2 and section 2 of this chapter, where the argument is referred to as "argument 3."

102. See chapter 2, section 3.1.2, where RNĀ (ĪSD 33.32–34.05) is discussed.

($H3a_1$).[103] The opponent further argued that since something's "being an effect" is not always observable, there will always be epistemically significant doubt about whether the reason property is excluded from dissimilar cases ($H3a_2$).[104] The opponent concluded from this that the *unrestricted* version of the reason property is defective, since both $H3a_1$ and $H3a_2$ are known to apply to it. By limiting the scope of the reason property, however, the opponent suggested that its pervasion with an intelligent agent could be established.[105] More specifically, it was suggested that the scope of the proposed reason property should be limited to a class of "specific effects" whose members are defined by the restrictive property "from the observation of which (both parties would agree) there could be an awareness of its having been made, even for one who did not observe its being made."[106] This restrictive property was meant to distinguish effects such as pots, for which an intelligent maker has been observed, from those such as growing grass, for which an intelligent maker has not been, and cannot be, observed.

Given this more restricted version of the reason property, the opponent suggested that pervasion with an intelligent maker could be established through observation and nonobservation, as required by the Nyāya theory.[107] After all, this restricted form of the reason property is not known to be present in a dissimilar case, and given that it is observable, there need not be epistemically significant doubt about its exclusion from dissimilar cases. It is possible, therefore, that the pervasion subcomponent of an instrument defined by it would be neither defeated by $H3a_1$ nor undermined by $H3a_2$. As the opponent pointed out, however, the problem with the restricted version of the reason property is that it is not present in the site of the inference, i.e., our world/the earth. In other words, it is defective because it is "unestablished in itself" (*svarūpāsiddha*, H1b).[108] The opponent's point is that the version of the reason property for which pervasion can be

103. See chapter 2, section 3.2.1, where RNĀ (ĪSD 36.26–36.27) is discussed.

104. See chapter 2, sections 3.2.2, where RNĀ (ĪSD 37.12–37.16) is discussed, and 3.2.3.

105. See chapter 2, section 3.2.3, where RNĀ (ĪSD 37.17–37.18) and RNĀ (ĪSD 37.20–37.26) are discussed.

106. See chapter 2, section 3.2.3, where RNĀ (ĪSD 37.27–37.29) is discussed.

107. Although this is not directly stated by the opponent, it is clear from his discussion, and Ratnakīrti's own interpretation of the argument, that this is what the opponent has in mind.

108. This is suggested at RNĀ (ĪSD 38.04–38.07). For a definition of this defect see KTBh 106.01, which is quoted and translated in the notes to chapter 2, section 2.3.1.

established cannot prove what the Naiyāyikas want to prove, because it is defeated by H1b, and the version of the reason property that could prove what the Naiyāyikas want to prove is defective because of H3a. In either case, one of the two subcomponents necessary for the instrument to be well-functioning—the site subcomponent or the pervasion subcomponent—is defective.

In the *Section on the Reason Property*, Ratnakīrti picks up the opponent's line of argument, by arguing that there needs to be a limiting property "*R*" that restricts the scope of the reason property "being an effect."[109] As mentioned earlier, one problem with the unrestricted version of the reason property is that since there are numerous loci in which this property is known to be present, and the target property, an intelligent maker, is known to be absent, it is inconclusive (H3a_1). Here Ratnakīrti cites the example of a lump of clay, in which the effects of drying and cracking are observed prior to the activity of a potter.[110] This example supports the opponent's earlier appeal to growing grass and Ratnakīrti's own reference to trees. Ratnakīrti's point is that since effects-in-general, such as the drying and cracking of a lump of clay, have not been observed to be caused by an intelligent maker, there cannot be pervasion between "being an effect'"—that is, effects-in-general—and "having an intelligent maker." A drying and cracking lump of clay, Ratnakīrti points out, is clearly a locus of deviation, since it is a locus in which the reason property "being an effect" is known to be present, but the target property "having an intelligent maker" is known to be absent. As a result of such examples, Ratnakīrti claims that the unrestricted version of the reason property deviates from the target property (H3a_1).

109. The structure of this section of Ratnakīrti's essay is somewhat complicated. In my discussion, therefore, I have chosen to reconstruct the Naiyāyikas' argument and Ratnakīrti's response to it by referring to ideas that are scattered throughout the section and discussed somewhat differently in different places. What "complicates" the structure of the section is that there are two (very helpful) "summary" passages, one in which the Naiyāyikas summarize their main points, RNĀ (ĪSD 52.11–52.21), and one in which Ratnakīrti reconstructs their argument and summarizes his own, RNĀ (ĪSD 52.22–53.20). Consider the following "outline" of the section: RNĀ (ĪSD 50.21–51.13), set up; RNĀ (ĪSD 51.14–52.11), the Naiyāyikas' trick; RNĀ (ĪSD 52.11–52.21), Nyāya summary; RNĀ (ĪSD 52.22–53.20), Ratnakīrti's summary and argument; RNĀ (ĪSD 53.20–54.01), Ratnakīrti's response (to miscellaneous parts of RNĀ [ĪSD 51.14–52.11] not discussed in his summary); and RNĀ (ĪSD 54.01–54.04), conclusion.

110. RNĀ (ĪSD 50.23–50.27). The example is referred to again at RNĀ (ĪSD 51.03–51.07).

In addition, according to Ratnakīrti, it cannot be shown that the absence of an effect-in-general—e.g., a pot—is due to the absence of an intelligent maker—e.g., the potter. This is because even though it can be shown that a pot is made by a potter, it cannot be shown that the absence of the pot is due to the absence of the potter. An observed instance of co-absence could be coincidental. Moreover, effects-in-general are not always observable. As a result, Ratnakīrti argues that negative concomitance cannot be established and that there will inevitably be epistemically significant doubt about the exclusion of the reason property from all dissimilar cases ($H3a_2$).[111] According to Ratnakīrti, the challenge for the Naiyāyikas is to identify a property "*R*" such that the subclass of effects-in-general defined by it can be known through observation and nonobservation to be pervaded by the target property. Such a property "*R*" would ensure that the reason property is neither inconclusive ($H3a_1$) nor one about which there is epistemically significant doubt about its exclusion from dissimilar cases ($H3a_2$). In addition, it must also be shown that the reason property that is restricted by "*R*" is present in the site of the inference; that is, that H1b does not apply.[112] If such a property could be found, it would restrict the reason property in such a way that C2.1, C2.2, and C2.3 could be satisfied. In arguing that such a property "*R*" has not been specified, Ratnakīrti seeks to show that H3a applies to the original reason property, effects-in-general. I will argue that in so doing Ratnakīrti also points to what he considers to be a more general problem with the Nyāya theory of instrument conditions and certification.

3.2. *Ratnakīrti and the Naiyāyikas' Trick*

Ratnakīrti's Naiyāyikas respond to the challenge of identifying "*R*" by making a distinction between two classes of effects: effects-in-general, and a class of effects for which an intelligent maker has been observed.[113] This more restricted class of effects is supposed to include subclasses of effects such as pots, cloth, and large buildings, but not effects like trees, mountains, growing grass, or drying and cracking.[114] The Naiyāyikas argue that since there is reasonable

111. RNĀ (ĪSD 51.09–51.13).

112. See RNĀ (ĪSD 51.15–51.16 and 52.11–52.14).

113. RNĀ (ĪSD 51.14–51.16).

114. RNĀ (ĪSD 51.18–51.21). This passage considers whether the class of specified effects

doubt about whether effects such as trees, mountains, growing grass, and drying and cracking have an intelligent maker, they should be included in the site of the inference, and so cannot be cited as counterexamples to pervasion.[115] Thus, as they see it, $H3a_1$ doesn't apply to this version of the reason property.

The Naiyāyikas then argue that there is a class of effects-in-general, a "sample class" of effects, for which an intelligent maker has been observed, and that for this class of effects pervasion with an intelligent agent can be established through observation and nonobservation, etc. They reason that no one can object to this, since in the case of well-known inferences, such as the inference of fire from smoke, pervasion is also established on the basis of a sample class. After all, it is not the case that each and every locus of smoke (and/or fire) has to be observed. On the basis of this parallel argument strategy, the Naiyāyikas reason that $H3a_2$ does not apply to their reason property either. Finally, they argue that even though trees, mountains, growing grass, and drying and cracking are not members of the sample class for which pervasion has been established, since they have not been *observed* to have an intelligent maker, they can nevertheless be included in the scope of the reason property "effects-in-general," since even Ratnakīrti would have to agree that they are effects. Thus H1b doesn't apply, and they can be inferred to have been made by an intelligent agent.[116] The Naiyāyikas conclude, therefore, that the reason property "effects-in-general"/"being an effect" does not need to be restricted, since in its unrestricted form it is a well-functioning instrument of awareness. Ratnakīrti refers to this line of reasoning as the "Naiyāyikas' trick" (*viḍambana*) and argues that it does not work.

3.2.1. Exposing the Trick

Ratnakīrti begins his analysis of the Naiyāyikas' trick by arguing against their grouping of effects into just two classes. He says,

---

refers to (1) those individual effects for which concomitance has been observed or (2) those effects from the observation of which there is an awareness of them having been made, even though the particular effect being observed may not itself have been observed to be made. My discussion considers (2). At RNĀ (ĪSD 57.29–57.31) Vācaspatimiśra points out the obvious problem with (1).

115. RNĀ (ĪSD 50.27–51.02, 52.14–52.18).

116. RNĀ (ĪSD 51.31–52.02, 52.03–52.04).

> (a) I don't accept that there are two classes of effects—one which includes all effects and another which includes things like pots, cloth, and large buildings, but excludes things like mountains. Instead, an effect belongs to multiple classes. Even if cloth is in the same class as things like large buildings, because of properties such as "being a thing," "having a particular shape," and "being an effect," it is still not the case that everyday perception can find out whether those properties are caused by an intelligent agent. This is because properties such as "being an effect" do not track with the negative concomitance of an intelligent agent. So how could there be the inference of an intelligent agent from seeing that things like large buildings and mountains are effects?[117]

Ratnakīrti continues by showing why it is legitimate to infer that things like pots are made by an intelligent agent, but illegitimate to infer that things like mountains are made by an intelligent agent. He explains that

> (b) In fact, it is said that for the collection of effects for which negative concomitance is established—namely, those belonging to the class "pots"—pervasion with an intelligent agent is proven on the basis of perception. Therefore, at a different place and time, there is of course the inference of an intelligent agent from things that belong to the class "pots." And when something that belongs to the class of large buildings is also ascertained, separately, in one locus, as being caused by an intelligent agent, then an intelligent agent is also established on the basis of things that belong to that class. It is in this way that the inference of an intelligent agent is not defective: collections of effects such as trays, buckets, carts, cloth, and bracelets—which belong to their respective classes—are ascertained, separately, as being made by an intelligent agent.
>
> (c) So, in this way, even though things such as pots, cloth, and mountains belong to the same class on the basis of properties such as "being an effect" or "being a thing," it is after recognizing a secondary

117. RNĀ (ĪSD 52.28–52.33): (a) *na hi kāryatvaṃ dvividham abhimatam | ekaṃ sarvakāryānuyogam aparaṃ parvatādivyāvṛttaṃ ghaṭapaṭaprāsādādyanuyāyīti | kintu kāryam anekajātīyakam | tatra yadi nāma paṭasya prāsādādibhiḥ saha vastutvasaṃsthānaviśeṣayogitvakāryatvādibhir dharmaiḥ sajātīyatvam asti tathāpi na tān dharmān buddhimatpūrvakān adhigacchati vyāvahārikaṃ pratyakṣam, kāryatvādīnāṃ buddhimadvyatirekānuvidhānābhāvāt | tat kathaṃ prāsādaparvatādiṣu kāryatvādidarśanād buddhimadanumānas tu.*

distinction between the classes "pot," "cloth," and "mountains" that pervasion-grasping perception functions for an ordinary person.[118]

In these passages Ratnakīrti explains that there are numerous properties on the basis of which classes of effects can be defined and individuated (passage *a*/passage *c*). This simple observation is important because, as Ratnakīrti explains, pervasion with an intelligent agent can be established for observed members of a subclass of effects on the basis of some properties but not on the basis of others (passage *b*/passage *c*). Moreover, as Ratnakīrti points out, a pervasion relation that is established for a sample class of effects on the basis of some property "*R*" (e.g., pots that have been seen to have been made by an intelligent maker) can be extended to effects beyond the original sample class only when those effects (e.g., pots that have not been seen to have been made by an intelligent maker) are also known to be defined by "*R*" (i.e., the property "being an pot").[119] The pervasion relation can be extended to include classes of effects not defined by "*R*" (e.g., carts, cloth, or bracelets) only if pervasion with an intelligent maker has been separately established for each one of them (passage *b*). Ratnakīrti explained earlier that this is because in order for there to be pervasion it must be known that the presence of the target property is *due to* the presence of the reason property and that the absence of the reason property is *due to* the absence of the target property. Moreover, as Ratnakīrti argues, "*R*" cannot be a property such as "being a thing," "being of a specific shape," or "being an effect," since pervasion has not been, and cannot be, determined by observation and nonobservation for a sample class of effects on the basis of those properties (passage *a*/ passage *c*). The Naiyāyikas' response is a "trick," according to

118. RNĀ (ĪSD 52.33–53.09): (b) *kiṇtu yasya ghaṭajātīyakāryacakrasya vyatirekasiddhis tasya buddhimadvyāptatvaṃ pratyakṣataḥ sidhyatīty uktam* | *tena deśakālāntare ghaṭajātīyād eva buddhimadanumānam* | *yadā tu prāsādajātīyakam api buddhimaddhetukam ekatra pṛthag avadhāryate tadā tajjātiyād api buddhimatsiddhiḥ* | *evaṃ tattajjātīyasarāvodañcanaśakaṭapaṭakeyūraprabhṛteḥ kāryacakrād buddhimatpūrvakatvena pṛthak pṛthag avadhāritād buddhimadanumānam anavadyam* | *{amum evārtham abhisandhāyācāryapādair abhihitam, siddhaṃ yādṛg adhiṣṭhātṛbhāvābhāvānuvṛttimat* | *sanniveśādi tad yuktaṃ tasmād yad anumīyate}* (c) *ity evaṃ ghaṭapaṭaparvatādīnāṃ kāryatvavastutvādibhir dharmaiḥ sajātīyatve 'pi avāntaraṃ ghaṭapaṭaparvatatvādijātibhedam ādāya lokasya vyāptigrāhakaṃ pratyakṣaṃ pravartata iti {darśayituṃ saṃvyavahārapragalbhapuruṣabuddhyapekṣayā yaddarśanād akriyādarśino 'pi kṛtabuddhir bhavatīty uktam}.*

119. Dharmakīrti seems to make a similar point at PVSV (3.09–3.19). My use of the phrase "on the basis of '*R*'" parallels Ratnakīrti's use of "due to/dependent upon" (*prayukta*).

Ratnakīrti, since they improperly extend the scope of the reason property to include effects that are defined by properties on the basis of which pervasion has not been and in some cases cannot be established (passage *a*). They violate what may be called "the extension principle."

The Naiyāyikas respond to this by pointing out that in every inferential argument the inference-warranting relation is extended beyond the sample class of objects (or property-possessors) for which it was originally established.[120] After all, they argue, there is always some dissimilarity between the sample class for which pervasion is established and the subject class to which the relation is extended. In Ratnakīrti's example of inferring that pots have an intelligent maker, the sample class of effects could be defined by the property "being an effect for which an intelligent maker has been observed" and the subject class by the property "being an effect for which an intelligent maker has not been observed." Thus, an inference-warranting relation that is established on the basis of a property "*R*" is extended to a non "*R*"-possessor. From this the Naiyāyikas conclude that, if correct, Ratnakīrti's argument would undermine all inferential reasoning. As they see it, Ratnakīrti's interpretation of the extension principle is just too rigid.

3.2.2. Preserving Intuitions

As both Ratnakīrti and the Naiyāyikas recognize, there are many cases in which an intelligent maker can be inferred from an effect.[121] The paradigmatic example is the inference of a potter from a pot. In addition, they also recognize that in every inferential argument an inference-warranting relation is extended beyond the sample class for which it was established. This feature of inferential reasoning is partially reflected in C2.1, which states that

---

120. RNĀ (ĪSD 52.18–52.21).

121. It is interesting to note that there has been a great deal of recent interest in such inferences. Philosophers of social science, for example, have become interested in how it can be known that an artifact has been made by a person. An early discussion of this is, of course, Paley 1890/1805 and his classic discussion of why intelligent design can be inferred when we discover a watch while walking across the heath, but not when we discover a stone. It should be clear that if the ground rules for such inferences could be understood, it would shed light on the argument for design and the Naiyāyikas' argument. Part of what is at stake in Ratnakīrti's argument are these ground rules. See Sober 1997 and Sober 2000 for a discussion of such ground rules and their relevance to the design argument. For more on this see section 5.2.

a reason property must be known to be present in the site of the inference—a locus that is not included in the sample class of either similar or dissimilar cases. In each and every inferential argument, therefore, the "scope" of the reason property and inference-warranting relation extends beyond the sample classes to at least the site of the inference.

What is specifically at issue in Ratnakīrti's argument are the conditions under which the scope of the reason property and pervasion relation can be extended from the sample class, on the basis of which pervasion is established, to unsampled members of the sample class, and finally to the site of the inference. What Ratnakīrti wants to show is that the conditions that the Naiyāyikas rely on are not consistent with our shared intuitions about the inference of intelligent makers. In response the Naiyāyikas argue that Ratnakīrti's point about the necessity of a restricting property "*R*" is not consistent with what we know about inferential reasoning more generally. In answering this charge, Ratnakīrti tries to show how on the basis of a property "*R*," the instrument conditions for an "*R*"-restricted version of the reason property can be satisfied for well-known inferences, but not for the Naiyāyikas' Īśvara-inference. In arguing this point, Ratnakīrti maintains that his version of the extension principle preserves our intuitions about maker-inferences and inferential reasoning more generally, and also explains why the Naiyāyikas' criticism of his earlier argument is not consistent with them. Interestingly, he does so by accusing the Naiyāyikas of allowing their intuitions to become "enslaved by philosophy" (*śāstra-paravaśa*).

In order to illustrate all of this, Ratnakīrti provides an example that brings his discussion back to the original property "*R*" suggested by the opponent—i.e., the property "from the observation of which there could be an awareness of its having been made, even for someone who did not observe its being made."[122] He writes,

> (d) In order to illustrate this, it is said that for a person gifted in common sense, there can be an awareness of something's having been made on the basis of seeing it, even though he did not see it being made. This is not the case, however, for a person whose awareness is enslaved by philosophy.
>
> (e) That is to say: A person who is gifted in common sense and free from the influence of philosophy determines that things that belong to

122. See chapter 2, section 3.2.2, and section 3.1 above.

> the class of temples are made by a person. He then enters a forest from the city. Upon seeing a temple, he has the awareness of its having been made, but does not have this awareness upon seeing a mountain—even though he saw neither of these things being made. Now, in virtue of being effects, both belong to a single class. But he is not able to establish either the absence or presence of the property "an awareness of having been made" without first relying on a secondary distinction in the class, defined by "being a mountain" and "being a temple." Once a difference in the class is established, pervasion is grasped for things that belong to the class of temples, but not for those that belong to the class of mountains. It is also not the case that pervasion is established for things that belong to the class of large buildings. So for those things there is not the inference of an intelligent maker. But once pervasion has been grasped, separately, for large buildings, then there can be the inference of an intelligent maker even for things that belong to that class. For things that belong to the class "being a mountain," pervasion cannot be grasped even in a dream.[123]

Consider, Ratnakīrti says, an ordinary person who has determined that there is pervasion between a sample class of temples in his city and the property "having an intelligent maker." Upon seeing, for the first time, a temple in a nearby forest, this person correctly infers that it has an intelligent maker. This is the case even though he did not see it being made, unlike the temples in his city. The reason the pervasion relation can be extended to include this object is because it is recognized as being a member of the class of objects on the basis of which pervasion was originally determined, that is, it is recognized as being a temple. The reason pervasion cannot be extended to include mountains (or even pots) is because they do not belong, in the relevant sense,

---

123. RNĀ (ĪSD 53.09–53.19): (d) *iti darśayitum saṃvyavahārapragalbhapuruṣabuddhyapekṣayā yaddarśanād akriyādarśino 'pi kṛtabuddhir bhavatīty uktam | na tu śāstraparavaśabuddhipuruṣāpekṣayā* | (e) *tathā hi, śāstra saṃskārarahitasya vyavahārapragalbhasya puruṣasya devakulajātīyakaṃ puruṣapūrvakatayāvadhāritavato nagarād vanaṃ praviṣṭasya parvatadevakulayor darśane tayor dvayor apy akriyādarśino 'pi devakule kṛtabuddhir bhavati na parvate | tad anayor devakulaparvatayoḥ kāryatvādinā ekajātitve kṛtabuddhibhāvābhāvau na tayoḥ parvatadevakulatvalakṣaṇāvāntarajātibhedam anavasthāpya sthātuṃ prabhavataḥ | jātibhede ca siddhe devakulajātīye vyāpter grahaṇān na parvatajātīyasya, na ca prāsādajātīyasya vyāptisiddhir iti na tato buddhimadanumānam | yadā tu prāsādasyāpi pṛthag vyāptigrahas tadā tajjātīyād api buddhimadanumānam astu | na kṣitidharādijātīyasya svapne 'pi vyāptigrahaḥ.*

to the same class as the originally sampled objects. As Ratnakīrti explains, objects that belong to "the same class" are only those objects that are known to share the property "*R*" on the basis of which pervasion was determined. This is the case even though there may be many other properties that they all share. In Ratnakīrti's example, the relevant property "*R*" is "being a temple" (or "being a large building"), but not "being a mountain" (or even "being a pot"). For a nonphilosopher, Ratnakīrti suggests, all of this is just good common sense.

As previously discussed, Ratnakīrti's implicit challenge to the Naiyāyikas was to discover a property "*R*" that redefined the scope of the reason property "being an effect" in such a way that on the basis of an "*R*"-restricted reason property, pervasion with an intelligent agent could be established on the basis of observation and nonobservation. The opponent's proposed property "*R*" was supposed to be just such a property. This property was supposed to restrict, and thereby redefine, the reason property in such a way that the three instrument conditions—C2.1, C2.2, and C2.3—could be satisfied. Ratnakīrti now returns to this original property "*R*" in order to show that, despite the Naiyāyikas' counterarguments, an "*R*"-restricted version of the reason property does account for our intuitions about the extension principle in accepted maker-inferences; support what we know about inferential reasoning more generally; and explain why the Naiyāyikas' response to the restricted scope argument is nothing but a trick (passage *e*).

In passage *e* Ratnakīrti asks us to consider the various subclasses of effects for which both Ratnakīrti and the Naiyāyikas agree that an intelligent maker has been observed for at least some members of each class—e.g., pots, cloth, bracelets, temples, large buildings, etc. For each of these subclasses of effects, pervasion with an intelligent maker can in principle be established on the basis of observation and nonobservation, as required by the Nyāya theory. Ratnakīrti suggests that these subclasses of effects are made up of members who have the property "*R*"—"being a member of a class of effects for which at least some members have been observed to have an intelligent maker."[124] It is not in virtue of their "being effects" that their pervasion by

124. Those subclasses of effects for which there may be disagreement—e.g., flint arrowheads, which only one party in the debate has ever seen being made—should be included in the site of the inference. Other objects, which both parties agree have been made but neither has seen being made—e.g., ballpoint pens or iPods—would, it seems, also have to be included in the site.

an intelligent maker is established, but rather in virtue of their being members of an "*R*"-restricted class of effects. This reveals that the proper form of the reason property in well-known inferences of an intelligent maker is not the unrestricted "being an effect," as the Naiyāyikas suppose. As Ratnakīrti has previously explained, if this were the case the reason property would be defeated by $H3a_1$ or $H3a_2$. Moreover, it is on the basis of being restricted by property "*R*" that pervasion is determined for the sample class of effects on the basis of which the Naiyāyikas establish pervasion. It is, therefore, only on the basis of "*R*" that the reason property can be extended to unobserved members of the sample class.

Thus it is the restricted form of the reason property that accounts for our shared intuitions regarding the inference of an intelligent maker from an effect. But, as the opponent originally pointed out, this restricted version of the reason property is not known to be present in the site of the Naiyāyikas' Īśvara-inference. After all, it is not the case that any members of the subclass "earth, mountains, or trees" were ever observed to have an intelligent maker. The reason property is, therefore, defeated by H1b and so cannot be a well-functioning instrument for the existence of Īśvara. Ratnakīrti's extension principle is thus supposed to explain our ability to infer an intelligent maker for effects such as pots and temples, but not for mountains or the earth.

It is important to note that Ratnakīrti does not need to show that there is no property "*R*" that could suitably restrict the reason property "being an effect" or that his property "*R*" best explains widely shared intuitions about maker-inferences. All that he needs to show is that without specifying some property "*R*," the Naiyāyikas cannot show that H3a does not defeat the pervasion subcomponent of their inference. In focusing attention on the need for some property "*R*," Ratnakīrti points to the extension principle that seems to support both the pervasion and site subcomponents in well-functioning instruments of inferential awareness. Without an extension principle based on some property "*R*," Ratnakīrti argues that the Naiyāyikas cannot establish pervasion, and so cannot show that $H3a_1$ and $H3a_2$ do not defeat or undermine the pervasion subcomponent in their Īśvara-inference. But without violating this extension principle, Ratnakīrti argues that they cannot show that H1b does not defeat the site subcomponent. Thus, as Ratnakīrti sees it, the Naiyāyikas cannot show that C2.1, C2.2, and C2.3 are all satisfied. As a result, they have failed to certify their argument for the existence of Īśvara by showing that H3a and H1b do not apply to "being an effect." At the very least, Ratnakīrti's argument shifts the burden of proof back to the Naiyāyikas.

3.3. *Conclusion: The* Section on the Reason Property

The property on the basis of which pervasion is determined is the only legitimate basis for extending the scope of the reason property and pervasion relation to include members of the class beyond those sampled—e.g., the site of the inference. As Ratnakīrti sees it, the Naiyāyikas' "trick" is to establish pervasion on the basis of one property and extend it on the basis of another. More specifically, in the Īśvara-inference pervasion is established for classes of effects for which at least some members have been observed to have an intelligent maker. In order to show that H1b does not apply, however, the Naiyāyikas must improperly extend the scope of the reason property to include classes of effects for which no members have been observed to have an intelligent maker—e.g., growing grass, trees, and other such "effects-in-general." While pervasion is established on the basis of a property "*R*," it is extended on the basis of a different property. Ratnakīrti's analysis suggests that this points to a more general problem with the Nyāya theory. According to Ratnakīrti, the Nyāya theory allows for this because it doesn't require that the presence of the target property be "due to" the presence of the reason property and/or that the absence of the reason property be "due to" the absence of the target property. Without a strict "due to" relation, the Nyāya extension principle is just too weak.

4. The *Section on the Target Property*

The presence of the defect called "opposed" (*viruddha*, H2) blocks the pervasion subcomponent of the instrument, inferential reasoning, by establishing that a reason property is known not to occur together with the target property in a single similar case.[125] This defect is usually defined in terms of a reason property that is known to be pervaded by a property that is "opposed to" the target property. In order to show that this defect does not apply to a particular reason property, it is sufficient to show that it is present in at least one similar case.

In their attempt to show that H2 does not apply to the reason property "being an effect," the Naiyāyikas considered three issues, each of which had

125. See chapter 2, sections 2.3.1 and 3.1.

to do with the target property.[126] The first concerned the proper description of the target property and the related issue of whether, once it had been properly described, its pervasion of the reason property could be established. A second issue had to do with whether the example cited in the inference (a pot) is really a similar case—i.e., a locus other than the site of the inference in which the target property is known to be present. The third issue had to do with how special, identifying characteristics of the target property could be established when pervasion is supposed to be established between a "generic form" of both the target property and the reason property. In chapter 2 this issue was discussed in terms of the scope of the reason property and the site subcomponent of the instrument.

In this section of his essay, Ratnakīrti assumes for the sake of argument that there is pervasion between "effects-in-general" (the generic form of the reason property) and "an intelligent agent-in-general" (the generic form of the target property), and instead directs his attention to the third issue described above. More specifically, he argues that the Naiyāyikas cannot show that the intelligent agent that is the target of their inference has the special characteristics that identify him as Īśvara. The significance of this is that without a satisfactory account of how special characteristics of this target property can be established, Ratnakīrti argues that the Naiyāyikas will not be able to satisfy certification condition C2.2, the certification condition defined by H2. This is because whether or not a locus counts as a similar case depends upon exactly how, in the final analysis, the target property is defined: if the target property is very specific—for example, a unique, eternal, and omniscient maker—things like pots would not count as similar cases, and as a result the Naiyāyikas would not be able to satisfy C2.2 by pointing to them.[127] If the target property is very general—for example, an intelligent agent-in-general—then (even if pervasion can be established) it appears as if the Naiyāyikas will not be able to show on the basis of satisfying C2.1 that the agent in question is Īśvara. In fact, their inference may actually prove that he is not. What follows is a brief discussion of Ratnakīrti's analysis of the Naiyāyikas' approach to the issue of special characteristics, and his specific arguments against its application to the Īśvara-inference.

---

126. See chapter 2, section 3.1.1.

127. That a precise understanding of the target property is necessary for distinguishing between the site, similarity class, and dissimilar cases is explicitly mentioned in the discussion at RNĀ (ĪSD 54.04–54.12).

4.1. Special Characteristics

If the inference-warranting relation between the reason property "an effect-in-general" and the target property "an intelligent agent-in-general" is assumed to have epistemic necessity and the reason property is known to be located in the site of the inference, the problem for the Naiyāyikas becomes how to prove that this intelligent agent, who is now known to be the maker of our world/the earth, has the special characteristics that uniquely identify him to be Īśvara.[128] These special characteristics include being unique, omnipresent, omniscient, and eternal.[129] In defending their argument, the Naiyāyikas argued that since the generic form of the target property—an intelligent agent-in-general—is known to be a property of the site of the inference, it is known that the intelligent agent-in-question is the one who made the earth. This entails, the Naiyāyikas argue, that this agent be unique and omniscient, and therefore that he must be Īśvara. Ratnakīrti rehearses the Nyāya argument before responding to it. He says,

> [The Naiyāyikas argue as follows:] Although pervasion by a general-term is well known, a special characteristic is proven through the force of being a property of the site of the inference—just as fire is proven [to be present on a mountain] through the exclusion of a nonconnection with the mountain.
>
> In response to this I say: A special characteristic is indeed proven through the force of being a property of the site of the inference, but not all [special characteristics are so proven]. This is because the characteristic that can be proven is that without which the reason property's location in the site of the inference could not occur—just as in the case of fire, the special characteristic is "being present on the mountain" and not "as beautiful as a five-colored crest jewel." Moreover, it is not the case that without a single, omnipotent, or omniscient maker, the mountains and trees will not be observed as being effects.[130]

---

128. In discussing this issue, Ratnakīrti turns his attention to what I referred to earlier as the "second step" of the Naiyāyikas' "hybrid argument." See the notes to chapter 2, section 2.1.

129. RNĀ (ĪSD 54.13–54.14).

130. RNĀ (ĪSD 54.17–54.27): *nanu sāmānyena vyāptau pratītāyām api pakṣadharmatābalād viśeṣasiddhiḥ | yathāgneḥ | parvatāyogavyavacchedādisiddhiḥ | {anyathā sarvānumānocchedaḥ |*

Although Ratnakīrti agrees with the Naiyāyikas that special characteristics can be proven through the force of the target property being a property of the site of the inference, he argues that there is actually only one characteristic that can be proven in this way—the characteristic that accounts for the target property being a property of the site. In the case of fire-in-general, the special characteristic that is proven is the property "being excluded from nonconnection with the mountain"—which Ratnakīrti somewhat imprecisely paraphrases as "being present on the mountain." Other special characteristics of this target property—such as having a particular color or being caused by grass or leaves, etc.—cannot be proven in this way.[131] Ratnakīrti argues that this position preserves well-known inferences and also points to a problem in the Naiyāyikas' argument for the existence of Īśvara. According to Ratnakīrti, all that the Naiyāyikas are entitled to prove on the basis of knowing that the target property, an intelligent agent, is a property of the site of the inference is that this agent is "excluded from nonconnection with the earth, mountains, and trees." As a result, according to him, the Naiyāyikas can only infer that the earth was made by an intelligent agent who is excluded from nonconnection with the earth, mountains, and trees. As Ratnakīrti sees it, this does not entail that this maker has the special characteristics that identify him to be Īśvara. In order to make this argument, Ratnakīrti argues that the Naiyāyikas cannot just rely on knowing that the target property is present in the site of the inference.

In response to this, the Naiyāyikas argue that if Ratnakīrti grants that there is pervasion between the generic form of the target property and the reason property, and also accepts that the special characteristic "the exclusion of nonconnection with the site of the inference" can be proven, then the following pair of inferences can prove that the intelligent maker of the earth, mountains, and trees has to be Īśvara. All that these inferences additionally require is that "intel-

---

anumānadveṣī hy evaṃ jalpati, anumānabhaṅgapaṅke 'smin nimagnā vādidantinaḥ | viśeṣe 'nugamābhāvaḥ sāmānye siddhasādhyatā || } atrocyate | sidhyaty eva pakṣadharmatābalato viśeṣaḥ | na tu sarvaḥ | yena hi vinā pakṣasthaṃ sādhanaṃ nopapadyate sa viśeṣaḥ sidhyatu | yathā vahner eva parvatavartitvādiviśeṣo na pañcavarṇaśikhākalāpakamanīyaḥ | na ca girīṇāṃ tarūṇāṃ kāryatvaṃ kartur ekatvavibhutvasarvajñatvādikam antareṇa nopapadyate, tad itareṣv api darśanāt | {tasmāt, pakṣāyogavyavacchedabhedamātre na dūṣaṇam | iṣṭasiddhyanvayābhāvād atirikte tu dūṣaṇam}. For a discussion of related issues see NKaṇ 149.18–150.15 and 153.29ff. Also see MTBh 45.05–45.12.

131. The example of fire that is fueled by grass and fire that is fueled by wood is discussed at MTBh 45.05–45.12.

ligent agent" refer to a maker who knows at least the material causes of the effect that is created. According to Ratnakīrti, the Naiyāyikas propose the following:

> [*Inference 1:*] "The subjects being discussed—bodies, mountains, and oceans, etc.—are made by an agent who knows their material causes and the like, on account of them being effects. Each and every effect—such as a large building—is made by an agent who knows its material cause and the like. The subjects being discussed—bodies, etc.—are like this. Therefore, they are so."

Ratnakīrti now explains that,

> Having thus proven, on the basis of this reason property, that there is a generic agent who knows material causes and the like, Vācaspati himself, in order to prove that this agent is omniscient, says: "Fine, first we prove that there is a generic agent who knows material causes, etc. And then, on the basis of a process of elimination (*pāriśeṣya*) inference, which is another name for an inference based on negative concomitance, we prove its special characteristics. That is to say,
>
> [*Inference 2:*] "A maker who knows the material causes of a body, the earth, and the like, is neither noneternal nor someone who does not know each and every object. This is because there would be the unwanted consequence that a maker of a body, etc., would not know its material causes, etc. For it is not the case that someone who knows the material causes of a body, etc., is like us. But, this maker does know the material causes of a body, etc. Therefore, he is like that."[132]

In inference 1 it is assumed that in the original Īśvara-inference the generic form of the target property is an agent who knows (at least) the material causes

---

132. RNĀ (ĪSD 55.04–55.14): *vivādādhyāsitās tanugirisāgarādaya upādānādyabhijñakartṛkāḥ | kāryatvāt | yad yat kāryaṃ tat tad upādānādyabhijñakartṛkam | yathā prāsādādi | tathā ca vivādādhyāsitās tanvādayaḥ | tasmāt tatheti | {evam ataḥ sādhanād upādānādyabhijñakartṛmātraṃ prasādhya tasya sarvajñasādhanāya vācaspatir eva punar idam āha} bhavatu tāvad upādānādyabhijñakartṛmātrasiddhiḥ | pāriśeṣyāt tu vyatirekidvitīyanāmno 'numānād viśeṣasiddhiḥ | tathā hi, tanubhuvanādyupādānādyabhijñaḥ kartā nānityāsarvaviṣayabuddhimān | tatkartus tadupādānādyabhijñatvaprasaṅgāt | na hy evaṃvidhas tadupādānādyabhijño yathāsmadādiḥ | tadupādānādyabhijñaś cāyam | tasmāt tatheti.*

of the effect being considered—namely, the earth. More specifically, what is assumed is that knowing material causes is necessary for being a maker of any effect. Given this assumption, and pervasion between the generic form of the target property and the reason property, the Naiyāyikas reason that the intelligent agent who made bodies, mountains, oceans, and the earth must be a maker who knew their material causes. Given this, they argue in inference 2 that unlike us this maker must be eternal and omniscient: he must be eternal, since for the Naiyāyikas the atoms out of which the earth is made are themselves eternal, and he must be omniscient, since only an omniscient being could have knowledge of all of the eternal atoms that were used to make it. With this pair of inferences, the Naiyāyikas show how they can argue from the special property that (even Ratnakīrti agrees) is directly proven through an inferential argument to those that are "entailed" by it. And, more specifically, they show how they can argue that the intelligent agent who made the earth has to be Īśvara.

Ratnakīrti chooses to respond to this pair of inferences by arguing that the Naiyāyikas have suppressed an important issue in their response—the issue of precisely how the target property in these inferences is to be interpreted. More specifically, Ratnakīrti argues that there are three likely interpretations: either there is supposed to be a single intelligent maker who knows the material causes of all of the numerous atoms from which, according to Nyāya ontology, the earth is created; or there is more than one maker who knows these material causes; or there are numerous makers, who in virtue of being spatially, temporally, and essentially remote from each other only know the material causes of their own respective objects.[133] Ratnakīrti dismisses each of these alternatives. He argues, for example, that the Naiyāyikas have not proved that there is a single maker.[134] In the inference of fire from smoke, for example, what is proved is that there is fire on the mountain, and not that there is only a single, unique fire on the mountain. Similarly, in the proposed Īśvara-inference, all that can be proven is that there is a maker of bodies and the earth, etc., and not that there is only one unique maker. As a result, Ratnakīrti argues that the Naiyāyikas need to provide a further argument to establish uniqueness. Ratnakīrti dismisses the second alternative by arguing that it is entirely possible that a number of different agents could

133. RNĀ (ĪSD 55.17–55.21).
134. RNĀ (ĪSD 55.21–55.29).

work together to produce a single effect.[135] Without further argument he reasons that there is no need to suppose that this is not the case. As a result, given this alternative, the Naiyāyikas cannot establish uniqueness either. Ratnakīrti dismisses the third alternative by arguing that if the Naiyāyikas were to agree that there were many agents who created the earth, etc., then there would not be any one agent who was omniscient.[136] Thus the third alternative cannot be accepted either.

According to Ratnakīrti, then, the proposed pair of inferences does not prove that Īśvara—an intelligent agent who is unique, omniscient, etc.—is the maker of things like bodies and the earth. As his arguments suggest, these inferences do not show that the inference of an agent-in-general, even one who knows the material causes of things like bodies and the earth, entails that this agent has the characteristics that identify him to be Īśvara.

4.2. The Site Component and H2

What is significant about Ratnakīrti's relatively brief remarks here is that they show that, according to him, the opponent's original worries about whether the Naiyāyikas can show that H2 does not apply to the reason property in their argument for Īśvara are well founded. While defending their argument, the Naiyāyikas tried to show that H2 did not apply to the reason property "being an effect" by showing that it is known to be present in a similar case, that is, in a locus in which the *generic form* of the target property is known to be present. The locus they cited was a pot. They then argued that in virtue of also knowing that the generic form of the target property is present in the site of the inference, special characteristics of the target property could be proven. As a result, they claimed to have shown that it is the case neither that the reason property is not present in a similar case—that is, that H2 applies to it—nor that the intelligent agent cannot be shown on the basis of this reason property to be Īśvara. Following the opponent, however, Ratnakīrti argues that even though the Naiyāyikas may have shown that the generic form of the target property may define a similar case, they have not shown how the special characteristics that identify this maker to be Īśvara—such as being unique or omniscient—can be established in virtue of it being

135. RNĀ (ĪSD 56.06–56.07).

136. RNĀ (ĪSD 56.14–56.29).

a property of the site of the inference. In other words, showing that the site subcomponent is not defective does not mean that the reason property has within its scope characteristics of the target property that identify the intelligent agent to be Īśvara. As a result, while it may be known that the earth was made by an intelligent agent, the Naiyāyikas have not shown that this maker is Īśvara.

Interestingly, Ratnakīrti does not directly relate these arguments to H2 or insist that the Naiyāyikas have not satisfied C2.2. Instead he argues that if all the Naiyāyikas can show is that the world has an intelligent maker, their argument will be rhetorically defective, since it will prove what is already accepted (*siddha-sādhana*) by those they are trying to convince.[137] If, on the other hand, the Naiyāyikas insist that the target property is an intelligent maker who is characterized by special characteristics such as omniscience, Ratnakīrti argues that their reason property will be inconclusive, since pervasion with such a maker has not been (and cannot be) established (issue 1).[138]

Although it is not made explicit in Ratnakīrti's analysis, it is clear that these arguments also relate to his earlier discussion of H2. If, for example, the Naiyāyikas are not able to show that the maker of the earth is specifically Īśvara, their strategy for showing that H2 does not apply to the reason property "being an effect" will not succeed. Their strategy depended on showing first that H2 did not apply to the reason property when similar cases were defined in terms of the generic form of the target property—i.e., an intelligent agent-in-general (issue 2). In support of this, they referred to the similar case of a pot, which everyone agrees is an effect made by an intelligent agent. This point was then supported by an argument that purported to show that special characteristics of this agent could also be proven (issue 3). It is through this two-part strategy that the Naiyāyikas tried to show that H2 does not apply to the reason property "being an effect." Without the second part, however, the overall strategy would be ineffective. As the opponent pointed out, in order to prove that Īśvara is the maker of the earth on the basis of the first part alone, a similar case would have to be defined in terms of a more specific form of the target property—e.g., a unique or omniscient agent. If the target property is not defined in this way then, as Ratnakīrti has

137. RNĀ (ĪSD 54.13–54.14, 56.28–56.29).

138. RNĀ (ĪSD 54.13–54.14, 56.28–56.29). See section 3 for a list of the three "issues."

argued, the Naiyāyikas will not be able to show that the intelligent maker-in-general has the special characteristics that identify him as Īśvara. Moreover, this will be the case even if pervasion is assumed. This argument is related to the site subcomponent of the inference-instrument, since, given pervasion, the issue is whether the scope of a reason property that is known to be present in the site of the inference includes those special characteristics. If the target property is defined in this way, however, then the Naiyāyikas will not have shown that the reason property is present in a similar case—that is, they will not have shown that H2 does not apply to the reason property "being an effect"—after all, a pot is not made by an omniscient agent and so cannot be considered a similar case.

4.3. *Conclusion: The* Section on the Target Property

According to Ratnakīrti, the Naiyāyikas' strategy for showing that H2 does not apply to the reason property "being an effect" points to two specific problems with the pervasion subcomponent of the Īśvara-inference, and to a more pervasive problem with the Nyāya theory of inferential reasoning. Both the specific and the general problems are interpreted by Ratnakīrti as having to do with precisely how the target property is supposed to be interpreted.

The two specific problems focus on how the pervasion subcomponent of the instrument is understood. The first problem is that since the Naiyāyikas insist that what is to be proven is not a generic form of the target property but a more specific form of it, they must show that there is pervasion between this more specific form of the target property and the reason property. Since this cannot be established for the terms in the Īśvara-inference, the pervasion subcomponent will be defeated by H3a. The second problem is that, given this, they cannot show that the reason property is present in a single similar case, and as a result they cannot show that H2 does not apply to their reason property. According to Ratnakīrti, then, the Naiyāyikas have not satisfied either C2.2 or C2.3, and so have not certified the Īśvara-inference.

A more pervasive problem, according to Ratnakīrti, has to do with their understanding of the site subcomponent of an inference and its significance. More specifically, according to Ratnakīrti, the Naiyāyikas' account of the special characteristics of the target property that can be proven in virtue of it being located in the site of the inference is not satisfactory. Even if pervasion is assumed, knowing that the reason property is present in the site of the inference—that is, knowing that the site subcomponent is well-functioning—cannot provide a basis for knowing special, unique characteristics of the target property. This is because the only special characteristic that is within the scope of the reason property is the characteristic of "exclusion of non-connection with the site of the inference." The kind of work that the Naiyāyikas require the site subcomponent to do far exceeds the kind of work that it can actually do. Thus the Nyāya understanding of the site subcomponent points to a problem in the Nyāya theory of inferential reasoning that is sure to affect other inferential arguments in much the same way as it affects the Īśvara-inference.

5. Conclusion: Is Īśvara the Maker of the World?

Ratnakīrti's reorganization of the Naiyāyikas' defense of the Īśvara-inference into subsections corresponding to pervasion (section 1 and section 2), the reason property (section 3), and the target property (section 4) is designed to look through the specific details of the Īśvara-inference to more fundamental problems in the Naiyāyikas' approach to the satisfaction of pervasion conditions C2.2, C2.3, and U, and the certification of inference-instruments more generally. While Ratnakīrti explicitly argues that the Naiyāyikas have not and cannot certify the Īśvara-inference, he sees their debate as extending to the epistemology of certification itself, and the Naiyāyikas' more general understanding of the metaphysics and epistemology of both the pervasion and site subcomponents of well-functioning inference-instruments. In criticizing the Īśvara-inference, Ratnakīrti thus points to the very basic philosophical intuitions and commitments that he thinks lead the Naiyāyikas astray.

Even within the relatively focused framework of Ratnakīrti's "Refutation of Arguments for Establishing Īśvara" it is clear that in order to determine whether Īśvara is the maker of the world a variety of philosophical problems need to be resolved. In concluding this chapter, and part 1 of this book, I want to briefly consider some of these problems, as a way of pointing to what Ratnakīrti and his Naiyāyikas tell us is at stake, both explicitly and implicitly, in their debate. I will do so by identifying two sets of philosophical problems on which the debate turns and explaining why (as Ratnakīrti and his Naiyāyikas recognize) these problems need to be resolved before the Naiyāyikas' inference, and the success of Ratnakīrti's critique, can be fully evaluated. Through this discussion I also hope to point to some of the competing philosophical commitments and intuitions that motivate the debate.

In this chapter thus far I have presented Ratnakīrti's critique in something like his own philosophical idiom and vocabulary. As in my conclusion to chapter 2, however, it may be helpful to reconsider my analysis in a somewhat different philosophical context. More specifically, I will reconsider Ratnakīrti's discussion of the pervasion subcomponent by drawing upon the conceptual vocabulary of debates between "regularity theorists" and "N-relation theorists" regarding the nature of scientific laws.[139] I will reconsider Ratnakīrti's discussion of the site subcomponent and extension principle by comparing it to what has been recently referred to as a "Galilean strategy."[140] These two contexts provide very different ways of framing the two central lines of argument that Ratnakīrti pursues in his critique: his arguments about the epistemology and metaphysics of pervasion, and those having to do with "remoteness," the ground rules for extending pervasion, and what we can learn about the target property on the basis of such an extension to the site. Both these lines of argument support and build upon my earlier discussion of the Naiyāyikas' "hybrid" argument. As before, this overall strategy seeks to make explicit, in a more familiar philosophical vocabulary and context, some of the philosophical issues on whose resolution the success of the Īśvara-inference and Ratnakīrti's critique depends. Before turning to these two new contexts, however, it may be helpful to briefly review the components of the Naiyāyikas' hybrid cosmological/design argument that I first discussed in chapter 2.

Recall that the Naiyāyikas' hybrid argument consists of three steps: (1) a statement of an existential fact; (2) a causal principle, which states a rule that in some relevant way is supposed to account for the existential fact in step 1;

---

139. The best-known contemporary version of "regularity theory" is probably the Ramsey 1978/Lewis 1973 account, according to which "laws are those universal generalizations that would be part of the overall systematization of our theories about the world that best combines simplicity and strength"; see Swoyer 2000. A classic statement of "N-relation theory" is Armstrong 1983:85, "Suppose it to be a law that *F*s are *G*s. *F*-ness and *G*-ness are taken to be universals. A certain relation, a relation of non-logical or contingent necessitation, holds between *F*-ness and *G*-ness. This state of affairs is symbolized as 'N(*F*, *G*).'" For a useful introduction to debates about "laws" see Carroll 2008, Cartwright et al. 2005, and Swoyer 2000.

140. This term is taken from the title of Kitcher 2001b.

and (3) a design argument, which functions as an explanatory argument to the effect that the fact expressed in step 1 is to be finally accounted for by the intentional actions of Īśvara. From my discussion in both chapters 2 and 3, it should be clear that the Naiyāyikas' "causal principle" is discussed in the context of the pervasion subcomponent of the Īśvara-inference and their "design argument" is discussed (primarily) in the context of the site subcomponent. My discussion will thus focus on the philosophical issues that frame Ratnakīrti and his Naiyāyikas' debate on these two subcomponents, and begins, in each case, with a restatement/reinterpretation of the Nyāya position.

5.1. Pervasion Subcomponent

According to Ratnakīrti's Naiyāyikas, the pervasion subcomponents of all well-functioning inference-instruments supervene on "natural relations." While such relations include those that are "causal," they are much broader in scope and clearly include those that are not.[141] Strictly speaking, then, it is this type of relation that accounts for the "causal principle" (or, more accurately, "inference-warranting relation") that supports the Naiyāyikas' hybrid argument for the existence of Īśvara. On the basis of Ratnakīrti's discussion, it is possible to distinguish between three levels of analysis, argument, and debate about these relations: the first focuses on the existence conditions for natural relations, the second on the pervasion conditions that define inference-warranting relations, and the third on the epistemology of satisfaction/certification.[142]

The "existence conditions" for natural relations can be described through a "nonepistemic" interpretation of the three pervasion conditions, C2.2, C2.3, and U. According to such an interpretation, the relation between a reason property and a target property is natural if and only if the reason property is present in a similar case (C2.2*), is excluded from all dissimilar cases (C2.3*), and has no additional conditions (U*). The nonepistemic fact on which inference-warranting relations are supposed to supervene can thus be described by the conjunction of C2.2*, C2.3*, and U*. It is this set of facts that describes the world-given connections between properties and property-

141. See, for example, the discussion in Oetke 1991:253–256.

142. While the terms "natural relation" and "inference-warranting relations" will be used to refer to ontological/metaphysical and epistemological dimensions of the pervasion subcomponent respectively, the term "pervasion" will be used more generically, as above.

possessing loci that Ratnakīrti's Naiyāyikas take to underwrite the pervasion subcomponent of well-functioning inference-instruments. These natural connections are supposed to be *nonvacuous*, in the sense that they are instanced in at least one locus, and *invariable*, in the sense that if a reason property *R* and its target property *T* are naturally related, all *R*-possessing loci are *T*-possessing loci.[143] As Ratnakīrti presents it, for his Naiyāyikas natural relations are supposed to be invariable regularities for which no overt appeal to specifically modal concepts (e.g., counterfactual conditionals) or modality-supplying entities (e.g., universals) is required.

While natural relations are defined by their existence conditions, inference-warranting relations are defined by their pervasion conditions—i.e., C2.2, C2.3, and U. Interestingly, C2.2 and U are the direct epistemic counterparts of existence conditions C2.2* and U*, but C2.3 is not a direct epistemic counterpart of existence condition C2.3*. This is because C2.3 is constituted by two epistemic facts, only one of which has a nonepistemic counterpart in C2.3*. Recall that there are two subtypes of defect H3a, the defect that defines C2.3—$H3a_1$ (the reason property is known to be present in a dissimilar case) and $H3a_2$ (there is doubt about the exclusion of the reason property from all dissimilar cases). Since only the absence of $H3a_1$ has a nonepistemic counterpart, it alone defines C2.3*.[144] Let us refer to the epistemic fact that does not have a nonepistemic counterpart in C2.3* as $C2.3a_2$, and the epistemic fact that has a nonepistemic counterpart in C2.3* as $C2.3a_1$. Strictly speaking, then, what supervenes on natural relations are inference-warranting relations defined by C2.2, $C2.3a_1$, and U. $C2.3a_2$ is thus an "added" epistemic condition, in the sense that it does not have a nonepistemic counterpart that is a part of the supervenience base. What $C2.3a_2$ seems to provide is *epistemic stability* to inference-warranting relations, in the sense that its satisfaction expresses that we *know* that we do not have epistemically significant doubt about pervasion. Interestingly, while U is a distinct pervasion condition

143. U* simply states that when a reason property *R* and its target property *T* are naturally related, there is no hidden property *U* such that all *T*-possessing loci are *U*-possessing loci but not all *R*-possessing loci are *U*-possessing. As an *existence* condition (but not a *pervasion* condition), U* is entailed by C2.2* and C2.3*. See Phillips and Tatacharya 2002:14–22. It is important to keep in mind that my discussion applies specifically to pervasion relations for which both C2.2 and C2.3 are supposed to be satisfied.

144. This is based on the idea that the absence of the reason property from all dissimilar cases is a nonepistemic fact, while the absence of doubt about this is not.

from C2.3, it does not, in and of itself, add anything to our awareness of C2.2 and C2.3. Since both C2.3a_1 and C2.3a_2 are associated with deviation, let us refer to their conjunction as epistemic fact "V." On my interpretation, according to Ratnakīrti's Naiyāyikas, if all of these epistemic conditions are satisfied—i.e., C2.2, V, and U—it is reflectively known that the inference-warranting relation is epistemically necessary, and therefore that the pervasion subcomponent is well-functioning. A central issue in Ratnakīrti's discussion of pervasion has to do with the source and nature of this necessity—that is, the source and nature of the modal force of inference-warranting relations in well-functioning inference-instruments, which thus far has not been explicitly accounted for in my interpretation of the Nyāya theory.

As discussed in both chapters 2 and 3, C2.2 and C2.3a_1 are satisfied through the observation of a reason property in similar cases and nonobservation/nonapprehension of it in dissimilar cases. What we come to know by satisfying C2.2 and C2.3a_1 is that a proposed reason property and its target are invariably associated with one another, in the sense that in addition to there being at least one locus in which both the reason property and the target property are known to be present, there is no locus in which the reason property is known to be present but the target property is known to be absent. Like its nonepistemic counterpart, this does not account for the modal force of the relation, since all it tells us (according to the Naiyāyikas) is that we know that any locus in which a proposed reason property is present is a locus in which its target property is present: it does not tell us that its target property must be present there.

In my view, it is through the *satisfaction* of V and U, and not just the epistemic facts themselves, that Ratnakīrti's Naiyāyikas account for the modal force in inference-warranting relations, and thus account for their epistemic *necessity*. In what follows, I want to provide an interpretation of the Naiyāyikas' attempt at satisfying V and U in order to support my interpretation of epistemic necessity, and provide a basis for reconsidering the significance of some of the arguments and counterarguments discussed in this chapter.

The overall argument schema that Ratnakīrti's Naiyāyikas use to satisfy both V and U can be helpfully interpreted as a version of the "argument from ignorance" (*argumentum ad ignorantiam*).[145] Such arguments generally

---

145. "Arguments from ignorance" are also known as "lack-of-knowledge arguments," "negative evidence arguments," and arguments based on "default reasoning." For a careful discussion of such arguments see Walton 1996, in which he surveys previous literature on

begin with a premise such as "It is not known that 's' is true (or false)" and on the basis of it conclude that "'S' is known to be false (or true)." Although such arguments are often assumed to contain defects, it is widely recognized that this is not always the case.[146] Interestingly, the three defining characteristics of such arguments are present in what I want to call the Nyāya version of it.

One characteristic feature of arguments from ignorance is that they have a "lack-of-knowledge" premise in which it is stated that some fact "s" is not known to be true (or false). In the Naiyāyikas' argument, there are two such facts: the fact that the reason property is present in a dissimilar case, in the case of V, and the fact that there is an additional condition, in the case of U. In the Naiyāyikas' version of the argument, this premise is the statement, "It is not known that the reason property is present in a dissimilar case" and/or "It is not known that there is an additional condition." For Ratnakīrti's Naiyāyikas, this is equivalent to the statement, "There is the nonapprehension (or nonobservation) of the reason property in dissimilar cases" and/or "There is the nonapprehension (or nonobservation) of an additional condition." That this is a part of the Nyāya approach to the satisfaction of V and U is clear from Ratnakīrti's presentation of the Nyāya theory.[147]

A second characteristic of such arguments is that they make use of what is called a "search premise." A search premise states that "If S were true (or false) it would be known to be true (or false)." In the Naiyāyikas' version of the argument this premise is something like "If a reason property were present in a dissimilar case it would be known/observed to be present in a dissimilar case" and/or "If an additional condition were present, it would be known/observed to be present." This parallels, almost exactly, the supportive role that suppositional reasoning (*tarka*) is supposed to play in the Nyāya account of how negative epistemic facts, such as the exclusion of a reason property from all dissimilar cases and the absence of an additional condition, are deter-

---

the subject, offers an interpretation of such arguments, and provides numerous examples of "good" and "bad" versions of it. My interpretation generally follows the one given by Walton. Both Walton (1996:141–142) and Ganeri (2001:122) have noted the relevance of this argument to Sanskrit philosophy. See Oetke 1996 for a discussion of the relevance of default reasoning to Sanskrit epistemology, and the more recent discussion in Taber 2004. Also see section 1.2.2, passage *b*, and 2.1.1.

146. Walton 1996.

147. See section 1.2.3.

mined.[148] Although this use of suppositional reasoning is not explicitly discussed in Ratnakīrti's account of the Nyāya argument, it is clearly suggested by Vācaspatimiśra's remark that "even after searching with great effort" a reason property is not discovered in a dissimilar case.[149] Moreover, this use of suppositional reasoning is explicitly noted by Ratnakīrti in his "Inquiry into Inference-Warranting Relations" (*Vyāptinirṇaya*).[150] Furthermore, the search premise captures, almost exactly, the significance of the Naiyāyikas' appeal to V and U. In fact, it seems to be the failure of just such a search that establishes these epistemic facts.[151]

The third characteristic of such arguments is that their general pattern follows *modus tollens*. This pattern is also evident in the Naiyāyikas' argument. Given this vocabulary, the Naiyāyikas' argument for V can be reconstructed as follows: "If a reason property were present in a dissimilar case, it would be known to be present in a dissimilar case (*search premise*), but it is not known to be present in a dissimilar case (*lack-of-knowledge premise*); therefore it is known that it is not present in a dissimilar case (by *modus tollens*)." And for U as: "If there were an additional condition, it would be known (*search premise*), but it is not known that there is an additional condition (*lack-of-knowledge premise*); therefore it is known that there is no additional condition (by *modus tollens*)."

The above argument pattern suggests that it is through *satisfying* V, and especially U, that an epistemic agent "upgrades" her awareness of the invariable association between the reason and target properties as defined by C2.2 and C2.3a_1, by conferring law-like or nomic status upon it. This is evident especially from the "search premise" in the argument, which suggests that for Ratnakīrti's Naiyāyikas both natural relations and inference-warranting relations are supposed to support counterfactuals, which is often taken to be a mark of law-like statements. It may be helpful to think of the Naiyāyikas' theory of inference-warranting relations, therefore, as a type of "regularity theory + X," according to which inference-warranting relations express (i)

148. See, for example, the notes to section 1.2.3 and the references contained therein.

149. See passage *a* in 2.1, where RNĀ (ĪSD 42.08–42.17) is discussed, and RNĀ (VN 107.14–107.15) where this same idea is repeated. In focusing his attention on the "lack of knowledge premise" Ratnakīrti makes the Nyāya argument appear weaker than it is. As will become clear, it is the "search premise" that is crucial to the success of such arguments.

150. RNĀ (VN 107.26–108.02).

151. See sections 1.2 and 2.1.

the invariable association of a reason property with its target property (i.e., "regularity"), plus (ii) the absence of epistemically significant doubt, as defined by the absence of defect $H3a_2$, and (iii) the law-like necessity that comes from the satisfaction of U (i.e., "X"). While the absence of an additional condition suggests that the relation supports counterfactuals, satisfaction of $C2.3a_2$ (the absence of $H3a_2$) provides an epistemic upgrade by eliminating epistemically significant doubt.

According to Ratnakīrti's Naiyāyikas, natural relations thus display law-like regularity and thereby underwrite only genuinely inference-warranting relations. They also have the added epistemic benefit that is based on the satisfaction of $C2.3a_2$. Their modal force, however, is due to U, whose satisfaction (like the satisfaction of V) is fallible, as Ratnakīrti's Naiyāyikas admit. When through the pattern of observation and nonobservation described above the pervasion conditions for a particular inference-instrument have been satisfied, Ratnakīrti's Naiyāyikas take the inference-warranting relation to be epistemically necessary and therefore to be underwritten by a class of natural relations. They thus move from the epistemology of satisfaction, to the satisfaction of the pervasion conditions, and finally to the presence of natural relations.

Against this background Ratnakīrti's arguments can be seen as challenging the Naiyāyikas' account of the source and nature of epistemic necessity, by targeting their understanding of the existence conditions, pervasion conditions, and epistemology of satisfaction for the pervasion subcomponents of well-functioning inference-instruments. Ratnakīrti's criticisms are informed by his own view that there are only two modes of pervasion, a production-mode, which is underwritten by causal relations, and an identity-mode, which is underwritten by what I have called "token-identity" relations. As Ratnakīrti's arguments suggest, he clearly thinks that these relations are epistemically necessary. In chapters 4 and 5 we will see that he takes them to hold between "universals."

According to Ratnakīrti, the existence conditions for natural relations do not define a class of relations that are known to exist (section 1.2). At best they define a class of "in some way other than" relations that are merely stipulated as being natural, and therefore stipulated as being strong enough to support inferential reasoning. These "in some way other than" relations are such that a reason property, *R*, is supposed to be invariably co-located with its target property, *T*. In the absence of an argument to show that there is such a class of world-given connections as the Naiyāyikas suppose, Ratnakīrti argues that such relations are nothing more than convenient fictions, as is the notion that they underwrite the pervasion subcomponents of only well-functioning inference-instruments. According to Ratnakīrti, the Naiyāyikas have an "identification problem" in that they have failed to adequately specify what a natural relation is and show that there are any.[152] This is, moreover, a general problem with the Naiyāyikas' theory of pervasion, one that extends well beyond the Īśvara-inference. As Ratnakīrti sees it, one fundamental problem that must be resolved before the Īśvara-inference (and any other inference) can be certified is whether there is a class of "natural relations" at all.

Ratnakīrti further argues that even if such relations did exist, they would be too weak to support only genuinely inference-warranting relations. Ratnakīrti suggests that existence conditions C2.2* and C2.3* merely define a class of universal generalizations (all *R*-possessing loci are *T*-possessing loci), each of which is instanced in at least one locus. For Ratnakīrti's Naiyāyikas, U* (but not U) is redundant. Even if C2.2*, C2.3*, and U* define a genuine class of world-given connections between things, Ratnakīrti argues that these conditions have not been shown to define a class of relations that has any modal properties. In addition to C2.2*, Ratnakīrti suggests that the absence of counterexamples (C2.3*) and additional conditions (U*) does not in and of itself account for nomic-necessity, as the Naiyāyikas clearly suggest. Ratnakīrti's argument is that there is nothing in the existence conditions themselves that entails that there is something about an object's having *R* that in any way makes it have *T*. As Ratnakīrti sees it, a fundamental philosophical problem with the Naiyāyikas' account has to do with whether there really is a class of world-given connections that can underwrite pervasion as they understand it. In his view, the Naiyāyikas have clearly not met their burden of proof to show that such connections exist. Moreover, even if such relations do exist, on the basis of their existence conditions there does not seem to be any reason to suppose that they have any modal features. As a result, the Naiyāyikas will be faced with the additional philosophical problem of explaining how the modal properties that they take to belong to inference-warranting relations can supervene on nonmodal ones.

---

152. My use of the term "identification problem" is derived from van Frassen 1989:72–76, 96, and his famous critique of a necessitarian conception of laws.

Like the existence conditions, Ratnakīrti argues that the Naiyāyikas' account of the pervasion conditions that define inference-warranting relations do not provide an epistemic solution to the "modality problem" either. After all, all that C2.3a_2 adds is the epistemic fact that there isn't any doubt about C2.3*. While this may add some epistemic force (perhaps in the sense of providing stability) to the inference-warranting relation, it doesn't account for its supposed modal features. Similarly, independent of any reference to how it is satisfied, U does not show that inference-warranting relations, and therefore natural relations, have any nomic features either. According to Ratnakīrti, the Naiyāyikas thus have an "inference problem" in that they have failed to show that either natural relations or inference-warranting relations can do the work that they are supposed to do.[153] As Ratnakīrti sees it, according to the Nyāya view of inference-warranting relations, the epistemic fact that, without exception, all *R*-possessing loci have been observed to be *T*-possessing does not entitle them to conclude that all *R*-possessing loci, even those that have not yet been encountered, will also be *T*-possessing. Ratnakīrti's point seems to be that if observed *R*-possessing loci are to be relevant to unobserved *R*-possessing loci there needs to be something about a locus possessing *R* that requires that it will also possess *T*. Without accounting for this "something"—which could serve as the source of modality—neither natural relations nor inference-warranting ones can be supposed to be epistemically necessary. Given the Naiyāyikas' understanding of them, Ratnakīrti takes such relations to be fallible, and therefore too weak to support only genuinely inference-warranting relations. A basic philosophical problem on which the success of the Īśvara-inference depends, then, has to do with whether fallible relations can be genuinely inference-warranting.

---

153. My use of the term "inference problem" is also attributable to van Frassen 1989:96–101, where he presents it as the second horn of the dilemma that he sees facing necessitarians. Lewis (1983:366) colorfully comments on Armstrong as follows: "Whatever *N* may be, I cannot see how it could be absolutely impossible to have *N(F,G)* and *Fa* without *Ga*. (Unless *N* just is constant conjunction or constant conjunction plus something else, in which case Armstrong's theory turns into a form of the regularity theory he rejects). The mystery is somewhat hidden by Armstrong's terminology. He uses 'necessitates' as a name for the lawmaking universal *N*; and who would be surprised to hear that if *F* 'necessitates' *G* and *a* has *F*, then *a* must have *G*? But if I say that *N* deserves the name 'necessitation' only if, somehow, it really can enter into the requisite necessary connections. It can't enter into them just by bearing a name, any more than one can have mighty biceps just by being called 'Armstrong.'"

Finally, Ratnakīrti also recognizes that the "identification problem" and the "inference problem" are related to one another and generate a kind of "tradeoff problem" for his Naiyāyikas.[154] His recognition of this is evident from his arguments against the Naiyāyikas' approach to the epistemology of satisfaction and certification. One extended line of argument that Ratnakīrti pursues throughout his critique of the Īśvara-inference is that the epistemology of satisfaction cannot result in the satisfaction of either V or U, as the Naiyāyikas' theory requires. The fundamental problem, as Ratnakīrti sees it, is that because of the possibility of "remoteness," the nonobservation of properties in individual loci is inadequate for detecting their absence in those loci, and this is the case even if the numerous problems having to do with "essential" remoteness are taken off the table. For example, as Ratnakīrti points out, a locus of deviation or an additional condition could be either temporally or spatially remote, or the set of causal conditions necessary for their observation could be, in some other way, incomplete. Ratnakīrti's point is that, even if a locus of deviation or an additional condition were present, there could still be the nonobservation of it. As a result, Ratnakīrti would clearly reject the Naiyāyikas' strategy of appealing to an *argumentum ad ignorantiam*, which, as he sees it, clearly depends on nonobservation/nonapprehension being able to establish absence. For him, the Naiyāyikas cannot satisfy either V or U, and the epistemic conditions that can be satisfied are weaker still, since they always leave open the possibility of epistemically significant doubt.

According to Ratnakīrti, the Naiyāyikas thus face an insurmountable "tradeoff problem": to achieve epistemic security, the conditions that define pervasion must be so weak that the inference-warranting relations defined by them will be too weak to support the pervasion subcomponent of only genuinely inference-warranting relations. But if one suitably strengthens the pervasion conditions (and the corresponding existence conditions), the Naiyāyikas' epistemology is not up to the task. Moreover, as Ratnakīrti sees it, not only does the Naiyāyikas' epistemology fail to satisfy their own set of pervasion conditions, but even if these conditions could be satisfied by the Naiyāyikas' epistemology, the relation that they define would be too weak to support genuinely inference-warranting relations. Ratnakīrti's point is that the Naiyāyikas' approach to certification (see argument 2) does not get them

154. My use of the term "tradeoff problem" comes from Swoyer 2000.

to what they want (which Ratnakīrti has argued is, in any case, inadequate to support inferential reasoning), let alone what they need, namely, a set of existence conditions, pervasion conditions, and supporting epistemology that enables them to pick out only those relations in which the presence of *R* in a particular locus is due to the presence of *T* in that locus.

As I have argued, the inference-warranting relation of pervasion functions as the Naiyāyikas' "causal principle" in their hybrid cosmological/design argument. In chapter 2, in defending their causal principle, Ratnakīrti's Naiyāyikas focused on the epistemology of satisfaction and argued on the basis of it to the presence of inference-warranting relations, and then to the metaphysics of natural relations. In contrast, in his own presentation of the Naiyāyikas' argument, Ratnakīrti argues from the metaphysics of natural relations to the epistemology that would be needed to detect them, and thus points to what he takes to be "gaps" between the metaphysics of natural relations, the epistemology of inference-warranting relations, and the epistemology of satisfaction. As I have argued, his target is the Naiyāyikas' understanding of epistemic necessity. Driving the different approaches and argument strategies that Ratnakīrti and his Naiyāyikas pursue are very different philosophical intuitions about inference-warranting relations. As a way of uncovering these differing intuitions, it may be helpful to return to the satisfaction of V and U in the Īśvara-inference, in the context in which I have just reframed my earlier discussion.

As I have presented it, a central feature of the Naiyāyikas' argument is their assumed right to presume that V are U are satisfied on the basis of the search premise in their *argumentum*. Ratnakīrti's Naiyāyikas take themselves to have met their epistemic obligations to show that V and U are satisfied to the extent that they (and their opponents) have searched for and failed to find either a dissimilar case in which the reason property is present or an additional condition. Assuming the lack of knowledge premise, they therefore assume the epistemic right to presume that V and U are satisfied. According to Ratnakīrti's Naiyāyikas, it is this "failure to find" that satisfies V and U, and through which they meet their epistemic obligations and in so doing shift the burden of proof back to their opponent.

In a number of different contexts, however, Ratnakīrti argues that in order to properly defend the search premise, the Naiyāyikas must show, through their search, that the reason property "being an effect" is excluded from *all* dissimilar cases and that there is *no* additional condition. According to him, this is the only way to establish V and U, and thereby show that neither $H3a_1$ nor $H3a_2$ applies to the reason property. As Ratnakīrti sees it, $C2.3a_1$ is not the fact that there is *no known* dissimilar case in which the reason property is present, but the fact that it is *known that there is no* dissimilar case in which the reason property is present. Similarly, U it is not the fact that there is *no known* additional condition, but the fact that it is *known that there is no* additional condition. It is not a negative epistemic fact that shows that $H3a_1$ and/or U does not apply, but a positive one.[155] Ratnakīrti's worry is that the standard that the Naiyāyikas have set for the search premise through their understanding of V and U is so weak that nearly anything could be inferred from anything. This worry is based on his conviction that the Naiyāyikas have not successfully explained why they are entitled to presume that something is true of every member of a domain without having first inspected each and every member of that domain.[156] Given that the Naiyāyikas have not inspected each and every effect, there is, according to Ratnakīrti, the ineliminable possibility that there is a locus of deviation somewhere in the domain. As a result, there will always be epistemically significant doubt about whether a reason property is excluded from *all* dissimilar cases. As he sees it, $C2.3a_2$ cannot be the fact that a locus of doubt is not known, but the fact that it is known that there is no locus of doubt. According to Ratnakīrti, a search premise that is based on this "correct" account of $C2.3a_2$ (and V more generally) cannot be adequately defended, since given his Naiyāyikas' own view on how such searches are conducted, they cannot explain how they can search all dissimilar cases.

The Naiyāyikas respond to this by arguing that Ratnakīrti's demand that they search *all* dissimilar cases and thereby guarantee that there are *no* additional conditions is unreasonable. As they see it, all that anyone needs to (and can) show is that there are no known dissimilar cases, loci about which there is doubt, or additional conditions. On the basis of their theory of epistemically significant doubt, they argue that once they have fulfilled their epistemic obligations, unobserved cases, loci, and potential additional conditions should not be considered a part of the knowledge base or domain. Their reasoning is that since such cases represent only possible, and not actual, objects of awareness, they cannot be reasonably included in the search domain. To insist that they be included in the domain is, according to them, an unreason-

---

155. This is, of course, just what the Naiyāyikas are trying to argue (unsuccessfully, according to Ratnakīrti) through their *argumentum ad ignorantiam*.

156. This is the case, even assuming that the relevant loci and properties are observable.

able demand, since it could never be satisfied. The Naiyāyikas' point is that Ratnakīrti's criticism of their argument places demands on the search premise that are just too strict. In responding to Ratnakīrti, they argue that the knowledge base should be "strongly closed"—that is, that the findings to date should be allowed to represent all the relevant facts from which a conclusion may be drawn.[157] Many of their arguments are designed to show therefore that, given the depth of their own search and that of their opponents, their point of closure is reasonable.

One underlying philosophical issue that emerges from this exchange has to do with whether and how an entire class of objects, including unobserved and unknown objects, can be the object of awareness, and therefore "sampled" or "searched." If such a class of objects can be an object of awareness then Ratnakīrti's demand that the search be exhaustive may not be unreasonable. If such an object cannot be an object of awareness, then, as the Naiyāyikas argue, Ratnakīrti's demand seems unreasonable. In chapter 4 we will see why Ratnakīrti thinks that this is not the case. A second underlying issue has to do with whether genuinely inference-warranting relations and/or the certification of the inference-instrument can be fallible. As Ratnakīrti sees it, the Naiyāyikas' account—which is based on regularities plus an epistemic upgrade—does not entail that there will not be a counterexample or an additional condition. His point is that there needs to be something about an object's being an *R-possessor* that will make it a *T-possessor*, on the basis of which examined cases can be related to unexamined ones. To eliminate doubt about negative concomitance, Ratnakīrti says specifically that what is necessary is to establish that the absence of *R* is "due to" the absence of *T*, and not just invariably associated with it. This is, Ratnakīrti argues, the only way to remove epistemically significant doubt about the presence of a counterexample or an additional condition (and, as I will discuss below, the only legitimate basis for extending the pervasion relation to "unobserved" loci).

According to Ratnakīrti, the Naiyāyikas' account of natural relations, inference-warranting relations, and the epistemology of satisfaction is such that pervasion is fallible. From his perspective, the problem with his Naiyāyikas' understanding of fallibility is that it specifically allows for epistemically significant doubt about negative concomitance, even in the case of well-known inferences such as the inference of a potter from pots. Moreover,

---

157. Walton 1996:264.

as Ratnakīrti sees it, for genuinely inference-warranting relations, satisfaction and certification cannot be fallible, since fallibility inevitably leads to epistemically significant doubt about whether a particular reason property is naturally related to its target. Ratnakīrti's Naiyāyikas obviously disagree. They argue that what Ratnakīrti says is epistemically significant doubt is in fact a form of unlocalized doubt and is not epistemically significant. Moreover, they argue that for them fallibility is appealed to only after reasonable and epistemically significant doubt has been removed. A stricter "infallibility" criterion of the sort proposed by Ratnakīrti would, they argue, undermine even well-known inferences and should be rejected. As they see it, it would let loose the "ghost of doubt." According to Ratnakīrti, however, this is not at all the case since, in his view, reasonable doubt can be the basis for rational action, even though this action would not be based on a knowing-event, as in the case of the long-life "inference."[158] The standards for what counts as a knowing-event are stricter than for awareness-events on the basis of which it is reasonable for us to act. As Ratnakīrti argues, it is only when there is no source of knowledge on which to base one's actions that fallibility, in the form of reasonable doubt, is acceptable. In the case at hand, however, the issue is precisely about whether a source of knowledge is certified, and thus fallibility, at any point in the certification process, is unacceptable. As Ratnakīrti presents it, an underlying issue that must be resolved before the success of the Īśvara-inference can be determined has to do with what counts as epistemically significant doubt, whether fallibility is ever acceptable, and if it is, under what conditions.

5.2. The Extension Principle and Site Subcomponent

As both Ratnakīrti and his Naiyāyikas accept, the Naiyāyikas' approach to the epistemology of satisfaction/certification cannot directly support pervasion relations that involve an "unobservable," as defined through the theory of remoteness. If such remote objects are to be included within the scope of a pervasion relation, an extension principle of some sort is necessary.[159] It is on the basis of such an extension principle that the Naiyāyikas' claim that an inference-warranting relation that is established for a sample class of objects

158. See section 2.1.2.

159. See also my discussion of the "search premise," which describes a rather different approach to this problem.

can be extended beyond the sample class to include remote, unsampled objects and eventually the site of the inference. "Unsampled" objects are either observed loci with an unobservable *property*, as is the case in the debate about C2.2/H2, or unobservable *loci* with an observable or unobservable property, as is the case in the debate about C2.3a/H3a.[160] It is also on the basis of such an extension principle that the analogical argument that was used to resolve the "gap problem" discussed in chapter 2 is based.[161] What I am calling the "second line" of argument in Ratnakīrti's critique of the Īśvara-inference has to do with the ground rules for this extension, and the closely related issue of what we can learn about the target property on the basis of it. Thus far I have discussed this issue primarily in terms of the site subcomponent of the inference, but given the close relationship between the site subcomponent and the pervasion subcomponent (which is clearly evident from debates about the scope of the reason property and target property) the ground rules for extension are also directly related to the metaphysics and epistemology of pervasion. One interesting (and I hope helpful) way of reframing the Naiyāyikas' argument and Ratnakīrti's critique of these ground rules is in terms of what is sometimes called a "Galilean strategy."[162]

A "Galilean strategy" is an argument that is designed to show that the methods we use to settle questions about noncontroversial, observable matters should be relied on to settle questions about controversial, unobservable matters.[163] Ratnakīrti's Naiyāyikas employ their own "analogical" version of

---

160. For C2.2/H2 see chapter 2, sections 2.3.1 and 3.1, and although it is less relevant, section 4 in this chapter. For C2.3/H3a see chapter 2, section 3.2, and sections 2 and 3 in this chapter.

161. See chapter 2, section 4.1.

162. Kitcher 2001a, Kitcher 2001b: chap. 2. The Naiyāyikas' "Galilean strategy" is, of course, different from the one discussed by Kitcher.

163. This is a restatement of the strategy that is based on Magnus 2003:465. Here "unobservable" refers both to things that we have not seen with our own eyes and things that we cannot see with our own eyes, such as the rings of Saturn or Īśvara. Kitcher (2001a:21) writes, "Methods of justification, like Galileo's telescope, can only be validated by examining the conclusions about observables to which they lead. It does not follow that the only conclusions licensed by those methods are conclusions about observables—any more than Galileo's demonstration on buildings and ships only show that the telescope is reliable in Venice. We need to consider whether there are good reasons for distinguishing a method's usage in its application to observables from its usage in application to unobservables." Also see Kitcher 2001b:175.

this strategy to support their extension principle. Their argument seems to be as follows: for a sampled set of objects (S), we can establish that "a property *R* is pervaded by a property *T*" on the basis of careful observation and nonobservation (as discussed above).[164] The sampled objects in this set are like the members of an unsampled set of remote objects (U) in that both have properties $P_1 \ldots P_n$ (which may include *R* and, in the case of negative concomitance, the absence of *T*). Therefore pervasion can be extended to include these unsampled objects. Let us refer to this method of establishing and extending pervasion as method *M*. The Naiyāyikas then deploy their analogical version of the Galilean strategy and argue: the pervasion subcomponents in well-known inferences, like the inference of a potter from pots or fire from smoke, are known to be well-functioning. In such cases pervasion is established and extended beyond a sampled set of similar and/or dissimilar cases to include all relevant cases on the basis of method *M*. The pervasion subcomponent in the Īśvara-inference is like the pervasion subcomponent in these well-known inferences, in that it too is established and extended on the basis of method *M*. Therefore the pervasion subcomponent in the Īśvara-inference is also well-functioning.[165]

---

164. Here "a property *R* is pervaded by a property *T*" means that each and every member of the set has property *R* and property *T*. What it means for an object to be "sampled" depends on the particular inferential argument. Here, a "sampled" object is one that is observed to have property *T*, while an "unsampled" object is one that is observed, but is not observed to have property *T*. "Unsampled" can also refer to objects that have not been observed. It is important to note that this argument can also be rephrased to make negative concomitance more explicit by specifying that "the absence of a property *T* is pervaded by the absence of a property *R*."

165. Magnus 2003 schematizes the Galilean strategy as follows: (1) *M*—e.g., Galileo's telescope—provides correct answers up to and along the vague boundary between matters we can check independently of *M* and ones that we cannot check; and (2) prevailing reasons for thinking that the boundary might make a difference to the reliability of *M* are mistaken. Magnus then strengthens it with (3) there is some significant positive reason to think that the success of *M* on matters we can check generalizes to matters that we cannot check; and concludes (4) *M* provides the correct answers for matters that we cannot check independently of *M*. In the context of the Īśvara-inference, *M* is the method, based on observation and nonobservation, that the Naiyāyikas use to establish and extend pervasion; "matters we can check independently" corresponds to well-known and noncontroversial maker-inferences; "matters we cannot check" corresponds to the Īśvara-inference; and "provides the correct answers" corresponds to a well-functioning pervasion subcomponent.

The Naiyāyikas' intuitions regarding method *M* are developed in two closely related contexts. In the first context pervasion is supposed to be extended from a sampled set of pots that are known, through observation and nonobservation, to be made by a potter (S) to an unsampled set of pots (U) on the basis of method *M*. In the second context pervasion is supposed to be extended from a sampled class of effect-loci that are known, through observation and nonobservation, to be made by an intelligent maker (S) to an unsampled class of effect-loci (U), also on the basis of method *M*.[166] In each of these contexts, what is specifically at issue is negative concomitance—i.e., the absence of a reason property, *R*, from all dissimilar cases, both sampled and unsampled.[167] Each of these noncontroversial contexts is supposed to support the Naiyāyikas' intuitions about the ground rules for extension-method *M*, which they then apply to the Īśvara-inference. Ratnakīrti attacks the Naiyāyikas' understanding of how and why extension works in these contexts by focusing on what he sees as two important ground rules for extension that are not recognized by his Naiyāyikas.

In the first context Ratnakīrti's Naiyāyikas argued that C2.3a_2 had been satisfied for the reason property "being an effect," since the inference-warranting relation in the Īśvara-inference was as strong as the inference-warranting relation in the inference of a potter from a pot (section 2.2.1). The Naiyāyikas' parallel argument strategy was to insist that their opponents cannot claim that H3a_2 applies to the reason property in the Īśvara-inference without also undermining the pervasion subcomponent in this well-known and widely accepted inference. In both cases his Naiyāyikas claim that negative concomitance is established and extended on the basis of method *M*. Ratnakīrti attacks this argument by focusing on the Naiyāyikas' assumed ground rules for extending pervasion in the inference of a potter from pots. In so doing he exposes what he takes to be a decisive disanalogy between well-known maker-inferences and the Īśvara-inference.

---

166. This context includes well-known maker-inferences in general.

167. Note that what is "unsampled" in the first context is the "absence of an observable (but spatially and/or temporally remote) maker" in observed loci, and in loci that are unobservable because of remoteness. In the second context what is "unsampled" is the "absence of a possibly unobservable maker" in observed loci, and also in loci that are unobservable because of remoteness.

Ratnakīrti argues that although the Naiyāyikas do not acknowledge it, method *M* requires that the properties that the objects in the sampled set (S) and unsampled set (U) share (i.e., $P_1 \ldots P_n$) must be relevant to the objects in the sampled set having the target property *T.* More specifically, he argues that what constitutes "being relevant" is that in the well-known inference of a potter from pots (or fire from smoke) it is known that, for the sampled objects, the presence of a reason property *R* in the sampled objects is ***due to*** the target property *T.* It is on the basis of this that he claims that extension is permitted to unsampled *R*-possessing loci, including the site. Earlier Ratnakīrti argued that the Naiyāyikas' method *M* does not establish this fact, and that, as a result, *M* does not really establish pervasion even in the case of well-known inferences. More specifically, Ratnakīrti argued that on the basis of the Naiyāyikas' method *M* one cannot show that the absence of a pot is ***due to*** the absence of a potter. Here, however, Ratnakīrti assumes that there is a method *M'*, based on a production-mode of pervasion, that can be used to establish pervasion in well-known inferences, in accordance with the ground-rule that he has just discussed. As he points out, however, *M'* is not the Naiyāyikas' method *M* and, as a result, there is a decisive disanalogy between well-known (and noncontroversial) inferences and the Īśvara-inference that permits extension in the first case but not in the second. As Ratnakīrti sees it, method *M* is not how pervasion is established in well-known maker-inferences, and therefore a Galilean strategy cannot be based on it. The ultimate success of Ratnakīrti's argument, however, depends upon the success of his own method *M'* (which I will briefly discuss in chapter 5) and its inapplicability to the Īśvara-inference.[168]

In the second context, Ratnakīrti's Naiyāyikas responded to the restricted scope argument by insisting that there is no need to restrict the scope of the reason property "effects-in-general" (section 3.1). They argued that when pervasion is established on the basis of a sampled set of specific

168. If *M* were a telescope, Ratnakīrti's Naiyāyikas might argue as follows: Our telescope also works for earthly objects other than those that we have independently seen. Earthly objects are like heavenly objects. So, our telescope works for heavenly objects (e.g., the rings of Saturn). Given this, the form of Ratnakīrti's argument would be as follows: Your telescope doesn't work for heavenly objects because it doesn't really work for earthly objects. Moreover, telescopes that really do work for earthly objects do not work for heavenly objects, because heavenly objects and earthly objects are very different, since earthly objects have been and can be independently seen (see next paragraph above).

"effects-in-general" that have been observed to have an intelligent maker, such as pots and cloth, it can be extended on the basis of method *M* to unsampled "effects-in-general" that have not been observed to have an intelligent maker, such as trees, the mountains, and the earth. In responding to the Naiyāyikas' counterargument, Ratnakīrti tries to make explicit another, and closely related, ground rule for the extension principle at work in noncontroversial maker-inferences, and thereby to show that there is another decisive disanalogy between these inferences and the Īśvara-inference.

According to Ratnakīrti, what is essential for inferring an intelligent maker of effects like pots or cloth is that, for a sampled set of such objects, we have *seen* that some of its members have been made by/are "due to" an intelligent maker. It is on the basis of having seen this that pervasion can be extended to include unsampled members of the set—e.g., unsampled pots, cloth, or bracelets, etc. However, we have never seen, for any member of a sampled set of things like trees, the mountains, or the earth, that it has been made by an intelligent maker. Thus in such cases pervasion cannot be extended to include such things. This is clear, Ratnakīrti argues, to anyone whose mind is not enslaved by philosophy. His point is that the relevant restrictive property on the basis of which pervasion is extended in well-known maker-inferences is "having *seen* that other members of the set have been made by (i.e., are due to) an intelligent maker." This fact is suppressed in the Naiyāyikas' account of method *M*. Moreover, once this is taken into account, Ratnakīrti argues that it reveals a second disanalogy between well-known maker-inferences and the Īśvara-inference.[169] As he sees it, the extension-method *M'* that accounts for well-known maker-inferences does not apply to the Īśvara-inference, since in well-known maker-inferences the maker is neither always spatially or temporally remote nor ever essentially remote. Here too the success of Ratnakīrti's argument depends on the success of method *M'*, which his Naiyāyikas would argue is too restrictive, since it seems to rule out what they would take to be noncontroversial maker-inferences for objects such as very old buildings and iPods, assuming that we have never seen either kind of object being made.

In his discussion of this disanalogy, Ratnakīrti also provides resources for generalizing the argument and specifying further what he means by

---

169. When it is known that the absence of *R* is due to the absence of *T*, Ratnakīrti argues that pervasion can be extended to observed loci in which the absence of *T* is unsampled and to unobservable loci that are themselves unsampled.

"such objects" and "other members of the set" (section 3.1). Ratnakīrti's argument seems to be based on the idea that there is a structured hierarchy of "intermediary" properties.[170] These (at least ersatz) properties are "structured," in the sense that higher-order properties are taken to be exemplified by lower-order properties.[171] For simplicity, let us suppose that there are three levels of such properties. In the context of the Īśvara-inference, suppose that the highest-order property is "being an effect-in-general," at level 1. Relative to this property are lower-level properties, at level 2, such as "being a pot," "being a piece of cloth," "being a tree," etc. At level 3 are properties such as "being a pot that has an observed intelligent maker" and "being a pot that has an unobserved intelligent maker." Notice that lower-level properties exemplify higher-order properties in the sense that the loci in which a lower-level property is located are loci in which the relevant higher-order property is also located.[172]

Ratnakīrti argues that given the Naiyāyikas' view about how pervasion conditions are satisfied, pervasion can be extended only to unsampled members of a set of objects ("being a pot that has an unobserved intelligent maker") when those objects exemplify the same relevant higher-order property ("being a pot") and are on the same level as the sampled members of the set on the basis of which pervasion was established ("being a pot that has an observed intelligent maker"). One way to understand the debate about restrictive property "*R*" is in terms of whether a higher-level and lower-level (i.e., "*R*" restricted) property pair can be specified such that pervasion can be established for a higher-level property, by sampling loci in which a lower-level property that exemplifies it is present, and then extended to include unsampled loci on that level in which that same higher-level property is present. As Ratnakīrti sees it, this can be specified for well-known maker-inferences, but not for the Īśvara-inference. The Naiyāyikas' trick is to extend pervasion to unsampled members of a set that do not exemplify the same relevant higher-order property for which pervasion is in fact established. The challenge, of course, is to provide an account of this structured hierarchy of

---

170. This is based on Ratnakīrti's use of the term "*avāntara*," which I translated in section 3.1, passages *c* and *e* as "secondary." Also see section 2.2.2.

171. For an excellent discussion of "properties" that is the source for much of my vocabulary in this paragraph see Swoyer 2000.

172. On my use of the term "property," a property, like a set, is extensional. For more on why Ratnakīrti might understand properties in this (rather unusual) way, see chapter 4.

properties, which Ratnakīrti seems to think are reflected in our most basic, pre-philosophical, intuitions and linguistic conventions. In chapter 4 I will discuss some of the philosophical resources that Ratnakīrti draws upon for developing such an account.

Interestingly, Ratnakīrti also uses this line of argument to undercut the Naiyāyikas' strategy for solving the "gap problem." He argues that the only additional property of the target that can be known on the basis of knowing that pervasion extends to the site of the inference is its "exclusion of a non-connection with the site." This is a property that is entailed by knowing both that the presence of the reason property in a particular locus is due to the presence of the target property in that locus, and that the reason property is located in the site. Ratnakīrti suggests that this is a consequence of the extension principle. As a result, all that Ratnakīrti claims can be known about the target property on the basis of an inferential argument is (1) that the reason property is "due to" it and (2) that it is excluded from a nonconnection with the site. Exactly what we learn on the basis of (1) depends on the scope of both the reason and the target properties. For example, if the reason property is "pot" we learn that the target is "potter" but not "weaver." If the reason property is "effect-in-general," however, even assuming pervasion, all we can learn is that the target is an "intelligent-agent-in-general." To learn more about the target, either a further inferential argument will be necessary, which just pushes the problem back to how the Naiyāyikas establish pervasion in the first place, or the scope of the reason property will have to be suitably restricted, which Ratnakīrti argues will result in either H1b or H3a. His point is that a correct understanding of the ground rules for extension exposes decisive disanalogies between solutions to the "gap problem" in well-known inferences and the Naiyāyikas' proposed solution for the Īśvara-inference. Thus the arguments that are used to support step 3 in the Naiyāyikas' hybrid argument cannot succeed.

Again, the success of Ratnakīrti's argument ultimately rests on his extension-method M' and, in this context, exactly what we can learn about the target property on the basis of it.

PART 2

Language, Mind, and Ontology

CHAPTER 4

The Theory of Exclusion, Conceptual Content, and Buddhist Epistemology

In looking through the Naiyāyikas' Īśvara-inference to uncover more basic problems in their account of inferential reasoning, Ratnakīrti presents himself as providing an "internal" critique of the Naiyāyikas' argument—that is, a critique based on arguments and philosophical principles that are supposedly acceptable to them. As I have suggested, however, Ratnakīrti's critique is also informed by his own philosophical views, as he brings to it very different ideas about the metaphysics and epistemology of inference-warranting relations (evident from his references to the "production" and "identity" modes of pervasion), the epistemology of certification and satisfaction, and the nature of reasonable doubt and acceptable level of epistemic risk. In this chapter and the next I will argue that what informs his thoughts on each of these issues is his version of the Buddhist theory of exclusion (*apoha*). His commitment to this theory provides the implicit philosophical context for his criticism of the Naiyāyikas' Īśvara-inference and motivates his position on the five issues most central to it, namely: (1) the nature of inference-warranting relations; (2) the relationship between the metaphysics and epistemology of such relations; (3) epistemic necessity; (4) the epistemology of certification and satisfaction (including the issue of epistemic risk); and (5) the extension principle.

In this chapter I will focus specifically (and narrowly) on Ratnakīrti's version of the theory of exclusion, as he presents it in his "Demonstration of Exclusion" (*Apohasiddhi*). I will argue that although he presents this theory as a theory of semantic value—that is, as a theory of what our words are about—it is best understood as a theory of mental content—that is, as a theory of what our thoughts are about and what our actions are directed toward. Building on my analysis in this chapter, I will argue in chapter 5 that the theory of exclusion provides the basic philosophical resources for Ratnakīrti's critique of the Īśvara-inference. When taken together, chapters 4 and 5 explain what Ratnakīrti's discussion of semantic value reveals about the contents of "inferential/verbal" awareness-events, especially those produced through inferential reasoning.[1] Part 2 of this book thus provides the immediate, but implicit, philosophical context for Ratnakīrti's critique of the Īśvara-inference.

Throughout this part of the book I will argue that in providing an account of what our words are about, Ratnakīrti seeks to explain how and why our thoughts are about what they are about. This effort is central to his debate with the Naiyāyikas since, according to him, the content of each and every conceptual awareness-event is an exclusion.[2] This includes the objects with which and about which we think when we reason inferentially—e.g., the site of an inference, reason and target properties, and the class of all dissimilar cases. Moreover, since the theory of exclusion also accounts for how exclusions are "related to" one another, it provides resources for thinking about the "location relations" (presence, absence, and pervasion) between such objects, and epistemic modality more specifically. As I will argue in chapter 5, the theory of exclusion is essential to Ratnakīrti's own views on inferential reasoning, and therefore to his critique of the Īśvara-inference.[3] In addition to using the theory of exclusion to support important parts of his critique of the Īśvara-inference, Ratnakīrti also recognizes that the

---

1. Since Buddhist philosophers like Ratnakīrti reduce testimony to inference, "verbal" states of awareness are, strictly speaking, inferential states of awareness. For convenience, therefore, I will use the label "inferential/verbal" to refer to awareness-events produced through "testimony," or inferential reasoning. For more on the reduction of testimony to inference see below, and chapter 5, section 2.4.1. For a useful discussion of this issue in Sanskrit philosophy more generally see Chakrabarti 1994 and Taber 1996.

2. My focus in this chapter will be on the content of conceptual awareness-events. I will discuss mental content, more generally, in chapter 5.

3. See chapter 5, section 5.

Naiyāyikas' Īśvara is incompatible with many of his other views. For example, in concluding his "Refutation of Arguments for Establishing Īśvara," Ratnakīrti remarks that what he has shown is that the Naiyāyikas have not, and perhaps cannot, prove the existence of Īśvara inferentially. As I have argued in chapters 2 and 3, Ratnakīrti sees his debate with the Naiyāyikas as being about justification, and the certification of the inference-instrument. Ratnakīrti recognizes, however, that in his "Refutation" he has not shown that Īśvara does not exist, and that in order to do so he would have to offer positive arguments that establish the *nonexistence* of Īśvara. Interestingly, he suggests that his inference to prove the Buddhist theory of momentariness (*kṣaṇikatva*) provides just such an argument since, as he notes, "momentariness is utterly incompatible with his defining characteristics."[4] Ratnakīrti clearly recognizes that aspects of his thought that are not discussed in his "Refutation" are relevant to the issue of Īśvara's existence. In drawing our attention to the theory of momentariness, Ratnakīrti explains that his views on ontology are particularly significant. More specifically, it is his view on what, what there is, is like that he thinks is the most relevant.[5]

Interestingly, the theory of exclusion also provides philosophical resources for thinking about Ratnakīrti's metaphysics and ontology. It does so by linking metaphysical and ontological issues with his theory of mental objects/images (*ākāra*). In chapter 5 I will build upon my discussion of exclusion in this chapter by discussing Ratnakīrti's theory of mental objects/images and explaining how, when linked with the theory of exclusion by means of the concept of determination (*adhyavasāya*), it explains Ratnakīrti's views

---

4. RNĀ (ĪSD 57.11–57.13): "So then, in this way, the matter of Īśvara's existence is rejected. But, with regard to the matter of [his] nonexistence, an argument based on a reason property such as existence—which establishes momentariness, which is utterly incompatible with his defining characteristics—must be made evident" (*tad evaṃ tāvad īśvarasya sadvyavahāro niṣedhaḥ | asadvyavahārārthaṃ tu tallakṣaṇavilakṣaṇakṣaṇabhaṅgasādhakaṃ sattādisādhanam eva draṣṭavyam iti*).

Ratnakīrti's inferential arguments for the theory of momentariness can be found at RNĀ (KSA 67–82), which is translated in Woo 1999, and RNĀ (KSV 83–96), which is translated in McDermott 1969. The secondary literature on the Buddhist theory of momentariness is extensive; see, for example, Gupta 1990, Halbfass 1997, Katsura 2003, Kyuma 2005, Laine 1998, Mimaki 1976, Mookherjee 1975, Rospatt 1995, Steinkellner 1968/1969, Tani 1996a, Tani 1996b, Tani 1997, Tani 2004, and Yoshimizu 1999.

5. MTBh 64.09–65.12 takes a similar approach to arguing against the Naiyāyikas' belief in the substance "soul" (*ātman*), of which Īśvara is said to be a special type.

on many of the metaphysical and ontological issues that inform his critique of the Īśvara-inference. Finally, in addition to uncovering the philosophical resources that lie hidden behind Ratnakīrti's "internal" critique of the Naiyāyikas' Īśvara-inference, chapters 4 and 5 discuss the philosophical resources that Ratnakīrti relies on to develop an alternative picture of the world and that point to the only kind of intelligent maker that he could agree creates it.

1. The Theory of Exclusion

The Buddhist theory of exclusion has long provided a context within which a broad range of philosophical issues are discussed. Given its prehistory in the work of the Sanskrit grammarians, the theory has been linked most closely with issues in semantics and the philosophy of language.[6] It was first developed by the Buddhist philosopher Dignāga (ca. 480–540), however, in response to more epistemological and ontological concerns.[7] What Dignāga noticed was that debates about meaning, reference, and semantic value could be related both to epistemological questions—regarding how the awareness of a reason property is supposed to produce awareness of its target—and to ontological questions—regarding exactly what it is that we are, and can be, aware of on the basis of inferential reasoning.[8] While Dignāga's primary

---

6. Bronkhorst 1999, Chakrabarti et al. (forthcoming), Deshpande 1992, Dravid 1972: chaps. 10–11, Ganeri 1995, Ganeri 1996, Ganeri 1999a, Hattori 1968, Hattori 1977, Hattori 1980, Hayes 1988: chaps. 1, 3, and 4, Herzberger 1986, Katsura 1991, Ogawa 1999, Pind 1991, Pind 1999, Raja 1986, Scharf 1996, and Siderits 2003:211–217.

The terms "philosophy of language" and "semantics" have a wide variety of meanings. I intend the term "philosophy of language" to be very general. By "semantics" I generally mean "descriptive semantics" (see below).

7. Although the term "exclusion" (*apoha*) is well known before Dignāga, the "theory of exclusion" seems to have been first developed by him. For pre-Dignāga mentions of "exclusion" see the references in note 6. The close connection between the theory of exclusion and Dignāga's epistemology (and ontology) is also well known, although the specific nature of this connection is not. For a translation of PS5 *ad* PS5.1–PS5.12 see Hattori 2000:137–146. For a complete translation see Hayes 1988: chap. 7. For an account of how the theory of exclusion developed in Dignāga's work see Frauwallner 1959, Hayes 1988: chaps. 3 and 5, Katsura 1983, and Katsura 1991:139.

8. Bronkhorst 1999:20, Frauwallner 1959:103, Ganeri 2001, Hattori 1968, Hattori 2000:137, Hayes 1986, Hayes 1988: chaps. 4 and 5, Matilal 1990:38, Pind 1991, and Pind 1999:324.

concern was to show that the epistemology of testimony could be reduced to that of inferential reasoning, subsequent Buddhist philosophers developed versions of the theory that were linked to their views on a variety of other philosophical issues.[9] In discussing the version of the theory developed by a particular Buddhist philosopher, therefore, it is important to keep in mind that philosopher's primary intellectual concerns. Attention to this is important, since an awareness of the immediate philosophical context in which a particular version of the theory of exclusion was developed can help us to discover exactly what that version of the theory was supposed to explain.

In his "Demonstration of Exclusion" Ratnakīrti develops a version of the theory that seeks to explain how and why our words are about what they are

---

On my use of the term, "semantic value" is neutral to whatever it is that a semantic theory associates with the expressions of the language it interprets. It is, in other words, the "object" that a semantic theory assigns to an expression. A "descriptive semantic theory" is a theory that (1) assigns semantic values to expressions of a language and (2) explains how the semantic values of complex expressions in that language are a "function" of the semantic values of its components. One such explanation is that the semantic value of a complex expression is just the propositional content or thought expressed by that expression and is not, strictly speaking, a function of its parts; see Stalnaker 1999:535. Many Buddhist philosophers, however, seem to work with what is known as "compositional semantics," that is, a semantic theory in which the semantic values of complex expressions are understood to be a function of their parts. In this chapter, my focus will be on (1).

9. That Dignāga was primarily concerned with the reduction of testimony to inference seems clear from the very first verse of his chapter on the "Exclusion of Others" in his *Compendium on the Sources of Knowledge* (*Pramāṇasamuccaya*), where he says that testimony is reducible to inference, since both the way in which verbal awareness is produced and what we come to know on the basis of it are inferential; see Hattori 2000:139. As is evident from his chapter on "Inference for Oneself," however, Dignāga also recognized how significant the theory was to inferential reasoning more generally. Dignāga's successors—Dharmakīrti, Dharmottara, Jñānaśrīmitra, Ratnakīrti, and Mokṣākaragupta—all discuss the relationship between exclusion and inferential reasoning, but also seem to expand its scope; see, for example, the numerous references to Dharmakīrti's PV and PVSV in Dunne 2004, Dharmottara's AP-D in Hattori 2006:63–68, Jñānaśrīmitra's AP in McCrea and Patil 2006, Ratnakīrti's AS in this chapter, and Mokṣākaragupta's MTBh in Kajiyama 1998. More specifically, Katsura (1986:172 n. 8) points out that Dharmakīrti also used the theory of exclusion to discuss causation in HB 9*.13–10*.04, and Meindersma (1991) has pointed to Dharmakīrti's discussion of exclusion in PV2 (vv. 88–102), where Dharmakīrti presents his argument for "other worlds" (*paraloka*). Also see Ganeri 1999b and Gillon 1999 for a discussion of "exclusion" and Dharmakīrti's account of the semantics of the particle "*eva*." For very recent work on exclusion, see the essays in Chakrabarti et al. (forthcoming).

about.[10] Although he is explicitly concerned with semantic value, it is very clear from his work that his theory is also about much more. As I will argue, Ratnakīrti's account of exclusion provides a general theory of conceptual content—that is, an account of the kind of object about which we speak and think and with respect to which we act.[11] According to Ratnakīrti, this object is best described as "a positive entity characterized by its exclusion of others" (*anyāpoha-viśiṣṭa-vidhi*) and is best understood as the content (*viṣaya*) of conceptual awareness-events (*vikalpa-buddhi*), such as those produced through inferential reasoning or verbal testimony (*śabda*).[12] This complex positive entity is also said to be the "meaning of a word" and the object that is "denoted by the term 'exclusion.'"[13]

2. What Exclusion Is Not

Ratnakīrti begins his essay by explaining how and why his version of the theory of exclusion is different from others. Two series of such remarks open his

---

10. For a minimally annotated translation of this text see Patil (forthcoming, b).

11. While the theory of exclusion does not directly provide an account of the content of nonconceptual awareness-events, it does contribute to our understanding of them and so may be thought of as a theory of mental content more generally. Also, my assertion that "conceptual content" is "what our physical activity is directed toward" may seem unwarranted. According to Ratnakīrti, however, there is sufficient similarity (and in some cases identity) between the objects about which we speak and think and the objects upon which we physically act. This has to do with his understanding of verbal, mental, and bodily activity and the objects of such activity. For a discussion of this see chapter 5.

12. These states of awareness will be discussed in greater detail in chapter 5.

13. See RNĀ (AS 58.01), where he states that "exclusion is the meaning of a word" (*apohaḥ śabdārtho {nirucyate}*) and RNĀ (AS 66.06–66.07) where he says that "this positive entity alone is expressed by the word 'exclusion,' and is the meaning of words" (*vidhiḥ | sa eva cāpohaśabdavācyaḥ śabdānām arthaḥ*). Like the word "meaning," the Sanskrit word "*artha*" has a broad semantic range and can be translated as "meaning," "object," "thing," "function," or "purpose." In discussions that focus on the philosophy of language, the term is sometimes translated as "meaning-*relatum*." I will generally translate the term "*artha*" as "meaning," "object," or "semantic value." On this use of the term, the "meaning" of a linguistic expression is whatever a competent speaker of a language understands from hearing that expression on a particular occasion of its use. The meaning of an expression will also be described in terms of the content of the state of awareness that is produced in the mind of such a speaker upon hearing it.

essay. The first takes place in the voice of an "opponent" who argues that there is no plausible interpretation of the exclusion theorist's slogan "Exclusion is the meaning of a word."[14] The second, which begins in Ratnakīrti's own voice, is used to explain how his interpretation of exclusion is different from the theories of the so-called positivists (*vidhi-vādin*) and negationists (*pratiṣedha-vādin*). What is important about the first few sections of Ratnakīrti's essay is that in briefly discussing how and why his interpretation of exclusion is different from these others, he introduces the issues that he thinks he will have to address in defending his version of the theory. It is also in these introductory remarks that Ratnakīrti begins to discuss his account of the relationship between semantic value and exclusion. Equally interesting about these introductory sections are the issues that Ratnakīrti does not choose to discuss—issues such as the precise nature of a "word" and the relationship between the meaning of a word and the meaning of more complex linguistic expressions such as sentences. In this section I want to consider what is and what is not discussed in Ratnakīrti's introductory remarks, in order to set the stage for a more detailed presentation and defense of his views in sections 3–4.

2.1. *Three Misinterpretations of "Exclusion"*

Ratnakīrti's "Demonstration of Exclusion" begins with an opponent who considers three possible interpretations of the statement "Exclusion is the meaning of a word."[15] In identifying "exclusion" with "meaning" the

---

14. This "slogan" is the first sentence of Ratnakīrti's "Demonstration of Exclusion." RNĀ (AS 58.01): "It is said that exclusion is the meaning of a word" (*apohaḥ śabdārtho nirucyate*).

On my reading, the introductory discussion at RNĀ (AS 58.01–59.03) is presented as a series of objections and responses by an opponent to the thesis, stated at RNĀ (AS 58.01), that "exclusion is the meaning of a word." This "opponent" is not necessarily an actual historical opponent or group of opponents, although many of the passages can be traced to specific authors, including some Buddhists (see below). In my view, Ratnakīrti uses previous (and well-known) discussions and criticisms of exclusion to create an imagined opponent whose criticism provides the immediate philosophical (and rhetorical) context for his own discussion.

15. RNĀ (AS 58.01–58.04): "But what is this exclusion? What is the reason for the grammatical analysis of 'exclusion' as 'this is excluded from other things' or 'from this other things are excluded' or 'in this other things are excluded'? Is what is intended (1) just an external object excluded from what belongs to a different class, (2) a mental image, or, (3) if exclusion means 'excluding,' the mere exclusion of other things? These are the three alternatives"

opponent assumes that exclusion theorists interpret "exclusion" as referring to either an excluded object or the process of exclusion itself. In the opponent's view, the theory of exclusion is a form of either what I will call "pure referentialism" or "pure nonreferentialism." On my use of these terms, "pure referentialism" is the view that semantic value can be completely specified in terms of some (positive) object "*x*." Following the opponent, my description of this view is neutral to the ontological status of this object, that is, to whether it is an "external" or an "internal" object, and whether it is a particular, a universal, or a complex object made up of particulars and universals. There can be, therefore, both realist and ideational versions of pure referentialism.[16] A realist version would be the view that the semantic value of an expression is the external object for which it stands.[17] The ideational version would be that it is the internal object or, more specifically, mental image (*buddhi-ākāra*) for which it stands.[18] Pure nonreferentialism, in contrast, is

---

(*nanu ko 'yam apoho nāma | kim idam anyasmād apohyate | asmād vānyad apohyate | asmin vānyad apohyata iti vyutpattyā* (1) *vijātivyāvṛttaṃ bāhyam eva vivakṣitam* | (2) *buddhyākāro vā* | (3) *yadi vāpohanam apoha ity anyavyāvṛttimātram iti trayaḥ pakṣāḥ*).

This grammatical analysis of exclusion (*apoha*) seems to have begun with Śākyabuddhi in his commentary on Dharmakīrti's *Pramāṇavārttika*, the *Pramāṇavārttika-ṭīkā* (See PVṬ *ad* PV v. 169). Karṇakagomin, another commentator on Dharmakīrti's text, also mentions it in his PVSVṬ, as do Śāntarakṣita and his commentator Kamalaśīla in their independent works (TS/TSP). For a parallel passage in the work of Ratnakīrti's teacher, Jñānaśrīmitra, see JNĀ (AP 202.12–212.14). For a discussion of Śākyabuddhi's analysis see Funayama 2000 and Dunne 2004:131ff. For a discussion of Karṇakagomin and Śāntarakṣita see Akamatsu 1981. For a reconstruction of a relevant portion of Śākyabuddhi's text based on Haribhadra Sūri's *Anekāntajayapatāka* (AJP), and a discussion of the threefold classification of exclusion, see Ishida (forthcoming).

16. These positions roughly correspond to the first and third interpretations of exclusion referred to by Śākyabuddhi; for a discussion of this see Funayama 2000, Dunne 2004, Ishida (forthcoming), and Katsura (forthcoming).

17. This phrase is from Ganeri 1999a.

18. I generally use the term "*mental* image" to translate the Sanskrit term "*ākāra*" (image), since according to Ratnakīrti all images are mental images. According to him, there can be both nonconceptual and conceptual mental images. Some Sanskrit philosophers argue that these mental images are "representations" of mind-independent external objects. Others, like Ratnakīrti, argue against this view on the grounds that there are no mind-independent external objects for these images to be representations of. Still others argue that these "images" are nothing more than real features of mind-independent external objects and, in fact, are not mental at all. For a useful discussion of "images" (*ākāra*) as interpreted by various Buddhist philosophers see Dunne 2004, Dreyfus 1997:331–344, and Kajiyama 1998:145–151.

the view that semantic value can be completely specified without reference to an object of any sort. On this view, semantic value is supposed to be completely specified by exclusion itself (*vyāvṛtti-mātra*).[19] Here, "exclusion" does not denote an object "*x*," but a process, capacity, or dispositional property.[20]

As plausible interpretations of "exclusion," however, both the realist and the ideational versions of pure referentialism and pure nonreferentialism are summarily dismissed by the opponent. Pure referentialism cannot be the proper interpretation of the theory since, the opponent reasons, it does not make sense of the obviously negative term "exclusion."[21] Pure nonreferentialism cannot be the proper interpretation either. According to the opponent, pure nonreferentialism is the view that exclusion itself is the meaning of a word. More specifically, it supposes that semantic value consists of nothing other than the property or process "excluding" (*apohana*). On this view, what a word such as "fire" really means is just an exclusion, i.e., an excluding of what is other than it (*anyāpoha*). The opponent rejects this view, by arguing that the self-examination of our own mental states reveals that the process of exclusion is, in fact, not the object of an inferential/verbal awareness-event. After all, the opponent remarks, it is obvious that when we hear the word "fire" our awareness is of a positive entity, "fire," and not "not non-fire." Since the proper description of the content of our awareness "There is fire here" is obviously not "There is not non-fire here," the opponent reasons that exclusion theorists cannot mean that exclusion itself is the content of inferential/verbal awareness.[22] Since neither pure referentialism nor pure nonreferentialism is a plausible interpretation of the theory of exclusion, the opponent concludes by asking how exclusion can be the meaning of a word.[23]

---

19. This positions roughly corresponds to the second interpretation of exclusion referred to by Śākyabuddhi. For a discussion of this see Funayama 2000, Dunne 2004, Ishida (forthcoming), and Katsura (forthcoming).

20. The idea is that the semantic value of a general term "F" is something like a quantifier-predicate expression such as $(y)\ (\sim Fy \rightarrow y \neq a)$ which is, of course, logically equivalent to Fa. See Ganeri 1999a:118 n. 15 and Siderits 1991.

21. RNĀ (AS 58.05): "Now then, it is neither of the first two alternatives since what is intended by the word 'exclusion' is just a positive entity" (*na tāvad ādimau* {i.e., 1 and 2} *pakṣau | apohanāmnā vidhir eva vivakṣitatvāt*).

22. RNĀ (AS 58.06–58.07): "Neither does the final one follow since it is rejected on the basis of [our] awareness" (*antimo 'py* {i.e., 3} *asaṅgataḥ, pratītibādhitatvāt*).

23. RNĀ (AS 59.03): "On what basis do you proclaim exclusion to be the meaning of word?" (*katham apohaḥ śabdārtho ghuṣyate*).

Before responding to the opponent's introductory remarks, Ratnakīrti introduces an interpretation of exclusion that I will call "sequentialism." Unlike pure referentialism and pure nonreferentialism, sequentialism asserts that there are two components of semantic value: one is taken to be the direct or primary semantic value of a term, and the other is taken to be its indirect or implied value. Ratnakīrti calls supporters of the view that a positive object (*vidhi*) is the direct semantic value of a term and exclusion (*apoha*) its implied value "positivists." Supporters of the view that exclusion is the direct semantic value of a term and a positive object its implied value are called "negationists."[24] These two views are also supposed to be neutral to the ontological status of the objects.

---

24. RNĀ (AS 59.07–59.09): "But as for the view of the positivists—when there is the awareness of a cow, exclusion is ascertained subsequently, by implication, with the thought that, 'What has this nature does not have the nature of another'—and the view of the negationists—when there is the awareness of exclusion from others, what is excluded from others is ascertained by implication—both are a mess" (*yat tu goḥ pratītau na tadātmā parātmeti sāmarthyād apohaḥ paścān niścīyata iti vidhivādinām matam anyāpohapratītau vā sāmarthyād anyāpoḍho 'vadhāryata iti pratiṣedhavādinām matam / tad asundaram*).

Mookherjee (1975) has famously argued that there are three distinct versions of the theory of exclusion: negativism, positivism, and synthesism. He identifies Dignāga and Dharmakīrti as "negativists," Śāntarakṣita and Kamalaśīla as "positivists," and Jñānaśrīmitra and Ratnakīrti as "synthesists."

In support of the possibility that Dignāga and Dharmakīrti are "negativists," Kajiyama (1998:125 n. 338), following Frauwallner, quotes the following remark by Śaṅkaramiśra: "*kīrtidignāgādibhir gaur ity ayam ityādi vikalpe vidhisphuraṇaṃ nāsty evety uktam | jñānaśrīyā tu vidhisphuraṇam adhyupagamya niṣedhasphuraṇam api tatra bhavantīti svīkṛtam | yad āha tatrāpohas tadguṇatvena gamyata iti.*" The last part of this remark is from JNĀ (AP 206). And although Hayes (1988) does not directly support or intend to support this view, there are a few places in his work where this interpretation is suggested. Against this identification Katsura (1986:171 n. 6) quotes PVSV (62.24–63.16): "*ayam arthāntaravyāvṛttyā tasya vastunaḥ kaścid bhāgo gamyate | śabdo 'rthāntaranivṛttiviśiṣṭān eva bhāvān āha.*" The latter half of this verse is PS5.36d. For a discussion of PS5.36d and Dharmakīrti's interpretation of it see Pind 1999; also see Raja 1986:190 n. 11. Pind (1999) has, in my view, shown that Dignāga should not be characterized as a negativist. In addition to the passages referred to above he quotes fragments from Dignaga's SāmP that are preserved in NCV (611.21–612) in Pind 1999:318 nn. 3–8, 319, fragments from his DvāṬ that are preserved in NCV (548.25) in Pind 1999:321 n. 13, and PS5.38 in Pind 1999:322. Interestingly, Pind also cites some passages that suggest that Dignāga is a sort of sequentialist and more specifically a negationist. He refers to PS5.34 quoted at TS 965 in Pind 1999:324 and to PVABh (265.23). For a discussion of Dharmakīrti's position see Dunne 1999: chap. 3. In support of the identification of Śāntarakṣita and Kamalaśīla as "positivists" see Katsura 1986a:174. In qualified support of this view see Siderits 1986a:196.

According to Ratnakīrti, each of these views—pure referentialism, pure nonreferentialism, and sequentialism—misrepresents his own position. He explains,

> (a) By the word "exclusion" I don't mean just a positive entity alone [pure referentialism] or even the mere exclusion of others [pure nonreferentialism], but rather that the meaning of a word is a positive entity characterized by its exclusion of others.[25]
>
> (b) Neither is it the case that having become aware of a positive entity one subsequently understands exclusion by implication ["positivist" interpretation of sequentialism] nor that having becoming aware of exclusion one understands that which is excluded from others ["negationist" interpretation].[26]

He says that this is the case because,

> (c) In becoming aware of that positive entity there is, at just that time, an awareness of exclusion, in virtue of it being a characteristic of it.[27]

According to Ratnakīrti, the problem with both pure referentialism and pure nonreferentialism is that semantic value is described in terms of a single component, either a positive entity of some sort or the exclusion of others (passage *a*). As Ratnakīrti explains, however, neither of these theories accurately describes his position since, according to him, semantic value is a complex object made up of both a positive component, the "positive entity," and a negative component, "exclusion" (passage *a*). As Ratnakīrti explains (in passage *b* and passage *c*), sequentialism also does not describe his view. One problem with sequentialism is that when we think about how it is we understand what it is we understand from hearing a token utterance of a term, it is clear that our awareness is not sequential (passage *b*). As Ratnakīrti sees it then, there is no reason to accept the idea that the content of our

---

25. RNĀ (AS 59.04–59.05): *nāsmābhir apohaśabdena vidhir eva kevalo 'bhipretaḥ | nāpy anyavyāvṛttimātram | kiṃ tv anyāpohaviśiṣṭo vidhiḥ śabdānām ārthaḥ |.*

26. RNĀ (AS 59.09–59.11): *na {hi} vidhiṃ pratipadya kaścid arthāpattitaḥ paścād apoham avagacchati | apohaṃ vā pratipadyānyāpoḍham.*

27. RNĀ (AS 60.16–60.18): *tatra vidhau pratīyamāne viśeṣaṇatayā tulyakālam anyāpohapratītir iti.*

awareness should be described in terms of two sequentially understood components of meaning.

Instead of sequentialism, Ratnakīrti suggests that the object of our awareness is a single complex entity. In his view, the "positive" and "negative" components of meaning that are identified by the sequentialists jointly constitute a complex object that is itself the single semantic value of a term. As he explains (passage *c*), sequentialism is an incorrect interpretation of his view since, according to him, there is always the *simultaneous* awareness of the "positive" component of semantic value and its "negative" characteristic, exclusion. According to Ratnakīrti, the meaning of a word is a "positive entity characterized by its exclusion from others" (passage *c*). It is this positive entity that is denoted by the term "exclusion" in the exclusion theorist's slogan, "exclusion is the meaning of a word." The central task of Ratnakīrti's essay is to clarify and defend this claim by providing a description of this positive entity and its negative characteristic, exclusion.

2.2. *Words, General Nominals, and Sentences*

Although in introducing his essay Ratnakīrti pays a great deal of attention to interpreting the term "exclusion," it is interesting that he does not explicitly discuss what he means by the term "word" or how word-meaning is related to sentence-meaning. Since these issues were considered in earlier discussions of exclusion, it is instructive to briefly consider them in the context of Ratnakīrti's analysis.[28]

Like the early exclusion theorist Dignāga, Ratnakīrti focuses his attention on so-called general nominal terms.[29] General nominal terms (*jāti-śabda*) denote common noun phrases and correspond, roughly, to the class of noncomplex descriptions in English. Common examples used by Ratnakīrti are "cow," "pot," "water," and "flower."[30] It is in specifying a semantic theory for these sorts of terms that Ratnakīrti, and almost all early Sanskrit philosophers of language, focused their effort. Such terms are usually the paradigmatic

---

28. For a treatment of these "earlier discussions" see Ganeri 1999a, Hattori 1968, Hayes 1988, Scharf 1996, and Siderits 1991.

29. See Hattori 2000 and Hayes 1988.

30. It is interesting to note that this list includes both "mass terms" (e.g., water) and "sortal terms" (e.g., cow).

example of a word in classical discussions of semantics. According to Buddhist philosophers, moreover, it was not even necessary to provide an independent analysis of the semantics for other sorts of terms since, according to them, adjectives, or quality-terms (*guṇa-śabda*), such as "white," verbal-terms (*kriyā-śabda*) such as "cook," substance-words (*dravya-śabda*) such as "horned," and proper names, or arbitrary-terms (*yādṛcchā-śabda*), such as "Ḍiṭṭa" could be understood on the model of general nominal terms.[31] Thus, by discussing the semantics of general nominal terms, Buddhist philosophers understood themselves to be offering a complete semantic theory. Although Ratnakīrti does not make this point directly, and although his illustrative examples are usually general nominal terms, it is clear that he too intends his analysis to be more general. This is implied in an interesting passage in his essay where he explains,

> In fact, exclusion is understood even in a sentence such as "This road goes to Śrughna," since it is easy to find an exclusion for each and every word: it is *just* "this," relative to roads other than the intended one; it is *just* "to Śrughna," relative to undesired places other than Śrughna; it *just* "goes," because it does not end, like a mountain path; and it is *just* a "road," in virtue of excluding caravans, messengers, etc.[32]

According to Ratnakīrti, exclusion (as indicated by the use of the word "just") also applies to parts of speech such as pronouns (e.g., "this"), nouns

---

31. Ganeri 1999a:82–83, Hattori 1968:85–86 n. 129, Hayes 1988:203, and Matilal 1971:35–37 all make this same point. On this view, even so-called singular terms—i.e., proper names and definite descriptions—were taken to share the semantic properties of general nominal terms (*jāti-śabda*). Dignāga mentions these five sorts of terms at PS1.3d. See Hayes 1988:203, Hattori 1968:25 nn. 26–28, and Matilal 1971:35. Incidentally, Matilal (1971:36 n. 19), contra Hattori, suggests that Dignāga's classification has more do to with Praśastapāda's fivefold classification of predicables (*viśeṣaṇa*) than with Patañjali's classification of terms.

32. RNĀ (AS 60.11–60.14): *eṣa panthāḥ śrughnam upatiṣṭhata ity atrāpy apoho gamyata eva | prakṛtapathāntarāpekṣayaiṣa eva* (|) *śrughnapratyanīkāniṣṭasthānāpekṣayā śrughnam eva | araṇymārgavad vicchedābhāvād upatiṣṭhata eva | sārthadūtādivyavacchedena panthā eveti pratipadaṃ vyavacchedasya sulabhatvāt*. This example appears in Uddyotakara's NV *ad* NS 1.1.33. Also see JNĀ (AP 206.06–206.14) and Kajiyama 1998:57 n. 132, where he traces the use of this example to Dharmottara, PVinṬ. This passage has also been discussed in Raja 1986:186.

(e.g., "road"), verbs (e.g., "goes"), and proper names (e.g., "Śrughna") and therefore to terms other than general nominals.

In this same passage Ratnakīrti almost incidentally also introduces the issue of whether exclusion applies to sentences. He explains that exclusion does apply to sentences, since the meaning of each and every word in a sentence can be understood through exclusion. It is as if a compositional theory of semantics is assumed to explain how word-meanings are related to sentence-meaning and vice versa. Unfortunately, Ratnakīrti does not explicitly discuss these issues in greater detail.[33] What Ratnakīrti seems to mean by the term "word," then, is both individual words and linguistic expressions more generally. General nominal terms are just the paradigmatic case of linguistic expression, and a historically convenient focal point for his analysis of exclusion. There is, however, another ambiguity concerning such terms that Ratnakīrti does not discuss.

General nominal terms are usually analyzed, in Sanskrit, as comprising a stem, which is derived from a nominal base, to which an inflection is added, indicating case, number, and gender. Since classical Sanskrit very rarely uses determiners, it is not always clear whether the inflected nominal is to be thought of on the model of an indefinite (e.g., a/some cow/s) or a definite description (e.g., the cow/s). In addition, it is also open as to whether the inflected noun is to be used generically or nongenerically.[34] Ratnakīrti, like many of his Buddhist, Mīmāṃsā, and Nyāya predecessors, does not clearly distinguish between these different uses of general nominal terms. In two of his examples, "Tie (a/the) cow" and "(Some/All) cows are grazing on (the/a) bank of (the/a) river," the general term "cow" is used to refer to an unspecified individual or group of individuals.[35] The term is being used, therefore,

33. The issue of how word-meaning is related to sentence-meaning is not discussed in detail in Ratnakīrti's essay. This is because this issue is subsumed under the general theory of exclusion, which is supposed to provide an account of all linguistic expressions. The theory is able to do so in part because, according to Ratnakīrti, the implied compositional principle just is exclusion.

34. There are, then, four possible uses of general nominal terms: (1) definite generic (e.g., "The cow has a dewlap, etc."), where the term "cow" is being used to denote the class or species; (2) definite nongeneric (e.g., "The cow belongs to Kauṇḍinya"), where the term "cow" is used to denote a specific individual; (3) indefinite generic (e.g., "A cow must not be kicked"); and (4) indefinite nongeneric (e.g., "Bring a cow"), where the term "cow" is used to denote an unspecified individual. These examples are from Ganeri 1999a:84, 84 n. 7.

35. RNĀ (AS 59.19–59.20), RNĀ (AS 63.10).

indefinitely and nongenerically. In another example, "This is a cow," the general term "cow" is used to refer to a specified class, and so is being used definitely and generically. Although distinguishing between various uses of general terms can be important, it does not seem to be so for Ratnakīrti, whose analysis is supposed to apply to all terms and all of the ways in which they can be used.[36]

3. Semantic Value

In the introductory sections of his "Demonstration of Exclusion" Ratnakīrti presents three rival interpretations of exclusion, and explains how they are different from his own view. Throughout his essay Ratnakīrti returns to the issues raised by proponents of pure referentialism, pure nonreferentialism, and sequentialism, in order to further clarify and defend his own view that a single complex entity is the best way to account for semantic value. In this section and the next I will consider Ratnakīrti's analysis of this complex entity in some detail.

According to Ratnakīrti, semantic value is a "positive entity characterized by its exclusion from others." This "positive entity" is a single complex object that is constituted by two analytically separable components that are nonsequentially and simultaneously brought to awareness. These components are the positive entity itself and its "negative" characteristic, the exclusion of others. Through his analysis of these two components Ratnakīrti addresses many of the issues that were raised in section 2. He clarifies, for example, what he means by "exclusion" and explains, in some detail, how, why, and in what sense it must be a component of semantic value. He also responds to questions about what sort of object the complex positive entity is supposed to be. For example, he considers the question of whether it is an "external object" or an "internal mental image" and whether it is best described as a particular (*svalakṣaṇa*), a universal (*sāmānya*), or some sort of imposed property (*upādhi*). Following Ratnakīrti, my discussion will begin with his account of the negative component of semantic value, the exclusion of others.

36. Although this is never explicitly stated, it seems to be the case.

3.1. *The Exclusion of Others*

3.1.1. Exclusion as a Characteristic/Property

According to Ratnakīrti, the exclusion of others is a component of semantic value in the sense that it is a characteristic (*viśeṣaṇa*) or property (*dharma*) of it. He says, for example,

> When, from the word "*Indīvara*"—which is introduced as referring to a blue lotus—there is an awareness of a blue lotus, it is undeniable that there is simultaneously the appearance of blue. In the same way, when, from the word "cow"—which is introduced as referring to what has been excluded from non-cows—there is an awareness of a cow, it is undeniable that there is, at just that time, the appearance of exclusion on account of it being a *characteristic*.[37]

More simply, he says,

> Therefore, what is understood from a word has the form of a positive entity with exclusion as a *property*: just as what is understood from the word "*Puṇḍarīka*" is a lotus characterized as white.[38]

Ratnakīrti asserts that exclusion is a component of semantic value in the sense that it is a necessary "characteristic" or "property" of the proper objects of inferential/verbal awareness. His argument is that upon hearing a token utterance of a word such as "*Indīvara*" or "*Puṇḍarīka*," the content of a competent speaker's awareness will, in part, have to be analyzed in terms of the characteristics "blue" and "white." This is the case even though the color component of the content may not be noticed by the hearer (she may not be attending to its color) and is not itself explicit in either name.[39] Ratnakīrti's point is that although the proper names "*Indīvara*" and "*Puṇḍarīka*" do not

37. RNĀ (AS 59.13–59.16): *yathā nīlotpale niveśitād indīvaraśabdān nīlotpalapratītau tatkāla eva nīlimasphuraṇam anivāryaṃ tathā gośabdād apy agavāpoḍhe niveśitād gopratītau tulyakālam eva viśeṣaṇatvād apohasphuraṇam anivāryam.*

38. RNĀ (AS 60.14–60.18): *tasmād apohadharmaṇo vidhirūpasya śabdād avagatiḥ puṇḍarīkaśabdād iva śvetimaviśiṣṭasya padmasya.*

39. This issue has been discussed by Siderits (1991: chap. 4) and Bhattacharya (1986:294).

explicitly name the color of the flower to which they refer, the awareness-event that is produced in the mind of a competent speaker from hearing a token utterance of these terms must be described in terms of a lotus flower that is either blue or white. The example reveals that there can be characteristics of the content of an awareness-event that are evident neither from the word itself nor from hearing a token utterance of it. According to Ratnakīrti, exclusion is just such a characteristic or property. Like the colors "blue" and "white" it is a component of the content of inferential/verbal awareness even though it may not be noticed as being so. Thus, exclusion is said to be a component of semantic value in the sense that it is a characteristic or property of it.

3.1.2. Exclusion as a Capacity

In order to further explain what sort of a characteristic or property the exclusion of others is, Ratnakīrti compares it with a capacity (*śakti*) that sense perception has to perceive "absence." What elicits this comparison is a question about how exclusion, which is considered by many to be a kind of absence or negation, can be present in awareness-events in which there seem only to be "positive" objects. Ratnakīrti says,

> Perception's grasping a nonimplicative form of absence is just its capacity to produce a conceptual awareness of absence. And this is just like our conceptual awareness of a positive entity: its grasping absence [i.e., exclusion] is said to be nothing other than its *capacity* to produce activity that conforms to it.[40]

---

40. RNĀ (AS 59.16–59.17): *yathā pratyakṣasya prasajyarūpābhāvagrahaṇam* abhāvavikalpotpādanaśaktir eva tathā vidhivikalpānām api tadanurūpānuṣṭhānadānaśaktir evābhāvagrahaṇam abhidhīyate.* In this passage the word "*abhāva*" (absence) is being used in two different senses. In its first two occurrences, "*prasajyarūpābhāva*" (nonimplicative form of absence) and "*abhāvavikalpa*" (conceptual awareness of absence), the term is being used in the sense of "negation." *Instead of "*prasajya-rūpa-abhāva-agrahaṇam*," I read "*prasajya-rūpa-abhāva-grahaṇam*," following mss. N1, N2, N3, and the parallel passage in MTBh; see Singh 1988:88.23.

As is well known, drawing on the resources of the Sanskrit grammatical tradition, Buddhist epistemologists make a distinction between two types of negation: nonimplicative negation (*prasajya-pratiṣedha*)—e.g., "It is not the case that there is a cow in the room"/"There is no cow in the room"—and implicative negation (*paryudāsa*)—e.g., "There is a non-cow in the room." Ratnakīrti is clearly referring to this here. In the compound "*abhāvagrahaṇam*" (grasping absence), however, the word "*abhāva*" (absence) is used in the sense of "*apoha*"

An example may help explain what I think Ratnakīrti has in mind. Ratnakīrti would analyze the awareness "There is nothing on the floor" as the awareness, "The floor is characterized by the absence of all other things."[41] In this paraphrase, "the floor" is the positive component of what is perceived, and "the absence of all other things" is a negative component. This "nonimplicative" form of absence is not itself an object of sense perception, only the floor is. The question is how the "absence of all other things" can be a part of that awareness-event. What we learn from this passage is that according to Ratnakīrti its presence in awareness is, like the presence of exclusion, due to a capacity that states of awareness have to construct objects, such as the concept "absence of all other things," and to produce object-consistent activity, such as not looking for a pot on that part of the floor. While in the earlier passages exclusion was compared to a characteristic/property of an object, here it is compared with a capacity belonging to awareness itself—the capacity of producing activity that is consistent with the content (or object) of a particular awareness-event. This raises the following questions: How does exclusion produce or contribute to object-consistent activity? What, if anything, does this have to do with its being a characteristic or property of semantic value? Attending to these two questions may help to further clarify the kind of characteristic, property, and capacity that exclusion is supposed to be, by focusing our attention on the relationship between the exclusion of others, semantic value, and object-consistent activity.

It is through thinking of the exclusion of others as a capacity of awareness that its role in Ratnakīrti's analysis of semantic value becomes apparent.[42] This is because, for Ratnakīrti, exclusion is linked very closely with our ability to mentally construct objects that are not themselves directly presented to or manifest in awareness. This ability or capacity is called "determination" (*adhyavasāya*).[43] The exclusion of others is, more specifically, the mechanism

---

(exclusion). This use of the term is not uncommon. See, for example, section 2.1.2. For more on the two types of negation see Staal 1962, Galloway 1989, and Kajiyama 1998:38–39 n. 62, 77 n. 202.

41. For Dharmakīrti's discussion see HB 4*.30–28*.03.

42. The following account is reconstructed from remarks made by Ratnakīrti in a number of different places in his work. What textual support there is can be found in the footnotes, both to this chapter and to chapter 5, where the process is discussed in greater detail. Also see section 3.3 for a translation of a number of relevant passages.

43. "Determination" (*adhyavasāya*) will be discussed in greater detail in chapter 5.

through which objects are determined. The link between determination, exclusion of others, and "object-consistent activity" is that determined objects are constructed through exclusion to be the objects about which we speak and think and toward which we act. Determined objects (*adhyavaseya*) are, then, the conceptual content of all inferential/verbal awareness-events. Semantic value is merely one such determined object. Exclusion of others "produces" (or contributes to) object-consistent activity in the sense that it is the mechanism whereby the objects of conceptual awareness-events are constructed from the images that are directly present or manifest in awareness. These constructed objects are often described as "universals," in part in order to distinguish them from the "particulars"—i.e., the nonconceptual, "manifest content"—from which they are constructed. This will be defended, and discussed in much greater detail, in chapter 5. For now, however, a series of examples may help to illustrate what I think Ratnakīrti has in mind.

According to Ratnakīrti, a "universal" is an object that is *excluded* from those that do not have its form.[44] There are two types of such universals. A "vertical universal" (*ūrdhva-sāmānya*) is an object that is *excluded* from those that belong to the same class (*sajātīya-vyāvṛtta*). A "horizontal universal" (*tiryag-sāmānya*) is an object that is *excluded* from those that belong to a different class (*vijātīya-vyāvṛtta*).[45] Interestingly, it is a "token," such as an

---

44. For example RNĀ (VN 109.17): "On the other hand, the determined object is a universal, a collection of particulars, which are excluded from those that do not have their form" (*adhyavaseyaṃ tu sāmānyam, atadrūpaparāvṛttasvalakṣaṇamātrātmakam*). RNĀ (VN 109.14–109.18) is quoted and translated in chapter 5.

The term "*mātra*," which I have here translated as "collection," deserves comment. Ratnakīrti uses this term quite often, and in both ordinary and more technical contexts, as he is doing here. When the term is used "technically," I translate it differently, even though it means roughly the same thing (especially when it is used to describe "universals"). I do so in order to preserve an ambiguity between "extensional" and "intensional" interpretations of terms for "universal." So, for example, "*x-mātra*" is translated as "*x*-in-general" or "generic-*x*" (abstract objects) and also as "a collection of *x*'s." See section 3.3.

45. For an interesting discussion of these two types of universals see Kajiyama 1998:58–59, where this passage is translated with a helpful set of notes. For a discussion of these two universals in Jaina texts, numerous references, and a discussion of JNĀ (VC 166.16–166.18) and RNĀ (CAPV 143.12–143.14)—where Ratnakīrti uses the terms "horizontal" and "vertical" in this way—see Balcerowicz 1999 and Balcerowicz 2001:180–183 n. 158. In contrast to these "universals," a particular (*svalakṣaṇa*) can be thought of as an object that is excluded both from those that belong to the same class and from those that belong to a different class

individual pot, that is often cited as a typical example of a "vertical universal" and a "type," such as "being a pot"/all pots, that is cited as a typical example of a "horizontal universal." In addition to being defined in terms of an exclusion, these universals are also associated with a mode of determination, in that both vertical and horizontal universals are understood to be constructed through a determination of singularity or nondifference (*ekatva-adhyavasāya*).[46] Furthermore, both types of universals are taken to be indirectly presented to awareness, since they are conceptually constructed from the manifest content of awareness through exclusion/determination.[47] What follows is an interpretation of how such universals are constructed through exclusion.

According to Ratnakīrti, what is directly present in or manifest to awareness is an object/image p (*tad*). Let us suppose that what individuates p is a set of identity conditions **I**. It may be helpful to think of p as a bundle of these identity conditions. Interestingly, Ratnakīrti himself does not specify exactly how **I** is defined or how p is constituted—e.g., whether it consists of tropes, properties, causal characteristics, etc.[48] Like his predecessors, however, he most often writes as if **I** is defined by causal characteristics. On this reading, what identifies p is a unique set of causes and potential effects:

(*sajātīya-vijātīya-vyāvṛtta*). Ratnakīrti does not himself use this expression. It is, however, used by Mokṣākaragupta. See MTBh 21.18–21.13.

46. RNĀ (CAPV 143.12–143.14), which is quoted and translated in chapter 5.

47. For Ratnakīrti "conceptualization," "exclusion," and "determination" name the same mental process. Like his teacher, Jñānaśrīmitra, Ratnakīrti recognizes that these terms have been used historically to mean slightly different things, and he himself uses the term "determination" only when he wants to speak about how a nonmanifest object is made into an object of activity. In using expressions such as "exclusion and determination" and "modes of determination," I do not mean to imply that there is a difference between the process of exclusion and the process of determination or that there are subvarieties of determination, since there is neither a real difference between exclusion and determination nor real subvarieties of determination. Any such differences or subvarieties are best thought of as being nominal ones. For a discussion of this see McCrea and Patil 2006 and Patil 2007. See also RNĀ (CAPV 135.31–136.02): "In the same way, conceptualization, superimposition, consideration, ascertainment, etc., are also like determination in that they are manifest only in that they terminate in their own image. They don't even bring any news of an external object. Thus they are of the same nature as determination, even though there is a difference in what occasions the use of those words" (*tathā vikalpāropābhimānagrahaniścayādayo 'py adhyavasāyavat svākāraparyavasitā eva sphuranto bāhyasya vārtāmātram api na jānantīty adhyavasāyasvabhāvā eva śabdapravṛttinimittabhede 'pi*).

48. See chapter 5, section 4.2.

nothing else has exactly the same causes and potential effects that it does.[49] It may be helpful to think of **I** as a "uniqueness class," and *p* as being constituted by it. Let **S**—a subset of **I**—define a set of "selection" conditions. This set of selection conditions is the basis for the construction of a dissimilarity class non-**P**, the set of objects that do not *satisfy* **S**; that is, the set of objects that exclusion theorists like Ratnakīrti refer to as "non-*p*'s"—i.e., as "not having that form/having the form of non-that" (*atadrūpa*). By excluding the dissimilarity class non-**P** from *p*, exclusion theorists argue that a similarity class like-**P** is constructed. This similarity class, like-**P**, consists of objects that satisfy **S**; that is, it consists of all "*p*'s"—i.e., all objects that "have that form" (*tadrūpa*). Here the construction process is described in terms of an "exclusion," which may be helpfully understood as the process of constructing the complement of non-**P**. On the basis of *p*, a set of selection conditions **S**, and two processes—one of which is an exclusion—Ratnakīrti argues that a similarity class, like-**P**, can be constructed.

What is most important to notice is that the similarity class, like-**P**, can be defined in terms of the dissimilarity class, non-**P**, and a relation of "nonintersection": like-**P** is just the class of things that do not intersect with the dissimilarity class non-**P**. Notice too that *p*/**I** is a member/subset of the similarity class like-**P**. All that is directly grasped (*grāhya*) by awareness, however, is *p*/**I**. The exclusion from *p*/**I** of the dissimilarity class, non-**P**, results in the construction of a new object that can be described alternately as the nonintersection (or complement) of the dissimilarity class non-**P**; the object that is constructed by the exclusion of "non-*p*'s"; the object that has been excluded from all those that are non-*p* (*atadrūpaparāvṛtta*); or the similarity class like-**P**.[50] What exclusion does, therefore, is construct a similarity class from *p*

49. This is, of course, not the only way to account for the individuation of *p*. One could, for example, individuate *p* by referring to its properties more generally. For Dharmakīrti's "effect-centered" account of the individuation of particulars see Dunne 1999 and Katsura 1991. Dunne's (1999: chap. 4) discussion of "property-*svabhāva*" and "nature-*svabhāva*" also provides references and resources for thinking about Dharmakīrti's view of this; see esp. Dunne 1999:181–183, 187 n. 37, 198, 228–231. It is important to note that although my account makes use of set-theoretic vocabulary, it is not intended to be completely consistent with it. For a useful discussion of set-theoretic vocabulary see Chierchia and McConnell-Ginet 1990. For a discussion of what he (appropriately) calls a "trope-theoretic" account see Ganeri 2001: chap. 4.

50. See section 3.1.5 for references to the variety of ways in which Ratnakīrti describes exclusion.

and its dissimilarity class. According to Ratnakīrti, it is this sort of similarity class that is often taken to be a "reạl" (rather than just a "constructed") universal and is in fact the kind of determined object that best accounts for the content of our inferential/verbal awareness-events, including semantic value.

Suppose, for example, that *p* is a single moment in a continuum of pot-moments. In such a case, the object constructed from *p* by excluding non-**P** would be defined by the bundle of causes and potential effects that are unique to this particular moment—that is, those that belong to its uniqueness class, **I**—and those other bundles that belong to its similarity class, like-**P**. Such an object/similarity class would be the complete continuum (*santāna*) of pot-moments, of which the directly grasped object *p* would be but a single moment. In other words, the constructed object would be an individual pot. This "token" pot, or vertical universal (*ūrdhva-sāmānya*), is also said to be constructed through a determination of singularity (*ekatva-adhyavasāya*) among the moments in that pot-continuum. In this context exclusion results in the construction of a difference (*bheda*), between moment-*p* and all of the momentary objects that are not a part of its continuum, and a nondifference (*abheda*), between the directly grasped moment-*p* and all of the other moments in its continuum. Importantly, Ratnakīrti also says that by directly grasping one characteristic/property of an object, it is possible to construct the entire object, in a similar way, through a determination of singularity. He asserts, for example, that by directly grasping only its unique color, it is possible to determine the pot of which the sensed color is a characteristic.[51]

Now suppose that *p* is a single pot, and not a single moment in a pot continuum. In this case, the object constructed from *p* by excluding non-**P**—that is, by excluding non-pots—would be defined by the bundles of causes and effects that are unique to that particular pot and those that belong to all other pots. Such an object would be a similarity class, the collection of all pots, or a pot-in-general. This "type," or horizontal universal (*tiryag-sāmānya*), is constructed through a determination of singularity among all pots. More specifically, in this context exclusion constructs a difference between the directly present pot and all non-pots and a nondifference between it and all other pots. In referring to exclusion as a capacity of awareness itself, Ratnakīrti thus highlights the process through which the objects of conceptual

51. See RNĀ (KSA 73.20–73.24), which is quoted and translated in chapter 5.

awareness-events are constructed. How this process applies specifically to semantic value will be discussed in section 3.3.

3.1.3. Exclusion as Selection

In addition to identifying its indispensable role in the construction of objects, Ratnakīrti provides an additional set of reasons for why exclusion is a necessary component of semantic value. In the following passage, for example, Ratnakīrti asserts,

> If the exclusion of what is other were not present when, on the basis of a word, we become aware of an object, how could one act by avoiding what is other? When ordered to tie up a cow one might then also tie up horses and the like.[52]

Without exclusion, Ratnakīrti argues, it would not be possible to explain why a competent speaker of English will tie up just a cow and not a horse when she obeys the command, "Tie up a cow." Ratnakīrti's claim is that it is necessary for exclusion to be a component of semantic value since otherwise we would be unable to explain our ability to successfully identify the appropriate objects for our intentional activity. Imagine that a competent speaker of English is looking out over a pasture in which cows, horses, and sheep are grazing and is told, "Bring a cow." Suppose further that the content of the awareness-event that is produced in the mind of this person upon hearing the word "cow" is to be described without the negative component, exclusion. In such a case, the content of this person's awareness could be described only in terms of a positive component such as "cow." The problem with this view, Ratnakīrti suggests, is that it cannot distinguish between awareness-events in which a "cow" is the *only* positive component of awareness and awareness-events in which, for example, "cow," "horse," "sheep," and "field" are positive components. While it is clear that the person in question has an awareness-event in which "cow" is *a* component, it has not been explained either why that awareness-event has to be one in which "cow" is the *only* relevant component or how a person who is aware of cows, horses, sheep, and field could

---

52. RNĀ (AS 59.18–59.20): *{anyathā} yadi śabdād arthapratipattikāle kalito na parāpohaḥ katham anyaparihāreṇa pravṛttiḥ | tato gāṃ badhāneti codito 'śvādīn api badhnīyāt*. Also see JNĀ 206.14–206.15 and Kajiyama 1998:125.

distinguish between the appropriate positive object, cow, and other positive objects of her awareness. Without accepting that exclusion is a negative component of semantic value, Ratnakīrti claims that one cannot explain why such a person does not instead/also bring a horse. The command "Bring a cow" has a deeper structure in which the semantic value of the word "cow" does not just have a positive component "cow" but also a negative component, "and not anything other than a cow"—i.e., not a horse, sheep, or field. As Ratnakīrti sees it, exclusion is needed in such a context to account for our ability to select an appropriate object (and only an appropriate object) for our actions.[53]

3.1.4. Properties and Property-Possessors

Why Ratnakīrti insists that exclusion, which has thus far been described as a capacity (or, perhaps, "dispositional property") of *awareness*, should also be described as a characteristic or property (*dharma*) of *semantic value* becomes apparent from his description of the relation between a property and a property-possessor and a characteristic and what is characterized by it. According to Ratnakīrti, our use of the terms "property" and "property-possessor" is based upon an "*imagined* difference"[54] (*kālpānika-bheda*) and the supposed relation between a characteristic and what is characterized is based on a "conceptually constructed difference" (*parikalpita-bheda*).[55]

---

53. "Selection" is only one mode of exclusion. In my typology there are three such modes: construction, selection, and abstraction. "Construction" accounts for the role that exclusion plays in constructing individuals (*piṇḍa, vyakti, vastu, svalakṣaṇa*), groups or classes of individuals, and universals (*jāti, sāmānya*). "Abstraction" accounts for the role that exclusion plays in abstracting out various features, such as properties, from constructed objects, and for the "abstraction" of individuals from classes or tokens from types. It is important to note that these three modes of exclusion can all be described in terms of the construction of a relevant set of differences and nondifferences.

54. RNĀ (AS 62.18): "In an authoritative text, however, it is established that 'There is a basis for an imagined difference, namely, our talk of a property and property-possessor'" (*kālpānikabhedāśrayas tu dharmadharmivyavahāra iti prasādhitaṃ śāstre*). It is clear from context that Ratnakīrti endorses this passage, even though it is a quotation. See JNĀ (AP 212.26–213.01).

55. RNĀ (AS 65.10–65.12): "In 'the pot possesses a nature' there can be a characteristic/characterized relation based on a conceptually constructed difference, namely, 'The individual possesses the universal cowness.' This is because the expression 'This is a cow' arises from the experience of what is excluded from non-cows" (*svarūpavān ghaṭa ityādivat gotvajātimān*

Ratnakīrti's point is that although it may be useful to speak of semantic value as having two different components, it is more precisely a single object that is only conceptually separable into a positive entity and exclusion. Whether one locates the property "exclusion of others" in awareness or in semantic value itself becomes, therefore, a matter of conceptual convenience. After all, semantic value is nothing but an object or mental image that is constructed out of awareness itself. Moreover, due to the nondifference between properties and property-possessors, and characteristics and what is characterized by them, the term "exclusion" can denote either the property, the exclusion of others, or its possessor, the excluded object. Ratnakīrti's point about these relations also applies to other conceptual objects that are constructed through exclusion, most notably those with which we think when we reason inferentially. Ratnakīrti's claim that the relation between a property/characteristic and its possessor is "imagined" or "constructed" suggests that, for him, the theory of exclusion may also be able to account for the relations between properties and their "locations"—i.e., relations such as presence and absence—and, perhaps, pervasion.[56]

Ratnakīrti's point about the relation between exclusion and what is excluded is also emphasized in another passage in which he responds to the objection that it is wrong to suppose that semantic value can be described as a complex entity consisting of both a positive and negative component.

> Once the use of the word "cow" has been agreed upon, it is right to refer to whatever remains with the word "non-cow." Furthermore, since there isn't mutual exclusion, there is neither a contradiction between what is excluded from others and its exclusion from others nor the destruction of the characteristic/characterized-relation. This is because, like a patch of ground and the absence of a pot, both share a locus. For it is well known to even a child that there is a contradiction between a positive entity and an absence/negation of itself, but not between it and the absence/negation of something else.[57]

---

piṇḍa iti parikalpitaṃ bhedam upādāya viśeṣaṇaviśeṣyabhāvasyeṣṭatvād {agovyāvṛttānubhavabhāvitvād gaur ayam iti vyavahārasya}). See JNĀ (AP 225.01–225.09).

56. This issue is discussed in chapter 5.

57. Two characteristics, e.g., "patch of ground" and "absence of pot," are said to "share the same locus" (*sāmānādhikaraṇya*), e.g., the awareness, "empty patch of ground," when they are co-referential.

The objection implicit in this passage is that conceptual content cannot be described as a positive entity characterized by its exclusion from others, since it is illogical to suppose that a single object of awareness can be constituted by both a positive component and a negative component that is its negation. Ratnakīrti's response is that, in his view, there isn't *really* a difference between the two components at all. They are nondifferent from one another, just as our positive awareness of an empty patch of ground is (as discussed earlier) nondifferent from our negative awareness of the absence of a pot there. Furthermore, the conceptually constructed pair of components in the awareness of, for example, "patch of ground" and "absence of a pot" are conceptually compatible with one another, and there is not an internal contradiction in supposing that semantic value is jointly constituted by these two nondifferent components.[58] The positive component is not, in Ratnakīrti's view, characterized by a negation of itself, but rather by the negation/exclusion of others. Again, as this discussion suggests, the relation between the two components is itself conceptually constructed through the exclusion process.

3.1.5. Descriptions of Exclusion

Before turning to Ratnakīrti's account of the "positive" component of semantic value, it may be helpful to briefly survey the variety of different expressions he uses to refer to exclusion. Attention to these expressions is important since they provide a somewhat different perspective from which to consider what Ratnakīrti means by the "exclusion of others."

Ratnakīrti uses at least ten different expressions to describe "exclusion of others" (*anyāpoha*).[59] Each of these expressions is itself a complex expression consisting of a term that denotes the process of excluding and one which denotes that which is excluded—that is, the dissimilarity class. In the

---

RNĀ (AS 60.08–60.11): *abhimate ca gośabdapravṛttāv agośabdena śeṣasyāpy abhidhānam ucitam | na cānyāpoḍhānyāpohayor virodho viśeṣyaviśeṣaṇabhāvakṣatir vā parasparavyavacchedābhāvāt | sāmānādhikaraṇyasadbhāvāt | bhūtalaghaṭābhāvavat | svābhāvena hi [vidher]** virodho na parābhāvenety ābālaprasiddham*. **On the basis of JNĀ (AP 206.01), I have inserted "*vidher*," which does not appear in the RNĀ passage.

58. Siderits (1991: chap. 4) also discusses this issue.

59. *anyāpoha* (AP 59.05), *para-apoha* (AP 59.19), *anya-parihāra* (AP 59.19), *atajjātīya-parāvṛtta* (AP 59.24), *atad-vyāvṛtti* (AP 59.25), *anya-vyāvṛtta* (AP 59.29), *vijātīya-vyāvṛtta* (AP 59.26), *atadrūpa-parāvṛtta* (AP 60.20), *viṣayāntara-parihāreṇa* (AP 65.26), *anya-abhāva* (AP 66.05).

phrase "exclusion of others," for example, the word "exclusion" denotes the process or capacity of excluding, while the word "others" denotes of what or from what there is exclusion. Ratnakīrti uses five different terms to denote the process of excluding: "exclusion" (*apoha*), "taking away" (*parihāra*), "separating out" (*vyāvṛtti*), "covering up" (*āvṛtti*), and "absence" (*abhāva*).[60] These terms are used synonymously and, with the exception of "absence," are consistently used to refer to exclusion. What these expressions suggest is that exclusion is the capacity of differentiating or selecting between elements in what could be multi-entitied awareness-events.[61] The elements from which there is exclusion are also described by Ratnakīrti in a number of different ways. He says, for example, that these entities are: "other than" (*anya*), "different from" (*para*), "non-that" (*atad*), those that "belong to a class which is non-that" (*atajjātīya*), those that "belong to a different class" (*vijātīya*), "other objects" (*viṣayāntara*), or those that "have the form of non-that" (*atadrūpa*).[62] What these expressions help clarify is the sense in which the elements from which there is exclusion are different or other; they are "different" or "other" in the sense that they have a different form or belong to a different class.[63] It is important to note that both terms in the complex expressions that Ratnakīrti uses to refer to the exclusion of others convey an idea of difference. In an important sense, exclusion of others is simply the construction of a relevant difference through exclusion.

According to Ratnakīrti, the content of inferential/verbal awareness-events is a conceptually complex entity constituted by two analytically separable components that are, in fact, nondifferent from each other. In providing a description of the semantic value of a term, however, it is necessary to make a conceptual distinction between a positive and a negative component, since without a conceptually distinct and negative component such as exclusion it

---

60. RNĀ (AS 59.05), RNĀ (AS 59.29), RNĀ (AS 59.24), RNĀ (AS 66.05).

61. It is not the case that every state of awareness needs to be understood as being "multi-entitied" in the manner described above. A state of awareness could be described, for example, as containing only one entity, e.g., a single cow. In such a case, one of the other two modes of exclusion (e.g., construction) would be appealed to in order to explain why exclusion must be a component of conceptual content.

62. RNĀ (AS 59.05), RNĀ (AS 59.19), RNĀ (AS 59.25), RNĀ (AS 59.24), RNĀ (AS 59.26), RNĀ (AS 65.26), RNĀ (AS 66.08).

63. Although it is not evident from the expressions themselves, the "differences" in form and class are mentally constructed in accordance with a particular set of expectations.

would not be possible, in Ratnakīrti's view, to explain how we are able to pick out, differentiate, and therefore act upon the relevant object in what could be complex awareness-events. Exclusion is the capacity or characteristic feature of conceptual content that constructs, selects, and determines the appropriate, and only the appropriate, intentional object. Moreover, since it is nondifferent from the positive component, the term "exclusion" denotes both the capacity to exclude—i.e., the exclusion of others—and the excluded object—i.e., that which is excluded from others. As Ratnakīrti explains in the introductory sections of his essay, his view cannot be classified as a version of either pure referentialism, pure nonreferentialism, or sequentialism.

3.2. *Positive Entity*

While Ratnakīrti's descriptions of exclusion as a property, characteristic, and capacity focus on an "active" feature of inferential/verbal awareness-events, his descriptions of exclusion as a positive entity focus on the more "passive" object that is actively constructed by these awareness-events through the exclusion of others. I have argued that these objects can be thought of as "constructed universals" or "similarity classes." In what follows, I want to consider what Ratnakīrti himself says about these objects and, more specifically, why he insists that they are both internal and external objects and why he thinks they can be neither particulars nor real universals.

3.2.1. Both Internal and External

Ratnakīrti's attention to how semantic value is constructed suggests that he might classify his theory as an ideational theory of meaning—that is, as a theory according to which meanings are just "in the head."[64] Interestingly, however, Ratnakīrti argues that the complex positive entity that he takes semantic value to be should be described as *both* an internal and an external object.[65] He explains, for example, that,

---

64. This phrase is from Putnam's famous remark, "Cut the pie any way you like it, meanings just ain't in the head." See Putnam 1975:144 for his statement of semantic externalism and Burge 1979 for an extension of Putnam's thesis. Stalnaker 1999: chap. 9 has a nice discussion of what is, and what is not, "in the head."

65. Ratnakīrti does not use the word "*āntara*" (internal) to refer to this object. He uses the word "*buddhyākāra*" (mental image), which in this context clearly refers to an internal

> What is meant by the word "positive entity" is, on the basis of determination, an external object excluded from those that do not have its form and, on the basis of manifestation, a mental image.[66]

In this passage Ratnakīrti clearly says that the complex positive entity that he identifies with semantic value is both an internal mental image—that is, an object that we, on the basis of its being manifest, take to be present in awareness, such as an exclusion—and an external object—that is, an object that we, on the basis of its being determined, take to be present in the external world, such as a cow.[67] In addition to the determination of "singularity," Ratnakīrti's analysis also depends upon a determination of "externality."[68] It is through this mode of determination that what are really internal mental images appear as if they are objects in the external world. These determined-to-be-external objects are the sorts of "external objects" that Ratnakīrti is referring to in this passage.[69] The question of whether an object of awareness is "internal" or "external" depends, therefore, upon whether we take it to be manifest in our awareness or externally determined by it. It is, then, how an object is present in awareness that determines whether it is properly described as an "internal" or an "external" one.[70] In a passage near the end of his essay, Ratnakīrti explains the

---

object. The word "*āntara*" (internal) is, however, used in a similar context by Jñānaśrīmitra. By the term "internal" I simply mean "mind-dependent."

66. RNĀ (AS 60.20–60.21): *vidhiśabdena ca yathādhyavasāyam atadrūpaparāvṛtto bāhyo 'rtho 'bhimato yathāpratibhāsaṃ buddhyākāraś ca.*

67. "Manifestation" (*pratibhāsa*) and "determination" (*adhyavasāya*) will both be discussed in much greater detail in chapter 5. For Jñānaśrīmitra's discussion of this see McCrea and Patil 2006:341–345.

68. This mode of determination should not be confused with Dharmottara's "superimposition theory," which Jñānaśrīmitra criticizes in his AP and Ratnakīrti dismisses at RNĀ (AS 65.23–65.24). One relevant difference between Dharmottara and Jñānaśrīmitra/Ratnakīrti's theories is that, for Dharmottara, the semantic value of a word comprises a superimposed liminal object that is neither a mental image nor an external object, since such an object is the only kind of thing that could belong to both the internal mental image that is produced upon hearing the word and the real external objects that we take that word to refer to. See Hattori 2006:63–68 for an insightful characterization of Dharmottara's view, based on passages from Jayanta Bhaṭṭa's NM.

69. RNĀ (AS 60.06), see passage *c*, which is quoted and translated above.

70. For more on the relativization of internality and externality see chapter 5, and McCrea and Patil 2006:338–340.

significance of this to the meaning of words and semantic value. He writes,

> A positive entity is definitely the meaning of a word. Furthermore, what is meant is both an external object and a mental image. Among these, there is neither affirmation nor negation of a mental image, either ultimately or conventionally, since it is known through reflexive awareness and is not determined. Neither is there the affirmation or negation of an external object, ultimately, since it does not appear in verbal awareness. Therefore, all things are ultimately inexpressible, since there is the absence of either manifestation or determination. It is for just this reason that there is only the affirmation or negation of an external object, conventionally. If this were not so, there would be the unwanted consequence of not being able to act at all.[71]

Initially, this passage may appear to contradict the one just discussed, since here Ratnakīrti seems to deny that we can ever make positive or negative statements about mental images. Ratnakīrti suggests that insofar as they are directly present in awareness, mental images are internal-particulars and are therefore perceptible through reflexive awareness. Since they are the manifest content of a perceptual awareness-event, they cannot be the conceptual objects of an inferential/verbal awareness-event.[72] According to Ratnakīrti, however, not all mental objects/images are *directly* present in awareness. As described earlier, mental objects/images can also be *indirectly* present, as a result of being constructed and determined.

In this passage Ratnakīrti argues that nondetermined mental images cannot be the objects about which we speak. They cannot be such objects, ultimately, since they are really just the momentary objects of reflexive-

---

71. RNĀ (AS 65.15–65.22): *{tad evaṃ} vidhir eva śabdārthaḥ | sa ca bāhyo 'rtho buddhyākāraś ca vivakṣitaḥ | tatra na buddhyākārasya tattvataḥ saṃvṛtyā vā vidhiniṣedhau svasaṃvedanapratyakṣagamyatvād anadhyavasāyāc ca | nāpi tattvato bāhyasyāpi vidhiniṣedhau tasya śābde pratyaye 'pratibhāsanāt | ata eva sarvadharmāṇāṃ tattvato anabhilāpyatvaṃ pratibhāsādhyavasāyābhāvāt | tasmād bāhyasyaiva sāṃvṛtau vidhiniṣedhau | anyathā saṃvyavahārahāniprasaṅgāt*. See JNĀ (AP 230.19–230.27). For an interesting discussion of "*sāṃvrta*" at PV 2.3 and "*saṃvṛtiḥ*" at PV 1.68–1.69 see Katsura 1993:67. For PVSV ad PV 1.68–1.69 see Dunne 1999:394.

72. See chapter 5.

awareness, and so are not available to inferential/verbal awareness. They cannot be such objects, conventionally, since they are not determined, and it is only through exclusion/determination that semantic value is constructed and presented to us as the kind of object with respect to which we can act. For Ratnakīrti, nondetermined mental images are not *actionable* by us. In this passage Ratnakīrti also explains why external objects cannot ultimately be the objects about which we speak. He argues that insofar as they are "external" to awareness—that is, determined—such objects are not present in that awareness-event and so cannot themselves really be the objects of it. Such objects thus fail to be *available* to inferential/verbal awareness. They fail what I will call the "epistemological constraint" on semantic value. Ratnakīrti concludes, therefore, that no nondetermined internal or external objects can be the objects of inferential/verbal awareness-events. According to him, all entities are ultimately "inexpressible."[73]

Despite this, however, Ratnakīrti argues that we can take determined external objects to be semantic value, conventionally. Without such a view, Ratnakīrti argues, it would be impossible to account for our ability to successfully speak, think about, or interact with objects in the "external" world. And although it is not made explicit in this passage, Ratnakīrti also believes that we can take determined internal objects to be the objects of inferential/verbal awareness-events, conventionally. Without such a view, it would be impossible to account for our ability to successfully speak and think about "internal" objects such as mental representations, concepts, or ideas. According to Ratnakīrti, then, his version of the theory of exclusion is neither a purely realist nor a purely ideational theory of meaning. Semantic value is a determined object regardless of whether it is taken to be an "external" or an "internal" one. Moreover, we are entitled to take a semantic value to be a determined object only "conventionally," since such objects are only *actionable* and not also *available*. The reason why neither a determined object nor an internal mental image are "ultimately" semantic value for Ratnakīrti is that neither can be both *actionable* and *available*.[74]

73. Interestingly, this conclusion seems to be much more important to Jñānaśrīmitra's discussion of exclusion. See Katsura 1986a:176 for a discussion of JNĀ (AP 231.21–231.22), where PVSV 92.23–93.01 is quoted. See also chapter 6.

74. This will be discussed in greater detail in chapter 5.

3.2.2. Neither Particular Nor Universal

Ratnakīrti continues his analysis of the positive component of semantic value by arguing that on neither description—i.e., neither as an "internal" nor an "external" object—and from neither perspective—i.e., neither conventionally nor ultimately—should this object be described as either a sensible-particular or a real universal.[75] What is specifically at issue in this discussion is the sort of object that this positive external or internal entity *cannot* be.

PROBLEMS WITH PARTICULARS

According to Ratnakīrti, neither the determined external nor the determined internal objects about which we speak can be sensible-particulars, since sensible-particulars are not manifest in conceptual awareness-events such as inferential/verbal awareness. Ratnakīrti begins his argument by explaining why the "external" objects about which we conventionally speak cannot be sensible-particulars. He argues,

> Among these, an external object is conditionally adopted to be what is expressed by a word only on the basis of determination, and not through the appearance of a particular. This is because a particular does not appear there as it does in perception—fixed with respect to place, time, and condition, and clearly manifest.[76]

---

75. To this list Ratnakīrti also adds "imposed properties" (*upādhi*). His discussion of these objects will not be considered here. It is also important to note that Ratnakīrti often uses the terms "sensible-particular" (*svalakṣaṇa*) and "universal" (*sāmānya*) to refer to semantic value and conceptual content. When he does so, however, he has his own interpretation of these terms in mind. In arguing against the view that sensible-particulars (*svalakṣaṇa*) or real universals (*sāmānya*) are the proper objects of inferential/verbal awareness he is assuming his opponents' understanding of these terms. On my use of the term, "sensible-particular" (*svalakṣaṇa*) refers to an object that can be perceived by sense perception and/or reflexive awareness. A "real universal" refers to a universal that is neither constructed nor mind-dependent.

76. RNĀ (AS 60.21–60.23): *tatra bāhyo 'rtho 'dhyavasāyād eva śabdavācyo vyavasthāpyate | na svalakṣaṇaparisphūrtyā | pratyakṣavad deśakālāvasthāniyatapravyaktasvalakṣaṇāsphuraṇāt.* See also JNĀ (AP 208.11–208.12). This passage is also used by Mokṣākaragupta. For a discussion of the history of "fixed with respect to place, time, etc." see Yoshimizu (forthcoming). For the variety of contexts in which this idea appears see the references in Kajiyama 1998:125.

It is only on the basis of determination that an external object can be semantic value. Ratnakīrti asserts that such determined-to-be-external objects cannot be sensible-particulars, since such objects do not appear in awareness-events in the same way that sensible-particulars do. According to him, this difference in phenomenology—that is, in what it is like for us to be aware of them—is the result of the fact that two different sorts of objects are appearing. In perceptual awareness-events, what appears is a sensible-particular that is vivid or clear (*spaṣṭa*) in its appearance, while in inferential/verbal awareness-events the objects that appear are less vivid and unclear (*aspaṣṭa*).[77] The clarity in perceptual awareness-events is said to result in part from the unique spatial, temporal, and structural specificity (*deśa-kāla-avasthā-niyata*) of the object of perception. The relative lack of clarity in inferential/verbal awareness-events is similarly due to the way its object appears.

An opponent argues, however, that Ratnakīrti's account of this asymmetry need not be the case, since perceptual and inferential/verbal awareness-events could merely present the same object differently. The proper explanation of the asymmetry noted by Ratnakīrti is, according to the opponent, that "there is a difference in the manifest-appearance of one and the same thing, because of a difference in the modes of awareness—one is sensory and the other is linguistic."[78] Ratnakīrti responds to this possibility by asserting that this is not the case, "since a difference between things is nothing but a difference in their forms and a difference in their forms in nothing but a difference in their manifest-appearance."[79] The opponent's argument is based on the idea that the difference between "clear" and "unclear" manifestations is due to the ways in which perception and inferential/verbal awareness-events present the same thing, and not because there is a difference in the thing presented. Ratnakīrti's response is based on his conviction that the difference in manifestations, correctly noted by the opponent, must be associated with and understood in terms of a difference in the things themselves. In the passage quoted above, Ratnakīrti presents a very strong formulation of this view by asserting that a difference in manifestations entails that there is a difference in things. The opponent immediately objects to Ratnakīrti's

---

77. See RNĀ (AS 61.03), quoted earlier.

78. RNĀ (AS 60.26): *indriyaśabdasvabhāvopāyabhedād ekasyaivārthasya pratibhāsabhedaḥ*. See also JNĀ (AP 208.19).

79. RNĀ (AS 61.01): *na hi svarūpabhedād aparo vastubhedaḥ | na ca pratibhāsabhedād aparaḥ svarūpabhedaḥ*. See also JNĀ (AP 208.24–209.01).

formulation by providing what he takes to be a counterexample. He points out that

> Even though in the case of one and the same tree, there is a difference between the clear manifest-appearance of someone standing nearby and the unclear manifest-appearance of someone standing far away, nevertheless there isn't a difference in the tree.[80]

Ratnakīrti responds by qualifying his earlier remarks,

> We don't say that a difference in manifest-appearance is invariably associated with different things, but rather that it is invariably associated with not having the same *object*. Therefore, when a difference in manifest-appearance is accompanied by a difference in pragmatic effect, etc., there are different *things*, such as a pot and a piece of cloth. If not, one invariably rejects there being a single object.[81]

Ratnakīrti's claim is that a difference in manifest-appearance is necessarily related to the absence of a single "object." In the proposed counterexample, therefore, the different manifestations "clear" and "unclear" necessarily imply that the two persons do not have the same object of awareness. What Ratnakīrti's qualifying remarks explain is that it is only when different manifestations are accompanied by a difference in their pragmatic effects that they are invariably associated with different things. Since the manifestations "clear" and "unclear" do not, in Ratnakīrti's example, lead the two people to different pragmatic results—they reach the same tree, for example—it is proper to conclude that the two people are seeing the same *thing*, but are not aware of the same *object*—that is, mental image. A difference in manifestations entails the absence of a single object of awareness (*ekaviṣayatva-abhāva*) but not the presence of more than one thing.

---

80. RNĀ (AS 61.03–61.04): *dūrāsannadeśavartinoḥ puruṣayor ekatra śākhini spaṣṭāspaṣṭapratibhāsabhede 'pi na śākhibheda {iti cet}*. See also JNĀ (AP 209.02).

81. RNĀ (AS 61.04–61.05): *na brūmaḥ pratibhāsabhedo bhinnavastuniyataḥ kintv ekaviṣayatvābhāvaniyata iti tato yatrārthakriyābhedādisacivaḥ pratibhāsabhedas tatra vastubhedo ghaṭapaṭavat* | anyatra punar niyamena ekaviṣayatāṃ pariharati.* *Following JNĀ (AP 209.13), I read "*ghaṭapaṭavat*" instead of the printed "*ghaṭavat*." JNĀ (AP 209.05–06, 209.12–13), JNĀ (AP 209.13–209.14).

Ratnakīrti is trying to show that a sensible-particular—the tree, in his example—cannot be the determined object of inferential/verbal awareness-events, since phenomenal differences between perceptual and inferential/verbal awareness-events entail that the objects of the awareness-events are different. Since a difference in manifestations only implies that the objects of awareness are different, and does not preclude the possibility that these different objects are associated with the same thing, Ratnakīrti's view is also consistent with the intuition behind the opponent's example. For Ratnakīrti then, it is on the basis of phenomenal differences between perceptual and inferential/verbal awareness-events that the objects of perception—sensible-particulars—cannot be the complex positive object that he takes semantic value to be. This suggests what I will refer to as a "phenomenal constraint" on semantic value.

A second set of arguments that Ratnakīrti uses to show that sensible-particulars cannot be semantic value is based upon what I am calling "The Argument from Indifference."[82] Ratnakīrti states the argument as follows,

> Furthermore, if a thing having the nature of a sensible-particular were expressed by a word, positive and negative statements about it would be irrelevant, since we would be aware of it in its entirety.[83] For if it really exists, it's pointless to say "It exists" and it is wrong to say "It does not exist." But if it reallv does not exist, it is pointless to say "It does not exist" and it is wrong to say "It exists." But we do use the words "It exists." Therefore, a verbal manifestation, being indifferent to cases where an external object exists and to where it does not, cannot have that as its object.[84]

Suppose that the semantic value of "tree" is a sensible-particular, e.g., a tree. Given this view, the object of the awareness-event produced in the mind of a

82. As Kajiyama (1998) notes, versions of this argument can be found in numerous Buddhist and Nyāya works. See, for example, PV 4.225–226, PVin 2.14–27, AP-D, NVTṬ 681.11 *ad* NS 2.2.66, JNĀ (AP 211.01–213.09), and MTBh 54.03–54.14. The JNĀ version is discussed in Katsura 1986a and both the JNĀ and PV4 versions are discussed in Siderits 1991: chap. 4.

83. JNĀ (AP 219.03–04).

84. RNĀ (AS 61.10–61.14): *kiṃ ca svalakṣaṇātmani vastuni vācye sarvātmanā pratipatter vidhiniṣedhayor ayogaḥ | tasya hi sadbhāve 'stīti vyarthaṃ nāstīty asamartham | asadbhāve tu nāstīti vyartham astīty asamartham | asti cāstyādipadaprayogaḥ | tasmāc chābdapratibhāsasya bāhyārthabhāvābhāvasādhāraṇyaṃ na tadviṣayatāṃ kṣamate*. See also JNĀ (AP 211.01–211.06).

competent speaker of English upon hearing the word "tree" would be a tree. Ratnakīrti's argument against this view is that this realist version of pure referentialism cannot account for an indisputable fact about the proper objects of inferential/verbal awareness, namely, that they are "indifferent to" or "the common objects of" both positive and negative existential statements. We may say about a particular tree, for example, both that "The tree exists" and that "The tree does not exist." The "tree" that we have in mind is, therefore, indifferent to claims about its existence: it is the same "tree" regardless of whether we say "It exists" or "It does not exist." Ratnakīrti's point is that if the semantic value of the term "tree" were an external tree, such as a presently existing tree, it would be redundant, and therefore pointless to say "The tree exists," since this would be equivalent to asserting that "The presently-existing-tree exists." It would also be incorrect to say "The tree does not exist," since this would be equivalent to asserting that "The presently-existing-tree does not exist."

Unlike the view being considered, Ratnakīrti's view is able to accommodate this fact about our use of language since for him it is only a determined particular, and not a sensible-particular, that is the object of inferential/verbal awareness.[85] Ratnakīrti's argument is also applicable to ideational versions of pure referentialism, since insofar as a mental image is an internal particular, it too is an object of perception, i.e., reflexive awareness. And insofar as it is an object of perception, we are "aware of it in its entirety."[86] As a result, such an object would not be indifferent to statements in which, for example, properties are predicated of it. If, for example, the internal particular has property *P*, the positive statement "It has *P*" would be redundant and the negative statement "It does not have *P*" would be incorrect.[87] If it does not have property *P*, the positive statement "It has *P*" would be incorrect and the negative statement "It does not have *P*" would be redundant. The objects of inferential/verbal awareness, however, are indifferent to such statements: we can ask, for example, whether the tree about which I am thinking or speaking is green,

---

85. Ratnakīrti's discussion includes much more than I have discussed here. For example, he offers possible strategies that his opponents could use to show that their views could account for indifference. See RNĀ (AS 61.10–63.09).

86. See RNĀ (AS 61.10–61.14), quoted earlier.

87. The JNĀ (AP 205.21–205.23, 219.03–219.27) version of this argument explicitly extends this to properties. While Ratnakīrti would clearly agree with what Jñānaśrīmitra has to say, he chooses not to discuss the issue in this way. See Siderits 1991: chap. 4.

tall, or exists. Ratnakīrti concludes from this that the proper objects of inferential/verbal awareness-events cannot be manifest internal-particulars. According to him, only determined particulars—whether "internal" or "external"—can be the objects of inferential/verbal awareness-events.[88] Only such objects meet what I will call the "representational constraint" on semantic value.

According to Ratnakīrti, then, neither internal nor external sensible-particulars can be the objects of inferential/verbal awareness-events. Since such objects are not determined, they are not the kinds of objects that we can act upon, and they thus fail the "phenomenal constraint" on semantic value. Since, unlike the proper objects of such states of awareness, they are not indifferent to the kinds of positive and negative statements that we routinely make about them, they also fail the "representational constraint."

PROBLEMS WITH UNIVERSALS

In addition to particulars, Ratnakīrti also argues that real universals do not appear in inferential/verbal awareness-events and therefore cannot be semantic value.[89] Through one set of arguments, Ratnakīrti tries to show that neither perception nor inference can establish that real universals are the proper objects of any awareness-event. These arguments focus on showing why his opponent's positive arguments in support of real universals fail. Although these arguments are interesting and important to Ratnakīrti's overall argument for exclusion, they do not help us to directly understand Ratnakīrti's own position and I have chosen not to discuss them here.[90]

Through a second set of arguments, however, Ratnakīrti explains how his view can account for features of semantic value that his opponents think can be explained only by real universals. He does so by further describing the complex object that he takes semantic value to be. Earlier I analyzed this object as a "similarity class" or "constructed universal." Through this second set of arguments, Ratnakīrti wants to show: that (1) this complex object has all of the explanatory power mistakenly attributed to real universals, and that (2) unlike a real universal, which cannot be proven by a well-functioning instrument of awareness, his complex object can be established through inferential reasoning. I will consider (1) in section 3.3 and (2) in section 4.

---

88. For Mokṣākaragupta's treatment of this issue see Kajiyama 1998:126. For an excellent discussion of "universal properties" in Sanskrit philosophy see Chakrabarti 2005b:580–587.

89. For Mokṣākaragupta's treatment of this issue see MTBh 54.15–57.06.

90. See RNĀ (AS 63.23–65.24) in Patil (forthcoming, b).

3.3. *Things-in-General*

Ratnakīrti's account of the complex positive entity that he takes semantic value to be can be reconstructed from the following four passages,

> (a) From the word "cow" in the sentence "There are cows grazing on the far bank of the river," dewlap, horns, tail, and the like appear, together with the form of the speech-sounds [that make up the word "cow"], as if "lumped together" because of inattention to differences between things that belong to the same class. And that [conglomeration of dewlap, horns, and tail] is definitely not a universal. . . . However, that very collection of dewlap, horns, and the like, although utterly distinct from every particular, is called a "universal" when it is made one with a particular.[91] Since an external object like that is not found, it is definitely erroneous, like the appearance of a net of hair [for someone with floaters].[92]
>
> (b) Everything that is verbally expressive has as its object a thing-in-general that is determined and excluded from those that do not have its form. . . .[93]
>
> (c) It is a conceptually constructed mental image that is externally determined to be as if shared by all such individuals . . .[94]
>
> (d) . . . enhanced by the co-operating cause of our memory of a previously seen individual, the total causal complex produces a specific awareness and brings about a conceptual awareness of a "universal" that is without an object.[95]

---

91. That is to say, when we link up this generic image with what we take to be in front of us, e.g., an individual cow. JNĀ (AP 220.07–220.08).

92. RNĀ (AS 63.10–63.16): *saritaḥ pāre gāvaś carantīti gavādiśabdāt sāsnāśṛṅgalāṅgūlādayo 'kṣarākāraparikaritāḥ sajātīyabhedāparāmarśanāt sampiṇḍitaprāyāḥ pratibhāsante | na ca tad eva sāmānyam | . . . | tad eva ca sāsnāśṛṅgādimātram akhilavyaktāv atyantavilakṣaṇam api svalakṣaṇenaikīkriyamāṇaṃ sāmānyam ity ucyate tādṛśasya bāhyasyāprāpter bhrāntir evāsau keśapratibhāsavat.* See also JNĀ (220.13–220.15).

93. RNĀ (AS 66.08–66.09): *{atra prayogaḥ |} yad vācakaṃ tat sarvam adhyavasitātadrūpaparāvṛttavastumātragocaraṃ {yatheha kūpe jalam iti vacanam}*. For other references to this example see Krasser 1991:57.

94. RNĀ (AS 60.06): *{tasmād} ekapiṇḍadarśanapūrvako yaḥ sarvavyaktisādhāraṇa iva bahiradhyasto vikalpabuddhyākaras {tatrāyaṃ gaur iti saṃketakaraṇe na itaretarāśrayadoṣaḥ}.*

95. RNĀ (AS 63.20–63.21): *{yataḥ} pūrvapiṇḍadarśanasmaraṇasahakāriṇātiricyamānaviśeṣapratyayajanikā sāmagrī nirviṣayaṃ sāmānyavikalpam utpādayati.* See also JNĀ (AP 221.11–221.14).

When taken together, these passages suggest the following: what a competent speaker of English understands from hearing a token utterance of a term such as "cow" is a "thing-in-general that is determined and excluded from those that do not have its form" (passage *b*). This object is a nonspecific collection (or bundle) of components that is constructed through exclusion (passage *a*). It is this "thing-in-general" that was described in section 2 as a "constructed universal" and "similarity class," and here is identified with semantic value.[96]

Since in these passages Ratnakīrti describes how this object is constructed, it will be useful to compare his analysis with my account of "Exclusion as Mental Construction" in section 3.1.2. In the above passages Ratnakīrti suggests that upon hearing a token utterance of the term "cow" a competent speaker of English first recalls an object that was previously, and invariably, associated with an earlier use of the term (passage *c* and passage *d*). The recollection of this previously observed individual is said to be a "co-operating cause" in the total causal complex that brings about the construction of the object. Insofar as this remembered individual is a "mental image," it is a mental particular that has its own unique causal history, i.e., no other particular has exactly the same set of causes and potential effects that it does. In virtue of being such a particular it can function as a basis for exclusion. It is functionally equivalent to what I earlier referred to as "*p*." Insofar as it can be taken to be constituted by components, however, it is also a collection. More specifically, this recalled object can be described as a specific collection of components that jointly constitute the object in question—that is, what I earlier referred to as "**I**." For a recalled cow, for example, the components are a specific set of dewlap, horns, and tail, etc. By ignoring the differences between a specific collection of these components (*p*) and other such collections (the dissimilarity class, non-**P**), a nonspecific

96. Although the term "semantic value" (*vācya*) is not explicitly used in these passages, it is clear from the context that this is what he is referring to. Elsewhere Ratnakīrti describes this collection as "an object that is characterized by its exclusion from others and excluded from those that belong to a different class" (*anyābhāva-viśiṣṭo vijātīyavyāvṛtto 'rthaḥ*); "a thing-in-general that is determined and excluded from those that belong to a different class" (*adhyavasita-vijātīyavyāvṛtta-vastumātra*); and "a determined external object" (*adhyavasita-bāhya-viśayatvam*). See RNĀ (AS 66.05–66.06), RNĀ (AS 66.13), and RNĀ (AS 66.20). A general term such as "cow" expresses the fact that in a particular context a specific conglomeration of components brings about a single set of effects, as a result of those components causally supporting each other in virtue of their "proximity."

collection or thing-in-general (the similarity class, like-**P**) is constructed (passage *a*).[97]

Elsewhere Ratnakīrti describes this process as the exclusion of a specific collection from those that belong to a different class.[98] It is clear, therefore, that the construction in question, the ignoring of relevant differences, is nothing other than exclusion. It is this nonspecific collection that is mistakenly taken by some to be a real universal, and is unconsciously associated with a group of particulars in which it is mistakenly thought to be instantiated. According to Ratnakīrti, this object is a positive entity that is neither a real particular nor a real universal. It is a thing-in-general that is constructed through its essential characteristic, exclusion, and is determined to be equivalent to semantic value. According to Ratnakīrti, it is this complex positive entity that best describes what is understood from hearing a token utterance of a term.

Following his description of this positive entity, Ratnakīrti defends his view from those who insist that real universals (and not just constructed ones) are necessary for explaining certain obvious and otherwise inexplicable features of verbally produced awareness-events. His strategy is to show that some of his opponents' criticism of his position are equally applicable to their own,[99] that, given their own view, real universals are unnecessary,[100] that real universals cannot be proven by either perception or inference,[101] and that the complex positive entity that he takes semantic value to be has all of the explanatory power mistakenly thought to belong exclusively to real universals. It is this final set of arguments that I will consider in what follows.

There are two features of verbally produced awareness-events that Ratnakīrti wants to show can be explained without relying upon real universals: their "specificity" and their "generality."[102] According to Ratnakīrti, both the "specificity" of a word—why a word such as "cow" applies to cows and

---

97. RNĀ (AS 63.11): "*sajātīyabhedāparāmarśana*" from passage *a*.

98. RNĀ (AS 66.05–66.06; 66.13).

99. RNĀ (AS 63.03–63.06).

100. RNĀ (AS 64.07–64.09), RNĀ (AS 64.26–64.29).

101. RNĀ (AS 63.26–63.28), RNĀ (AS 65.01–65.14).

102. RNĀ (AS 63.30–64.03). The arguments in this section of Ratnakīrti's text are rather short, and it is often helpful to read the parallel passages at JNĀ (AP 221.11–223.27). Ratnakīrti's discussion is not, however, the same as the discussion in JNĀ, and so the JNĀ discussion must be used with some care.

only to cows (and not to horses)—and its "generality"—why a word such as "cow" can apply to cows and not just a particular cow—can be explained in terms of the process through which similarity classes, Ratnakīrti's "universals," are constructed.[103] As mentioned earlier, according to Ratnakīrti, a similarity class is the "thing-in-general" that is constructed from a particular through exclusion. The construction of this "universal" is therefore dependent upon a specific individual, since it is a recalled individual that provides the basis for the selective exclusion that generates it.[104] According to Ratnakīrti, his account of how similarity classes are constructed from this specific individual provides all of the conceptual resources necessary for explaining the "specificity" and "generality" of semantic value.

Suppose, for example, that someone is told "Bring a brown cow," i.e., any brown cow. Suppose further that upon hearing this utterance of the term "brown cow" the object that is recalled is a specific cow, *p*, that has a unique brown color, dewlap, horns, and tail—its "identity" conditions, **I**. Based on this specific collection of color, dewlap, horns, and tail, it is possible, according to Ratnakīrti, to construct a generic collection of things having the relevant components. It is, in other words, possible to construct a similarity class, like-**P**. Like-**P** is constructed by excluding those things that do not have what we take to be the relevant set of components—that is, that do not

---

103. Strictly speaking, there is not a single opponent. I have grouped together objections that are raised by a variety of opponents for the sake of brevity and clarity. For concerns about "generality" see RNĀ (AS 63.20–63.22), for "specificity" see RNĀ (AS 63.26–63.28), and for both see RNĀ (AS 64.07–64.08). To these objections could be added concerns about the awareness of "continuity" or "consistency" (*anuvṛtti-pratyaya*). See, for example, RNĀ (AS 64.15ff).

104. See RNĀ (AS 65.26–66.03): "Although everything is ungrasped, there is activity with respect to water and the like. This is because our conceptual awareness has a specific object, since it is produced by a specific causal complex, has a specific mental image, and has a specific capacity. It is like smoke's producing an awareness of a fire that is beyond the range of our senses: for things that have specific capacities and whose natures have been established by valid awareness are not liable to questions about the mixing up of their capacities. Therefore, because of association with a specific image, 'determining it' just is 'producing activity with respect to it'" (*yady api viśvam agṛhītaṃ tathāpi vikalpasya niyatasāmagrīprasūtatvena niyatākāratayā niyataśaktitvān niyataiva jalādau pravṛttiḥ | dhūmasya parokṣāgnijñānajananavat | niyataviṣayā hi bhāvāḥ pramāṇapariniṣṭhitasvabhāvā na śaktisāṅkaryaparyanuyogabhājaḥ | tasmāt tadadhyavasāyitvam ākāraviśeṣayogāt tatpravṛttijanakatvam*). See RNĀ (KS 74.07–74.12) and (CAPV 137.09–137.10), which are quoted and translated in chapter 5, note 39.

satisfy the selection set **S**. This set of things is the dissimilarity class, non-**P**. The similarity class, like-**P**, that is constructed by excluding this dissimilarity class, non-**P**, is what is understood from hearing the utterance of the term "brown cow" in this example. The reason this utterance of the term cannot be used to correctly refer to horses is that its semantic value is in part based upon a specific causal process, a specific individual, and an intentionally determined or "selective" process of exclusion: it is almost impossible, for example, given the selective exclusion described above, that someone would construct the mental image of a horse from either the observation of a brown cow or a recalled brown cow. Similarly, neither the observation of a horse nor a recalled horse could, through the selective exclusion described above, correctly lead to the awareness "brown-cow." Thus, the "specificity" in the correct use of the word "cow" in this context can be explained. The theory can account for why "cow" refers to cows and nothing but cows.[105]

According to Ratnakīrti, his theory can also account for why an exclusion that is based upon a recalled individual can apply to more than the individual on which it is based. Suppose we are told, for example, to bring a cow, i.e., any cow and not just a brown cow.[106] Suppose further that the recalled object is the specific brown cow, *p*. As mentioned above, from its specific collection of color, dewlap, horns, and tail—**I**—it is possible to construct a similarity class like-**P** that includes all brown cows. It is also possible, however, to selectively focus on just its specific collection of dewlap, horns, and a tail, and thereby construct a new selection set, **S.** In this case, the color component would not be considered since it is not relevant to the person's specific interests, as determined by the context in which the term "cow" is uttered. Things that do not satisfy **S** define the dissimilarity class, non-**P.** By excluding non-**P** from *p*, what will be constructed is the collection of things that satisfy **S**—that is, those things that we take to have a dewlap, horns, and a tail. Such a similarity class would include all cows, regardless of their color. Ratnakīrti argues, therefore, that his account of what is understood from hearing a token utterance of a term can also account for "generality."

---

105. See chapter 5, section 3.3 for an extended discussion of this issue.

106. This example is not discussed explicitly in RNĀ. It is, however, discussed in a parallel section of text at JNĀ (AP 221.26–222.02): "if in the case of a horse there isn't the awareness 'cow' because of exclusion from a particular brown cow, then there shouldn't be [such an awareness] even in the case of a spotted cow, since particulars are never distributed" (*{athāpi syād} yadi bāhuleyapiṇḍābhāvāt turage na gobuddhiḥ śābaleye 'pi mā bhūt svalakṣaṇasya kvacid ananvayāt*).

4. Ratnakīrti's Inferential Argument

In arguing against the idea that real universals are needed to account for semantic value, Ratnakīrti tried to show that they could not be established by any accredited instrument of valid awareness. In explaining why exclusion is necessary for an account of semantic value, however, Ratnakīrti has not shown that his view is supported by either of the two instruments of valid awareness that are accepted by him, namely, perception and inference.[107] In concluding his essay, Ratnakīrti provides an inferential argument to support his view. His decision to conclude his essay in this way is important, because it brings together the various subarguments used throughout his essay and does so in a more "formal" context. What Ratnakīrti's argument seeks to prove is that the semantic value of a word is a positive entity characterized by its exclusion from others. He says,

> Here is the argument: Everything expressive has as its object a thing-in-general that is determined and excluded from those that do not have its form, like the expression, "There is water here in this well." And what is expressive here has the form of a word such as "cow." Thus the reason property is of the same nature as [its target].[108]

In this argument, the site of the inference is something that "has the form of a word such as 'cow.'" Here, this "something" is the inferential/verbal awareness-event produced in the mind of a competent speaker of a language upon hearing a token utterance of an expression in that language. The reason property is the property "being expressive," which may be helpfully thought of as "being expressive of semantic value." As Ratnakīrti explains, this property is supposed to be "of the same nature" as its target, and so is supposed to be related to it through the "identity-mode" of pervasion. Ratnakīrti's argument is that awareness-events produced through testimony,

---

107. According to Ratnakīrti, there are two accredited instruments for valid awareness, perception (*pratyakṣa*) and inferential reasoning (*anumāna*). A discussion of why there are only two such instruments can be found at RNĀ (PAP 96.01–105.19). Much of this material is cited in MTBh 5.03–11.15; for a translation see Kajiyama 1998:30–40.

108. RNĀ (AS 66.06–66.10): *atra prayogaḥ | yad vācakaṃ tat sarvam adhyavasitātadrūpaparāvṛttavastumātragocaram | yatheha kūpe jalam iti vacanam | vācakaṃ cedaṃ gavādiśabdarūpam iti svabhāvahetuḥ*. A portion of this passage is also quoted in section 3.3 above.

such as the awareness-event produced in the mind of a competent speaker of English upon hearing the word "cow" (the site of the inference), take as their objects a thing-in-general that is determined and excluded from those that do not have its form (the target property), since they express semantic value (the reason property). Elsewhere, Ratnakīrti described this "object" as a complex positive entity, an object characterized by its exclusion from others, an object that is excluded from those that belong to a different class, a thing-in-general that is determined and excluded from those that belong to a different class, and a determined external object.[109] As discussed above, this object is neither a particular nor a universal. It is a thing-in-general that is constructed through its essential component, exclusion, and is determined to be the object to which we refer. Earlier I referred to these objects as "similarity classes" and "constructed universals."

There are two steps in Ratnakīrti's argument: (1) the statement of pervasion (the "pervasion subcomponent" of the inference): "Everything expressive has as its object a thing-in-general that is determined and excluded from those that do not have its form, like the expression, 'There is water here in this well'"; and (2) the statement that the reason property is a property of the site of the inference (the "site subcomponent" of the inference): "What is expressive here has the form of a word such as 'cow.'" In order to defend this argument, Ratnakīrti must show that neither subcomponent is defective. He does so by showing that the reason property is neither unestablished (H1), opposed (H2), nor inconclusive (H3). Since the site subcomponent is assumed by both Ratnakīrti and his opponents to be free from any defects, Ratnakīrti focuses his attention on the pervasion subcomponent. It is interesting to note that in terms of the certification conditions discussed in chapters 2 and 3, Ratnakīrti focuses only on the instrument conditions—that is, C2.1, C2.2, and C2.3. It should come as no surprise, then, that in defending his argument he considers only those defects that were earlier said to defeat the functioning of the instrument.

4.1. The Site Subcomponent: Unestablished (H1)

In defending this inferential argument, Ratnakīrti first argues that the reason property is not unestablished-in-itself (H1)—that is, that it is known to

---

109. RNĀ (AS 66.08–66.09), RNĀ (AS 66.05–66.06), RNĀ (AS 66.13), RNĀ (AS 66.20).

exist (and so can be shown to be present in the site of the inference).[110] He says, for example, that

> This is because, by the previously stated rule,[111] everyone who acts in the world must accept that even though an expressed-expressor relation doesn't really exist, one is in fact constructed through determination. Otherwise, there would be the unwanted consequence of not being able to act at all.[112]

Earlier in his essay Ratnakīrti argued that what is reflected in our use of indispensable pairs of concepts such as "property" and "property-possessor," and by extension "expressor" and "expressed," is an "imagined" or "conceptually constructed" difference.[113] The reason property "being expressive" is established, therefore, through a form of conceptual construction.[114] Although the property "being expressive" does not *really* exist, in virtue of its being indispensable for explaining our ordinary practices it has a kind of conceptual existence that is sufficient for the purposes of an inferential argument. As a result, Ratnakīrti concludes that it is not "unestablished-in-itself."

---

110. In this context Ratnakīrti is referring to what I earlier called a "subtype" of the defect "unestablished" (H1) (*asiddha*). Both Ratnakīrti and the Naiyāyikas call this subtype "unestablished-in-itself" (*svarūpāsiddha*). See the notes to chapter 2 for the Naiyāyikas' discussion of this defect. For a Buddhist discussion of this defect see NB 3.6.1, RNĀ (KSA 67.15–67.20), and MTBh 61.03–62.03, where it is explained that there are two ways in which a reason property may be unestablished: there may be (epistemically significant) doubt about its existence or there may be (epistemically significant) doubt about the existence of the site of the inference. On the basis of either form of doubt, it cannot be known that the reason property is present in the site of the inference, and so the reason property is defective. In this context, Ratnakīrti is referring to doubt about the existence of the reason property itself. For a very similar discussion of this defect in Ratnakīrti's work see RNĀ (KSA 67.15–67.20).

111. This seems to be referring to what precedes "*iti sthitam*," RNĀ (AS 66.06–66.07).

112. RNĀ (AS 66.10–66.12): *{nāyam asiddhaḥ | pūrvoktena nyāyena}* pāramārthikavācyavācakabhāvasyābhāve 'py adhyavasāyakṛtasyaiva sarvavyavahāribhir avaśyaṃ svīkartavyatvāt | anyathā sarvavyavahārocchedaprasaṅgāt.* *This is referring to the "rule" (*nyāya*) at RNĀ (AS 66.06–66.07).

113. See 2.1.4, where this is discussed in detail.

114. According to my typology, this form of construction is "abstraction."

4.2. The Pervasion Subcomponent: Opposed (H2) and Inconclusive (H3)

Ratnakīrti next asserts that the reason property is not opposed since it is known to be present in a similar case.[115] According to Ratnakīrti, this is obvious since the reason property "being expressive" is well known to be present in inferential/verbal awareness-events other than those produced upon hearing the word "cow." His point is that in order to show that the defect opposed does not apply, all that he has to do is show that other inferentially/verbally produced awareness-events are expressive of semantic value. As a result, Ratnakīrti argues that it is obvious that the reason property is not opposed. Earlier, this was described as satisfying pervasion condition C2.2.

In arguing that the reason property is not inconclusive (H3)—i.e., that it is *not* present in a dissimilar case—Ratnakīrti tries to satisfy pervasion condition C2.3. He argues that

> The reason property "being expressive" is excluded from [all] dissimilar cases, since it is excluded from a pervader of the target property "having an object," on the basis of there not being a different kind of expressed object. Thus pervasion is established.[116]

Through this very short argument, Ratnakīrti asserts that he has established negative concomitance, and thereby shown that the reason property is not inconclusive, since if negative concomitance can be established the reason property will be known to be excluded from all dissimilar cases. There are three components to Ratnakīrti's argument: (1) the reason property, "being expressive"; (2) dissimilar cases—that is, loci (in this case, awareness-events) in which the reason property is present but the target property is not, such as an inferential/verbal awareness-event that has as its object an object that is different from the sort of object described by Ratnakīrti; and (3) a "pervader"—that is, a property that is known to pervade both the target property and the reason property. Here the pervading property is the

115. For a similar discussion see RNĀ (KSA 67.20–70.08).

116. RNĀ (AS 66.19–66.21): *{tad evaṃ} vācyāntarasyābhāvād viṣayavattvalakṣaṇasya vyāpakasya nivṛttau vipakṣato nivartamānaṃ vācakatvam adhyavasitabāhyaviṣayatvena vyāpyata iti vyāptisiddhiḥ.*

property "having an object," which is known to pervade the target property, since any awareness-event that has an object like the one specified by Ratnakīrti must have an object. This property is also known to pervade the reason property, since according to Ratnakīrti it is not possible for there to be awareness-events that are expressive but objectless.[117] Ratnakīrti's argument against the reason property being inconclusive can be understood in terms of these components.

Ratnakīrti first states that the pervading property "having an object" is excluded from all dissimilar cases, that is, from all inferential/verbal awareness-events in which either a particular or a real universal is supposed to be its content.[118] We know this to be the case since, as Ratnakīrti has shown earlier in his essay, inferential/verbal awareness-events cannot have either particulars or real universals as their objects. Given that these two objects are assumed to exhaust the possibilities, it is then known that the property "having an object" is excluded from states of awareness in which "objects" other than the complex positive entity described by Ratnakīrti are supposed to be present. Given that the property "having an object" is also known to pervade the reason property "being expressive," it is also known that the reason property is excluded from all dissimilar cases. As a result, negative concomitance is proven, and the reason property is known not to be inconclusive. By showing that C2.2 and C2.3 are satisfied, Ratnakīrti takes it that he has shown that the pervasion subcomponent is well-functioning. Interestingly, Ratnakīrti's essay concludes, somewhat abruptly, with this argument.

5. Conclusion: Jñānaśrīmitra's Three Questions

The best summary of Ratnakīrti's conclusions about semantic value can be found in a passage that concludes his teacher Jñānaśrīmitra's "Monograph

---

117. Ratnakīrti does not defend this view here. For a very brief discussion of arguments in favor of such a position see MTBh 69.11–69.18. Also see Kajiyama 1965.

118. I have simplified this discussion by assuming, as I have done earlier, that these are the only possibilities other than Ratnakīrti's complex positive entity. As mentioned earlier, Ratnakīrti himself discusses other possibilities such as "imposed properties" (*upādhi*). Ratnakīrti's discussion (and dismissal) of these other possibilities can be found in his very brief discussion of the defect "inconclusive" (*anaikāntika*), at RNĀ (AS 66.12–66.18).

on Exclusion" (*Apohaprakaraṇa*). At the end of this essay Jñānaśrīmitra answers three questions about the theory of exclusion. He says,

> So, when one is asked (1) "How is exclusion expressed by a word?," we answer "as a characteristic of [semantic value]," the meaning of which is as described. If the question is (2) "Why is neither a mental image, a particular, nor an imposed property expressed?," it is dispensed with by saying, "Because of the absence of determination, the absence of appearance, and the absence of both." But, if the question is (3) "What is it that is expressed by words?," then, having set out these options—(i) on the basis of appearance, (ii) on the basis of determination, or (iii) really—the answer is, respectively, (i) "The image that is excluded from what is other and is present in conceptual awareness"; or (ii) "The particular which is excluded from what is other"; or (iii) "Nothing."[119]

5.1. How Is Exclusion Expressed by a Word?

According to both Jñānaśrīmitra and Ratnakīrti, exclusion is the object of inferential/verbal awareness in the sense that it is an essential characteristic of the objects that are constructed by those awareness-events. As Ratnakīrti has explained, exclusion may also be thought of as the inherent capacity or dispositional property of inferential/verbal awareness to construct such positive entities/semantic values. Since the objects of inferential/verbal awareness-events are nothing but mental objects (and so are nothing but awareness itself), it is helpful to think of exclusion as an essential component, characteristic, or property of each and every constructed mental object. It is in this sense that Ratnakīrti argues that exclusion is only an analytically separable component of the complex objects that are constructed by inferential/verbal awareness. Thus exclusion is expressed by a word since it is, necessarily, a feature of the object that we take that word to refer to.

---

119. JNĀ (AP 232.05–232.10): *{tad evaṃ} katham apohaḥ śabdavācya iti praśne tadguṇatvena yathoktārthenety uttaram | atha buddhyākāraḥ svalakṣaṇam upādhayo vā kasmān na vācyā iti praśnaḥ tadadhyavasāyasya pratibhāsasya ubhayasya cābhāvād iti krameṇa visarjanāni | yadā tu śabdaiḥ kiṃ vācyam ity anuyogas tadā pratibhāsād arthādhyavasāyād yad vā tattvata iti vikalpasya vikalpastho* 'nyāpoḍhākāraḥ | anyāpoḍhasvalakṣaṇaṃ na kiṃcid iti prativacanāni krameṇaivety uktaṃ bhavati.* *I read *vikalpastho* instead of *vikalpasthe*.

5.2. Why Is Neither a Manifest Nor an External Particular Expressed?

Directly present (i.e., nondetermined/unconstructed) mental images cannot be the proper objects of inferential/verbal awareness-events because without being determined, such objects cannot be the objects upon which we linguistically act. Such objects are not *actionable*. Without being determined, these internal mental images would be momentary particulars and would, in this sense, not really be "objects" at all. They would simply be conceptually and linguistically inaccessible, manifest particulars. Just as exclusion is necessary for constructing semantic value, determination is necessary for us to take that value as an object about which we can think (e.g., a concept) or upon which we can linguistically act by referring to it (e.g., a physical object). On the other hand, an external particular cannot be the proper object of verbally produced awareness-events either, since insofar as it is an external object it cannot be present in an awareness-event and is vulnerable to the "Argument from Indifference." This is the case regardless of whether this object is supposed to be a real universal or a real particular or some other kind of object.

Ultimately, then, neither manifest internal objects nor external objects can be the objects of inferential/verbal awareness-events. All such determination-independent objects are ultimately inexpressible, since insofar as they are determination-independent they are *unavailable* to conceptual thought.

5.3. What Is Expressed?

The best account that can be given of semantic value identifies it as either a determined mental image such as the concept "tree" or a determined-to-be-external-object such as a tree. Each of these objects is constructed through exclusion and determination and can be described as a positive entity characterized by its exclusion of others. These objects are the constructed universals or similarity classes that both Jñānaśrīmitra and Ratnakīrti take semantic value to be. Since these objects are constructed through exclusion, they are present in inferential/verbal awareness in a way that makes them invulnerable to the "Argument from Indifference." Since these objects are determined, they are the kinds of objects about which we can speak and are, therefore, *actionable*. Furthermore, given the way in which they are constructed, they account for the "specificity" and "generality" of semantic value, and thus have the explanatory scope that an account of semantic value requires.

In this chapter I have focused on Ratnakīrti's version of the theory of exclusion by closely following the structure of his "Demonstration of Exclusion." In taking this approach, I have developed an interpretation of his theory in terms of similarity classes, and have emphasized that Ratnakīrti thinks that semantic value is constructed through the process of selective exclusion and determination. Attending to this aspect of Ratnakīrti's theory is especially important for seeing how and why the theory of exclusion is relevant not only to Ratnakīrti's philosophy of language, but also to nearly every aspect of his thought. In arguing in support of his account of semantic value, and against those who think that particulars, real universals, or complex entities made up of particulars and universals are the best way to account for semantic value, Ratnakīrti quietly introduces the conceptual vocabulary that marks mental construction and implicitly identifies three constraints on what he thinks semantic value should be—what I have called the "phenomenal," "epistemological," and "representational" constraints on semantic value.

The conceptual vocabulary that Ratnakīrti uses to refer to the "exclusion of others," and the closely related term "determination," makes it relatively easy to identify where Ratnakīrti thinks that exclusion is at work. By attending closely to this conceptual vocabulary, I will show in chapter 5 that Ratnakīrti understands exclusion to apply directly to each and every conceptual awareness-event, including those produced through perception and inferential reasoning. As he sees it, the content of each and every conceptual awareness-event is a determined object—that is, an object constructed through exclusion. In extending the scope of the theory in this way, I argue that Ratnakīrti's account of what our words are about is also an account of what our experiences and thoughts are about. And given that perception and inference are, for him, the only accredited instruments for valid awareness, the theory of exclusion also provides the basis for what, and how, Ratnakīrti thinks we can know. If the theory of exclusion can be extended in this way, then the constraints on semantic value are constraints on whatever is constructed through exclusion—that is, all conceptual content/determined objects. In chapter 5 I will show how all of this is relevant to Ratnakīrti's critique of the Īśvara-inference, by explaining, in detail, the significance of Ratnakīrti's theory of exclusion to his theory of mental content, his ontology, and finally, his epistemology.

Before turning to this discussion, however, it is worth noting that Ratnakīrti's theory of exclusion also provides new philosophical resources for arguing against the Naiyāyikas' conception of Īśvara. Even if the Naiyāyikas' Īśvara-inference were not defective, for example, given the theory of exclusion, all that we could infer would be the similarity class or constructed object "Īśvara." While this object would be Īśvara, it would not be the mind-independent being who is the maker of the world and about whom the Naiyāyikas believe they can speak and think. Such an argument does not show that there is not an Īśvara, but only that if there were he would be either "inexpressible" or a determined mind-dependent object. While this is an argument that Ratnakīrti does not make explicitly, we will see in chapter 5 that it is one to which he indirectly refers.

CHAPTER 5
Ratnakīrti's World
Toward a Buddhist Philosophy of Everything

LIKE MANY OF HIS PREDECESSORS IN THE SO-CALLED Yogācāra philosophical tradition, Ratnakīrti has no room in his ontology for mind-independent external objects (*bāhyārtha*).[1] For him, what we take to be mind-independent objects are nothing but mental objects/images. It is through his theory of mental objects/images that Ratnakīrti accounts for our experiences and thoughts about the world and the success of our "reality-involving" practices, such as sense perception and inferential-reasoning.[2] Our use of language is also such a reality-involving practice and, as explained in chapter 4, semantic value is one such mental object. For Ratnakīrti, it is the theory of exclusion that provides the philosophical resources

1. While I take it as unproblematic that "Yogācāra" philosophers have no room in their final ontology for mind-independent objects, there is some controversy about this. See, for example, the recent discussion of Lusthaus 2002 by Schmithausen (2005). It is worth noting that there were Buddhist epistemologists who accepted the existence of external objects, such as Śubhagupta (ca. 720–780) and his pupil Dharmottara (ca. 740–780). For a brief discussion of this issue see McCrea and Patil 2006:332 n. 72 and the references contained therein.

2. By "reality-involving practices" I mean any activity that we take to involve things that are a part of our world, and usually things that are "external" to ourselves.

for understanding how such objects are constructed from the images that directly appear in awareness.[3]

By appealing to the conceptual vocabulary that Ratnakīrti himself relies upon in his discussion of exclusion (especially the closely linked concept of determination), I will argue in this chapter that the theory of exclusion is used by him to explain how *all* determined objects—that is, all similarity classes—are constructed. This includes not only semantic value, but also perceptual and inferential value, that is, the determined objects of perceptual and inferential/verbal awareness-events (the objects that we "see" and "infer"). In explaining how such determined objects are constructed, Ratnakīrti also explains what they are constructed from—that is, the directly present or manifest image *p*. When linked with his account of mental objects/images, the theory of exclusion thus becomes a general theory of mental content, a theory of what all of our experiences and thoughts—that is, what all of our awareness-events—are about.[4]

The primary purpose of this chapter is to reconstruct Ratnakīrti's theory of mental content by providing an interpretation of his scattered remarks on the nature and status of mental objects/images. Since this chapter does not focus on a single text or set of arguments, and does not present Ratnakīrti's position as he himself presented it, it is the most speculative of the substantive chapters in this book. What is important about such a reconstruction is that it helps to connect Ratnakīrti's critical remarks on Nyāya epistemology (discussed in chapter 2 and chapter 3) with his own theory of semantics (discussed in chapter 4), in such a way that it becomes possible to see how his own philosophical views inform and support his critique of the Īśvara-inference. In my reconstruction I will pay particular attention to how Ratnakīrti accounts for inferential reasoning in terms of his inventory of mental objects/images. An added benefit of such an approach is that it gives one a

3. Ratnakīrti is not consistent in his use of the terms "object" and "image." This is in part because some mental objects (*viṣaya*)—O1 and O3—are identical to the images (*ākāra*) with which they are associated, while others—O2 and O4—are not. When this difference is significant, I will refer to the relevant images as I1, I2, I3, and I4. In general, when this distinction is important to Ratnakīrti I will use "image" to refer to the manifest-content of an awareness-event and "object" to refer to the determined-content of an awareness-event. Since this distinction was not relevant to my discussion in chapter 4, I did not highlight it there.

4. The terms "mental content" or "contents of awareness" may refer to images, objects, or both, depending on the context.

perspective on Ratnakīrti's overall philosophical project, which in my view is to show how what we generally take to be mind, language, and world together create mind, language, and world. It also helps us to see why such a project may have been important to him. I will discuss this issue in chapter 6.

The chapter begins with a very brief discussion of Ratnakīrti's inventory of mental objects/images in order to introduce the conceptual vocabulary on which my reconstruction will rely.[5] In the three sections following, I will then provide a more detailed account of the mental objects/images that make up what I am calling "Ratnakīrti's World." The chapter concludes with a discussion of the relevance of this reconstruction to my analysis of Ratnakīrti's arguments against the existence of Īśvara.

1. An Inventory of Mental Objects/Images

According to Ratnakīrti, the contents of our awareness-events can be completely described in terms of four different kinds of mental objects.[6] These

---

5. The textual support for my reconstruction will be provided in footnotes to the text, where the relevant Sanskrit passages will be cited and translated. Given the nature of this chapter, selected portions of some of these passages will be cited and translated more than once.

6. The four-object model of awareness comes from Dharmottara. In his innovative commentary on Dharmakīrti's *Nyāyabindu*, NBṬ 70–72 *ad* NB1.12, he says: "For the object of valid awareness is two-fold: a grasped object whose image is produced, and an attainable object that one determines. For the grasped object is one thing and the determined is something else, since for perception what is grasped is a single moment but what is determined—through a judgment that arises by the force of perception—can only be a continuum. And only a continuum can be the attainable object of perception because a moment cannot be attained. So too for inference: it *grasps* a nonentity, because, even though its own appearance is not a [real] object, there is activity through the determination of an object. But, since this imposed thing [i.e., the nonentity] that is grasped is *determined to be a particular*, in inference, a determined particular is the object of activity. But what is grasped is a nonentity. So here, showing the *grasped object* of this mode of valid awareness, he says that a particular is the object of perception" (*dvividho hi viṣayaḥ pramāṇasya grāhyaś ca yadākāram utpadyate, prāpaṇīyaś ca yam adhyavasyati | anyo hi grāhyo 'nyaś cādhyavaseyaḥ | pratyakṣasya hi kṣaṇa eko grāhyaḥ | adhyavaseyas tu pratyakṣabalotpannena niścayena santāna eva | santāna eva ca pratyakṣasya prāpaṇīyaḥ | kṣaṇasya prāpayitum aśakyatvāt | tathānumānam api svapratibhāse 'narthe 'rthādhyavasāyena pravṛtter anarthagrāhi | sa punar āropito 'rtho gṛhyamāṇaḥ svalakṣaṇatvenāvasīyate yataḥ, tataḥ svalakṣaṇam avasitaṃ pravṛttiviṣayo 'numānasya | anarthas tu grāhyaḥ | tad atra pramāṇasya grāhyaṃ viṣayaṃ darśayatā pratyakṣasya svalakṣaṇaṃ viṣaya*

four objects are differentiated from one another by the state of awareness in which they appear and the mode through which they appear in them.[7] According to Ratnakīrti, there are two such states of awareness, perceptual and inferential/verbal. Each is constituted by two awareness-events and each has a direct and an indirect object. The "direct" object of awareness is the object that appears, through a process called "manifestation" (*pratibhāsa*), in the first of the two awareness-events (*buddhi*, *jñāna*) that make up that state of awareness. This object is most often referred to as the object that is directly "grasped" (*grāhya*) by awareness. It may also be thought of—at least for the time being—as the nonconceptual content of awareness. What makes it "nonconceptual" is that it is the "manifest" content of awareness. To be nonconceptual is simply to be manifest in awareness. In contrast, the indirect object of awareness appears through determination (*adhyavasāya*). This object is most often referred to as the object that is "determined" (*adhyavaseya*) by awareness. It is these determined objects—my "similarity classes"—that are constructed from the directly grasped objects—the "manifest" image, *p*—through exclusion.[8] This

---

uktaḥ). For a discussion of this model in its historical context see McCrea and Patil 2006:325–333.

7. Ratnakīrti describes this basic model in a number of different places in his work, and he is clearly committed to it. Consider, for example: RNĀ (VN 109.14–109.18): "This is because what manifests in awareness is grasped, but that with respect to which it [i.e., awareness] operates is determined. Among these, the grasped object of perception is a particular, but the determined object is a universal, i.e., a genericized-particular excluded from those that do not have its form. For inference, it is the reverse" (*yaddhi yatra jñāne pratibhāsate tad grāhyam | yatra tu tat pravartate tad adhyavaseyam | tatra pratyakṣasya svalakṣaṇaṃ grāhyam | adhyavaseyaṃ tu sāmānyam, atadrūpaparāvṛttasvalakṣaṇamātrātmakam | anumānasya viparyayaḥ*). RNĀ (CAPV 131.04–131.05): "The objects of awareness are of two sorts, grasped and determined. Those that are manifest in awareness are grasped. Those that are determined are the objects of positive activity, even though they are not grasped" (*iha dvividho vijñānānāṃ viṣayo grāhyo 'adhyavaseyaś ca | pratibhāsamāno grāhyaḥ | agṛhīte 'pi pravṛttiviṣayo 'dhyavaseyaḥ*); more of this passage is quoted in section 5.1. RNĀ (KSA 73.20–73.21): "This is because the object of perception is twofold, grasped and determined" (*dvividho hi pratyakṣasya viṣayaḥ, grāhyo 'dhyavaseyaś ca*).

8. That the determined object of an inferential/verbal awareness-event (O4) is constructed through exclusion should be clear from chapter 4. That the determined object of a perceptual awareness-event (O2) is also constructed through exclusion is made explicit by Ratnakīrti at RNĀ (VN 109.17), which was quoted and translated in the previous footnote. In this passage it is stated explicitly that the determined object of perceptual states of awareness is *actionable*, even though it is not manifest in awareness. As I argued in chapter 4, the only way for objects to be determined/actionable is to be constructed through exclusion; see chapter 4, section 3.2.1.

object may also be thought of as the "conceptual content" of awareness. What makes it "conceptual" is that it is the "determined" content of awareness. To be conceptual is just to be determined by awareness. Both direct and indirect objects can also be understood as mental objects/images, which are nothing more than "formations" or "facets" (*ākāra*) of awareness itself.

For Ratnakīrti, the world, and our experiences and thoughts about it, can be completely described in terms of these four kinds of mental objects (*viṣaya*) and/or images (*ākāra*): the direct objects of perception (O1), the indirect objects of perception (O2), the direct objects of inferential/verbal awareness (O3), and the indirect objects of inferential/verbal awareness (O4).

In addition to differentiating between the objects of perception—O1 and O2—and the objects of inferential/verbal awareness—O3 and O4—by indicating whether they are the manifest- or determined-content of each type of awareness, Ratnakīrti also says that they can be distinguished from each other by whether they are "particulars" (*svalakṣaṇa-s*) or "universals" (*sāmānya-s*). For him, O1 and O4 are "particulars" and O2 and O3 are "universals."[9] More accurately, O1 is a manifest particular and O4 a determined particular.[10] O2 is a determined universal and O3 a manifest

9. See RNĀ (VN 109.14–109.18), which is quoted and translated in n. 7.

10. These terms are not actually used by Ratnakīrti, even though they could have been. That O1 can be referred to as a "manifest particular" is clear from the fact that it is said to be "manifest" and a "particular." That O4 can be referred to as a "determined particular" is clear from the fact that it is said to be a "particular" (see below) and from Ratnakīrti's remark at RNĀ (KS 73.11), where, in the context of describing O4, he says that with respect to inferential/verbal awareness-events "only the particular is determined" (*adhyavaseyatvaṃ svalakṣaṇasyaiva*). It is worth noting, however, that the term "determined particular" (*svalakṣaṇam avasitam*) is used by Dharmottara; see NBṬ *ad* NB 1.12, which is quoted in n. 6.

RNĀ (CAPV 137.27–137.30): "For there are two ways to talk about objects: on the basis of manifestation and on the basis of determination. So here it is said that even though it is not manifest, a particular, which is excluded from what is other, etc., is an object simply on the basis of determination" (*dvividho hi viṣayavyavahāraḥ, pratibhāsād adhyavasāyāc ca | tad iha pratibhāsābhāve 'pi parāpoḍhasvalakṣaṇāder adhyavasāyamātreṇa viṣayatvam uktam*); see also JNĀ (AP 225.17–225.18). RNĀ (KSA 73.09): "Being determined means being made into an object of positive activity, even though [it is] not manifest. And this 'being determined' applies only to particulars and not to the other one [i.e., the universal], since the positive activity of someone who wants [something] is due to a desire for a pragmatically effective [particular]" (*apratibhāse 'pi pravṛttiviṣayīkṛtatvam adhyavaseyatvam | etac cādhyavaseyatvaṃ svalakṣaṇasyaiva yujyate, nānyasya, arthakriyārthitvād arthipravṛtteḥ*).

universal.[11] There are, therefore, three pairs of concepts that are used to classify the contents of awareness: "perceptual" or "inferential/verbal," which indicate the kind of awareness-event in which a particular object/image appears; "manifest" or "determined," which indicate the way in which it appears; and "particular" or "universal," which indicate (in retrospect) what appears.

While objects like O1–O4 are necessary for explaining the content of our experiences and thoughts about the world, Ratnakīrti argues that under the most rigorous philosophical description only objects like O1 really exist. In the final analysis, neither mind-independent external objects nor mind-dependent "internal" objects like O2, O3, and O4 *really* exist. Trying to understand exactly what Ratnakīrti means by this, and how he is able to account for reality-involving practices such as sense perception and inferential reasoning in terms of his four-object model of mental content, is the central task of this chapter. What follows is a more detailed reconstruction of Ratnakīrti's account of "reality," a discussion of the four objects and ten concepts used in its construction, and an account of why under the most rigorous philosophical description only objects like O1 really exist.[12] To a significant degree, this chapter is simply an extended explanation and interpretation of Ratnakīrti's inventory of objects, and an account of its relevance to his critique of the Īśvara-inference.

2. The Contents of Perception

2.1. Object O1: The Direct Object of Perception

Object O1 is the direct object of perception. As such, it is the only object of an awareness-event that is not necessarily associated with some form of mental

11. These terms are also not used by Ratnakīrti, even though they could have been. That O2 is a "determined universal" is clear from that the fact that it is said to be "determined" (*adhyavaseya*) and a "universal" (*sāmānya*). That O3 is a "manifest universal" is clear from the fact that it is said to be "manifest" (*pratibhāsa*) and a "universal" (*sāmānya*). See the passages quoted earlier in notes 7 and 10.

12. The 10 concepts are "manifestation" (*pratibhāsa/prakāśa*), "determination" (*adhyavasāya*), "grasped" (*grāhya*), "determined" (*adhyavaseya*), "exists" (*sat*), "does not exist" (*asat*), "particular" (*svalakṣaṇa*), "universal" (*sāmānya*), "activity" (*pravṛtti*), and "mental object/image" (*ākāra*).

construction (*vikalpa*). Because the perceptual awareness-event in which the indirect object of perception appears, and both inferential/verbal awareness-events, are necessarily associated with some form of mental construction, it is only the first awareness-event in the perceptual process that is, strictly speaking, said to be free from conceptual construction (*nirvikalpa*).[13] As the direct object of perception, O1 is both manifest in and grasped by awareness. I will refer to it as the "manifest-content" of perception.

In his "Debating Multifaceted Nonduality" (*Citrādvaitaprakāśavāda*), Ratnakīrti defends the following inferential argument and indirectly tells us more about the manifest-content of perception. He argues that whatever directly appears in or is manifest to (*pra+√kāś*) awareness is a single (*eka*), nondual (*advaita*) image.[14] He explains further that this image is a complex and dynamic collection of many seemingly different mental images, such as the color "white," the note "*ga*," the taste "sweet," the smell "fragrant," the touch "soft," and the feelings "pleasure" and "pain." Since this complex collection directly appears in awareness, however, Ratnakīrti infers that it is a multifaceted nonduality (*citrādvaita*)—that is, a single, unitary image. As he tries to show, any image that directly appears in awareness must be single, nondual, and multifaceted.[15] Ratnakīrti's description of this complex image/object suggests that the "subimages" that constitute O1 are the most basic or ontologically primitive objects of perception, even though they are supposed

---

13. The idea that "perception is free from conceptual construction" (*pratyakṣaṃ kalpanāpoḍham*) is one of the foundational tenets of the Buddhist epistemological tradition. For a discussion of this see chapter 6, section 3.1, and the references contained therein.

14. Ratnakīrti uses a number of different terms to mean "appears in" or is "present in" awareness. Most often, he uses the term "manifests" (*pratibhāsa*), and other terms derived from the verbal root √*bhās*, to mean "*directly appears in* an awareness-event." In some contexts, however, such as this one, he also uses the term "*prakāśa*" to mean "manifests/directly appears in." Ratnakīrti is not always consistent in his terminology, and it is important to keep in mind when he is using a term to mean "manifests/directly appears in" and when he is using it to mean "appears in."

15. RNĀ (CAPV 129.19–129.21): "Whatever manifests [in awareness] is single, just as the image 'blue' that exists in the midst of a collection of diverse images. [This is the pervasion subcomponent of the inference]. And this collection of diverse images, namely, white, the note '*ga*,' sweet, fragrant, soft, happiness and its opposite, etc., is manifest. [This is the site subcomponent]" (*yat prakāśate tad ekam | yathā citrākāracakram adhyavartī nīlākāraḥ | prakāśate cedaṃ gauragāndhāramadhurasurabhisukumārasātetarādivicitrākārakadambakam iti svabhāvahetuḥ*).

to be nondifferent from O1.[16] I will refer to these "subimages" as "O1s." In addition, since under the most rigorous philosophical description only these "subimages" really exist, all of the other objects in Ratnakīrti's ontology can be reduced to, and thus accounted for, in terms of them.[17]

Unfortunately, Ratnakīrti does not say more about these "subimages" or the single, nondual, multifaceted image with which they are identical. This is in part because in his "Debating Multifaceted Nonduality" Ratnakīrti is primarily concerned with showing that it is conceptually consistent to maintain that O1 is both multifaceted (*citra*) and nondual (*advaita*).[18] He does not choose, therefore, to provide a more detailed discussion of O1 and its many facets/subimages or the awareness-event that it is the content of. From his remarks, however, it seems as though O1 is dynamic and, metaphorically at least, in motion. This is suggested by his use of wheel imagery to describe O1 and is implied by his views on how its seemingly diverse facets/subimages are related to everyday sensory modalities (see above).[19] His references to O1 also suggest that although its subimages form a single complex, they can still be individuated, insofar as they can be identified as subimages of it.

In addition to this account of O1, Ratnakīrti also provides a "functional" description of O1. That is, in addition to the single, nondual, multifaceted O1 object, Ratnakīrti also indicates that it is appropriate to refer to each and every object that directly appears in a perceptual-awareness event as an "O1." This is important, since by definition only O1 objects can be the direct objects of perception. Moreover, according to Buddhist philosophers like Ratnakīrti, each and every object of awareness can be the manifest-content of a

---

16. Feelings such as "happiness and its opposite" are most probably the objects of reflexive-awareness (*svasaṃvedana*), a subtype of perception. See, for example, MTBh 14.05–20.01, where four types of perception are discussed.

17. The existential status of these objects will be discussed in section 3.

18. RNĀ (CAPV 129.16–129.17): "Therefore, due to the mistaken view that this—i.e., 'being multifaceted'—is incompatible with 'being non-dual' there is indeed a dispute about nonduality. Thus, in order to correct this, this inferential argument was stated" (*tasmāc citrateyam advaitavirodhinīti vyāmohād ekatva eva vipratipattir iti tatra prasādhanaṃ sādhanam ucyate*). For the "inferential argument" that is being referred to see n. 15 above.

19. There is no direct textual support for the claim that O1 is "dynamic," although Ratnakīrti occasionally uses wheel imagery (*cakra*) to refer to the single complex of images. It is this imagery that suggests to me an "active" quality to the content of this awareness-event. See RNĀ (CAPV 141.08) and RNĀ (CAPV 129.19).

special type of perception called "reflexive-awareness" (*svasaṃvedana*).[20] Thus in this sense any of them could be a direct object of perception, and therefore an "O1." Functionally, O1 is the manifest-content of a perceptual awareness-event, including a reflexive perceptual awareness-event. In much of what follows, it is this sense of O1 that it is most important to keep in mind.

It is also important to note that on neither description of O1 is the O1 object (or "O1" objects) noticed, that is, it doesn't seem like anything to us to be aware of them. Our awareness of O1 objects—the manifest-content of perception—does not have phenomenal character.[21] It is, therefore, only in "retrospect," by looking back on them from our awareness of the O2 object that has been constructed from them, that we can say anything about them.

2.2. *Object O2: The Indirect Object of Perception*

Unlike O1, O2 is an object of a conceptual awareness-event, an awareness-event necessarily associated with some form of mental construction. More specifically, it is the indirect object of perception. Ratnakīrti characterizes such objects as "universals." And like all indirect objects, O2 objects appear in perceptual awareness-events as a result of determination. They are, therefore, the *determined-content* of perception—that is, what we take "perceptual value" to be.[22]

According to Ratnakīrti, determination is a capacity inherent in all constructing awareness-events through which *actionable* objects—objects that appear to us as though we can act upon them (O2/O4)—are constructed from those that are manifest in awareness but cannot be acted upon since, for example, they don't have phenomenal character (O1/O3). Since determination is inherent in constructing awareness-events, regardless of whether they are part of perceptual or inferential/verbal states of awareness,

---

20. As the contents of awareness-events, O1–O4 are referred to as both objects and images. Since they are usually taken to be manifest, O1 and O3 are best thought of as "images," while O2 and O4 are best thought of as "objects"—that is, as the kinds of things that we generally take ourselves to be acting upon. However, it is important to keep in mind that O2 and O4 are also "images" in the sense that underlying each object is a mental image which is the manifest-content of reflexive-awareness. For more on reflexive-awareness see MTBh 15.18–19.09. It is worth noting that for Ratnakīrti, since reflexive-awareness is a type of perception, it too must have two objects.

21. For more on "phenomenal character" see Alter and Walter 2007.

22. See the passages cited in the notes to section 1.

it is impossible for there to be a constructing awareness-event without determination.[23]

According to Ratnakīrti, there are two ways in which objects are determined.[24] It is through these "modes" of determination that determined objects (O2/O4) are constructed from what directly appears in, and is grasped by, awareness (O1/O3). Another way of putting this is to say that the determined-content of a state of awareness is constructed from its manifest-content. The first mode of determination is the construction of an individual or token. Ratnakīrti sometimes refers to this as the capacity to determine singularity (*ekatva-adhyavasāya*).[25] He explains what this means through the following examples. Given that all existing things are momentary,

---

23. It is worth noting that the qualifying phrase "for example" is necessary, since there are other reasons that only determined objects are said to be "actionable." The relationship between having phenomenal character and being actionable that is implied in this sentence is also not explicitly stated by Ratnakīrti. An interesting "limit case" is what Jñānaśrīmitra calls "entirely habitual action" (*atyantābhyāsa*), or reflex action. See JNĀ (AP 230.27–231.02), which is quoted and translated below.

For a discussion of the history of "determination" (*adhyavasāya*) in the Buddhist epistemological tradition see McCrea and Patil 2006 and the references contained therein. For a discussion of the concept of determination in the work of Dharmakīrti see Katsura 1993 and Dunne 2004. The simplest account that Ratnakīrti gives of determination is as follows: RNĀ (AS 65.25–65.26): "What is the meaning of 'it is determined by it'? What it means is that 'although it is not manifest, it is made into an object of positive activity'" (*tadadhyavasitam iti ko 'rthaḥ | apratibhāse 'pi pravṛttiviṣayīkṛtam iti yo 'rthaḥ*). See also RNĀ (KS 73.09): *apratibhāse 'pi pravṛttiviṣayīkṛtam adhyavaseyatvam,* and RNĀ (CAPV 140.0): *apratibhāse 'pi pravṛttiviṣayīkṛtam ity arthaḥ.*

24. See also chapter 4, section 3.1.2, where this issue was also discussed.

25. RNĀ (CAPV 143.12–143.14): "For a vertical universal there is, because of ignorance, a determination of singularity, even though different moments are known through sense perception. In the same way, for a horizontal universal as well there is, just on the basis of ignorance, a determination of difference, even though what is known through reflexive-awareness is a nondifference in images" (*yathordhvam indriyapratyakṣataḥ kṣaṇabhede pratīte 'py avidyāvaśād ekatvādhyavasāyas tathā tiryak svasaṃvedanapratyakṣeṇākārābhede 'dhigate 'py avidyāvaśād eva bhedāvasāyaḥ*). Note the relationship in this passage between "vertical universals" and the "determination of singularity" and "horizontal universals" and the "determination of difference." In both cases, ignorance conceals what is directly present to our awareness and determination results in what is actionable by us. The determination of singularity results in the construction of an individual/token from different moments. The determination of difference results in the construction of an individual/token, by abstracting it out from its universal/type.

the determination of singularity describes the construction of a single continuum (*santāna*) from the direct awareness of one discrete moment (*kṣaṇa-grahaṇa*).[26] It is, in other words, the construction of a persisting individual from a series of discrete moments. The determination of singularity is also at work in the construction of an individual from its various constituents/components. For Ratnakīrti, an individual is nothing more than a collection (*samudāya*) of components. From the direct awareness of only one of its components, Ratnakīrti argues that an individual collection can be constructed. He explains, for example, that by directly sensing only its color it is possible to determine the pot of which the sensed color is a component.[27] It is, moreover, this determined pot or pot-continuum that is said to be the actual object of sense perception.[28]

Regardless of whether it is understood as a continuum or as a collection, the determination of singularity is, as these two examples suggest, the determination or construction of an individual/token from the directly grasped object of perception.[29] Let us refer to this object as O2.1. More details about how this object is constructed will be given below. The second mode of determination is the construction of a set, type, or collection of tokens. Let us

---

26. RNĀ (KSA 73.24): "It is like coming to know a continuum from grasping a moment" (*kṣaṇagrahaṇe santānaniścayavat*).

27. RNĀ (KSA 73.24–73.25): "It is like coming to know a pot that is made up of color, taste, smell, and touch from grasping only its color" (*rūpamātragrahaṇe rūparasagandha-sparśātmakaghaṭaniścayavac ca*).

RNĀ (VN 109.18–109.19): "And therefore, given our ordinary, everyday sources of knowledge, even though it is only the color component of a pot—which is made up of a collection of color, taste, smell, and touch components—that is grasped, it is accepted that the collection is known on the basis of perception" (*tataś ca sāṃvyavahārikapramāṇāpekṣayā rūparasagandhasparśasamudāyātmakasya ghaṭasya rūpabhedamātragrahaṇe 'pi pratyakṣataḥ samudāyasiddhivyavasthā*).

28. This is clear from RNĀ (CAPV 143.13) and RNĀ (VN 109.18–109.19), where the term "perception" (*pratyakṣa*) is used, and from RNĀ (KSA 73.24–73.25), where the term "sense perception" (*indriyapratyakṣa*) is used to refer to awareness-events in which these constructed tokens are objects. In addition, in RNĀ (KSA 73.20–73.23), which is the passage immediately preceding the examples cited above, Ratnakīrti explains that the tokens described in the examples are supposed to be the objects of perception.

29. In principle, the "determination of singularity" (*ekatva-adhyavasāya*) can also describe the construction of types such as the collection of all pots. In this case, the part or component that is being directly grasped may be an individual pot. Components and collections are, therefore, defined relative to one another.

refer to such a collection as O2.2. From a number of different contexts, it is clear that the set of individual pots or types, such as pot, smoke, and fire, are examples of O2.2 objects.[30] It is also clear that these objects are supposed to be the indirect objects of perception.[31]

2.2.1. Universals and Particulars

Ratnakīrti's understanding of the distinction between particulars (*svalakṣaṇa*) and universals (*sāmānya*) helps to explain this a bit further, and provides some of the conceptual resources necessary for understanding how these two modes of determination bring about the construction of such objects. While Ratnakīrti most often refers to O2 objects as being determined objects, he also describes them as being universals (*sāmānya*), and says specifically that the determined object of perception is a universal—that is, an object that is "excluded from those that do not have its form" (*atadrūpaparāvṛtta*).[32] This is, of course, exactly how semantic value was described in chapter 4. It should be clear, therefore, that for Ratnakīrti both exclusion and determination are necessary for explaining how the indirect objects of both perception and inferential/verbal awareness are constructed. This general description of the determined object of perception can be made more precise by specifying the meaning of the phrase "those that do not have its form." More specifically, as discussed in chapter 4, a universal is either an object that is excluded from those that belong to the same class (*sajātīya*) or an object that is excluded from those that belong to a different

30. RNĀ (KSA 73.21–73.23): "The entire collection of things that is excluded from those that do not have its form cannot be the grasped object of sense perception, since it is not directly manifest. But it is without a doubt the determined object, since when one component of it is grasped, conceptualization is produced that ascertains pervasion between two such collections" (*sakalātadrūpaparāvṛttavastumātraṃ sākṣād asphuraṇāt pratyakṣasya grāhyo viṣayo mā bhūt | tadekadeśagrahaṇe tu tanmātrayor vyāptiniścāyakavikalpajananād adhyavaseyo viṣayo bhavaty eva*).

31. See RNĀ (KSA 73.21–73.23), which is quoted and translated in the previous note.

32. RNĀ (VN 109.17): "But the determined object is a universal, i.e., a genericized-particular excluded from those that do not have its form" (*adhyavaseyaṃ tu sāmānyam, atadrūpaparāvṛttasvalakṣaṇamātrātmakam*). The passage of which this sentence is a part is quoted and translated in notes 7 and 27. Also see RNĀ (KSA 73.21–73.23), which is quoted and translated in note 30.

class (*vijātīya*).[33] These two sorts of exclusion, which are identified as forms of determination, result in the construction of two different sorts of universals.

In chapter 4 the first sort of universal was called a "vertical universal" (*ūrdhva-sāmānya*): an object that is excluded from those that belong to the same class.[34] Tokens, such as an individual pot or pot-continuum, are examples. Object O2.1 is understood to be a vertical universal. The second sort of universal was called a "horizontal universal" (*tiryak-sāmānya*): an object that is excluded from those that belong to a different class.[35] A type, such as the class or set of pots, is an example of this sort of universal. O2.2 is understood to be a horizontal universal. As the indirect objects of perceptual states of awareness, it is important to keep in mind that both O2.1 and O2.2 are perceptible. In perceptual states of awareness, then, universals are determined, and are therefore the indirect objects of that state of awareness. Furthermore, they are constructed through the different modes of determination from the direct objects of that state of awareness, i.e., O1. According to Ratnakīrti, it is therefore possible to perceive universals regardless of whether they are vertical universals, such as a pot, smoke, or cow-tokens, or horizontal universals, such as kind properties or classes.

In this context, O1s, the objects from which O2.1 and O2.2 are constructed, are referred to by a number of different terms. They are said to be parts (*deśa*), pieces (*bheda*), special properties (*viśeṣa*), and also particulars (*svalakṣaṇa*).[36] According to Ratnakīrti, particulars are conceptually differentiated from universals in that they are neither just excluded from those that belong to the same class nor just excluded from those that belong to a different class. Although Ratnakīrti never describes them in this way, a

---

33. The terms "those that belong to the same class" (*sajātīya*) and "those that belong to a different class" (*vijātīya*) are quite common in RNĀ, and are used in a number of different contexts. See, for example, RNĀ (KSA 81.26), where they occur together. Although the term "excluded from those that belong to the same class" does not seem to occur, the term "excluded from those that belong to a different class" (*vijāti/vijātīya-vyāvṛtta*) is not uncommon. See RNĀ (AP 58.03, 59.26, 64.02, 66.13).

34. RNĀ (CAPV 143.12), quoted above.

35. RNĀ (CAPV 143.12), quoted above. Ratnakīrti uses the term "excluded from a different class" (*vijātivyāvṛtta*) to refer to dissimilarity classes at RNĀ (AS 66.05–66.06) and RNĀ (AS 66.13). Although he is discussing semantic value in these passages, his remarks also apply to perceptual value, since both are the determined objects of their respective states of awareness.

36. RNĀ (KSA 73.22, 73.24), RNĀ (VN 109.19), RNĀ (KSA 74.07), RNĀ (VN 109.16–109.17), and RNĀ (KSA 73.25–73.29), respectively.

particular may be thought of as an object that is excluded from those that belong to the same class *and* those that belong to a different class (*sajātīya-vijātīya-vyāvṛtta*).[37] Ratnakīrti understands such particular objects to be the basic objects from which determined objects are constructed. In the context of perceptual states of awareness, it is O1s that are said to be particulars. From Ratnakīrti's examples, it is clear that the individual moments of a continuum and the individual components of a collection are also O1s.

2.2.2. Constructing O2.1 and O2.2

The concepts described thus far make it possible to reconstruct Ratnakīrti's view of how O2.1 and O2.2 objects are constructed from O1. Although there are a variety of contexts in which Ratnakīrti describes this process, one of the more detailed descriptions is in his "Demonstration of Momentary Destruction" (*Kṣaṇabhaṅgasiddhi*).[38] Here Ratnakīrti explains that even though each and every component part that constitutes an O2 object is utterly distinct from every other such part, a relevant set of parts—that is, O1s/subimages—are nevertheless associated with one another prior to the construction of O2. They are associated with one another in the sense that they are brought together within O1 by a sufficiently similar—for all practical purposes the "same"—causal complex (*sadṛśasāmagrīprasūta*) and they bring about sufficiently similar—for all practical purposes the "same"—effects (*sadṛśakāryakārin*).[39] There is, therefore, a linked set of component O1s/

37. This description of a particular is given at MTBh 21.12.

38. RNĀ (KSA 67.03–82.17). This text has been critically edited and translated, with annotations, in Woo 1999.

39. RNĀ (KSA 74.07–74.15): "Now perception grasps a single particular [but] leads to the establishment of a collection of particulars, which are excluded from those that do not have their form. It does so by bringing about the ascertainment/determination of a thing-in-general that is excluded from those that do not have its form, on the basis of a connection, that is to say (*iti*), in virtue of *all* of those particulars (*viśeṣa*) being similar, since they were produced by a similar total causal complex and bring about a similar effect. This is just like establishing that perception grasps a pot: it grasps only a color-component, which is invariably related to a single total causal complex, [but] brings about the ascertainment/determination of the pot. If this were not the case, neither 'pots' nor a pot-continuum could be established through perception, since neither is grasped in its entirety (*sarvātmanā*). Moreover, 'grasping one part of it' is not different in the case of a thing excluded from those that do not have its form. Given this, it should be the case that through this very method there

subimages that is individuated by its causes and potential effects. One of these causally linked components is the particular, functional O1 object, such as the grasped moment of a continuum or the color-component of a pot, from which the universal O2 will be constructed.

Although all of the mental images that constitute the one multifaceted nondual O1 image are inseparable, there is a process whereby specific groups of its constituent images, which are here called "particulars," or O1s, come to be associated with one another. While Ratnakīrti does not say very much about this, it seems as though what brings about this grouping is an unending series of latent *karmic*-impressions (*anādivāsanā*). His remarks suggest that it is the ripening of *karmic* seeds that begins the process of individuating, constructing, and determining objects.[40] The specific details are never mentioned. What seems likely, however, is that appealing to *karmic*-impressions is a way of accounting for at least some of the factors that regulate the exclusion process, such as why a specific linked-image *p* (rather than some image *q*) is the manifest-content of a particular perceptual state of awareness.[41]

Having shown that particular O1s can be linked together in this way, Ratnakīrti then explains how an O2 object can be constructed. He points out that even though only one particular O1 is the direct object of perception, by grasping it, it is possible to be "in touch with" all of the other particulars with

---

can also be an awareness of the pervasion of all particulars, as in the relation of characteristics [e.g., the color-component of a pot] with what is characterized [e.g., the pot]" (*atha teṣāṃ sarveṣām eva viśeṣāṇāṃ sadṛśatvāt sadṛśasāmagrīprasūtatvāt sadṛśakāryakāritvād iti pratyāsattyā ekaviśeṣagrāhakaṃ pratyakṣam atadrūpaparāvṛttamātre niścayaṃ janayad atadrūpaparāvṛttaviśeṣamātrasya vyavasthāpakam | yathaikasāmagrīpratibaddharūpamātragrāhakaṃ pratyakṣaṃ ghaṭe niścayaṃ janayad ghaṭagrāhakaṃ vyavasthāpyate | anyathā ghaṭo 'pi ghaṭasantāno 'pi pratyakṣato na sidhyet, sarvātmanāgrahaṇābhāvāt | tadekadeśagrahaṇaṃ tv atadrūpaparāvṛtte 'py aviśiṣṭam | yady evam anenaiva krameṇa sarvasya viśeṣasya viśeṣaṇaviśeṣyabhāvavad vyāptipratipattir apy astu*). For parallel passages see PVSV 158.20, JNĀ (KBhA 52.03–52.09), and PVSVṬ 562.10, where the term "*pratyāsattyā*" is glossed with the term "*sādṛśyena.*"

40. At RNĀ (CAPV 138.14–138.16), for example, Ratnakīrti explains: "We do not say that there is positive activity through superimposition, but rather that what leads to positive activity toward an external object, even one that is not seen, is an awareness-event that is produced by the ripening of latent karmic impressions. This is, of course, the error that is inherent in everyday life" (*na vayam āropeṇa pravṛttiṃ brūmaḥ | kiṃ tarhi, svavāsanāparipākavaśād upajāyamānaiva sā buddhir apaśyanty api bāhyaṃ bāhye pravṛttim ātanoti, iti viplutaiva saṃsārātmikā ca*). See also RNĀ (AS 66.04), where the second part of this passage is quoted, and MTBh 68.07–68.08.

41. These "factors" will be discussed in greater detail below.

which it is linked in a specific causal context. Object O1 is the manifest image *p* that is individuated by its identity conditions **I**, defined here in terms of causes and potential effects. By excluding this "subimage" from what does not have its form (*atadrūpaparāvṛtta*)—where "having its form" defines the selection set **S**—there is also the exclusion of the subimages with which it is linked. Thus, if a linked set of images is excluded from the linked sets of images that belong to the "same class," a vertical universal or individual token (O2.1) will be constructed. If, however, the set is excluded from those that belong to a "different class," a horizontal universal or type (O2.2) will be constructed.

Consider, for example, an O2.1 object such as a blue pot. According to Ratnakīrti this individual pot is simply a specific collection of directly sensible particulars. For simplicity, suppose it is a collection of just the color "blue," the shape "round," and the smell "earthy." By grasping the particular color "blue"—which, in this case, is the O1 object, *p*—perception is also in touch with all of the other particulars with which this particular color "blue" is linked, i.e., the particular shape "round," the particular smell "earthy," etc. By excluding this particular color "blue" from all of the things that are not linked in the relevant way with non-this-blue-particulars—that is, the dissimilarity class non-**P**—what remains is the similarity class like-**P**, which is made up of this particular color "blue" and all of the other particulars with which it is linked. In other words, what remains is an individual blue pot, i.e., a vertical universal like object O2.1. Now suppose that what is grasped is this blue pot. By excluding this particular blue pot, *p*, from those things that do not have a "blue" color-particular, a "round" shape-particular, and an "earthy" smell-particular—that is, the dissimilarity class non-**P**—what remains is all of the things that have the linked particulars, the color "blue," the shape "round," and the smell "earthy." In other words, what remains is the similarity class like-**P**, the set of blue pots, i.e., a horizontal universal, like object O2.2. Thus, according to Ratnakīrti, both vertical and horizontal universals are perceived, in the sense that they are constructed through exclusion to be the determined-content of perception.

2.2.3. Determining Externality: O2E

In addition to its essential role in the construction of O2 objects, determination also seems to account for the phenomenality of perception, most importantly our sense that the objects of sense perception are in some sense external to us and therefore actionable. For Ratnakīrti, determination includes the capacity of awareness-events to externally place or project an O2 object. Let us refer to such an externally projected (*bahir-adhyasta*) object as O2e. O2e objects are the seemingly "subject-independent" objects that we purport to see, hear, taste, smell, touch, act upon, etc. More specifically, for Ratnakīrti, an O2e object is an externally projected mental image that only appears to be independent of us.[42] O2e is the kind of "external" object that we generally take to be the object of sense perception. Like all O2 objects, however, it is actually a similarity class or constructed universal that, despite appearing in awareness, appears to us as if it were present in the external world. It is the result of our (mis)taking what appears in awareness as something that does not. This is the case whether O2e is a projection of an O2.1 or an O2.2 object.

There is another sense in which O2 objects are also considered to be "external" by Ratnakīrti. Not only are O2 objects "external" in the sense that they are taken to be subject-independent, but they are also "external" in the sense that they are external to the image that directly appears in that awareness-event. For example, when we see a tree, the tree that we take ourselves to be seeing is something that we think is external to us.[43] It is an object like O2e. This is also the case with the semantic value of the word "tree." What we understand by the word "tree" is generally something that we think is external to us. It too is an object like O2e. Suppose, however, I choose to reflect upon the *mental image* of the tree that I (mis)take to be external to me. In this case, the object that I am reflecting upon is not the mental image itself, which is the manifest-content of reflexive awareness, but the relevant determined object that I can "mentally" act upon. According to Ratnakīrti, this object is, strictly speaking, "external," in the sense that like O2e it is external to the awareness-event in which it appears.[44]

---

42. See RNĀ (AS 60.06), discussed in chapter 4, where the phrase "conceptually constructed mental image that is externally projected/determined" (*bahiradhyasta vikalpabuddhyākāra*) is used to refer to O4e. That Ratnakīrti would agree to describe O2e in the same way is, I think, clear from his numerous descriptions of determination as "that through which an object of activity is constructed." For two very clear cases where this description is used, specifically in cases of perception, see RNĀ (KSA 73.09–73.18), which is partially quoted and translated in note 10. For a clear case where this description is meant to apply to both perceptual and inferential/verbal awareness see RNĀ (VN 109.13–109.23), which is also partially quoted and translated in note 7.

43. See chapter 4, section 3.2.

44. JNĀ (AP 229.07–229.10): "Therefore, just as on the basis of determination an external tree is conditionally adopted as what is denoted by the word 'tree,' in the same way it is

2.3. *Intentional Activity*

Once this aspect of determination is in view, it becomes clear why Ratnakīrti describes O2 objects as being the objects of activity (*pravṛtti-viśaya*).[45] In fact, for him, determined objects are by definition the only kinds of objects that we can act upon. Ratnakīrti explains further that there are three sorts of activity (*vṛtti*): bodily (*kāyikī*), verbal (*vācikī*), and mental (*mānasī*). The objects of these various forms of activity are the objects that we in some way physically act upon, e.g., pots, cows, trees, etc; those that we linguistically act upon, e.g., semantic value; and those that we are aware of mentally, e.g., concepts such as "pot," "cows," "trees," etc. In his "Debating Multifaceted Nonduality" Ratnakīrti briefly illustrates the relationships between determination, these three forms of activity, and their objects.[46] He explains, for example, that the determination that there is fire in a particular place can lead to all three forms of activity. For a person who instinctively withdraws her hand after touching the flames of a campfire, the fire that she touches and from which she withdraws her hand is a determined O2e object of her bodily activity. Determining that there is fire in a particular place can also produce linguistic activity in the form of a sentence such as "I know that there is fire in that place." In this sentence, the semantic value of the word "fire" is the object of the speaker's linguistic activity. It is important to keep in mind that even though, as a result of determination, perceptual awareness-events may involve conceptualization, they

---

only on the basis of determination that one talks about affirming or denying [any] external object. Even when, due to certain circumstances, one examines a mental image, having brought it to mind by means of another conceptualization, then too there is affirmation and denial of what is external to this conceptualization" (*tasmād yathā vṛkṣaśabdena bāhyo vṛkṣo 'dhyavasāyād abhidheyo vyavasthāpitaḥ, tathādhyavasāyād eva bāhyasya vidhir niṣedho vā vyavahriyate | yadāpi kutaścit prakaraṇād buddhyākāraṃ kañcid vikalpāntareṇādāya parīkṣā, tadāpi tadvikalpād bāhya eva vidhiniṣedhau*).

45. While this term is only used once, at RNĀ (CAPV 139.18), the concept is clearly referred to in many other places. For some of these references, see below.

46. RNĀ (CAPV 139.17–139.19): "Just as the determination 'There is fire here' leads to bodily activity, it also leads to verbal activity, i.e., 'Fire has been apprehended by me,' and to mental activity as well, in the form of the reflective awareness of this mental image" (*ihāgnir atrety adhyavasāyo yathā kāyikīṃ vṛttiṃ prasūte tathāgnir mayā pratīyata iti vācikīm api prasūte, etadākārānuvyavasāyarūpāṃ mānasīm api prasavati | evaṃ ca sati yathā vikalpenāyam artho gṛhīta iti niścayaḥ*). For a parallel passage see JNĀ (AP 226.25–227.01).

never involve language.[47] As a result, no object of a perceptual awareness-event can ever be the object of verbal activity. The object of verbal activity must be, therefore, the determined object of an inferential/verbal state of awareness. These O4 objects will be discussed in section 3. Finally, according to Ratnakīrti, the determination that there is fire in a particular place can also produce mental activity, in the form of one's reflective awareness of the image or concept of the fire that we take to be the object of our bodily or verbal activity.

Other than this brief illustration, Ratnakīrti does not discuss the three forms of activity in detail. He also does not provide a detailed analysis of the objects of these forms of activity. What is clear from his remarks, however, is that determined objects such as O2 (and O4) are the kinds of objects that we act upon. O2s should be described, therefore, not only as "universals" and the "determined-content" of perception, but also as the objects of activity. Insofar as they are mental objects, e.g., concepts or ideas, Ratnakīrti understands them to be the determined objects of reflexive awareness and so the objects of specifically mental activity. Insofar as we (mis)take such objects to be subject-independent, however, they are like O2e, and so the objects of bodily or linguistic activity.

2.4. *Inferential Reasoning: Part 1*

Ratnakīrti tries to show that his account of the contents of perception, more than just serving as the basis for a general account of intentional activity, can also be used, successfully, to explain reality-involving practices that his opponents, while agreeing that they depend upon perception, do not think can be explained exclusively in terms of objects like O1, O2.1, O2.2, and O2e. One such practice is the process of establishing an inference-warranting relation. By considering this practice in the context of making an inference-for-one's-own-sake (*svārthānumāna*), it is possible to see how Ratnakīrti might use such an account to explain other reality-involving practices involving perception.[48] Attention to this issue also begins to address the question of how Ratnakīrti applies the theory of exclusion and his account of mental objects/images to philosophical problems that are more specific to inferential reasoning.

---

47. See Patil 2007 and chapter 6, section 3 for a discussion that somewhat complicates this.

48. Since we are considering perceptual states of awareness it is necessary to consider an inference-for-one's-own-sake and not an inference for another, which is said to be linguistic in nature. See MTBh 24.02–24.08; and for a short discussion of this see Tillemans 2000:xv–xvi.

Consider, for instance, the standard example, introduced in chapter 2, of inferring that there is fire (the target property) on a particular mountain (the site of the inference) by seeing smoke (the reason property) rising up from it.[49] The thought process that results in the inference that there is fire on that mountain is understood by Buddhist philosophers like Ratnakīrti to take place in two stages.[50] The first stage involves seeing "smoke rising up from a particular mountain." Earlier this was referred to as the "site subcomponent" of the inference-instrument.[51] The second stage requires remembering that "wherever there is smoke there is fire." This was referred to earlier as the "pervasion subcomponent" of the inference-instrument.[52] This two-part process is said to result immediately in the awareness that "there is fire on that mountain." One way to analyze this process is in terms of the following objects: the perceived object, the horizontal universal/token "smoke-on-that-mountain-at-a-particular-time" (O2.1/O2e); the two invariably concomitant objects, the vertical universals/types "fire-in-general" and "smoke-in-general" (O2.2); and the contents of inferential/verbal awareness: its manifest-content, the universal "fire-in-general" (O3), and its determined-content, the particular "fire-on-that-mountain-at-this-time." (O4e). For Ratnakīrti, these are the "objects" involved in the inferential process.

Given Ratnakīrti's inventory of mental objects/images, the perceived object "smoke-on-that-mountain-at-a-particular-time" is clearly the determined-content of sense perception. As such, it is a similarity class, like the vertical

---

49. See chapter 2, section 1.4.

50. MTBh 24.02–24.04 describes an inference-for-one's-own-sake (*svārthānumāna*) as follows: "An inference that is 'for oneself' is one that is 'for one's own sake.' It is of the nature of awareness. After he sees smoke on a property-possessing location such as a mountain, an awareness of fire is produced in a certain inquirer. An object that is beyond the range of the senses is made known to him, and to no other, through that awareness. This is an inference 'for one's own sake'" (*svasmai yat tat svārtham anumānaṃ jñānātmakam | parvatādau dharmiṇi dhūmādikaṃ dṛṣṭvā yasya pratipattur vahnijñānam utpadyate, sa eva tena jñānena parokṣam arthaṃ pratipadyate nānya iti svārtham anumānam*).

The two steps of an inferential argument are described at MTBh 27.12–27.13 as follows: "For Buddhists, the statement of an inferential argument has only two parts: pervasion and the property of being located in the site of the inference" (*vyāptipakṣadharmatāsaṃjñakaṃ dvyavayavam eva sādhanavākyaṃ saugatānām*).

51. See chapter 2, section 2.3, where the idea is first discussed, and chapter 3, section 3, where the term is first used.

52. See chapter 2, section 2.3, where the idea is first discussed, and chapter 3, section 1, where the term is first used.

universal O2.1, but externally projected. It is an object that appears to us as being subject-independent. In other words, it is an O2e object.

Unlike the O2.1 and O2e objects that I described earlier, however, this object is described as being spatially and temporally located.[53] According to Ratnakīrti, objects can be identified by their spatial, temporal, and image-specifying coordinates (*deśa-kāla-ākāra-niyata*).[54] "Image-specifying" coordinates refer to all of the identity conditions of an object other than its spatial and temporal coordinates. Thus O2e objects can be described as mental objects that are constructed through exclusion and determined to be present in a particular locus "*l*" and at a particular time "*t*." While Ratnakīrti is not explicit about how to account for the spatial and temporal coordinates of an object, they do not seem to be a part of the one dynamic and complex collection that is O1.[55] It seems therefore that the spatial and temporal features of an object are supposed to be explained by the various "factors" that are built into the idea that latent *karmic*-impressions are essential for the construction of objects. If this is the case, spatio-temporal features are reflected in both **I** and **S**, and are bundled into the constructed O2 object by exclusion and determination. For now, what is important is that for the perceived token "smoke-on-that-mountain-at-a-particular-time," a set of three individuating characteristics can be specified. Thus, what we see when we see "smoke-on-that-mountain-at-a-particular-time" is, according to Ratnakīrti, an O2e object. This is in part how the content of the first stage in the process of

---

53. See section 2.2.

54. Ratnakīrti usually prefers the equivalent phrase "*deśa-kāla-svabhāva-niyama*." For some examples of how he uses this term see RNĀ (ISD 41.12), RNĀ (ISD 48.07), and RNĀ (KSA 69.03). There are far too many uses of this term to list them all here. See also MTBh 21.08–21.09, where the more familiar term "*deśa-kāla-svabhāva-niyata*" is used to describe the coordinates of a particular (*svalakṣaṇa*) pot. For more on the specificity of such particulars see, for example, RNĀ (KSA 73.12–73.18) and RNĀ (KSA 74.07–74.15), which are quoted and translated in note 39. For an excellent discussion of the history of this triad see Yoshimizu (forthcoming).

55. Ratnakīrti refers to temporality briefly at RNĀ (CAPV 142.29–142.32): "All sense perceptions—erroneous and nonerroneous, with conceptual construction and without conceptual construction, white and black—are nondifferent awareness-events, since they are grasped together. But priority and posteriority cannot be known at all" (*bhramābhramākalpanakalpanāni, śātāsitādīny akhilākṣajāni | jñānāny abhinnāni sahopalabdheḥ, pūrvāparatvaṃ tu na vedyam eva*). Other than the first metrical foot, this is a quotation of JNĀ (SSS 458.14–458.17).

inferring something for oneself can be understood in terms of Ratnakīrti's account of mental objects/images.[56]

The second stage in the process of inferring something for oneself is the act of remembering that given the presence of smoke, the presence of fire is epistemically necessary.[57] In order to remember this, however, it is necessary to have previously established that smoke and fire are related to one another through the "production-mode" of pervasion, and that they are therefore invariably concomitant.[58] As Ratnakīrti explains, this amounts to establishing that the horizontal universal/type "smoke" is invariably concomitant with the horizontal universal/type "fire." For Ratnakīrti, inference-warranting relations are supposed to be relations between universals, and in the case of the production-mode of pervasion, between horizontal universals.[59] The issue that I want to consider is how, given his inventory of mental objects/images, Ratnakīrti accounts for this.[60]

According to Ratnakīrti, establishing that the production-mode of pervasion obtains in a specific case—for example, between smoke and fire—is possible through a sequence of three awareness-events, whose objects seem to be vertical universals/tokens like O2.1 that are (mis)taken to be O2e. Ratnakīrti describes two sequences of such awareness-events.[61] The first is described as follows: (1) the nonapprehension of smoke and fire in a single locus—such as a kitchen; (2) the perception of fire in that locus, and nothing new other than fire; and finally (3) the perception of smoke in that locus. Through this procedure the positive concomitance of smoke with fire—i.e., that there is smoke only where there is fire—is supposed to be established.[62]

---

56. For a discussion of relations such as "on" (that is, "presence") see section 5.2.

57. See chapter 2, section 1.4.

58. See chapter 2, section 3.2.2.

59. There are a number of places where Ratnakīrti makes it clear that pervasion is established between "types" or "similarity classes." See, for example, RNĀ (KSA 73.11–73.23), RNĀ (KSA 74.07–74.13), and RNĀ (VN 109.13–109.36), which are partially quoted and translated in notes 68, 39, and 7, 27, and 32, respectively.

60. For an excellent discussion of the history of this issue, and some of the philosophical problems that are raised by it, see Gillon 1991, Inami 1999, Kajiyama 1963, Lasic 1999, Lasic 2003, and Woo 1999:180–181. See also MTBh 28.02–28.15, where this issue is discussed.

61. For a discussion of this approach see Kajiyama 1963, Inami 1999, Lasic 1999, and Lasic 2003.

62. RNĀ (VN 111.02–111.03): "Someone who sees, in sequence, two things that were not seen before or does not see, in sequence, two things that were seen knows the nature of a

The second sequence of awareness-events is described as follows: (1') the perception of both smoke and fire in a single locus (along with all of the other things that are present in that locus); (2') the nonapprehension of fire in that locus, and nothing other than fire; and finally (3') the nonapprehension of smoke in that locus. Through this procedure the negative concomitance of smoke with fire—i.e., that there is the absence of smoke only where there is the absence of fire—is supposed to be established.[63]

Given the episodic nature of awareness-events (each awareness-event can have one and only one object) and his inventory of mental objects/images, Ratnakīrti faces two challenges with this proposed method for establishing inference-warranting relations: he must show not only that this procedure makes sense given the episodic nature of awareness-events, but also that awareness-events whose objects are unrelated tokens can lead to an awareness-event of a relation between types.

In responding to an opponent who argues that because awareness-events are episodic in nature, it is not possible for this procedure to result in the awareness of a relation between *two* things, Ratnakīrti provides a more detailed account of how relational-awareness, specifically the awareness that some *e* is the effect of some *c* (and so invariably concomitant with it), is possible.[64] Here is Ratnakīrti's description of how positive concomitance is established: assuming an awareness-event A1, in which neither a thing *c* nor a thing *e* is apprehended in a locus, *l*, Ratnakīrti explains that in a subsequent awareness-event, A2, a thing *c*, which is the determined-content of perception, appears. According to Ratnakīrti, this awareness-event also projects an

---

cause and effect, for otherwise it would be never-ending" (*prāgadṛṣṭau kramāt paśyan vetti hetuphalasthitim | dṛṣṭau vā kramaśo 'pasyann anyathā tv anavasthitir iti*). For parallels see JNĀ (VC 169.02), which is also quoted at JNĀ (KKBhS 319.22).

JNĀ (VC 165.5–165.7): "If someone knows that there is the absence of smoke when there is the absence of fire, then, when there is only the absence of fire <2>, the nonobservation of smoke <3>, which is preceded by the joint apprehension [of fire and smoke] <1>, can be used to prove a connection [between effect and cause]" (*yadāgnyabhāve dhūmābhāvaṃ pratyeti, tadā sahopalambhapūrvakam* <1> *agnimātrābhāve* <2> *dhūmādarśanam* <3> *upayuktaṃ pratibandhasiddhau*).

63. See JNĀ (KKBhS 317.03–317.05), where he briefly outlines both approaches. This passage is cited and commented upon in Kajiyama 1963:5 and Inami 1999:140. See also JNĀ (VC 165.08–165.10).

64. For this objection see RNĀ (SSD 116.15–116.16) and Inami 1999:146, where he quotes a similar objection from PVSVṬ 98.13–98.15.

impression of *c* into a subsequent awareness-event A3. Along with the impression of *c*, there is, in awareness-event A3, the awareness of a single new thing, *e*. Awareness-event A3 is thus supposed to lead to the awareness of positive concomitance, namely, that given *e* in locus *l*, there is *c* in locus *l*.[65] Here is a parallel description of how "negative concomitance" is established: Assuming an awareness-event A1', in which both a thing *c* and a thing *e* are apprehended in a single locus, *l*, Ratnakīrti explains that in an awareness-event A2', the absence of a thing *c* in locus *l* is determined (as a result of perceiving *l*). This awareness-event also projects an impression of the absence of *c* in locus *l* into awareness-event A3'. Along with the impression of the absence of *c* in awareness-event A3', there is the awareness of the absence of *e* in locus *l*. Awareness-event A3' thus leads to the awareness of negative concomitance, namely, that given the absence of *c* in locus *l*, there is the absence of *e*.[66] In both A3 and A3' two "objects" appear to be in relation to each

---

65. RNĀ (KSA 72.11–72.17): "Moreover, it is not the case, even given momentariness, that our awareness of causal capacity is struck down. That is to say: The judgment/determination of positive concomitance—i.e., 'given the presence of *e*, *c* is present'—is produced by an awareness-event [A3]. A3 grasps the effect [*e*] as the primary effect of an awareness-event [A2] that grasps a cause [*c*]. A3 also contains within it an impression [of *c*] that has been projected [into it] by A2. In just this way, the judgment/determination of negative concomitance—i.e., 'given the absence of *c*, there is an absence of *e*'—is produced by an awareness-event [A3']. [A3'] grasps, relative to an effect [*e*], an empty patch of ground as the primary effect of an awareness-event [A2'] that grasps the empty patch of ground relative to a cause [*c*]. A3' also contains within it an impression [of 'the empty patch of ground relative to *c*'] that has been projected [into it] by [A2']" (*na ca saty api kṣaṇikatve sāmarthy-apratītivyāghātaḥ | tathā hi kāraṇagrāhijñānopādeyabhūtena kāryagrāhiṇā jñānena tadarpitasaṃskāragarbheṇāsya bhāve asya bhāva ity anvayaniścayo janyate | tathā kāraṇāpekṣayā bhūtalakaivalyagrāhijñānopādeyabhūtena kāryāpekṣayā bhūtalakaivalyagrāhiṇā jñānena tad-arpitasaṃskāragarbheṇa asyābhāve 'syābhāva iti vyatirekaniścayo janyate*).

For another example of how this procedure is put to work see RNĀ (SS 3.21–3.29), where he explains that this procedure can be used to show that the production mode of pervasion obtains in the case of the reason property—a "mental image associated with meditative practice"—and its target—a "clear and distinct manifestation"—just as it can in the case of pot and potters or the image of a young woman and its manifestation in the mind of her lovesick lover. See Bühneman 1980:8 and MTBh 61.15–62.03, quoted in Kajiyama 1963:488. This argument is discussed in chapter 6, section 2.

66. See the relevant part of RNĀ (KSA 72.11–72.15), which is quoted and translated in note 65, and the very similar description at RNĀ (SSD 125.14–125.20): "That is to say: This conditionally adopted position is easily established, even with [us] relying on a [momentary] mental continuum, which subsists in the relation of a primary cause and primary effect. So, why bring

other: what actually appears in awareness-event A3, however, is a single "object"—*e* as produced by/due to *c*—and in A3' the absence of *e* produced by/due to the absence of *c*. According to Ratnakīrti, putting together two previously grasped objects, *e* and *c* or the absence of *e* and the absence of *c*, in this way is just one of the features of mental construction.[67]

---

back a persisting self? [An] awareness of an effect-cause relation is consistent with this. In this case the judgment/determination that 'given the existence of *e*, *c* exists' is produced through an awareness-event [A3]. [A3 grasps] an 'existing-thing' [*e*] as the primary effect of an awareness-event [A2] that ascertains an 'existing-thing' [*c*]. A3 contains within it an impression [of *c*] that is projected [into it] by A2. In the same way, negative concomitance is ascertained/determined—i.e., 'given the nonexistence of *c*, *e* cannot exist' by an awareness-event [A3']. [A3'] ascertains/determines an empty patch of ground, relative to an 'existing-thing' [*e*], as the primary effect of an awareness-event [A2'] that ascertains/determines the empty patch of ground relative to an 'existing-thing' [*c*]. A3' also contains within it an impression [of 'the empty patch of ground relative to *c*'] that has been projected [into it] by [A2']" (*tathā hi, upādānopādeyabhāvasthitacittasantatim apy āśrityeyaṃ vyavasthā sustheti katham ātmānaṃ pratyujjīvayatu | tatra kāryakāraṇabhāvapratītis tāvad anākulā | tathāpi, prāgbhāvivastuniścayajñānasyopādeyabhūtena tadarpitasaṃskāragarbheṇa paścādbhāvivastujñānenāsmin satīdaṃ bhavatīti niścayo janyate | tathā prāgbhāvivastvapekṣayā kevalabhūtalaniścāyakajñānopādeyabhūtena tadarpitasaṃskāragarbheṇa paścādbhāvivastvapekṣayā kevalabhutalaniścāyakajñānenāsminn asatīdaṃ na bhavatīti vyatirekaniścayo janyate*). This is similar to how the process is described at MTBh 28.02–28.15.

67. RNĀ (KSA 72.20): "Given that this is the case, it is this conceptualization alone that brings the two grasped objects together. This is because it brings together the objects grasped in the two serial perceptual awareness-events, i.e., the two things that are related as primary cause and primary effect" (*evaṃ sati gṛhītānusandhāyaka evāyaṃ vikalpaḥ | upādānopādeyabhūtakramipratyakṣadvayagṛhītānusandhānāt*).

See RNĀ (SSD 127.01–127.06) for more on conceptualization as a "bringer together" (*anusandhāyaka*) of what is grasped: "Even though there cannot be a direct experience of a previous and subsequent moment related as cause and effect in just one awareness-event, [their] being a cause and being an effect [respectively] is definitely grasped by a pair of sequential awareness-events, which are the primary cause and effect. This [cannot be directly experienced] because, since there isn't an effect when the cause arises, we do not see the [actual] effect, even though we grasp its capacity [i.e., the capacity of the cause, e.g., a seed] to have it [i.e., the effect; e.g., a sprout] as an object. It is only when there is the determination of it that someone who has not acted is led to act by 'seeing the effect.' In the same way, when an effect is seen, its being an effect of that [cause] is definitely not grasped: it is brought together [with its cause] through conceptualization" (*yato hetuphalabhūtayoḥ pūrvottarakṣaṇayor ekaikena jñānenānanubhave 'py upādānopādeyabhūtābhyāṃ kramijñānābhyāṃ hetuphalatve gṛhīta eva | kevalaṃ hetukāle phalābhāvāt tadviṣayasāmarthyagrahaṇe 'pi phalādarśanāt tadavasāya evāpravṛttaḥ kāryadarśanena pravartyate | tathā phalāvalokane 'pi tatkāryatāgṛhītaiva vikalpenānusandhīyate*).

If Ratnakīrti's account can explain how an awareness of a "relation" is possible, the question that remains is how he can claim that the relation is one of concomitance between types. There are a number of places in his work where Ratnakīrti provides just such an explanation. In his "Inquiry Into Inference-Warranting Relations" (*Vyāptinirṇaya*) and his "Demonstration of Momentary Destruction" (*Kṣaṇabhaṅgasiddhi*), Ratnakīrti explains not only that pervasion is a relation between types, but also how the perception of objects that appear to be tokens—objects like *e* and *c*—can lead to an awareness involving types.[68] Here Ratnakīrti draws on his theory of exclusion. He

---

68. Consider the following passages: (1) RNĀ (KSA 73.18–73.23): "Even though it is in actuality impossible for a single thing to persist over time, perception [still] grasps pervasion between a reason property and a target property, which are excluded from those that do not have their form and [so are] present in all places and at all times. The reason for this is that the object of perception is twofold, grasped and determined. An 'entire collection of things that is excluded from what does not have its form' cannot be the grasped object of perception, since it is not directly manifest. But it is, without a doubt, the determined object [of perception], since when one component of it is grasped, it produces a conceptualization that can ascertain pervasion between two such collections. It is like coming to know a continuum from grasping a moment and like coming to know a pot, which is made up of color, taste, smell, and touch, from grasping only its color. If this were not the case, there would be the unwanted consequence that all inferential reasoning would be impossible" (*nānākālasyaikasya vastuno vastuto 'saṃbhave 'pi sarvadeśakālavartinor atadrūpaparāvṛttayor eva sādhyasādhanayoḥ pratyakṣena vyāptigrahaṇāt | dvividho hi pratyakṣasya viṣayaḥ, grāhyo 'dhyavaseyaś ca | sakalātadrūpaparāvṛttavastumātraṃ sākṣād asphuraṇāt pratyakṣasya grāhyo viṣayo mā bhūt | tadekadeśagrahaṇe tu tanmātrayor vyāptiniścāyakavikalpajananād adhyavaseyo viṣayo bhavaty eva | kṣaṇagrahaṇe santānaniścayavat, rūpamātragrahaṇe rūparasagandhasparśātmakaghaṭaniścayavac ca | anyathā sarvānumānocchedaprasaṅgāt*). For some interesting parallel passages to this, see JNĀ (VC 166.11–166.21), NBhū 140.22–140.25, and RNĀ (KS 74.07–74.13, which is partially quoted and translated in note 39, and VN 109.13–109.19, which is partially quoted and translated in notes 7 and 27).

(2) RNĀ (VN 109.18–109.26): "And therefore, even though, relative to our everyday sources of knowledge, what is grasped is only the color-component of a pot, which is constituted by a collection of color-, taste-, smell-, and touch-components, it is the collection that is conditionally adopted. In this way, even though a single thing excluded from those that do not have its form is grasped, it is correct that pervasion is grasped between a target-property-in-general and a reason-property-in-general. Both are things-in-general that are excluded from those that do not have their form and both become objects of awareness through the exclusion of a nonconnection" (*tataś ca sāṃvyavahārikapramāṇāpekṣayā rūparasagandhasparśasamudāyātmakasya ghaṭasya rūpamātragrahaṇe 'pi pratyakṣataḥ samudāyasiddhivyavasthā | tathaikasyātadrūpaparāvṛttasya grahaṇe 'pi sādhyasādhanasāmānyayor atadrūpaparāvṛttavastumātrātmanor ayogavyavacchedena viṣayabhūtayor vyāptigraho yukta eva*). Note that RNĀ (VN 109.13–109.18) is quoted in note 7.

argues that just as an individual collection—a vertical universal/token—can become the object of a perceptual awareness-event by directly grasping only one of its components, a horizontal universal/type can become an object of a perceptual awareness-event by directly grasping only one of its component tokens.[69] This is possible in Ratnakīrti's view since tokens and types are constructed through two different modes of determination from the same directly perceived object.[70] There is in his view nothing special about perceiving tokens rather than types since both are just similarity classes constructed through exclusion and determination.

Insofar as both *c* and *e* are the objects of sense perception, they are O2e objects and, more specifically, O2.1 objects that have been externally projected. Given exclusion, however, they can also be perceived as types, that is as O2.2 objects. For example, in awareness-event A1' the object of awareness is a locus, *l,* in which both smoke and fire are present. Here the perceived smoke, *e*, and fire, *c*, are externally projected O2.1 objects. In awareness-event A2' the object of awareness is the absence of fire, *c*, which, according to Ratnakīrti, is nothing other than the perception of locus *l*—an O2e object—characterized by the absence/exclusion of fire. In this case, the "fire" is an O2.2 object. What is absent is not just a fire token, but all fire. What is projected into awareness-event A3' is therefore an impression of an O2.2 object. In awareness-event A3' the object of awareness is the absence of smoke—another O2.2 object—which, because of the impression from A2', appears not just as an awareness of the absence of smoke—the O2.2 object "all smoke"—but as the awareness that the absence of smoke is accompanied by/due to the absence of fire—the O2.2 object "all fire." In perceiving O2 objects, one perceives not only O2.1 but also O2.2.[71]

Ratnakīrti argues that inference-warranting relations such as pervasion can be established through the perception of types, like object O2.2. One thing that differentiates these objects from tokens is that they do not have spatial or temporal coordinates. They are differentiated from other types, either through the perceived component from which they were constructed or from the perceived token through which the type comes to be perceptible. For these objects, only one of the three individuating coordinates, the image-specifying coordinate, can be described. They are, in this sense, not

69. See chapter 3 and section 2.2.1.

70. See chapter 3 and section 2.2.1.

71. See Lasic 2003:192, where he briefly discusses this issue.

spatio-temporally located. They are also different from O2.1 in their phenomenal character—whatever it is like to be aware of them is clearly different from what it is like to be aware of an object like O2.1.

What is remembered in the second step of an inference-for-one's-own-sake is what was originally perceived, namely, that the type "smoke" and the type "fire" are invariably concomitant. Unfortunately, Ratnakīrti does not discuss either memory or the objects of memory in detail. It is clear, however, that what are remembered are not mind-independent external objects and that memories themselves are mental objects/images. As a result, all of the objects involved in the perception of smoke and the establishment of the concomitance between fire and smoke can be explained as mind-dependent objects. By showing how both stages in the thought process leading up to the inference of "fire on that mountain" can be completely explained in terms of these objects, Ratnakīrti protects his account from the charge that it is unable to explain sense perception and the establishment of concomitance. Since the "fire" that is inferred in this inferential argument is an object of inferential/verbal awareness, it will be discussed in section 3. Before we turn to inferential/verbal awareness-events, however, it will be useful to discuss how Ratnakīrti accounts for testimony and verbal conventions in terms of O2 objects.

According to Buddhist philosophers like Ratnakīrti, testimony is reducible to inference: both the way in which we come to know things through testimony and the contents of awareness-events produced by it are like inferential reasoning and the contents of inferential awareness-events.[72] As a result, testimony and the contents of verbal awareness are reducible to inferential reasoning and the contents of inferential awareness. Thus, if Ratnakīrti can account for inferential reasoning through his four-object model of awareness, he should also be able to account for testimony. As discussed in chapter 4, in his "Demonstration of Exclusion" Ratnakīrti provides an inferential argument that makes explicit the inferential nature of verbal testimony.[73] In this argument Ratnakīrti seeks to show that anything that is expressive takes as its object a thing-in-general that is determined and excluded from those that do not have its form. The relationship between a word and its semantic value is thus defined in terms of the inference-warranting relation in this argument. Recall that the site subcomponent of this inference is

72. See the notes to chapter 4, section 1.

73. See chapter 4, section 4.

defined by the location of the reason property "being expressive" in the site of the inference, i.e., "an inferential/verbal awareness-event which has the form of a word such as cow." The pervasion subcomponent of the inference is defined by the inference-warranting relation "everything expressive takes as its object a thing-in-general that is determined and excluded from those that do not have its form." Unlike in the inference of fire from smoke, however, this inference-warranting relation is supposed to be an example of the "identity-mode" of pervasion.[74] Moreover, unlike the inference of fire from smoke, where the issue was how Ratnakīrti could account for our awareness of causation, in this case pervasion is based on a verbal convention. What is at issue is how verbal conventions for a particular word, in this case "cow," can be established. A successful account of how verbal conventions are established is necessary not only for Ratnakīrti's inferential argument, but also for his defense of his worldview. It also provides an interesting context in which to explore Ratnakīrti's account of the identity-mode of pervasion. What follows is a reconstruction of Ratnakīrti's account of how verbal conventions are established in terms of his inventory of mental images.[75]

---

74. See chapter 2, section 3.2.2.

75. This reconstruction is based on JNĀ (AP 204.08–204.16): "{If you say this, then in the same way, if the form of the conventional association were stated with words of this sort, 'The word "cow" refers to what is excluded from non-cows,' then there would be this problem.} But what possible problem could there be if: (a) The language learner has, with respect to the individuals intended by the speaker, a reflective awareness containing a single image, and (b) On the basis of context, he is caused to form a determinate awareness of them, and then (c) The speaker makes the conventional association 'This is a cow'? For that language learner understands that all of the individuals that fall within the scope of his own conceptual awareness (which are themselves excluded from all individuals that do not belong to that class, without relying on words such as 'excluded from non-cows') are expressed by the word 'cow.' Therefore, by the word 'cow,' he refers only to those individuals in which he apprehends the exclusion of what does not belong to that class. And in virtue of this, the statement that 'The word "cow" refers to what is excluded from non-cows' is just a gloss on the empirically established fact and is not the form of the convention itself. This is because it is only when this application of the word 'cow' has been accepted that everything else can be denoted by the word non-cow. However, whether the shared image that is excluded from what does not belong to that class is the appearance of a universal in conceptual awareness or is the real nature of the individual will be determined later. But it is established that there is no circularity. And just as upon hearing the word 'Puṇḍarīka' one is aware of a white lotus flower, so too when one hears the word 'cow' one is aware of something that is excluded from non-cows. {Therefore, it is established that even those who believe in real class-

Suppose that someone who has no idea what a cow is is being taught the semantic value of the word "cow." Let us refer to the person who is being taught the convention as "the student" and the other person as "the teacher." Although the student does not know anything about cows, it is important to note that she is a competent speaker of English, and so knows about many other things. Now suppose that the teacher and the student are looking out over a field in which there are cows, horses, and sheep—O2e objects. Suppose further that the teacher points to three of these objects and says "Look at that, that, and that," and then says, "Cows." Here is how, Ratnakīrti argues, the student learns the convention regarding the semantic value of the word "cow." On the basis of sequentially perceiving the three things that the teacher points to, the student constructs a single image—more specifically, a generic image or similarity class—on the basis of the three *p* images that were manifest to her awareness. The generic image that she constructs is the determined-content of perception—that is, an O2.2 object. On the basis of the teacher saying "cows," she then understands that the semantic value of the term "cow" is this determined generic image. Although the teacher may have said "cow" only once, as in the examples of fire and smoke, the student does not think that she is being taught the semantic value of this token utterance of the term "cow." As a result, it is a generic utterance "cow" that she takes the convention to be about—that is, an O2.2 object. The convention, therefore, is between two O2.2 objects. Now suppose that sometime later someone tells the student, "Bring a cow." In this case, she hears a token utterance of the term "cow," recalls pervasion, and infers semantic value. In this case, the manifest-content of her inferential/verbal awareness will be O3. The determined-content will be O4.

---

properties (*jāti*) must accept that a positive object (*vidhi*) is necessarily linked with awareness of exclusion as a qualifier of it}" (*{evaṃ tarhi yady agavāpoḍhe gośabda itīdṛśākāraṃ saṅketākārakīrtanaṃ tadā 'yaṃ doṣaḥ} yadā tu vivakṣitavyaktiṣv ekākārapratyavamarśavartini prakaraṇād avadhārite pratipattari saṅketakaraṇam ayaṃ gaur iti, tadā kva doṣāvakāśaḥ? sa hi svavikalpatalpaśāyinīḥ sakalavyaktīr agovyāvṛttādy akṣaram anapekṣya svayaṃ tadvijātīyāśeṣavyaktivyāvṛttā gośabdavācyāḥ pratipadyamāno yatraiva vijātīyavyāvṛttiṃ pratipadyate tā eva gośabdena vyavaharatīti, tāvatāgovyāvṛtte gośabda iti siddhāntānuvāda eva na saṅketākāraḥ, abhimate gośabdavṛttāv agośabdena śeṣasyābhidhātuṃ śakyatvāt | sa tu vijātīyavyāvṛttaḥ sādhāraṇākāro vikalpe sāmānyasya pratibhāso vyakter vā svātmaiveti paścān niścesyate | itaretarāśrayas tu nāstīti siddham | siddhaṃ ca puṇḍarīkaśabdaśrutau śvetaśatapatrapratipattivad gośabdaśrutāv apy agavāpoḍhapratītau {jātivādināpy avaśyābhyupagantavyam apohaviśeṣaṇaśemuṣīnāntarīyakatvaṃ vidher iti}*). See also the passages cited in chapter 4, section 3.3.

In this inferential argument the inference-warranting relation of pervasion is between two O2.2 objects, which are said to be related to one another through the identity-mode of pervasion. It may be helpful to think of these O2.2 objects as being "token-identical" in that there is no location/awareness-event in which the reason property is present and the target property is not.[76] As Ratnakīrti has argued, any awareness-event in which the reason property "being expressive" is located is an awareness-event that is about an actionable object. Since the only actionable objects are determined objects—i.e. "things-in-general that are determined and excluded from those that do not have its form"—the reason property will always be co-located with it. More specifically, on the token-identity model, every expressive token is identical with some token "thing-in-general that is determined and excluded from those that do not have its form." Attention to the inferential nature of testimony thus suggests that Ratnakīrti has philosophical resources to protect himself from the charge that his account of the content of perceptual-awareness events cannot account for the identity-mode of pervasion and our ability to establish verbal conventions.

3. The Contents of Inferential/Verbal Awareness

Inferential/verbal states of awareness are understood to be different from perceptual states of awareness. Not only is inferential/verbal awareness produced through a different instrument of awareness, namely, inferential reasoning or verbal testimony, but its manifest- and determined-contents are described differently. Unlike the contents of perception, the manifest-content of inferential/verbal awareness is said to be a "universal" while its determined-content is said to be a "particular."[77] In addition, there is also a difference in the phenomenal character of the determined-content of perception and inference: relative to what we "see," what we infer—or come to understand from hearing a word—is less "vivid" or fine-grained. Strictly

---

76. Consider the following: The type "being a cow"—whose tokens are the set {Śābaleya, Bāhuleya, Bessie}—and the type "being an animal"—whose tokens are the set {Śābaleya, Bāhuleya, Bessie, Mr. Ed <a horse>, Lassie <a dog>, Stuart <a mouse>}. Since the set of cows is a subset of the set of animals, cows and animals are "token-identical" in that every token cow is identical to some token animal.

77. See section 1.

speaking, perceptual and inferential/verbal states of awareness do not share any of the same objects or mental images. But, as should be clear from the role that perception plays in inferential reasoning and, therefore, testimony, inferential/verbal awareness is dependent upon perception for its contents.

3.1. Object O3: The Direct Object of Inferential/Verbal Awareness

O3 is the manifest-content of inferential/verbal awareness. Unlike the manifest-content of perception, but like its determined-content, O3 is said to be a "universal." Given Ratnakīrti's view that universals are similarity classes, constructed universals, or generic images constructed through exclusion, it might appear as though O3 is a "constructed" object. Insofar as O3 is the manifest-content of a state of awareness, however, it is directly present in awareness and cannot be "constructed." This contradiction, which seems to be generated by the conceptual vocabulary that Ratnakīrti uses to describe mental objects/images, is only apparent, and can be resolved by focusing on what Ratnakīrti means by the term "universal."

As mentioned above, for Ratnakīrti particulars and universals are defined relative to one another—there is no object that is in and of itself either a "particular" or a "universal."[78] The image that appears in the first stage of the perceptual process is not a "grasped object of perception" because it is a particular, but rather it is a "particular" because it is the grasped object of perception. In the same way, the image that appears in the first stage of the inferential process is not a "grasped object of inference" because it is a universal, but rather it is a "universal" because it is the grasped object of inference. Objects/images are labeled as "particulars" or "universals" only in relation to a subsequent determination. Thus for Ratnakīrti "particular" and "universal" are not really ontological categories at all. Instead, they are defined contextually. Objects/images are categorized as either one or the other depending on the role that they are made to play by subsequent acts of conceptualization. A particular is something that is made into a universal—regardless of whether that particular is a component/property of an individual or an individual—by the determination of singularity. A universal is something that is made into a particular by what Ratnakīrti once calls the determination of difference (*bhedāvasāya*).[79]

78. See section 1.

79. RNĀ (CAPV 143.14), which is quoted and translated above in section 2.2.

Thus O3 is a "universal" not in the sense that it is constructed, but in the sense that it will be deconstructed or particularized. Insofar as O3 is the manifest-content of inferential/verbal awareness it is not constructed, and may be thought of as the nonconceptual/manifest-content of such states of awareness.

Although this is the primary sense in which mental objects/images are identified as being either "particulars" or "universals," there is another reason O3 objects are "universals" that is not explicitly discussed by Ratnakīrti but is suggested by the reconstruction of the inferential process described above. Given that O3 is the direct object of inferential/verbal awareness, it is the image that directly appears in inferential/verbal awareness as a result of inferential reasoning/verbal testimony. It is, in other words, the immediate output of this process. Given my reconstruction of the inferential process in terms of the contents of perception, it may seem as though the immediate output of the inferential process is an O2 object. More specifically, it is the O2 object that defines the target property in the recalled pervasion relation. Whether this object is an O2.1 or an O2.2 object will depend on the inferential context. For example, in the inference of fire from smoke, what is directly and nonconceptually manifest in inferential/verbal awareness may seem to be an O2.2 object like the constructed universal "fire-in-general"; so too in the inference of the semantic value of the word "cow," where what seems to be directly and nonconceptually manifest is an object like the constructed universal "cow-in-general." It is also possible to come up with examples where the object seems to be like O2.1—e.g., the inference of the semantic value of the proper name "Ratnakīrti." These O3 objects are, however, different from O2 objects in that they are manifest in inferential/verbal awareness-events. It should be clear that despite the role that the content of perception seems to play in the production of the manifest-content of inferential/verbal awareness, O3 objects cannot be O2 objects.[80]

As the manifest-content of inferential/verbal awareness, O3 is the object from which both inferential and semantic value are constructed through exclusion and determination. It is, in other words, the object *p* that is the basis for exclusion. As I have argued, O3—and therefore *p*—can be described as either a vertical or a horizontal universal. What is most important, however, is that regardless of whether O3 is a vertical or a horizontal universal, it

80. It should be noted that there is no clear textual support for this view, other than what can be inferred from the passages cited in section 1.

is a "universal," in the sense that the determined-content of inferential/verbal awareness is a "particular" that is constructed from it. Although O3 is a "universal," there are two important differences between it and the determined-content of perception (O2), which is also said to be a "universal." Unlike the determined-content of perception, O3 is a universal because it is deconstructed into one of its components, which is, by definition, a "particular." Unlike the determined-content of perception, because O3 is manifest, it does not have phenomenal character. It doesn't seem like anything to us to be aware of it. In fact, what we are able to say about O3 is primarily what we, in hindsight, come to learn about it on the basis of the O4 object that is constructed from it.

3.2. Object O4: The Indirect Object of Inferential/Verbal Awareness

Object O4 is an indirect object of an inferential/verbal state of awareness. As such it is an object that is constructed through exclusion and determination from the O3 object that is manifest in awareness. Given that O4 is the determined-content of inferential/verbal awareness, it is an object of activity. More specifically, it is an object of inferential and verbal activity, in the sense that it is what we take both inferential and semantic value to be. It is therefore the object that we take ourselves to act upon.[81] Unlike the determined object of perception, however, O4 is said to be a "particular" and, more accurately, a "determined/excluded particular."[82] As mentioned above, a "particular" is an object that is constructed from a universal—in this case, O3—through exclusion and determination. Inferential value and semantic value are the paradigmatic examples of determined/excluded particulars. O4e is just the external projection of O4. Examples of O4e objects are the "real" fire that we infer to be present on the mountain and the "external" referent of a word.

As a particular, O4 is an object that is excluded from both those that belong to the same class and those that belong to a different class.[83] What distinguishes the use of the term "particular" when it is applied to O1 and when it is applied to O4 is not its general description—rather, it is the nature of the object to which it is related through determination. In the context of

---

81. See earlier references in section 1.

82. See RNA (CAPV 137.25–137.33), where the term "*parāpoḍhasvalakṣaṇa*" is used. This passage is quoted and translated in note 91. Also see section 1.

83. See chapter 4, section 3.1.2.

perceptual states of awareness, particulars are constructed into universals. In inferential/verbal states of awareness universals are constructed into "particulars." The mechanism of construction is, however, the same: exclusion constructs the object with reference to a relevant set of "similarities" and "differences."

Consider, for example, the inference of fire from smoke. The manifest-content of inferential awareness is O3. Based on how this O3 is produced—that is, the specific inferential process, including the context that prompts the inference—it may be helpfully thought of as a generic fire-image, like the horizontal universal "fire-in-general." This O3 image is what results from a perceptual awareness-event in which the determined image that appears, "smoke-on-that-mountain," is conditioned by the recollection of the pervasion of smoke by fire. What we infer, however, is not fire-in-general—that is, the target property—but rather that "there-is-now-fire-on-that-mountain." The determined-content of perception is not a specific fire token like O2.1/O2e, nor is it a type, which like O2.2 is neither spatially nor temporally specified. What is inferred is a universal fire, which is more general than the specific fire-token that could be perceived and yet more specific than the perceived type "fire." It is in other words not the fire that is actually there on that mountain at that particular time "*t*," but rather whatever fire could be there on that mountain at a particular time "*t*." Moreover, what we take ourselves to be inferring the presence of is not a mental image, but an object that we take to be subject-independent—that is, O4e. As will be discussed below, it is through exclusion and determination that O4/O4e is constructed from O3.

Suppose O3 is the horizontal universal, "fire-in-general." This is the object *p* that is the manifest-content of inferential/verbal awareness. Like all such objects, it is defined by a set of identity conditions, **I**. **I** will include conditions that specify its "image" coordinates as well as its spatio-temporal ones.[84] Given the context, the selection set **S** will be defined, at least in part, by the spatial coordinates of the site of the inference—the mountain—and an appropriate set of temporal coordinates. The dissimilarity class non-**P** will contain the set of objects that do not satisfy **S**—e.g., fire-tokens that existed in

84. This point depends on my argument that O3 does not have the same image specifying coordinates as O2. Since there isn't clear textual support for my position, it is likely to be controversial. If O3 does have the same image-specifying coordinates as O2, then spatio-temporal coordinates will not be a part of **I**.

the past or fire-tokens that "share" the appropriate temporal coordinates but not the relevant spatial ones. By excluding the dissimilarity class, non-**P**, from *p*, one constructs its complement, the similarity class, like-**P**, which includes all of the objects that we take to satisfy **S**, in this case, the token "fire-that-is-now-on-that-mountain."

3.3. *Intentional Activity: Regulating Inferential/Semantic Value*

Although Ratnakīrti gestures to the various factors that influence and regulate the construction of O3 and O4 objects, he neither provides a systematic account of them nor explains in any detail how we can account for the apparent success of our reality-involving practices and the seemingly high degree of intra- and intersubjective agreement that they generate. In what follows I want to present a generic version of Ratnakīrti's approach to the construction of mental images, as a way of highlighting how their construction is supposed to be regulated. This reconstruction of Ratnakīrti's theory of exclusion and determination also provides the framework within which to approach the question of what it means for Ratnakīrti to say that inference is a source of knowledge.

Given what has been said so far, there seem to be three steps in the construction of mental images through exclusion and determination:

Step 1: Start with some object *p* with identity conditions **I**, where **I** is the set of (causal) conditions that individuate *p*—the "manifest-content" of awareness.

Step 2: Take **S**—a subset of **I**—to define the set of "selection" conditions. This set of selection conditions is the basis for the *construction* of a dissimilarity class, non-**P**—the set of objects that do not *satisfy* **S**; that is, the set of objects that we take to be "non-*p*'s."

Step 3: Finally, construct the similarity class like-**P** by the *exclusion* of the dissimilarity class non-**P**. The similarity class, like-**P**, consists of objects that satisfy **P**; that is, it consists of all "*p*'s." Here, the construction process is described in terms of an exclusion, which is akin to constructing the complement of non-**P**. Like-**P** is the "determined-content" of awareness.

"Object *p*" is the manifest-content of a state of awareness. Relative to the awareness-event in which it nonconceptually appears, it is either said to be a "particular" or a "universal." With "hindsight"—that is, on the basis of what is supposed to be constructed from it—*p* can be characterized as a moment, a property, an individual, or a class.[85]

Based on Ratnakīrti's scattered remarks about *p*, there seem to be four factors that affect why a specific *p* (rather than some object *q*) appears in awareness when it appears. These "factors" may be helpfully thought of as accounting for *p*'s identity conditions—that is, what makes *p* what it is. Often Ratnakīrti appeals to subject-specific factors such as those encoded in one's latent *karmic* dispositions to explain why, in a particular case, we start with the *p* that we start with. Let us refer to these "*karmic*" factors as F1. Although not much is said about it, F1 seems to be a very broad category that overlaps with and/or includes three other sets of factors that can be at least conceptually distinguished from it. To account for the manifest-content of awareness, Ratnakīrti sometimes points to (F2) contextual factors—such as one's current interests/concerns, the conversational or inferential context in which one finds oneself, etc.; (F3) well-established social conventions or norms—including social facts such as the semantic value of "cow" and, perhaps, shared biological facts such as the fact that water can quench our thirst; and (F4) features of the object(s) that in some sense produced the image. Often each of these factors is given a causal interpretation such that **I** is defined as a set of causes and potential effects. In an important sense F1–F4 define the total causal complex that produces *p* and determines its identity coordinates.

Selection set **S** is a subset of **I**, and is the basis for the construction of the dissimilarity class non-**P**. The factors that account for why, in a particular case, a specific set **S** (rather than a different subset of **I**) is the "selection" set seem to be transmitted, at least in some cases, from those that result in *p*, e.g., our current interests or concerns. In general, the kinds of factors that account for *p* also seem to be the kinds factors that account for **S**. Let us refer to any nontransmitted factors, if and when there are any, as F5. It is on the basis of **S** that the dissimilarity class non-**P** is constructed. Non-**P** is defined by those objects that do not satisfy **S**—that is, those objects that we would take to be "non-*p*'s." "Non-*p*'s" are therefore the objects that, according to us, would not function within the expectation parameters encoded in **S**. The phrases "that *we* take to be" and "according to *us*" are supposed to highlight

85. In the case of the manifest-content of inferential/verbal awareness, "foresight" may also tell us something about *p*.

the fact that there are intersubjective constraints on what satisfies **S** in a particular context. For example, in the context of determining semantic value, F3 provides one such constraint.[86]

Finally, through the exclusion of non-**P**, a similarity class "like-**P**" is constructed. Like-**P** is the complement of the dissimilarity class non-**P**. According to Ratnakīrti, it is clear that like-**P** is a mental object/image (*ākāra*). Most often Ratnakīrti describes this mental object/image as a positive object characterized by its exclusion of others; as a thing-in-general separated out from things that are non-that; and a generalized image. This object is understood to be constituted by two components that are only analytically or conceptually separable from one another: the so-called positive component, the mental image, and the so-called negative component, the exclusion process through which it was produced. It is claimed that this object accounts for conceptual content, since it is what we end up taking to be the object (or patient) of any act—whether linguistic, mental, or physical. It is in other words the only sort of "actionable" object. It is never the case that what we experience/notice/think there to be in awareness is, in fact, what there really is. There is always a "mismatch" between what is ***available*** and what is ***actionable***. According to Ratnakīrti, the gap between what is available—that is, what is directly present in/manifest to awareness—and what is actionable—that is, conceptual content—is bridged by determination, which is nothing but another feature of exclusion.[87]

Thus on the basis of *p*, a set of selection conditions **S**, and two processes—the construction of a dissimilar class non-**P** and exclusion—Ratnakīrti supposes that a similarity class like-**P** can be constructed. Given this account, F1–F4 are the factors that an exclusion theorist can appeal to in order to explain why we start with the *p* that we start with and, with the addition of F5, why this *p* provokes or triggers the construction of the image that it does. The reason the exclusion process is not arbitrary is that F1–F5 are supposed to regulate it. In the vocabulary of Ratnakīrti's inventory of mental images, *p* is the manifest-content of awareness—that is, O1 or O3—and the similarity class, like-**P**, is the determined-content of awareness—that is, O2 or O4.

86. It is worth noting that unlike *p*, however, non-P is not taken to be an object or mental image at all. It is not itself the content of an awareness-event. Instead, the construction of non-P seems to be a subprocess in the overall process of exclusion.

87. For more on the relationship between "conceptualization" and "determination" see Patil 2007.

3.4. *Inferential Reasoning, Part 2*

With this generic account of the construction of mental images in place, it becomes possible to continue the discussion of the inference of fire from smoke that I began in section 2.4. Let us suppose that the inference-for-one's-own-sake discussed there was made by a forest-ranger, sitting in a fire-tower in the midst of a mountain range. As mentioned above, the smoke that the ranger "sees" is an O2.1 object that has been constructed from an object *p* and externally projected to be an O2e. This ranger comes to construct the smoke-image that she constructs through a causal complex that is defined by (or at the very least includes) F1–F5. It is this same causal complex that accounts for triggering her memory of pervasion between smoke-in-general and fire-in-general, two O2.2 objects. As a result of this, an O3 object, fire-in-general, is manifest in inferential/verbal awareness.[88] Moreover,

---

88. RNĀ (AS 65.25–66.05): "You may argue: If in determination a determined real thing does not appear, then, what does it mean to say 'it is determined by it'? You say it means, 'Even though it does not appear it is made into an object of activity.' But how are we to act with respect to a specific object by excluding other objects when there are no distinctions without manifestation? We reply: Although everything is ungrasped, there is activity with respect to water and the like. This because our conceptual awareness has a specific object, since it is produced by a specific causal complex, has a specific mental image, and has a specific capacity. It is like smoke's producing an awareness of a fire that is beyond the range of our senses. For things that have specific capacities and whose natures have been established by valid awareness are not liable to questions about the mixing up of their capacities. Therefore, because of association with a specific image, 'determining it' is simply 'producing activity with respect to it.' Moreover, we do not say that there is activity because there is the superimposition of similarity, such that there would be an opportunity to criticize us for imposing the external object on the image or the image on the external object. What then? The awareness that arises purely as the result of the maturation of its own karmic traces, even without seeing the external object, produces activity with respect to the external object" (*nanv adhyavasāye yady adhyavaseyaṃ vastu na sphurati tadā tad adhyavasitam iti ko 'rthaḥ | apratibhāse 'pi pravṛttiviṣayīkṛtam iti yo 'rthaḥ | apratibhāsāviśeṣe viṣayāntaraparihāreṇa kathaṃ niyataviṣayā pravṛttir iti cet | ucyate | yady api viśvam agṛhītaṃ tathāpi vikalpasya niyatasāmagrīprasūtatvena niyatākāratayā niyataśaktitvān niyataiva jalādau pravṛttiḥ | dhūmasya parokṣāgnijñānajananavat | niyataviṣayā hi bhāvāḥ pramāṇapariniṣṭhitasvabhāvā na śaktisāṃkaryaparyanuyogabhājaḥ | tasmāt tadadhyavasāyitvam ākāraviśeṣayogāt tatpravṛttijanakatvam | na ca sādṛśyād āropeṇa pravṛttiṃ brūmaḥ, yenākāre bāhyasya bāhye vākārasyāropadvāreṇa dūṣaṇāvakāśaḥ | kiṃ tarhi svavāsanāvipākavaśād upajāyamānaiva buddhir apaśyanty api bāhyaṃ bāhye pravṛttim ātanoti*). See also RNĀ (KSA 73.12–73.18), which was partially quoted and translated in notes 10 and 23, and RNĀ (CAPV 138.01–138.12), which is quoted and translated in note 89.

as the manifest-content of inferential/verbal awareness, O3 is an object *p* that has a set of identity conditions **I**, which, it is important to note, are also determined by F1–F5. O3, which is described as a "universal," is, however, different from the O2.2 "fire-in-general"-image that is the target property in the pervasion relation. Unlike this O2.2 object, the appearance of O3 has a slightly different causal history—after all, it is the result of a specific inferential process (and not perception or memory).

According to Ratnakīrti, the total causal complex that accounts for the O3 object that is the manifest-content of the ranger's inferential/verbal awareness includes elements of the causal complex that produced O2e and triggered the memory of the specific O2.1 and O2.2 objects that she, at one time, perceived. These "remembered" objects are causally related to the specific O2e object, smoke, that she perceives on the mountain. This is because the set of causal factors that result in her perceiving smoke on the mountain is a subset of the causal factors that result in her remembering concomitance and inferring O3. This causal complex is in turn a subset of the causal factors that result in her associating the O3 object she infers with the concept "fire," and so is itself a subset of the causal factors that result in the construction of the determined-contents O4 and O4e. The O2e object that she perceives on the mountain is causally related, therefore, to the O4e object toward which she eventually acts. This causal relationship between these facets of awareness underlies and regulates the inferential process, so that under normal conditions the perception of smoke will lead to the inference of fire and not, for example, to the inference of water.[89]

---

89. RNĀ (CAPV 138.01–138.12): "About this we say: If a determined object isn't grasped, no 'thing' is grasped either. Still, [we] act only with respect to specific objects, and not everything. This is because [our] conceptual awareness has a specific capacity in virtue of its specific image, which is due to the force of an immediately preceding awareness which is of that sort. Since things that have specific capacities have natures that are completely known through valid awareness, they are not liable to questions about their capacities being mixed up. This is because, even though no 'thing' exists, *only* a sprout is produced from a seed, [unlike] production from a nonexistent. This is because the [seed] is ascertained through valid awareness as having [causal] capacity only with respect to a [sprout]. It is just like this here: a person who seeks the pragmatic effects of cooking on fire and the like has a memory of [fire]. [His] conceptual awareness contains a fire-image [and], as known through valid awareness, has the capacity to [generate] activity that is directed only to fire. How could this capacity fall prey to overextension? Furthermore, when we consider the connection (*pratyāsatti*) between them, both the *real* fire and the one that is depicted in our conceptual awareness have a blazing and

Suppose further that the forest-ranger decides to seek out the fire that she infers to be there. In this context the word "fire" refers to its external referent, i.e., an O4e object. As the object toward which she physically acts, O4e is an object of her bodily activity. One consequence of this view is that the fire that she seeks, the O4e object, and the fire that she eventually reaches, the O2e object, are not the same. Strictly speaking, then, she does not infer the existence of what she eventually perceives. In Ratnakīrti's account, however, the inferential process is tightly regulated, and it is this that accounts for the reliability or success of inferential reasoning. More specifically, its reliability is due to the nature of the relationship between the O2e object (i.e., the smoke she is currently perceiving), the O2 objects she perceived while establishing the concomitance between fire and smoke, the O3 object she infers, and the O4e object toward which she acts. Built into the process of exclusion, then, are the mechanisms that are supposed to account for the success and failure of our reality-involving practices.

4. Nonexistence, Existence, and Ultimate Existence

It is through his account of the contents of awareness-events that Ratnakīrti seeks to explain reality, our reality-involving practices, and our experiences and thoughts about the world. According to him, however, the contents of these awareness-events do not have the same existential status. As I will argue, for him only O1 objects *really* exist. Attending to Ratnakīrti's remarks about the ways in which things "exist" thus provides a context for understanding what is special about O1 objects and, interestingly, also what it

---

radiant image. Thus, due to this, a conceptual awareness of fire has the capacity to cause one to act only with respect to fire, and not with respect to water and the like" (*atra brūmaḥ | yady adhyavaseyam agṛhītaṃ viśvam apy agṛhītam, tathāpi niyataviṣayaiva pravṛttir na sarvatra, tathābhūtasamantarapratyayabalāyātaniyatākāratayā niyataśaktitvād vikalapasya | niyataśaktayo bhāvā hi pramāṇapariniṣṭhitasvabhāvāḥ, na śaktisāṅkaryaparyanuyogabhājaḥ, asadutpattivat sarvatrāsattve 'pi hi bījād aṅkurasyaivotpattiḥ, tatraiva tasya śakteḥ pramāṇena nirūpaṇāt | tathehāpi hutavahākārasya vikalpasya dāhapākādyarthakriyārthinas tatsmaraṇavato hutavahaviṣayāyām eva pravṛttau sāmarthyaṃ pramāṇapratītaṃ katham atiprasaṅgabhāgi | pratyāsatticintāyāṃ ca tāttvikasyāpi vahner jvaladbhāsvarākāratvaṃ vikalpollikhitasyāpīti, tāvatā tatraiva pravartanaśaktir jvalanavikalpasya na jalādau*). For parallel phrases see JNĀ (AP 226.02–226.03), JNĀ (AP 220.07), and JNĀ (AP 226.06–226.09). See also JNĀ (AP 65.26–66.03), which is quoted and translated in chapter 4, section 3.3.

means for him to say that perception and inference are sources of knowledge. By returning to Ratnakīrti's inventory of the contents of awareness-events, this time with a focus on their existential status, I hope to provide an account of Ratnakīrti's ontology of mental images.

4.1. The Determined-Contents of Awareness: O4/O4e, O2/O2e

The determined-contents of awareness-events include both perceptual (O2) and inferential/semantic value (O4). As discussed above, perceptual value and inferential/semantic value are positive entities characterized by their exclusion of others. They are most often referred to as the determined-content of their respective awareness-events. It is only insofar as they are determined by awareness that they are "objects," that is, the kinds of things that we can act upon, either physically, verbally, or mentally. It is also in virtue of being determined that these objects are said to be "external." Insofar as such positive entities are manifest in awareness, however, they are said to be mental images and are not, strictly speaking, "objects" at all.

In what follows, it will be important to keep in mind that although these positive entities appear in conceptual awareness-events, insofar as they are mental images, they are the objects of reflexive-awareness and are, therefore, the manifest-content of a nonconceptual awareness-event. In other words, they are functionally O1s. As such, they neither have phenomenal character nor are the determined objects that we act upon. They are not, therefore, the kinds of things that we normally consider our experiences and thoughts to be about. Insofar as they are mental images, they are not "actionable." On the other hand, insofar as they comprise the determined-content of their respective awareness-events—awareness-events produced through perception or inference (O2/O4)—they are actionable and the "objects" of our awareness. In what follows I will refer to O2 and O4 as "objects" and their underlying "images" as I2 and I4.[90]

---

90. Ratnakīrti often refers to the images that underlie determined objects as the "very nature," "real nature," or "own-form" of the object. See, for example, RNĀ (CAPV 131.33), which is quoted and translated in note 97. For the idea that only mental images are manifest in nonconceptual awareness-events and are the objects of reflexive-awareness, see RNĀ (CAPV 132.28): "Now then, in nonconceptual awareness, other than the mental image itself, which is established through reflexive-awareness, dissimilar cases and the like are not manifest" (*nirvikalpe tāvat svasaṃvedanasiddhasvākāram antareṇa vipakṣādayo na parisphuranti*).

In a number of interesting passages in his "Debating Multifaceted Nonduality" Ratnakīrti explains that there are three sorts of determined objects: those that "exist," such as pots (O2), smoke (O2), and fire (O4); those whose existential status has not yet been determined (O2/O4); and those "non-things" that do not exist, such as the soul (O2/O4), nonmomentary things (O2/O4), Īśvara (O4), the horns of a rabbit (O2), and things like the imaginary net-like apparitions that people sometimes see when they close their eyes (O2).[91] Like all determined objects, each of these sorts of "things" is

---

For a discussion of I2/O2 see RNĀ (CAPV 131.11–132.03), which is quoted and translated in note 97. For I4/O4 see JNĀ (AP 220.07–220.08): "For one and the same bare image—blazing and radiant—although it is utterly distinct from every particular, when it is being made one with a particular, is called a 'universal.' But that [image] is not itself a universal belonging to those particulars, because it recurs elsewhere as a mental image" (*tad eva hi jvaladbhāsurākāramātram akhilavyaktāv atyantavilakṣaṇam api svalakṣaṇenaikīkriyamāṇaṃ sāmānyam ity ucyate | na tu tatsāmānyam eva tāsām, buddhyākāratvenānyatrānugamāt*). See the parallel discussion at RNĀ (AP 63.10–63.19).

91. RNĀ (CAPV 137.25–137.33): "This is because, on the basis of determination, it is not the case that even if there isn't the *manifestation* of a real external thing, such as a piece of cloth; a thing whose existence as a real thing [is] in doubt because of a defeater, such as a moment; or a non-thing such as a hare's horn, even Brahmā can condemn the established connection [between what is manifest and what we know, i.e., the 'object' that we are aware of]. This is because there are two ways of talking about objects: on the basis of manifestation and on the basis of determination. So here, even though it is not manifest, the particular that is excluded from what is other is said to be an 'object' merely on the basis of determination. And so of course it follows that 'what is made known by awareness is not manifest in that awareness-event.' This is because, even if there isn't a relation between what is manifest and what makes something manifest, there can be a relation between an object and what it is the object of, also through the relation between determination and what determines something" (*na hy adhyavasāyād bāhyasya paṭāder vastuno bādhakāvatārāt pūrvasandigdhavastubhāvasya kṣaṇikāder avastuno vā śaśaviṣāṇāder asphuraṇe 'pi siddhipratibandho brahmaṇāpi pratividhātuṃ śakyaḥ | dvividho hi viṣayavyavahāraḥ, pratibhāsād adhyavasāyāc ca | tad iha pratibhāsābhāve 'pi parāpoḍhasvalakṣaṇāder adhyavasāyamātreṇa viṣayatvam uktam, sarvathā nirviṣayatve pravṛttinivṛttyādisakalavyavahārocchedaprasaṅgāt | tataś ca tena ca tat pratipādyate na ca jñāne tatprakāśa iti saṅgatir asty eva, prakāśyaprakāśakabhāvābhāve 'py adhyavasāyādhyavasāyakabhāvenāpi viṣayaviṣayibhāvopapatteḥ*). For parallel phrases see JNĀ (AP 225.17–225.18) and JNĀ (AP 225.14–225.15).

RNĀ (CAPV 140.04–140.09): "Therefore, a real thing, such as a pot, cloth, and the like; an uncertain thing, which has not been proven or disproven; and a non-thing, such as the soul, space, time, or something nonmomentary, are said to be 'determined.' This means that even though it is not manifest, it is made into an object of activity. And as all this is known from authoritative texts, this is the meaning of 'imposition,' 'making one,' 'determination,' 'grasping nondifference,' etc. Thus, because determination is associated with a specific mental

constructed from the manifest-content of the relevant state of awareness. According to Ratnakīrti, insofar as these sorts of things are supposed to be external to awareness—that is, actionable objects—it is possible to determine their existential status by determining whether or not they are capable of being pragmatically effective.[92] For him, to say that such objects exist means just that they are capable of being pragmatically effective. To be "capable of being pragmatically effective" an object must be capable of functioning within the expectation parameters of the awareness-event of which it is an object. Another way of putting this is to say that pragmatically effective objects are the determined-contents of *valid* awareness.

According to Buddhist philosophers like Ratnakīrti, the validity of a state of awareness and its pragmatic efficacy (*arthakriyā*) are closely linked.[93] A state

---

image [it has] the property 'capable of causing activity [towards an object] even though [the object] is not grasped.' It is in virtue of this that there is a grasped/grasper relation between the external object and determination. Since, on the basis of [our] conventions, this is very difficult to deny, the relation between an object and what it is an object of is also secure. Thus it is correct to say that there is the relation between an object and what it is an object of, merely through determination" (*tasmād vastu vā ghaṭapaṭādi sandigdhavastu vā sādhakabādhakātikrāntam, avastu vātmadikkālākṣaṇikādikam adhyavasitam iti, apratibhāse 'pi pravṛttiviṣayīkṛtam ity arthaḥ | ayam eva cāropaikīkaraṇādhyavasāyābhedagrahādīnām arthaḥ sarvatra śāstre boddhavyaḥ | tasmād adhyavasāyasyākāraviśeṣayogād agṛhīte 'pi pravartanayogyatā nāma yo dharmas tayā bāhyādhyavasāyayor grāhyagrāhakabhāvaś cet saṃvṛtyā duṣparihāraḥ, tadā viṣayiviṣayabhāvo 'pi labdha ity adhyavasāyamātreṇa viṣayaviṣayitvam uktam iti yuktam*). For other references to this basic division between objects see RNĀ (KSA 89.01–89.12) and RNĀ (KSA 89.20–89.23).

92. RNĀ (CAPV 132.21–132.29): "'Manifestation is indeed an accredited instrument for establishing the existence of a thing. But it is not the case that when that accredited instrument is not functioning, an object is absent. Rather, existence is the capacity for being pragmatically effective. And it is not the case that this is incompatible even with something that is not manifest.' If this is your argument, it is correct. This is because, given the view that there are external objects, I can accept that even what is not manifest can have that capacity. This is because, if a net-like apparition is manifest, the nonexistence of the determined object is established only on the basis of its not being capable of pragmatic efficacy. But if no external objects exist, since awareness does not deviate from manifestation, it [exists] just in virtue of that. With regard to existence, what is the point of pragmatic efficacy?" (*nanu prakāśo nāma vastunaḥ sattāsādhakaṃ pramāṇam | na ca pramāṇanivṛttāv arthābhāvaḥ | arthakriyāśaktis tu sattvam | tac cāprakāśasyāpi na virudhyata iti cet | satyam etat | bahirarthavāde 'prakāśasyāpi sāmarthyābhyupagamāt | keśoṇḍukādipratibhāse 'dhyavasitasyārthakriyāśaktiviyogād evābhāvasiddheḥ | sarvathā bahirabhāve tu jñānasya prakāśāvyabhicārāt tāvataiva sattve kim arthakriyayā*).

93. For a discussion of this concept in Dharmakīrti's work see Nagatomi 1967, Mikogami 1979, Katsura 1984, Franco 1997, Dunne 2004, McCrea and Patil 2006.

of awareness is "valid" (*pramāṇa*) insofar as any activity that we undertake on the basis of it can lead us to results that are consistent with the specific expectations that we form (and could form) on the basis of it.[94] This does not mean that our expectations must be met in every case, but only that the objects toward which we are prompted to act could function within these expectation parameters.[95] Valid states of awareness must then direct us toward objects that are *capable* of meeting our expectations, i.e., toward objects that have the capacity to be pragmatically effective, regardless of whether our expectations are actually met in any specific case. Thus, for an object to be the determined-content of *valid* awareness it must be capable of being pragmatically effective, and so must exist. It is because of this criterion of pragmatic efficacy that: (1) we can say that "non-things" do not exist: according to Ratnakīrti, neither Īśvara, the soul, nor the horns of a rabbit can exist, since they are not the determined-contents of a *valid* awareness-event; (2) we are right to be agnostic about the existential status of things whose capacity for pragmatic efficacy cannot be determined; and (3) we can say that the "things" that we perceive (such as pots) and that we infer (such as the fire on the mountain) "exist."

According to the criterion of pragmatic efficacy, the existential status of these three sorts of things is different. Nevertheless, they are all determined objects: they are all mental images (I2/I4) that we (mis)take to be objects of one sort or the other (O2/O4). Insofar as they are mental images they are, like all mental images, manifest in awareness, in the sense that they are the

---

94. See, for example, RNĀ (PAP 97.21–97.22).

95. A central concept here is Dharmakīrti's idea of "*arthakriyāsthiti*" in PV 2.1. For translations see Vetter 1964, Nagatomi 1967, van Biljert 1989, Franco 1997, Kellner 2001:507, and Dunne 2004. As I understand it, the term does not mean simply the "existence" of pragmatic efficacy, but its persistence or consistency. The test for the validity of awareness is that its object continues to behave within the expected parameters, as defined by our interests. This is not limited to cases in which we actually want this object and successfully obtain it. It also includes cases in which we wish to avoid a particular object or, according to some, cases in which we are indifferent. This is recognized by authors in the tradition who take *arthakriyā* to include avoidance (*hāna*) as well as obtaining (*upādāna*). An awareness is said to be valid, therefore, if the object that we come to know on the basis of it behaves in conformity with the expectations that we form on the basis of that awareness. It is worth noting that others in the tradition, such as Vinītadeva (NBṬ [Vi: 39.4ff]), but not Dharmottara (NBṬ 30.2), add to "avoidance" and "obtaining/acquisition," "neglect/indifference" (*upekṣā/upekṣaṇīya*). See Krasser 1997 and Kellner 2001:511 n. 32 for a short but interesting discussion of this point.

manifest-content of a reflexive-awareness event. As the manifest-content of an awareness-event, these images are like O1 and, as I will explain below, even more like O3. According to Ratnakīrti, while the criterion for determining the existence of an *object* is pragmatic efficacy, the criterion for determining the existential status of an *image* is manifestation: determined objects and manifest images are said to exist for very different reasons.

4.2. *The Manifest-Content of Awareness: O1, I2, O3, I4*

Unlike the determined-contents of states of awareness, the manifest-contents of awareness are not "objects" in the sense that they are not the kinds of things that we can act upon. According to Ratnakīrti, to say that such images exist means simply that they are manifest in awareness. He says explicitly that being manifest in awareness is the mark of existence, since existence (*sattā*) is pervaded by manifestation (*prakāśa*) and the absence of manifestation (*aprakāśa*) is pervaded by nonexistence (*asattā*).[96] He also suggests that what it means for something to be manifest is that it is incapable of being defeated—manifest-content cannot be shown to be false. One consequence of this is that, for Ratnakīrti, existing things cannot be defeated (and nonexisting things cannot be manifest). Moreover, since actionable objects, i.e., the determined-contents of awareness, can be shown to be "false," it is only the manifest-contents of awareness that can really exist.[97]

---

96. RNĀ (CAPV 132.19–132.20): "It is because it is known that existence is pervaded by manifestation and nonmanifestation by nonexistence" (*prakāśavyāptatvāt sattāyāḥ | aprakāśasyāsattayā grastatvāt*).

97. RNĀ (CAPV 131.31–132.01): "The fourth option {1.4} is also not possible, since there is a contradiction between 'manifestation' and 'nonexistence,' and it is not tenable that a manifesting thing is false. That is to say: What do you mean by the manifestation of something that does not exist? Is what you mean the manifestation of a nonexistent thing like Īśvara {1.4.1}; or a manifest mental image that doesn't exist {1.4.2}; or that no existing thing is manifest {1.4.3}? Among these, {1.4.1} How can something whose own form is completely manifest not exist? Living beings need to understand this. This is because even though the manifest mental image 'net-like apparitions' is shown to be false with respect to its having the form of an external object, as the Ācārya has explained, it is an object in virtue of its having the form of awareness since, [if this were not the case] there would be the unwanted consequence that even imageless manifestion, which is supposed to grasp things, would be said to be 'nonexistent'" (*{1.4} na caturtho 'pi prakāraḥ sambhavati, asatprakāśayor virodhāt, sphurato 'līkatvāyogāt | tathā hy asatprakāśa iti kim asadīśvarādeḥ khyātiḥ {1.4.1}, bhāsamāno vākāro 'san {1.4.2}, san vā na kaścit khyātīti {1.4.3} vivakṣitam | tatra {1.4.1} yasya padārthasya*

The relationship between "being manifest," "being actionable," "being shown to be false," and "existing" is explained further in a passage in which Ratnakīrti considers the objection that while manifestation may be a mark of existence (in that existence pervades it), it is not the case that the absence of manifestation is pervaded by the absence of existence.[98] In other words, while there may be positive concomitance between the two, there doesn't seem to be negative concomitance, since, for example, objects such as pots, which are not manifest in awareness, appear to exist. The force of the objection is to suggest that pragmatic efficacy may be in fact a better mark of existence than manifestation, since there is both positive and negative concomitance between it and existence. Ratnakīrti responds to this by saying that on the view that there are external objects, it is correct to say that even things that are not manifest in awareness are capable of pragmatic efficacy, and to conclude therefore that they exist. With respect to external objects he agrees that there is both positive and negative concomitance between existence and pragmatic efficacy.

As an example of negative concomitance he cites the example of net-like apparitions and argues that given the manifestation of net-like apparitions (I2) one can prove that they do not exist only by discovering that the corresponding determined object (O2e) is not pragmatically efficacious. Notice that it is the determined object and not the manifest image whose nonexistence (or existence) can be established on the basis of pragmatic efficacy. As far as the manifest image (I2) is concerned, Ratnakīrti explains that it is manifestation alone that establishes its existence. Moreover, given that in his view there are no nondetermined external objects, manifestation is the only criterion for existence, and so there is no point in appealing to pragmatic efficacy.

4.3. *Conventional and Ultimate Existence*

There are then two different criteria for determining existence, one that applies to the determined-contents of awareness (that is, to "objects") and the other that applies to manifest-content (that is, to "images"). For Ratnakīrti, however, the criterion of manifestation is philosophically superior to the crite-

---

svarūpaparinirbhāsaḥ sa katham asann iti prāṇadhāribhir abhidhātavyaḥ | sphurataḥ keśoṇḍukākārasya bāhyarūpatayā bādhyatve 'pi jñānarūpatayārthatvasyācāryeṇa pratipāditatvād grāhakābhimatanirākāraprakāśasyāpy asattvābhidhānaprasaṅgāt).

98. RNĀ (CAPV 132.21–132.25), which is quoted and translated in note 92.

rion of pragmatic efficacy. As a result, things that are said to exist because they are pragmatically effective are taken to exist only "conventionally," while things that are said to exist because they are manifest in awareness are taken to "really" exist or exist "ultimately." As explained above, to say that something "really"/"ultimately" exists is simply to say that it cannot be defeated—that is, that it cannot be shown to be false.

In his "Demonstration of Exclusion" Ratnakīrti makes explicit the conceptual connection between what is really the case (*tattvataḥ*) and the manifest-contents of awareness and what is conventionally the case (*saṃvṛti*) and the determined-contents of awareness. He does this in a passage near the end of his essay in which he explains why even though semantic value must be the determined-content of verbal awareness we can take this to be the case only conventionally, and not ultimately.[99] As I have argued in this chapter, since semantic value is the determined-content of an awareness-event, the significance of Ratnakīrti's remarks can be extended to include not just semantic value, but also perceptual and inferential value as well. In making his point about the determined-contents of awareness, Ratnakīrti also explains why even though they ultimately exist, the manifest-contents of awareness are neither conventionally nor ultimately the contents of either sense perception or inference. By interpreting this passage in the light of Ratnakīrti's discussion of pragmatic efficacy and manifestation, it becomes possible to extend its scope to include the contents of all awareness-events and not just inferential/verbal ones.

According to Ratnakīrti, the manifest-content of an awareness-event is an object of reflexive-awareness. Since the manifest-content of an awareness-event is not determined, it does not have phenomenal character and so cannot be what we take perceptual, inferential, or semantic value to be. Insofar as it is manifest, it is not an object that we can act upon and is not, therefore, what we conventionally think of as the objects of our experiences and thoughts. Such objects do not function within expectation parameters, since

99. RNĀ (AP 65.15–65.22), which is quoted and translated in chapter 4, section 3.2.1. This point is nicely summarized in a verse that Ratnakīrti cites immediately following this passage at RNĀ (AP 65.21–65.22): "There is no way of *really* affirming either the mental image or the external object. *Conventionally* there is affirmation only of externals, whereas even conventionally there is no affirmation of the mental image" (*nākārasya na bāhyasya tattvato vidhisādhanam | bahir eva hi saṃvṛtyā saṃvṛtyāpi tu nākṛteḥ*). This verse is also quoted in JNĀ (AP 229.03–229.04) and JNĀ (SSS 443.13–443.14).

we cannot have the relevant sorts of expectations about them. They are not, in other words, pragmatically effective, and therefore cannot exist conventionally. Since they are manifest, however, they do exist. But, as Ratnakīrti explains, the mental images that are manifest in awareness are the manifest-content of reflexive-awareness and not the manifest-content of the state of awareness in question. Thus the mental image (I4/I2) that is mistaken to be either inferential/semantic value (O4) or perceptual value (O2) is not itself an object or image of that inferential/verbal or perceptual awareness-event. It is, in a sense, inaccessible to those awareness-events and so, for philosophical reasons, just cannot be what inferential/verbal or perceptual awareness-events are ultimately about. Although these images are not ultimately the objects of either sense perception or inference, since they are manifest in awareness they do exist: they are the manifest-content of reflexive-awareness. Moreover, in virtue of manifest images like I2 and I4 (and also O1 and O3) being "inaccessible" to sense perception and inference, they neither can be what these awareness-events are about nor can they be defeated by them. As the manifest-content of reflexive-awareness—that is, as O1s—such images not only exist, but since they cannot be defeated, they exist ultimately. So for Ratnakīrti, although mental images really exist, they are not the content of sense perception or inference, either conventionally or ultimately. They are the objects of reflexive awareness, which Ratnakīrti says is ultimately the only accredited source of knowledge.[100]

Unlike the manifest-contents of awareness, the determined-contents of awareness (O2/O2e, O4/O4e) are actionable objects and are therefore the kinds of thing that can be pragmatically effective. They are the kinds of objects that can function within expectation parameters, and therefore are the kinds of objects that we have experiences of and thoughts about. As a result, it is the determined objects of awareness-events that we are conventionally entitled to say exist. It is also the determined objects of perceptual and inferential/verbal states of awareness that we are conventionally entitled to take to be the objects of perception and inference. If we do not speak and take things in this way, Ratnakīrti argues, we will not be able to explain the success of any of our reality-involving practices. Of course, not all determined objects exist conventionally. According to Ratnakīrti, for example,

100. RNĀ (CAPV 143.25): "reflexive-awareness itself is the only mode of valid awareness" (*{vijñānavāde tv anātmaprakāśābhāvāt} svasaṃvedanam evaikaṃ pramāṇam*).

neither mirages nor Īśvara should be said to exist even conventionally, since neither is the object of a valid awareness-event. For Ratnakīrti, while only the determined-contents of awareness can be pragmatically effective, we are only conventionally entitled to take those determined objects that are the objects of valid awareness-events to exist.

Implicit in Ratnakīrti's remarks is also an argument for why we are only conventionally, and not ultimately, entitled to take the determined-contents of awareness to be the pragmatically effective objects of perception or inference. As Ratnakīrti sees it, a philosophically rigorous account of mental content must be one according to which the content of an awareness-event **E** is both "available" to it and "actionable" by it. To be "available to awareness" means that an object/image must be internal to it. If the content of awareness-event **E** is not internal to **E**, Ratnakīrti suggests that it cannot be the content of **E**, even though it might be the content of some other awareness-event. O1, I2, O3, and I4 are, according to Ratnakīrti, "available" to their respective awareness-events: sense perception, reflexive-awareness, and inference. To be "actionable by awareness" means that an object/image must be the kind of thing that can be acted upon by someone on the basis of that awareness-event. Since O1, I2, O3, and I4 are not determined, they cannot be acted upon. Only O2 and O4 objects are "actionable" by the awareness-events in which they appear. However, these objects are not "available" to these awareness-events, since they are not "internal" to them. They are the result of mistaking what is internal to them, namely O1, I2, O3, or I4, to be something else. As a result, Ratnakīrti considers them to be, strictly speaking, "external" to the relevant awareness-event. For Ratnakīrti, then, what is available is not actionable and what is actionable is not available. Since what we want to mean by the content of awareness must be both, and there isn't any such thing, we are only conventionally entitled to say that determined objects are the contents of our thoughts and experiences. The reason we are entitled to say that they exist only conventionally is a bit different.

According to Ratnakīrti, all determined objects are constructed through exclusion and determination and are therefore external to the awareness-event in which their manifest image appears. It is because of this that we come to mistake the manifest-content of awareness with the determined object that we construct. Ratnakīrti concludes from this that all such objects are the result of an error, even though only some of them—like mirages and Īśvara—can be defeated through sense perception or inferential-reasoning. As discussed in chapter 4, Ratnakīrti argues that error is the result of taking something to be an "*x*" when a "non-*x*" is given.[101] Since determination constructs an object "*x*" when a "non-*x*" is given—e.g., it constructs an O2/O4 object from O1/O3—Ratnakīrti asserts that determination is nothing other than error itself. This means that even though it may not be possible to prove that specific O2–O4 objects are false, or that they will be defeated by another awareness-event in the future, they are still the product of error, as a result of being determined. Thus they do not really exist and are not ultimately real.

For Ratnakīrti, then, to exist conventionally something must be the determined-content of a valid awareness-event—i.e., an awareness-event produced through either perception or inferential reasoning. To exist ultimately, something must be the manifest-content of reflexive-awareness, and therefore be immune from defeat. According to this criteria, O2 and O4 objects may exist conventionally while O1, I2, I4, and O3 objects exist ultimately.[102] Although this seems to be Ratnakīrti's final position, I will argue that there is a difference between O1 and I2, I4, and O3 that suggests that for Ratnakīrti only O1 really exists. More specifically, O1 seems to be the only object not dependent upon mental construction for its appearance in a state of awareness.

4.4. O1

From Ratnakīrti's point of view, it is clear that objects O2 and O4 are constructed from O1 and O3 through the various modes of determination. As determined objects they do not really exist. However, the images that are mistaken to be these objects—that is, images I2 and I4—really are manifest in their respective states of awareness and so, according to Ratnakīrti's analysis, really exist. Although I2 and I4 are not yet determined to be O2 and O4, their presence in awareness is nevertheless the result of construction from O1 and O3 through exclusion. In this sense, these images are constructed, even though they are manifest. In my view, this is also the case with O3. Like I2 and I4, O3 is manifest in awareness. Also like I2 and I4, O3 is a constructed image in the sense that it could not be manifest in awareness without some

101. RNĀ (CAPV 137.03–137.04): "Since when a non-'*x*' is manifest, determination grasps an '*x*' in place of a 'non-*x*' and makes what is seen and what is determined into a single thing, it is said to be 'error'" (*{śāstre ca} atasmins tadgrahāt svapratibhāse 'narthe 'rthādhyavasāyād dṛśyavikalpyayor ekīkaraṇād bhrāntir uktā*). Also see chapter 4, section 4.2.

102. See RNĀ (CAPV 138.01–138.12), which is quoted and translated in note 89.

form of mental construction. Although it is strictly speaking not constructed, it is not the case that it is not due to construction. The extent to which this is true should be clear from my reconstruction of the inferential process described above. In the end, the only object that is not dependent on any mental construction is O1 and so, by Ratnakīrti's criteria, it alone ultimately exists.

5. The Īśvara-Inference, Revisited

Ratnakīrti's account of the contents of awareness-events clearly demonstrates that the philosophical reach of the theory of exclusion extends well beyond the semantic context in which it was originally developed. As I have argued, for Ratnakīrti the theory of exclusion is best understood as a theory of the contents of awareness-events and the nature and existential status of mental objects/images like O1–O4. As we have seen, the theory of exclusion is at the center of Ratnakīrti's account of how these objects are constructed and related to one another. Furthermore, as discussed in sections 2.4 and 3.4, the theory is directly relevant to Ratnakīrti's account of inferential/verbal awareness, and can be used to map the inferential process onto Ratnakīrti's theory of mental objects/images. As I now hope to show, the theory of exclusion also quietly informs important parts of Ratnakīrti's critique of the Naiyāyikas' Īśvara-inference and supplies some of the important philosophical resources that he relies upon in his critique of it.

5.1. Pervasion Subcomponent

As discussed in chapter 3, especially sections 1 and 2, one of the focal points for Ratnakīrti's critique of the Īśvara-inference is pervasion condition C2.3—a reason property must be known to be excluded from all dissimilar cases. Satisfying C2.3 shows that neither $H3a_1$, which *defeats* pervasion, nor $H3a_2$, which *undermines* it, applies to the reason property in question.[103] In his critique of the Īśvara-inference, Ratnakīrti argues that the Naiyāyikas

103. Recall that $H3a_1$ (a subtype of the defect "inconclusive") *defeats* pervasion through the identification of a locus in which the reason property is known to be present and the target property is known to be absent. $H3a_2$ *undermines* pervasion by raising epistemically significant doubt about whether the reason property is excluded from *all* dissimilar cases. See chapter 2, sections 2.3.2, 3.2.1, and 3.2.2, and chapter 3, sections 2.1 and 2.2.

cannot satisfy C2.3 because of fundamental problems in their account of certification and satisfaction.

According to Ratnakīrti there are two specific, and closely related, problems with the Naiyāyikas' approach to the satisfaction of C2.3. The first is that they cannot explain how, on the basis of observation and nonobservation, one can be aware of *all* dissimilar cases. The second is that they cannot rule out the possibility of there being deviation, since they are unwilling to consider "potential" dissimilar cases as being relevant to the satisfaction of C2.3 (e.g., objects of awareness that are spatially or temporally remote at the time of observation and nonobservation). According to Ratnakīrti, each of these "problems" results in epistemically significant doubt about the satisfaction of C2.3, and it is partially on the basis of this that he argues that the reason property in the Īśvara-inference is undermined by $H3a_2$. As I argued in chapter 3, this argument can be extended to the certification of many other inferences as well and, according to Ratnakīrti, exposes a fundamental problem in the Naiyāyikas' approach to the satisfaction of C2.3 and the certification of the inference-instrument.

In responding to this criticism, Ratnakīrti's Naiyāyikas argue that his interpretation of C2.3, and his understanding of the conditions necessary for its satisfaction, place unreasonable demands on the certification of any inference-instrument and in effect render inferential reasoning impossible. They insist, further, that their approach to the satisfaction of C2.3 can rule out "epistemically significant" doubt about the exclusion of a reason property from all dissimilar cases and that it is Ratnakīrti's demands that generate "paralyzing doubt" about the satisfaction of C2.3. Although it is far from explicit in his discussion of C2.3, the theory of exclusion supports Ratnakīrti's arguments and helps to explain why he thinks that the demands he places on certification and satisfaction are not unreasonable.[104]

5.1.1. All Dissimilar Cases

In providing an account of how similarity classes are constructed from the manifest-content of awareness, the theory of exclusion provides an account

---

104. My discussion here picks up on issues 2 and 4, discussed in the opening section of chapter 4.

of how it is possible to be aware of all dissimilar cases by observing only a few of them. More specifically, for Ratnakīrti, a similarity class of all dissimilar cases (which includes those that are spatially or temporally remote) is a determined O2.2 object that is constructed from the manifest-content of a perceptual awareness-event through exclusion and determination. According to Ratnakīrti, it is therefore possible for us to be aware of *all* dissimilar cases, and thereby to determine (at least in principle) whether or not a reason property is excluded from them.

In an interesting passage in "Debating Multifaceted Nonduality," Ratnakīrti says this explicitly, while explaining to an opponent that even though the class of all dissimilar cases is not *manifest* in awareness, it can be *determined* by it. He says,

> Awareness-episodes have two sorts of objects—grasped and determined. A grasped object is one that is manifest. A determined object is an object of activity, even though it is not grasped. For someone making an inference there cannot be the manifestation of all dissimilar cases, unless he is omniscient. Therefore, between these two, we don't say that dissimilar cases are objects in virtue of being grasped, since there would be the unwanted consequence that all inferences would fail. The reason for this is that since there is never the manifestation of all dissimilar cases, the exclusion of the reason property from them could not be established. Moreover, if there were manifestation—that is, the direct presentation of all dissimilar cases independent of space, time, and nature—the poor target property itself could be known so much better, and thus inferential reasoning would be useless. Therefore, the exclusion of smoke and the like from dissimilar cases can be ascertained, because even though they are not manifest, they are definitely established through determination. . . . Now, if they were not even determined, it would be right to say that negative concomitance could not be ascertained, since there isn't an everyday way of acting with respect to each and every object.[105]

105. RNĀ (CAPV 131.04–131.13): *{iha} dvividho vijñānānāṃ viṣayo grāhyo 'dhyavaseyaś ca | pratibhāsamāno grāhyaḥ | agṛhīto 'pi pravṛttiviṣayo 'dhyavaseyaḥ | tatrāsarvajñe 'numātari sakalavipakṣapratibhāsābhāvān na grāhyatayā vipakṣo viṣayo vaktavyaḥ, sarvānumānocchedaprasaṅgāt, sarvatra sakalavipakṣapratibhāsābhāvāt tato vyatirekāsiddheḥ | pratibhāse ca deśakālasvabhāvāntaritasakalavipakṣasākṣātkāre sādhyātmāpi varākaḥ sutarāṃ pratīyata ity anumānavaiyarthyam |*

In this passage Ratnakīrti explains to an opponent why, even though in his view the class of all dissimilar cases is not *manifest*, it is still possible to satisfy C2.3 by showing that $H3a_2$ does not undermine the reason property being discussed. Ratnakīrti argues that he is able to do so because in his view the class of all dissimilar cases is a *determined* O2.2 object that one can be aware of. Even those objects that the Naiyāyikas dismiss as being merely "potential objects of awareness" can be actual objects of awareness and are therefore relevant to the satisfaction of C2.3. It is because constructed similarity classes such as the class of all dissimilar cases can be the actual objects of awareness-events that Ratnakīrti argues that the demand that he places on the Naiyāyikas is not unreasonable. What the Naiyāyikas insist is "paralyzing doubt" is, in fact, "epistemically significant." Ratnakīrti's argument against C2.3 is clearly supported by his theory of exclusion, and its success depends, at least in part, on the success of his version of this theory. The theory of exclusion is thus at the center of Ratnakīrti's debate with the Naiyāyikas over pervasion and the level of epistemic risk that one can assume in inferential reasoning.

5.1.2. Ratnakīrti's Modal Conventionalism

The significance of the theory of exclusion, however, extends beyond issues having to do with the epistemology of certification and satisfaction (and the related issue of acceptable epistemic risk). In my view, it also extends to Ratnakīrti's views on the nature of epistemic necessity itself, and related issues regarding the nature of inference-warranting relations and the relationship between the metaphysics and epistemology of such relations.[106] While I have shown in this chapter how Ratnakīrti's version of the theory of exclusion is relevant to the construction of "epistemic objects" and "epistemic relations" (especially the production- and identity-modes of pervasion), and therefore to Ratnakīrti's account of inferential reasoning as a "reality-involving" practice, I want to now suggest that Ratnakīrti's theory of exclusion also accounts for his views on the metaphysics and epistemology of modality

---

tasmād apratibhāse 'py adhyavasāyasiddhād eva vipakṣād dhūmāder vyatireko niścitaḥ | {tat kimartham atra vipakṣapratibhāsaḥ prārthyate} | yadi punar asyādhyavasāyo 'pi na syāt tadā vyatireko na niścīyata iti yuktam, pratiniyataviṣayavyavahārābhāvāt.

106. This second cluster of issues corresponds to issues 3, 1, and 2 mentioned in the opening section of chapter 4.

itself—and more specifically, the modality of inference-warranting relations.[107]

Recall that in such relations a reason property is taken to be *pervaded* by a target property, on the basis of either the production- or the identity-mode of pervasion. When such relations obtain, the presence of a reason property in a particular locus is taken to "epistemically necessitate" the presence of the target property in that locus. It is the source of this necessity in inference-warranting relations that I briefly want to explore. Although Ratnakīrti is not explicit about this, I want to suggest that Ratnakīrti is a "conventionalist" about modality, and further that this thesis is grounded in his theory of exclusion.[108] More specifically, my suggestion is that Ratnakīrti's "modal conventionalism" is based on his view that modal truths are attributable for the most part to the conventions on the basis of which we construct objects.[109] In many cases these conventions will simply be linguistic conventions about the semantic value of words. Since there are no mind-independent objects or relations between objects, modality itself is for the most part entirely the result of such conventions. For Ratnakīrti, there is no mind-independent world whose world-given connections could account for the modality of pervasion relations, for example.

---

107. "Modality" most generally refers to the way in which a statement (or proposition) describes its subject matter and, by extension, to the nature of the states of affairs described by such statements. My use of the term to discuss the modality of inference-warranting relations includes *alethic*, *causal,* and *epistemic* modalities.

108. My discussion of this issue is rather preliminary, and is meant to be suggestive but not conclusive. A detailed treatment of modal conventionalism is well beyond the scope of this chapter. For an excellent discussion of contemporary forms of modal conventionalism see Sidelle 1989, Sidelle 1998, and Thomasson (forthcoming). For criticism of this view see Elder 2004, Elder 2007, and Sider 2003. What is not relevant to my discussion is the "possible worlds" approach to modality made famous in Lewis 1986. According to one account of "modal conventionalism," the most general modal principles are analytic, including the most fundamental identity and persistence conditions. Such a position has been forcefully defended by Alan Sidelle, who argues that basic modal truths (e.g., that whatever a human being's actual biological origin is, he necessarily has that origin) are discoverable through conceptual analysis, even though empirical inquiry may also be needed to fill in the details (e.g., that Margaret Truman is Bess Truman's daughter) and result in our awareness of modal statements (e.g., that Margaret is necessarily Bess's daughter). See Sidelle 1989:34 n. 20, 75–76, discussed in Thomasson (forthcoming).

109. The qualification "for the most part" seems necessary since it is not entirely clear whether F1–F5 are all "mind-dependent" in the relevant sense.

As my reconstruction of Ratnakīrti's theory of exclusion suggests, the fundamental identity and persistence conditions for objects—i.e., determined objects such as O2 and O4—are built into the process of their construction through exclusion, through their being a subset of selection set **S**.[110] Such conditions are only a subset of **S**, since **S** may also contain conditions that are not in any way "fundamental" to what we take to be the identity and persistence conditions of that object. Built into the construction of an object then are our expectations about what sorts of changes the object in question could undergo while still being the "same"/"same kind of" object, and also our expectations about what makes that object the "kind" of object that it is. If this is the case, then whether two "objects" are in fact related to one another through the identity-mode of pervasion, for example, will be built into the construction of each object. This doesn't mean, however, that our awareness of a pair of objects guarantees that we will be aware of the relationship between them.

As Ratnakīrti points out in his discussion of the production-mode of pervasion, establishing that fire causes smoke requires a series of observations and nonobservations, even for those who know what fire is and what smoke is. Even though we may know the basic identity and persistence conditions of smoke and fire, we must still appeal to putatively empirical facts to learn that they are related to one another through the production-mode of pervasion. In this case, the production-mode of pervasion may be helpfully thought of as an *a posteriori* necessity. This doesn't change the fact, however, that the modality of the relation itself is built into the conventions that govern our construction of the objects. This is also the case with the identity-mode of pervasion (at least in some cases). The identity-mode of pervasion, however, may be thought of as an *a priori* necessity. For example, if we know the semantic value of "oak" (a reason property) and the semantic value of "tree" (its target property), we can infer that because something (the site of the inference) is an "oak," it is a "tree."

Ratnakīrti's modal conventionalism is relevant to his critique of the Īśvara-inference, since it supports both his skepticism regarding his Naiyāyi-

110. It seems important to specify both identity and persistence conditions, since there are kinds whose identity/membership conditions do not double as their persistence conditions. See Elder 2007 for a discussion of this.

kas' insistence that natural relations (and the regularities that they capture) have sufficient modal force to underwrite inference-warranting relations, and his confidence that the production- and identity-modes of pervasion (since they are relations between similarity classes/constructed universals) can underwrite the modality of such relations. Similarly, his conventionalism supports his skepticism of his Naiyāyikas' claims to "modal knowledge" and his confidence in his own claims to it.[111]

5.2. The Extension Principle and the Site Subcomponent

In addition to the issues discussed in relation to the pervasion subcomponent of the Naiyāyikas' Īśvara-inference, Ratnakīrti also raised a series of arguments in his *Section on the Reason Property* (chapter 3, section 3) and *Section on the Target Property* (chapter 3, section 4) having to do with the scope of the reason property "being an effect" and the target property "an intelligent maker."[112] More specifically, his attention to the scope of the reason property led to an important argument against the Naiyāyikas' "Extension Principle," while his attention to the target property led to a series of arguments, one of which had to do with the site subcomponent of the inference. More specifically, this argument had to do with the "special characteristics" of the target property that could be established on the basis of the Naiyāyikas' inference, such as uniqueness, omniscience, etc. Interestingly, each of these arguments is also informed by Ratnakīrti's theory of exclusion.

5.2.1. Exclusion and the Extension Principle

In defending the Īśvara-inference, Ratnakīrti's Naiyāyikas stated that the reason property "being an effect" should be interpreted as "effects-in-general," so as to include all effects. Ratnakīrti argued, however, that this *unrestricted* version of the reason property is defective, since there are numerous loci in which an "effect-in-general" is known to be present and the

---

111. There is, of course, much more work that needs to be done on these issues. What I have tried to do in this section is simply to outline a proposal based on my work in chapters 4 and 5.

112. My discussion here picks up on issue 1 of the opening section of chapter 4.

target property "an intelligent maker" is known to be absent. The examples he cited were trees, mountains, growing grass, and a drying and cracking lump of clay.

In addition to its being defeated by H3a_1, Ratnakīrti argued that the *unrestricted* reason property is also undermined by H3a_2, since it is inevitable that there will be epistemically significant doubt about its exclusion from all dissimilar cases: "effects-in-general" are not always observable. As a result, Ratnakīrti challenged the Naiyāyikas to specify a property "*R*" that restricts the scope of the reason property in such a way that the subclass of effects-in-general defined by it can be known, through observation and nonobservation, to be pervaded by the target property. This *R*-restricted reason property must also be known to be present in the site of the inference, since if it were not, H1b would apply. Ratnakīrti proposed the property "from the observation of which (both parties would agree) there could be an awareness of its having been made, even for one who did not observe its being made." It was agreed that locations about which there was disagreement would be a part of the site of the inference. Ratnakīrti then argued that given the Nyāya theory of inferential reasoning, the only way the Naiyāyikas could make this *R*-restricted reason property work is by violating the "extension principle"—the principle that specifies the conditions under which the scope of the reason property can be extended from a sample class, on the basis of which pervasion is established, to unsampled members of that class, and finally to the site of the inference.

According to Ratnakīrti, the specific property on the basis of which pervasion is determined is the only legitimate basis for extending the scope of the reason property to include what is beyond the sample class. The Īśvara-inference, however, violates this rule: pervasion is established for a class of *R*-restricted effects but is extended to the site of the inference on the basis of a different property, i.e., effects-in-general. Ratnakīrti went on to explain how his version of the extension principle not only preserves our intuitions about maker-inferences—e.g., a potter from a pot, a temple-builder from a temple (but not Īśvara from growing grass)—but also exposes the "Naiyāyikas' trick." Although it is not explicit, Ratnakīrti's extension principle is supported by his theory of exclusion.

Consider the classes of *R*-restricted effects-in-general that Ratnakīrti and his Naiyāyikas agree have an intelligent maker—pots, cloth, bracelets, temples, etc. According to Ratnakīrti, these are O2e objects. Given the Naiyāyikas' observability requirement, Ratnakīrti argues that pervasion cannot be established for the entire class of *R*-restricted effects-in-general (as the Naiyāyikas suppose). Instead, he argues, pervasion with an intelligent maker can be established only for "subclasses" of this *R*-restricted class—for classes of pots, cloth, bracelets, etc. To explain this, let us consider how the pervasion relation between pots and the potter who made them is established.

The selection set $\mathbf{S}_1$ for the construction of the O2e pot that is first observed to have an intelligent maker is constituted by a set of image-specifying coordinates, a spatial coordinate, and a temporal coordinate. The selection set $\mathbf{S}_2$ for a second O2e pot that is observed to have a maker is constituted by a different set of image-specifying coordinates, as well as different spatial and temporal coordinates. The same would be the case for the selection set $\mathbf{S}_3$ of a third O2e pot, and so on. What counts as a set of "pot"-image-specifying coordinates is determined by convention, as is what counts as an "intelligent maker." On the basis of these O2e objects it is possible to construct an O2.2 object by creating a new selection set **S** in which any spatial and temporal coordinates are ignored. Ratnakīrti suggests that this O2.2 object is "pots-in-general, from the observation of which there could be an awareness of having been made." It is this O2.2 object that is known to be pervaded by the target property. According to Ratnakīrti, the scope of this O2.2 reason property can be clearly extended to, and in fact includes, unsampled O2e pots—that is, other members of the class "pots-in-general." The legitimacy of this extension is based on **S** and the fact that the image-specifying coordinates of **S** are consistent with "*R*." While unsampled pots are clearly included in O2.2, the scope of this reason property cannot be extended to either cloth or bracelets, or trees, mountains, growing grass, a drying and cracking lump of clay, etc.

Given the observability requirement, it is the O2e objects that are actually observed to have an intelligent maker that supplies the relevant "image-specifying coordinates" that serve as the basis for the construction of the O2.2 "pots-in-general." It is this O2.2 object that is the basis for pervasion. Thus, while it is the case that pervasion could also be established for "cloth" and "bracelets," and a larger class of pervaded O2.2 objects could be constructed, nevertheless it is still the case that pervasion is based on the image-specifying coordinates of the members of each distinct subclass of O2e objects for which an intelligent maker had been observed. As a result, Ratnakīrti argues that in the Īśvara-inference the Naiyāyikas improperly extend the scope of their reason property to the site of the inference. And although I will not go into it here, many of the same considerations regarding the construction of the target property enter into Ratnakīrti's discussion in chapter 3, section 4.

5.2.2. Exclusion and the Site Subcomponent

Another important issue in Ratnakīrti's discussion of the site subcomponent in the Naiyāyikas' Īśvara-inference had to do with the scope of the target property. In a subsection of his *Section on the Target Property*, Ratnakīrti assumed (for the sake of argument) that the Naiyāyikas could show both that there is pervasion between "effects-in-general" and "an intelligent agent-in-general" and that the reason property "effects-in-general" is known to be present in the site of the inference. Given this, however, Ratnakīrti argued that the Naiyāyikas could still not establish that the intelligent agent who is now known to be the intelligent maker of the earth has the special characteristics that uniquely identify him as Īśvara. Ratnakīrti's argument was based on what he took to be the illegitimacy of the Naiyāyikas' claim that "although pervasion with a general-term is well known, special characteristics are proven through the force of being a property of the site of the inference." Recall that Ratnakīrti's Naiyāyikas argued that in virtue of knowing that the target property is present in the site of the inference, they could determine the special characteristics of the agent in question that identify him as Īśvara, such as omniscience etc. Ratnakīrti's rejection of this is based on his understanding of the location-relation "presence," which he defines through the theory of exclusion.

According to Ratnakīrti, "presence" is nothing more than the "exclusion of nonconnection." Thus the target property's "presence" in the site of the inference can be interpreted as its being characterized by the "exclusion from nonconnection with the site of the inference." According to Ratnakīrti, what this means is that on the basis of knowing that the target property is "present" in the site of the inference, all that one can conclude is that it is "excluded from nonconnection with it." On the basis of this, Ratnakīrti concludes that the only characteristic that can be proven on the basis of knowing that the target property is present in the site of the inference is this one. Thus, in the inference of fire from smoke what we learn on the basis of the inference is that fire is excluded from nonconnection with the mountain.

We do not learn anything more about the fire other than those characteristics that are entailed by its exclusion from nonconnection with the mountain. We can learn, for example, that it is the kind of fire that produced the smoke on the mountain, but not its color or specific fuel-source.

Similarly, Ratnakīrti explains that the most we can expect from the Naiyāyikas' inference is to establish that our world has an intelligent maker of some sort or the other. We cannot conclude that this maker is Īśvara. Moreover, Ratnakīrti says that if all that the Naiyāyikas are trying to establish is that our world has some sort of an intelligent maker, they are trying to prove something that he already accepts (see section 6). If they are trying to establish an omniscient maker, however, then, as discussed in chapter 3, their inference-instrument would not be certified. Again, it should be clear that Ratnakīrti's argument is supported by the theory of exclusion.

6. Conclusion: Who Created the World?

When taken together, Ratnakīrti's remarks on what there is provide yet another perspective from which to consider his critique of the Naiyāyikas' argument for the existence of Īśvara. Just as his theory of exclusion provided resources for understanding his account of epistemic objects and relations, his ontology helps us to understand how these objects are related to one another. His account of O1–O4 thus provides a kind of "ontological structure" on which to map his theory of content and his epistemology. For example, while the theory of exclusion tells us that universals are constructed from particulars, Ratnakīrti's ontology helps us to see that many of those particulars are themselves the result of construction. Similarly, while his theory of exclusion suggests that he is a conventionalist about epistemic necessity, his ontology helps us to see that in the final analysis nothing about what our thoughts are about is due to the external world in which we are supposed to live. Most interestingly perhaps, his remarks on the status of external objects show us that even though an intelligence-possessing maker like Īśvara is not the maker of the world, there is still an intelligence-possessing (or mental) maker of the world: that maker is not the Naiyāyikas' Īśvara, but rather mental construction, exclusion, and determination. In this he supports the longstanding Buddhist commitment to there being a conscious maker of our world, while also showing that such a maker need not be the single, permanent, omniscient maker whose existence his Naiyāyikas have worked so hard to establish.[113] Behind both of these points are, as I have argued, his theory of exclusion and the variety of philosophical commitments and resources reflected in it.

113. For an excellent discussion of "creation" in Buddhist philosophy see Steinkellner 2006:15–45, Lindtner 1999, and Schmidt-Leukel 2006:111–177. Mokṣākaragupta makes this same argument at MTBh 60.12–61.22.

Conclusion

CHAPTER 6

The Values of Buddhist Epistemology

In introducing this book I began with a discussion of its subject matter (*abhidheya*), my reasons for writing it, including what I hoped to accomplish in doing so (*prayojana*), and how I hoped to achieve these ends (*sambandha*).[1] It seems appropriate, therefore, to conclude with how Ratnakīrti himself might answer such questions about his own work and, more specifically, with how he understood its value. My discussion of Ratnakīrti's interest in the Naiyāyikas' argument for the existence of Īśvara (in chapters 2–3) and my analysis of the broad range of philosophical resources that he relies upon in criticizing it (in chapters 3–5) reveal how Ratnakīrti practiced philosophy. By describing the conceptual resources that he uses to fashion and respond to arguments and analyzing the language and style in which he argues, I have tried to provide a picture of how Ratnakīrti

---

1. For a discussion of how Sanskrit philosophers themselves theorized the ideas expressed in this sentence, and discussed the terms "subject matter" (*abhidheya*), "purpose" (*prayojana*), and "relation between the two" (*sambandha*), see Kumārila's ŚV, *Pratijñāsūtra* 11–25, where the latter two terms are discussed. For a discussion of all three in the work of a Buddhist epistemologist see Dharmottara's NBṬ 5.01–16.02 and Arcaṭa's HBṬ 1.18–3.03. For an excellent discussion of this issue, and numerous additional references, see Funayama 1995.

engaged with his opponents, both explicitly and implicitly. In the texts discussed in these chapters, however, Ratnakīrti does not tell us what he hoped to gain in critically engaging his opponents in this way and, more generally, how he understood the value of philosophy, as defined by his work.[2] In this chapter I want to argue that Ratnakīrti's understanding of the value of philosophy, and epistemology more specifically, is implicit in his practice of it—a practice that both subtly gestures to, and draws from, a "two-dimensional framework of value" that he shares with his text tradition.[3]

This two-dimensional framework of value is defined in terms of the two kinds of rationality that I hope to show are evident in Ratnakīrti's work, namely, epistemic rationality and instrumental rationality.[4] On my use of the term, "epistemic rationality" is the kind of rationality that one displays when one's belief "that *p*" is based on reasons that are taken to be neither defeated nor undermined. Epistemic rationality is also displayed when one refrains from believing "that *p*" on the basis of reasons that are taken to be defeated or undermined. Given this, "epistemic reasons" are often thought to have categorical normative force—that is, to be binding on any rational agent, regardless of that agent's interests or goals.[5] Many of the reasons that Ratnakīrti and his opponents appeal to in their debate about the Īśvara-inference seem to be epistemic in this sense. In contrast, "instrumental rationality" is the kind of rationality that one displays when one takes the means to one's ends. Thus, "instrumental reasons" are often thought to have hypothetical force—that is, to be binding on a rational agent who possesses the goal or

2. For an excellent study of such questions in the work of Śāntarakṣita (ca. 725–788) and his "commentator," Kamalaśīla (ca. 740–795), see McClintock 2002: esp. chap. 1, section 4; chap. 2; and chap. 6. For an interpretation of how the Buddhist epistemologist Mokṣākaragupta might answer such questions see Griffiths 1999b. For additional references to relevant work on the Buddhist epistemological tradition, see Funayama 1995, Kellner 2004b, Krasser 2004, and the references contained therein. See also Eltschinger 2007b.

3. For more on the idea of a "text tradition" see McCrea and Patil (forthcoming).

4. For a discussion of these, and an extended argument against the reduction of epistemic rationality to instrumental rationality, see Kelly 2003, where he argues against the idea that epistemic rationality is simply a species of instrumental rationality—that is, instrumental rationality in the service of some cognitive goal. For a typology of different "varieties" of rationality see Plantinga 1993a:132–137, and for an argument against the philosophical utility of "rationality" see Goldman 1986:27.

5. See Kelly 2003:614.

goals in question.[6] In much of this chapter, I am going to focus on Ratnakīrti's goals and will be concerned primarily with instrumental reasons. What I am most interested in, however, is the relationship between such reasons and specifically epistemic ones. Associated with each kind of reason is also a kind of value that I will refer to as "epistemic value" and "instrumental value," respectively.[7] It is these two kinds of value that define the two-dimensional framework of value that I will argue is present in Ratnakīrti's work.

In much of what follows I will be arguing that for Ratnakīrti philosophy is of instrumental value, since it is indispensable for those who seek to understand the nature of the Buddhist path and to make progress along it. My argument in support of this conclusion has three parts. In section 1 I will briefly discuss the philosophical goals and ideals of the Buddhist epistemological tradition, as understood by Dignāga and Dharmakīrti (and some of their commentators), in order to show how from the very beginning the tradition was methodologically self-conscious and reflected upon the value of philosophy. In section 2 I will show that Ratnakīrti himself shared the framework of value that was constructed by his text tradition. In section 3 I will discuss how Ratnakīrti's teacher, Jñānaśrīmitra, incorporated these goals and ideals into a framework in which philosophy as an intellectual practice and philosophy as a form of religious education were brought together. In the final two sections of this chapter I will show how all of this relates to epistemic value and the two-dimensional framework of value described above.

1. Foundational Figures and Foundational Texts

1.1. Dignāga

From the opening verse of Dignāga's (ca. 480–540) *Compendium of the Sources of Knowledge* (*Pramāṇasamuccaya*)—the text upon which the Buddhist epistemological tradition is founded—the tradition's self-consciousness

6. For a discussion of the terms "hypothetical" and "categorical" in a similar context see Papineau 2003.

7. See Foley 1987:11–12, where the link between kinds of reasons and kinds of value is also made.

regarding the role of philosophy, and especially epistemology, is evident.[8] In this opening verse, and his own commentary on it, Dignāga very clearly explains that he composed his work in order to refute his opponents' views on the instruments of valid awareness (*pramāṇa*) and to establish his own.[9] He explains further that this is an important task, because there is a great deal of confusion about these instruments and many competing claims have been made about them. Since our account of *what* we know depends upon our account of *how* we know, Dignāga goes on to say that it is important to argue against mistaken views of these instruments, in order to show one's opponents that what they conclude on the basis of them is also mistaken. Establishing correct

---

8. Dignāga is said to have been born into a Brahmin family from Kāñci in South India and to have lived and worked, at least for a time, at the Buddhist monastic and educational complex of Nālanda, which was located in North India, in the modern state of Bihar. For more on what we know of Dignāga's life see Frauwallner 1933 and Hattori 1968:1–11, and the references contained therein. For a helpful discussion of Nālanda see Mullens 1994:49–68. With the discovery of two Sanskrit manuscripts of Jinendrabuddhi's commentary on the PS, it is now possible to reconstruct large parts of Dignāga's PS and PSV. As this work is published, it is sure to revolutionize our understanding of Dignāga and the history of Buddhist epistemology in India. See Steinkellner et al. 2005:xvii–lii for a discussion of these manuscripts and Katsura 2004 and Katsura and Steinkellner 2004 for a taste of what is to come with regard to important elements in Dignāga's theory of inferential reasoning.

9. PS 1.1: "With great reverence to the teacher who exists as a source of knowledge; who seeks the well-being of the world; who is accomplished; and who is our protector, I compose this *Compendium,* on the basis of my own thoughts, which are scattered about here and there, in order to establish the sources of knowledge" (*pramāṇabhūtāya jagaddhitaiṣiṇe praṇamya śāstre sugatāya tāyine | pramāṇasiddhyai svamatāt samuccayaḥ kariṣyate viprasṛtād ihaikataḥ*). PSV 1.10–1.13: "With great reverence to the teacher who has such qualities, I will compose this *Compendium of the Sources of Knowledge* by bringing together material from my other works, such as the *Nyāyamukha*, in order to reject the sources of knowledge of my rivals and promote my own, since an awareness of what can be known depends upon the sources of knowledge, and there are many competing claims made about them" (see Hattori 1968:23–24, Kellner 2004b:148) (*evaṃguṇaṃ śāstāraṃ praṇamya pramāṇasiddhyai svaprakaraṇebhyo nyāyamukhādibhya iha samāhṛtya pramāṇasamuccayaḥ kariṣyate parapramāṇapratiṣedhāya svapramāṇaguṇodbhāvanāya ca, yasmāt pramāṇāyattā prameyapratipattir bahavaś cātra vipratipannāḥ*). Also see PSṬ 20.14–22.13. For an extremely important discussion of the phrase that I have translated as "exists as a source of knowledge" (*pramāṇabhūta*) see the excellent discussion in Krasser 2001 and the references contained therein. For a discussion of why Dignāga and Śākyabuddhi interpret the "as" in this phrase to mean "is," while Prajñākaragupta takes it to mean "like," see Kellner 2004b, and for a somewhat different interpretation, Iwata 2004. For a discussion of the variety of ways in which the term "accomplished" (*sugata*) is interpreted by Dignāga see Hattori 1968:23.

views about the instruments of valid awareness is, therefore, also a way of establishing what is in fact the case.

From Dignāga's rather brief remarks in the opening section of his *Compendium*, it is clear that his work has a dual purpose: it is meant to "reject the instruments of others" (*parapramāṇapratiṣedha*)—and thereby reject the conclusions that they draw on the basis of them—and to "make public the virtues of one's own account of the instruments" (*svapramāṇaguṇodbhāvana*)—and thereby support one's own conclusions.[10] This dual purpose is also explicit in the structure of Dignāga's text: each chapter includes both an account of his own position and a detailed refutation of rival views.[11] Implicit in his introductory remarks is also his view about the value of epistemology. From what Dignāga says in the opening section of his *Compendium*, what seems to be of value is being right, both about how one knows and what one knows. And, as Dignāga suggests, it is through critical reflection upon the instruments of valid awareness that one is able to determine this. Dignāga also makes it clear that this is not simply a personal affair: it is essential to his

10. In the following passage Dignāga's own words are printed underlined, while his commentator Jinendrabuddhi's are not. My reason for citing this passage is to support my point that built into Dignāga's "dual purpose" are not just the "instruments," or sources of knowledge, but also the "conclusions," or objects of knowledge/valid awareness.

PSṬ ms. B258b1–4 (as cited in Krasser 2004:141 n. 32): "It is not the case that only in chapters such as the 'Investigation of Nyāya' are the objects of knowledge refuted, since it is seen that in this [section] too they are [refuted] by implication. . . . In [response to the question]—But why can't this be known through perception?—he says, 'things are imagined by them,' etc. Since, in virtue of their being imperceptible, the existence of things such as the material basis for the world, the passive principle of consciousness, space, time, and inherence are established on the basis of a reason property, they can be known only through [such] reasoning. 'It is not the case that it is worth touching' means 'It isn't worthy of thought.' And he has explained the ways in which they do not stand up to thought. 'For this reason' means 'since.' Thus reasoning cannot be the basis for an investigation. Therefore it should be known that it is definitely the case that here too the objects of knowledge, which are supposed to be known through reasoning, are refuted by implication" (*na kevalaṃ nyāyaparīkṣādiṣu prameyapratiṣedhaḥ kṛtaḥ, ihāpy arthataḥ kṛta iti darśanāt. {sarveṣāṃ cetyādi}. kasmāt punaḥ pratyakṣagamyaṃ na bhavatīty āha—tatparikalpitapadārthānām ityādi. pradhānapuruṣadikkālasamavāyādīnām apratyakṣatayā liṅgenāstitvavyavasthāpanāt tarkagamyatvam. na vimardakṣama iti na vicāram arha ity arthaḥ, yathā ca vicāraṃ na sahate, tathā pratipāditam, ata iti. yasmād evaṃ na parīkṣākṣamas tarkaḥ, tasmāt tadgamyasya prameyasyāpy arthataḥ pratiṣedho 'tra kṛta eva veditavya iti*).

11. For an introduction to this text and a discussion of its organizing principles see Hattori 1968 and Hayes 1988.

work, as he understands it, to argue against those who disagree with him and, as we will see, to convince them that their views are mistaken and that his are not. Why any of this should be of value, and what special significance if any it has for a Buddhist philosopher, is not discussed by Dignāga here.

In the concluding sections of his *Compendium*, however, Dignāga explicitly links the dual purpose of his text to the teachings of the Buddha, and thereby explains further why this way of "being right" is itself of value.[12] He says that his opponents' views on the instruments of valid awareness, and the conclusions that they draw on the basis of them, are not well-established (*durvihita*) and so are distant from (*viprakṛṣṭa*) the real nature of *dharma* as taught by the Buddha. He also explains that it is because their conclusions do not stand up to critical analysis—and instead are transformed and altered by it—that they are so distant. This implies that what makes something well-established is the degree to which it can withstand critical philosophical analysis, and further that being able to withstand such analysis is an indicator of proximity to *dharma*. But, as Dignāga (and the tradition before him) also points out, the real nature of *dharma* is not itself accessible to such analysis (*atarkagocara*).[13] As a result, his purpose is not (and cannot be) to

12. PSṬ ms. B258b4ff. For quoted fragments (*pratīka*) from PS/PSV see Krasser 2004:131, nn. 10, 11, 15, where he quotes and translates the passage. What follows is based on Krasser's translation. The Tibetan text is Kanakavarman's translation (PSV/no. 5702 of the Peking edition of the Tibetan canon, 176b8–177a2): "I composed this [work] in order to turn those who adhere to the views of non-Buddhists away from them, since they are without essence because the sources of knowledge (*pramāṇa*) and their objects (*prameya*) [as taught by non-Buddhists] are not properly fixed (*durvihitatvena*). However, by just this (*iyatā*), I do not expect them to enter in to the teaching of the Tathāgata, since his *dharma* is not within the realm of reasoning. But those who have turned away (*vyāvṛttās tu*) [from the views of non-Buddhists] can more easily understand [the *dharma*] after hearing it, since it is very far [from their views] and close to his (*viprakṛṣṭāntaratvāt*)" (*tshad ma kun las btus par yaṅ | tshad ma daṅ gźal bya ñe bar brjod pa ñid kyis mu stegs pa 'i 'dod pa sñiṅ po med pa 'i phyir | der źen pa rnams ldog pa 'i don du 'di brtsams pa yin gyi | 'di tsam gyis de bźin gśegs pa 'i bstan pa la gźug pa 'i don du ni ma yin te | de 'i chos ni rtog ge 'i yul ma yin pa 'i phyir ro || ldog pa las ni ston pa 'i chos ñid thos nas 'bad pa med par rtogs par 'gyur te | bar du ma bskal ba 'i phyir ro*). It is worth noting that according to Jinendrabuddhi this section—which is quoted by Bu ston Rin chen grub in his *History of Buddhism* (*chos 'byuṅ*)—states Dignāga's "secondary"/"more distant" (*vyavahita*) purpose, while his "primary"/"immediate" (*sākṣāt*) purpose is indicated in PS 1.1. For a very careful analysis of this passage see Krasser 2004:131–135. As Krasser notes, the passage is also translated in Obermiller 1931:46.

13. For a very helpful list of such passages see Krasser 2004:139 n. 28.

teach his opponents the *dharma* itself, but rather to turn them away from their false views so that it will be easier for them to eventually realize it. The reason for critically analyzing the teaching of the Buddha is to ensure that it is understood correctly and to show that, unlike the teachings of those who oppose or misunderstand the Buddha, it stands up to philosophical analysis. Even though what is established through such analysis is not *dharma* itself, it is nevertheless conducive for realizing it one day.

In his commentary on this section of Dignāga's text, Jinendrabuddhi (ca. 750–800) confirms this reading of Dignāga and states explicitly what is otherwise only implicit in Dignāga's own words. Jinendrabuddhi explains that Dignāga's reference to "philosophical analysis" is a synecdoche for conventionally valid sources of knowledge, i.e., perception and inferential reasoning.[14] He also says that the kinds of things that non-Buddhists think can be established through philosophical analysis, such as the soul, cannot stand up to such analysis, since such things do not exist as these non-Buddhists suppose.[15] In contrast, the kinds of things established by Buddhists, such as

---

14. PSṬ ms. B258b6–7 (as cited in Krasser 2004:135 n. 18): "Thus Dignāga says: 'Because the Buddha's *dharma* is not accessible to reasoning.' The reference to 'reasoning' is as a synecdoche for the conventional sources of knowledge. What this means is that since the Buddha's *dharma*—which each individual seeks to know—is an object of only the ultimate source of knowledge, it is not an object of the conventional ones" (*ity āha, taddharmasyātarkagocaratvāt. tarkagrahaṇaṃ vyāvahārikapramāṇopalakṣaṇārtham. lokottarasyaiva hi pramāṇasya viṣayo bhagavato dharmaḥ pratyātmavedyaḥ, na vyāvahārikasyety arthaḥ*).

15. PSṬ ms. B259b2–6 (as cited in Krasser 2004:134 n.16), where he suggests that the underlined words are from Dignāga's verse. Here is the "verse" extracted from the context of the commentarial passage: "Those who seek the essence of *dharma* by way of reasoning have fallen far from the Buddha's teachings. Still, the defining features of the Buddha's *dharma* should be investigated, since perhaps they may undergo change." Here is the passage in full: "Because they have set out on the wrong path, he says, 'But, they have fallen very far.' Those who investigate the nature of *dharma* by the path of reasoning have fallen very far from the teaching of the Buddha, since the nature of *dharma* is not an object of reasoning. Even though this is the case, he says, 'Still the defining features of the Buddha's *dharma* should be investigated, since perhaps it may undergo change'—like the things conceived of by non-Buddhists. He said that this means that although they are accepted as being the objects of reasoning, the kinds of things that are critically reflected upon through reasoning by non-Buddhists, such as the soul and the like, 'undergo change' in the sense that they do not remain as they were established in a philosophical text. The teachings (*dharma*) that are made known by the Buddha are of the opposite nature: [their nature] is selflessness and the like, which does not 'change' when it is critically reflected upon. This means that it is apprehended in itself, just as it appears through a conventional [source of knowledge]. Therefore,

selflessness (*nairātmya*), can withstand philosophical analysis, in the sense that what is known on the basis of the instruments of valid awareness as understood by Buddhists is never defeated. He also explains that even though *dharma* itself is inaccessible to philosophical analysis, things that are known through such analysis can help one to realize it.

Dignāga thus identifies the analysis of the instruments of valid awareness as the primary purpose of his *Compendium* and stakes out a position as to why this is of value. He says that by exposing mistakes in rival accounts of these instruments and establishing one's own position it is possible to turn one's opponents toward the *dharma*, which despite being inaccessible to such analysis can nevertheless be approached through it. It is important to keep in mind four features of Dignāga's account: (1) the dual purpose of his text; (2) his suggestion that being right is of value in that it brings one closer to *dharma*; (3) the claim that *dharma* itself is inaccessible to philosophical analysis; and (4) his conviction that despite this fact philosophical analysis is conducive to one day realizing *dharma*. These four themes are taken up in various ways by Dignāga's successor, Dharmakīrti, and, as I will argue, are clearly present in Ratnakīrti's own work.

1.2. Dharmakīrti

Dignāga's successor, Dharmakīrti (ca. 600–660), is arguably the most influential Buddhist philosopher in Indian philosophical history (and among the most important Sanskrit philosophers).[16] In his works, Dharmakīrti picks up on each of the four themes discussed above, as does the extensive commentarial tradition on his *Ascertainment of the Sources of Knowledge* (*Pramāṇavi-*

---

although reasoning cannot have ultimate truth as its object, still, in teaching [us about] a thing as it is established in its generic form, it is helps [us to] realize what is really the case. This is what is taught" (*sudūranaṣṭās tv iti, unmārgapravṛttatvāt. sudūraṃ naṣṭās te munīndraśāsanāt, ye tarkapathena dharmatāṃ niścinvanti, tasyā atarkaviṣayatvāt. yady apy etad evaṃ tathāpi tathāgatadharmalakṣaṇaṃ parīkṣyatāṃ yady upayāti vikriyāṃ tirthikaparikalpitapadārthavat. etad uktaṃ bhavati, tarkaviṣayatvenābhyupagatā api tīrthikair ātmādayaḥ padārthās tarkeṇa vicāryamāṇā vikriyante, yathā śāstre teṣāṃ vyavasthāpitās tathā nāvatiṣṭhanta ity arthaḥ. tathāgatapraveditadharmāṇām aviparītah svabhāvo nairātmyādir vicāryamāṇo na vikriyate, yathā darśito vyāvahārikeṇātmanā tathaivopalabhyata ity arthaḥ. etena yady api tarkaḥ paramārthaviṣayo na bhavati, tathāpi yathāvasthitaṃ vastu sāmānyarūpeṇa sūcayaṃs tattvādhigamānukūlo bhavatīti sūcitam*).

16. For a brief introduction to Dharmakīrti's life and works see Steinkellner 1998.

niścaya) and his *Commentary on the Compendium of the Sources of Knowledge* (*Pramāṇavārttika*).[17]

In the introductory verse of his *Ascertainment of the Sources of Knowledge*, Dharmakīrti explains that he has composed the text in order to teach those who do not already know that in order to consistently acquire what is helpful (*hita*) and avoid what is unhelpful (*ahita*) it is necessary to know what correct/valid awareness (*samyagjñāna*) really is.[18] What is emphasized in this verse is the close connection between a correct account of the instruments of valid awareness and what is helpful, and incorrect accounts of these instruments and what is unhelpful. That there is a direct relationship between valid awareness and what we take to have value—that is, what we take to be helpful or unhelpful—is clearly expressed, as is Dharmakīrti's pedagogical intent. How this relates to the teachings of the Buddha is made clear in a passage that concludes the first chapter of his *Ascertainment*.[19]

---

17. For bibliographic references to his texts, and corresponding secondary scholarship, see Steinkellner and Much 1995. For discussions of his thought see Dreyfus 1997 and Dunne 2004, and the numerous references contained therein.

18. PVin 1 (introductory passage before PV 1.1) (as quoted in Krasser 2004:142 n. 36): "I have undertaken this work in order to explain what valid awareness is to those who do not know, since acquiring what is beneficial and avoiding what is harmful is invariably due to it" (*hitāhitaprāptiparihārayor niyamena samyagjñānapūrvakatvād aviduṣāṃ tadvyutpādanārtham idam ārabhyate*). See also Vetter 1966:30 n. 1.

19. PVin 1.59: "'How can he say that an awareness-event with a distorted mental impression is not valid and one that is other than that is valid? Since he denies that any awareness-event has an object, there isn't a difference between them.' Seeing that for the unenlightened too there is a lack of confidence in ordinary activity, since there is the problem that distorted mental impressions are not connected, he says that one of them is not valid. The other is said to be valid awareness. This is because, in virtue of its mental impressions standing firm, its connection is unbroken as long as *saṃsāra* endures. Relative to its not disappointing us in our ordinary activities it is valid awareness for us here. And this is what he says is the form of a conventionally valid source of knowledge. About this too, those others—who are fools—lead the world astray. But those who continuously seek out wisdom produced through reflection come face to face with the ultimately valid source of knowledge, which is clear, since it is error free, and does not change" (*so 'pi kathaṃ sarvajñānānāṃ viṣayaṃ vyatirecayann upaplavetarayoḥ pramāṇetaratāṃ brūyāt. upaplavavāsanāvisandhidoṣād aprabuddhasyāpy anāśvāsikaṃ vyavahāram utpaśyann ekam apramāṇam ācakṣīta, aparam ā saṃsāram aviśliṣṭānubandhaṃ dṛḍhavāsanatvād iha vyavahārāvisaṃvādāpekṣayā pramāṇam. sāṃvyavahārikasya caitat pramāṇasya rūpam uktam, atrāpi pare mūḍhā visaṃvādayanti lokam iti. cintāmayīm eva tu prajñām anuśīlayanto vibhramavivekanirmalam anapāyi pāramārthikapramāṇam abhimukhīkurvanti*). As Krasser notes, this probably refers back to PVin 1.28 and PVin 1.29–1.31,

In this passage Dharmakīrti clarifies some of what he says in his introductory verse and picks up on many of the themes discussed by Dignāga. He first explains, for example, what he means by "valid" and "invalid" awareness. In explaining how the two are to be distinguished from one another, he also provides an account of what it means to say that valid awareness is "helpful." More specifically, Dharmakīrti argues that those who have a correct account of valid awareness say that acting on the basis of an awareness-event that has a distorted image is not reliable—in the sense that acting on the basis of it will not reliably lead to results that are consistent with the kinds of expectations that we form on the basis of it. As a result, he says, there is a genuine basis for such philosophers to say that such an awareness-event is "not valid." Similarly, according to Dharmakīrti, they also say that acting on the basis of an awareness-event that has a firmly established image is reliable—and will be so as long as the world goes around. As a result of this, he says that there also is a basis for such philosophers to say that such an awareness-event is "valid." Valid awareness is "helpful" in the sense that it is reliable and does not disappoint us or lead us astray.[20] According to Dharmakīrti, this is an essential part of a correct account of conventionally valid awareness.

Dharmakīrti goes on to say that those who are confused about this end up leading the world astray, in the sense that they prevent others from accurately understanding what conventionally valid awareness is, and so distance them from ultimately valid awareness—that is, awareness of *dharma* itself.[21] In contrast, those who focus their attention and meditate upon what is conventionally valid have the chance to realize what is ultimately valid. Although Dharmakīrti is not explicit about this, it is clear that he shares the dual objectives outlined by Dignāga, namely, of arguing against one's opponents—that is, those who lead the world astray—and in support of one's own position. It is also implicit in Dharmakīrti's remarks that his reason for doing so is to put people on the right path for realizing *dharma* by

---

which according to Vetter 1966:74 n. 3–4 correspond to PV 282, 285. The passage is quoted from Krasser 2004:143, following Steinkellner's forthcoming edition of PVin 1 and 2; it has also been noted by Mikogami (1993:99 n. 34 and translated on p. 93) and Dunne (2004:315–317, 315 n. 35).

20. For a discussion of "validity" in the work of Dharmakīrti, see Katsura 1984, van Biljert 1989, and Dunne 2004. For an excellent discussion of some of the issues raised by Dharmakīrti's account see Krasser 1995. See also McCrea and Patil 2006.

21. See notes 18 and 19.

bringing them closer to it—even though *dharma* itself is inaccessible to conventionally valid awareness and our ordinary sources of knowledge.

In concluding this passage, Dharmakīrti refers to his commentary on an earlier passage, in which he also discusses the relationship between epistemology, conventionally valid awareness, and the path to ultimately valid awareness.[22] In this earlier passage he says that even for Yogis—and so, by implication, for everyone else too—it is only after understanding what has been taught through "awareness based upon what has been heard" and then establishing that what has been heard is fact the case through "awareness based upon reflection"—that is, conventionally valid awareness—that one can put oneself in a position to cultivate the kind of clear, nonconceptual, and ultimately valid awareness that results from meditation and gives one awareness of *dharma* itself. Again, although it is not explicit, the reason those who are mistaken about the nature of valid awareness lead the world astray is that they mislead us all on the basis of their mistaken epistemology, and thus prevent us from arriving at what is conventionally valid. Since an understanding of what is conventionally valid is a prerequisite for ultimately valid awareness—that is, knowledge of the *dharma* itself—a mistaken epistemology necessarily distances us from it.

Ideas very similar to these are also explicitly stated by the Buddhist philosopher Dharmottara (ca. 740–800) in his commentary on this section of Dharmakīrti's text.[23] According to Dharmottara, Dharmakīrti analyzes

---

22. PVin 1.28 (in Krasser 2004:144 n. 42, following Steinkellner's forthcoming edition of PVin 1 and 2): "By the power of mental cultivation/meditation, it manifests clearly, like fear, etc. That awareness-event which does not disappoint [us] is perception free from conceptualization. Even for Yogis, mental cultivation should follow from understanding things through the awareness of what is heard, followed by their adoption through awareness produced by reflection—that is, reasoning. When complete, there is clear manifesting awareness, as in the case of fear. It is nonconceptual and does not deviate from its object. It is the source of knowledge, perception. It is like the perception of the noble truths as analyzed in my *Pramāṇavārttika*" (*bhāvanābalataḥ spaṣṭaṃ bhayādāv iva bhāsate | yaj jñānam avisaṃvādi tat pratyakṣam akalpakam. yogināṃ api śrutamayena jñānenārthān gṛhītvā yukticintāmayena vyavasthāpya bhāvayatāṃ tanniṣpattau yat spaṣṭāvabhāsi bhayādāv iva, tad avikalpakam avitathaviṣayaṃ pramāṇaṃ pratyakṣam, āryasatyadarśanavad yathā nirṇītam asmābhiḥ pramāṇavārttike*). See also Vetter 1966: n. 74, referring to a parallel passage at PVABh 327.16–327.18, and Vetter 1966:73–15, 73 n. 1–3. See also PV 3.285, quoted in Funayama 2005:7 n. 26, where he compares it with Kamalaśīla's *Bhāvanākrama* II.

23. PVinṬ *ad* PVin 1.59=D167b6–181a1=Peking no. 196a2–5: "Even ultimately valid awareness is not without a cause—and there is no cause other than mental cultivation/meditation.

conventionally valid sources of knowledge in great detail, since it is only by meditating on an object that has been established through a conventionally valid source of knowledge that one can realize ultimate truth. Meditating on what is incorrect, and not so established, will not be effective. Thus, for Dharmottara, setting out on the Buddhist path requires both excluding error and establishing what is the case.

While in his *Ascertainment of the Sources of Knowledge* Dharmakīrti is self-conscious about the importance of epistemology (i.e., both perception and inference) and its relation to *dharma*, the commentarial tradition on Dharmakīrti's *Commentary* provides some insight into why specifically inferential reasoning is thought to be of value. The context for this discussion is the order of the chapters in Dharmakīrti's text, which is itself supposed to be a "commentary" on Dignāga's *Compendium*.[24] One group of commentators takes the chapter titled "Inferential Reasoning for Oneself" (*svārthānumāna*)—the only chapter of the text on which Dharmakīrti himself comments—to come first.[25] Another group of commentators takes the chapter "Establishing the Sources of Knowledge" (*pramāṇasiddhi*) to be first, in part because

---

Moreover, mental cultivation/meditation takes as its object what has been ascertained by conventionally valid awareness. And so the conventionally valid sources of knowledge have been analyzed completely. They become the cause of ultimately valid awareness. . . . For those things that have been made into objects through invalid awareness—imagined as mental images of eternal things, etc.—are not a prerequisite for ultimately valid awareness. But things imagined as momentary mental images are a prerequisite. Therefore, a person who has excluded error will set out on the way to ultimate truth, since this error takes as its object a gross form. Reaching ultimate truth is preceded by ending this error" (*pāramārthikam api pramāṇaṃ na nirhetukam. na ca bhāvanāvyatirikto hetuḥ. bhāvanā ca sāṃvyavahārikapramāṇaparicchinnārthaviṣayā. tataś ca tat saṃvyavahārikaṃ pramāṇaṃ samyaṇ nirūpitaṃ pāramārthikajñānahetuḥ sampadyate. {tatas tadviṣayo yatnaḥ paramārthaviṣaya eva.} mithyājñānena hi viṣayīkṛtā bhāvā nityādibhir ākārair bhāvyamānā na pāramārthikajñānanibandhanaṃ bhavanti. anityādibhis tv ākārair bhāvyamānā nibandhanaṃ bhavanty eva. tasmād ato vyāmohaṃ vyāvartya paramārthanaye 'vatārayitavyo janaḥ, sthūlaviṣayatvād asya vyāmohasya. etadvyāmohanivṛttipūrvikā ca paramārthaprāptiḥ*). The quoted text follows Krasser 2004:144–145 n. 44, who notes that this passage is quoted in the *Dravyālaṃkāraṭīkā*. See Jambuvijayaji 2001:77.19–77.25 and Lindtner 1984:157 n. 23. For PVin 1.59 see earlier notes. Also see D167b2–3=Peking no. 195b4–5, and Krasser's paraphrase in Krasser 2004:144.

24. For a discussion of this issue see Ono 1997 and Kellner 2004b.

25. This group includes Devendrabuddhi (ca. 630–690), Śākyabuddhi (ca. 660–720), Karṇakagomin (fl. 800), and, for different reasons, Ravigupta (fl. ninth century) and Yamāri (fl. eleventh century).

it is organized in terms of Dignāga's description of the qualities of the Buddha in the introductory verse of his *Compendium* and can be seen, therefore, as an extended commentary on the first half of it.[26] Both groups of commentators seem to understand questions about the sequence of chapters as being about the relative importance of providing an account of inferential reasoning at the beginning of a text like Dharmakīrti's *Commentary*, in comparison with providing an account of the qualities of the Buddha.[27] It is worth noting, however, that there is no disagreement about whether these chapters are important or even about the ways in which they are important. What is at issue seems to be their relative importance. In what follows I will focus on the first group of commentators and, more specifically, the remarks of Śākyabuddhi (ca. 660–720) and Karṇakagomin (fl. 800).

In the opening section of his auto-commentary on the "Inference" chapter of his *Commentary*, Dharmakīrti himself explains that inferential reasoning is the basis for distinguishing between what is useful (*artha*) and what is useless (*anartha*). As a result of this, and since there are also many conflicting opinions about it, he says that a correct account of inferential reasoning is important.[28] Śākyabuddhi, in commenting on this line—as a part of his explanation of an earlier commentator's remarks on the order of Dharmakīrti's chapters—explains that what Dharmakīrti means by "useful" is Dignāga's account of the sources of knowledge, and that what he means by "useless" is the account provided by non-Buddhists.[29] As Śākyabuddhi says, the reason

26. This group includes Prajñākaragupta (fl. 800), indirectly, and Jayanta (fl. eleventh century).

27. For a discussion of the structure of the *pramāṇasiddhi* chapter (PV1), see Nagatomi 1959, and Inami and Tillemans 1986.

28. PVSV 1.08–1.09: "He says, 'in order to establish it [i.e., inference] because there is disagreement about it,' since inference is the basis for distinguishing between what is helpful and what is harmful" (*arthānarthavivecanasyānumānāśrayatvāt tadvipratipattes tadvyavasthāpanāyāha*).

29. PVṬ D5b7ff/Q5b3ff, which is parallel to PVSVṬ 6.2–6.5 (as quoted in Kellner 2004b:153 n. 14): "'Helpful' refers to the descriptions of the sources of knowledge, etc., that were set down by the teacher Dignāga, because they are correct. 'Unhelpful' refers to those set down by non-Buddhists, because they are incorrect. Distinguishing which is which is established through their correctness and incorrectness, [and] inference is the basis of that. For it is on the basis of inference alone, and not perception, that the correctness or incorrectness of those descriptive statements can be established. This is because [perception] is nondiscerning" (*ācāryadignāgapraṇītaṃ pramāṇalakṣaṇādikam artho yuktatvāt, tīrthikapraṇītaṃ na yuktatvād anarthaḥ. tayor vivecanaṃ yuktāyuktatvena vyavasthāpanam, tasyānumānāśrayatvāt. anumānam*

Dignāga's account is said to be of value, and the opponents' is not, is that only what Dignāga says is correct (*yukta*). He goes on to say that since for Dharmakīrti perception cannot be used to demonstrate this, it is only on the basis of inferential reasoning that we can distinguish between what is actually correct and what is incorrect. As a result, a correct account of inferential reasoning is a prerequisite for any kind of philosophical analysis, and so Dharmakīrti chooses to discuss it as an independent topic at the beginning of his text, even though Dignāga himself did not.

In a closely related passage, Śākyabuddhi adds to this earlier explanation by saying that a correct account of inferential reasoning is, more specifically, a prerequisite for Dharmakīrti's discussion of the Buddha's teachings, since it is only on the basis of inferential reasoning that we can arrive at a correct understanding of fundamental aspects of what the Buddha taught—e.g., the five aggregates (*skandha*) that constitute living beings, the sensory spheres (*āyatana*), and the eighteen elements (*dhātu*).[30] Śākyabuddhi says that since, in the chapter in which the qualities of the Buddha are discussed, Dharmakīrti wants to show that only the teachings of the Buddha are correct, he needs to first provide an account of inference, on the basis of which he will then be able to show that the Buddha's teachings are correct and the teachings of non-Buddhists are not. As Śākyabuddhi sees it, the dual purpose that Dignāga outlined in the beginning of his *Compendium* is also shared by Dharmakīrti, and presumably by Śākyabuddhi himself.[31] It is also clear from

eva hy āśritya lakṣaṇavākyānāṃ yuktāyuktatvaṃ vyavasthāpyam, na pratyakṣam, tasyāvicārakatvād iti).

30. PVṬ D71b1/Q86a6, parallel to PVKP 517.29–518.02 (as quoted in Kellner 2004b:155 n. 18): "The five aggregates, sensory spheres, and eighteen elements are defined in the three baskets—the teaching of the Buddha, which is [what Devendrabuddhi] meant by 'a text of definitions.' Moreover, that is a source of knowledge, since it does not disappoint. And so 'text of definitions' means a 'text of definitions of the sources of knowledge,' i.e., the words of the Buddha. . . . This is what that means" (*lakṣyante skandhadhātvāyatanāni yena śāstreṇa tal lakṣaṇaśāstraṃ tripiṭakam. pramāṇaṃ ca tad, avisaṃvāditvāt, lakṣaṇaśāstraṃ ceti pramāṇalakṣaṇaśāstraṃ bhagavatpravacanam . . . iti bhāvaḥ*). For a more detailed and contextually grounded analysis of this passage see Kellner 2004b:152–156.

31. VṬ D71a5/Q86a1, parallel to PVKP 517.05–517.06 (as quoted in Kellner 2004b:155 n. 17): "Inference is a prerequisite for that elucidating commentary in which [Dharmakīrti] explains [the meaning of Dignāga's *Compendium*] in the proper manner, after setting aside the false explanations of previous commentators and the false views of non-Buddhists" (*pūrvaṭīkākārāsadvyākhyāṃ tīrthikavimatiṃ cāpanīya yathāsthitavyākhyānaṃ vyākhyā. tasyā nibandhanam anumānam*).

Śākyabuddhi's analysis that being right about the sources of knowledge, and specifically inferential reasoning, is important for having access to the path.

Interestingly, while commenting on this line, Karṇakagomin rejects Śākyabuddhi's claim that for Dharmakīrti, inferential reasoning is of special importance because it is only through inferential reasoning that we can determine what is useful and what is useless. Although Karṇakagomin doesn't disagree that inferential reasoning is *a* basis for making such determinations, he thinks that in certain cases perception is too. For Karṇakagomin, what is uniquely important about inferential reasoning is that it is only through inferential reasoning that we can come to know, conventionally, the four noble truths, and thus hope to make progress on the path. Like his predecessors, he believes that the four noble truths, which constitute *dharma*, cannot be known through perception. For Karṇakagomin, when Dharmakīrti says "useful" what he means is the cessation of suffering and the path that leads to it—that is, the third and fourth noble truths—while when he says "useless" what he means is suffering and its causes—the first and second noble truths. Like Dharmottara, Karṇakagomin also explains that it is only after someone has come to know the four noble truths inferentially, and has meditated upon them, that ultimately valid awareness is possible.[32]

Dharmakīrti and many of the commentators on his *Ascertainment of the Sources of Knowledge* and *Commentary on the Compendium of the Sources of Knowledge* pick up on, and in some cases extend, Dignāga's treatment of the four

---

32. PVSVṬ 7.23–7.28 *ad* PVSV 1.8 (as quoted in Kellner 2004b:157 n. 20): "And the Buddha has said that 'liberation arises by seeing the four noble truths.' Moreover, 'seeing' them is the result of repeated meditation, and [one] engages in meditation by ascertaining the four noble truths. And since [they] are supersensory, their ascertainment is possible only on the basis of inference. Thus [Dharmakīrti says] that inference is the only basis for distinguishing between what is helpful and what is harmful. 'Helpful' means the path toward cessation, because that is to be sought out. 'Harmful' means suffering and its causes, because they are to be abandoned. Alternatively, 'helpful' is ultimate truth [and] 'unhelpful' is conventional truth" (*muktiś {ca} caturāryasatyadarśanād bhavatīti bhagavatoktam. taddarśanaṃ ca bhāvanābhyāsato niṣpadyate. bhāvanāyāṃ pravṛttiś ca caturāryasatyaniścayena. tanniścayaś ca parokṣatvād anumānād eva bhavatīty arthānarthavivecanāśrayatvam anumānasyaiva. artho nirodhamārgāv upādeyatvād, anartho duḥkhasamudayau, tyājyatvāt. yad vā 'rthaḥ paramārthasatyam anarthaḥ saṃvṛttisatyaṃ*). Kellner reads Śākyabuddhi as understanding the role of inference to be "outward" whereas she reads Karṇakagomin as taking its significance to be "inward"; see Kellner's excellent summary at Kellner 2004b:157.

issues that structure his account of the purpose and value of Buddhist epistemology in his *Compendium*. There is, for example, widespread agreement that there is a dual purpose in the work of the Buddhist epistemologists—namely, to argue both against their opponents' account of the sources of knowledge and in support of their own. There is also widespread agreement that a correct account of the sources of knowledge brings one closer to understanding and realizing the *dharma*, even though *dharma* itself is inaccessible to philosophical analysis. One of the reasons given for this is that the realization of *dharma* requires meditating upon an object—specifically, the teaching of the Buddha—that has been established on the basis of conventionally valid sources of knowledge—most relevantly, inference. Establishing an object in this way seems to fix it in awareness in the way that is required for successful meditation. What is important is not just that one is aware of an object that can, for example, withstand critical philosophical analysis, but that this object is fixed in awareness as a result of a conventionally valid awareness-event. There is little doubt that the Buddhist epistemological tradition, as inherited by Ratnakīrti, views philosophy, and epistemology more specifically, as having value, in that it can turn one away from incorrect views and toward the kind of view that can lead one to the realization of *dharma* itself.

2. The Soteriological Significance of Epistemology

Unlike his predecessors, Ratnakīrti is rarely explicit about his commitment to the ideals of his text tradition regarding the soteriological significance of epistemology. As I will argue, however, he is clearly committed to these ideals and views his own work in support of them. As a way of illustrating this, I will focus on aspects of Ratnakīrti's discussion of the inference for omniscience, as presented in his "Demonstration of Omniscience" (*Sarvajñasiddhi*), in which he tries to prove that meditating (*bhāvanā*) upon a conceptually constructed mental object—in particular, the four noble truths—can lead to omniscience, the ultimately valid awareness of *dharma* itself.[33] I will argue

33. This text is edited and translated in Bühneman 1980 and Goodman 1989. For an excellent discussion of omniscience in Buddhist philosophy see McClintock 2002.

Here is Ratnakīrti's inference as presented at RNĀ (SS 1.20–1.24): "Every mental element that is accompanied by repeated reflection that is sincere, uninterrupted, and continues for a long period of time [the reason property] is capable of becoming manifest [target

further that his discussion of this inference provides a new perspective on his other work, by revealing his otherwise implicit commitment to the ideals of his text tradition and his own understanding of their significance.

2.1. *Dual Purpose*

In setting up his inference for proving the omniscience of the Buddha, Ratnakīrti indirectly indicates the dual purpose of his work. Following Dharmakīrti, he says that he will prove the omniscience of the Buddha in order (1) to argue against his opponents, who reject the possibility of anyone being able to have direct knowledge of ***dharma***, and (2) to establish that it is possible for someone to know ***dharma*** itself—that is, to have direct, noninferential awareness of what is to be given up, what is to be sought out, and the means of accomplishing both.[34] Unlike Dignāga, however, Ratnakīrti does

---

property], like the mental image of a young woman for her lover [a similar case]. And these mental images, whose objects are the four noble truths [the site of the inference], are mental elements that are accompanied by repeated reflection, as stated above" (*yo yaḥ sādaranirantaradīrghakālābhyāsasahitacetoguṇaḥ sa sarvaḥ sphuṭībhāvo yogyaḥ | yathā yuvatyākāraḥ kāminaḥ puruṣasya | yathoktābhyāsasahitacetoguṇāś cāmī caturāryasatyaviṣayā ākārā iti {svabhāvo hetuḥ}*). Ratnakīrti describes the components of the inference at RNĀ (SS 4.31–4.32): "So here the site of the inference is the complete complex of the mental image of the four noble truths together with meditation upon them. The reason property is the complete complex of a mental element in general which is characterized by meditation. The target property is the capacity to be manifest" (*tad atrābhyāsasahitacaturāryasatyākāraḥ samagro dharmī sāmagryam abhyāsaviśiṣṭacetoguṇatvamātraṃ hetuḥ sphuṭībhāvayogyatāsādhyam*).

34. That there is a dual purpose to his "Demonstration of Omniscience" (SS) is evident from RNĀ (SS 1.11–1.14), where Ratnakīrti explains Dharmakīrti's "intentions"—and in this way his own—in arguing against his opponents' views and in support of his own. In this case, Ratnakīrti identifies the "opponent" as the Mīmāṃsaka, Kumārila; see RNĀ (SS 1.7). Also see RNĀ (SS 1.11–1.15), where—while discussing the views of Dharmakīrti—Ratnakīrti indicates that the Buddha is one who "knows the truth of what is to be given up, what is to be sought out, and the means of accomplishing both" (*saparikaraheyopādeyatattvajña*)—that is, the four noble truths. Ratnakīrti makes this identification at RNĀ (SS 2.07–2.09), where he says that the "mental image of the four noble truths is defined by what is to be given up, what is to be sought out, and the means of accomplishing both" (*saparikaraheyopādeyātmakasya caturāryasatyākārasya*). For a further discussion of this see Bühneman 1980:92 n. 7. For some other references see PVABh 52.16–52.20, PVV 20.22ff. For more on this type of inference, see Steinkellner 1999 and Eltschinger 2007b. For more on Ratnakīrti's inference see Moriyama 2004 and Taber (forthcoming).

not directly say that he will be arguing against his opponents' views on the sources of knowledge and in support of his own. Nevertheless, since it is on the basis of his opponents' understanding of these sources that Ratnakīrti argues against their conclusions, and on the basis of his own understanding of these sources that he argues in support of his conclusions, it is clear that there is a direct relationship between the dual purpose of his text, as stated here, and the sources of knowledge.[35]

2.2. *Proximity to the* Dharma

Unlike many of his predecessors, Ratnakīrti does not directly say that a proper account of conventionally valid awareness and the sources of knowledge that produce it is soteriologically significant since on the basis of it people who are "distant" from the teachings of the Buddha can be brought "closer" to it. This is, however, something that is implied by his work. For Ratnakīrti, the relevant teachings of the Buddha are the "four noble truths" (*caturāryasatya*), which he suggests are themselves related to the underlying truth of selflessness (*nairātmya*)—the view that there is no enduring self.[36] As Ratnakīrti sees it, discontent (*duḥkha*)—the first noble truth—is defined in terms of the five psycho-physical aggregates (*skandha*) that are thought to be constitutive of living beings.[37] The cause of this discontent (*samudaya*)—the second noble truth—is, as Ratnakīrti says, the false belief that these five psycho-physical aggregates constitute an enduring self (*ātmadṛṣṭi*).[38] That

---

35. For more on this point see section 2.4.

36. For the idea that the four noble truths are what is relevant see RNĀ (SS 20.07–20.08). For a defense of the claim that the four noble truths are related to the view that there is no enduring self and momentariness, see below.

37. See RNĀ (SS 2.17), where Ratnakīrti says that discontent (*duḥkha*) "is just the five current psycho-physical aggregates" (*vārtamānikapañcaskandhātmaka*). A similar formulation is repeated at RNĀ (SS 2.22), where it is said that the "effect" (*kārya*)—that is, discontent—is "defined by the five psycho-physical aggregates that migrate through existence" (*sāṃsārikapañcaskandhalakṣaṇa*). That discontent (*duḥkha*) is to be identified as "what is to be given up" is suggested at RNĀ (SS 2.07–2.10, 2.11).

38. See RNĀ (SS 2.20), where, in responding to the objection at RNĀ (SS 2.4) that the cause (*hetu*) of "what is to be given up" (*heya*) is not known, Ratnakīrti says that it has been ascertained that "with respect to discontent, the cause is identified as the view that there is an enduring self, along with actions whose efficacy in worldly life is due to error and desire" (*duḥkhe viparyāsatṛṣṇāpravṛttiśaktikarmabhiḥ sahitasyātmadṛṣṭilakṣaṇasya hetoḥ*). This idea is

the cessation of this discontent (*nirodha*) is possible—the third noble truth—is directly explained in terms of selflessness, which Ratnakīrti says is an antidote to the false belief in an enduring self.[39] The path to the cessation of discontent (*mārga*)—the fourth noble truth—is said to be nothing other than the conventionally valid awareness of selflessness, which is itself established by proving that all existing things are momentary.[40]

In arguing that meditation on the four noble truths can lead to the direct manifestation of *dharma* itself, Ratnakīrti is in effect saying that meditation on selflessness can lead to its direct manifestation, which he says is just what omniscience is.[41] Ratnakīrti further identifies selflessness and the thesis that all existing things are momentary as the unique teachings of the Buddha, and thus suggests that they alone are the proper objects for meditation.[42] In his "Demonstration of Omniscience" Ratnakīrti switches back and forth between referring to the objects of meditation as "the four noble truths," "selflessness," and "momentariness." Since, as I have argued, the four noble truths can be reduced to selflessness, and selflessness is itself established

---

also repeated at RNĀ (SS 2.27) in a verse that Steinkellner (1977) suggests is from Jñānaśrīmitra's now lost "Demonstration of Omniscience" (*Sarvajñasiddhi*).

39. See RNĀ (SS 2.31), where Ratnakīrti explains that discontent can come to an end "because it is possible to see that selflessness is an antidote to the ignorance that takes the form of the view that there is an enduring self" (*ātmadṛṣṭirūpāyā avidyāyāḥ pratipakṣabhūtasya nairātmyadarśanasya saṃbhavāt*). Also see RNĀ (SS 2.29), where Ratnakīrti says that "it is by arguing against the idea of a self that the error in the view that there is a self is seen" (*ātmadarśanasya cāvidyātvam ātmapratikṣepato draṣṭavyam*).

40. See RNĀ (SS 3.01), where Ratnakīrti responds to the objection, at RNĀ (SS 2.04), that there is no known defeater (*bādhaka*) of the view that there is a self, by saying that this is not the case "since it is validly ascertained that the selflessness thesis is denoted by the term 'path'" (*nairātmyadarśanasya mārgaśabdavācyasya pramāṇato niścitatvāt*). See also Trilocana's account of the Buddhist position at RNĀ (SS 14.16–14.22)—especially where the "path" is said to be defined by momentariness as the object of contemplation. Also see JNĀ (KKBhS 323.03–323.05), which is translated in Kajiyama 1998:54 n. 128.

41. See RNĀ (SS 21.20), where Ratnakīrti says that "meditation on the truth of the path is how omniscience is established" (*mārgasatyābhyāsāt siddhaḥ sarvajñaḥ*).

42. See RNĀ (SS 6.11–6.12), where he says that for those who want to know not about an omniscient person in general, but about a particular omniscient person, "the Lord Buddha, who is omniscient, [is] the only one who taught momentariness and selflessness in accordance with the sources of knowledge" (*pramāṇopapannakṣaṇikanairātmyavādina eva sugatasya bhagavataḥ sarvajñatā*). That the teachings of the Buddha are the only proper objects of meditation follows from RNĀ (SS 19.17–19.21) and (SS 21.14–21.20), which are quoted and translated below.

through (and often identified with) momentariness, I will refer to the object of meditation as "selflessness/momentariness."[43]

In an interesting passage in his "Demonstration," Ratnakīrti discusses the relationship between the conventionally valid awareness of selflessness/momentariness and the teachings of the Buddha, and suggests why he thinks that being right about epistemology is of value. In this passage Ratnakīrti suggests that to be distant from the teachings of the Buddha is to be distracted (*vikṣepa*), by being turned away from the truth of selflessness/momentariness.[44] Since what distracts or confuses people is their false belief in an enduring self, successfully arguing against this view is, he suggests, conducive to turning people toward the truth of selflessness/momentariness. More specifically, it removes an impediment to successfully following the path.[45] Elsewhere Ratnakīrti also suggests that it is necessary to show that one's view, which in this context is the view that all existing things are momentary, is properly established. Ratnakīrti provides two reasons for this: First, he suggests that since the awareness that all things are momentary is itself an antidote to the false view that there is an enduring self, arguing in support of it helps to turn people away from their false views. Second, and more important for Ratnakīrti, the proper object of meditation must be an object of conventionally valid awareness—that is, an object that has been established on the basis of a source of knowledge. Furthermore, it seems as though it must also be known to be so.[46] A

---

43. This pairing is very common, both in Ratnakīrti's text and in the tradition that he inherits. See, for example, McClintock 2002.

44. In this passage, RNĀ (SS 21.14–21.20), Ratnakīrti is responding to an earlier objection by Vācaspatimiśra—RNĀ (SS 15.20–15.27)—in which he argues that since, according to Buddhist philosophers like Ratnakīrti, awareness-events can have only a single object/image, our thoughts can never be really distracted. As a result, he says, there should be no need to practice meditation in order to eliminate "distractions" and focus our minds on a single object. In his response to this objection Ratnakīrti explains that this is not the case since "any [awareness] at all that is turned away from the truths of selflessness, etc., is distracted [and any awareness] that is directly presented with those truths, through meditation, is focused" (*nairātmyāditattvaparāṅmukhasya sarvasyaiva vikṣiptatvāt | bhāvanābalena tattvasākṣātkāriṇaḥ samāhitatvāt*).

45. This idea is expressed a few lines later in the same passage—RNĀ (SS 21.16–21.18)—where Ratnakīrti says that even in everyday life the apparent difference between a grasping subject and grasped objects is how the "productive practice of the path is obstructed" (*mārgābhyāsapravṛttir abhyāhateti*).

46. These two reasons are suggested by RNĀ (SS 19.17–19.21), which is also a part of Ratnakīrti's response to Vācaspatimiśra's objections, and more specifically, to the objection—

proper account of such awareness is therefore necessary and of soteriological significance.

It is interesting that Ratnakīrti doesn't say why the proper object of meditation must be an object of conventionally valid awareness or explain in what sense his opponents' belief in an enduring self is "false." While he does not address this issue directly, it is possible to reconstruct Ratnakīrti's views by drawing upon the resources of his text tradition and the nature of his other work. As I have argued in chapters 2 and 3, there are two senses in which Ratnakīrti thinks that his opponents' views on the existence of Īśvara are "false." What they say about Īśvara is "false," on the one hand, because by their own lights they have not certified the Īśvara-inference and cannot do so. As an object of awareness, the existence of Īśvara cannot withstand philosophical analysis and in fact crumbles in the face of it. Moreover, as discussed in chapter 5, for Ratnakīrti, awareness-events that are not valid are not pragmatically effective and thus "mislead" us with respect to their content. In a slightly different sense, the Naiyāyikas' view is also "false" in that it is incompatible with the claim that all existing things are momentary, a conclusion that Ratnakīrti thinks he has established inferentially. He thinks that the momentariness thesis, unlike the existence of Īśvara, can withstand philosophical analysis, and remains firm in the face of it. Insofar as momentariness is known to be the object of a conventionally valid awareness-event, there is also certainty about it that adds to its stability.

In part, then, what seems to make an object of conventionally valid awareness a proper object of meditation is that, unlike objects that are not

---

which is not necessarily Vācaspatimiśra's—at RNĀ (SS 19.15–19.17), where the issue of the proper object of meditation is raised. In his response, Ratnakīrti explains that he does not say that "the sense-faculty of the mind, along with meditation on an object that has been fixed by a source of knowledge, leads to an awareness-event in which the nature of the object itself is grasped—but rather that it is meditation on the real nature of all things, which is defined by momentariness and selflessness, that opposes the ignorance constituted by false views" (*{na hi vayaṃ} pramāṇadṛṣṭavastubhāvanāsahitaṃ mana indriyam arthasvarūpagrāhijñānaṃ janayatīti brūmaḥ, api tv asaddṛṣṭilakṣaṇāvidyāparipanthikṣaṇikanairātmyalakṣaṇasarvavastutattvabhāvanāsahitam*). He goes on to say that the "real nature of all things" (*sarvavastutattvam*) is "just momentariness and selflessness, which has been made known by establishing momentary destruction" (*kṣaṇikanairātmyam eveti kṣaṇabhaṅgaprasādhanataḥ pratipāditam iti*). The same point is also made, in almost the exact same language, a few pages later at RNĀ (SS 20.18–21.21).

conventionally valid and/or known to be so, it is epistemically stable. In addition, and perhaps more importantly, only conventionally valid awareness-events are pragmatically effective and capable of effectively leading us to their objects. It is important to note that for Ratnakīrti, it is only by meditating on selflessness/momentariness that the clear manifestation of *dharma* itself is possible.[47] This is because, for Ratnakīrti, selflessness/momentariness is the nature of reality, and by meditating on it, it is possible for reality itself to be manifest in awareness, just as a lovesick man's meditating on the form of his lover can result in her becoming manifest to him.[48]

2.3. "Dharma" *and the* Dharma *Itself*

Ratnakīrti is very clear that the proper objects of meditation are mental objects—and more specifically, mental objects whose representational content is the four noble truths or, as I have argued, selflessness/momentariness. As Ratnakīrti emphasizes, it is necessary that what is meditated upon be proven by a conventionally valid source of knowledge, in this case inferential reasoning. Although what is proven through inferential reasoning is an O4 object, what is meditated upon is an object that one can focus one's attention upon, like the form of a woman for her lover. Unlike the form of the woman, which is based on sense perception, the object of meditation is not (and cannot be) based on sense perception. As Ratnakīrti explains, momentariness—and therefore the four noble truths—is not an object of sense perception. In this sense it is like any other inferred object, such as the "fire" that is inferred in the standard inference of fire from smoke.

One way to think of the object that is meditated upon may be in terms of an inferred O4 object as it is subsequently brought to mind (perhaps through memory). As such, this object will be—like the form of the woman or the concept "fire"—an O2 object that one can mentally act upon. Like the concept of the inferred object "fire," which is capable of leading us to a "real" fire on

47. See prior note, where RNĀ (SS 19.15–19.17) is discussed. It is important to note that Ratnakīrti also says, at RNĀ (SS 20.07, 4.24–4.28), that as the objects of valid awareness-events, the four noble truths and selflessness are proper objects for meditation. As I have argued, however, they are all, in the relevant sense, equivalent to momentariness.

48. Again see note 46, where RNĀ (SS 19.15–19.17) is discussed. Ratnakīrti also argues this point in a number of other places.

the mountain that we can perceive through sense perception, the object of meditation is also supposed to be capable of leading us to a clear manifest awareness of momentariness—that is, the *dharma* itself. According to Ratnakīrti, as a result of meditation it is possible for us to directly "see" the *dharma* itself, through a special kind of perception called "yogic perception."[49] Like his predecessors, Ratnakīrti does not think that the *dharma* itself is accessible to our conventional sources of knowledge. What is accessible are only constructed O2/O4 objects such as the "four noble truths," "selflessness," and "momentariness." But, as Ratnakīrti argues in this essay, meditating on these constructed O2 objects can lead to the manifestation of *dharma* itself.[50]

Ratnakīrti's discussion of the omniscience-inference provides an interesting new framework within which to view his work as a whole, and also my analysis of his argument against the existence of Īśvara (chapters 2 and 3) and theory of mental images (chapters 4 and 5). One of the threads running through these four chapters has been the question of Ratnakīrti's purpose, and more specifically what is at stake for him in the various arguments that he makes and the counterarguments to which he responds. It is interesting that Ratnakīrti never mentions that his technical arguments against the existence of Īśvara are relevant to the path taught by the Buddha or discusses in any detail why epistemology itself is of importance. When it is viewed from within the framework of his remarks in his "Demonstration of Omniscience," however, I will argue that much of Ratnakīrti's work can be viewed in relation to his text tradition's shared ideals regarding the soteriological significance of epistemology.

It is clear from the nature of Ratnakīrti's work as a whole that the dual purpose that he alludes to in setting up his "Demonstration of Omniscience" is not restricted to this text. Of the ten extant texts by Ratnakīrti, two are devoted to arguing against his opponents' views, five focus on establishing his own, and the remaining three argue against rival positions while also supporting his own.[51] Some of these texts can be seen, therefore,

---

49. RNĀ (SS 19.17–19.21), discussed above, and RNĀ (SS 20.05–20.11).

50. In two very interesting passages, Ratnakīrti explains how the omniscience-inference is different from inferences like the inference of fire from smoke; see RNĀ (SS 4.24–4.28) and RNĀ (SS 5.04–5.10). See also Eltschinger 2007b and Steinkellner 1999.

51. RNĀ (ĪSD) and RNĀ (SSD) are devoted to arguing against his opponents. RNĀ (SS), RNĀ (AS), RNĀ (KSA), RNĀ (KSV), and RNĀ (CAPV) focus on establishing his

as extended arguments against the conclusions of his opponents, while others can be seen as attempts at establishing his own positive views. As I have argued in this book, what is at stake in these texts is much more than just the particular position being argued for or against. What is at stake is also the epistemological framework within which such arguments are presented and defended. Thus, in arguing against his opponent's conclusions and in support of his own, he is arguing against their understanding of the sources of knowledge and in support of his own. As I have argued, this is evident from the nature of Ratnakīrti's critique of the Īśvara-inference and the close relationship between this critique and his theory of exclusion and mental images. While much of this was only implicit in Ratnakīrti's criticism of the Īśvara-inference, what Ratnakīrti says in his "Demonstration of Omniscience" supports my argument explicitly. For Ratnakīrti, as for his predecessors, one's philosophical work serves a dual purpose: to argue against one's opponents' conclusions and the epistemology that supports them, and to argue in support of one's own view and the epistemology that supports it.

Attending to Ratnakīrti's "Demonstration of Omniscience" helps us to see that for him too this dual purpose is of soteriological significance. In this context, what is especially important about his critique of the Īśvara-inference is that Īśvara is generally taken to be the paradigmatic example of an enduring self. Exposing inherent problems in the Īśvara-inference is therefore extremely important for turning (some) of his opponents away from their false view of an enduring self. A similar point can also be made about his arguments against the claim that entities endure through time and in support of his momentariness thesis. In the interpretive framework provided by his "Demonstration of Omniscience," Ratnakīrti's extensive discussion of this issue takes on new significance. His arguments in support of momentariness can be seen as an attempt at turning his opponents away from their false views and bringing them closer to the *dharma*, by establishing the "object" that he will show is the proper object of meditation. As I have argued, his support of the theory of exclusion, mental images, and pervasion can also be viewed in terms of its soteriological significance. By establishing his own position on each of these issues, Ratnakīrti develops the philosophical resources that support his critique of his opponents and the epistemology for

---

own views. RNĀ (PAP), RNĀ (SD), and RNĀ (VN) do both. For the full titles with translations see chapter 1 and the list of abbreviations in the front matter.

his own positive conclusions. When taken together, the theory of exclusion and his account of mental images support a theory of content according to which there is ultimately no "object" of awareness. These texts thus (1) turn his opponents away from all of their false views, by showing them that the epistemology that is used to support them is not adequate; and (2) turn them toward his own views, by showing them that his epistemology overcomes the inherent weaknesses in theirs, without any added cost.

3. Jñānaśrīmitra on Epistemology as Pedagogy

As I have argued in this chapter, the insights provided by Ratnakīrti's text tradition—as defined by the work of Dignāga, Dharmakīrti, and their commentators—make it possible to see clearly what is implicit in Ratnakīrti's work that might otherwise pass unnoticed. Ratnakīrti's greatest intellectual debts, however, are to his teacher Jñānaśrīmitra, whose own work is the direct source of many of his arguments and provides the detailed blueprints for much of his corpus.[52] Ratnakīrti's work is in no small part a deliberate, careful, and strategic reconstruction of many of his teacher's texts and arguments.[53] The very high degree to which Ratnakīrti is faithful to his teacher's work, however, also highlights areas of difference. Just as what is understated in Ratnakīrti's work can sometimes be brought to the surface by viewing it from within its broader intellectual context, so too can what he chooses

52. Comparing the titles of Ratnakīrti's texts with those of his teacher illustrates this nicely. Jñānaśrīmitra's extant works are as follows: "A Study of Moment by Moment Destruction" (*Kṣaṇabhaṅgādhyāya*), "Analysis of Pervasion" (*Vyāpticarcā*), "Examination of 'Difference and Nondifference'" (*Bhedābhedaparīkṣā*), "The Mystery of Nonapprehension" (*Anupalabdhirahasya*), "Investigation of the Total Absence of Sound" (*Sarvaśabdābhāvaparīkṣā*), "Monograph on Exclusion" (*Apohaprakaraṇa*), "Debating God" (*Īśvaravāda*), "Proof of the Cause-Effect Relationship" (*Kāryakāraṇabhāvasiddhi*), "Monograph on the Discernment of Yogis" (*Yoginirṇayaprakaraṇa*), "Monograph on the Drop of Nonduality" (*Advaitabinduprakaraṇa*), "A Treatise Proving That Awareness Contains an Image" (*Sākārasiddhiśāstra*), and "A Verse Summary on the Possession of an Image" (*Sākārasaṃgrahasūtra*). In addition to these texts, Jñānaśrīmitra also wrote a work on poetic meter (see Hahn 1971 and Hahn 1989) and a lost "Demonstration of Omniscience" (*Sarvajñasiddhi*) (see Steinkellner 1977).

53. For a very clear example of this compare Lasic 2000a with Lasic 2000b. Also see Steinkellner 1977 and the references in Bühneman 1980.

to suppress. In this section I want to discuss a concept that is central to Jñānaśrīmitra's "Monograph on Exclusion" (*Apohaprakaraṇa*), but that is deliberately written out of Ratnakīrti's own "Demonstration of Exclusion."

The concept of a "conditionally adopted position" (*vyavasthā*) is the basis for Jñānaśrīmitra's account of why his predecessors (and sometimes he himself) argue in support of philosophical positions that are strictly speaking not correct.[54] For Jñānaśrīmitra, attending to the use of "conditionally adopted positions" is also crucial for understanding the pedagogical role that he takes his text tradition to assign to epistemology. I will argue that in writing this concept out of his work, Ratnakīrti, while agreeing with the pedagogical role of epistemology as understood by Jñānaśrīmitra, shifts its focus, and in so doing reveals not only what he takes to be of primary importance about it, but also where his view differs from that of his teacher. As I hope to show, what Jñānaśrīmitra says about conditionally adopted positions helps us to see what is implicit and suppressed both in Ratnakīrti's own work regarding the pedagogical role of epistemology, and in philosophy more generally.

3.1. A Multiple-Content Model of Awareness

The philosophical context for Jñānaśrīmitra's discussion of conditionally adopted positions is the multiple-content model of awareness that Ratnakīrti shares with him.[55] Recall that according to this model, each state of awareness has two objects: a grasped object, which is directly present in awareness, and a determined object, which is conceptually constructed through exclusion. What is so striking about this model is that it seems to fly in the face of what is arguably their text tradition's most basic tenet and characteristic feature: the claim that perception is free from conceptual construction.[56] For many Buddhist and non-Buddhist philosophers alike, this tenet was taken to be the foundational insight of Dignāga and Dharmakīrti. Before turning to how Jñānaśrīmitra accounts for what appears to be his radical departure from Dignāga and Dharmakīrti's account of the content of

---

54. Much of my discussion in this section is based on Patil 2007. See also McCrea and Patil 2006.

55. For a detailed discussion of Ratnakīrti's version of this model see chapter 5.

56. See chapter 5, section 1, where Dharmottara's NBṬ 70–72 *ad* Dharmakīrti's NB 1.12 is quoted and translated.

perception, it will be helpful to briefly review the multiple-content model of awareness, by focusing on what Jñānaśrīmitra says about it.

Like Ratnakīrti, Jñānaśrīmitra says that each state of valid awareness must have two objects, a grasped object and a determined object.[57] In his "Analysis of Pervasion" (*Vyāpticarcā*), in a debate specifically about the nature of the object of perception, Jñānaśrīmitra states this very clearly. He says,

> Now, for us, both modes of valid awareness have both objects, because of the distinction between what is grasped and what is determined. For that which is manifest in an episode of awareness is what is grasped, but that with respect to which it [i.e., the episode of awareness] functions is what is determined. Now, for perception, what is grasped is a particular and what is determined is a universal. But for inference it is the reverse.[58]

Just as for Ratnakīrti, in both perception and inference both manifestation and determination are necessary. This is because each mode of awareness must have two objects, a grasped object, the object that is manifest in awareness,

---

57. Although Jñānaśrīmitra adopts the structure of Dharmottara's model of valid awareness and its objects, he criticizes him in a number of places in his work. See, for example, JNĀ (AP 205), on the issue of implicative negation (*paryudāsa*); JNĀ (AP 228), on imposition (*āropa*); JNĀ (KKBhS 322), on causality (*kāryakāraṇabhāva*); JNĀ (YN 332), on supernormal perception (*yogipratyakṣa*); the references in Woo 2001 to Jñānaśrīmitra's KBhA; and the references in Kellner 1997a to his AR. There are also important differences between Jñānaśrīmitra and Dharmottara's version of the two-object model of perception and inference. For a discussion of some of these differences see McCrea and Patil 2006 and below.

58. JNĀ (VC 166.13–16) and Lasic 2000a:13*.02–13*.06 (note that Lasic [2000a:13*.03] corrects Thakur *-adhyavaseyabhedena* from *adhyavasāyabhedena*): *asmākaṃ tāvad ubhayam api pramāṇam ubhayaviṣayam, grāhyādhyavaseyabhedena. yaddhi yatra jñāne pratibhāsate, tad grāhyam. yatra tu tat pravartate, tad adhyavaseyam. tatra pratyakṣasya svalakṣaṇaṃ grāhyam, adhyavaseyaṃ ca sāmānyam. anumānasya tu viparyayaḥ.* See also JNĀ (AP 225.17): *dvidhā viṣayavyavahāraḥ pratibhāsād adhyavasāyāc ca* ("There are two ways of talking about objects: On the basis of appearance and on the basis of determination"). The idea is also discussed in JNĀ (KBhA 137.15–137.18). It is worth noting that Jñānaśrīmitra, unlike Dharmottara, explicitly identifies the determined object of perception as a universal (*sāmānya*) in order to provide a basis for distinguishing between the two different kinds of universals that can be constructed from the grasped moment in the perceptual process. See also JNĀ (VC 166.14–166.21) and Lasic 2000a:13*.06–14*.14. JNĀ (VC 166.16–19) is also discussed and translated in Balcerowicz 1999:212.

and a determined object, the object that we take ourselves to be acting with respect to.[59] In the case of perception, the grasped object is generally called a "particular" and the determined object a "universal," while in inferential/verbal awareness the grasped object is generally called a "universal" and the determined object a "particular."[60] Thus, to properly account for the contents of perception and inference (and their validity) both manifestation and determination are necessary.[61]

Equally important to Jñānaśrīmitra's basic picture is his insistence that the determined objects of both perception and inference are conceptualized. In other words, like determination, conceptualization (*vikalpa*) is an equally important and essential part of both perception and inference. When confronted with an objector who presses him to explain why Dharmakīrti himself appears to use the terms "conceptualization" and "determination" contrastively in his *Short Study of the Reason Property* (*Hetubindu*),[62] he says,

---

59. In this passage Jñānaśrīmitra just states his view. He argues in support of his position that both appearance and determination/conceptualization are necessary at JNĀ (AP 230.08–231.02).

60. The qualification "generally called" is necessary when describing Jñānaśrīmitra's view since, according to him, the terms "particular" and "universal" do not really refer to ontologically distinct entities. For him, these two terms are defined relative to the mental process that follows the appearance of what we take to be a particular or a universal. See, for example, JNĀ (AP 220.02–220.09) for a discussion of this. This passage and a related passage about Jñānaśrīmitra's relativization of the terms "internal" and "external" are discussed in McCrea and Patil 2006.

61. JNĀ (AP 230.24–230.27): "Whatever does not appear in a certain episode of awareness or is not determined by it is not the object of that awareness, just as a horse [is not the object] of the awareness 'cow.' And a particular does not appear in verbal awareness, and a mental image is not determined by it. Thus [in each case] a pervading factor is missing. Since a necessary relation has been established [between being both manifest in appearance and determined, and being an object of awareness], [this inferential reason] is not inconclusive" (*yatra jñāne yan na pratibhāsate yena vā yan nāvasīyate sa na tasya viṣayo yathā gojñānasyāśvaḥ | na pratibhāsate ca śābdajñāne svalakṣaṇam, nāvasīyate cānena buddhyākāra iti vyāpakānupalabdhiḥ | pratibandhasādhanān nānaikāntikaḥ*).

62. The opponent's discomfort with Jñānaśrīmitra's position is clearly stated at JNĀ (AP 225.19–225.26), where the opponent quotes a fragment from Dharmakīrti, HB 3*.14–3*.15, to support his view that these terms are used contrastively. This fragment is quoted again at JNĀ (AP 227.10–227.11), which is quoted below.

> "Conceptualization" and "determination" refer to the same thing. It's just that the [use of the] word "conceptualization" is occasioned by connection with words and the like, while "determination" is occasioned by suitability for activity, even with respect to [an object] that is not grasped [by awareness].[63]

According to Jñānaśrīmitra, determination is really nothing but conceptualization and conceptualization is really nothing but determination. The only meaningful difference between them is that the word "conceptualization" is generally used when we want to say that the object of our awareness is inextricably bound up with the form of the word that is used to refer to it—that is, in inferential and verbal contexts.[64] On the other hand, the word "determination" is generally used when we want to talk about the objects of our awareness as if they were objects that we could act upon—that is, in contexts of intentional activity (which includes activity based on perception and inferential/verbal awareness).[65] For Jñānaśrīmitra, however, the terminological distinction between conceptualization and determination is neither based on, nor reveals, a real difference in the mental processes to which the two terms refer. Rather, it is the result of a fictional difference that is indexed

---

63. JNĀ (AP 226.01–226.03): *satyam ekārthau vikalpādhyavasāyau kevalaṃ vikalpaśabdaḥ śabdādiyojanānimittakaḥ | adhyavasāyas tv agṛhīte 'pi pravartanayogyatānimittaḥ.*

64. This is, of course, completely consistent with the way(s) in which Dignāga and Dharmakīrti describe conceptualization. As is well known, at PS 1.3d Dignāga explains that conceptualization (*kalpanā*) is "association with a name, class character, etc." (*nāmajātyādiyojanā*). Dharmakīrti expresses a similar idea at PVin 1.4b–c, where he says that "a conceptual state of awareness is a state of awareness associated with words" (*abhilāpinī pratītiḥ kalpanā*), and at NB 1.5 (=PVin 1.40.6–8), where he says that "conceptualization is a state of awareness in which a mental image is associated with words" (*abhilāpasaṃsargayogyapratibhāsā pratītiḥ kalpanā*). For an extremely interesting and thorough discussion of this see Funayama 1992:44–48; 59 n. 38, 39; 75 n. 116; 77 n. 121. See also the excellent discussion in Franco 1984.

65. This is also consistent with what Dharmakīrti has to say. Consider, for example, the famous quotation at PVin 2.8, where he says, "because even though its image is not an object there is activity through the determination of an object" (*svapratibhāse 'narthe 'rthādhyavasāyena pravartanāt*). For a discussion of this concept and term, see Katsura 1984, Katsura 1993, and the references in Dunne 2004. It may be worth noting that in McCrea and Patil 2006 we argue that Dharmakīrti uses the term "determination" only when discussing inferential and verbal states of awareness and that it may not be helpful, therefore, to think of determination as a form of "perceptual judgment." For Jñānaśrīmitra's account of intentional activity as including physical, verbal, and mental activity see JNĀ (AP 226–227).

to how the terms happen to be used.[66] Given my analysis in chapters 4 and 5, it should be clear that the "two mental processes" are not really different, since they are both nothing other than exclusion.

For Jñānaśrīmitra, as for Ratnakīrti, the objects of awareness fall into two neatly defined and mutually exclusive categories—those that are grasped, and therefore free from conceptual construction, and those that are determined, and therefore conceptualized. As is clear from this basic model, perception and inference must have both objects. Thus, according to Jñānaśrīmitra and Ratnakīrti, perception cannot be free from conceptual construction. Since for Jñānaśrīmitra it is clear that conceptualization is a part of the perceptual process, the problem for him is how to make sense of the traditional claim that "perception is free from conceptual construction." His approach is to insist that this problem is not really a philosophical one about the contents of perception, but rather an exegetical and historical one. It is in response to this exegetical and historical imperative that Jñānaśrīmitra appeals to his theory of conditionally adopted positions.

3.2. *Conditionally Adopted Positions*

In the following passage, Jñānaśrīmitra develops his theory of conditionally adopted positions (*vyavasthā*). He says,

> By relying on a little bit of the truth, a certain conditionally adopted position is constructed for a specific purpose in one way, even though the actual state of affairs is different, just as in examples such as the "self." . . . By relying on [a little bit of the truth, namely,] the conceptual construction of a single continuum, [we conventionally say]: "Who else will experience the [result of an] action done by this very person?," in order to frustrate the deceptive view that there is the passing away of what has been done and the onset of what has not been done.[67]

---

66. The reason Jñānaśrīmitra thinks that the two terms refer to the same mental process is that, according to him, conceptualization is just a form of determination. When we "conceptually" apprehend something by associating it with a word, for example, we are simply acting upon it verbally. Verbally (vs. nonverbally) referring to objects is a form of activity and is therefore to be included under the broader heading of determination.

67. JNĀ (AP 204.26–205.03): *atra brūmaḥ | iha kācid vyavasthā tattvaleśam āśritya prayojanaviśeṣād anyathā sthitāv apy anyathā kriyate, yathātma{tadutpāda iti | utpādo hi prāgabhāvaviśiṣṭa-*

A conditionally adopted position is a kind of philosophically sanctioned "white lie"—a statement that is only partially true and is used only for specific, and philosophically legitimate, purposes. Jñānaśrīmitra explains how conditionally adopted positions work by providing an example: in explaining the theory of karma, a Buddhist philosopher may legitimately say that a person will experience in the future the karmic results of actions that (s)he now performs. Yet this is not really true, because there is no "person" who endures through time. The statement is, however, based on a "little bit of the truth," namely, that people generally do construct a mental continuum that they (mis)take to be an enduring "person/self." Jñānaśrīmitra explains that it is even legitimate for this partially true statement to be used in contexts where one needs to expose as false the view that our current actions do not have karmic consequences (or the view that we may experience karmic consequences that are not the result of *our* previous actions). While the statement that there is an enduring self is strictly speaking false, in certain contexts it may serve an important pedagogical function. In this context, for example, its function is to disabuse people of the idea that there is no karma. Elsewhere Jñānaśrīmitra points out that ordinary people cannot function without such convenient fictions and that asking them to do so—by insisting, for example, that they no longer make use of concepts such as a self—would just leave them mentally exhausted.[68]

Jñānaśrīmitra makes it absolutely clear that this theory of conditionally adopted positions and his earlier discussion of conceptualization and determination are directly relevant for understanding what Dignāga and Dharmakīrti have to say about perception. He says,

---

sya vastunaḥ sata eva dharmaḥ | atha ca prāgabhāvalakṣaṇatattvaleśam āśrityāsata iti vyavasthāpyate satkāryavādaśaṅkāsaṅkocāya} yathā vā 'nenaiva kṛtaṃ karma ko 'nyaḥ, pratyanubhaviṣyatīty ekasantānaprajñaptim āśritya kṛtanāśākṛtābhyāgamavañcanā vimohāya. For hints of such an idea in the work of his predecessors see PV 3.218–3.219, quoted in Dreyfus 1997:104 n. 71 and Dunne 2004:55 n. 5; see also Dreyfus 1997:83, 99. For Devendrabuddhi and Śākyabuddhi's commentary on PV 3.194–224, see Dunne 2004:396–411.See also PVABh *ad* PV 3.218–220 (p. 289) for a seemingly explicit parallel to this idea. Dunne 2004 also points to Ratnāvalī 61.94–97, BCA 9.3–9.4, De Breet 1992, and Pye 2003. For a discussion of this idea in the work of Bhartṛhari see Houben 1995:16–18. See also Kajiyama 1978, cited in McClintock 2002:70.

68. This is clearly implied in a number of different places. See, for example, JNĀ (AP 227.10–227.11), which is quoted in note 78, and JNĀ (AP 231.07–231.10), which is quoted in note 80. Ncte Dunne 2004:66, where, in commenting on Dreyfus 1997:49, he says, "one can bend beings' minds just so far before they snap."

> It is for this very same reason[69] that—with a view toward the practically oriented person whose mind has [already] worn itself out with the mistaken idea [that conceptualizing a thing and apprehending its name are the same]—the qualifier "free from conceptual construction" is included in the definition of perception [by Dignāga and Dharmakīrti], and that in the authoritative text [i.e., Dharmakīrti's *Short Study of the Reason Property*] there is separate mention [of conceptualization and determination] with the words "on the basis of conceptual awareness . . . by determination."[70]

According to Jñānaśrīmitra, both the claim that perception is free from conceptual construction and Dharmakīrti's statement in his *Short Study of the Reason Property*, where the terms "conceptualization" and "determination" are used contrastively, are just conditionally adopted positions—that is, they are white lies. They must be, Jñānaśrīmitra thinks, because it is just not the case that perception is free from conceptual construction, since, as he has pointed out, perception and inference each have a nonconceptual *and* a conceptual (i.e., determined) object.[71] Similarly, it is not the case that conceptualization and determination are different: at best, the two terms just pick out two different ways of referring to the same mental process, namely, exclusion. According to Jñānaśrīmitra, what Dignāga and Dharmakīrti have to say about perception cannot be literally true: neither can really mean what he says. In order to account for their words, therefore, one has to realize that they are just stating conditionally adopted positions, that is, philosophically sanctioned white lies. In the passage just cited, Jñānaśrīmitra only gestures to why such white lies are told: they are told, he says, for the sake of a person who just can't get his mind around the idea that conceptualization can be decoupled from language. Trying to persuade someone of this (at least at

---

69. The phrase "this very same reason" (*ata eva ca*) refers to JNĀ (AP 227.01–227.04), where Jñānaśrīmitra explicitly states that the assumed difference between conceptualization and determination is just a conditionally adopted position. Given its context, it is clear that in this passage Jñānaśrīmitra is also identifying the traditional claim that "perception is free from conceptual construction" as a conditionally adopted position. JNĀ (AP 227.01–227.04) is quoted in note 73 and is discussed, in context, in McCrea and Patil 2006. It is worth noting that JNĀ (AP 227.05–227.09) is a restatement of the famous summary verse of the AP.

70. JNĀ (AP 227.10–227.11). The reference is to HB 3*.14–3*.15, quoted at JNĀ (AP 225.18–225.19): *ata eva ca tadabhimānamlānamānasaṃ vyavahārikaṃ prati pratyakṣalakṣaṇe kalpanāpoḍhaviśeṣaṇam upādīyate, sūtrato 'pi vikalpād adhyavasāyeneti.*

71. For a discussion of Jñānaśrīmitra's arguments in support of this position see Patil 2007.

this point in her philosophical education) is just too much trouble and in general would be counterproductive. In the final few pages of his *Monograph on Exclusion*, Jñānaśrīmitra explains this in greater detail.

3.3. *The Pedagogical Significance of Dharmakīrti's White Lies*

Jñānaśrīmitra is aware that his discussion of conditionally adopted positions is likely to raise (perhaps troubling) questions for philosophers in his text tradition: Why, for example, did Dharmakīrti need to tell white lies? Why did he speak as if conceptualization and determination are really different? Why does he say that perception is free from conceptual construction when it is not? Jñānaśrīmitra's answer to these questions is based on his idea that what motivates Dharmakīrti's statement that perception is free from conceptual construction is his recognition of the deeply entrenched view that since conceptualization is inextricably linked with language it must be different from determination, which instead has to do with an object's being more generally actionable. Because of this, people do not generally think that the perceptual process involves (or even could involve) conceptualization. After all, don't prelinguistic infants perceive? Thus, as Jñānaśrīmitra sees it, it makes sense for Dharmakīrti to try to use these deeply entrenched views, rather than argue against them directly, even though he knows that they are not strictly speaking correct. For Jñānaśrīmitra, Dharmakīrti's accommodation of these ideas is just a conditionally adopted position. In the following passages Jñānaśrīmitra states this explicitly, and points to the "little bit of the truth" (*tattvaleśa*) on which each of these views is based and identifies the specific "purpose" (*prayojana*) that is served in adopting them.

About the view that conceptualization and determination are really different, Jñānaśrīmitra explains that,

> Just as one concludes that an object has been apprehended through conceptualization, likewise [one concludes that it has been] bound up with the word [that is used to refer to it]. This is because, like the partial image of a thing [in perception][72], [in "conceptual" awareness] too the image of a

72. The conceptual state of awareness that immediately follows "perception" classifies what is being looked at by picking out one aspect of it. To conceptualize what one is looking at as "smoke" (rather than as "gray" or "cloudlike") is for that conceptual state of awareness to contain just an aspect or part of what was grasped by the preceding nonconceptual awareness.

> word appears. Therefore, the conditionally adopted position regarding conceptualization [namely, that it is different from determination] is not based in reality, but is simply indexed to the judgment that "insofar as a person conceives of himself as apprehending a thing, to that extent he likewise conceives of himself as apprehending it together with its name."[73]

For Jñānaśrīmitra, the terminological distinction between conceptualization and determination reveals only that people generally associate the object that they "conceptually" apprehend with the word that they use to refer to it. It is because of this that they mistakenly believe that conceptually apprehending an object and associating it with its name are one and the same thing.[74] When taken together with what Jñānaśrīmitra said in the passage cited earlier, it is clear that it is in order to accommodate this little bit of the truth that Dignāga, Dharmakīrti, and others in the Buddhist epistemological tradition speak as if "conceptualizing" an object (i.e., apprehending it in association with a word that is used to refer to it) and "determining" it (i.e., apprehending it as an object that one can act upon) are different, even though they are one and the same.[75] The "little bit of the truth" on which this conditionally adopted position is based is a truth about how these terms are generally understood. And as Jñānaśrīmitra implies in this and the earlier passage, the specific "purpose" that is served in adopting this position is that by strategically conforming to the way in which these terms are generally used it will eventually become possible to correct people's false ideas about perception.[76]

This usually takes place in conjunction with the memory of prior instances of smoke and in some cases the word "smoke," etc. For a discussion of selectivity in conceptualization see chapters 4 and 5, and Dunne 2004, Kellner 2004a, and Patil 2003.

73. JNĀ (AP 227.01–227.04): *yathā vikalpenāyam artho gṛhīta iti niścayas tathā śabdena saṃyojya ity api, arthākāraleśavac chabdākārasyāpi sphuraṇāt | tasmād yāvad arthagrahaṇābhimānavān ?mānavas tāvad abhidhānasaṃyuktagrahaṇābhimānavān apīty avasāyānurodhād eva vikalpavyavasthā na tattvataḥ.*

74. However, as Jñānaśrīmitra suggests, by way of comparison with the "partial image of the thing [in perception]," what is most important about "conceptualization" is that it makes what is grasped by awareness phenomenally available to us, and this is equally true for both perception and inferential/verbal states of awareness. The two modes of awareness are really parallel processes in that appearance and conceptualization/determination are a necessary part of both.

75. This is supposed to explain Dharmakīrti's contrastive use of these terms in his HB.

76. See JNĀ (AP 231.07–231.10). To get an better idea of how conditionally adopted posi-

Jñānaśrīmitra is now in a position to explain why the statement "perception is free from conceptual construction" is also a conditionally adopted position. According to Jñānaśrīmitra, underlying the—strictly speaking—false statement that "perception is free from conceptual construction" is also a little bit of the truth, namely, that perception does in fact have a nonconceptual object that is grasped in the first part of the perceptual process. Jñānaśrīmitra seems to believe that the reason Dignāga and Dharmakīrti state only this partial truth is that for people who take conceptualization to be necessarily implicated in language, it will be too difficult to accept the idea that conceptualization is a necessary part of perception too. Dignāga and Dharmakīrti therefore work around this limitation by formulating a definition of perception that takes the first step toward clearly identifying the two objects of perception. According to Jñānaśrīmitra, this is the specific purpose that is served in saying that "perception is free from conceptual construction." Although it is just a conditionally adopted position, Dignāga and Dharmakīrti's one-object model of perception (and inference) is still an important step for an ordinary person who, Jñānaśrīmitra suggests, is already "worn out" by having to understand even this much.[77]

An objector soon argues that if all of this is supposed to be for the benefit of ordinary people, then Jñānaśrīmitra's insistence that the one-object model of perceptual awareness is actually supposed to lead the way to a two-object model is just wishful thinking. According to the opponent, ordinary people will never be able to grasp the distinction between what is "perceived"—namely, the grasped object of perception—and what is "conceptualized"—namely, the determined object of perception. As a result, they will be able to understand neither that the phrase "perception is free from conceptualization" is merely a conditionally adopted position nor that the two-object model is philosophically superior. Jñānaśrīmitra writes,

---

tions about the objects of awareness have been used see JNĀ (AP 205.03–205.09), where Jñānaśrīmitra explains how the conditionally adopted position that exclusion is the object of inferential/verbal states of awareness is used.

77. I take the analysis in this passage to be supported by the two passages cited above and the scattered references to perception in his AP. See JNĀ (AP 231.10–231.16), which is quoted below, and the discussion that leads up to it at JNĀ (AP 230.27–231.10), which is discussed, briefly, in the final section of section 3.

> Now, if you say—"For an ordinary person, there is surely a failure to grasp even the difference between what is perceived and what is conceptualized. Thus, a determined fire is just the same as the one that appears"—we say, "no." This is because, [since the determined fire] is due to the recollection of other appearances [of fire, people] make the mistake that there is the appearance of that [determined fire]. In perception, it is possible to show that the appearance of the thing [before one] is in fact different from a conceptual appearance and likewise that this [conceptual appearance] is different from the perceptual appearance, because it is only there[, in perception,] that one can settle on the appearance of a thing. Thus, for [modes of awareness that are] different from that [perception—i.e., language and inference], it is better to deny that [anything—either the grasped or determined object—] is the appearance of a thing. Therefore, it was rightly said that "[This is] conditionally adopted. But really, nothing at all is expressed."[78]

While acknowledging that ordinary people do not usually distinguish between "grasped" and "determined" objects of perception, Jñānaśrīmitra nevertheless argues that it is not difficult to show such a person that there is a clear difference between the grasped image of a perceived object, such as a campfire that is a few meters in front of one, and the conceptual image/object that appears when one recalls or imagines "fire."[79] Furthermore, one can show that many of the properties that we think belong to the fire that we "see"—e.g., its capacity to heat things up—are not directly presented in the grasped visual image, but rather are derived from our memory of previous experiences with fire. Therefore it can be clearly demonstrated that the "fire" that we take ourselves to see—the "fire" that is phenomenally available to us—is actually made up of what is visually present to us (the grasped object that appears in awareness) and what we conceptually construct on the basis

78. JNĀ (AP 231.10–231.16), quoting JNĀ 203.04: *atha pṛthagjanasya dṛśyavikalpyayor apy abhedagraho niyata evety avasito vahniḥ pratibhāsita eveti cet. na, pratibhāsāntarasmaraṇena tatpratibhāsabhramabhraṃśasya kṛtatvāt | yathā ca vikalpapratibhāsād anya eva vastupratibhāso darśayitum adhyakṣe śakyaḥ, tathā nādhyakṣapratibhāsād anyo 'stīti tatraiva vastupratibhāsaviśrāmāt tadvijātīyasya vastupratibhāsatāvyudāsaḥ śreyān | tasmād yuktam uktam, sthāpyo vācyas tattvato naiva kaścit.*

79. For a similar strategy in the work of Dharmottara see Krasser 1995 and the references in Krasser 1991 to Dharmottara's LPrP.

of our previous experiences (the determined object). Thus, in perception, one can point to a clear distinction between grasped and determined "objects." As a result, even an ordinary person can be shown that perception has both a nonconceptual and a conceptual object and that the phrase "perception is free from conceptual construction" is nothing but a white lie. So, despite the opponent's worries, it is possible to show an ordinary person that the one-object model of perception is a convenient fiction when compared to the philosophically superior two-object model. Thus a specific and philosophically legitimate purpose is served by conditionally adopting the partial truth that perception is free from conceptual construction.

While the one-object model is an important step toward the two-object model of perception, Jñānaśrīmitra confesses near the end of his "Monograph on Exclusion" that the two-object model is itself a white lie. More specifically, he says that although the two-object model is an improvement over Dignāga and Dharmakīrti's "lower-order convention" (*adhara-samvṛti*), it is itself still conventional.[80] Jñānaśrīmitra explains that when speaking to an ordinary person who believes that the (momentary) object that is manifest to him and the (temporally extended) object that he takes to be the object of his subsequent activity are one and the same, it is important to say that perception really has two objects, a nonconceptual one (the grasped moment) and a conceptually constructed one (the determined continuum).[81] But at the end of the day Jñānaśrīmitra explains that perception, like inferential/

---

80. JNĀ (AP 231.07–231.10): "About this, I say: What I have stated is a conditionally adopted position about the way things are. There is 'being an object' only in virtue of the existence of both [manifestation and determination]. The convention is said to be 'the way things really are' just relative to a lower-order convention. This is because for the practically oriented person things are not destroyed at each moment, since pragmatic activity breaks down when one gets down to the division between moments. Even with perception there is really no possibility of both. Thus there is no problem" (*atrocyate | tattvavyavasthām āha, ubhayasaṃbhavenaiva viṣayatvam, kevalaṃ sāṃvyavahārikāpekṣayā saṃvṛter evādharasaṃvṛtim apekṣya tattvam iti vyavahriyate, kṣaṇabhedāvatāre saṃvyavahāravilopād vyāvahārikaṃ prati pratikṣaṇakṣīṇatāyā abhāvāt, tattvataḥ pratyakṣeṇobhayasaṃbhavābhāvaḥ, iti na doṣaḥ*). For an extremely interesting discussion of higher and lower orders of conventional truth see JNĀ (KBhA 6.09–7.24).

81. This is the purpose that is served in conditionally adopting the two-object model. The little bit of the truth on which this model is based is that it is philosophically better to treat perception and inference as parallel processes having two objects each.

verbal awareness, cannot have a real object at all. This is because in order for something to be a genuine object of an awareness-event it must be both available (that is, grasped by that awareness-event) and actionable (that is, determined by it to be an object of activity).[82] This is philosophically the only way to capture our intuitions about what an object of an awareness-event must be. But, as Jñānaśrīmitra argues, nothing can be both grasped *and* determined.[83] Thus, while the two-object model of perception is for philosophical reasons an improvement on the "lower-order convention" of the one-object model, it is still "conventional," and is adopted only conditionally.

3.4. Philosophy and Pedagogy

Jñānaśrīmitra's discussion of Dharmakīrti's white lie provides an interesting framework for understanding his perspective on the pedagogical significance of Buddhist philosophy.[84] According to Jñānaśrīmitra, his predecessors in the Buddhist epistemological tradition used convenient fictions and partial truths to philosophically educate those who they felt were in error. This is clear from Jñānaśrīmitra's example of how the idea of an enduring self can be used to argue against those who do not accept karma. By standing on a rung of the philosophical stepladder higher than that of their targeted audience, Jñānaśrīmitra's predecessors were able to reach down and help people up to the next philosophical rung, even if (according to Jñānaśrīmitra) they themselves realized that this next rung was not the final one. It is because of their privileged position on the ladder that Jñānaśrīmitra seems to think that Dignāga and Dharmakīrti were able to clearly see, and therefore affect, what was going on below. The situation is no different for Jñānaśrīmitra himself. It is from a philosophical vantage point one step up the ladder that he is able to identify and expose Dharmakīrti's white lies and conditionally adopted positions to those who are not already aware of them.

According to Jñānaśrīmitra, the way that one learns to move up from rung to rung of this ladder is by discovering conceptual problems inherent in how we speak about awareness and its objects. By discovering specific conceptual problems with the one-object model, for example, Jñānaśrīmitra

82. For a discussion of this see chapter 4 and chapter 5.

83. JNĀ (AP 231.07–231.10).

84. See Dreyfus 1997:443–462.

expects us to move up to his two-object model. Similarly, by coming to see conceptual problems inherent in how we speak about awareness and its objects from within the two-object model, he expects us to move up to his no-object model. In both cases conceptual problems become apparent through discovering how each model is based on a partial truth about the nature of awareness and its objects. It is important that the philosophical issues at stake have to do with the nature of awareness and the kinds of mental objects and processes that best account for it. Given the subordination of ontology to the philosophy of mind in Jñānaśrīmitra's text tradition, this is also just what one would expect.[85] Philosophy, then, is of pedagogical significance, since it is through philosophical analysis and argumentation that a teacher like Jñānaśrīmitra is able to help his "students" move up from rung to rung of a philosophical stepladder.[86] For Jñānaśrīmitra too, philosophy is supposed to change people's minds by turning them away from their false or partially true views and toward those that are more correct.[87]

The internal logic of Jñānaśrīmitra's account of conditionally adopted positions suggests that there are at least three levels of analysis (or rungs on the philosophical stepladder), in addition to a basement level of false views.[88] The first level is the one on which Jñānaśrīmitra discovers there to be a conditionally adopted position. In Jñānaśrīmitra's "Monograph on Exclusion," this first level is characterized by Dignāga and Dharmakīrti's statements about valid states of awareness and their object(s). More specifically, on level 1, perception is said to be free from conceptual construction and to have only

---

85. I think that Dreyfus (1997) is right to emphasize the relative importance of issues in epistemology (and the philosophy of mind) over those having to do with ontology. Cf. the analysis in Dunne 2004:61–63.

86. It is worth noting that this is only one reason that Jñānaśrīmitra thinks that philosophy is of value.

87. Cf. Griffiths 1999a.

88. See Dreyfus 1997:83–105, McClintock 2002:68–72, and Dunne 2004:53–79 for three very interesting accounts of this model. For a critical discussion of these accounts see Kellner (forthcoming) and Kyuma (forthcoming). The strategy that I am describing here has been described in the context of Dharmakīrti's work as a "strategy of ascending scales of analysis" (Dreyfus 1997; cf. Phillips 1987:243ff.) and "sliding scales of analysis" (Dunne 2004:53, McClintock 2002:68–76, 203, 139ff,). In these models four levels of analysis are usually identified. Dreyfus and Dunne describe them as follows: level 1: common sense/beliefs of ordinary people; level 2: alternative interpretation/*abhidharma* typology; level 3: standard interpretation/external realism (Sautrāntika); level 4: *yogācāra*/epistemic idealism.

a real particular as its object. Similarly, according to Jñānaśrīmitra, it is also a conditionally adopted position to say that inferential/verbal states of awareness are inherently conceptual and have only an exclusion as their object.[89] Like perception, inferential/verbal states of awareness also have two objects.[90] In this numbering scheme, the views that Dignāga and Dharmakīrti themselves argue against—e.g., the views of non-Buddhists—are in the "basement," at level 0. This is also the level on which Jñānaśrīmitra himself seems to place such views.[91] Unlike the philosophical claims made on level 1, however, the claims made on level 0 are not white lies, but only falsehoods.

Level 2 is the level on which a position is conditionally adopted by Jñānaśrīmitra himself: this is the level of Jñānaśrīmitra's own conditionally adopted two-object model of valid awareness. On this level, it is clear that perception is not free from conceptual construction, since it can be shown that it has two objects—a grasped object and a determined/conceptualized one.[92] Similarly, it is clear that inferential/verbal awareness does not have just an exclusion as its object, since it too has two objects—a grasped object and a determined/conceptualized one. It is, moreover, only from the vantage point of level 2 that the position adopted on level 1 can be seen to be just a conditionally adopted one.[93] Level 2 is also the level that Jñānaśrīmitra relies upon in criticizing his opponent's views, such as the existence of Īśvara, and on the basis of which he establishes his own philosophical positions, such as selflessness/momentariness and the efficacy of the Buddhist path. The top level is level 3, the level from which Jñānaśrīmitra's own conditionally adopted position on level 2 can be identified as such, and on which no position is itself adopted conditionally. This is the level of Jñānaśrīmitra's view that neither perception nor inference really has an object at all.

Jñānaśrīmitra's theory of conditionally adopted positions also suggests that for him the second of the three levels of analysis is the highest level of conventional truth and that the levels below it are just lower-order conventions.[94] This is confirmed by Jñānaśrīmitra himself, who clearly believes that

---

89. JNĀ (AP 202.21–203.25), (AP 205.03–205.09).

90. JNĀ (AP 225.17), (VC 166.13–166.15).

91. For example, see Kyuma 2005:lxxx–lxxxiv, 77–79 n. 99.

92. JNĀ (AP 225.17), (VC 166.13–166.15).

93. JNĀ (AP 226.01--226.03).

94. JNĀ (KBhA 6.09–7.24). For a translation and discussion of this see Kyuma 2005, esp. p. 77 n. 99.

the second level of analysis provides the philosophically most rigorous way for us to speak about perception and inference and their objects. According to him, his two-object model thus provides the best philosophical theory of perception and inference. Although it is the most philosophically rigorous way for us to understand states of awareness and their objects, it is still a white lie, since awareness-events do not really have an "object" at all. Thus, the best philosophical account that can be given of the contents of perception and inference is ultimately still not the case. Relative to level 1, it is just a higher-order convention (*uttara-saṃvṛtti*).[95] As his discussion makes clear, an analysis of the two-object model of awareness reveals that it too is a white lie and that it is, in fact, a no-object model of awareness that provides the most rigorous philosophical account of awareness and is, therefore, what is ultimately the case. The pedagogical purpose of Jñānaśrīmitra's multiple-content model of awareness is thus to first turn people away from their false/partially true views on level 1 and then, after providing them a place to rest, lead them to level 3.[96]

4. Ratnakīrti's Framework of Values

In his "Demonstration of Exclusion," Ratnakīrti effectively writes out Jñānaśrīmitra's discussion of conditionally adopted positions, and in so doing reveals an important difference between himself and his teacher. While Jñānaśrīmitra is deeply concerned with accounting for apparent inconsistencies between his work and that of the foundational figures of his text tradition,

---

95. Kyuma 2005:lxxx–lxxxiv and the references contained therein.

96. What this model suggests is that within a single philosophical text an author may choose to argue from various philosophical perspectives that are not his own in order to win a particular argument. The philosophical (and soteriological) hierarchy of these various perspectives is supposed to ensure that this approach is not philosophically dishonest, since in making arguments that are rhetorically effective a philosopher who adopts this strategy hopes to persuade members of his target audience to give up philosophical positions that he thinks are not only genuinely mistaken, but mistaken for the reasons that he provides. Since different audiences are likely to be persuaded by arguments from different philosophical perspectives, however, it may appear as if a philosopher who adopts this method is deeply confused. But when it is understood that what he is trying to do is to philosophically educate someone by helping him make better and better mistakes—until he comes to the "right" or "maximally correct" answer—the charge of being confused loses its force.

Ratnakīrti is not. Relative to Jñānaśrīmitra, Ratnakīrti is indifferent to such historical and exegetical concerns. Instead, Ratnakīrti's arguments are devoted almost exclusively to the dual purpose discussed above. While Jñānaśrīmitra too has this dual purpose in view, he infuses it with a level of historical sensitivity and interest that Ratnakīrti does not seem to share. Jñānaśrīmitra also adds to it an explicitly intra-Buddhist concern. When Ratnakīrti does argue against other Buddhists in his own work—e.g., Dharmottara (but not Dignāga or Dharmakīrti)—he treats their views in the same way as he treats those of non-Buddhists. Their views are not white lies or partial truths: they are just falsehoods. This is not to say that Ratnakīrti would not agree with what Jñānaśrīmitra has to say about conditionally adopted positions, but only that he chooses to suppress such questions in order to focus on others. That this was a conscious decision on his part is obvious when one compares Jñānaśrīmitra's "Monograph on Exclusion" with Ratnakīrti's "Demonstration of Exclusion." It is precisely the passages in which Jñānaśrīmitra develops the idea of conditionally adopted positions that Ratnakīrti skips over in his reconstruction of his teacher's text.

While Ratnakīrti suppresses the idea of conditionally adopted positions, he seems to accept the pedagogical role that Jñānaśrīmitra assigns to epistemology on the basis of it. Ratnakīrti's work can thus be seen in terms of a tripartite pedagogical structure, but one that is rather different in character from that of his teacher's. For Ratnakīrti, the *first level* of analysis is defined by the views of his opponents, both Buddhist and non-Buddhist. As I have argued, this level includes both the specific philosophical positions that are being argued for and the epistemology that supports them. This corresponds to Jñānaśrīmitra's "basement"—that is, level 0 (which is also how I will refer to it when discussing Ratnakīrti's tripartite pedagogical structure). Ratnakīrti's *second level* of analysis includes his own philosophical views—e.g., momentariness—and the epistemology that supports them. As I have argued, it is by looking down from this level, and subtly drawing from it, that Ratnakīrti fashions his "internal critique" of positions on level 0. This is in contrast with Jñānaśrīmitra, who looks down from this level not only to level 0 but also to level 1 (a level that Ratnakīrti all but ignores). As with Jñānaśrīmitra, for Ratnakīrti too, the *third level* is defined by the view that neither perception nor inference really has an "object" at all.

In Ratnakīrti's work what is emphasized is the transition from level 0 to level 2. While Ratnakīrti ignores level 1, the transition from level 2 to level 3 is acknowledged, but deemphasized. This is consistent with Ratnakīrti's understanding of the dual purpose of his work, which is to argue (1) against the views of others, in order to turn them away from level 0, and (2) in support of his own, so that he may bring them up to level 2, the highest level of conventional truth. It is on level 2 that the selflessness/momentariness-thesis is located and the efficacy of the path is established through the omniscience-inference.

Where then does this leave us with respect to the question of how Ratnakīrti understood why epistemology, and philosophy more generally, was of value? As I have argued in this chapter, Ratnakīrti inherits a framework of value from his text tradition that he both builds upon and modifies, in part, by embedding it in a pedagogical framework that he takes from his teacher Jñānaśrīmitra. Ratnakīrti's framework is built around four identifiable goals: (1) to refute his opponents' philosophical views and the epistemology that supports them; (2) to establish his own philosophical views and the epistemology that supports them; (3) to establish, more specifically, his selflessness/momentariness thesis; and (4) to establish that meditating upon selflessness/momentariness can lead to omniscience—that is, the direct awareness of *dharma* itself.[97]

Ratnakīrti's acceptance of Jñānaśrīmitra's pedagogical framework, which envisions philosophy (at least in part) as an instrument for moving up from level to level on the philosophical stepladder of the Buddhist epistemological tradition, suggests that these four goals are interlinked. Success in goal 1, for example, is a prerequisite for success in goal 2. Without having refuted the philosophical views of his opponents that are incompatible with his own, it seems unlikely that Ratnakīrti would be in a position to convince someone of his own views. In the case of the Naiyāyikas, for example, without arguing successfully against the existence of Īśvara—the paradigmatic example of an enduring self—it seems unlikely that Ratnakīrti would be in a position to convince them that all existing things are momentary. Arguing against an opponent's epistemology supports this effort by undermining the basis for any of the opponent's conclusions. It thus creates a context in which an alternative epistemology might be considered. Success in goal 1 is supposed to turn someone away from their false views (on level 0) and thereby encourage them to seek an alternative by looking up to level 2. Goal 2 is somewhat different

---

97. Since goal 3 and goal 4 can easily be included in goal 2, the structure of Ratnakīrti's goals are clearly in line with the "dual purpose" of his text tradition.

from goal 1, in that it requires Ratnakīrti to establish his own epistemology, and at least some of the philosophical views that it supports. Success in this goal is supposed to bring someone up to level 2, and thus make success in goals 3 and 4 possible. Without being able to establish the epistemological principles on the basis of which his own philosophical views are founded, it seems unlikely that Ratnakīrti would be in a position to support his views. More specifically, without establishing his own views on pervasion and inferential reasoning more generally, how could he establish momentariness? Success in goal 2, like success in goal 1, puts the opponent/student in a new epistemic position. Just as goal 1 is a prerequisite for goal 2, goal 2 is a prerequisite for goal 3. And given that goal 3 has been reached, all of the pieces are finally in place to reach goal 4, and thus climb up to level 3. In the pedagogical structure that is implied by Ratnakīrti's work, the goals are clearly sequential.[98]

It is in relation to these four goals that both the instrumental and the epistemic value of philosophy becomes apparent. Given that Ratnakīrti seeks to refute his opponents' philosophical views and the epistemology that supports them (goal 1), I have argued that it is instrumentally rational for him to argue against those views and their supporting epistemology by internally criticizing them. As I discussed in chapters 2 and 3, this is exactly what Ratnakīrti tries to do in his arguments against the Īśvara-inference. In the context of goal 1, these arguments can be seen as having instrumental value for him insofar as he thinks they will turn his opponents away from their false views about the Īśvara-inference and the epistemology that supports it. Similarly, in his other work Ratnakīrti seeks to establish his own views and the epistemology that supports them (goal 2).[99] As I argued in chapters 4 and 5, in the context of this goal it is instrumentally rational for him to fashion his arguments against the Īśvara-inference by gesturing to and drawing upon his own philosophical views. Adopting this strategy in the context of goal 1 clearly supports Ratnakīrti's interest in achieving goal 2. Finally, given that he seeks to establish both his momentariness thesis and the omniscience-inference (goals 3–4), it is instrumentally rational for him to write the texts

98. It is worth noting that achieving goal 4 is supposed to lead to action on the part of the student, which is different from the results of achieving goals 1–3. Achieving goals 1–3 leads to new views and not to any specific action, per se.

99. See the texts referred to in section 2.4.

that he does, and to highlight the connections between them. For Ratnakīrti, the instrumental value of epistemology and philosophy more generally is based on his view that it is the only way to achieve goals 1–4.[100]

Instrumental rationality and instrumental value are, however, insufficient for explaining how Ratnakīrti understands the value of his work. For example, as I have argued, instrumental rationality explains why Ratnakīrti tries to criticize the Naiyāyikas on their own terms, by showing them that they have not and cannot certify the inference-instrument in the Īśvara-inference. Given that Ratnakīrti has the goal of refuting his opponents and turning them toward his own views, "instrumental rationality" can help us to understand why Ratnakīrti argued in the way that he did and why he thought it was of value. What it does not explain, however, is why Ratnakīrti thinks any of his arguments will work, especially since his opponents do not share any of the same relevant goals.

In my view, Ratnakīrti does not think that it is *instrumentally* rational for his Naiyāyikas to accept his analysis. Rather, he thinks that it is *epistemically* rational for them to do so. Consider, for example, Ratnakīrti's analysis of the defect "inconclusive" (H3). Given Ratnakīrti's cognitive goals, it is instrumentally rational for him to find a counterexample to the pervasion relation in the Īśvara-inference.[101] Responding to the counterexample itself, however, cannot be supposed by Ratnakīrti to be instrumentally rational for his opponents—rather it must be epistemically so. We are not told of any goal that they possess in relation to which accepting that their Īśvara-inference is defeated would be instrumentally rational. While Ratnakīrti possesses the goal of turning his Naiyāyikas away from their false views, and thus possesses the goal of identifying a counterexample to the pervasion relation in their Īśvara-inference, his Naiyāyikas do not. Yet it is clear from Ratnakīrti's analysis (especially given the "dual purpose" of his work) that he expects his Naiyāyikas to accept his counterexample, even though it is clear that doing

100. That this is the *only* way for him to achieve goals 1–4 is never stated explicitly. I take this to be the case, however, since according to him the only proper object of meditation is one that has been established by a conventionally valid source of knowledge, which suggests that epistemology, and philosophy more generally, is necessary, at least for achieving goals 2–4. While philosophy may not be necessary for goal 1, the only way that Ratnakīrti seeks to achieve it in his written work is through philosophy.

101. This corresponds to goal 1, discussed above.

so would hinder them from achieving their own cognitive goals.[102] He expects his analysis to have categorical normative force—that is, to be binding on any rational agent regardless of that agent's interests or goals.[103] While it is instrumentally rational to find a counterexample, he takes it to be epistemically rational for him, and for his Naiyāyikas, to accept the counterexample as a counterexample to pervasion.[104] While one might argue that accepting this is instrumentally rational for Ratnakīrti, since it is in service of his cognitive goals, it is certainly not the case that Ratnakīrti thinks that his Naiyāyikas will accept this because they take it to be in service of some cognitive goal that they possess. Similarly, given that Ratnakīrti has the cognitive goal of turning his opponents toward the *dharma*, it is instrumentally rational for him to establish the epistemology that supports his own philosophical views and, more specifically, his selflessness/momentariness thesis and omniscience-inference.[105] However, if his tripartite pedagogical structure is to work, his opponents must also accept his arguments, even though they may not (yet) share any of the goals that motivate Ratnakīrti or are implicit in his version of the stepladder.[106] It seems clear, therefore, that Ratnakīrti takes himself to be providing compelling, categorical reasons for his views, and not just reasons that are compelling for those who may possess the right sort of goals.[107] Thus Ratnakīrti sees his philosophical work as exhibiting both instrumental and epistemic rationality and as having both instrumental value and epistemic value. Unlike the instrumental value of his work, which is indexed to the achievement of his goals, its epistemic value is a kind of "final value"—it is valuable for its own sake, and not just for some end.

---

102. See Kelly (forthcoming), which is a response to Leite (forthcoming).

103. One might object that while accepting Ratnakīrti's analysis might hinder and frustrate some of the Naiyāyikas' goals, it is still in service of their more general and overarching cognitive and epistemic goal of having more correct views than incorrect ones. On such an "instrumentalist" response, epistemic rationality would be reduced to a species of instrumental rationality.

104. Whether any Naiyāyika would actually accept his analysis is a different matter. What is relevant here is only that Ratnakīrti expects them to do so.

105. This corresponds, roughly, to goals 2–4, discussed above.

106. Once they are on level 2 and have achieved goal 2, and perhaps goal 3, however, it seems as though they are expected to shift from being "opponents" to being "students."

107. See Kelly 2003:621.

5. Conclusion: Religious Reasoning as Religious Practice

The two-dimensional framework of value that I have argued Ratnakīrti shares with his text tradition contributes to our understanding of how Buddhist epistemologists (and perhaps Buddhist philosophers more generally) understood the nature of their work and its value. As I have argued, this framework and the pedagogical structure in which it is embedded provides us with an important perspective on what members of this text tradition took their work to be all about. Although there has been a great deal of skepticism (if not outright hostility) to the idea that Buddhist epistemology is important for understanding "Buddhism," it should be clear that the Buddhist epistemological tradition itself saw a very close relationship between philosophical work and the Buddhist path, as they understood it.[108] Ratnakīrti's work further suggests that, at least for him, the essence of the Buddha's teaching can be captured in the momentariness/selflessness thesis.[109] As I have tried to show in this chapter, thinking that broader religious concerns did not inform the technical philosophical work of Buddhist epistemologists like Ratnakīrti is, simply put, a mistake.[110]

Although Ratnakīrti and his text tradition agree that *dharma* itself is inaccessible to "reasoning," they still insist that philosophical work is necessary for realizing *dharma*. The primary reason for this is that it is *only* through philosophical analysis—and inferential reasoning, more specifically—that momentariness can be established as the proper object of meditation. Simply accepting the momentariness thesis on other grounds is insufficient, since in such cases it will crumble in the face of critical analysis. Only when

---

108. See Krasser 2004, Steinkellner 1982, and Kapstein 2001:22–23 n. 13 for a discussion of how earlier scholars understood this issue. See also Davidson 2002:102–105.

109. This view is of course not just restricted to Ratnakīrti. In addition, see for example TS vv. 1–6 and TSP *ad* TS vv. 1–6, which are beautifully translated in Kapstein 2001:10, 14, and MMK vv. 1–2 and MMK 24.18a–b, which are also translated in Kapstein 2001:24 n. 22, 23. See also Kapstein 2001:13, 15 for a brief description of Śāntarakṣita's "dual purpose" and the relationship between it and momentariness and omniscience. For the importance of omniscience and its centrality to the path, see McClintock 2002:1, 5, where she strongly underscores this point.

110. Krasser (2004) makes this same point, with specific reference to the Buddhist epistemological tradition. For excellent work on Dharmakīrti as a philosopher of religion see Eltschinger 2005a, Eltschinger 2005b, Eltschinger 2007b. Some of this work has also been discussed in Eltschinger 2007a. For work on Śāntarakṣita see Funayama (forthcoming).

it is the object of a conventionally valid awareness-event will it be fixed enough in one's mind to serve as a proper object of meditation/cultivation.[111] One way to understand Ratnakīrti's confidence in this claim is to see that for him it is *both* instrumentally and epistemically rational to accept the momentariness thesis. It is, therefore, the categorical normative force of his inferential arguments that seems to be the source of his confidence. What is important is not just an awareness of momentariness, but a certified valid awareness of it, which is only possible by working within the sources of knowledge framework of the Buddhist epistemological tradition as understood by Ratnakīrti.

When embedded in Ratnakīrti's tripartite pedagogical structure, the two-dimensional framework of instrumental and epistemic values also helps us to understand exactly what Ratnakīrti hoped to gain in criticizing his opponents as he did. Attending to Ratnakīrti's use of instrumental rationality (as defined by his four goals) in the context of his pedagogical framework shows that Ratnakīrti expected his arguments to be persuasive—to actually turn his opponents away from their false views and bring them closer to the *dharma*, by convincing them that all existing things are momentary and that it is possible, by meditating on momentariness, for the *dharma* itself to be manifest in awareness.[112] The fact that his critique of the Īśvara-inference is phrased as an internal one that targets both the inference itself and the epistemology that supports it is, therefore, not at all insignificant. As I have argued, given his goals, it is instrumentally rational for him to argue in just this way. The reason he expects his specific arguments to work is because of their epistemic rationality. As I have argued, Ratnakīrti expects his arguments to have categorical normative force, that is, to be binding on any rational agent, regardless of that agent's interests or goals.[113] To think that Ratnakīrti understood his work, and by extension the work of others in his

111. See McClintock 2002: chaps. 1, 3, 5, and 8.

112. See Griffiths 1999a and Griffiths 1999b for an extended argument against this view in Buddhist philosophy more generally and in the work of the Buddhist epistemologist Mokṣākaragupta more specifically.

113. It is, of course, a separate question whether such arguments were in fact effective. See Griffiths 1999b:517–519 for a discussion of this point, and a short response in McClintock 2002:31 n.14. See also McClintock 2002:38–42 for a discussion of how such "rational agents"—whom she refers to as "judicious persons" (*prekṣāvant*)—were conceived of by Śāntarakṣita and Kamalaśīla. Also see her discussion of Griffiths 1999a and Griffiths 1999b in McClintock 2002:31–38.

text tradition, as being part of an entirely (or even primarily) "tradition internal conversation" not only disregards what Ratnakīrti himself says about it but denies that his work displays epistemic rationality.[114] As I have argued, attention to epistemic rationality helps us to see that Ratnakīrti expected his arguments not only to lead to valid awareness-events but to be persuasive because of it.

The pedagogical stepladder that I have argued is implicit in Ratnakīrti's work also reveals the importance of a "problems and arguments" approach to philosophical work, even within a structured hierarchy that culminates in a call for action (in the form of cultivation/meditation).[115] Each rung on Ratnakīrti's stepladder is constituted by his engagement with very specific philosophical problems. His sustained and detailed arguments against the Īśvara-inference are hardly atypical, and in fact are characteristic of much of his critical work (on level 0). His arguments in support of his theories of pervasion, exclusion, and mental images (on level 2) similarly display his commitment to detail and philosophical rigor. This is not at all surprising since, as I have argued, these theories are the cornerstones of his own epistemology. Even more extensive is his defense of his momentariness thesis (also on level 2). As I have argued, on each of these levels Ratnakīrti tries to provide compelling, categorical reasons for his views and thus seeks to improve his opponent's epistemic position with respect to a structured set of goals that Ratnakīrti has, but his opponents do not.[116] Moreover, it is his

---

114. This term is from Griffiths 1999a. In Griffiths 1999b:506, Griffiths argues that the arguments of the Buddhist epistemologist Mokṣākaragupta were not intended by him to be persuasive; Griffiths' essay suggests, also, that this is a typical characteristic of such arguments. For a powerful argument in support of his view see Griffiths 1999a.

115. This phrase is from Kapstein 2001:5.

116. This is certainly the case with respect to level 1. With respect to level 2, it may be the case that some of Ratnakīrti's opponents have now become students and so share his goals. Even so, it is by responding to Ratnakīrti's epistemic reasons that they can improve their epistemic position with respect to their own goals. Kelly (2003:634) explains this with the following example: "Suppose that I hear a strange and unexpected sound behind me, and, seeking to find out the source of this noise, I turn around. Here, the reason I have to turn around is an instrumental reason—I have the (cognitive) goal of finding out what is responsible for the relevant noise, and given this goal, it is instrumentally rational for me to change my epistemic position in a certain way. Suppose further that, upon turning around, I discover the source of the noise: a cat has entered the otherwise-empty room. Finding myself face-to-face with the cat, it is now epistemically rational for me to believe that a cat was responsible for the noise."

commitment to these arguments, especially those having to do with the nature of awareness-events and their "objects" that leads him to the no-object model of awareness (on level 3). In my view, it is clear from Ratnakīrti's work that he thought that solving philosophical problems and defending his solutions to them were among his most important intellectual tasks.

While the rungs of Ratnakīrti's stepladder are constituted by philosophical problems and arguments and are focused on improving his opponent's epistemic position with respect to a set of goals, its structural hierarchy is determined by both philosophical and soteriological concerns that are informed by Ratnakīrti's understanding of the Buddhist path. In relation to soteriological concerns and goals, philosophical activity is clearly taken to be a form of religious practice in which it is instrumentally rational (and in fact necessary) to engage. Attention to Ratnakīrti's framework of values and tripartite pedagogical structure thus enables us to see exactly what sort of a practice it is, and exactly how Ratnakīrti thinks it is relevant to the Buddhist path. From Ratnakīrti's work, philosophical activity, as a form of religious practice, improves one's epistemic position with respect to a soteriological goal, by both removing one's false views and fixing the right views in one's mind through very detailed and deliberate philosophical analysis.[117] Built into this work is the expectation that once in this new epistemic position one will display epistemic rationality and accept Ratnakīrti's conclusions. On Ratnakīrti's model, religious reasoning is a "hybrid virtue" that requires that one be sensitive to both instrumental and epistemic reasons.[118]

Ratnakīrti's work thus provides a model for religious reasoning according to which, by responding to both instrumental and epistemic reasons, a truly rational agent is able to climb up a philosophical stepladder, and thus put herself in a proper epistemic position to one day become omniscient and

117. Exactly how this sort of development is related to *philosophia*, as famously suggested by Hadot (1995), is not obvious. For a discussion of this issue in the work of Śāntarakṣita and Kamalaśīla see Kapstein 2001:7–11, 19–20 and McClintock 2002:6–8. The comparison of *philosophia* with Buddhist philosophy as practiced within what Kapstein (2001) refers to as a "Madhyamaka architecture" seems more appropriate than with the work of Ratnakīrti and others in his text tradition. This is in part because the explicit discussion of philosophy as a kind of therapy is nearly absent from Ratnakīrti's work, and certainly is not emphasized.

118. I take this from Kelly 2003:637.

see *dharma* itself. Ratnakīrti's arguments against the existence of Īśvara can thus be seen as the first step in the philosophical and religious education of his Nyāya opponents. While religious reasoning is necessary for progressing on the path, and is therefore a form of religious practice, it is itself insufficient for realizing *dharma*. As Ratnakīrti explains, meditation/cultivation is also necessary. What is necessary for this practice to be successful, however, is something about which Ratnakīrti's texts are interestingly (and perhaps importantly) silent.[119]

---

119. For an excellent discussion of how Kamalaśīla's account of the relevance of philosophy to the path relates to what we generally take to be a more traditional understanding of Buddhist "practice," see Funayama 2005 and Funayama (forthcoming), where he explores the connection between the process that I have described in this chapter and the "realms/ stages of a Boddhisattva" (*boddhisattvabhūmi*), especially the first (*pramudita-bhūmi*). Also note BhK3 30.03–30.08, where Kamalaśīla equates this first stage on the Boddhisattva path to the "path of seeing" (*darśanamārga*). For an explicit equation of Ratnakīrti's "fourth goal" with such "practice" see Vinītadeva's commentary to Dharmakīrti's NB, NBṬ-Vi 47.4–47.12, e.g., where he explains that in the practice that "leads to insight" (*nirvedhabhāgīya*) the object of meditation is the four noble truths. As noted in Funayama 2005:4 n. 11, Kamalaśīla's account in BhK1 224.7–224.10 is different: he takes the object of meditation in the practice that leads to insight to be a type of nonduality. Funayama's analysis suggests that Ratnakīrti too would take success in his fourth goal to lead to just the first of the ten stages on the Boddhisattva path. Far from being the end of one's soteriological journey, this is just the beginning. For a discussion of Kamalaśīla's *Bhāvanākrama*, see Adam 2002.

REFERENCES

Adam, Martin T. 2002. "Meditation and the Concept of Insight in Kamalaśīla's *Bhāvanākramas*." Ph.D. diss., McGill University.

Akamatsu, A. 1981. "Karṇakagomin and Śāntarakṣita: On the Thirteen *Kārikās* Common to the *Pramāṇavārttikasvavṛttiṭīkā* and the *Tattvasaṃgraha*." *Indological Review* 3:53–58.

Alston, William P. 1989. *Epistemic Justification: Essays in the Theory of Knowledge*. Ithaca: Cornell University Press.

Alter, T., and S. Walter. 2007. *Phenomenal Concepts and Phenomenal Knowledge: New Essays on Consciousness and Physicalism*. New York: Oxford University Press.

Armstrong, David. 1983. *What Is a Law of Nature?* Cambridge: Cambridge University Press.

Arnold, Daniel A. 2005. *Buddhists, Brahmins, and Belief: Epistemology in South Asian Philosophy of Religion*. New York: Columbia University Press.

Asher, F. M. 1975. *Vikramaśīla Mahāvihāra*. Bangladesh: Lalitkala Dhaka.

Athalye, Yashwant Vasudev, and Mahadev Rajaram Bodas. 1974. *Tarka-Saṃgraha*. Rev. and enl. 2nd ed. Bombay Sanskrit and Prakrit Series 55. Poona: Bhandarkar Oriental Research Institute.

Bagchi, S. 1953. *Inductive Reasoning: A Study of Tarka and Its Role in Indian Logic*. Calcutta: Munishchandra Sinha.

Balcerowicz, Piotr. 1999. "How Could a Cow Be Both Synchronically and Diachronically Homogenous?; or, On the Jaina Notions of *Tiryak-Sāmānya* and *Ūrdhva-Sāmānya*." In *Approaches to Jaina Studies: Philosophy, Logic, Rituals, and*

Symbols, ed. N. K. Wagle and Olle Qvarnstrom, 211–235. South Asian Studies Papers 11. Toronto: University of Toronto, Centre for South Asian Studies.

—. 2001. *Jaina Epistemology in Historical and Comparative Perspective: Critical Edition and English Translation of Logical-Epistemological Treatises: Nyāyāvatāra, Nyāyāvatāra-vivṛti and Nyāyāvatāra-Ṭippaṇa with Introduction and Notes.* Alt- und neu-indische Studien 53. Stuttgart: Steiner.

Bantly, Francisca Cho. 1990. *Deconstructing/Reconstructing the Philosophy of Religions: Summary Reports from the Conferences on Religions in Culture and History, 1986–89, the Divinity School, the University of Chicago.* Chicago: Divinity School.

Bechert, Heinz, Hellmuth Hecker, and Duy Tu Vu. 1966. *Buddhismus, Staat und Gesellschaft in den Ländern des Theravada-Buddhismus.* Schriften des Instituts für Asienkunde in Hamburg 17. Frankfurt: Metzner.

Behe, M. 2001. "The Modern Intelligent Design Hypothesis: Breaking Rules." *Philosophia Christi* 3:165–179.

Bennett, Jonathan Francis. 2001. *Learning from Six Philosophers: Descartes, Spinoza, Leibniz, Locke, Berkeley, Hume.* Oxford: Clarendon Press.

Bhargava, Dayanand. 1973. *Mahopādhyāya Yaśovijaya's Jaina Tarka Bhāṣā: With Translation and Critical Notes.* Delhi: Motilal Banarsidass.

Bhattacharya, B. 1974. *Siddhāntakaumudi of Bhaṭṭoji Dīkṣita: Edited with an Elaborate English Exposition and Annotations.* Calcutta: Sanskrit Pustak Bhandar.

Bhattacharya, Gopikamohan. 1961. *Studies in Nyāya-Vaiśeṣika Theism.* Calcutta Sanskrit College Research Series 5.14. Calcutta: Sanskrit College.

—. 1986. "Ratnakīrti on Apoha." In *Buddhist Logic and Epistemology: Studies in the Buddhist Analysis of Inference and Language,* ed. B. K. Matilal and R. D. Evans, 291–298. Dordrecht: Kluwer Academic.

Bhattacharya, Gopinath. 1976. *Tarkasaṃgraha-Dīpikā on Tarkasaṃgraha.* Calcutta: Progressive Publishers.

Bhattacharya, S. 1996. *Gaṅgeśa's Theory of Indeterminate Perception (Nirvikalpakavāda),* Part I. New Delhi: Indian Council of Philosophical Research.

Biardeau, Madeleine. 1964. *Vakyapadiya Brahmakanda.* Publications de l'Institut de civilisation indienne 8.24. Paris: de Boccard.

BonJour, Laurence. 1985. *The Structure of Empirical Knowledge.* Cambridge, MA: Harvard University Press.

BonJour, Laurence, and Ernest Sosa. 2003. *Epistemic Justification: Internalism Versus Externalism, Foundations Versus Virtues.* Great Debates in Philosophy. Malden, MA: Blackwell.

Bowlin, John R. 1999. *Contingency and Fortune in Aquinas's Ethics.* Cambridge Studies in Religion and Critical Thought 6. Cambridge: Cambridge University Press.

Bronkhorst, Johannes. 1989. "Review of *'Ich' und das Ich:* Analytische Untersuchungen zur Buddhistische-Brahmanischen Atmankontroverse." *Wiener Zeitschrift für die Kunde Südasiens und Archiv für Indische Philosophie* 33:223–225.

—. 1993. *The Two Sources of Indian Asceticism.* Schweizer Asiatische Studien 13. Bern: P. Lang.

——. 1996. "God's Arrival in the Vaiśeṣika System." *Journal of Indian Philosophy* 24:281–294.

——. 1999. "Nagārjuna and Apoha." In Katsura 1999:17–24.

Brueckner, Anthony, and M. Oreste Fiocco. 2002. "Williamson's Anti-Luminosity Argument." *Philosophical Studies* 110:285–293.

Bühneman, Gudrun. 1980. *Der allwissende Buddha: Ein Beweis und seine Probleme: Ratnakīrtis Sarvajñasiddhi.* Wiener Studien zur Tibetologie und Buddhismuskunde 4. Vienna: Arbeitskreis für Tibetische und Buddhistische Studien, Universität Wien.

Bulcke, C. 1947. *The Theism of Nyāya-Vaiśeṣika: Its Origin and Early Development.* Delhi: Motilal Banarsidass.

Burge, T. 1979. "Individualism and the Mental." *Midwest Studies in Philosophy* 4:73–121.

Cabezón, José Ignacio. 1994. *Buddhism and Language: A Study of Indo-Tibetan Scholasticism.* Albany: State University of New York Press.

——. 2006a. "The Discipline and Its Other: The Dialectic of Alterity in the Study of Religion." *Journal of the American Academy of Religion* 74.1:21–38.

——. 2006b. "In Defense of Abstraction: A Reply to William Schweiker." *Journal of the American Academy of Religion* 74.1:45–46.

Cardona, G. 1974. "Pāṇini's Kārikās: Agency, Animation, and Identity." *Journal of Indian Philosophy* 2:231–306.

Carman, John Braisted. 1994. *Majesty and Meekness: A Comparative Study of Contrast and Harmony in the Concept of God.* Grand Rapids, MI: Eerdmans.

Carroll, John W. 2008. "Laws of Nature." *Stanford Encyclopedia of Philosophy.* http://plato.stanford.edu/archives/spr2008/entries/laws-of-nature/.

Cartwright, Nancy D., with Anna Alexandrova, Sophia Efstathiou, Andrew Hamilton, and Ioan Muntean. 2005. "Laws." In *Oxford Handbook of Contemporary Philosophy*, ed. F. Jackson, 792–818. New York: Oxford University Press.

Chadha, Monima. 2001. "Perceptual Cognition: A Nyāya-Kantian Approach." *Philosophy East and West* 51.2:197–209.

Chakrabarti, Arindam. 1989. "From the Fabric to the Weaver: The Cosmological Argument in Indian Philosophy." In *Indian Philosophy of Religion*, ed. R. Perrett, 21–34. Studies in Philosophy and Religion. Dordrecht: Kluwer Academic.

——. 1992. "I Touch What I Saw." *Philosophy and Phenomenological Research* 52.1:103–116.

——. 1994. "Testimony: A Philosophical Survey (Review Essay)." *Philosophy and Phenomenological Research* 54.4:965–972.

——. 1997. *Denying Existence: The Logic, Epistemology, and Pragmatics of Negative Existentials and Fictional Discourse.* Synthese Library 261. Dordrecht: Kluwer Academic.

——. 1998. "Experience, Concept-Possession, and Knowledge of a Language." In *The Philosophy of P. F. Strawson*, ed. L. E. Hahn, 315–324. Chicago: Open Court.

——. 2000. "Against Immaculate Perception: Seven Reasons for Eliminating Nirvikalpaka Perception from Nyāya." *Philosophy East and West* 50.1:1–8.

—. 2003. "Perception, Apperception and Non-Conceptual Content." In *Perspectives on Consciousness*, ed. A. Chatterjee, 89–107. New Delhi: Munshiram Manoharlal.

—. 2004. "Seeing Without Recognizing? More on Denuding Perceptual Content." *Philosophy East and West* 54.3:365–367.

—. 2005a. *Ādhunika-Pratīcya-Pramāṇa-Mīmāṃsā.* Contemporary Western Theories of Knowledge. R. S. Vidyapeeth: Tirupati.

—. 2005b. "Universal Properties in Indian Philosophical Traditions." In *Encyclopedia of Philosophy,* ed. Donald M. Bachert, 580–587. 2nd ed. Detroit: Macmillan.

Chakrabarti, Arindam, Mark Siderits, and Tom Tillemans, eds. Forthcoming. *Apoha Semantics and Human Cognition.*

Chakrabarti, Kisor Kumar. 1999. *Classical Indian Philosophy of Mind: The Nyāya Dualist Tradition.* Albany: State University of New York Press.

Chatterjee, Satischandra. 1978. *The Nyāya Theory of Knowledge: A Critical Study of Some Problems of Logic and Metaphysics.* Calcutta: University of Calcutta.

Chattopadhyaya, Debiprasad. 1969. *Indian Atheism: A Marxist Analysis.* Calcutta: Manisha.

Chattopadhyaya, Debiprasad, and Alaka Chattopadhyaya. 1970. *Taranatha's History of Buddhism in India.* Simla: Indian Institute of Advanced Study.

Chemparathy, G. 1965. "The Testimony of the Yuktidīpikā Concerning the Īśvara Doctrine of the Pāśupatas and Vaiśeṣikas." *WZKSO* 9:119–146.

—. 1968. "The Īśvara Doctrine of Praśastapāda." *Vishveshvaranand Indological Journal* 6:65–87.

—. 1969a. "Two Little-Known Fragments from Early Vaiśeṣika Literature on the Omniscience of Īśvara." *Adyar Library Bulletin* 33:117–134.

—. 1969b. "Two Early Buddhist Refutations of the Existence of Īśvara as the Creator of the Universe." *Wiener Zeitschrift für die Kunde Süd und Ostasiens und Archiv für Indische Philosophie* 12/13:85–100.

—. 1972. *An Indian Rational Theology: Introduction to Udayana's Nyāyakusumāñjali.* Publications of the de Nobili Research Library 1. Vienna: Gerold and Co.

Chierchia, Gennaro, and Sally McConnell-Ginet. 1990. *Meaning and Grammar: An Introduction to Semantics.* 2nd ed. Cambridge, MA: MIT Press.

Clooney, Francis. 1997. "What's a God? The Quest for the Right Understanding of Devata in Brahmanical Ritual Theory (Mīmāṃsā)." *International Journal of Hindu Studies (Quebec)* 1.2:337–385.

—. 1999. "The Existence of God: Reason and Revelation in Two Classical Hindu Theologies." *Faith and Philosophy* 16.4:523–543.

Collins, R. 2003. "Evidence for Fine-Tuning." In *God and Design*, ed. N. Manson, 178–199. New York: Routledge.

Collins, Steven. 1998. *Nirvana and Other Buddhist Felicities: Utopias of the Pali imaginaire.* Cambridge Studies in Religious Traditions 12. Cambridge: Cambridge University Press.

Craig, William Lane. 1980. *The Cosmological Argument from Plato to Leibniz.* London: Macmillan.

Craig, William Lane, and Walter Sinnott-Armstrong. 2004. *God?: A Debate Between a Christian and an Athiest*. Point/Conterpoint Series. Oxford: Oxford University Press.

Davidson, Ronald M. 2002. *Indian Esoteric Buddhism: A Social History of the Tantric Movement*. New York: Columbia University Press.

Davis, Lawrence. 1981. "Tarka in the Nyāya Theory of Inference." *Journal of Indian Philosophy* 9:105–120.

De Breet, Jan A. 1992. "The Concept of *Upāyakauśalya* in the *Aṣṭasāhasrikā Prajñāpāramitā*." *WZKS* 36:203–216.

Dembski, William A. 1998. *The Design Inference: Eliminating Chance Through Small Probabilities*. Cambridge Studies in Probability, Induction, and Decision Theory. Cambridge: Cambridge University Press.

—. 2002. *No Free Lunch: Why Specified Complexity Cannot Be Purchased Without Intelligence*. Lanham, MD: Rowman and Littlefield.

Deshpande, Madhav. 1992. *The Meaning of Noun: Semantic Theory in Classical and Medieval India=Nāmārtha-Nirṇaya of Kauṇḍabhaṭṭa*. Studies of Classical India 13. Dordrecht: Kluwer Academic.

Dravid, N. S. 1995. *Ātmatattvaviveka of Udayanācārya with Translation, Explanation, and Analytical-Critical Survey*. Shimla: Indian Council of Philosophical Research.

—. 1996. *Nyāyakusumāñjali of Udayanācārya, vol. 1, with Translation and Explanation*. New Delhi: Indian Council of Philosophical Research.

Dravid, Raja Ram. 1972. *The Problem of Universals in Indian Philosophy*. Delhi: Motilal Banarsidass.

Dretske, Fred I. 1981. *Knowledge and the Flow of Information*. Cambridge, MA: MIT Press.

Dreyfus, Georges. 1997. *Recognizing Reality: Dharmakīrti's Philosophy and Its Tibetan Interpretations*. SUNY Series in Buddhist Studies. Albany: State University of New York Press.

Dunne, John D. 1999. "Foundations of Dharmakīrti's Philosophy: A Study of the Central Issues in His Ontology, Logic, and Epistemology with Particular Attention to the *Svopajñavṛtti*." Ph.D. diss., Harvard University.

—. 2004. *Foundations of Dharmakīrti's Philosophy*. Boston: Wisdom Publications.

Elder, Crawford. 2004. *Real Natures and Familiar Objects*. Cambridge, MA: MIT Press.

—. 2007. "Realism and the Problem of *Infirmae species*." *American Philosophical Quarterly* 44:111–127.

Eltschinger, V. 2005a. "Recherches sur la philosophie religieuse de Dharmakīrti, 1: Le Bouddha comme Śāstṛ et comme Sugata." *Études Asiatiques/Asiatische Studien* 59.2:395–442.

—. 2005b. "Recherches sur la philosophie religieuse de Dharmakīrti, 2: L'āśrayaparivṛtti." *Journal Asiatique* 293.1:151–211.

—. 2007a. *Penser l'autorité des écritures: La polémique de Dharmakīrti contre la notion brahmanique orthodoxe d'un Veda sans auteur*. Vienna: Verlag der Österreichischen Akademie der Wissenschaften.

——. 2007b. "On Seventh- and Eighth-Century Buddhist Accounts of Human Action, Practical Rationality, and Soteriology." In *Pramāṇakīrtiḥ: Papers Dedicated to Ernst Steinkellner on the Occasion of His 70th Birthday,* part 1, ed. H. K. B. Kellner, M. T. Much, and H. Tauscher, 135–162. Wiener Studien zur Tibetologie und Buddhismuskunde 70. Vienna: Arbeitskreis für Tibetische und Buddhistische Studien, Universität Wien.

Fitelson, B., C. Stephens, and E. Sober. 1999. "How Not to Detect Design: A Review of William Dembski's *The Design Inference." Philosophy of Science* 66:472–488.

Foley, Richard. 1987. *The Theory of Epistemic Rationality.* Cambridge, MA: Harvard University Press.

Franco, Eli. 1984. "Studies in the Tattvopaplavasiṃha, II: The Theory of Error." *Journal of Indian Philosophy* 12:105–137.

——. 1997. *Dharmakīrti on Compassion and Rebirth.* Wiener Studien zur Tibetologie und Buddhismuskunde 38. Vienna: Arbeitskreis für Tibetische und Buddhistische Studien, Universität Wien.

Franco, Eli, and Karin Preisendanz, eds. 1997. *Beyond Orientalism: The Work of Wilhelm Halbfass and Its Impact on Indian and Cross-Cultural Studies.* Poznan Studies in the Philosophy of the Sciences and the Humanities 59. Atlanta, GA: Rodopi.

Frauwallner, Erich. 1933. "Zu den Fragmenten Buddhistischer Logiker im Nyāyavārttikam." *WZKS* 40:281–304.

——. 1937. "Beitrage zur Apohalehre II Dharmottaras." *WZKM* 44:233–287.

——. 1959. "Dignāga, sein werk und seine Entwicklung." *WZKSO* 3:83–164.

Fumerton, Richard A. 2006. *Epistemology.* First Books in Philosophy. Malden, MA: Blackwell.

Funayama, Toru. 1992. "Study of Kalpanāpoḍha: A Translation of the Tattvasaṃgraha vv. 1212–1263 by Śāntarakṣita and the Tattvasaṃgrahapañjikā by Kamalaśīla on the Definition of Direct Perception." *Zinbun* 27:33–128.

——. 1995. "Arcaṭa, Śāntarakṣita, Jinendrabuddhi, and Kamalaśīla on the Aim of a Treatise (*Prayojana*)." *WZKS* 39:181–201.

——. 2000. "Mental Cognition in Kamalaśīla's Theory of Direct Perception." *Journal of Philosophical Studies* 569:105–132.

——. 2005. "Perception, Conceptual Construction, and Yogic Cognition According to Kamalaśīla's Epistemology." *Chun-Hwa Buddhist Journal* 18:273–297.

——. Forthcoming. "Kamalaśīla's View on Yogic Perception and the Boddhisattva Paths."

Gajendragadkar, A. B., and R. D. Karmarkar. 1934. *The Tarkabhāṣā of Keśavamiśra.* Poona: Aryabhushan Press.

Gale, Richard. 1991. *On the Nature and Existence of God.* Cambridge: Cambridge University Press.

——. 2000. "Why Traditional Cosmological Arguments Don't Work, and a Sketch of a New One That Does." In *Contemporary Debates in Philosophy of Religion*, ed. M. Peterson, 114–130. Malden, MA: Blackwell.

——. 2007. *On the Philosophy of Religion.* Wadsworth Philosophical Topics. Australia: Thomas Wadsworth.

Gale, R., and A. Pruss. 1999. "A New Cosmological Argument." *Religious Studies* 35:461–476.

——. 2003. *The Existence of God*. International Research Library of Philosophy 28. Aldershot: Ashgate.

——. 2005. "Cosmological and Teleological Arguments." In *Oxford Handbook of Philosophy of Religion*, 116–137. Oxford: Oxford University Press.

Galloway, Brian. 1989. "Some Logical Issues in Madhyamaka Thought." *Journal of Indian Philosophy* 17:1–35.

Ganeri, Jonardon. 1995. "Vyāḍi and the Realist Theory of Meaning." *Journal of Indian Philosophy* 23:403–428.

——. 1996. "Meaning and Reference in Classical India." *Journal of Indian Philosophy* 24:1–19.

——. 1999a. *Semantic Powers: Meaning and the Means of Knowing in Classical Indian Philosophy*. Oxford Philosophical Monographs. Oxford: Clarendon Press.

——. 1999b. "Dharmakīrti's Semantics for the Particle *Eva*." In Katsura 1999:101–116.

——. 2001. *Philosophy in Classical India: An Introduction and Analysis*. New York: Routledge.

——. 2007. *The Concealed Art of the Soul: Theories of Self and Practices of Truth in Indian Ethics and Epistemology*. Oxford: Oxford University Press.

Gangopadhyaya, Mrinalkanti. 1971. *Vinītadeva's Nyāyabindu-ṭīkā. Sanskrit Original Reconstructed from the Extant Tibetan Version with English Translation and Annotations*. Calcutta: Indian Studies, Past and Present.

Ghosh, A. 1989. *An Encyclopedia of Indian Archaeology*. New Delhi: Munshiram Manoharlal Publishers.

Gillon, Brendan S. 1991. "Dharmakīrti and the Problem of Induction." In Steinkellner 1991a:53–58.

——. 1999. "Another Look at the Sanskrit Particle *Eva*." In Katsura 1999:117–130.

Gillon, Brendan, and R. P. Hayes. 1991. "Introduction to Dharmakīrti's Theory of Inference as Presented in *Pramāṇavārttika Svopajñavṛtti* 1–10." *Journal of Indian Philosophy* 19:1–73.

Glasenapp, Helmuth von. 1954. *Buddhismus und Gottesidee: Die Buddhistischen Lehron von den überweitlichen Wesen und Machten und ihre Religionageschichtlichen Parallelan*. Mainz: Akademie der Wissenschaften und der Literatur.

Gnoli, R. 1960. *The Pramāṇavārttikam of Dharmakīrti: The First Chapter with the Autocommentary*. Rome: Instituto italiano per il Medio ed Estremo Oriente.

Goekoop, C. 1967. *The Logic of Invarible Concomitance*. Dordrecht: Kluwer Academic.

Gokhale, Pradeep P. 1992. *Inference and Fallacies Discussed in Ancient Indian Logic, with Special Reference to Nyāya and Buddhism*. Bibliotheca Indo-Buddhica Series 107. Delhi: Sri Satguru Publications.

Gold, Jonathan C. 2007. *The Dharma's Gatekeepers: Sakya Paṇḍita on Buddhist Scholarship in Tibet*. Albany: State University of New York Press.

Goldman, Alvin I. 1986. *Epistemology and Cognition*. Cambridge, MA: Harvard University Press.

——. 1992. *Liaisons: Philosophy Meets the Cognitive and Social Sciences.* Cambridge, MA: MIT Press.

——. 1999. *Knowledge in a Social World.* Oxford: Clarendon Press.

Gonda, Jan. 1968. "The Concept of a Personal God in Ancient Indian Religious Thought." *La réalité suprême dans les religions non-chrétiennes* 17:111–136.

Goodman, S. 1989. "A Buddhist Proof for Omniscience: The *Sarvajñasiddhi* of Ratnakīrti." Ph.D. diss., Temple University.

Granoff, P. E. 1978. *Philosophy and Argument in Late Vedānta: Śrī Harṣa's Khaṇḍanakhaṇḍakhādya.* Studies of Classical India 1. Boston: Reidel.

Griffiths, Paul J. 1986. *On Being Mindless: Buddhist Meditation and the Mind-Body Problem.* La Salle, IL: Open Court.

——. 1999a. *Religious Reading: The Place of Reading in the Practice of Religion.* New York: Oxford University Press.

——. 1999b. "What Do Buddhists Hope for from Antitheistic Arguments?" *Faith and Philosophy* 16.4:506–523.

——. 2006a. "On the Future of the Study of Religion in the Academy." *Journal of the American Academy of Religion* 74.1:66–74.

——. 2006b. "Reply to Armour." *Journal of the American Academy of Religion* 74.-1:77–78.

Gupta, Rita. 1990. *Essays on Dependent Origination and Momentariness.* Calcutta: Sanskrit Pustak Bhandar.

——. 2006. *The Buddhist Concepts of Pramāṇa and Pratyakṣa.* New Delhi: Sundeep Prakashan.

Gutting, Gary. 1982. *Religious Belief and Religious Skepticism.* Notre Dame, IN: University of Notre Dame Press.

Habermas, Gary R., Antony Flew, and John Ankerberg. 2005. *Resurrected?: An Atheist and Theist Dialogue.* Lanham, MD: Rowman and Littlefield.

Hadot, Pierre, and Arnold Ira Davidson. 1995. *Philosophy as a Way of Life: Spiritual Exercises from Socrates to Foucault.* Oxford: Blackwell.

Hahn, Michael. 1971. *Jñānaśrīmitra's Vṛttamālāstuti: Ein Beispielsammlung zur altindischen Metrik.* Wiesbaden: Harrassowitz.

——. 1989. *Shivasvāmin's Kapphinābhyudaya; or, The Exaltation of King Kapphina.* New Delhi: Aditya Prakashan.

Halbfass, Wilhelm. 1992. *On Being and What There Is: Classical Vaiśeṣika and the History of Indian Ontology.* Albany: State University of New York Press.

——. 1997. "Arthakrīyā und Kṣaṇikatva: Eine Beobachtungen." In *Bauddhavidyāsudhākara: Studies in Honor of Heinz Bechert on the Occasion of His 65th Birthday,* 233–247. Swistall-Odendort: Indica et Tibetica.

Hattori, Masaaki. 1968. *Dignāga, On Perception; Being the Pratyakṣapariccheda of Dignāga's Pramāṇasamuccaya from the Sanskrit Fragments and the Tibetan Versions.* Harvard Oriental Series 47. Cambridge, MA: Harvard University Press.

——. 1977. "The Sautrāntika Background of the Apoha Theory." In *Buddhist Thought and Asian Civilization: Essays in Honor of Herbert V. Guenther on His Sixtieth Birth-*

day, ed. H. V. Guenther, L. S. Kawamura, and K. Scott, 47–58. Emeryville, CA: Dharma Pub.

——. 1980. "Apoha and Pratibhā." In *Sanskrit and Indian Studies: Essays in Honour of Daniel H. H. Ingalls*, ed. M. Nagatomi, 61–73. Dordrecht: Kluwer Academic.

——. 2000. "Dignāga's Theory of Meaning: An Annotated Translation of the *Pramāṇasamuccayavṛtti*: Chapter V: *Anyāpoha-parīkṣā* (I)." In *Wisdom, Compassion, and the Search for Understanding: The Buddhist Studies Legacy of Gadjin M. Nagao*, ed. J. A. Silk, 137–146. Honolulu: University of Hawai'i Press.

——. 2006. "The *Apoha* Theory as Referred to in the *Nyāyamañjarī*." *Acta Asiatica* 90:55–70.

Hayes, Richard P. 1986. "An Interpretation of *Anyāpoha* in Diṅnāga's General Theory of Inference." In *Buddhist Logic and Epistemology: Studies in the Buddhist Analysis of Inference and Language*, ed. B. K. Matilal, 31–58. Dordrecht: Kluwer Academic.

——. 1988. *Dignāga on the Interpretation of Signs*. Studies of Classical India 9. Dordrecht: Kluwer Academic.

Heil, John. 1999. "Belief." In *A Companion to Epistemology*, ed. J. D. Sosa and E. Sosa, 45–48. Malden, MA: Blackwell.

Herzberger, Radhika. 1986. *Bhartṛhari and the Buddhist: An Essay in the Development of Fifth- and Sixth-Century Indian Thought*. Studies of Classical India 8. Dordrecht: Kluwer Academic.

Hintikka, Jaakko. 1962. *Knowledge and Belief: An Introduction to the Logic of the Two Notions*. Ithaca: Cornell University Press.

Holdrege, Barbara. 2000. "What's Beyond the Post? Comparative Analysis as Critical Method." In *A Magic Still Dwells: Comparative Religion in the Postmodern Age*, ed. K. C. Patton, B. C. Ray, M. D. Eckel, D. L. Eck, and L. E. Sullivan, 77–91. Berkeley: University of California Press.

Houben, Jan E. M. 1995. *The Sambandha-Samuddeśa (Chapter on Relation) and Bhartṛhari's Philosophy of Language*. Groningen: Egbert Forsten.

Inami, M. 1999. "On the Determination of Causality." In Katsura 1999:131–155.

Inami, Masahiro, and Tom J. F. Tillemans. 1986. "Another Look at the Framework of the *Pramāṇasiddhi* Chapter of *Pramāṇavārttika*." *WZKS* 30:123–142.

Inden, Ronald B. 1990. *Imagining India*. Oxford: Basil Blackwell.

Ingalls, Daniel Henry Holmes. 1951. *Materials for the Study of Navya-nyāya Logic*. Harvard Oriental Series 40. Cambridge, MA: Harvard University Press.

Ishida, H. Forthcoming. "On the Classification of *Anyāpoha*."

Iwata, Takashi. 2004. "The Negative Concomitance (*Vyatireka*) in the Case of Inconclusive (*Anaikāntika*) Reasons." In Katsura and Steinkellner 2004:91–134.

Iyengar, Rangaswami H. H., ed. 1952. *Tarkabhāṣā and Vādasthāna of Mokṣākaragupta and Jitāripāda with a Foreword by Mahopadhyāya Vidhuśekhara Bhattāchārya*. Mysore.

Jackson, Roger. 1986. "Dharmakīrti's Refutation of Theism." *Philosophy East and West* 36.4:315–348.

Jacobi, H. 1923. *Die Entwicklung der Gottesidee bei den Inden: Und Deren Beweise für das Dasein Gottes*. Geistesströmungen des Ostens 1. Bonn: K. Schroeder.

Jambuvijayaji, Muni, ed. 1966–1988. *Dvādaśāraṃ Nayacakram of Ācārya Śrī Mallavādī Kṣamāśramaṇa with the Commentary Nyāyāgamānusāriṇī of Śrī Siṃhasūri Gaṇi Vādi Kṣamāśramaṇa.* 3 vols. Bhavnagar: Sri Jain Atmanand Sabha.

——. 2001. *Dravyālaṃkāraṭīkā*. Ahmedabad.

Jetly, J. S. 1971. *Praśastapādabhāṣyam: with the Commentary Kiraṇāvalī of Udayanācārya.* 1st ed. Gaekwad's Oriental Series 154. Baroda: Oriental Institute.

——. 2003. *Śivāditya's Saptapadārthī, with a Commentary by Jinavardhana Sūri.* L. D. Institute of Indology Series 134.1. Ahmedabad: L. D. Institute of Indology.

Jhalakīkar, Bhīmācārya, ed. 1996. *Nyāyakoṣa; or, Dictionary of Technical Terms of Indian Philosophy.* Bombay Sanskrit and Prakrit Series 49. Pune: Bhandarkar Oriental Research Institute.

Kajiyama, Yūichi. 1963. "*Tripañcakacintā,* Development of the Buddhist Theory on the Determination of Causality." *Miscellanea Indologica Kiotiensia* 4–5:1–15.

——. 1965. "Saṃtānāntradūṣaṇa of Ratnakīrti." *IBK* 25:9–24.

——. 1966. *An Introduction to Buddhist Philosophy: An Annotated Translation of the Tarkabhāṣā of Mokṣākaragupta.* Memoirs of the Faculty of Letters of Kyoto University 10. Kyoto.

——. 1978. "Later Mādhyamikas on Epistemology and Meditation." In *Mahāyāna Buddhist Meditation: Theory and Practice*, ed. M. Kiyota, 114–143. Honolulu: University of Hawai'i Press.

——. 1989. *Studies in Buddhist Philosophy.* Kyoto: Rinsen.

——. 1998. *An Introduction to Buddhist Philosophy: An Annotated Translation of the Tarkabhāṣā of Mokṣākaragupta.* Wiener Studien zur Tibetologie und Buddhismuskunde 42. Vienna: Arbeitskreis für Tibetische und Buddhistische Studien, Universität Wien.

Kāpādia, H. R. ed. 1940/1947. *Anekāntajayapatākā: With His Own Commentary and Municandra Sūri's Supercommentary.* Gaekwad's Oriental Series 88.105. Baroda: Oriental Institute.

Kapstein, Matthew. 2001. *Reason's Traces: Identity and Interpretation in Indian and Tibetan Buddhist Thought.* Boston: Wisdom Publications.

Katsura, Shoryu. 1983. "Dignāga on Trairūpya." *Journal of Indian and Buddhist Studies* 32:15–21.

——. 1984. "Dharmakīrti's Theory of Truth." *Journal of Indian Philosophy* 12:215–235.

——. 1985. "On *Trairūpya* Formula." In *Buddhism and Its Relation to Other Religions. Essays in Honour of Dr. Shozen Kumai on His Seventieth Birthday*, ed. K. S. H. Kunenkai, 161–172. Kyoto.

——. 1986a. "Jñānaśrīmitra on Apoha." In *Buddhist Logic and Epistemology: Studies in the Buddhist Analysis of Inference and Language,* ed. R. D. Evans, 171–184. Dordrecht: Reidel.

——. 1986b. "On The Origin and Development of the Concept of Vyāpti in Indian Logic." *Tetsugaku: Journal of Hiroshima Philosophical Society* 37:1–16.

——. 1991. "Dignāga and Dharmakīrti on *Apoha*." In Steinkellner 1991a:129–146.

——. 1992a. "*Pramāṇavārttika* IV.202–206—Towards the Correct Understanding of *Svabhāvapratibandha*." *Journal of Indian and Buddhist Studies* 40.2:35–40.

—. 1992b. "Dignāga and Dharmakīrti on Adarśaṇamātra and Anupalabhdi." *Asiatische Studien/Etudes Asiatiques* 46.1:222–231.

—. 1993. "On Perceptual Judgment." In *Studies on Buddhism in Honour of Professor A. K. Warder*, ed. N. K. Wagle and F. Watanabe, 66–75. Toronto: University of Toronto, Centre for South Asian Studies.

—, ed. 1999. *Dharmakīrti's Thought and Its Impact on Indian and Tibetan Philosophy. Proceedings of the Third International Dharmakīrti Conference, Hiroshima, November 4–6, 1997.* Vienna: Verlag der Österreichischen Akademie der Wissenschaften: Beiträge zur Kultur- und Geistesgeschichte Asiens.

—. 2003. "Some Cases of Doctrinal Proofs in the *Abhidharma-kośa-bhāṣya*." *Journal of Indian Philosophy* 31:105–120.

—. 2004. "The Role of *Dṛṣṭāṇa* in Dignāga's Logic." In Katsura and Steinkellner 2004:135–174.

—. Forthcoming. "The Apoha Theory as an Approach to Understanding Human Cognition."

Katsura, S., and E. Steinkellner, eds. 2004. *The Role of the Example (Dṛṣṭānta) in Classical Indian Logic.* Vienna: Arbeitskreis für Tibetische und Buddhistische Studien, Universität Wien.

Kellner, Birgit. 1997a. "Non-cognition (*Anupalabdhi*)—Perception or Inference? The View of Dharmottara and Jñānaśrīmitra." *Tetsugaku* 49:121–134.

—. 1997b. *Nichts bleibt nichts: Die buddhistische Zurückweisung von Kumārilas Abhāvapramāṇa: Übersetzung und Interpretation von Śāntarakṣitas Tattvasaṅgraha vv. 1647–1690, mit Kamalaśīlas Tattvasaṅgrahapañjikā, sowie Ansätze und Arbeitshypothesen zur Geschichte negativer Erkenntnis in der indischen Philosophie.* Wiener Studien zur Tibetologie und Buddhismuskunde 39. Vienna: Arbeitskreis für Tibetische und Buddhistische Studien, Universität Wien.

—. 1999. "Levels of (Im)perceptibility: Dharmottara on the *Dṛśya* in *Dṛśyānupalabdhi*." In Katsura 1999:193–208.

—. 2001. "Negation—Failure or Success? Remarks on an Allegedly Characteristic Trait of Dharmakīrti's *Anupalabdhi*-Theory." *Journal of Indian Philosophy* 29:495–517.

—. 2004a. "Why Infer and Not Just Look?" In Katsura and Steinkellner 1994.

—. 2004b. "First Logic, then the Buddha? The Controversy About the Chapter Sequence of Dharmakīrit's *Pramāṇavārttika* and the Soteriological Relevance of Inference." *Hōrin* 11:147–167.

—. 2007. *Jñānaśrīmitra's Anupalabdhirahasya and Sarvaśabdābhavacarcā: A Critical Edition with a Survey of His Anupalabdhi-theory.* Wiener Studien zur Tibetologie und Buddhismuskunde 67. Vienna: Arbeitskreis für Tibetische und Buddhistische Studien, Universität Wien.

—. Forthcoming. "Dharmakīrti's Exposition of *Pramāṇa* and *Pramāṇaphala* and the Sliding Scale of Analysis."

Kelly, T. 2003. "Epistemic Rationality as Instrumental Rationality: A Critique." *Philosophy and Phenomenological Research* 66.3:612–640.

—. 2005. "The Epistemic Significance of Disagreement." In *Oxford Studies in Epistemology*, ed. Tamar Szabo Gendler, 167–196. Oxford: Clarendon Press.

—. Forthcoming. "Evidence and Normativity: Reply to Leite."

Kielhorn, Franz, ed. 1962–1973. *The Vyākaraṇa-Mahābhāṣya of Patañjali*. Bhandarkar: Oriental Research Institute.

Kiparsky, P., and Staal, F. 1969. "Syntactic and Semantic Relations in Pāṇini." *Foundations of Language* 5:83–117.

Kitcher, Philip. 2001a. *Science, Truth, and Democracy*. Oxford Studies in Philosophy of Science. New York: Oxford University Press.

—. 2001b. "Real Realism: The Galilean Strategy." *Philosophical Review* 110:151–197.

Klein, Peter. 1996. "Warrant, Proper Function, Reliabilism, and Defeasibility." In *Warrant and Contemporary Epistemology*, ed. J. Kvanvig, 97–130. Lanham, MD: Rowman and Littlefield.

Koons, R. 1997. "A New Look at the Cosmological Argument." *American Philosophical Quarterly* 34:193–211.

—. 2001. "Defeasible Reasoning, Special Pleading, and the Cosmological Argument: A Reply to Oppy." *Faith and Philosophy* 18:192–203.

Krasser, Helmut. 1991. *Laghuprāmāṇyaparīkṣā of Dharmottara*. Vienna: Österreichische Akademie der Wissenschaften.

—. 1995. "Dharmottara's Theory of Knowledge in His *Laghuprāmāṇyaparīkṣā*." *Journal of Buddhist Ethics* 23:247–271.

—. 1997. "Zur Buddhistischen Definition von gültiger Erkenntnis (*Pramāṇa*) in Jayantabhaṭṭas Nyāyamañjarī." *Studien zur Indologie und Iranistik* 21:105–132.

—. 1999. "Dharmakīrti and Kumārila on the Refutation of the Existence of God." In Katsura 1999:215–224.

—. 2001. "On Dharmakīrti's Understanding of *Pramāṇa-bhūta* and His Definition of *Pramāṇa*." *WZKS* 45:173–199.

—. 2002. *Śaṅkaranandanas Īśvarāpākaraṇasaṅkṣepa: Mit einem anonymen Kommentar und weiteren Materialien zur buddhistischen Gottespolemik*. Beiträge zur Kultur- und Geistesgeschichte Asiens 39. Vienna: Verlag der Österreichischen Akademie der Wissenschaften.

—. 2004. "Are Buddhist Pramāṇavādins non-Buddhistic? Dignāga and Dharmakīrti on the Impact of Logic and Epistemology on Emancipation." *Hōrin* 11:129–146.

Krasser, Helmut, and Ernst Steinkellner. 1989. *Dharmottaras Exkurs zur Definition gültiger Erkenntnis im Pramāṇaviniścaya: (Materialien zur Definition gültiger Erkenntnis in der Tradition Dharmakīrtis 1): Tibetischer Text, Sanskritmaterialien und Übersetzung*. Beiträge zur Kultur- und Geistesgeschichte Asiens 2. Vienna: Verlag der Österreichischen Akademie der Wissenschaften.

Krishna, Daya, M. P. Rege, R. C. Dwivedi, and Mukund Lath, eds. 1991. *Saṃvāda: A Dialogue Between Two Philosophical Traditions*. Delhi: Indian Council of Philosophical Research.

Kyuma, T. 2005. *Sein und Wirklichkeit in der Augenblicklichkeitslehre Jñānaśrīmitras. Kṣaṇabhaṅgādhyāya I: Pakṣadharmatādhikāra*. Sanskrittexte und Ubersetzung 62. Vienna: WSTB.

—. Forthcoming. "On the Perceptibility of External Objects in Dharmakīrti's Epistemology."

Laine, Joy. 1993. "Some Remarks on the Guṇaguṇibhedabhaṅga Chapter on Udayana's Ātmatattvaviveka: Defense of Nyāya Epistemo-Logical Realism Against Buddhist Idealism." *Journal of Indian Philosophy* 21:261–294.

——. 1998. "Udayana's Refutation of the Buddhist Thesis of Momentariness in the Ātmatattvaviveka." *Journal of Indian Philosophy* 26:51–97.

Lasic, Horst. 1999. "Dharmakīrti and His Successors on the Determination of Causality." In Katsura 1999:233–242.

——. 2000a. *Jñānaśrīmitra's Vyāpticarcā: Sanskrittext, Übersetzung, Analyse*. Wiener Studien zur Tibetologie und Buddhismuskunde 48. Vienna: Arbeitskreis für Tibetische und Buddhistische Studien.

——. 2000b. *Ratnakīrti's Vyāptinirṇaya: Sanskrittext, Übersetzung, Analyse*. Wiener Studien zur Tibetologie und Buddhismuskunde 49. Vienna: Arbeitskreis für Tibetische und Buddhistische Studien.

——. 2003. "On the Utilisation of Causality as a Basis of Inference: Dharmakīrti's Statements and Their Interpretation." *Journal of Indian Philosophy* 31:185–197.

Leite, A. Forthcoming. "Epistemic Instrumentalism and Reasons for Belief: A Reply to Tom Kelly's 'Epistemic Rationality as Instrumental Rationality: A Critique.'"

Le Poidevin, Robin. 1996. *Arguing for Atheism: An Introduction to the Philosophy of Religion*. London: Routledge.

Leslie, John. 1988. "How to Draw Conclusions from a Fine-Tuned Cosmos." In *Physics, Philosophy, and Theology: A Common Quest for Understanding*, ed. Robert Russell, 297–312. Vatican City State: Vatican Observatory Press.

Lewis, David. 1973. *Counterfactuals*. Cambridge, MA: Harvard University Press.

——. 1983. *Philosophical Papers*. New York: Oxford University Press.

——. 1986. *On the Plurality of Worlds*. New York: Basil Blackwell.

Lindtner, Christian. 1984. "Marginalia to Dharmakīrti's Pramāṇaviniścaya I–II." *WZKS* 28:149-175.

——. 1999. "Madhyamaka Causality." *Hōrin* 6:55–63.

Lusthaus, Dan. 2002. *Buddhist Phenomenology: A Philosophical Investigation of Yogācāra Buddhism and the Ch'eng Wei-shih lun*. Curzon Critical Studies in Buddhism. London: RoutledgeCurzon.

Mack, Burton. 1996. "On Redescribing Christian Origins." *Method and Theory in the Study of Religion* 8:247–269.

Mackie, J. L. 1982. *The Miracle of Theism: Arguments For and Against the Existence of God*. Oxford: Clarendon Press.

Magnus, P. D. 2003. "Success, Truth, and the Galilean Strategy." *British Journal for the Philosophy of Science* 54.3:465–474.

Malvania, D., ed. 1971. *Dharmottara-pradīpa: Paṇḍita Durveka Miśra's Dharmottara-pradīpa [Being a Sub-commentary on Dharmottara's Nyāya-bindu-ṭīkā, a Commentary on Dharmakīrti's Nyāya-bindu]*. Patna: Kashi Prasad Jayaswal.

Manson, N. 2000a. "Anthropocentrism and the Design Argument." *Religious Studies* 36:163–176.

——. 2000b. "There Is No Adequate Definition of 'Fine-Tuned for Life.'" *Inquiry* 43:341–351.

——. 2003. *God and Design*. London: Routledge.

Matilal, Bimal Krishna. 1968. *The Navya-nyāya Doctrine of Negation: The Semantics and Ontology of Negative Statements in Navya-nyāya Philosophy*. Harvard Oriental Series 46. Cambridge, MA: Harvard University Press.

——. 1970. "Reference and Existence in Nyāya and Buddhist Logic." *Journal of Indian Philosophy* 1:83–110.

——. 1971. *Epistemology, Logic, and Grammar in Indian Philosophical Analysis*. Janua Linguarum, series minor 111. The Hague: Mouton.

——. 1977. *Nyāya-Vaiśeṣika*. A History of Indian Literature 6.2. Wiesbaden: Harrassowitz.

——. 1985. *Logic, Language, and Reality: An Introduction to Indian Philosophical Studies*. Delhi: Motilal Banarsidass.

——. 1986. *Perception: An Essay on Classical Indian Theories of Knowledge*. Oxford: Clarendon Press.

——. 1990. *The Word and the World: India's Contribution to the Study of Language*. Delhi: Oxford University Press.

——. 1998. *The Character of Logic in India*. SUNY Series in Indian Thought. Albany: State University of New York Press.

——. 2002. *Mind, Language, and World: The Collected Essays of Bimal Krishna Matilal*. Philosophy, Culture, and Religion. Ed. J. Ganeri. New Delhi: Oxford University Press.

Matilal, Bimal Krishna, Jonardon Ganeri, and Heeraman Tiwari. 1998. *The Character of Logic in India*. Albany: State University of New York Press.

McClintock, Sara L. 2002. "Omniscience and the Rhetoric of Reason in the Tattvasaṃgraha and the Tattvasaṃgrahapañjikā: A Thesis." Ph.D. diss., Harvard University.

McCrea, L., and P. G. Patil. 2006. "Traditionalism and Innovation: Philosophy, Exegesis, and Intellectual History in Jñānaśrīmitra's *Apohaprakaraṇa*." *Journal of Indian Philosophy* 34:303–366.

——. Forthcoming. *Buddhist Philosophy of Language in India: Jñānaśrīmitra's Monograph of Exclusion*.

McDermott, A. C. Senape. 1969. *An Eleventh Century Logic of "Exists": Ratnatkīrti's Kṣaṇabhaṅgasiddhiḥ Vyatirekātmikā*. Dordrecht: Reidel.

——. 1970. "Empty Subject Terms in Late Buddhist Logic." *Journal of Indian Philosophy* 1:22–29.

McPherson, Thomas. 1972. *The Argument from Design*. London: Macmillan.

Meindersma, T. E. 1991. "A Brief Reference to *Apoha* Theory in the Section on *Paralokasiddhi* in *Pramāṇavārttika* II." In Steinkellner 1991a:169–174.

Mellor, D. H. 1969. "God and Probability." *Religious Studies* 5.2:223–234.

Mikogami, E. 1979. "Some Remarks on the Concept of *Arthakriyā*." *Journal of Indian Philosophy* 7:79–94.

——. 1993. "Śubhagupta's Theory of Sense-Perception: Disputes Between Realists and the Vijñānavādins." In *Studies on Buddhism in Honour of Professor A. K.*

Warder, ed. N. K. Wagle and F. Watanabe, 86–99. Toronto: University of Toronto Centre for South Asian Studies.

Mimaki, Katsumi. 1976. *La réfutation bouddhique de la Permanence des Choses (Sthirasiddhidūṣaṇa) et la Preuve de la Momentanéité des Choses (Kṣaṇabhaṅgasiddhi)*. Paris: Institut de civilisation indienne.

Mishra, Umesh. 1934. *Smṛti Theory According to Nyāya-Vaiśeṣika*. Poona: Bhandarkar Oriental Research Institute.

——. 2006. *Nyāya-Vaiśeṣika: Conception Matter in Indian Philosophy*. Delhi: Bharatiya Kala Prakashan.

Miyasaka, Y. E. 1971/72. "Pramāṇa-vārttika-kārikā (Sanskrit and Tibetan), Chapters 2, 3, 4." *Acta Indologica* 2:1–206.

Mohanty, Jitendranath. 1966. *Gaṅgeśa's Theory of Truth: Containing the Text of Gaṅgeśa's Prāmāṇya (jñapti) vāda*. Santiniketan: Centre of Advanced Study in Philosophy Visva-Bharati.

——. 1992a. *Reason and Tradition in Indian Thought: An Essay on the Nature of Indian Philosophical Thinking*. Oxford: Clarendon Press.

——. 1992b. "On Matilal's Understanding of Indian Philosophy." *Philosophy East and West* 42.3:397–406.

——. 1999. *Logic, Truth, and the Modalities: From a Phenomenological Perspective*. Synthese Library 278. Dordrecht: Kluwer Academic.

Mookherjee, Satkari. 1975. *The Buddhist Philosophy of Universal Flux: San Exposition of the Philosophy of Critical Realism as Expounded by the School of Dignāga*. Delhi: Motilal Banarsidass.

Moriyama, Shinya. 2004. "Is the Proof of the Omniscient Buddha Possible?" *Hōrin* 11:183–197.

Mullens, James G. 1994. "Principles and Practices of Buddhist Education in Asaṅga's *Boddhisattvabhūmi*." Ph.D. diss., McMaster University.

Nagatomi, M. 1959. "The Framework of the *Pramāṇavārttika*, Book One." *JAOS* 79:262–266.

——. 1967. "Arthakriyā." *Adyar Library Bulletin* 31/32:52–72.

Nenninger, Claudius. 1992. *Aus gutem Grund: Praśastapādas anumāna-Lehre und die drei Bedingungen des logischen Grundes*. Philosophia indica 1. Reinbek: Dr. Inge Wezler Verlag für Orientalische Fachpublikationen.

Neville, Robert C. 2001a. *The Human Condition*. The Comparative Religious Ideas Project. Albany: State University of New York Press.

——. 2001b. *Ultimate Realities*. The Comparative Religious Ideas Project. Albany: State University of New York Press.

——. 2001c. *Religious Truth*. The Comparative Religious Ideas Project. Albany: State University of New York Press.

Nieuwendijk, Arthur. 1992. "Semantics and Comparative Logic." *Journal of Indian Philosophy* 41:377–418.

Nozick, Robert. 1981. *Philosophical Explanations*. Cambridge, MA: Harvard University Press.

Nyman, Patrik. 2005. "On the Meaning of *Yathārtha*." *Journal of Indian Philosophy* 33:553–570.

Oberhammer, G. 1964. "Der Svābhāvika-sambandha: Ein geschichtlicher Beitrag zur Nyāya-Logik." *WZKS* 8:131–181.

—. 1965. "Zum Problem des Gottesbeweises in der Indischen Philosophie." *Numen* 12.1:1–34.

Obermiller, E. 1931. *The History of Buddhism in India and Tibet by Bu ston*. Heidelberg: Harrassowitz.

Oetke, Claus. 1988. *"Ich" und das Ich: Analytische Untersuchungen zur buddhistisch-Brahmanischen Atmankontroverse*. Alt- und neu-indische Studien 33. Stuttgart: Steiner.

—. 1991. "*Svabhāvapratibandha* and the Types of Reasons in Dharmakīrti's Theory of Inference." In Steinkellner 1991a:243–268.

—. 1993. "Controverting the Ātman-Controversy and the Query of Segregating Philological and Non-philosophical Issues in Studies on Eastern Philosophies and Religions: Comments on Some Remarks of J. Bronkhorst." *Studien zur Indologie und Iranistik* 18:191–212.

—. 1994a. "Praśastapāda's Views on the 'Antinomic Reason' and Their Consequences for a Theory of Default Reasoning." *Asiatische Studien/ Studien Asiatique* 48.2:845–865.

—. 1994b. *Studies on the Doctrine of Trairūpya*. Wiener Studien zur Tibetologie und Buddhismuskunde 33. Vienna: Arbeitskreis für Tibetische und Buddhistische Studien Universität Wien.

—. 1996. "Ancient Indian Logic as a Theory of Non-Monotonic Reasoning." *Journal of Indian Philosophy* 24:447–539.

Ogawa, H. 1999. "Bharṭhari on Representations (*Buddhyākāra*)." In Katsura 1999:267–287.

Ono, M. 1997. "A Reconsideration of the Controversy About the Order of the Chapters of the *Pramāṇāvārttika*—The Argument by Indian Commentators of Dharmakīrti." In *Tibetan Studies: Proceedings of the 7th Seminar of the International Association for Tibetan Studies, Graz 1995*, ed. M. T. Much, 701–716. Vienna: Verlag der Österreichischen Akademie der Wissenschaften.

Oppy, Graham Robert. 2006a. *Philosophical Perspectives on Infinity*. Cambridge: Cambridge University Press.

—. 2006b. *Arguing About Gods*. Cambridge: Cambridge University Press.

Owen, R. 1843. *Lectures on the Comparative Anatomy and Physiology of the Invertebrate Animals, Delivered at the Royal College of Surgeons, in 1843*. London: Longman, Brown, Green, and Longman.

Paley, William. 1890/1805. *Natural Theology; or, Evidences of the Existence and Attributes of the Deity, Collected from the Appearances of Nature*. 10th ed. London: R. Faulder.

Pandeya, Raghavendra. 1984. *Major Hetvābhāsas: A Formal Analysis, with Reference to Nyāya and Buddhism*. Delhi: Eastern Book Linkers.

Papineau, D. 2003. *The Roots of Reason: Philosophical Essays on Rationality, Evolution, and Probability*. New York: Oxford University Press.

Patil, Parimal G. 2003. "On What It Is That Buddhists Think About—*Apoha* in the *Ratnakīrti-nibanbdhāvalih*." *Journal of Indian Philosophy* 31:229–256.

—. 2007. "Dharmakīrti's White-Lie." In *Pramāṇakīrtiḥ: Papers Dedicated to Ernst Steinkellner on the Occasion of His 70th Birthday, Part 2*, ed. B. Kellner and H. Tauscher, 597–619. Vienna: Wiener Studien zur Tibetologie und Buddhismuskunde.

—. Forthcoming, a. "History, Philology, and the Philosophical Studies of Sanskrit Texts." *Journal of Indian Philosophy*.

—. Forthcoming, b. "Without Brackets: A Minimally Annotated Translation of Ratnakīrti's *Apohasiddhi*." In *Apoha Semantics and Human Cognition*, ed. Arindam Chakrabarti, Mark Siderits, and Tom Tillemans.

Perry, Bruce. 1995. "An Introduction to the Nyāyacaturgranthikā: With English Translations." Ph.D. diss., University of Pennsylvania.

Phillips, Stephen H. 1987. "Dharmakīrti on Sensation and Causal Efficiency." *Journal of Indian Philosophy* 15:231–259.

—. 1995. *Classical Indian Metaphysics: Refutations of Realism and the Emergence of "New Logic."* Chicago: Open Court.

—. 2001. "There's Nothing Wrong with Raw Perception." *Philosophy East and West* 51:104–113.

Phillips, Stephen H., and N. S. Ramanuja Tatacharya. 2002. *Gaṅgeśa on the Upādhi, the "Inferential Undercutting Condition": Introduction, Translation, and Explanation*. New Delhi: Indian Council of Philosophical Research.

—. 2004. *Epistemology of Perception: Gaṅgeśa's Tattvacintāmaṇi, Jewel of Reflection on the Truth (about Epistemology): The Perception Chapter (Pratyakṣa-khaṇḍa)*. Treasury of the Indic Sciences. New York: American Institute of Buddhist Studies.

Pietroski, Paul M. 1998. "Actions, Adjuncts, and Agency." *Mind* 107:73–111.

—. 2000. *Causing Actions*. Oxford: Oxford University Press.

Pind, Ole. 1991. "Dignāga on *Śabdasāmānya* and *Śabdaviśeṣa*." In Steinkellner 1991a:269–280.

—. 1999. "Dharmakīrti's Interpretation of Pramāṇasamuccayavṛtti V 36: *Śabdo 'rthāntaranivṛttiviśiṣṭān eva bhāvān āha*." In Katsura 1999:317–332.

Plantinga, Alvin. 1993a. *Warrant and Proper Function*. New York: Oxford University Press.

—. 1993b. *Warrant: The Current Debate*. New York: Oxford University Press.

Pollock, Sheldon. 1989. "Mīmāṃsā and the Problem of History in Traditional India." *Journal of the American Oriental Society* 109:603–610.

—. 2004. "The Meaning of Dharma and the Relationship of the Two Mīmāṃsās: Appayya Dīkṣita's 'Discourse on the Refutation of a Unified Knowledge System of Pūrvamīmāṃsā and Uttaramīmāṃsā.'" *Journal of Indian Philosophy* 32:769–811.

—. 2006. *The Language of the Gods in the World of Men: Sanskrit, Culture, and Power in Premodern India*. Berkeley: University of California Press.

Poole, Fitz, and John Porter. 1986. "Metaphors and Maps: Towards Comparison in the Anthropology of Religion." *Journal of the American Academy of Religion* 54:411–457.

Potter, Karl H. 1977. *Indian Metaphysics and Epistemology: The Tradition of Nyāya-Vaiśeṣika up to Gaṅgeśa*. Encyclopedia of Indian Philosophies 2. Delhi: Motilal Banarsidass.

——. 1984. "Does Indian Epistemology Concern Justified True Belief?" *Journal of Indian Philosophy* 12:307–327.

——. 1993. *Indian Philosophical Analysis: Nyāya-Vaiśeṣika from Gaṅgeśa to Raghunātha Śiromaṇi*. Encyclopedia of Indian Philosophies 6. Delhi: Motilal Banarsidass.

Prets, Ernst. 1992. "On the Development of the Concept of Parārthānumāna." *WZKS* 36:195–202.

Priest, Graham. 1981. "The Argument from Design." *Australasian Journal of Philosophy* 59:422–443.

Pruss, Alexander R. 2006. *The Principle of Sufficient Reason: A Reassessment*. Cambridge Studies in Philosophy. New York: Cambridge University Press.

Putnam, Hilary. 1975. "The Meaning of 'Meaning.'" In *Language, Mind, and Knowledge*, ed. K. Gunderson, 131–193. Minneapolis: University of Minnesota Press.

Pye, Michael. 1978. *Skillful Means: A Concept in Mahayana Buddhism*. London: Duckworth.

Quinn, Phillip L. 1996. "The Cultural Anthropology of Philosophy of Religion." In *God, Philosophy, and Academic Culture: A Discussion Between Scholars in the AAR and the APA*, ed. W. J. Wainwright. Atlanta, GA: Scholars Press.

Raja, K. K. 1986. "*Apoha* Theory and Pre-Diṅnāga Views on Sentence Meaning." In *Buddhist Logic and Epistemology: Studies in the Buddhist Analysis of Inference and Language*, ed. B. K. Matilal and R. D. Evans, 185–192. Dordrecht: Kluwer Academic.

Ramachandran, Murali. 2006. "How Believing Can Fail to Be Knowledge." *Theoria* 56:185–194.

Ramsey, Frank Plumpton. 1978. *Foundations: Essays in Philosophy, Logic, Mathematics, and Economics*. International Library of Psychology, Philosophy, and Scientific Method. Atlantic Highlands, NJ: Humanities Press.

Ratzsch, Del. 2003. "Perceiving Design." In *God and Design: The Teleological Argument and Modern Science*, ed. N. Manson, 121–144. New York: Routledge.

Ray, Gangasagar, ed. 1993. *Ślokavārttikam*. Varanasi: Ratna Publications.

Reichenbach, Bruce. 1972. *The Cosmological Argument: A Reassessment*. Springfield, Ill: Charles C. Thomas.

——. 2004. "Cosmological Argument." *Stanford Encyclopedia of Philosophy* (fall 2006 edition), ed. Edward N. Zaltah. http://plato.stanford.edu/archives/fall2006/entries/cosmological-argument.

Rorty, Richard. 1989. "Review of Gerald J. Larson and Eliot Deutsch: *Interpreting Across Boundaries: New Essays in Comparative Philosophy*." *Philosophy East and West* 39.3:332–337.

———. 1992a. "Philosophers, Novelists, and Intercultural Comparisons: Heidegger, Kundera, and Dickens." In *Culture and Modernity: East-West Perspectives*, ed. Eliot Deutsch. Honolulu: University of Hawai'i Press.

———. 1992b. "A Pragmatist View of Rationality and Cultural Difference." *Philosophy East and West* 42.4:581–596.

Rosenberg, Jay F. 2002. *Thinking About Knowing*. Oxford: Oxford University Press.

Rospatt, Alexander von. 1995. *The Buddhist Doctrine of Momentariness: A Survey of the Origins and the Early Phase of this Doctrine up to Vasubandhu*. Alt- und neu-Indische Studien 47. Stuttgart: Steiner.

Rowe, William L. 1975. *The Cosmological Argument*. Princeton: Princeton University Press.

———. 1978. *Philosophy of Religion: An Introduction*. Encino, CA: Dickenson.

———. 1997. "Cosmological Arguments." In *A Companion to Philosophy of Religion*, ed. C. Taliaferro, 331–337. Malden, MA: Blackwell.

Rowe, William L., William J. Wainwright, and Robert L. Ferm. 1998. *Philosophy of Religion: Selected Readings*. 3rd ed. Fort Worth: Harcourt Brace.

Ruegg, D. S. 1986. "Does the Madhyamika Have a Thesis?" In *Buddhist Logic and Epistemology*, ed. R. D. Evans, 229–238. Dordrecht: Kluwer.

Sāṃkṛtyāyana, Rāhula, ed. 1938–1940. "Dharmakīrti's Pramāṇavārttika with Commentary by Manorathanandin." *Appendix to the Journal of the Bhandarkar Oriental Research Institute* 24–26.

———. 1943. *Ācārya-Dharmakīrteḥ Pramāṇavārttikam (Svārthānumānaparicchedaḥ) Svopajñavṛttyā Karṇakagomiviracitayā Taṭṭīkayā ca sahitam*. Allahabad.

———. 1953. *Prajñākaragupta's Pramāṇavārttikālaṅkārabhāṣyam; or, Vārttikālaṅkāraḥ of Prajñākaragupta (Being a Commentary on Dharmakīrti's Pramāṇavārtikam)*. Tibetan Sanskrit Work Series 1. Patna: Kashi Prasad Jayaswal Research Institute.

Sanghavi, S. 1949. *Hetubinduṭīkā of Bhaṭṭa Arcaṭa: With the Sub-commentary Entitled Āloka of Durveka Miśra*. Baroda: Oriental Institute.

Sartwell, Crispin. 1992. "Why Knowledge is Merely True Belief." *Journal of Philosophy* 89:169–180.

Śāstri, Sāmbaśiva, and V. A. Rāmasvāmi Śāstri, eds. 1926–1943. *Mīmāṃsāślokavārttikaṃ Sucaritamiśra-praṇītayā Kāśikākhyayāṭīkayā sametam*. 3 vols. Trivandrum.

Scharf, Peter M. 1996. *The Denotation of Generic Terms in Ancient Indian Philosophy: Grammar, Nyāya and Mīmāṃsā*. Transactions of the American Philosophical Society 86.3. Philadelphia: American Philosophical Society.

Schmidt-Leukel, Perry. 2006. *Buddhism, Christianity, and the Question of Creation: Karmic or Divine?* Burlington, VT: Ashgate.

Schmithausen, L. 2005. *On the Problem of the External World in the Cheng wei shi lun*. Studia Philologica Buddhica 13. Tokyo: International Institute for Buddhist Studies.

Schopen, Gregory. 1987. *Bones, Stones, and Buddhist Monks: Collected Papers on the Archaeology, Epigraphy, and Texts of Monastic Buddhism in India*. Studies in the Buddhist Traditions. Honolulu: University of Hawai'i Press.

Shah, Nagin J. 1992. *A Study of Jayanta Bhaṭṭa's Nyāyamañjarī: A Mature Sanskrit Work on Indian Logic*. Sanskrit-Sanskriti Granthamālā 1. Ahmedabad.

Sharma, Aryendra, ed. 1969–1985. *Kāśika: A Commentary on Panini's Grammar by Vamana and Jayaditya*. Hyderabad: Osmania University, Sanskrit Academy.

Shastri, Dwarikas. 1972. *Vādanyāyaprakaraṇa of Ācārya Dharmakīrti with the commentary Vipañcitārthā of Ācārya Śāntarakṣita and Sambandhaparīkṣā with the commentary of Prabhācandra*. Bauddha Bharati 8. Varanasi: Bauddha Bharati.

—, ed. 1981. *Tattvasaṃgraha of Ācārya Shāntarakṣita with the Commentary 'Pañjikā' of Shri Kamalashīla*. 2 vols. Varanasi: Bauddha Bharati.

—. 1984. *Nyāyabindu of Ācārya Dharmakīrti with the Commentaries by Ārya Vinītadeva and Dharmottara and Dharmottara-Ṭīkā-Ṭippaṇa*. Varanasi: Bauddha Bharati.

—. 1988. *Bodhicaryāvatāra of Ārya Śāntideva with the Commentary Pañjikā of Shri Prajñākaramati and Hindi Translation*. Varanasi: Bauddha Bharati.

Shukla, Bradrinath. 1991. "On Propositions." In *Saṃvāda: A Dialogue Between Two Philosophical Traditions*, ed. R. D. Krishna, R. C. Dwivedi, and M. Lath, 191–213. Delhi: Motilal Banarsidass.

Sidelle, Alan. 1989. *Necessity, Essence, and Individuation: A Defense of Conventionalism*. Ithaca: Cornell University Press.

—. 1998. "A Sweater Unraveled: Following One Thread of Thought for Avoiding Coincident Entities." *Noûs* 32:423–448.

Sider, Ted. 2003. "Reductive Theories of Modality." In *The Oxford Handbook of Metaphysics*, ed. D. W. Zimmerman, 180–208. Oxford: Oxford University Press.

Siderits, Mark. 1986a. "Was Śāntarakṣira a Positivist?" In *Buddhist Logic and Epistemology: Studies in the Buddhist Analysis of Inference and Language*, ed. B. K. Matilal and R. D. Evans, 193–206. Dordrecht: Reidel.

—. 1986b. "Word Meaning, Sentence Meaning, and Apoha." *Journal of Indian Philosophy* 13:133–151.

—. 1991. *Indian Philosophy of Language: Studies in Selected Issues*. Studies in Linguistics and Philosophy 46. Dordrecht: Kluwer Academic.

—. 1999. "Apohavāda, Nominalism, and Resemblance Theories." In Katsura 1999:341–348.

—. 2003. *Personal Identity and Buddhist Philosophy: Empty Persons*. Aldershot: Ashgate.

—. 2004. "Perceiving Particulars: A Buddhist Defense." *Philosophy East and West* 54.3:367–382.

Singh, B. N. 1988. *Bauddhatarkabhāṣā of Mokṣākaragupta*. Varanasi: Asha Prakashan.

Smart, J. J. C., and J. J. Haldane. 2003. *Atheism and Theism*. Malden, MA: Blackwell.

Smith, Jonathan Z. 1971. "*Adde Parvum Parvo Magnus Acervus Erit*." *History of Religions* 11:67–90.

—. 1980. "Fences and Neighbors: Some Contours of Early Judaism." *Approaches to Early Judaism, Brown Judaic Studies* 9.2:1–25.

—. 1982. *Imagining Religion: From Babylon to Jonestown*. Chicago Studies in the History of Judaism. Chicago: University of Chicago Press.

—. 1986–1987. "The New Liberal Arts." *International Journal of Social Education* 1:7–17.

—. 1988. "'Religion' and 'Religious Studies': No Difference at All." *Soundings* 71:231–244.

—. 1990. *Drudgery Divine: On the Comparison of Early Christianities and the Religions of Late Antiquity.* Jordan Lectures in Comparative Religion 14. London: School of Oriental and African Studies University of London.

—. 2000. "Epilogue: The 'End' of Comparison: Redescription and Rectification." In *A Magic Still Dwells: Comparative Religion in the Postmodern Age*, ed. K. C. Patton, B. C. Ray, M. D. Eckel, D. L. Eck, and L. E. Sullivan, 237–242. Berkeley: University of California Press.

—. 2004. *Relating Religion: Essays in the Study of Religion*. Chicago: University of Chicago Press.

Sober, E. 1993. *The Philosophy of Biology*. Boulder, CO: Westview.

—. 1997. "The Design Argument." In *A Companion to Philosophy of Religion*, ed. C. Taliaferro, 472–488. Cambridge: Blackwell.

—. 2000. "How Not to Detect Design: A Review of William Dembski's 'The Design Inference' (with B. Fitelson and C. Stephens)." *Philosophy of Science* 66:472–488.

—. 2004. "The Design Argument." In *Debating Design—From Darwin to DNA*, ed. W. Dembski and M. Ruse, 98–129. New York: Cambridge University Press.

Sosa, Ernest. 1991. *Knowledge in Perspective: Selected Essays in Epistemology*. Cambridge: Cambridge University Press.

—. 1997. "Reflective Knowledge in the Best Circles." *Journal of Philosophy* 94:410–430.

—. 2003. *Epistemic Justification: Internalism vs. Externalism, Foundations vs. Virtues.* Great Debates in Philosophy. Malden, MA: Blackwell.

—. 2007. *A Virtue Epistemology*. Oxford: Clarendon Press.

Staal, F. 1962. "Negation and the Law of Contradiction in Indian Thought." *Bulletin of the School of Oriental and African Studies* 25:52–71.

Stalnaker, Robert. 1999. *Context and Content: Essays on Intentionality in Speech and Thought*. Oxford Cognitive Science. Oxford: Oxford University Press.

Steinkellner, Ernst. 1967. *Dharmakīrti's Hetubinduḥ*. Veröffentlichungen der Kommission für Sprachen und Kulturen Süd- und Ostasiens 4–5. Graz: Böhlau in Kommission.

—. 1968/1969. "Die Entwicklung des *Kṣaṇikatvānumānam* de Dharmakīrti." *Wiener Zeitschrift für die Kunde Südasiens* 12/13:361–377.

—. 1971. "Wirklichkeit und Begriff bei Dharmakīrti." *WZKS* 15:179–211.

—. 1973. *Dharmakīrti's Pramāṇaviniścaya 2 Kapitel: Svārthānumāna*. Viena: Verlag der Österreichischen Akademie der Wissenschaften.

—. 1974. "On Interpretation of the *Svabhāvahetu*." *WZKS* 18:117–129.

—. 1977. "Jñānaśrīmitra's *Sarvajñasiddhi*." In *Prajñāpāramitā and Related Systems: Studies in Honor of Edward Conze*, ed. L. Lancaster, 383–393. Berkeley: University of California Press.

—. 1982. "The Spiritual Place of the Epistemological Tradition in Buddhism." *Nanto Bukkyō* 49:1–18.

—. 1988. "Remarks on *Niścitagrahaṇa*." In *Orientalia Iosephi Tucci memoriae dicta*, ed. G. Gnoli and L. Lanicotti, 1427–1444. Rome: Istituto italiano per il Medio ed Estremo Oriente.

—, ed. 1991a. *Studies in the Buddhist Epistemological Tradition. Proceedings of the Second International Dharmakīrti Conference*. Vienna Österreichischen Akademie der Wissenschaften: Philosophisch-historischen Klasse, Denkschriften 222. Vienna: Verlag der Österreichischen Akademie der Wissenschaften.

—. 1991b. "On the Logic of *Svabhāvahetu* In Dharmakīrti's *Vādanyāya*." In Steinkellner 1991a:311–344.

—. 1992. "Lamotte and the Concept of *Anupalabdhi*." *Asiatische Studien/ Études Asiatiques* 46.1:398–410.

—. 1998. "Dharmakīrti." In *Routledge Encyclopedia of Philosophy*, ed. E. Craig, 51–53. London: Routledge.

—. 1999. "Yogic Cognition, Tantric Goal, and Other Methodological Applications of Dharmakīrti's *Kāryānumāna* Theorem." In Katsura 1999:349–362.

—. 2006. "Hindu Doctrines of Creation and Their Buddhist Critiques." In *Buddhism, Christianity, and the Question of Creation: Karmic or Divine?*, ed. P. Schmidt-Leukel, 15–32. Burlington, VT: Ashgate.

Steinkellner, Ernst, and Michael Torsten Much. 1995. *Texte der erkenntnistheoretischen Schule des Buddhismus*. Systematische Übersicht über die buddhistische Sanskrit-Literatur 2. Göttingen: Vandenhoeck and Ruprecht.

Steinkellner, E., H. Krasser, and H. Lasic. 2005. *Jinendrabuddhi's Viśālāmalavatī Pramāṇasamuccayaṭīkā: Chapter 1*. Beijing/Vienna: China Tibetology/Austrian Academy of Sciences.

Stern, Elliot M., ed. 1998. "'Vidhivivekah' of Mandanamiśra, with commentary 'Nyāyakaṇika,' of Vacaspatimiśra, and Supercommentaries, Jusadhvankarani, and Svaditankarani of Parameśvarah, Critical and Annotated Edition." Ph.D. diss., University of Pennsylvania.

Strawson, P. F. 1998. "Reply to Arindam Chakrabarti." In *The Philosophy of P. F. Strawson*, ed. L. E. Hahn, 324–329. Chicago: Open Court.

Swinburne, Richard. 1968. "The Argument from Design." *Philosophy* 43:199–211.

—. 1979. *The Existence of God*. Oxford: Clarendon Press.

—. 1994. *The Christian God*. Oxford: Clarendon Press.

Swoyer, Chris. 2000. "Properties." In *Stanford Encyclopedia of Philosophy*, ed. E. N. Zalta. http://plato.stanford.edu/archives/win2000/entries/properties/.

Taber, John. 1986. "Utpaladeva's *Īśvarasiddhi*." *Adyar Library Bulletin* 50:106–173.

—. 1992. "What Did Kumārila Bhaṭṭa Mean by *Svataḥ Prāmāṇya*?" *Journal of the American Oriental Society* 112.3–4:204–221.

—. 1996. "Is Verbal Testimony a Form of Inference?" *Studies in Humanities and Social Sciences* 3.2:19–31.

—. 2001. "Much Ado About Nothing: Kumārila, Śāntaraksita, and Dharmakīrti on the Cognition of Non-being." *Journal of the American Oriental Society* 121.1:72–88.

—. 2004. "Is Indian Logic Nonmonotonic?" *Philosophy East and West* 54.2:143–170.

——. 2005. *A Hindu Critique of Buddhist Epistemology: Kumārila on Perception. The "Determination of Perception" Chapter of Kumārila Bhaṭṭa's Ślokavārttika*. RoutledgeCurzon Hindu Studies. London: RoutledgeCurzon.

——. Forthcoming. "Yoga and Our Epistemic Predicament."

Tachikawa, Musashi. 1971. "A Sixth-Century Manual of Indian Logic (A Translation of the *Nyāyapraveśa*)." *Journal of Indian Philosophy* 1:111–129.

Taliaferro, Charles. 2005. *Evidence and Faith: Philosophy and Religion Since the Seventeenth Century*. Evolution of Modern Philosophy. Cambridge: Cambridge University Press.

Tani, Tadashi. 1996a. "Jñānaśrīmitra's Proof of Momentary Destruction of Existence." *Bulletin of Kochi Technical College* 35:1–16.

——. 1996b. "Jñānaśrīmitra's Proof of Momentary Existence by Perception." *Bulletin of Kochi Technical College* 40:17–36.

——. 1997. "Problems of Interpretation on Dharmottara's Kṣaṇabhaṅgasiddhi (1), (2). and (3)." *Bulletin of Kochi Technical College* 41:19–77.

——. 2004. "Jñānaśrīmitra's Proof of the Momentary Destruction of Existence: A Philosophical Investigation from the Standpoint of Intuitionistic Logic." In *Three Mountains and Seven Rivers: Professor Musashi Tachikawa's Felicitation Volume*, ed. S. Hino and T. Wada, 375–392. Delhi: Motilal Banarsidass.

Tatacharya, N. S. Ramanuja. 2005. *Śābdabodhamīmāṃsā: An Inquiry Into Indian Theories of Verbal Cognition*. New Delhi: Rashtriya Sanskrit Sansthan.

Thakur, Anantalal. 1975. *Ratnakīrti-nibandhāvaliḥ: Buddhist Nyāya Works of Ratnakīrti*. Tibetan Sanskrit Works 3. Patna: Kashiprasad Jayaswal Research Institute.

——. 1987. *Jñānaśrīmitranibandhāvali*. Patna: Kashiprasad Jayaswal Research Institute.

——. 1996a. *Nyāyavārttikatātparyaṭīkā*. Delhi: Indian Council of Philosophical Research.

——. 1996b. *Nyāyavārttikatātparyaṭīkāpariśuddhi*. Delhi: Indian Council of Philosophical Research.

——. 1997a. *Nyāyavārttika*. Delhi: Indian Council of Philosophical Research.

——. 1997b. *Nyāya-sūtra. Gautamīyanyāyadarśana with Bhāṣya of Vātsyāyana*. Delhi: Indian Council of Philosophical Research.

Thomasson, A. Forthcoming. "Modal Conceptualism."

Tillemans, Tom J. F. 1984. "Sur le parārthānumāna en logique bouddhique." *Études Asiatiques/Asiatische Studien* 38:73–99.

——. 1995. "Dharmakīrti and Tibetans on Adṛśyānupalabdhihetu." *Journal of Indian Philosophy* 23:129.

——. 2000. *Dharmakīrti's Pramāṇavārttika: An Annotated Translation of the Fourth Chapter (Parārthānumāna)*. Sitzungsberichte/Österreichische Akademie der Wissenschaften, philosophisch-historische Klasse. Vienna: Verlag der Österreichischen Akademie der Wissenschaften.

Toulmin, Stephen. 1973. "Rationality and the Changing Aims of Inquiry." In *Proceedings of the Fourth International Congress for Logic, Methodology, and Philosophy of Science*, 885–903. Amsterdam: North-Holland.

Tucci, Guiseppe. 1986. *Minor Buddhist Texts, Parts One and Two.* 1st Indian ed. Delhi: Motilal Banarsidass.

van Biljert, Vittorio A. 1989. *Epistemology and Spiritual Authority: The Development of Epistemology and Logic in the Old Nyāya and the Buddhist School of Epistemology, with an Annotated Translation of Dharmakīrti's Pramāṇavārttika II (Pramaṇasiddhi) vv. 1–7.* Wiener Studien zur Tibetologie und Buddhismuskunde 20. Vienna: Arbeitskreis für Tibetische und Buddhistische Studien, Universität Wien.

Van den Bossche, F. 1998. "Jain Arguments Against Nyāya Theism." *Journal of Indian Philosophy* 26:1–26.

van Frassen, Bas C. 1989. *Laws and Symmetry.* Oxford: Oxford University Press.

Varadachari, V. 1977. "Nyāyaratna." In *Indian Metaphysics and Epistemology: The Tradition of Nyāya-Vaiśeṣika up to Gaṅgeśa*, ed. Karl H. Potter, 669–682. Princeton: Princeton University Press.

Varadacharya, K. S., ed. 1969/1983. *Nyāyamañjarī of Jayantabhaṭṭa with Ṭippaṇī-Nyāyasaurabha by the Editor.* 2 vols. Mysore.

Vattanky, John. 1984. *Gaṅgeśa's Philosophy of God: Analysis, Text, Translation, and Interpretation of Īśvaravāda Section of Gaṅgeśa's Tattvacintāmaṇi with a Study of the Development of Nyāya Theism.* Adyar Library Series 115. Madras: Adyar Library and Research Centre.

—. 1993. *Development of Nyāya Theism.* New Delhi: Intercultural Publications.

Vetter, Tilmann. 1964. *Erkenntnisprobleme bei Dharmakīrti.* Vienna: H. Bölaus.

—. 1966. *Pramāṇaviniścayaḥ, 1. Kapitel: Pratyakṣam. Einleitung, Text der tibetischen Übersetzung, Sanskritfragmente.* Veröffentlichungen der Kommission für Sprachen und Kulturen Süd- und Ostasiens 3. Graz: Böhlau.

—. 1997. "Atheistische un theistische Tendenzen im Buddhismus." In *Gott im Spiegel der Weltreligionen. Christliche Identität und interreligiöser Dialog*, ed. E. Klinger, 22–35. Regensburg.

Wada, Toshihiro. 1990. *Invariable Concomitance in Navya-Nyāya.* Delhi: Sri Satguru Publications.

—. 2007. *The Analytical Method of Navya-Nyāya.* Gonda Indological Studies 14.8. Groningen: Egbert Forsten.

Wainwright, William J. 1996. *God, Philosophy, and Academic Culture. A Discussion Between Scholars in the AAR and the APA.* Reflection and Theory in the Study of Religion 11. Atlanta, GA: Scholars Press.

Walton, Douglas. 1996. *Arguments from Ignorance.* University Park: Penn State University Press.

Weatherson, Brian. 2004. "Luminous Margins." *Australasian Journal of Philosophy* 82:373–383.

Williamson, Timothy. 2000. *Knowledge and Its Limits.* Oxford: Oxford University Press.

—. 2007. *The Philosophy of Philosophy. Blackwell/Brown Lectures in Philosophy*, vol. 2. Malden, MA: Blackwell Pub.

Woo, Jeson. 1999. "The Kṣaṇabhaṅgasiddhi-Anvayātmika: An Eleventh-Century Buddhist Work on Existence and Causal Theory." Ph.D. diss., University of Pennsylvania.

—. 2001. "Incompatibility and the Proof of the Buddhist Theory of Momentariness." *Journal of Indian Philosophy* 29:423–434.

Yogindrananda, S., ed. 1968. *Śrīmadācāra-Bhāsarvajña-praṇītasya Nyāyasārasya svopajñaṃ vyākhyānaṃ Nyāyabhūṣaṇam.* (Ṣaḍdarśanaprakāśanagranthāmālā 1). Vārāṇasī: Ṣaḍdarśanaprakāśanapratiṣṭhānam.

Yoshimizu, Chizuko. 1999. "The Development of Sattvānumāna from the Refutation of a Permanent Existent in the Sautrāntika Tradition." *WZKS* 43:231–254.

—. Forthcoming. "Buddhist Inquiries Into the Nature of an Object's Determinate Existence in Terms of Space, Time, and Defining Essence."

Zagzebski, Linda T. 1999. "What Is Knowledge?" In *Blackwell Guide to Epistemology,* ed. E. Sosa, 92–116. Malden, MA: Blackwell.

—. 2000. "From Reliabilism to Virtue Epistemology." In *Knowledge, Belief, and Character: Readings in Virtue Epistemology*, ed. Guy Axtell, 113–123. Maryland: Rowman and Littlefield.

INDEX